Social Memory Theory and Conceptions of Afterlife in Jewish and Christian Antiquity

Studies in Cultural Contexts of the Bible

Edited by

Sandra Huebenthal (Passau),
Anselm C. Hagedorn (Osnabrück),
Jacqueline Eliza Vayntrub (New Haven),
Zeba Crook (Ottawa)

VOLUME 8

Thomas R. Hatina, Jiří Lukeš (Eds.)

Social Memory Theory and Conceptions of Afterlife in Jewish and Christian Antiquity

TUTA SUB AEGIDE PALLAS · 1683 ·

BRILL
SCHÖNINGH

Cover illustration: Sixth-century mosaic of the Raising of Lazarus, church of Sant'Apollinare Nuovo, Ravenna, Italy.

Bibliographic information published by the Deutsche Nationalbibliothek.

The Deutsche Nationalbibliothek lists this publication in the Deutsche Nationalbibliografie; detailed bibliographic data available online: http://dnb.d-nb.de

www.schoeningh.de

Cover design: Evelyn Ziegler, Munich
Production: Brill Deutschland GmbH, Paderborn

ISSN 2629-9224
ISBN 978-3-506-79621-9 (hardback)
ISBN 978-3-657-79621-2 (e-book)

Contents

Preface

This volume is the culmination of a project initiative on the relationship between social memory theory and Jewish and Christian conceptions of afterlife in antiquity, which was spearheaded by Jiří Lukeš, Sandra Huebenthal, and Thomas Hatina during a series of doctoral seminars in Prague on Social Memory Theory and early Christianity in May 2017. The initiative led to the organization of two related international conferences over the span of two years. The first was held at the 2018 Society of Biblical Literature meeting in Denver. Gratitude is extended to the steering committee of *The Bible in Ancient and Modern Media* section which graciously agreed to dedicate one full day to the launch of this project. The second conference was held in May 2019 over two days in Prague at both the Hussite Theological Faculty of Charles University and The House of the Professed which is a beautifully decorated early baroque building that houses the faculty of Mathematics and Physics. In the preparation of this volume, we would like to thank Naomi Rey for her careful editing and the editorial staff at Brill. We are also grateful to all the organizers, the participants at the conferences, and the contributors to this volume. For several, engagement with social memory theory is a recent undertaking and we are appreciative for their willingness to meet the challenge in a spirit of mutual learning. We would particularly like to acknowledge Prof. Petr Pokorny who presented a paper entitled "Social Memory Theory and *Formgeschichte*." His sad passing before he could convert his notes into a structured paper did not allow us to include his contribution. We would like to honor his participation—alongside his immense scholarly influence and gentle spirit—by dedicating this volume to his memory.

Abbreviations

Abbreviations for primary sources follow *The SBL Handbook of Style* (2d ed.; Atlanta, Ga.: SBL Press, 2014).

AB	Anchor Bible
ABD	*Anchor Bible Dictionary*. Edited by D. N. Freedman. 6 vols. New York. 1992
AGJU	Arbeiten zur Geschichte des antiken Judentums und des Urchristentums
ANET	*Ancient Near Eastern Texts Relating to the Old Testament*. Edited by J. B. Pritchard. 3d ed. Princeton, 1969
BETL	Bibliotheca ephemeridum theologicarum lovaniensium
Bib	*Biblica*
BibInt	*Biblical Interpretation*
BibInt	Biblical Interpretation Series
BibSem	The Biblical Seminar
BIS	Biblical Interpretation Series
BL	*Bibel und Liturgie*
BSIH	Brill's Studies in Intellectual History
BTB	*Biblical Theology Bulletin*
BTS	Biblical Tools and Studies
BZAW	Beihefte zur Zeitschrift für die alttestamentliche Wissenschaft
BZNW	Beihefte zur Zeitschrift für die neutestamentliche Wissenschaft
CBQ	*Catholic Biblical Quarterly*
CBQMS	Catholic Biblical Quarterly Monograph Series
CC	Continental Commentaries
CEJL	Commentaries on Early Jewish Literature
CH	*Church History*
CJR	*Contemporary Justice Review*
COS	The Context of Scripture. Edited by W. W. Hallo. 3 vols. Leiden, 1997–
CurBR	*Currents in Biblical Research*
CV	*Communio viatorum*
DCL	Deuterocanonical and Cognate Literature
DJD	Discoveries in the Judaean Desert
ECL	Early Christianity and Its Literature

EKK	Evangelisch-katholischer Kommentar
ETL	*Ephemerides Theologicae Lovanienses European Studies*
FAT	Forschungen zum Alten Testament
FRLANT	Forschungen zur Religion und Literatur des Alten und Neuen Testaments
GSC	Die griechischen christlichen Schriftsteller der ersten Jahrhunderte
HdO	Handbuch der Orientalistik
HTS	Harvard Theological Studies
HvTSt	*Hervormde teologiese studies*
ICC	International Critical Commentary
JAAR	*Journal of the American Academy of Religion*
JBL	*Journal of Biblical Literature*
JECS	*Journal of Early Christian Studies*
JETS	*Journal of the Evangelical Theological Society*
JR	*Journal of Religion*
JRA	*Journal of Roman Archaeology*
JSHJ	*Journal for the Study of the Historical Jesus*
JSHRZ	*Jüdische Schriften aus hellenistich-römischer Zeit*
JSJ	*Journal for the Study of Judaism in the Persian, Hellenistic, and Roman Periods*
JSJSup	Supplements to the Journal for the Study of Judaism
JSNT	*Journal for the Study of the New Testament*
JSNTSup	Journal for the Study of the New Testament Supplement Series
JSOTSup	Journal for the Study of the Old Testament Supplement Series
JSP	*Journal for the Study of the Pseudepigrapha*
JTS	*Journal of Theological Studies*
KEK	Kritisch-exegetischer Kommentar über das Neue Testament (Meyer-Kommentar)
KTU	*Die keilalphabetischen Texte aus Ugarit.* Edited by M. Dietrich, O. Loretz, and J. Sanmart.n. AOAT 24/1. Neukirchen-Vluyn, 1976. 2d enlarged ed. of *KTU: The Cuneiform Alphabetic Texts from Ugarit, Ras Ibn Hani, and Other Places.* Edited by M. Dietrich, O. Loretz, and J. Sanmartín. Münster, 1995 (= *CTU*)
LCL	Loeb Classical Library
LNTS	Library of New Testament Studies
MDAI	*Mitteilungen des Deutschen archäologischen Instituts*
NedTT	*Nederlands theologisch tijdschrift*

Neot	*Neotestamentica*
NHMS	Nag Hammadi and Manichaean Studies
NICNT	New International Commentary on the New Testament
NIGTC	New International Greek Testament Commentary
NTD	Das Neue Testament Deutsch
NTOA	Novum Testamentum et Orbis Antiquus
NTS	*New Testament Studies*
NovT	*Novum Testamentum*
NovTSup	Novum Testamentum Supplements
OECS	Oxford Early Christian Studies
PAWB	Potsdamer Altertumswissenschaftliche Beiträge
PHSC	Perspectives on Hebrew Scriptures and Its Contexts
PIBA	Proceedings of the Irish Biblical Association
PRSt	*Perspectives in Religious Studies*
RBS	Resources for Biblical Study
RivB	*Rivista Biblica*
SAAA	Studies on the Apocryphal Acts of the Apostles
SBLEJL	Society of Biblical Literature Early Judaism and Its Literature
SBLSP	*Society of Biblical Literature Seminar Papers*
SBLSymS	Society of Biblical Literature Symposium Series
SBT	Studies in Biblical Theology
SecCent	*Second Century*
SemeiaSt	Semeia Studies
SNTSU (*SNTU.A*)	Studien zum Neuen Testament und seiner Unwelt
SPhiloA	The Studia Philonica Annual
SSEJC	*Studies in Early Judaism and Christianity*
STAC	Studien und Texte zu Antike und Christentum
TBT	*The Bible Today*
TDNT	*Theological Dictionary of the New Testament*. Edited by G. Kittel and G. Friedrich. Translated by G. W. Bromiley. 10 vols. Grand Rapids, 1964–1976
TPQ	*Theologisch-praktische Quartalschrift*
TU	Texte und Untersuchungen
TUGAL	Texte und Untersuchungen zur Geschichte der altchristlichen Literatur
VCSup	*Vigiliae Christianae* Supplements
VTSup	Vetus Testamentum Supplements
WBC	Word Biblical Commentary

WMANT	Wissenschaftliche Monographien zum Alten und Neuen Testament
WUNT	Wissenschaftliche Untersuchungen zum Alten und Neuen Testament
ZÄS	*Zeitschrift für ägyptische Sprache und Altertumskunde*
ZNW	*Zeitschrift für die neutestamentliche Wissenschaft und die Kunde der älteren Kirche*
ZPE	*Zeitschrift für Papyrologie und Epigraphik*

Introduction

The Afterlife in Jewish and Christian Antiquity: Navigating Competing Conceptions as Products of Social Memory

Thomas R. Hatina and Jiří Lukeš

Combining social memory theory and conceptions of afterlife may at first appear to be a strange or even random undertaking. It certainly has not been a common link for historians of antiquity or biblical scholars. At first glance, one might ask, what do memories of the past have to do with hopes and fears about the future? This question, however, assumes a popular view of memory as recollection, retrieval, or reminiscence, which restricts the process of remembering to a backward-looking activity. In this sense, there would be little relevance for personal or communal constructs of the afterlife, apart from cause-and-effect processes whereby, for example, perceived good and evil actions in the past lead to predetermined post-mortem outcomes. As is discussed below, this cavalier use of memory is limiting and does not represent the primary concerns of social memory theorists who focus on the role of the present in constructs of the past. While the present conditions of an ancient author certainly shape how he or she thought about the afterlife, at the same time that present can never be separated from a mediated past that involves a complex process such as selection, arrangement, invention, and forgetting. Conceptions about the future, namely the afterlife, likewise affect how the past is remembered, and vice versa. Cognitive psychologists together with social memory theorists reinforce the dynamic interplay that accounts for the dynamic process that gives content to human hopes and fears.[1]

In this volume, conceptions of afterlife are viewed as products of mnemonic processes that involve degrees of remembering and forgetting by groups who identify (or are acquainted) with Judaism and/or Christianity in antiquity, spanning approximately from the earliest receptions of Israelite traditions within early Judaism to the Patristic/Rabbinic period. It represents a period that acutely fuses what we might today call historical remembrance, family remembrance and religious remembrance. The primary aim of this introduction is to provide contexts for the subsequent essays that focus on social

1 Endel Tulving and Martin Lepage, "Where in the Brain is the Awareness of One's Past?" in *Memory, Brain and Belief*, ed. Daniel L. Schacter and Elaine Scarry (Cambridge: Harvard University Press, 2000), 208–28.

 | DOI:10.30965/9783657796212_002

memory theory as an explanatory hermeneutic and even an organizing principle for various conceptions of the afterlife. This introductory and descriptive essay consists of four parts that are not intended to be directly integrated, but aim to establish the multidimensionality of the contexts. First, we selectively survey the diversity of conceptions. Second, we point to myth as the language most appropriate to afterlife imagery. Third, we focus on both the context of social memory theory and its hermeneutical function. Finally, we explain the aim of this project and provide brief summaries of its contributions.

Conceptions of Afterlife in Jewish and Christian Antiquity

When attempting to understand conceptions of afterlife in Jewish and Christian antiquity, we are immediately struck by two general observations. The first is that these conceptions were diverse, often addressing varying experiences of injustice in relation to the fate of those who are associated with either good or evil actions. The second observation is that our primary medium is the surviving written material. We first turn to the diverse constructs which cannot simply be bifurcated based on Jewish or Christian (or early Christ-followers) identity. They were prevalent within both groups. Smaller communities of Jews, such as Pharisees, Sadducees, Essenes, and a host of diaspora communities throughout the Mediterranean basin, much like contemporary groups that professed to follow Christ, differed among themselves on conceptions such as death, the post-mortem body, the resurrected state, the interval between death and afterlife, the preconditions of afterlife, and the fate of the condemned. There simply was no overarching view of the afterlife in either Jewish or Christian antiquity. The following survey of afterlife conceptions is descriptive and aims to offer an entry into that fascinatingly diverse world.

Diversity of Constructs

Jewish and Christian conceptions of rewards and punishments in the afterlife did not originate in a vacuum. Scholars have often pointed to the influence of Homer's *Iliad* and *Odyssey*. Apart from being widely known in Greek and Roman cultures, these writings contained imaginative tales of afterlife that contrasted from the otherwise mundane and meaningless ideas that were commonplace in the pre-Platonic Greek world. Although death is categorically final for mortals in Homer's writings, the *psychē* ("soul" or "breath") survives the body in the underworld where it exists as a form or "shade" of the body, but does not experience bodily sensations and functions of any kind. It simply exists forever as an immaterial shade. The *Odyssey* is particularly interesting because it contains stories of Odysseus' encounters in Hades with the dead who are unconscious, helpless, and without purpose. Later re-presentations of Homer's imagery (e.g., in Virgil's *Aeneid*, Book 6) alongside the development of afterlife ideas among philosophers, like Plato, laid a foundation for conceptions that are widely believed today. It is impossible to reconstruct the details of popular beliefs about the afterlife since most people in antiquity were illiterate and did not leave a written record, but according to the tombstones that are still legible, the post-mortem existence of the soul appears to have been widely believed. Nevertheless, if we only rely on the surviving literature, one could argue that belief in the soul, the principle of equitable punishment and reward, and spatial notions of heaven and hell in both Judaism and Christianity were influenced by pagan imagination about life beyond this one.

In the Hebrew Bible, the finality of death is lamented and life is seen as fleeting (e.g., Ps 37:20; 1 Chron 29:15; 2 Sam 14:14). Unlike in Greek thought (as represented by the Homeric and Platonic traditions), the ancient Hebrews did not believe in the immortality of the soul. Humanness was understood as the unification of the physical body and the *nephesh*, which was the "life force" or "breath" residing in the neck. In Gen 2:7, God forms Adam from the dust of the earth and breaths life into him, but the breath is not a substance in a dualistic portrayal of humanness. Adam is a unitary being. Consequently, in this text, death is a permanent return to dust. On numerous occasions in the Hebrew Bible, the term *Sheol* is used to refer to humanity's ultimate destination, but it is not a reference to hell or heaven.[2] Neither eternal punishment nor eternal reward are found in the Hebrew Bible. In most uses of the term, it refers to the grave where the corpse is buried. Since the Hebrew Bible expresses religious ideas that span centuries, it is not surprising to find a few deviations from the norm where death is not the end of existence. For example, occasional references to sorcerers (Deut 18:10–11; 1 Sam 28:15) who have the ability to contact the dead imply that death was not viewed as the end of the human story. But the dead in these exceptions do not emerge from *Sheol*. They appear to be spiritual beings who are recognizable. Another example concerns the fate of Israel as a nation which is believed to survive death. Several prophetic writings convey hope that despite Israel's demise, viewed as punishment for sin, the nation will survive (or attain a new lease on life). A prominent example is Ezekiel 37 which metaphorically refers to Israel being buried in the valley of dry bones and then raised to life by God, reminiscent of the creation of Adam. Although the passage refers to Israel's disobedience, exile and return to God, it is often thought to be a precursor to the idea of a national resurrection.

2 See the article in this volume by Craig C. Broyles.

The same afterlife implications can be found in those passages that refer to God's prophets restoring the dead (e.g., 1 Kings 7:17–24) or those where *Sheol* is averted altogether (2 Kings 2:1–12).[3] In light of these deviations, and the many objects of commemoration found from the time of the Iron Age (e.g., everyday objects, food, jewelry, figurines, lamps), it is possible that conceptions of the afterlife were much more diverse than the Old Testament might imply.[4]

Centuries later, during the Maccabean period, some Jews anticipated a day of resurrection that included all of the faithful members of Israel who had unjustly suffered for their faith. Unlike the earlier prophetic literature, the resurrection of individuals appears to overshadow the resurrection of the nation. Their belief in a bodily resurrection of the faithful at the end of the age, as a solution for the injustices they suffered, became the direct influence for the teachings of Jesus and his followers. The book of Daniel (12:1–3), which was influenced by the Maccabean revolt, is the only writing in the Hebrew Bible that anticipates a resurrection of the dead at the end of the age. As in contemporary (non-canonical) Jewish texts of the time (e.g., *1 Enoch; 2 Maccabees*), the idea of just reparations in the afterlife appears to have replaced the traditional explanation of suffering as punishment by God for disobedience. This represented a dramatic shift from the earlier beliefs of a post-mortem nonexistence. Despite the prosperity of the wicked and the suffering of the righteous in this life, it was believed that God will distribute punishments and rewards respectively in the next. Where the initial ideas of resurrection originated is, however, open to debate. In the past, many scholars pointed to Zoroastrianism, but that is less certain today. Nevertheless, conceptions of resurrection varied. Some groups believed that both the righteous and the wicked will be raised to face judgment (e.g., *Pss. Sol.* 13:11) at the end of the age. Other Jews believed that only the righteous will be raised on the Day of Judgment, but the wicked will simply be annihilated at death (*2 Macc.* 7:14). A few believed that a preliminary judgement at the time of death occurs as a prelude to a final Day of Judgment and resurrection (e.g., *4 Ezra; Testament of Abraham*). Others still imagined only one judgement for all to which all are raised immediately after death (*4 Macc.* 18:22–23).[5]

---

3 See, for example, the essays in Jacob Neusner and Alan J. Avery-Peck, eds., *Judaism in Late Antiquity. Part Four: Death, Life-After-Death, Resurrection and the World-to-Come in the Judaisms of Antiquity*, HdO 49 (Leiden: Brill, 2000).

4 Elizabeth Bloch-Smith, *Judahite Burial Practices and Beliefs about the Dead*, JSOTSup 123 (Sheffield: JSOT Press, 1992), 63–115, 140–42.

5 Stefan Alkier, *The Reality of the Resurrection the New Testament Witness* (Waco: Baylor University Press, 2013), 97. If the Mishnah is an accurate representation of early rabbinic

While it appears that most Jews in the Second Temple period believed in some variation of post-mortem resurrection, not all did. Note two prominent examples. First, the Sadducees did not believe in the resurrection (Matt. 22:23; Acts 23:8), nor did they believe in the survival of the soul after death. According to Josephus, they believed that the soul dies with the body (*Ant.* 18:16), and thus by implication, there is no vengeful torture of the soul in the underworld (*War* 2:165), which reflects a more traditional conception of the afterlife. Second, if Philo is representative of Hellenistic Judaism (at least in Egypt), then post-mortem existence looks different still. Since Philo was influenced by Middle Platonism and Stoicism, he believed in a soul that was metaphorized as a shadow, which was an image (of the former glory) of the deceased in the underworld, reminiscent of what we find in Sophocles.[6] While the conceptions lack an eschatological goal, the soul's aim is to transcend the limits of the created cosmos so it can reach the uncreated being. The emphasis of afterlife existence is not so much placed on a location, but on an existence of mind.[7]

Among the early Christians, afterlife conceptions were also diverse. For some Christians, who were less apocalyptically oriented like the evangelist Luke, an immediate post-mortem judgment was assumed (e.g., 23:43; Acts 7:56). Others, like the evangelist Mark, who were rooted in a conception of a cosmic struggle between good and evil, anticipated an imminent (though not immediate) resolution on the Day of Judgment when the righteous (including Jews and Gentiles) would be exalted and the sinners (including Jews and Gentiles) destroyed (e.g., Mark 9:1; Matt 20:16; 23:12). While not eschatological in the same sense, the evangelists John appears to coincide with a delay (e.g., 14:2–3), but also includes references to an already realized judgment (e.g., 5:24–25). What is consistent in the New Testament is that the condemned appear neither to go to hell nor experience eternal torment. Frequently, the righteous are promised resurrection and eternal dwelling with God, but the sinners are promised annihilation, which is often depicted as a process of dying. Justice is preserved on the grounds that the living are presented with a choice. They can either take a narrow path which leads to the way of life or they can take a wider path which leads to destruction (Matt 7:13–14). In contrast to the blissful reward promised to the righteous in God's kingdom, the latter is associated

---

Judaism, then we can say that bodily resurrection became fundamental to its belief in the second century (e.g., *m. Sanh.* 10.1).

6 Cecilia Deutsch, "Visions, Mysteries, and the Interpretive Task: Text Work and Religious Experience in Philo and Clement," in *Experientia, Volume 1: Inquiry into Religious Experience in Early Judaism and Christianity*, ed. Frances Flannery, Colleen Shantz and Rodney A. Werline, SBLSymS 40 (Leiden: Brill, 2008), 83–103, esp. 85, 88, 99–101.

7 Geza Vermes, *The Resurrection* (New York: Penguin Books, 2008), 47.

with fatal imagery such as weeping, teeth grinding, and casting into the fire/furnace. These images do not describe anguish for eternity, but rather the process that leads to annihilation. Even Jesus' reference to Gehenna (often wrongly translated as "hell"), which was associated with a rubbish dump where the "fires never end" and the "worm never dies" (e.g., Isa 66:24), should likewise be viewed as a place where everything decays and not where the decaying process lasts forever (Matt 10:28). Gehenna, called a "valley of curse" in *1 Enoch* 27, was long associated with the place of judgment, the slaughter of Israel's enemies, and even pagan sacrifice before the time of Jesus and not with eternal torment. The same can be said about the judgment of the "goats" in Matt 25:46 which are condemned to "eternal punishment" in contrast to the "sheep" which receive "eternal life." If the contrast is meant to be an antithetical parallelism, then "life" is the opposite of death (not ceaseless torment) which is likely implied by the use of "punishment." This reading is consistent with other Jesus-sayings in the Gospels about the destruction of sinners. While similar divisions of the "saved" and "condemned" are found in other New Testament writings, they differ in that adherence to the significance of Jesus' death and resurrection (and exaltation as the Son of God) becomes the central condition for eternal life. This view is well represented in the Pauline tradition, for example. Similarly, in the Johannine tradition, eternal life is predicated on the testimony that Jesus is the Christ, which again differs from the Synoptic tradition.

The role of baptism in Paul's letters provides another variation. Similar to the baptism of Jesus in Mark's Gospel, which appears to inaugurate Jesus' ministry and identity as God's son, in Romans 6 Paul describes the baptism of the believer as a mystical event that likewise changes one's identity. The baptized are no longer "in Adam," but "in Christ," and thereby participate in his death and eventually his resurrection, escaping the destruction of sinners on the day of God's wrath. Paul views baptism as the beginning of a new life that is united with Christ. It is, in a sense, a taste of the resurrected life before death. Apart from drawing a general parallel to the inauguration of Jesus' ministry and identity, the role of baptism as a precondition to resurrection in the afterlife in Paul's teaching differs considerably. Centuries later, the lack of baptism is viewed as a precondition for eternal torment, irrespective of one's virtues (e.g., Chrysostom, *Hom. Jo.* 5.29).

For Paul, the raising of the righteous does not seem to occur at death, but at the imminent return of Christ when the buried dead are raised just prior to the living who "will be caught up in the clouds together with them to meet the Lord in the air" (1 Thess 4:17). Nothing, unfortunately, is said about the Day of Judgment, the interim state, or those who are not raised to meet the Lord. Their fate is simply described as "sudden destruction" on the "Day of the Lord"

(1 Thess 5:3). Though, in 2 Cor 5:10 Paul says that on the Day of Judgment, everyone will stand before Christ, which indicates that sinners are also raised and then annihilated (as in 1 Cor 15:24, 26). They appear to die a second time after seeing the righteous rewarded, but Paul does not say that they are condemned to eternal torment. During the interim state, the saved appear to be in the presence of Christ, while the unsaved are not. The portrayal leaves one pondering whether the dead are in a non-existent state during the interim period. Or are they just bodiless (i.e., "naked") souls as might be implied in 2 Cor 5:2–4? Are the souls of both the saved and unsaved returned to their bodies at the return of Christ? It is vague.

When it comes to understanding Paul's view of the state of the raised body, the text of choice is 1 Corinthians 15 where Paul strenuously responds to the Corinthians' misunderstanding of the resurrection. It can be surmised from Paul's lengthy response that many of the congregants did not believe in the resurrection of the dead because they saw themselves as already living in a resurrected state. They may have viewed their charismatic experiences, like speaking in tongues and prophesying, as expressions of the resurrected life and in turn may have considered their questionable behaviour as inconsequential. Or, they may have simply been influenced by a Platonic idea that separated the perishable body from the immortality of the soul. Nevertheless, by exaggerating their resurrected state, they separated the pneumatic substance from the physical and thereby considered the actions that were done "in the body" as having no impact on their communal life "in Christ." Paul conceives of resurrection as a transformation that does not allow for the retention of an earthly body, which directly confronts the Corinthian belief. He explains that the nature of Christ's resurrected body should serve as a precedent for what will happen to the believer's body in the imminent resurrection of the dead (1 Cor 15:20). Paul argues that Christ was transformed from having a perishable "flesh (*sarx*) and blood" body to a non-perishable "spiritual body" (*sōma pneumatikon*) when he was raised (1 Cor 15:42–50, also Phil 3:11, 20–23).[8] While Christ's pneumatic body still retained its physicality since his earthly form was recognizable to his followers, it is hard to know how Paul conceived of that physicality and its heavenly state. Did he believe that Jesus' corpse of flesh (*sarx*) and blood was still in the grave while his body (*sōma*) was with the Father? He makes no mention of an empty tomb. The Corinthians may have been the earliest Christian group to have speculated on the nature of the

8 The common translation "spiritual" body is problematic since it does not adequately express the concept of pneumatic substance in antiquity. See Dale B. Martin, *The Corinthian Body* (New Haven: Yale University Press, 1995).

resurrected state. When closely reading the resurrection accounts in Matthew, Luke, and John, it is not clear if the conception of the resurrected state is the same since they contain empty tomb stories. In Luke, for example, the resurrected Jesus avers that he is not a spirit (*pneuma*), but rather a form that has "flesh (*sarx*) and bones" which can digest fish (24:39). Should we presume that Luke thought that Christ's resurrected body had a digestive system? Although both Paul and Luke agree that Jesus was raised bodily, they appear to have different conceptions of that body.[9]

Historians have regularly found that early Christian conceptions of resurrection is a variegated world of ambiguity that even envelops concepts of death. For example, Outi Lehtipuu has convincingly shown that the resurrection of the dead was not always conceived as a physical phenomenon nor was it always limited to post-mortem existence (e.g., John 5:25–29).[10] It also referred to a transformed existence, and not always to the ultimate goal of humanity. As mentioned above, one of the ways that early Christian conceptions incorporated a temporal paradox that enabled them to participate in resurrection, while still alive, was through baptism, which Paul associated with a new life freed from the bondage of sin before resurrection. Some of his followers, however, viewed baptism not just as a taste, but as a realized participation in the resurrected life (Col 2:12–13; Eph 2:1–6), like the aforementioned Corinthians. Other followers of Paul, however, appeared to have opposed the idea that "the resurrection has already taken place" (2 Tim. 2:16–18). Given these early variances and Platonic influences concerning the immortality of the soul, the nature of the resurrected form dominated the debate in some sectors of early Christian thought. Later so-called gnostic Christian communities that separated the spirit from the body and by-passed an apocalyptic eschatology altogether (e.g., *Gos. Thom.* §2) appear to align with some of the early sentiments about a realized resurrection targeted in, for example, 1 Corinthians, Colossians, and the Pastorals. In the second and third centuries, there were still Christians and Jews who were repulsed by the idea of a physical body being united with the soul in the resurrection (e.g., Celsus in Origen, *Cels.* 5, 14; Simon and Cleobius in *3 Corinthians*). In response to these views, considered heretical, many among the proto-orthodox groups advocated strongly for the

9 Note the discussion in Daniel A. Smith, "Seeing a Pneuma(tic) Body: The Apologetic Interests of Luke 24:36–43," *CBQ* 72 (2010): 752–72.

10 Outi Lehtipuu, *Debates over the Resurrection of the Dead: Constructing Early Christian Identity* (Oxford: Oxford University Press, 2015). See also, for example, Bruce D. Chilton, *Resurrection Logic: How Jesus' First Followers Believed God Raised Him from the Dead* (Waco: Baylor University Press, 2019); Dale C. Allison Jr., *Resurrecting Jesus: The Earliest Christian Tradition and Its Interpreters* (London: T & T Clark, 2005).

resurrection of the actual buried body of flesh by pointing to the precedent of Jesus' bodily resurrection. Deniers of this view were threatened with endless conscious torment in the afterlife while adherents were promised eternal bliss in the presence of God. Tertullian, as a representative of proto-orthodox sentiment, even developed a detailed explanation about the fate of souls after death. He was convinced that while the souls of martyrs go directly to paradise, the souls of both the righteous and sinners go to their allocated locations in Hades where they await judgment at the resurrection when souls are united with the same bodies they had at the point of death. Variations on the reward of martyrs continued well beyond Tertullian, including the belief that they became angels just before death (e.g., *Mart. Pol.* 2.3).

The Hellenistic period was also influential for later Jewish and Christian apocalyptic conceptions of cosmic entities that were believed to be responsible for much of the sin in the world. These opponents of God, who were led by the Satan (variously called Beelzebul, the Devil, Mastema, etc.) and his demons, played a significant role in explaining suffering in the context of the cosmic battle between good and evil. While "the Satan" (lit. "accuser" or "adversary") appears a number of times in the Hebrew Bible as a designation for human adversaries, he only appears as a cosmic entity in Job and Zechariah. In both cases, the Satan is not the purely evil instigator of calamity in the world as one finds in the Roman period, but rather he is respectively a divine counselor, albeit not too amicable to humans, and a prosecutor. The belief in God's ultimate victory and the banishment of the evil entities, which was believed by Jesus and his earliest followers, contributed to later developments (mostly from the second century CE onward) of hell and eternal torment at the oversight of Satan and his minions.

Guided by the principles of retribution and vindictiveness, Jews and Christians believed that behaviour (and not just belief) in this life affected one's outcome in the next (e.g., Matt 25:31–46; Rom 2:6–11). While faith in the accomplishments of Jesus should not be minimized, where it is emphasized (e.g., Romans 3, John), the sense is closer to faithfulness as an activity and attitude rather than cognitive belief. In the post-New Testament environment, though already captured in Revelation and possibly Luke (as noted below), the purveyors of righteousness must have derived a great deal of satisfaction in the cause of justice leveled against their brutal oppressors to envision their enemies brutally tormented for eternity (e.g., Cyprian, *Demetr.*17, 24; *Apocalypse of Peter* [discussed below]; *Apocalypse of Paul*). Select Christian writings from the first three centuries list numerous sins that are deserving of eternal torment, but sexual sins are particularly noticeable. By contrast, chastity, purity, and martyrdom become dominant preconditions for reward in the afterlife. As noted earlier, prior to the early Patristic period, however, eternal punishment as torture rarely appears. One of two possible exceptions is the punishment of the Rich Man in Luke 16 who appears to be tormented by fire in Hades forever. Although this story is presented as a parable about helping the needy, it may convey an early localized idea about the afterlife. The other exception is the series of references to an eternal "lake of fire" where "the Beast" and "the false prophet" (Rev 19:20) are ceaselessly tormented. The human followers, however, are killed by the sword (Rev 19:21) and appear to be annihilated. After the final judgement, a thousand years later, the devil joins "the Beast" and "the false prophet" in Hades where they roast forever. The sinners are also thrown into the lake of fire along with "death" and "Hades, but there are no references to their eternal torment. Theirs is a "second death," which refers to extermination (Rev 20:14).[11]

In addition to its paucity in the New Testament, eternal torment is not mentioned in the Hebrew Bible. Even Daniel and its contemporary non-canonical Jewish writings that mention the resurrection of the dead do not include it. While there are references to the wicked being forever reviled and put to shame, their ultimate fate is annihilation, not eternal torment (e.g., *Pss. Sol.* 15:11–13; 4 Ezra 7:61). There are indications in 4 Maccabees (e.g., 9:8–9; 12:11–12; 13:14–15), which is influenced by Greek philosophy, that eternal torment of the soul was beginning to take shape in the early part of the second century CE. This time frame coheres with the rise of similar sentiments about the perpetual fate of sinners in Christianity. In particular, an obsession developed about the gruesome and painful experiences of those who were deemed condemned. While most theologians in the Patristic period believed that divine punishment lasted forever, some like Origen did not. Instead, quoting 1 Cor 15:25, he argued that punishment was a temporary purge of sin that leads all people, even the devil and his demons, to an existence of submission to God (e.g., *Princ.* 1.6.1; 2.10.3).

Without surveying the many varieties of torment imagery in early Christianity, we point to the second-century *Apocalypse of Peter* as a representation. The author graphically writes that after a cataclysmic end to the world, which includes its burning and the melting of the stars, all people will be raised, judged, and divided into two groups. The righteous will reap eternal reward and the sinners will reap eternal punishment which is particularly imaginative, gruesome and extensive. For example, in the Ethiopic text, those

11 See the discussion of "eternal" in Ilaria L. E. Ramelli, *The Christian Doctrine of Apokatastasis: A Critical Assessment from the New Testament to Eriugena*, VCSup 120 (Leiden: Brill, 2013). Ramelli argues that the Bible never uses αἰών or αἰώνιος to refer to "eternal" unless it is used in reference to God (e.g., pages 26–27).

who blasphemed the righteous are hanged by their tongues over "unquenchable flames." Seductive women are hanged by their hair over eternal fire. The seduced men are hanged by their genitals. Women who had abortions are thrown into a deep pit filled with excrement overseeing their aborted children who pierce their mothers' eyes with flashes of lightening. The slanderers of the righteous chew their tongues and are tormented by fiery irons which burn their eyes. Others have their lips cut off and have fire put into their mouths and anuses.

The diversity of afterlife conception in apocryphal Christian texts extends well beyond descriptions of punishments, which can partly be explained due to their broader temporal and geographical representation, but it may also be due to their possible entertainment value. A segment of their audiences may have viewed these writings as fictional, but the extent to which that may have been the case is difficult to ascertain. The imaginative expansions certainly exceed the New Testament. For example, they include post-mortem appearances by apostles (*Mart. Paul* 116), prayers celebrating resurrection and immortality (*Acts John* 207–8), the disappearance of the body of a deceased apostle and its appearance three days later (*Acts John* 115b), resurrections of the dead and visions of sinners' souls in the afterlife (*Acts Thom.* 170–74; *Revelation of Peter*—Greek 21–4, Ethiopic 7–10), the raising of dead animals (*Acts Pet.* 13), and the ascension of the apostles to the ninth heaven (*The Coptic Gnostic Apocalypse of Paul*).

Throughout the long period that is covered in this volume, the process of reception in both Judaism and Christianity that resulted in the transformation of prior teachings and beliefs was a constant. Cultural changes and social demands led to the retellings of received traditions and the inventions of new ones. As the essays in this volume propose, the remembrances of the past, be they traditions, events, or figures, were shaped by the tellers' experiences in their present and their quests for relevance that extended to the future. The survival of the traditions depended on their circulation and adaptability. Often, the experiences entailed suffering, deep loss, torture and privation of justice. A contextualized explanation of this process follows in the next two major sections of this introduction.

Limitations of the Medium

The second observation when studying conceptions of afterlife in Jewish and Christian antiquity is that, apart from funerary inscriptions and artistic expressions (e.g., sarcophagi reliefs, catacomb frescoes, and iconic images), our primary medium is the surviving written material which is contextualized within the peripheries of the literary works and the social conditions they express.

To put it succinctly, the language in which these conceptions are expressed is mythical and the process that contributed to the written expressions is mnemonic.

We are fortunate to have an extensive array of literature from antiquity in which writers creatively engage with their group's origins, identity, destiny, and literary heritage. On occasion, these writers give us glimpses of imagined existence that transcends what we might today call the physical or material world. Yet, these are only windows into their imaginations at certain points in space and time. They are suspended expressions that are usually generated by hopes and fears in tumultuous contexts. In addition, they are restrained by their literary contexts. For us, they are glimpses into a world that was imagined in a vastly different way. But accessibility into that world through them remains limited. Much, if not all, of the written material is representative of scribal elites and we are not sure how influential it was beyond their spheres of influence. We are also not sure about the extent to which popular belief influenced the educated class. While some writings, like Paul's authentic letters, appear to be more broadly representative, again we are unsure about their reach. It is also important to note that written texts were not the usual authoritative medium for normative religious practice and belief.[12] Their meanings were certainly not considered to be fixed since the literary environment in which they were written placed great value on the creativity of retelling. Our treatment of them as archival data banks is problematic if we do not at the same time view them as snapshots of a flowing river.[13]

Conceptions of afterlife are perhaps the pinnacle of human imagination in its struggle to achieve a perceived justice, belonging, and meaning which have profound significance on social values and structures. Imagination by its very nature is creative, fluid, and inventive, but it is always pressured by its reflections on inherited traditions. The process of narrativizing conceptions of afterlife is a merging of the past and present that necessarily involves a remythologizing process if the inherited traditions are to address ever-changing demands. The survival of inherited ideas is contingent on this evolutionary process.

12 Michael Satlow, *How the Bible Became Holy* (New Haven: Yale University Press, 2014), 136–53.

13 Note for example Ben Sira's (24:30) characterization of his work as "a canal from a river" as developed by Eva Mroczek, *The Literary Imagination in Jewish Antiquity* (Oxford: Oxford University Press, 2016), 86–113.

Language of Afterlife

Although the present volume targets the explanatory value of social memory theory for making sense of competing conceptions of afterlife, the process of mythmaking, or mythopoesis, is seamlessly complementary because (1) its narrativized meaning-making function shares in the constitutive elements of the cultural dialectic between past and present, (2) it has a cohesive function among its adherents, (3) it presupposes an integrative transcendent reality as a framework for its drama, and (4) most importantly, it aims at an ideological legitimacy of a group's identity vis–à–vis competing pressures. Myth theorists, like their social memory counterparts, are attuned to the processes of utility, selection, and invention, recognizing that history narrativizes the past in order to create new meanings compelled by the present. Mythmaking, like memory, is not primarily defined by its product or substance, but by its function. Instead of being an object to be studied, it is a form of argumentation or persuasion that legitimizes re-presented embodiments of the past.

Among the several theories of myth on offer, Northrop Frye's concept is particularly suitable for understanding the diversity of afterlife conceptions in written media that reflect temporally overlapping groups.[14] Frye not only views the ideological understanding of mythmaking as identity formation and legitimization, but he also recognizes myth's poetic and imaginative features and functions. In Frye's theory there is no gap between the archetype's origin and its occurrence in consciousness, and hence expression in language, because the archetypes are the structures in language. Since Frye is leery about an "unconscious" that is somehow known, the separation between one's body and mind is more of a distinction whereby the physical is at the same time the ground of language and the source of archetypal form.[15] One of the particular features in Frye's conception that has given it an enduring function and congruence with social memory theory, is its rootedness in the unification of sense perception (called "the literal") and consciousness (which constitutes "the imagination"). Another way of putting it is that it is an integration of material and spiritual aspects of a culture more generally or of a group in particular. Myth expresses the whole of life as a single mental form that attempts to transform the totality of human experience into symbol or art, which expresses

---

14 E.g., Northrop Frye, *Fearful Symmetry: A Study of William Blake* (Princeton: Princeton University Press, 1947); *Words with Power: Being a Second Study of 'The Bible and Literature'* (Toronto: Penguin, 1992).

15 Glen Robert Gill, *Northrop Frye and the Phenomenon of Myth* (Toronto: University of Toronto Press, 2006), 187.

narration that is cohesive for establishing truth and reality. It is as Frye puts it, "the language of belief" out of which literature is existentially commissioned and received.[16] The poet's connection with the past, through various means of retelling, allusion, or quotation, is a maneuver that garners authority by a kind of osmosis whereby the old accepted wisdom, be it expressed by Homer, the Jewish prophets, or the evangelists, finds both a new context and a new veracity in the present. Thus, the poet's particular attribute is not so much a knowledge of *style*, but a broad knowledge of *data* stemming from an understanding of what we might call a mythopoeic history and is closely related to Jan Assmann's "menmohistory."[17]

Apart from the potential benefit that myth has for understanding the process of remembrance (and vice versa), its main value pertains to the function of its language. Viewing conceptions of afterlife as glimpses of mythmaking steers us away from an analogous function of an imagined reality toward a metaphorical one. While the former is more descriptive, detached, and distant, the latter conveys integration of the subject and object, which is more in keeping with processes of embodiment. To speak metaphorically about the spiritual realm is to reveal how subjects prioritize and are unified with (while at the same time alienated from) particular aspects of constructed realities. Here, the medium can only be symbol as it is traversed within social remembrance. The efficacy of symbol is contingent on its cultural familiarity, fluidity, frequency, and utility. As such, traditional theological language is more constrained than what we might find in literary studies which has always appeared to be more comfortable with imagination and invention. Frye distances himself from theological language because it must rely on subjects and objects even when speaking about God, and by extension the afterlife, as immanent or transcendent which leaves language in a more restricted state. Whenever humans are the subject and God is the object, the distance seems unbridgeable even in the use of analogy. Instead of analogy, Frye finds more cohesion in *identity*, which is the principle behind metaphor and imagination, and ultimately myth. Thus, paradoxical claims that two different things are the same, such as "God is man," or "Christ is a lamb" is at the heart of both religious and poetic language, which

16 Northrop Frye, *The Critical Path: An Essay on the Social Context of Literary Criticism* (Bloomington: Indiana University Press, 1971), 36.

17 Jan Assmann, *Moses the Egyptian: The Memory of Egypt in Western Monotheism* (Cambridge, Harvard University Press, 1997), 8–9. Assmann explains, "Unlike history proper, mnemohistory is concerned not with the past as such, but only the past as it is remembered. It surveys the story-lines of tradition, the webs of intertextuality, the diachronic continuities and discontinuities of reading the past." Mnemohistory's aim, then, he says, "is not to ascertain the possible truth of traditions."

resist habitual thinking, expand the mind, and incline toward the imaginative. Frye concisely writes, "I think the real conception 'God' must start in typological metaphor: God is the existential reality of the 'all one body we' metaphor."[18] Identity as the principle of myth is clearly seen in the earliest stories of creation and redemption wherein the gods were identified with the particulars of a created order, such as the sun, the moon, rivers, oceans, plants, and the cycle of life and death. These stories allowed for the identification of individuals and people groups with the world and its life cycle. The identification process in myth occurs within the historicizing of the stories. In other words, because of events that have happened in a distant past, we are who we are and we will be who we will be even in the afterlife. The present and the past are brought together in myth, though never apart from the universal human narrative whose plot extends from creation to apocalypse.[19] Afterlife conceptions are integrated within these broader narrations.

Myth as an identity narration still includes ideology. However, instead of viewing myth as the narrativizing of ideology, as suggested for example by Bruce Lincoln,[20] Frye argues that ideology is subordinate to myth. Myth creates ideology, which in turn selects, adapts, historicizes, and applies myth in the formation of a social belief system. Myth in this context provides an identity and a shared knowledge proclaiming what must be known.[21] The belief is akin to adherence, obedience, and at times even fact, and is often reinforced by a power structure. Since ideology, according to Frye, is monological and exclusive, it is very guarded in permitting competing ideologies to be dialogue partners. To restrict dialogue that potentially challenges existing ideologies is for Frye a controlling tendency that is authoritative and aggressive. The mythic underpinnings become especially visible when an ideology is enforced or advanced in extreme ways.[22] Divergence from the dominant ideology also has political consequences at the institutional level. Myth is potentially threatening to the foundations of societal structure because it elicits new visions of reality for this life and the next. This process is particularly noticeable in more

18 Robert D. Denham, ed., *Northrop Frye's Notebooks and Lectures on the Bible and Other Religious Texts*, Collected Works of Northrop Frye, Volume 13 (Toronto: University of Toronto Press, 2003), 350.

19 Robert D. Denham, *Northrop Frye: Religious Visionary and Architect of the Spiritual World* (Charlottesville: University of Virginia Press, 2004), 9; Northrop Frye, *Myth and Metaphor: Selected Essays, 1974–1988*, ed. Robert D. Denham (Charlottesville: University of Virginia Press, 1990), 115.

20 Bruce Lincoln, *Theorizing Myth: Narrative, Ideology, and Scholarship* (Chicago: University of Chicago Press, 1999).

21 Frye, *Words with Power*, 31.

22 Frye, *Words with Power*, 23–24.

institutionalized notions of the resurrection and eternal punishment in the patristic period.

Remembrance of Afterlife: Setting the Context for Social Memory Studies

The interpretation of biblical and cognate texts from the perspective of social memory has been a welcomed development in recent years, which has impacted how they are approached hermeneutically, methodologically, historically and exegetically. The interest reflected in scholarly organizations (notably the European Association of Biblical Studies, the Society of Biblical Literature, and the Society of New Testament Studies) and the expanding list of publications shows no signs of waning. Within the fields of the Hebrew Bible, its textual traditions (e.g., LXX), Second Temple literature, and even early Rabbinic writings, practitioners of social memory theory have commonly engaged with the ground-breaking work of Jan and Aleida Assmann who have provided hypothetical explanations of processes that span from archived memories to functional memories. Their work has contributed to a better understanding of how and why received traditions are (and need to be) altered, invented and even forgotten.[23] Remembrance has served as an explanatory tool, beyond the earlier work of Gerhard von Rad, for understanding the pragmatic processes that accounted for Israel's conceptions of the past as representations of identity.

Interest in social memory has been particularly robust in early Christian studies. Within the last two decades, appropriations of social memory theory have challenged the way we think about the Gospels, their underlying oral traditions, historiography, the methods in historical Jesus research, reconstructions of Paul, and more broadly our understanding of the reception process in the expansion of Christian thought well beyond the first century. At the core of the challenges are the assumptions of transmission operative in form

23 E.g., Aleida Assmann, *Erinnerungsräume: Formen und Wandlungen des kulturellen Ged. chtnisses* (Munich: C. H. Beck, 1999); Assmann, *Moses the Egyptian*. See also the important work of Ehud Ben Zvi, *Social Memory among the Literati of Yehud*, BZAW 509 (Berlin: de Gruyter 2019); Diana V. Edelman and Ehud Ben Zvi, eds., *Leadership, Social Memory and Judean Discourse in the 5th–2nd Centuries BCE*, Worlds of the Ancient Near East and Mediterranean (London: Equinox, 2016); Diana V. Edelman and Ehud Ben Zvi, eds., *Remembering Biblical Figures in the Late Persian & Early Hellenistic Periods: Social Memory and Imagination* (Oxford: Oxford University Press, 2013); Ehud Ben Zvi and Christoph Levin, eds., *Remembering and Forgetting in Early Second Temple Judah*, FAT 85 (Tübingen: Mohr-Siebeck, 2012).

criticism, redaction criticism, the criteria of authenticity, and generally the long tradition of German Protestant hermeneutics. The so-called Third Quest (and inherited elements of the New Quest) of Jesus research is considered to be over by proponents of social memory theory. While a few propose that we are now in a new "No Quest" period, many suggest that we are at the beginning of a "memory approach," claiming that the past of Jesus, which is called the "mediated past," is knowable *through* or is contained *within* the memory process, not *behind* it or *apart* from it.[24] In relation to mediated transmission, the "memory approach" is not entirely new. The work, for example, of Birger Gerhardsson (interestingly siding with form critics), which focused on the process of transmission in Tannaitic and Amoraic Judaism, along with the later work of Werner Kelber, which opened a new dimension of research focused on the transition from oral discourse to textuality in earliest Christianity, became important building blocks for today's conversations.[25] While there has been a more deliberate reliance in recent years on the reception constructs of social memory theorists such as the Assmanns, Barry Schwartz and Jeffrey Olick, there are still unresolved comparisons and contrasts with post-World War II influences stemming from literary criticism, history, philosophy, psychology, and sociology. Nevertheless, today's appropriations of social memory theory often coincide with postmodern epistemological assumptions in the humanities and social sciences.

Interdisciplinary Milieu of Social Memory Studies

The study of memory in the European context can be traced all the way back to Plato, Aristotle, the Greek and Roman rhetoricians, ancient rhapsodies, and oral poetry. More directly, however, the theoretical underpinnings of current issues related to remembering, forgetting, identity formation, and the role of the collective lie in the modernist and emerging postmodernist thinking among philosophers like René Descartes, Gottfried Leibniz, John Lock, Henri Bergson, Giambattista Vico, Friedrich Nietzsche, Georg Hegel,

---

24 E.g., Jens Schröter, Rafael Rodríguez, Chris Keith and Anthony Le Donne. Note especially the essays in Chris Keith and Anthony Le Donne, eds., *Jesus, Criteria, and the Demise of Authenticity* (London: T & T Clark, 2012).

25 Birger Gerhardson, *Memory and Manuscript: Oral Tradition and Written Transmission in Rabbinic Judaism and Early Christianity* (Lund: C. W. K. Gleerup, 1961). Werner H. Kelber, *The Oral and the Written Gospel: The Hermeneutics of Speaking and Writing in the Synoptic Tradition, Mark, Paul, and Q* (Philadelphia: Fortress Press, 1983). Note also the earlier awareness of mediated transmission in Rudolf Bultmann, *Die Geschichte der synoptischen Tradition* (Göttingen: Vandenhoeck & Ruprecht, 2011); Martin Dibelius, *Die Formgeschichte des Evangeliums* (Tübingen: J. C. B. Mohr, P. Siebeck, 1933).

Immanuel Kant, Wilhelm Dilthey, Friedrich Schleiermacher, Theodor Adorno and Walter Benjamin.[26]

Today's widespread interest in social memory theory can be traced to French sociologists, notably Émile Durkheim (1858–1917) and Maurice Halbwachs (1877–1945). Their probes into how social contexts affect remembrances of the past was limited to the field of sociology, but this is no longer the case. The implications of the relationship between the present and the past, both in relation to remembering and forgetting, have been far-reaching. Although Halbwachs' use of "collective memory" and "social memory" at times overlaps, each conveys a distinct aspect. Collective memory refers to a shared cultural past that individuals recall and constantly shape; whereas social memory refers to the influence of the social framework on the individual's memory.[27] Today, the terminology is used inconsistently. What is more, social memory is redefined further in relation to temporality, as is discussed below. Nevertheless, the act of social remembrance contributes to social cohesion that not only delineates societal boundaries between those who are members of a group and those who are not, but also helps a social group to identify itself through shared recollection of its past in relation to the larger world around it. As a meaning-making phenomenon, it is essentially hermeneutical, performative and process-oriented.

Social memory theory, as it was conceived by Halbwachs, paid particular attention to the function of religion in society. One of Halbwachs' key observations on the function of memory within religious frameworks is that recollections of the past are assimilated within the frameworks of the present. While the past is continually (re)shaped and (re)collected so as to have meaning in the present, the present is continually informed and guided by the past, especially if the tradition is older and its adoption is widespread. The function of religion was fruitful ground for Halbwachs' contemporaries as well, such as Durkheim whose conception of "collective consciousness"[28] overlapped with

26 Manfred Weinberg, "Historický přehled," in *Paměť a trauma pohledem humanitních věd*, trans. Alexander Kratochvíl (Praha: Karolinum, 2015), 12–30, esp. 20–25. Originally published as "Trauma—Geschichte, Gespenst, Literatur – und Gedächtnis," in *Trauma. Zwischen Psychoanalyse und kulturellem Deutungsmuster*, ed. Elisabeth Bronfen, Birgit R. Erdle, and Sigrid Weigel (Köln: Böhlau, 1999), 173–206.

27 See Sandra Huebenthal, "Social and Cultural Memory in Biblical Exegesis: The Quest for an Adequate Application," in *Cultural Memory in Biblical Exegesis*, ed. Pernille Carstens, Trine Hasselbalch, and Niels Peter Lemche, Perspectives on Hebrew Scriptures and its Contexts 17 (Piscataway: Gorgias Press, 2012), 191–216.

28 Émile Durkheim, *Sociologie a filosofie* (Praha: Sociologické nakladatelství, 1998), 38, 44–45.

Karl Marx's "class consciousness."[29] The focus on religion allowed for deeper examinations of the expressions of collective ideals communicated through various media to different levels of society.[30] Benedetto Croce well examined the deep structure of historical consciousness of idealism which highlighted the crisis of historicism and led to the undermining of historians' demands for objectivity, scientism, and realism.[31]

The early ideas have undergone considerable development in their engagements with a wide array of disciplines such as history, literary criticism, and most recently cultural studies, computer science (computer, as externalized memory) and neurology.[32] Reflecting on the causes that have contributed to the growing interest in memory, Jan Assmann and Pierre Nora have highlighted the technological transformation of (Western) society, the declining number of holocaust witnesses, and our changing relationship to the traditional conceptions of the past.[33] For instance, historians attuned to memory studies have contributed to the criticism of official versions of history and prioritized unofficial versions that are sometimes referred to as the "cancelled or confiscated past,"[34] which impacted new conceptions of historiography through the lens of New Historicism.[35] From a slightly different angle, Jay Winter identifies contemporary memory studies as being built upon and interacting with the first two generations of "memory booms" within the last century. The first boom, spanning from the 1890s to the 1920s, focussed on the formation of identities, particularly national identities, though not to the exclusion of social, cultural and individual identities. The remembrances of the fallen after the Great War figured prominently in the first boom. The second boom, according to Winter, emerged in the 1960s and 70s when considerable attention was paid to the remembrances of World War II and the Holocaust. The second boom penetrated many of the national narratives of the first boom, resulting in "memory"

29 Hayden White, *Metahistory: The Historical Imagination in Nineteenth-Century Europe* (Baltimore: The Johns Hopkins University Press, 1973), 38–42.

30 Břetislav Horyna and Helena Pavlincová, *Dějiny religionistiky* (Olomouc: Nakladatelství Olomouc, 2001), 131–32.

31 White, *Metahistory*, 40–41.

32 Assmann, *Erinnerungsräume*, 16.

33 Pierre Nora, "L'avènement Mondial de la mémoire," in: *Tr@nsit online* 22/2002, 19 April 2002—*EUROZINE*: https://ez.gridworks.sk/lavenement-mondial-de-la-memoire/?pdf, 1–9. See also Weinberg, "Historický přehled," 12.

34 Nora, "L'avènement Mondial de la mémoire," 1. Roman Rakowski, "Postmodernismus jako nekonečná rozmanitost," *Filosofický časopis* 67 (2019): 227–40, esp. 228–29.

35 Hayden White, *Tropics of Discourse: Essays in Cultural Criticism* (Baltimore: The Johns Hopkins University Press, 1978), 121–25.

being used metaphorically for finding a "useable past" or what Nora calls *lieux de mémoire*.[36]

While biblical studies is a latecomer, it had formed a favourable foundation given its selective pockets of interest in history, sociology, philosophy and a wide range of literary criticism including formalism, structuralism, poststructuralism, and New Criticism.[37] Today, we are witnessing a fragmentation whereby scholars who are influenced by some of these approaches clash hermeneutically with more traditional historical approaches that are built on the "Schleiermacher-Gadamer" foundations, traditional German historiography, and phenomenology.[38] One of the most debated topics, for example, is the question of what constitutes continuity and discontinuity of a mediated tradition when it is viewed as memory. Tangentially, this topic interacts with well-established discussions about the relationship between memory and history. The so-called end of the philosophy of history, the resignation of the topic of "Truth," the beginning of the era of "emotivism" as a social way of behaving, and the advancement of cultural studies also play a role in current divisions. Often (and often unknowingly in biblical studies) the debates are rooted in a hermeneutical divide between the reductionisms advocated within structuralist conceptions and the intertextual "uncertainties" of poststructuralism.[39]

As one might already infer, it is impossible to capture the nuances of the current state of hermeneutics in biblical studies in this brief overview, but we can say that its interdisciplinary engagement in select pockets is a reflection of the current (hypermodern) epoch which views the transformation of historical consciousness into social consciousness where the explanatory value of memory studies thrives.[40]

Given the pervasive function of memory at every level of human existence, numerous disciplines have contributed to the development of what is today called "memory studies." In the field of sociology, inquiry into the relationship between collective and personal identity in relation to memory and

---

36 Jay Winter, *Remembering War: The Great War Between Memory and History in the Twentieth Century* (New Haven: Yale University Press, 2006), 17–40.

37 Elizabeth A. Clark, *History, Theory, Text: Historians and the Linguistic Turn* (Cambridge: Harvard University Press, 2004), 9.

38 The main problem today is not the fragmentations that have led to hermeneutical trajectories, which has been a healthy examination of what exegesis is about. Rather, the problem is the lack of communication among the fragmented interest groups. The uniqueness of biblical studies, in contrast to many other disciplines, is its close relationship with highly theologized and ideologized interests.

39 Jonathan Culler, *Literary Theory: A Very Short Introduction* (New York: Oxford University Press, 2000), 42–44.

40 Nora, "L'avènement mondial de la mémoire," 1, 6–7.

society—advocated, for example, by Charles Cooley, George Mead, Erving Goffman, Peter Berger, Thomas Luckmann, and Klaus Eder—remains a vital component to this day.[41] Attention to memory and its implications for interpretation also appeared in modernist literature like that of Marcel Proust, who is responsible for the opposition between free and involuntary memory, and James Joyce, who addresses the relationship between music and Irish cultural memory.[42]

The field of psychology was particularly influential for the development of social memory theory. Psychological or individual memory was not rejected by Halbwachs, but was viewed as an expression of the social patterning of an individual's social group. Halbwachs argued that no memories are independent from social frameworks.[43] Ironically, early critique of individual memory in the works, for example, of Sigmund Freud and Carl Jung, has led to mutually beneficial interactions. Today, memory studies have a significant impact on psychology, neurology (as well as genetics), and their tangential applications such as socio-cognitive and socio-scientific inquiry into early Christianity.

In modern history, the study of social memory has been well established. It has been connected with the study of orality and the transmission of memories across generations. One of the key insights that continues to be widely held is that the past is always mediated. Appropriations of social memory theory by some biblical scholars (as mentioned above) is an expression of a much broader and ongoing debate about the relationship between what is considered as history among professional historians and what is considered as memory. Wulf Kansteiner captures one aspect of the debate when he writes,

> Collective memory is not history, though it is sometimes made from similar material. It is a collective phenomenon but it only manifests itself in the actions and statements of individuals. It can take hold of historically and socially remote events but it often privileges the interests of the contemporary. It is as much a result of conscious manipulation as unconscious absorption and it is always mediated.[44]

---

41 Jakub Mlynář, "Vztah paměti a identity v soudobé sociologii," in *Kolektivní paměť. K teoretickým otázkám*, ed. Nicolas Maslowski and Jiří Šubrt (Praha: Karolinum, 2014), 257–76, esp. 262–66.

42 Weinberg, "Historický přehled," 25. Assmann, *Erinnerungsräume*, 236–40, 270–71.

43 Maurice Halbwachs, *On Collective Memory*, trans. Lewis A. Coser (Chicago: University of Chicago Press, 1992). Originally published as *Les Travaux de L'Année Sociologique* (Paris, F. Alcan, 1925), 43, 50–51.

44 Wulf Kansteiner, "Finding Meaning in Memory: A Methodological Critique of Collective Memory Studies," *History and Theory* 41 (2002): 179–97, here 180.

Similarly, studies of ancient literature and non-literary material have shown that historical knowledge can no longer be classified into individual disciplines (without significant reduction). Formerly narrow terms like "archaeology" or "archive" have become integrated with multidisciplinary research.[45] This shift has been well articulated by both Jan and Aleida Assmann, who began to apply the term "archaeology" to their understanding of ancient mnemonic practices since the 1970s.[46] Their synthesis allowed for a historical study of ancient texts in pre-literacy epochs. However, the notion of "history" seemed too reductive because it expanded inquiry to include the medium of writing, memory, tradition, techniques of accumulation of knowledge, orality, the technology of recording and of the transmission of information, culture, methods of communication, and so on. In the 1960s and 70s, research by the "Toronto School" contributed to the synthesis, notably by Marshall McLuhan whose work brought further attention to the social role of orality (especially among Milman Parry, Albert Lord, William Whallon) and its impact on writing (as in the work of Jack Goody). At the same time, in philosophy there was a vigorous discussion among structuralists and poststructuralists (expanded into literary theory) which likewise brought considerable attention to the medium of writing, language systems, text perceptions, and authorial intention (e.g., Michel Foucault, Roland Barthes, Jacques Lacan, and Jacques Derrida).[47] The interdisciplinarity has freed scholars to move from one field to another. Previously distinct fields such as ethnology, anthropology, religion, and archeology can now be seen as important contributors to literary studies.[48]

The ancient religious text, as a suspended expression in time and space, is inseparable from the question of its "extended situation" given its connections with tradition, oral culture, cultural transformation, cultural continuity, cultural coherence, rituals, holidays, and remembrance.[49] The interdisciplinary questions find a common denominator in social memory, which provides a structuring matrix for understanding the numerous manifestations of human society. Memory is both a medium experienced and acquired through transmission and structured by social or cultural frameworks that continually change. Thus, memory can transmit values and information that are found in

45 Michel Foucault, *Archeologie vědění* (Praha: Herrmann & synové, 2016), 201. Originally published as *L'archéologie du savoir* (Editions Gallimard, 1969).

46 E.g., Aleida and Jan Assmann, "Exkurs: Archäologie der literarischen Kommunikation," in *Einführung in die Literaturwissenschaft*, ed. Miltos Pechlivanos, Stefan Rieger, Wolfgang Struck, and Michael Weitz (Stuttgart: Verlag J. B. Metzler, 1995), 200.

47 A. and J. Assmann, "Exkurs: Archäologie der literarischen Kommunikation," 201.

48 A. and J. Assmann, "Exkurs: Archäologie der literarischen Kommunikation," 202.

49 A. and J. Assmann, "Exkurs: Archäologie der literarischen Kommunikation," 203.

traditions, textual records, social conditions, social moods, national identities, diverse interactions, and personal experiences or preferences that affect our preconceptions and orientations in the world. Attention to memory (and forgetting) is an irreplaceable hermeneutical step that reveals value judgments about the analyzed texts and its testimonies. As part of that hermeneutical step, memory also reflects the critic and his or her location in the academic quest. For example, trends in literary criticism, social thought, or epistemology in either European or North American universities play a role in conceptions of the present from which analysis takes place. In addition, varied conceptions of social memory will determine aims and conclusions.[50]

The Community and the Text

Collective memory can foster as well as dampen changes in a group's sense of identity and character as it relates itself to a past.[51] Its distinction from that of historical memory goes back to Halbwachs whose focus on the present has undoubtedly been influential, but his ill-defined concept of "the past" has left his theory deficient in this regard. While Halbwachs accepted that the past is a prior cause of memory, it is not what we might call "the actual past." Halbwachs' ambivalence toward the past has proven to be unsatisfying for current social memory theorists working with ancient literature, notable Jan and Aleida Assmann in Germany and Barry Schwartz in the United States. Building on Halbwachs, contemporary social memory theorists view memory as a sign (or effect) of communal affiliation. For instance, Aleida Assmann broadens the distinction by claiming that, "Die Gedachtnistheorien von Nietzsche, Halbwachs oder Nora betonen den konstruktivistischen, identitatssichernden Charakter der Erinnerung und affirmieren deren Recht gegeniiber einer objektiven und neutralen historischen Geschichtswissenschaft" ("Nietzsche's, Halbwachs', and

50 Marie-Claire Lavabre ("Historiography and Memory," in *A Companion to the Philosophy of History and Historiography*, ed. Aviezer Tucker [Chichester: Blackwell Publishing, 2009], 362–70, here. 363) writes, "A general synthesis would be unwieldy. Today, it appears that three main conceptual approaches to memory co-exist. The first is that of 'realms of memory' (*lieux de mémoire*), a term coined by Pierre Nora; the second is that of 'the working through of remembering' (*travail de mémoire*), associated with Paul Ricoeur. The third is that of 'frameworks of memory' (*cadres de la mémoire*) which emerged from Maurice Halbwachs' thoughts on the social conditions of the construction and evocation of memory. Although these three approaches co-exist and often overlap, they were nonetheless elaborated at different periods, are anchored in different disciplines, and focus on different objects."

51 Aleida Assmann, *Prostory vzpomínání. Podoby a proměny kulturní paměti*, trans. Jakub Flanderka, Světlana Ondroušková and Jiří Soukup (Praha: Karolinum, 2018), 149. Originally published as *Erinnerungsräume*.

Nora's memory theories emphasize the constructivist nature of memory that ensures its identity-formative character, and affirm objections to an objective and neutral historical science").[52] Her observation addresses the tension that persists between memory and history (developed below). Unlike traditional conceptions of collective memory that stem from the Renaissance, today's theorist is no longer concerned with individual experience, but rather with groups and communities.[53] While metanarratives that have served as interpretive guides for history no longer have legitimacy among postmodern thinkers, the emphasis now lies on "smaller" stories of everyday life since these include more accurate information about both individuals and their memberships in communities.[54]

Contemporary approaches to social memory and its relationship to community requires several distinctions, which have not always shared the same terminology among theorists. As a result, definitions are always required. To reiterate, we use *social* memory as a generic term to cover the varied temporal distinctions simply for the sake of convenience.[55] When the time frame of reception is under consideration, most critics refer to three different stages of memory. *Communicative* memory is a designation used for the daily oral interactions within the first generation of reception. *Collective* (sometimes *social*) memory is used as a designation for the memories that have endured (roughly within the 30–70-year timeframe) within more iconic or mythic frameworks shared by the broader culture. This is not just the sum of the memories of the members of a group, but a shaped account that reflects the distinctive character of the group which contributes to its unification.[56] The collective identity derives from it. Collectives stabilize memories, just as memories stabilize groups. Finally, *cultural* memory refers to longstanding and established memories that can include customs, memorials, rituals, important texts, and fixed

52 Assmann, *Erinnerungsräume*, 133.

53 Nora, "L'avènement Mondial de la mémoire," 6–7.

54 Jean-François Lyotard, *O postmodernismu* (Praha: Filosofický ústav AV ČR, 1993), 30. Originally published as *Le condition postmoderne* (Paris: Editions de Minuit 1979). See also Jean-François Lyotard, *Le postmoderne expliqué aux enfants* (Paris: Editions Galilée 1986).

55 This differs from Halbwachs' use of "collective memory" and "social memory." Each conveys a distinct aspect. For him, collective memory refers to a shared cultural past that individuals recall and constantly shape; whereas social memory refers to the influence of the social framework on the individual's memory.

56 "Memory is said to be collective not because it is the memory of the group as such, but because the collective, or the social, is the state in which individuals exist. It should be added that any reflection on this interaction must take the multiple loyalties of individuals into account." Lavabre, "Historiography and Memory," 368.

memory points from the past.[57] These memories represent a community's concretized values, practices and structures.[58]

As a communal product, a written text in antiquity is not just a projection of its author's ideals, memories, and thought constructions. The text also reflects the needs and identity of the author's community, which then listens to the text and extends its reach. A text that endures to the stage of cultural memory is received as a contributor to a concretized identity.[59] The process is influenced by variable pressures of the present together with backward projections onto past events, which results in making some memories (intentionally) irrelevant and forgotten while others are given space for incorporation, sometimes leading to new interpretations of the past or even shifts in communal identity. Irrelevant memories can take the form of *concord-fictions* that create the illusion of collective experience.[60] The fiction of conformity fills vacuums with meaning. They are unpredictably fluid. They are not refutable even by means of falsification, and their status depends on the recipients' attitudes toward them.[61] Thus, processes of memory can both reduce meanings and simultaneously incorporate new ones even if they are not based on real experiences or events.

The Hermeneutical Framework

As was already stated several times, the growing popularity of memory studies has been impacted by the paradigmatic shift in approaches to history and historiography which significantly impacts the study of ancient Jewish and Christian writings. Today, many biblical scholars who appropriate social

57 Harald Welzer, "Co je to komunikativní paměť a z čeho se skládá," in *Paměť a trauma pohledem humanitních* věd, ed. Alexander Kratochvíl (Praha: Karolinum, 2015), 73–89, esp. 75. Originally published as "Das kommunikative Gedächtnis und voraus ae besteth," in *Arbeit am Gedächtnis*, ed. Michael Frank and Gabriele Rippl (München: Fink, 2007), 47–62.

58 On nomenclature, especially with reference to biblical studies, see Sandra Huebenthal, "Social and Cultural Memory in Biblical Exegesis: The Quest for an Adequate Application," in *Cultural Memory in Biblical Exegesis*, ed. P. Carstens et al., Perspectives on Hebrew Scriptures and its Contexts 17 (Piscataway: Gorgias, 2012), 191–216; "'Frozen Moments'—Early Christianity through the Lens of Social Memory Theory," in *Memory and Memories in Early Christianity*, ed. Simon Butticaz and Enrico Morelli, WUNT 398 (Tübingen: Mohr Siebeck, 2018), 17–43.

59 Jan Assmann, "Collective Memory and Cultural Identity," *New German Critique* 65 (1995): 125–33, esp. 125, 127–28.

60 Frank Kermode, *The Sense of an Ending: Studies in the Theory of Fiction* (New York: Oxford University Press 2000), 53–54, 58–59.

61 Wolfgang Iser, *The Fictive and the Imaginary: Charting Literary Anthropology* (Baltimore: The Johns Hopkins University Press, 1993), 89–93, esp. 90–91.

memory theory agree that the actual past is not accessible, but is mediated at every level of reception. Yet, at the same time, there remains a pervasive historical positivism that is more optimistic about reconstructions that can reveal the actual past. When narratives about the past (and from the past) are viewed as remembrances, they invite hermeneutical queries that span from the assumed author to his/her implied readers and beyond to levels of reception that include the contemporary critic. Since every level of reception is mediated, the process of memory can tell us much more about competing conceptions (and the identities of those groups who hold them) of the past than the actual past itself. This realization did not arise in a vacuum, but in addition to the interdisciplinary influences addressed above, the main impetus has come from the intersection of literary criticism and history, to which we now turn.[62] Since ancient written texts are preservations of memories in specific times and places, an analysis of how that medium is perceived is of vital importance for understanding the mnemonic process at every stage of reception.

These shifts in how history and historiography are perceived are especially well documented in the works of Hayden White and Aleida Assmann.[63] At a theoretical level, the dominant influence was the growing interest in New Historicism, which gained momentum especially in the United States since the 1980s. As a literary theory, New Historicism approaches literature from varied historical perspectives that bring to the forefront the hermeneutical premise that the wider historical context includes not only how the author reflects his own times, but also how the critic's conclusions reflect his or hers as well. It draws close connections in the interrelationship between literature and history, creating suspicions of positivist links between history and the actual past.[64] For New Historicists, history is a construct in which the past and the present reflect each other through a narrated medium.[65] It is commonly proposed that there are only texts and their various connections (described as intertextuality). Thus, the historian (of literature) has no history at his disposal. He or she only has literature that can be compared and contrasted as

62 In New Testament studies, note the intersection of social memory theory, history, and narrative criticism in Huebenthal, *Reading Mark's Gospel.*

63 E.g., Hayden White, *Tropics of Discourse: Essays in Cultural Criticism* (Baltimore: The Johns Hopkins University Press, 1986), 123–25. Assmannová: *Prostory vzpomínání*, 53–56.

64 Jean E. Howard, "The New Historicism in Renaissance Studies," *English Literary Renaissance* 16 (1986): 13–43. Terry Eagleton, *Literary Theory: An Introduction* (Minneapolis: University of Minnesota Press, 2008), 115–16.

65 Antoine Compagnon, *Démon teorie. Literatura a běžné myšlení* (Brno: Host 2009), 232. Originally published as *Le Démon de la théorie. Littérature et sens commun* (Paris: Editions du Seuil 1998).

fragmentary discourses that are connected by the author/editor/community and allocated to various chronologies.[66] At the advent of New Historicism, efforts were in play to overcome the familiar reading techniques associated with close reading, which was the standard approach that dominated the Anglo-Saxon world. Adherents of this New Criticism, which was more concerned with how texts present ideas, have been debating with adherents of a positivist literary historiography since the 1930s and 1940s about reconstructions of authorial intentions.[67] New Criticism was foundational for later New Historicism which reacted against viewing a text, its historical context, its readers and its criticism in isolation.

New Critics approached literary works by using their own categories and concepts.[68] They were built on the principle that there are no "innocent" readers just as there are no "objective" texts, writings, or readings since so-called "natural" processes and past critical endeavors only masked political or economic ideology.[69] According to the New Critics, writing cannot be treated as a spoken language since the written text does not depend on the presence of a speaker.[70] Meaning is viewed as the creation of generally shared labeling systems that is captured in the slogan, "writing writes, not authors."[71] The longstanding concern for reconstructing authorial intention began to dissolve, especially in light of the work of Foucault and Barthes (which, despite considerable differences with New Criticism, displaced the authority of the author).[72] The author was replaced by speech, and attention was focused on the text or subject in a grammatical or linguistic sense. Texts were perceived as autonomous and ahistorical objects constructed of quotations.[73] The aim of the critic

66 Compagnon, *Démon teorie*, 232.

67 Michael Weitz, "Zur Karriere des Close Reading: New Criticism, Werkästhetik und Dekonstruktion," in *Einführung in die Literaturwissenschaft*, ed. Miltos Pechlivanos, Stefan Rieger, Wolfgang Struck, and Michael Weitz (Stuttgart: Verlag J. B. Metzler, 1995), 354–65, esp. 356–57.

68 Terence Hawkes, *Structuralism and Semiotics* (London: Routledge, 1992), 125–33, esp. 126–27.

69 Hawkes, *Structuralism and Semiotics*, 127–28.

70 Hawkes, *Structuralism and Semiotics*, 132–33. Bruce A. Rosenberg, "The Complexity of Oral Tradition," *Oral Tradition*, 2.1 (1987): 73–90, esp. 74–75.

71 Hawkes, *Structuralism and Semiotics*, 132–33. Eagleton, *Literary Theory*, 93–94.

72 Peter Szondi, *Úvod do literární hermeneutiky* (Brno: Host 2003), 53. Originally published as *Einführung in die literarische Hermeneutik* (Frankfurt am Main: Suhrkamp Verlag, 1975). Compagnon, *Démon teorie*, 50.

73 Compagnon, *Démon teorie*, 51. The theory of intertextuality also played a role in their cause, which views literature as a fabric of intertwined texts that do not form a continuous series of successive works, but the interrelationships of various texts. Shamma Schahadat, "Intertextualität: Lektüre—Text—Intertext," in *Einführung in die Literaturwissenschaft*,

was to reveal information that is only offered in the text itself.[74] It was proposed that the unity of the text is created not by the author (or the text's origin), but by the reader (to whom the text is oriented).[75] However, the reader is no longer personal, "but transforms into a mere function," and the same fate meets the author who becomes an "authorial function," according to Foucault.[76] In addition to the French critics, the aforementioned American New Critics, who also eliminate the author to ensure the independence of literary criticism from a positivist sense of history, came into play.[77] While New Critics at least acknowledged that literature offered some knowledge of the world, Northrop Frye pushed the boundaries even further and fenced literature off from the contamination of a positivist sense of history as an "autonomous verbal structure" that did not refer to a reality beyond its boundaries.[78]

Historiography was interrelated with these currents in literary criticism since authors writing about the past were likewise viewed as reflecting their contexts and even universal systems.[79] The influence of deconstruction, through the work of Jacque Derrida and its popularizing in America through the Yale School, impacted literary critics who gradually began to incorporate into their conceptions of interpretation an emphasis on the encounter with culture since its assumed unity was believed to reveal the unity of texts.[80] Disagreements about presumptions of what constituted the "canon of literary works" emerged (in the 1990s), and with it came the emphasis on cultural interpretations that targeted "reminders, directed against unjust forgetfulness."[81] These deconstructive readings were conceived by some as analyses of cultural memory (even of the critic).[82] The idea that the historian has access to objective reality and can independently access facts within a structuralist framework has led to tensions between memory and historiography.[83] The New Historicism influenced by Foucault, who described culture as a web of (knowledge) power relations, was influenced by Marxist analysis and incorporated sociological tools

ed. Miltos Pechlivanos, Stefan Rieger, Wolfgang Struck, and Michael Weitz (Stuttgart: Verlag J. B. Metzler, 1995), 366–77, esp. 366.

74 Weitz, "Zur Karriere des Close Reading," 356.

75 Compagnon, *Démon teorie*, 51.

76 Compagnon, *Démon teorie*, 51, 53, 54.

77 Compagnon, *Démon teorie*, 48–52, esp. 48.

78 Eagleton, *Literary Theory*, 80–81.

79 Eagleton, *Literary Theory*, 80–81.

80 Clifford Geertz, *The Interpretation of Cultures* (New York: Basic Books, 2017), 3–33, esp. 26–31.

81 Culler, *Literary* Theory, 47–49. Weitz, "Zur Karriere des Close Reading," 364.

82 Weitz, "Zur Karriere des Close Reading," 365.

83 Eagleton, *Literary Theory*, 94. Mlynář, "Vztah paměti a identity v soudobé sociologii," 269.

into its interpretive arsenal,[84] which played a powerful role. According to Terry Eagleton, this was an adaptation of historiography for postmodern times.[85] In the process, so-called subaltern cultures have come to the fore, and there is growing interest today in the experiences of those who have been excluded from the so-called dominant culture.[86] Historical events are treated as textual phenomena, and historiography is viewed as only a form of narration determined by the narrator's prejudices. Eagleton characterizes New Historicism's view of history as a tangled tangle of incoherent narratives, none of which are more important than the others. Knowledge of the past is distorted by current interests and desires.[87] Thus, ideological aspects enter the viewfinder of literary history which has no uniform objective meaning.

There are interesting parallels here with Hayden White's observations of historical writing prior to the French Revolution, when "historiography was widely perceived as a literary art, specifically as an offshoot of rhetoric, and its 'fictional' character was generally recognized." He further notes that writing was still judged from either a literary or scientific point of view, but the key distinction was based on categories of "truth" and "error" and not on "fact" and "imagination."[88] The situation was similar in the rhetorical historiography in antiquity, when *inventio* was connected with *memoria* and *imaginatio/phantasia*. There was no *phantasia* apart from a tradition (e.g., canon of classical authors) that coincided with collective memory.[89] Imagination was not freewheeling, but was engaged with collective and cultural memory. In some respects, there are more parallels between ancient historiography and postmodern conceptions of it than is often recognized. Alternatively, one could speculate that the optimism of positivist historiography is/was a temporary interval.

White further observes that at the beginning of the nineteenth century, a turning point occurred when truth began to be identified among historians with reality (with fact) as opposed to fiction, leading to clearer distinctions

84 Compagnon, *Démon teorie*, 231. Stefan Rieger, "Memoria und Oblivio. Die Aufzeichnung des Menschen," in *Einführung in die Literaturwissenschaft*, ed. Miltos Pechlivanos, Stefan Rieger, Wolfgang Struck, and Michael Weitz (Stuttgart: Verlag J. B. Metzler, 1995), 378–92, esp. 380–81. Eagleton, *Literary Theory*, 197–98.

85 Eagleton, *Literary Theory*, 198.

86 Compagnon, *Démon teorie*, 231.

87 Eagleton, *Literary Theory*, 197.

88 White, *Tropics of Discourse*, 123.

89 Uwe Hebekus, "Topik/Inventio," in *Einführung in die Literaturwissenschaft*, ed. Miltos Pechlivanos, Stefan Rieger, Wolfgang Struck, and Michael Weitz (Stuttgart: Verlag J. B. Metzler, 1995), 82–96, esp. 85, 87.

between historical writing and the novel.[90] Since the historian saw it necessary to eliminate all fictional elements, he distinguished himself from the style of poets, orators, and novelists.[91] Reacting to the perceived shortcomings of their predecessors who were charged with distortions and omissions of factual data, historians were commonly under the illusion that historical treatises could be written without fictional content and style.[92] However, they did not realize that the facts did not speak for themselves. Facts still need to be selected, assembled, arranged and prioritized from among the surviving fragments.[93] Ironically, the process resembled the novelist who used similar tropological techniques.[94]

Due to the shift in hermeneutical awareness, most historians today are sensitive to the relationship between their present and its impact on their perceptions of the past. Facts, or memories of them, are viewed within cultural frameworks that provide coherence. Influenced by the phenomenology of Edmund Husserl and the hermeneutics of Martin Heidegger, Hans Robert Jauss is viewed as one of the foremost voices associated with reception theory, which privileges the active function of the audience as the agent that gives life to a literary work. In the Gadamerian spirit, Jauss tries to point out the importance of various moments of historical reception which take precedence over the author's interests, influences, and literary trends.[95] The reception process in Jauss' thought, which views the reader within a "horizon of expectation" (i.e., the framework of expectations that allows the worlds of the author and reader to merge) that is socially conditioned, overlaps with that of collective and cultural memory, which likewise attends to social and merging frameworks. Jauss' approach to reception has influenced a wide array of disciplines over the last two decades, including biblical studies.[96] Given reception theory's focus on the role of the reader, it has had considerable impact among literary critics like Wolfgang Iser, who emerged out the "Constance School" (which Jauss founded). On the other side of the Atlantic, similar ideas were circulated by critics like Stanley Fish for whom reading is not a disclosure of the meaning

90 White, *Tropics of Discourse*, 124.
91 White, *Tropics of Discourse*, 124.
92 White, *Tropics of Discourse*, 125.
93 White, *Tropics of Discourse*, 126.
94 White, *Tropics of Discourse*, 126–28.
95 Eagleton, *Literary Theory*, 69, 73–75.
96 Note for example, Brennan W. Breed, *Nomadic Text: A Theory of Biblical Reception History* (Bloomington: Indiana University Press, 2014), 9–13, 52–74.

of the text, but a process in which we experience what the text does to us.[97] "Interpretive strategies" are associated with the things that readers share.[98] Again, the communal nature of interpretation was prioritized over that of authorial intent or even textual trends and coherence because individuals are products of their communities. While Fish's reading may suffice for fiction, it has raised questions in relation to historiography or biography which may preserve aspects of the past, albeit in a mediated way. According to White, reception theory brings us back to the world of historiography before the French Revolution. While these "non-fiction" genres can contain authentic representations of the past, they are always mediated through the process of collective memory which shapes the "truth" judgments of readers/listeners.

For biblical and cognate studies, social memory theory offers an alternative hermeneutic (and correlated methods that can benefit from their use in other disciplines) to that of historical-criticism which primarily approaches written texts as archives and traditions without the complexity of reception. It allows the study of ancient Jewish and Christian texts to no longer be guided by reconstructions of the actual past(s) or quests for their reliability or unreliability. There is no question that historical criticism continues to yield tremendous results in its mining of data from the ancient world, but its interpretation of data requires engagement with contemporary hermeneutical insights that social memory theory can offer. The outcome for our purposes in this volume is the recognition that memory is not a tool for reconstructing the past, but rather a tool of explaining how the past was perceived within an ongoing process of relevance resulting in text productions that express competing conceptions and perceptions.

Linking Social Memory and Conceptions of Afterlife: The Current Project

As explained in the Preface, the following studies in this volume represent the culmination of a two-year project initiative on the relationship between social memory theory and Jewish and Christian perceptions of afterlife in antiquity. While all of the contributors locate their scholarship within the literature of Jewish and/or Christian antiquity, many are recent arrivals to social memory theory, which is not unusual given the relative newness of this approach. The

97 Stanley Fish, *Is There a Text in the Class: The Authority of Interpretive Communities* (Cambridge: Harvard University Press, 1980).

98 Eagleton, *Literary Theory*, 74.

studies provide a window into the various ways social memory theory is being appropriated for understanding the competing conceptions of afterlife in relation to the identity constructs of their corresponding communities. The ambitious aim of the collection is to explore and hopefully establish social memory as a hermeneutic that can contribute to innovative approaches to the exegetical task.

The papers are divided into three sections. The first section contains four studies on the conceptions of afterlife in ancient Judaism, spanning from the earliest receptions of Israelite traditions to the Rabbinic period. In the first study, Craig Broyles proposes that the idea of the dead (also "rephaim") descending to the underworld/*Sheol* was problematic for Yahwism. Given the ancient Near Eastern parallels, especially those found at Ugarit, he argues that these beliefs are best understood, not as a tradition generated within Yahwism itself, but as memories inherited—subjectively and even unconsciously—within Israel's broader Semitic culture. Since they were regarded as incompatible with Yahwism, the Old Testament contains a variety of counter-memories, such as Yahweh redeeming the dead from *Sheol*. Broyles argues that these counter-memories first circulated orally in ancient Israel as soundbites and fostered imaginative glimpses of hope until they were combined, enhanced, and inscribed in later apocalyptic texts like Daniel 12. In the second study, Jiří Janák and Michael Sommer provide a cautious analysis of how the Egyptian concept of the Judgement of the Dead may have been influential in the shaping of Jewish apocalyptic texts. In particular they focus on the *Apocalypse of Sophonias* and the *Testament of Abraham*. Next, David Cielontko compares and contrasts the meaning-making activity in 2 and 4 Maccabees. He argues that both accounts reframe the story of the Maccabean martyrs (i.e., Eleazar, the seven sons, and their mother) in their own cultural contexts which results in different collective memories that reflect and affect the respective identities of two audiences. Both stories of the martyrs, who are rewarded for their bravery, offer insights into the afterlife conceptions of two distinct communities. In the final study of this section, Brad Anderson explores the reception in Jewish tradition of the *Aqedah* (Genesis 22) in which Isaac dies and is resurrected on Moriah, even though the biblical text seems to state clearly that Isaac did not in fact die. This study traces a number of key elements in the Jewish reception of the *Aqedah* which point to Isaac's death and resurrection in the account of Genesis 22—from traditions concerning Isaac's blood and ashes to those focusing on the merits of the fathers. Drawing on these examples, as well as the work of Jan and Aleida Assmann, Anderson offers some reflections on how Isaac's death and resurrection might contribute to our understanding of the relationship between cultural memory and reception history.

The second section of the volume consists of studies on conceptions of afterlife in early Christianity ranging from the early Pauline tradition to the Patristic period. The first four studies focus on the New Testament. First, Anthony Le Donne explores the ways that resurrection became associated with water symbolism in Christian commemorative activity and thereby contributed to its multivalent impact. Touchstones include discussions of ritual, symbol, and myth. Le Donne introduces a concept that he calls "mnemonic cross-pollination" and illustrates its applicability to several New Testament texts that concern resurrection. In the second study, Kyle Parsons argues that Colossians, as a pseudepigraphon, was a counter-memory produced by a reputational entrepreneur (the actual author) who reconstructed an image of Paul in order to legitimize a new "Pauline" conception of resurrection that would satisfy the (actual) audience's present identity needs. Continuing with the Pauline tradition, Frederick Tappenden poses the question: How are the bodies of the deceased remembered by those who commemorate them? In answering the question, Tappenden focusses on the mnemonic frames for commemorating the apostle's "body" in early Christ-believing communities. He begins with an examination of Paul's "body" in the undisputed letters. He then turns to the many ways Paul's "body" is remembered within the late-first and second centuries. He concludes with reflection on how the memory of Paul's "body" both reflects and grounds certain kinds of early Christian identities and discourses. In the third study, comparing Mark's Gospel to a symphony, Sandra Huebenthal explores how its readers at different times dealt with its abrupt ending in 16:8. She observes that there were two ways of addressing the problem. Readers either added further notes to the seemingly unfinished symphony or performed it in its current state as a meaningful piece. Huebenthal argues that both variations can be evaluated as expressions of the situational needs experienced by groups for whom Jesus' afterlife provided solutions.

The subsequent three studies in the same section concentrate on the post-New Testament period. Jiří Lukeš focuses on the theme of restraint and purity in connection with the resurrection in the *Acts of Paul and Thecla*. His study contrasts the image of Paul in the canonical Acts of the Apostles (similar to that of Cicero) with the one presented in the *Acts of Paul and Thecla*, which was a product within a cultural framework that saw a developing interest in the genre of fiction. Lukeš argues that Thecla's social protest is an important underlying theme which offers Christianity a connection between defiance against the powerful men of the Roman Empire and sexual austerities that are important for eternal life. In the subsequent study, Tobias Nicklas focusses on the *Apocalypse of Peter*, which contains perhaps the earliest detailed description of hell as "another space" and "place of punishment." Nicklas argues that while the author probably used source material which is no longer extant (and/or was taken from already existing cultural memory), his appropriation of it can be understood as an expression of a particular form of collective memory that aims to lead its readers to a special perception of this world and of their identity as the group that follows the "way of righteousness." Christian Handschuh then discusses the *Passio Perpetuae et Felicitatis*, which has attracted considerable attention and yielded variant readings in both history and Church history over the last few decades. His close examination of the text and its reception reveals its mnemonic and identity-formative function among early Christians living in and around Carthage. In particular, he argues that the three famous visions in the *Passio* contain biblical and apocryphal features which are connected with the authoritative status of the martyrs. In effect, the redactor's text production expresses his own perception of the inherited memories.

The three studies in the final section could have been also included in the previous one since they focus on New Testament texts and traditions. However, given their extensive discussions of hermeneutics and method, they are placed in their own section for the purposes of drawing attention to the philosophical and historical implications of social memory theory in the exegetical process. In the first study, Zeba Crook interacts with the common complaint among memory theorists working in current historical Jesus research that since conventional indebtedness to form criticism by and large omits memory studies, it should be abandoned. In response, Crook compares the functions of form-critical thinking and memory theory in relation to early Christian narratives about the resurrection of Jesus. He argues that on the topic of the resurrection, memory theory refines form-critical thinking and does not contradict or correct it. In the next study, Stu Talené interacts with Alexey Somov's monograph on the representations of the afterlife in Luke-Acts.[99] In particular, he addresses Somov's observation that Luke seems comfortable including differing, and even conflicting, representations of the afterlife. Finding Somov's approach incomplete (which is rooted in Cognitive Metaphor Theory) because it does not adequately address the process of transmission and reception, Talené proposes that the insights of social memory theory and in particular those of Henri Bergson offer a more complete explanation. In the final study, Thomas Hatina contrasts conventional historical-critical approaches to the risen saints in Matt 27:52–53 by conceiving of the episode as a memory text. He argues that this hermeneutic in conjunction with a Deleuzian conception of process leads to an alternate set of questions and a re-prioritizing of exegetical methods. While this may not always

99 Alexey Somov, *Representations of the Afterlife in Luke-Acts*, LNTS 556 (London: Bloomsbury, 2017).

lead to alternate readings, the results are based on a different set of exegetical priorities which particularly impinge on how we might understand Matthew's conception of the raised saints walking around Jerusalem in relation to competing conceptions of resurrection in early Christianity.

Bibliography

Allison Jr., Dale C. *Resurrecting Jesus: The Earliest Christian Tradition and Its Interpreters*. London: T & T Clark, 2005.

Alkier, Stefan. *The Reality of the Resurrection the New Testament Witness*. Waco: Baylor University Press, 2013.

Assmann, Aleida. *Erinnerungsräume: Formen und Wandlungen des kulturellen Ged. chtnisses*. Munich: C. H. Beck, 1999. Czech translation: *Prostory vzpomínání. Podoby a proměny kulturní paměti*. Translated by Jakub Flanderka and Světlana Ondroušková a Jiří Soukup. Praha: Karolinum, 2018.

Assmann, Aleida und Jan. "Exkurs: Archäologie der literarischen Kommunikation." Pages 200–206 in *Einführung in die Literaturwissenschaft*. Edited by Miltos Pechlivanos, Stefan Rieger, Wolfgang Struck, and Michael Weitz. Stuttgart: Verlag J. B. Metzler, 1995.

Assmann, Jan. "Collective Memory and Cultural Identity." *New German Critique* 65 (1995): 125–33.

———. *Moses the Egyptian: The Memory of Egypt in Western Monotheism*. Cambridge, Harvard University Press, 1997.

Ben Zvi, Ehud. *Social Memory among the Literati of Yehud*. BZAW 509. Berlin: de Gruyter 2019.

Ben Zvi, Ehud, and Christoph Levin, eds. *Remembering and Forgetting in Early Second Temple Judah*. FAT 85. Tübingen: Mohr-Siebeck, 2012.

Bloch-Smith, Elizabeth. *Judahite Burial Practices and Beliefs about the Dead*. JSOTSup 123. Sheffield: JSOT Press, 1992.

Breed, Brennan W. *Nomadic Text: A Theory of Biblical Reception History*. Bloomington: Indiana University Press, 2014.

Bultmann, Rudolf. *Die Geschichte der synoptischen Tradition*. Göttingen: Vandenhoeck & Ruprecht, 2011.

Chilton, Bruce D. *Resurrection Logic: How Jesus' First Followers Believed God Raised Him from the Dead*. Waco: Baylor University Press, 2019.

Clark, Elizabeth A. *History, Theory, Text: Historians and the Linguistic Turn*. Cambridge: Harvard University Press, 2004.

Compagnon, Antoine. *Le Démon de la théorie. Littérature et sens commun*. Paris: Editions du Seuil 1998. Czech translation: *Démon teorie. Literatura a běžné myšlení*. Brno: Host 2009.

Culler, Jonathan. *Literary Theory: A Very Short Introduction*. New York: Oxford University Press, 2000.

Denham, Robert D, ed. *Northrop Frye's Notebooks and Lectures on the Bible and Other Religious Texts*, Collected Works of Northrop Frye, Volume 13. Toronto: University of Toronto Press, 2003.

——. *Northrop Frye: Religious Visionary and Architect of the Spiritual World*. Charlottesville: University of Virginia Press, 2004.

Deutsch, Cecilia. "Visions, Mysteries, and the Interpretive Task: Text Work and Religious Experience in Philo and Clement." Pages 83–103 in *Experientia, Volume 1: Inquiry into Religious Experience in Early Judaism and Christianity*. Edited by Frances Flannery, Colleen Shantz and Rodney A. Werline. SBLSymS 40. Leiden: Brill, 2008.

Dibelius, Martin. *Die Formgeschichte des Evangeliums*. Tübingen: J. C. B. Mohr, P. Siebeck, 1933.

Durkheim, Émile. *Sociologie a filosofie*. Praha: Sociologické nakladatelství, 1998.

Eagleton, Terry. *Literary Theory: An Introduction*. Minneapolis: University of Minnesota Press, 2008.

Edelman, Diana V. and Ehud Ben Zvi, eds. *Remembering Biblical Figures in the Late Persian & Early Hellenistic Periods: Social Memory and Imagination*. Oxford: Oxford University Press, 2013.

——, eds. *Leadership, Social Memory and Judean Discourse in the 5th–2nd Centuries* BCE, Worlds of the Ancient Near East and Mediterranean. London: Equinox, 2016.

Fish, Stanley. *Is There a Text in the Class: The Authority of Interpretive Communities*. Cambridge: Harvard University Press, 1980.

Foucault, Michel. *L'archéologie du savoir* (Editions Gallimard, 1969). Czech translation: *Archeologie vědění*. Praha: Herrmann & synové, 2016.

Frye, Northrop. *Fearful Symmetry: A Study of William Blake*. Princeton: Princeton University Press, 1947.

——. *The Critical Path: An Essay on the Social Context of Literary Criticism*. Bloomington: Indiana University Press, 1971.

——. *Myth and Metaphor: Selected Essays, 1974–1988*. Edited by Robert D. Denham. Charlottesville: University of Virginia Press, 1990.

——. *Words With Power: Being a Second Study of 'The Bible and Literature.'* Toronto: Penguin, 1992.

Geertz, Clifford. *The Interpretation of Cultures*. New York: Basic Books, 2017.

Gerhardson, Birger. *Memory and Manuscript: Oral Tradition and Written Transmission in Rabbinic Judaism and Early Christianity*. Lund: C. W. K. Gleerup, 1961.

Gill, Glen Robert. *Northrop Frye and the Phenomenon of Myth*. Toronto: University of Toronto Press, 2006.

Halbwachs, Maurice. *Les Travaux de L'Année Sociologique*. Paris, F. Alcan, 1925. English translation: *On Collective Memory*. Translated by Lewis A. Coser. Chicago: University of Chicago Press, 1992.

Hawkes, Terence. *Structuralism and Semiotics*. London: Routledge, 1992.

Hebekus, Uwe. "Topik/Inventio." Pages 82–96 in *Einführung in die Literaturwissenschaft*. Edited by Miltos Pechlivanos, Stefan Rieger, Wolfgang Struck, and Michael Weitz. Stuttgart: Verlag J. B. Metzler, 1995.

Howard, Jean E. "The New Historicism in Renaissance Studies." *English Literary Renaissance* 16 (1986): 13–43.

Horyna, Břetislav, and Helena Pavlincová. *Dějiny religionistiky*. Olomouc: Nakladatelství Olomouc, 2001.

Huebenthal, Sandra. "Social and Cultural Memory in Biblical Exegesis: The Quest for an Adequate Application." Pages 191–216 in *Cultural Memory in Biblical Exegesis*. Edited by Pernille Carstens, Trine Hasselbalch, and Niels Peter Lemche. Perspectives on Hebrew Scriptures and its Contexts 17. Piscataway: Gorgias Press, 2012.

———. "'Frozen Moments'—Early Christianity through the Lens of Social Memory Theory." Pages 17–43 in *Memory and Memories in Early Christianity*. Edited by Simon Butticaz and Enrico Morelli. WUNT 398. Tübingen, Mohr Siebeck, 2018.

Iser, Wolfgang. *The Fictive and the Imaginary: Charting Literary Anthropology*. Baltimore: The Johns Hopkins University Press, 1993.

Kansteiner, Wulf. "Finding Meaning in Memory: A Methodological Critique of Collective Memory Studies." *History and Theory* 41 (2002): 179–97.

Kelber, Werner H. *The Oral and the Written Gospel: The Hermeneutics of Speaking and Writing in the Synoptic Tradition, Mark, Paul, and Q*. Philadelphia: Fortress Press, 1983.

Keith, Chris, and Anthony Le Donne, eds. *Jesus, Criteria, and the Demise of Authenticity*. London: T & T Clark, 2012.

Kermode, Frank. *The Sense of an Ending: Studies in the Theory of Fiction*. New York: Oxford University Press 2000.

Lavabre, Marie-Claire. "Historiography and Memory." Pages 362–70 in *A Companion to the Philosophy of History and Historiography*. Edited by Aviezer Tucker. Chichester: Blackwell, 2009.

Lehtipuu, Outi. *Debates over the Resurrection of the Dead: Constructing Early Christian Identity*. Oxford: Oxford University Press, 2015.

Lincoln, Bruce. *Theorizing Myth: Narrative, Ideology, and Scholarship*. Chicago: University of Chicago Press, 1999.

Lyotard, Jean-François. *Le postmoderne expliqué aux enfants*. Paris: Editions Galilée 1986.

———. *Le condition postmoderne*. Paris: Editions de Minuit 1979. Czech translation: *O postmodernismu*. Praha: Filosofický ústav AV ČR, 1993.

Martin, Dale B. *The Corinthian Body*. New Haven: Yale University Press, 1995.

Mlynář, Jakub. "Vztah paměti a identity v soudobé sociologii." Pages 257–76 in: *Kolektivní paměť. K teoretickým otázkám*. Edited by Nicolas Maslowski and Jiří Šubrt. Praha: Karolinum, 2014.

Mroczek, Eva. *The Literary Imagination in Jewish Antiquity*. Oxford: Oxford University Press, 2016.

Neusner, Jacob, and Alan J. Avery-Peck, eds. *Judaism in Late Antiquity. Part Four: Death, Life-After-Death, Resurrection and the World-to-Come in the Judaisms of Antiquity*. HdO 49. Leiden: Brill, 2000.

Nora, Pierre. "L'avènement Mondial de la mémoire," in: Tr@nsit online 22/2002, 19 April 2002—EUROZINE: https://ez.gridworks.sk/lavenement-mondial-de-la-memoire/?pdf, 1–9.

Rakowski, Roman. "Postmodernismus jako nekonečná rozmanitost." *Filosofický časopis* 67 (2019): 227–40.

Ramelli, Ilaria L. E. *The Christian Doctrine of Apokatastasis: A Critical Assessment from the New Testament to Eriugena*. VCSup 120. Leiden: Brill, 2013.

Rieger, Stefan. "Memoria und Oblivio. Die Aufzeichnung des Menschen." Pages 378–92 in *Einführung in die Literaturwissenschaft*. Edited by Miltos Pechlivanos, Stefan Rieger, Wolfgang Struck, and Michael Weitz. Stuttgart: Verlag J. B. Metzler, 1995.

Rosenberg, Bruce A. "The Complexity of Oral Tradition." *Oral Tradition*, 2.1 (1987): 73–90.

Satlow, Michael. *How the Bible Became Holy*. New Haven: Yale University Press, 2014.

Schahadat, Shamma. "Intertextualität: Lektüre—Text—Intertext." Pages 366–77 in *Einführung in die Literaturwissenschaft*. Edited by Miltos Pechlivanos, Stefan Rieger, Wolfgang Struck, and Michael Weitz. Stuttgart: Verlag J. B. Metzler, 1995.

Smith, Daniel A. "Seeing a Pneuma(tic) Body: The Apologetic Interests of Luke 24:36–43." CBQ 72 (2010): 752–72.

Somov, Alexey. *Representations of the Afterlife in Luke-Acts*. LNTS 556. London: Bloomsbury, 2017.

Szondi, Peter. *Einführung in die literarische Hermeneutik*. Frankfurt am Main: Suhrkamp Verlag, 1975. Czech translation: *Úvod do literární hermeneutiky*. Brno: Host 2003.

Tulving, Endel, and Martin Lepage. "Where in the Brain is the Awareness of One's Past?" Pages 208–28 in *Memory, Brain and Belief*. Edited by Daniel L. Schacter and Elaine Scarry. Cambridge: Harvard University Press, 2000.

Vermes, Geza. *The Resurrection*. New York: Penguin Books, 2008.

Weinberg, Manfred. "Trauma—Geschichte, Gespenst, Literatur – und Gedächtnis." Pages 173–206 in *Trauma. Zwischen Psychoanalyse und kulturellem Deutungsmuster*. Edited by Elisabeth Bronfen, Birgit R. Erdle, and Sigrid Weigel. Köln: Böhlau, 1999. Czech translation: "Historický přehled." Pages 12–30 in *Paměť a trauma pohledem humanitních věd*. Praha: Karolinum, 2015.

Weitz, Michael. "Zur Karriere des Close Reading: New Criticism, Werkästhetik und Dekonstruktion." Pages 354–65 in *Einführung in die Literaturwissenschaft*. Edited by Miltos Pechlivanos, Stefan Rieger, Wolfgang Struck, and Michael Weitz. Stuttgart: Verlag J. B. Metzler, 1995.

Welzer, Harald. "Das kommunikative Gedächtnis und voraus ae besteth." Pages 47–62 in *Arbeit am Gedächtnis*. Edited by Michael Frank and Gabriele Rippl. München: Fink, 2007. Czech translation: "Co je to komunikativní paměť a z čeho se skládá." Pages 73–89 in *Paměť a trauma pohledem humanitních* věd. Praha: Karolinum, 2015.

White, Hayden. *Metahistory: The Historical Imagination in Nineteenth-Century Europe*. Baltimore: The Johns Hopkins University Press, 1973.

———. *Tropics of Discourse: Essays in Cultural Criticism*. Baltimore: The Johns Hopkins University Press, 1978.

Winter, Jay. *Remembering War: The Great War Between Memory and History in the Twentieth Century*. New Haven: Yale University Press, 2006.

I.

Afterlife in Ancient Judaism

The Nightmare of Sheol and the Counter-Memories of Yahwism

Craig C. Broyles

Afterlife within the Old Testament's Frame of Reference

The horizons of the stage on which the Old Testament (OT) is played mostly extend to this life only. "And he died" or "he lay down with his fathers" are the usual phrases marking the end of a human's story (starting with Adam, Gen 5:5). The spotlight is focused on Israel's fidelity to Yahweh and to the blessings and consequences during one's lifespan. This observation brings to light the OT's frame of reference. The eschaton in the OT is not the resurrection of individual believers to an eternal afterlife in heaven, but the postexilic restoration of later generations of corporate Israel in the land. In our study of afterlife in the OT, we would be remiss to focus on a small selection of disparate passages that happen to touch on death and afterlife, without first observing and respecting the fact that the OT itself gives little attention to the subject.

The OT's frame of reference can be illustrated in the Deuteronomistic History, which is intent on judging whether or not each king did what is "evil" (הָרַע) or "right" (הַיָּשָׁר) "in the eyes of Yahweh." When each king dies of natural causes—whether doing what is right (like David in 1 Kgs 2:10 or Hezekiah in 2 Kgs 20:21) or what is evil (like Jeroboam in 1 Kgs 14:20, Ahab in 1 Kgs 22:40, or Manasseh in 2 Kgs 21:18)—he simply "lay down with his fathers" (וַיִּשְׁכַּב ... עִם־אֲבֹתָיו)—end of story. There is no afterlife or distinction in their destiny.

*After*life appears to be an *after*thought. There is no such doctrine developed in the OT. It is not a central topic of interest in its own right, but a spinoff from Israel's developing theology of Yahweh. As their identity and connection with God develop, so does their understanding of an afterlife. In other words, it grows as a consequence of prior theological developments. The OT says little about a heavenly reward in the afterlife—what is sometimes called "pie-in-the-sky." Those of us who have grown up in Western culture, influenced as it is by a Christian world view, should not impose on the OT the assumption that God owes humans an afterlife or that death is a flaw in the system.

This study will explore a variety of OT passages touching on death and afterlife to clarify *what* beliefs are represented and *how* they developed in ancient Israelite society and in their scriptures. During the investigation, we will also

 | DOI:10.30965/9783657796212_003

assess the tools of tradition history criticism and social memory theory to see which provides the best lens for conceptualizing the data

The Nightmare of Sheol

Pre-exilic Psalms: The Dead Cannot Worship Yahweh

The OT characteristically refers to death as the end of one's story in descriptive narrative accounts and legal material. Some passages, however, show a persistent belief in human existence beyond the grave (קֶבֶר) in the underworld, usually specified as "Sheol,"[1] the "pit," or "Abaddon" (אֲבַדּוֹן, place of the lost/perishing). Most instances occur in poetic passages and in reported speech in narratives.[2]

In the Yahwistic source of the Pentateuch (J), the underworld surfaces in Jacob's laments over the apparent death of Joseph and the potential death of Benjamin (Gen 37:35; 42:38; 44:29, 31) and in Moses's threat of judgment on Korah and kin (Num 16:29–33). It appears in Wisdom literature, some 19 times in the poetic speeches of the book of Job and 14 times in Proverbs (including 3 to the Rephaim). In the Prophets it is used as an image of threat in judgment oracles (e.g., Isa 5:14), especially in those against foreign nations (Babylon in

---

1 "Sheol" is a term peculiar to ancient Israel. Its etymology has been heavily debated. The two most probable options are that שְׁאוֹל derived from the root שׁאל, "to ask," thus reflecting the popular, though taboo, practice of consulting the dead, or from the root שׁאה, "to be desolate." The suffixed *lamed* could be understood in the same sense as כַּרְמֶל, "orchard," derives from כֶּרֶם, "vineyard."

2 For details see Philip Johnston, *Shades of Sheol: Death and Afterlife in the Old Testament* (Downers Grove: InterVarsity Press, 2002), 70–73. Scholars have long debated about the referential reality of Sheol in the minds of the ancient Hebrews and whether or not they believed it was humanity's default destination, whether righteous or wicked. Biblical narratives frequently refer to death as a natural process, but they never matter-of-factly refer to Sheol as the location of the dead. It occurs in laments, where the rhetorical function is evident in the rhetorical questions that suggest Yahweh's dismissal of the petitioner's cry would be counterproductive: Yahweh would lose a worshiper. Sheol violates the worshiper's right to "praise" and Yahweh. The image of Sheol can either amplify the desperation of the lament (Ps 30:9) or heighten Yahweh's praise (Ps 30:3). In wisdom and prophetic texts these expressions portray graphic images of impending consequences. The answer to the question "did Sheol refer to a real place or did it function as an image of diminished existence?" probably lay in the mind of the beholder. As commentators of texts, I do not think we can be certain what was in the minds of the ancient psalmists and worshipers. See further Jon D. Levenson, *Resurrection and the Restoration of Israel: The Ultimate Victory of the God of Life* (New Haven: Yale University Press, 2006), 67–81.

Isa 14:9–20; Tyre in Ezek 26:20; 28:8; and Egypt, along with Assyria and Sidon in Ezek 31:14–18; 32:18–32).

The most frequent references to the underworld occur in the lament language of the Psalms, some 30 times. Of particular interest is the repeated claim that the dead cannot praise Yahweh.

> For in death there is no *remembrance* of you,
> in Sheol who gives you thanks? (Ps 6:5)
>
> ... my life draws near Sheol.
> I am reckoned with those who descend to the pit ...
> Released among the dead, like the slain who lie down in the grave,
> whom you *remember* no more ...
> For the dead do you work wonders,
> or do the shades (רְפָאִים) rise and give you thanks?
> Is your loyalty recounted in the grave,
> your faithfulness in Abaddon?
> Are your wonders known in the darkness,
> and your righteousness in the land of *forgetfulness*? (Ps 88:3b–5, 10–12)

The clearest evidence that Sheol is at odds with Yahwism lies here: Sheol destroys the possibility of memory: Yahweh's memory of his worshiper (*Gedächtnis*) and the worshiper's remembering/memorializing Yahweh (*Erinnerung*). The issue of memory is fundamental to Yahweh's worshipers because it is fundamental to their identity, and death/Sheol is its most decisive threat. Similar expressions are found in Psalm 30:9 (where Yahweh's praise is characterized as his "holy remembrance," v. 4), Psalm 115:16–18, and in Hezekiah's psalm in Isaiah 38:18–19.

To what attributes of Yahweh do these petitioners near death appeal? Which divine attributes are seen to be at odds with the notion of Sheol?

> Turn, Yahweh, deliver my life;
> save may *for the sake of your loyalty.*
> For in death there is no commemoration of your name;
> and Sheol who will give you thanks? (Ps 6:4–5)

In each of these passages, Yahweh's "loyalty" (חֶסֶד, Pss 6:4–5; 88:12; also 13:5 ["lest I sleep the death"]; חָסִיד, 16:10) and "fidelity" (אֱמֶת or אֱמוּנָה, Pss 30:9; 88:12; Isa 38:18–19) are spotlighted—not his justice or promises of blessing. Sheol seems incompatible with Yahweh's values.

We can make more sense of the psalmic language once we *hear* it imaginatively in the *visual* spaces of the temple, where many of the psalms were performed. The underworld/Sheol forms the antithesis of the temple mount.

Table 2.1 Temple vs. Sheol/Underworld

Temple	**Sheol/Underworld**
Mt. Zion	Valley of Hinnom (Gehenna)
Sacred mountain	Underworld
Singing, shouting, music	Silence
Light, lamps	Darkness
Commemoration, testimony	Forgetting
Broad, stable place	Narrow place ("distress"), snares, cords

In the late seventh century, King Josiah and the prophet Jeremiah discredited the ritual practice of making one's child "pass through the fire to Molech," an underworld deity, in the Valley of Hinnom. Thereafter, this valley became associated with fire, the underworld, and a place of burial for the dead.

> He defiled Topheth [→ cooking hearth], which is in the valley of Ben-hinnom, so that no one would make a son or a daughter pass through fire as an offering to Molech (2 Kgs 23:10, NRSV; cf. Isa 30:33).
>
> And they go on building the high place of Topheth, which is in the valley of the son of Hinnom, to burn their sons and their daughters in the fire—which I did not command, nor did it come into my mind. Therefore, the days are surely coming, says the Lord, when it will no more be called Topheth, or the valley of the son of Hinnom, but the valley of Slaughter: for they will bury in Topheth until there is no more room. The corpses of this people will be food for the birds of the air, and for the animals of the earth; and no one will frighten them away (Jer 7:31–33, NRSV; cf. Jer 19:1–14; 31:40 [הָעֵמֶק הַפְּגָרִים]; 32:35).

This language of the psalms echoes the geographic symbolism of the temple on Mt. Zion and its proximity to the Valley of Hinnom (גֵּי־הִנֹּם) or, as it is better known from the Greek transliteration, "Gehenna" (γέεννα). As worshipers stood on the sacred temple mount, they could look southward down into Gehenna, the burial ground and entry into the underworld.

A Memory Inherited from the Semitic Culture

Death as a Descent to the Underworld

We are fortunate that archaeologists have uncovered the royal and priestly archives in the Late Bronze city of Ugarit, on the Mediterranean coast in modern-day Syria. Although not technically in the land of Canaan, it does appear to represent the West Semitic culture of the Levant. The correspondences between the OT and Ugarit regarding death and the underworld are remarkable.

In Act III of the Baal myth, Mot, the god of death and the underworld, invites his rival Baal as a guest and—ironically—as his main course, saying, "surely you will descend into Divine Mot's throat" (KTU 1.5:1:6–7). Baal is then given these instructions:

And descend to the House of Release in the underworld,	*wrd.btḫpṯt/arṣ.*
Be counted among the those who descend to the underworld.	*tspr.by/rdm.arṣ*
And you will know, O god, that you are dead (KTU 1.5:5:14–17; cf. KTU 1.4:8:7–9).	*wtdʿilm/kmtt.*

Baal's death is described as a "descent" to "the House of Release" in the "earth" or underworld.[3]

Over 40 times the Law, the Prophets, and the Writings describe death as a "descent" (ירד) to the pit or Sheol (e.g., Pss 22:29; 28:1; 30:3, 9; 55:15, 23; 115:17; 143:7). Baal's death as a "descent" into the underworld is remarkably similar to the poetic description of death in Psalm 88.

I am reckoned with those who descend to the pit …,	נֶחְשַׁבְתִּי עִם־יוֹרְדֵי בוֹר
Released among the dead, like the slain who lie down in the grave … (Ps 88:4–5).	בַּמֵּתִים חָפְשִׁי כְּמוֹ חֲלָלִים שֹׁכְבֵי קֶבֶר

Many commentators have found the term, חָפְשִׁי ("set free, released"), in Ps 88:5 problematic and have thus attempted to emend it. But the parallel Ugaritic cognate phrase, *bêta ḫupṯîti*, confirms חפשי as original and not a corruption, thus making this parallel all the more compelling. The term is likely a euphemism for "release" from normal human life and contact.[4]

3 In another text, the god El/*ʾIlu* becomes, as it were, dead drunk: "*ʾIlu* falls as though dead, *ʾIlu* falls like those who descend into the earth" (*iʾl . km mt // iʾl . k yrdm . aʾrṣ*, KTU 1.114:21–22). In the OT, אֶרֶץ can refer to the "underworld" (Exod 15:12; Ps 22:29; 71:20; Jer 17:13; Jonah 2:6).

4 An even closer parallel to the Ugaritic phrase, "the House of Release" (*btḫpṯt, bêta ḫupṯîti*), appears in biblical narrative where the leprous king Uzziah spent his remaining days in בֵּית הַחָפְשִׁית (2 Kgs 15:5 = 2 Chr 26:21). See further Mark S. Smith and Wayne T. Pitard, *The Ugaritic Baal Cycle: Introduction with Text, Translation and Commentary of KTU 1.3–1.4* (Leiden: Brill, 2009), 2.714–16. The Gilgamesh Epic from Mesopotamia echoes a similar

Dust as the Location of the Dead

"Dust" as a place of the dead is an image attested at Ugarit (*'pr*, KTU 1.2:4:5; 1.17:1:27–28; 1. 161:21–22) and in the Bible (עפר, Job 7:21; 17:16; 20:11; 21:26; Ps 22:15, 29, emended; 30:9; Isa 26:19; Dan 12:2; cf. Gen 2:19).

Death as "Sleep"

At Ugarit, death could be likened to sleep: Aqhat's lying in his "grave" (qbr) is a parallel expression to "his sleep" (šnt, KTU 1.19:3:44–45). This metaphor surfaces in most sections of the biblical canon: Psalms (Pss 13:3; 22:29, emended), Wisdom (Job 3:13; 14:12), Prophets (Jer 51:39, 57), apocalyptic (Dan 12:2), and is implied in historical narrative (1 Sam 28:15).

The Dead as "Rephaim"

Another compelling link between the OT and Ugarit is the puzzling group called the Rephaim (רְפָאִים, Rapiuma). Eight times the OT refers to the Rephaim, often rendered "shades," where the term is collocated with the "dead" (מות) and Sheol (Job 26:5; Ps 88:11; Prov 2:18; 9:18; 21:16; Isa 14:9; 26:14, 19). At Ugarit the Rapiuma are the "ancient dead" and, most notably, their deified kings, who have "descended into the earth, ... into the dust" (KTU 1.161:21–22). They are quite active, and the term likely means "healthy ones" or possibly "healers," thus derived from the West Semitic root, רפא.[5]

The OT usage, however, likely exploiting a polemical twist points to the root, רפה, meaning "those who drop/grow slack, the weak" or "the shades" (see esp. Isa 26:14). The closest parallel to the phenomena described in the Ugaritic texts appears in Isaiah 14:9–21.

Before proceeding, we must highlight two important points. First, these parallels, though we observe them as texts, were not transmitted textually by scribes. They cannot be intertextual allusions. Ugarit was destroyed by the Sea Peoples near the end of the Late Bronze period (ca. 1180 BCE). So, its library was inaccessible to the Hebrew settlers who entered the Canaanite highlands in the Iron Age. These parallels must be explained as "oral tradition"—if we use the historical-critical terminology of tradition criticism (Traditionsgeschichte) and transmission history (Überlieferungsgeschichte)—or more accurately,

---

portrayal of "the House of Darkness, ... the house which none leave who have entered it, On the road from which there is no way back, To the house wherein the dwellers are bereft of light, Where dust is their fare and clay their food" (*ANET*, 87).

5 Dennis Pardee, *Ritual and Cult at Ugarit*, Writings from the Ancient World 10 (Atlanta: Society of Biblical Literature, 2002), 282. Further references to the Rephaim can be found in sarcophagus inscriptions of fifth-century Sidonian kings (*COS* 2.56–57), whose burial is described as a "resting-place" from which they do not want to be "disturbed" (cf. 1 Sam 28:15).

I believe, as "cultural memory."[6] Second, the infelicities that Sheol has with Yahwism, as will be shown, indicate that Israel's default images of death and Sheol were not generated within Yahwism, but were a memory that Israel inherited within its common Semitic culture.

Sheol: Cosmic Map and Deity Map

This inherited memory of the dead in the underworld was part of a broader Semitic memory, which we may call the cosmic map of the geography of the universe. The Bible's default map can be visualized from the priestly creation account in Genesis 1, along with poetic passages. The earth is "founded" upon the waters (Pss 24:2; 102:25; 104:5; Job 38:4–7), both those in the oceans and in the underworld below, by "pillars" (1 Sam 2:8; Ps 75:3; Job 9:6), the tops which can be seen in the mountains. Below the earth is the underworld of Sheol. Keeping the waters in the skies above from flooding the earth is the solid metal plate of the "firmament" (Job 37:18). The heavenly lamps—including the sun, moon, and stars—are secured in the skies above by their installation *in* the firmament.

The deity who established this world order was "the God of the skies," who vanquished the chaotic deep. Throughout the Semitic world, he did so by vanquishing the chaotic seas, after which he is acclaimed king over all the gods. The "reign" of this cosmic king is manifest in the "rain" that he dispenses for the agricultural economy of the ancient world. As king, he then has his palace/temple constructed upon his sacred mountain: Zaphon in Ugarit and Zion in Israel.

In the ancient Near East, corresponding to this cosmic map of the geography of the universe was the deity map of their respective domains. The religions of the ancient Near East can be characterized as "naming the powers," whereby the forces and regions of nature were named as gods and personified. At Ugarit, El was the old patriarch of the gods, the supreme authority, and "creator of creatures." Baal/Hadad was the younger, vigorous warrior, known as

6 See esp. Jan Assmann, "Collective Memory and Cultural Identity," *New German Critique* 65 (1995): 128–33; Jan Assmann, "Memory and Culture," in *Memory: A History*, ed. Dmitri Nikulin (Oxford: Oxford University Press, 2015), esp. 330–42; Sandra Huebenthal, "Social and Cultural Memory in Biblical Exegesis: The Quest for an Adequate Application," in *Cultural Memory in Biblical Exegesis*, ed. Pernille Carstens, Trine B. Hasselbalch, and Niels Peter Lemche, PHSC 17 (Piscataway: Gorgias, 2012), 183. Huebenthal is correct that OT literature deals primarily with "*kulturellem Gedächtnis*," in contrast to the NT, which operates primarily as "*kommunikatives Gedächtnis*" (192).

"Cloud Rider," the god of the skies. His arrows and lance were lightening, and his voice was thunder. Mot was the god of death and the underworld.

Within this Semitic cultural framework, ancient Israel's theologies, or memories of Yahweh, were formed by the processes of assimilation and differentiation, whereby Yahweh assimilated the various job descriptions and portfolios of the deities of the ancient world, but also differentiated himself from Baal, Molech, and the other so-called gods (personified powers).[7] Yahweh actually takes on El's name, as evident in the people Isra-El, the city Beth-El, and divine epithet El Shaddai. He adopts Baal's role as "Cloud Rider" (God of the skies), while simultaneously dissociating himself from Baal and becoming his rival. However, it would seem, Israel could never bring itself to the point to ascribe Mot's role as an underworld deity (chthonic) to Yahweh. The OT never embraces Sheol as Yahweh's domain.

This issue of Yahweh's domain applies not only to the cosmic and deity maps of the ancient world but also to the physical geography map. OT passages reflecting the early Iron Age suggest that Yahweh's sovereignty and domain was limited to the boundaries of Israel. When Saul pursues David to the border of Israel, he says,

> Now therefore let my lord the king hear the words of his servant. If it is the Lord who has stirred you up against me, may he accept an offering; but if it is mortals, may they be cursed before the Lord, for *they have driven me out today from my share in the heritage of the Lord, saying, 'Go, serve other gods.'* Now therefore, do not let my blood fall to the ground, *away from the presence of the Lord*; for the king of Israel has come out to seek a single flea, like one who hunts a partridge in the mountains" (1 Sam 26:19–20, NRSV, emphasis mine).

Other passages also imply this limitation on Yahweh's domain (Judg 11:24, Josh 24:15, Num 21:29, and Deut 32:8–9; cf. Mic 4:5). We should note also the perspectives of Absalom ("Yahweh in Hebron," 2 Sam 15:7–8) and Naaman (2 Kgs 5:17–19). But once Israel's political perspectives shift from petty states in the Levant to the Assyrian Empire in the second half of the eighth century, and later the Babylonian and Persian Empires, the extent of Yahweh's estate is reevaluated and expanded, as we shall see.

To be clear on the frame of reference of the OT, we must recalibrate our statement of the problem. The problem is not one of "life versus afterlife" or "mortality versus immortality" or "time versus eternity"; the problem for ancient Israel was one of geography. It was perceived not as an anthropological

7 See further Mark S. Smith, *The Early History of God: Yahweh and the Other Deities in Ancient Israel*, 2nd ed. (Grand Rapids: Eerdmans, 2002), 7–9.

problem regarding the soul, but a theological one regarding divine domain. Death signals a loss of contact with Yahweh. To my knowledge, Sheol has no genesis in the OT. Yahweh never creates it, nor does he engineer it as a prison to which the wicked are sentenced after judgment. It is notably absent from the cosmic map portrayed in the priestly account in Genesis 1. In the Yahwistic Garden of Eden account (Genesis 2–3), the human lifecycle is from אדמה to אדם and back to אדמה, from the ground to the human and back to the ground—dust to dust—or what science calls the carbon cycle. There is no afterlife, and the possibility of "living forever" (וָחַי לְעֹלָם) is contingent on access to "the tree of life" (Gen 3:22–24). Sheol is a loose end within Israelite monotheism. Its genesis does not lie within Yahwism; it was a memory inherited from its Semitic cultural environment or, more to the point, it was a nightmare incompatible with Yahwism.

Yahwism's Counter-Memories

The popular perceptions of death and the "afterlife" in Sheol formed a memory that Israel inherited within their Semitic culture. Death for the Israelites, as for all humanity, was the great unknown. But their problem was compounded because death and Sheol seemed incompatible with Yahwism.

In what follows we shall see that the biblical writers addressed this problem by applying to this great *unknown* what they *knew* of Yahweh from the collective memories of their experiences in this life. In short, they believed that Yahweh, who has shown himself to be "faithful," will somehow transcend death—in a way yet to be disclosed. What I see operating here is what I would call "reasoned revelation," that is, revelation by inference and analogy—a kind of empirical process based on experience. They reasoned, for example, as Yahweh has been our savior and redeemer, especially from Egypt, then he can and indeed must redeem us from Sheol.

Early Poetry: Yahweh's Capacity

Many scholars believe that the earliest literature contained in the Hebrew Bible can be found in some archaic poems. Among them are the Song of Moses (Deuteronomy 32) and the Song of Hannah (1 Samuel 2).[8]

---

8 Other archaic poems are two tribal blessings—one in the mouth of Jacob (Genesis 49), another in the mouth of Moses (Deuteronomy 33)—two victory songs—the Song of the Sea

Much of the Song of Moses concerns Israel's defection to other gods. Its theological perspective is henotheistic, where Israel is uniquely Yahweh's "allotted heritage" while other nations have their own patron deities (vv. 8–9). Israel is to worship Yahweh exclusively, but the poem later asserts that Yahweh is incomparable on the deity map (see also v. 43 in 4QDeut[q]).

> See now, I even I am he,
> and there is no god besides me;
> I put to death (impf.) and I bring (back) to life (impf.);
> I wounded (pf.) and I will heal (impf),
> And there is none who delivers from my hand (Deut 32:39).

To undergird this claim, the poem predicates actions of Yahweh that assert divine powers in opposite pairs. Chief among them is his *power* over death and life. The poem also highlights the extent of Yahweh's *reach*.

> For a fire is kindled in my anger,
> and it burns to lower Sheol,
> and devours the earth and its produce,
> and it blazes the foundations of the mountains (Deut 32:22).
> It does not go so far, however, as to claim that Sheol lies within his *domain* or realm.
> The Song of Hannah (1 Samuel 2) appears in the context of reversal, where Hannah, long barren, gives birth to a child.
> The barren has borne seven,
> but the woman of many sons languishes.
> Yahweh puts to death (ptc.) and brings (back) to life (ptc.),
> brings down (ptc.) to Sheol and brings up (vav-consecutive) (1 Sam 2:5b–6).

This song, a hymn inserted and transposed (note the mention of "his king," v. 10) to Hannah's experience, hints of Yahweh's wider powers of social reversal. The word order of both of these ancient poems suggests that Yahweh's "bringing (back) to life" is an act of "reviving" from death, as healing must follow wounding. The vav-consecutive in the Song of Hannah is clear that Yahweh's act of "raised up" is subsequent to his "bringing down to Sheol." Yahweh is not only sovereign over whether or not one faces a premature death, but he has the power or capacity to bring people up from Sheol.

To be clear, these early poems do not treat afterlife as an independent subject. Yahweh is the principal subject. Revival after death illustrates Yahweh's

---

(Exodus 15) and the Song of Deborah (Judges 5)—and two poems from the early monarchy—David's Thanksgiving (Psalm 18 = 2 Samuel 22) and the Song of Hannah (1 Samuel 2).

power of reversal and his divine incomparability. No specific testimony is adduced that Yahweh has actually performed a revival after death. These hymns simply assert his capacity to do so.

Psalms: Yahweh as the Levite's "Portion"

When facing the inevitability of death, two psalms uniquely claim Yahweh as the worshiper's "portion" (חֵלֶק).

> Yahweh is the allotment of my portion (חֵלֶק) and my cup;
> you hold my lot.
> The boundary lines have fallen for me in pleasant places;
> my heritage (נַחֲלָה) is pleasing for me (Ps 16:5–6).

> My flesh and my heart are finished,
> God is the rock/mountain of my heart and my portion (חֵלֶק) forever (Ps 73:26).

Elsewhere in the OT, this claim is exclusive to the Levites (Deut 10:9; 18:2) and the Aaronic priests (Num 18:20). While Levitical psalmists may have composed psalms from their distinctive traditions, they become democratized by the public performance of their psalms. This appropriation is evident in Pss 119:57; 142:5; Lam 3:24. Psalm 16 goes on to claim,

> For you will not abandon my soul to Sheol;
> you will not allow your faithful one (חָסִיד) to see the pit.
> You (will) make known to me the path of life;
> fullness of joy is with your presence/face;
> delights are in your right hand forever (Ps 16:10–11).

One could argue that, given the majority view among the Psalms, verse 10 simply refers to the avoidance of premature death and verse 11 to the joy of temple worship. But, at the very least, the phrasing opens a new potential for belief in an inheritance with Yahweh that transcends death.

The same may be said of Psalm 73. Both psalms claim that Yahweh "holds" worshipers (16:5, תמך, and 73:23, אחז) during their threatened existence.

> With your counsel you guide me,
> and afterword (with) glory you take/receive me.
> My flesh and my heart are finished;
> God is the rock/strength of my heart and my portion to remote time (Ps 73:24, 26).

At the moment of the failure of his own body, the worshiper claims Yahweh as his "portion" and the enduring "rock" of his heart. The logic appears to be that, though I am mortal, my "inheritance" and relationship with Yahweh will endure.

The interpretive crux lies in how we construe לְעוֹלָם ("to remote time" or "forever") and אַחַר ("after" what?). I have argued elsewhere that because the worshiper's pivotal discovery occurs at the moment of "entering the sanctuary of God" (v. 17), the psalm should be read in light of the rites of temple entry known from other psalms (esp. Psalms 15 and 24).[9] If so, Yahweh's "guiding" this worshiper may align with Yahweh's "guiding" his pilgrims to the temple (Pss 5:8; 23:3; 43:3; 61:2; cf. 27:11; 31:3; 32:8; 139:24). Yahweh's "receiving" the worshiper with "glory" may refer to the pilgrim's reception into "the place where your glory dwells," that is, the sanctuary (Ps 26:8).

Nevertheless, both Psalms 16 and 73 may take on new meaning when read alongside other canonical passages where God's "taking" (לקח) a worshiper cheats death itself (Gen 5:24; Ps 49:15). To this question we shall return.

Pre-exilic Psalms: "Awaking" and "Seeing God" in Temple Ritual

Psalms 7 and 17 are suggestive of a cultic rite of incubation (a night vigil) for those accused of a crime, where in the absence of clear evidence a petitioner appeals to the supreme court of Yahweh (שׁפט in 7:6, 8, 11; 17:2, דין in 7:8).

> From your presence/face may my judgment come forth;
> May your eyes behold equity.
> You have assayed my heart, you have called me to account *at night*;
> you have refined me and found nothing ...
> I, in righteousness, I will behold your face;
> I shall be satisfied, upon *awaking*, (with) your manifestation (Ps 17:2–3a, 15).

During this rite the petitioner takes an oath or self-curse ("if I have done this ... let an enemy pursue my soul," Ps 7:3–5), requesting Yahweh, "the assayer of hearts and kidneys," to "judge me" (vv. 8–9). Should the petitioner survive the night under Yahweh's scrutiny, he will "awake" and "behold Yahweh's face in righteousness." This metaphor likely refers to God's vindication of the innocent, not to a beatific vision in the afterlife (similarly Ps 27:4, 13).[10]

---

9 Craig C. Broyles, *Psalms* (Grand Rapids: Baker Books, 2012), 302–304.

10 Given the eastern orientation of Israelite and ANE temples, this "manifestation" upon "awaking" (Ps 17:15) could be symbolized by the appearance of the sun at dawn (Ps 46:5). Thus, morning (Ps 5:3; 57:8) at the start of the "day" (Pss 7:11; 88:9; 145:2) is the preferred time of prayer, when the joy that God brings arrives (Ps 30:5). As Psalms 7 and 17 refer to a

Psalm 11 also speaks of taking "refuge" in Yahweh, who dwells "in his holy temple" and whose eyes "behold" and "assay" (בחן) all humanity (Ps 11:1, 4–5). This psalm speaks more in terms of the corporate interests of "the righteous" and closes with the confession, "the upright shall behold his face" (v. 7), thus echoing the climax of Psalm 17. With the emerging expectations in postexilic period, however, this imagery of "awaking" and "seeing God" (also mentioned in Ps 16) will become ripe for re-application.

Eighth-Century Prophets: Yahweh's Reach (לקח) and Yahweh as Savior

We now arrive at the prophetic books of Amos and Hosea, whose ministries correlate with Tiglath-pileser's transformation of Assyria from a localized kingdom to an empire spanning the Fertile Crescent—just when Israel and Judah are about to lose their political independence. With the political encroachment of Assyria, the extent of Yahweh's sovereignty needed clarification. Will Yahweh be overshadowed by Asshur, the patron god of Assyria, and later by Marduk, the patron god of Babylon?[11] Both of these prophets address the northern kingdom of Israel and both repeatedly appeal to the memory of the exodus when Yahweh brought his people up from Egypt (Amos 2:10; 3:1; 9:7; Hos 2:15; 11:1; 12:9, 13; 13:4). Given the precedent of Yahweh's power over Egypt, one could reason that he can overpower the superpowers of Assyria and Babylon. These prophets chart out Yahweh's power not only on the geo-political map but also the cosmic map.

In a judgment oracle (Amos 9:1–10), Yahweh highlights his inescapable judgment on Israel (vv. 1, 8–10). It begins with his cosmic reach.

> If they dig into Sheol,
> from there my hand will take/snatch (לקח) them;
> if they ascend to the skies/heavens,
> from their I will bring them down (Amos 9:2).[12]

---

specific ritual for individuals experiencing false accusation (how many cases would there have been in ancient Israel anyway?), we might suppose this image of sleeping, awaking, and seeing God had limited circulation. But Pss 3:5; 4:8; 13:3 testify to a general belief that it was Yahweh who sustains people during their sleep.

11 The 8th–7th century Assyrian crisis and the 6th century Babylonian crisis precipitated "breakdowns in tradition" that accelerated shifts in "memory media," which in ancient Israel included prophets and scribes (see Huebenthal, "Social and Cultural Memory in Biblical Exegesis," 184.

12 Amos 9:1–10 then extends Yahweh's reach further in geographic-cosmic locations: from the top of Mount Carmel to the seabed and its "serpent" (v. 3), and then to Israel's captivity in a foreign land (v. 4). After a doxology of Yahweh as the God of the skies (vv. 5–6),

Once again, the issue is not afterlife *per se*, but the extent of Yahweh's reach and capacity.

In another judgment oracle highlighting the certainty and extent of Yahweh's judgment on Israel, Hosea affirms Israel's death sentence—from a stillborn at the womb (13:13) to their death in Sheol (13:14).

> From the hand of Sheol should I ransom (פדה) them,
> from death should I redeem (גאל) them?
> Where are your plagues, O Death?
> Where is your sting, O Sheol?
> Compassion is hidden from my eyes (Hos 13:14).

The Hebrew imperfect verbs are best rendered in a modal sense ("should") for two reasons. First, the verse's closing line and the context of the passage focus on Yahweh's inevitable and inescapable impending judgment. Second, elsewhere the prophet uses the same verbal construction (אֶפְדֵּם) where it should be rendered in a modal sense, as it simply raises the possibility.

> And I would redeem them,
> but they have spoken lies against me (Hos 7:13).

Yahweh seems to raise the possibility of redeeming the Israelites, only to say this will not happen. Once again, Hosea 13:14 is not a claim that Yahweh characteristically redeems humans from Sheol, but simply that he has the capacity to do so. Moreover, the prophet does not hereby disclose a new revelation about Yahweh's abilities. The rhetorical question works only if there is already a shared assumption with Hosea's audience that Yahweh can redeem Israelites from Sheol. The verbal choice of "redeem/ransom" implies that Sheol marks the extent of Yahweh's reach, but not his domain or realm as such.[13]

In chapter 6, Hosea mimics a liturgy of repentance, which includes a series of reversals that echo the Song of Moses (Deut 32:39; cf. the Song of Hannah, 1 Sam 2:6).

Yahweh asserts his engineering the geographic migrations of people groups beyond the Israelites (v. 7).

13 Though not mentioned in either Hosea or Amos, גאל and פדה are the verbs of choice to describe Yahweh's redemption of Israel from Egypt (Exod 6:6; Deut 7:8; 9:26; 13:5; 15:15; 24:18; 2 Sam 7:23 = 1 Chr 17:21; Mic 6:4), as is לקח (Deut 4:20; cf. Exod 6:7). Yahweh overpowers Egypt, but Egypt is not identified as Yahweh's domain.

Come, and let us (re)turn to Yahweh,
for he has torn, so he may *heal* us;
and he has struck, so he may bind us up.
He will *bring* us *to life* after two days;
on the third he will raise us up,
so we may live before him (Hos 6:1–2).

I put to death and I *bring to life*;
I wounded and I will *heal* (Deut 32:39).

In Hosea, we must be clear that this action of "revival" occurs after wounding, not putting to death. And it applies to corporate restoration, not individual resurrection. But we shall see how this pre-exilic oracle will be adapted in the postexilic period.

Psalm 49 uses the same verbs as found in the pre-exilic prophets Hosea (13:14, פדה) and Amos (9:2, לקח).[14]

But God will ransom (פדה) my life from the hand of Sheol,
for he will take (לקח) me (Ps 49:15).

Most commentators have identified Psalm 49 as a wisdom psalm, and so it may be but we should not presume to segregate Israel's social circles too narrowly.[15] Most view it as a late psalm, though we cannot be certain or precise. The petitioner's chief concern is "those who trick" him. Although they "trust in their wealth" (vv. 5–6), even they cannot afford to pay the "ransom," "so they could yet live forever and never see the pit" (vv. 7–9; cf. Ps 89:48). Indeed, "graves are their home forever, their dwellings to all generations" (v. 11), and "like sheep they are appointed to Sheol" (v. 14). Given the petitioner's contrasting destiny, it seems unavoidable to read this claim as God's deliverance from Sheol after death, not merely a deliverance from premature death. This may be our first clear reference in the OT to deliverance out of Sheol and an afterlife with God.

14 The psalm's pairing of these key verbs shared with these prophetic oracles need not indicate textual dependence. As psalms and oracles were first published orally, Yahweh's actions of ransoming, redeeming, and taking are probably stock phrases reflecting oral propagation. On the bard's memory of "a float of themes and formulas" see Walter J. Ong and John Hartley, *Orality and Literacy: The Technologizing of the Word*, 3rd ed. (New York: Routledge, 2012), 58, 60, 64.

15 The intention to convey "wisdom," a "proverb," and a "riddle" (vv. 3–4) and the familiar word pair of "the wise" and "the fool" (v. 10) echo the wisdom tradition. We should note, however, that Psalm 78 introduces itself with the same word pair of "parable" and "riddle" (v. 2, also "teaching," v. 1), but it clearly does not derive from the wisdom sages but from Levitical psalmists that recite a lengthy historical recital derived from Deuteronomic traditions.

Exilic Prophets: Corporate Resurrection and the Servant

The OT's clearest reference to resurrection, as an intervention of God, is Ezekiel's vision of the valley of dry bones (Ezek 37: 1–14). The problem for these "bones" is not that they lie in Sheol, but that they lack "flesh" (בשׂר) and "breath" (רוח). Fortunate for Ezekiel, a priest, Yahweh did not require him to lay his hands on the bones, but simply to prophesy twice. Yahweh's action is to "bring breath" and "flesh" to the bones, after which "they lived and stood on their feet" (vv. 5–6, 10).

In the closing verses interpreting this vision (vv. 11–14), Yahweh clarifies, "these bones are the whole house of Israel," making clear this portrays corporate resurrection from exile. Yet although this instance is metaphoric, it has rhetorical force only if it were thought literally possible for Yahweh to resurrect bones. In this case, the bones speak and lament, "our bones are dried up and our hope is lost." The intervention is also described differently. Yahweh says, "I will open your graves and I will raise you from your graves." The promise, "I will bring you to the ground of Israel," clarifies that this vision is an image of Israel's postexilic restoration to the land, not a promise of bodily resurrection.

No passages of the Bible have been more hotly contested than the so-called Servant Songs found in Second Isaiah (with their additions, Isa 42:1–4 + 5–9; 49:1–6 + 7–12; 50:4–9 + 10–11; 52:13–53:12). What is his identity and role? Does he in fact die and then see resurrection? In the exilic context of Second Isaiah, I believe he embodies a segment of "Israel," whom Yahweh commissions "to restore Jacob/Israel to him" and "raise up the tribes of Jacob/Israel" (Isa 49:3, 5–6). In all likelihood this segment of Israel is the Babylonian exiles. Second Isaiah begins with Yahweh's commission to "my people":

> Comfort (pl), comfort, my people,
> says your God.
> Speak to the heart of Jerusalem … (Isa 40:1–2).

"My people" is not the direct object of the verb but the vocative commanded to speak to Jerusalem. "My people" are the exiles, who run as "Zion's herald of good news" announcing Yahweh's appearance to Jerusalem and Judah's cities (40:9; also 52:7).

The Servant Songs likely served as a model for the exiles to emulate. Their job description is the antitype to that of Cyrus, the Persian king. Cyrus' commission was to restore the exiles to a rebuilt Jerusalem (44:26–28), while the Servant was to restore them to Yahweh. Cyrus' modus operandi was to "trample on rulers as on mortar, as the potter treads clay" (41:25), but the Servant "will not lift his voice …, nor break a crushed reed" (42:2).

In the narrative sequence of the fourth song the servant is described as "cut off from the land of the living." He is given "his grave ... in his death." And "his life" is described as "a guilt offering" (Isa 53:8–10a). Yet he will subsequently "see his seed," "prolong his days," and "see light" (53:10–11, reading אור with 1QIsa[a], 1QIsa[b], 4QIsa[d], LXX.). Yahweh then "will allot him ... spoil" (v. 12). Whether this Servant was understood—in the original historical context—as an individual or corporate group, and whether or not he was actually dead, buried, and subsequently raised, need not deter us now. Our ultimate interest is how this passage is subsequently reinterpreted in the postexilic period.

The Priests: Death and Ritual Impurity

The priestly materials and traditions in the Hebrew Bible appear to say little, if anything, about an afterlife. The book of Leviticus exhibits a priestly preoccupation with ritual purification, which is most often occasioned by the flow of blood, female menstrual fluids, or male semen—all of which signified loss of life and thus potentially death. Contact with a corpse also brought impurity (Num 19:11, 14; Lev 11:31–32; 21:11). In ritual sacrifice, the separation of the blood and the fat symbolized death.

Given the OT's preoccupation of forbidding idolatry in the worship of other gods, it is striking that the book of Leviticus says relatively little about this (19:4; 26:1, 30), except that it singles out the forbidden worship of Molech, a deity of the dead and the underworld (Lev 18:21; 20:2–5). These efforts likely reflect the priests' zeal to ban the so-called cult of the dead and ancestor worship. A consequence of these efforts, however, was to dissociate Yahweh from the dead in ancient Israel. I would suggest, therefore, that, in effect, the priests suppressed affirmations and hopes for an afterlife with Yahweh.[16] Their influence in shaping the Hebrew Bible was considerable, as evident in P, the redaction of the Pentateuch, Ezekiel, Ezra, and 1–2 Chronicles.

Peculiar to P is the phrase "gathered to his people," when describing death: Abraham, Ishmael, Isaac, Jacob (Gen 25:8, 17; 35:29; 49:29, 33) Aaron (Num 20:24), and Moses (Num 27:13; 31:2, which is picked up in Deut 32:50). Although this expression highlights the importance of kinship bonds in the ancient world, it sidesteps saying anything about their status vis-à-vis Yahweh.

---

16 Jacob Milgrom, *Leviticus*, CC (Minneapolis: Fortress Press, 2004), 66–67, agrees: "the concept of an afterlife was deliberately suppressed. The reason, I submit, is that it was associated with ancestor worship".

There is one instance, however, where the priestly writers may have inadvertently provided hope for an afterlife with God. The priestly genealogy in Genesis 5 appears to mimic the Sumerian King List. Both highlight the seventh member of the list and both are interrupted by "the flood".[17] The seventh king, Enmeduranki, ruled 21,000 years. "Shamash and Adad called him to their assembly,"[18] where he learned divination practices with oil and liver.[19] His counsellor also "ascended into heaven."[20] The seventh listed in the priestly "scroll of the generations of Adam" is Enoch.

In Gen 5:24, "Enoch walked with God, and he was not, for God took (לקח) him." The point of the priestly genealogy is to highlight the figure of Enoch. The verb choice "took" (לקח), once the Hebrew Scriptures were formed, invited a reinterpretation of the same verb found in our two key passages in the Psalms.

> With your counsel you guide me,
> and after (death) with glory you take (לקח) me (Ps 73:24).
>
> But God will ransom my soul from the hand of Sheol,
> for he will take (לקח) me (Ps 49:15).

Read canonically, these passages could now signify that God will "take" or "snatch" his devoted one from death and Sheol!

Apocalyptic: Death Devoured and Awaking from Sleep

Apocalypses are among the latest material in the OT. Most scholars date Isaiah's little apocalypse (Isaiah 24–27) to the postexilic period.[21] Isaiah 25:6–8

17 *ANET*, 265–266.

18 Nicolas Wyatt, *Space and Time in the Religious Life of the Near East*, BibSem 85 (Sheffield: Sheffield Academic Press, 2001), 195.

19 William W. Hallo and K. Lawson Younger, *The Context of Scripture* (Leiden: Brill, 1997–), 1.421.

20 Kenton L. Sparks, *Ancient Texts for the Study of the Hebrew Bible: A Guide to the Background Literature* (Peabody: Hendrickson Publishers, 2005), 346. See further Kenton L. Sparks, *God's Word in Human Words* (Grand Rapids: Baker Academic, 2008), 217–18; John Day, "The Development of Belief in Life after Death in Ancient Israel," in *After the Exile: Essays in Honour of Rex Mason*, ed. John Barton and David J. Reimer (Macon: Mercer University, 1996), 237.

21 Although prophecy and (proto-)apocalyptic may share similar motifs, apocalypses exhibit a heightened portrayal of cataclysmic events and a final, universal judgment of earthly and heavenly powers (Isa 24:21–22) and retribution beyond death. J. J. M. Roberts, on the basis of historical allusions but not generic characteristics, offers an intriguing

promises that Yahweh will prepare a lavish banquet "on this mountain," apparently Mount Zion in Jerusalem (24:23; 27:13), at which time "he will swallow up … the shroud that enwraps all the peoples." And most importantly for this study,

> He will swallow up death forever,
> and the Lord Yahweh will wipe away tears from all faces,
> and the reproach of his people he will remove from all the earth,
> for Yahweh has spoken (Isa 25:8).

The image of swallowing seems to indicate that Yahweh's menu for the banquet will come as a notable surprise. The direct objects of the same verb, shroud and Death, suggest that a burial shroud is intended.[22] Yahweh's devouring of death is strangely reminiscent of Mot's devouring Baal in the Ugaritic library.[23] What this entails about physical death and afterlife is not entirely clear. While the feast is "for all peoples," "his people," that is Yahweh's, are particularly in view throughout this apocalypse (note also v. 9). "Tears" may still exist but Yahweh will wipe them away.

Subsequent verses likewise echo the mythological memories of Israel's West Semitic culture, only to strip the Rephaim of any power, life, or memory.

> Yahweh our God, lords besides you have ruled (verb בעל, "baal") us,
> but your name alone we commemorate.
> The dead they will not live; the Rephaim they will not arise,
> … you have destroyed their memory (Isa 26:13–14).

By contrast for the people of Yahweh,

> Your dead shall live; their corpses shall arise.
> Awake and shout for joy, O dwellers in the dust,
> for your dew is the dew of lights,
> and the earth/underworld shall give birth to (lit. let drop) the Rephaim (Isa 26:19).

Although this passage is often hailed as one of the clearest references to resurrection in the OT, we must be struck that no action is predicated of Yahweh.

---

argument for a late 7th-early 6th century date, thus aligning it with Ezekiel's vision of resurrection (*First Isaiah: A Commentary*, ed. Peter Machinist, Hermeneia [Minneapolis: Fortress Press, 2015], 306–307).

22 Roberts, *First Isaiah*, 323.

23 Mot, whose appetite is voracious (KTU 1.5:1:14, 19), promises to devour Baal (KTU 1.5:1:6–8). Baal then enters his enormous mouth (KTU 1.5:2:2–6), and Mot devours him "like a lamb in my mouth" (KTU 1.6:2:21–23). Cf. Isa 5:14; Hab 2:5.

He does not intervene or resurrect. Instead, afterlife is depicted as "awaking" from sleep "in the dust." In effect, afterlife becomes conceivable because death is reduced to a form of sleep, from which awaking is a natural process, as are "dew" and "light" in the morning.

The second image of afterlife is even more bizarre. The language refers to another natural process: Mother earth lets her baby "drop" (תַּפִּיל) from the womb. Moreover, her baby is identified as the "Rephaim," the ancient mythological identifier for the "shades" of the dead.

Mythological memories, evidenced in the Ugaritic library (KTU 1.5:1:1–4), are center stage once again in Isaiah's apocalypse.

> In that day Yahweh with his severe, great, and strong sword will punish Leviathan the fleeing serpent, Leviathan the twisting serpent, and he will slay the dragon in the sea (Isa 27:1).

Given the extraordinary claim of resurrection, we should inquire about its antecedents. To our surprise, the strongest parallels occur in Ugaritic literature and its biblical echoes. "Dust" as a place of the dead is an image attested at Ugarit (*ʿpr*, KTU 1.2:4:5; 1.17:1:27–28; 1. 161:21–22) and in the Bible (עפר, Job 7:21; 17:16; 20:11; 21:26; Ps 22:15, 29, emended; 30:9; Isa 26:19; Dan 12:2; cf. Gen 2:19). While "your dead live" (היה, Qal) in Isaiah's apocalypse, Yahweh himself does not "bring them to life" (היה, Piel), as in the archaic poems (Deut 32:39; 1 Sam 2:6), nor does he "redeem" or "take" them (גאל, פדה, לקח) as in the Prophets (Amos 9:2; Hos 13:14) and Psalms (49:15; 73:24). Nor does Yahweh give them "breath" and "flesh" and "raise" (עלה, Hiph) them from their graves, as in Ezekiel's vision (Ezek 37:1–14).[24]

So, we have now come full circle. The mythological memory that Israel inherited from its Semitic culture was the nightmare for Yahwism. But Isaiah's apocalypse, which banishes the nightmare, is strangely framed in mythological

24 John Day posits eight parallels between Hosea 13–14 and Isaiah 26–27 and argues that Isa 26:19 is "certainly dependent" on Hos 13:14 ("The Development of Belief in Life after Death in Ancient Israel," 244–45). Some of his alleged parallels, however, occur in disparate oracles within these chapters and others are hardly distinctive (e.g., affirmations of Yahweh alone, the need for discernment, and the condemnation of idolatry). Common images need not indicate *literary* dependence. Most importantly, the possibility of afterlife for Israel is denied in Hosea but asserted in Isaiah. Hosea foregrounds Yahweh's intervention as redemption from death, but Isaiah's apocalypse likens bodies rising to awaking from sleep and to the appearance of dew and light in the morning. I do not perceive a clear flag in the Isaiah passage that alerts the listener/reader to Hosea's. The most that could be said is the possibility of "influence" (see Jon Levenson's assessment of Day's parallels in his *Resurrection and the Restoration of Israel*, 202–4).

terms, not in terms that are characteristic of Yahwism and Yahweh's saving interventions.[25] The OT does not demystify and demythologize the Rephaim away and revert to a dust-to-dust paradigm. Logic and theology alone cannot expunge a nightmare, so the Semitic cultural imagination is employed to awaken hope in God's people. Memories are not erased and replaced; they are reimagined.

Another apocalyptic passage, Daniel 7, illustrates how ancient "memories" survive over centuries and among diverse people groups. Anyone familiar with the Baal myth cannot help but experience déjà vu between Daniel's "Ancient of Days" and the deity El and between the "Son of Man" coming from "the clouds of heaven" and the Cloud Rider Baal. These echoes can be explained only in terms of "cultural memories," not on the basis of genetic textual links.[26] The Late Bronze period library at Ugarit was buried long before the emergence of ancient Israel's canonical library. Yet these memories appear a millennium later in the postexilic period.

Arguably the clearest passage about afterlife in the OT is found in the second-century apocalypse of Daniel 12.

> ... but at that time your people shall be delivered, each who is found written in the book. And many of those who sleep in the ground of dust will awake, these to everlasting life and these to taunts and everlasting abhorrence. And the wise/ enlighteners will be bright like the brightness of the firmament, and those who lead the many to righteousness, like the stars forever and ever (Dan 12:1b–3).

We might imagine that the OT invoked belief in an afterlife because Yahweh's retributive justice was not evident in this earthly life. But this late apocalyptic passage is the first to distinguish the destinies of the righteous and those deserving judgment in an afterlife.[27] Prior to this, death and Sheol were problematic

---

25 Further on the prevalence of mythic images in apocalyptic literature, see John J. Collins, *The Apocalyptic Imagination: An Introduction to Jewish Apocalyptic Literature*, 2nd ed. (Grand Rapids: Eerdmans, 1998), 17–19, 24.

26 Paul G. Mosca attempts to connect the Baal Myth and Daniel 7 by linking Psalm 89 (esp. vv. 5–13, El incomparable among the "sons of El" who rules Yam and crushed Rahab) and Psalm 8 ("son of man"). See his "Ugarit and Daniel 7: A Missing Link," *Bib* 67.4 (1986): 496–517. But he does not succeed in addressing the problem that he raises himself, namely finding an inner-biblical link connecting the heavenly figures "the Ancient of Days" and the "son of man." Nothing especially links these two psalms. Yahweh/El's rule is cosmic, and the earthly "son of man's" (which is not a figure or title, but simply a parallel idiom for humanity) rule is over animals.

27 Also, a late postexilic testimony, Qoheleth highlights the infelicity in divine retribution when he laments "the one event [of death] for the righteous and for the wicked" (Eccl 9:2–3; cf. 2:16).

for Yahwism, not because Yahweh's justice was in question, but because they cut off contact with Yahweh. According to the developing testimony of the OT, Israel's central value was an enduring relationship with Yahweh. The primary concern was with Yahweh's faithfulness (אֱמֶת, חֶסֶד) and secondarily with his justice (מִשְׁפָּט). So Jon Levenson is indeed correct when he argues that "the language and symbolism of resurrection were present and available, perhaps even abundant, long before the literal expectation" in Daniel 12:1b–3.[28]

Unlike the previous passages we have examined, this one appears to be textually derived from other passages in the OT, first from Isaiah's apocalyptic passage. Yet even here the echoes are subtle, without clear flags referring readers to prior authoritative texts.

Table 2.2 Echoes in Daniel 12 and Isaiah 26

Daniel 12:1–3	**Isaiah 26:19**
many of those who sleep in the ground of dust (עָפָר) will awake (קיץ)	Awake (קיץ) …, O dwellers in the dust (עָפָר)

Once again, we note that this OT passage does not describe resurrection as an act of God, but simply as "awaking" from sleep in the "dust."

In 1953 Harold Ginsberg argued that the "oldest interpretation of the suffering servant" in Isaiah 53 was this passage in Daniel, which also draws from other texts in the OT.

Table 2.3 The "suffering servant" in Daniel 12 and Second Isaiah

Daniel 12	**Second Isaiah**
3 the wise/enlighteners (שׂכל, Hiph)	52:13 Behold, my servant shall be wise/enlighten (שׂכל, Hiph)
2 And many (רַבִּים) of those who sleep in the ground of dust will awake, these to everlasting life … 3 the wise/enlighteners …, those who lead the many (הָרַבִּים) to righteousness (צדק, Hiph)	53:11 … in his knowledge, a righteous one, my servant will lead the many (לָרַבִּים)[29] to righteousness (צדק, Hiph) 53:12 Therefore, I will apportion to him with the many (בָּרַבִּים) … spoil … but he bore the sin of many (רַבִּים) …

28 Levenson, *Resurrection and the Restoration of Israel*, 185.

29 The "many" are also referenced at the beginning of this servant song (Isa 52:14–15).

Table 2.3 The "suffering servant" in Daniel 12 and Second Isaiah (*fortges.*)

Daniel 12	**Second Isaiah**
3 the enlighteners will shine	53:11 he will see light
2 these to taunts and everlasting abhorrence (דראון)	66:24 And they shall go out and look upon the corpses of the men who transgressed against me, for their worm will not die, and their fire will not be quenched, and they will be an abhorrence (דֵּרָאוֹן) to all flesh.

If Daniel 12 is in fact the oldest interpretation of the Suffering Servant, it clearly offers a corporate interpretation and identifies "my servant" as the "wise/ enlighteners" (*maskilim*, cf. 11:33, 35; 12:10).[30] While we might debate whether or not Isaiah's Suffering Servant experienced the "light" of resurrection, it is clear that Daniel's "enlighteners" must be counted among the "many" who were "sleeping in the ground of the dust," but "awoke ... to everlasting life."

Daniel 12 draws from another passage in Isaiah, one that closes the scroll with observers seeing corpses (פֶּגֶר) and unquenchable "fire." This scene likely picks up Jeremiah's scene of Topheth (cooking hearth) in the Valley of Hinnom, where the Israelites made their children pass through "fire" and which they would later fill with corpses (נְבֵלָה, Jer 7:31–33). (Here we see the developing image of Gehenna.)

Table 2.4 Jeremiah's scene of Topeth in Daniel 12

Daniel 12	**Psalms**
2 those who sleep in the ground of dust (יְשֵׁנֵי אַדְמַת־עָפָר)	Ps 22:29 All the sleepers[31] (יְשֵׁנֵי) of the earth shall eat and worship; before him shall kneel all who descend to the dust (עָפָר), even whose soul cannot stay alive.

30 The "son of man" in Daniel 7 is similarly portrayed as an individual figure who is interpreted as a corporate body.

31 Reading יְשֵׁנֵי, instead of the MT's דִּשְׁנֵי־.

Table 2.4 Jeremiah's scene of Topeth in Daniel 12 (*fortges.*)

Daniel 12	Psalms
2 many of those who sleep in the ground of dust will awake (קיץ) 2 those who lead the many to righteousness (צדק)	Ps 17:15 I, in righteousness (צדק), I will behold your face; I shall be satisfied, upon awaking (קיץ), (with) your manifestation.

The closest phrasing to Daniel's "those who sleep in the ground of dust" (מִיְּשֵׁנֵי אַדְמַת־עָפָר) can be found in the reconstructed text of Psalm 22:29 (יְשֵׁנֵי־אֶרֶץ). In my commentary on the Psalms, I have argued that these five verses closing this psalm were likely a postexilic addition, which adapted the preceding individual lament to serve as a corporate lament of the exilic and postexilic communities. The psalm's closing section (vv. 27–31) is unlike anything that precedes but is akin to the psalms of Yahweh's kingship (i.e., the enthronement psalms, Psalms 47; 93; 96–99). In this reapplication of Psalm 22, the community of Israel laments the Babylonian exile, and then celebrates Yahweh's deliverance from exile in the subsequent thanksgiving. The final section that celebrates "all the ends of the earth" (כָּל־אַפְסֵי־אָרֶץ) "turning to Yahweh" echoes Second Isaiah's vision of "all the ends of the earth" (כָּל־אַפְסֵי־אָרֶץ) "turning" to Yahweh (Isa 45:22) and "seeing the salvation of our God" (Isa 52:10)—in the events of the postexilic restoration.

The key term for resurrection in both Isa 26:19 and Dan 12:2 employs the image of "awaking" (קיץ) from sleep in the dust. "Awaking" is also the decisive moment of vindication for the falsely accused in the Psalms, as they underwent a cultic rite of being tested at night in the sanctuary (Ps 17:15). There may appear little to connect these apocalyptic passages with the Psalms, but both point to a trial by God. The two psalms use the language of judgment (שפט in 7:6, 8, 11; 17:2, דין in 7:8). Daniel 12 refers to "the book" that records those who shall "be delivered" (12:1). Daniel's earlier vision referred to "books" that are "opened" as God's "court sat" for trial (דִּינָא, 7:10, 22, 26). The Psalms elsewhere refer to "the book of the living" (69:28; cf. 87:4–6; 139:16). In both Ps 17:15 and Dan 12:1–3, Yahweh's judgment hinges on the quality of "righteousness."

Conclusions and the Benefits of Social Memory Theory

Theory of memory—of which I am clearly a novice. It began as an attempt to interpret the OT data regarding death and afterlife. Along the way I have discovered that memory studies may be a more appropriate tool than tradition history for studying the phenomena and processes operating in Israelite religion and the OT. How should scholars conceptualize ancient Israel's beliefs and how they developed? As traditions or memories?

Cultural Memories: Subjectively and Unconsciously Received

Both the Bronze Age Ugaritic tablets and the OT share the following depictions of the dead: death as a descent to the underworld; dust as the location of the dead; death as sleep; and the dead as Rephaim.

As argued above, the notion of diminished existence in Sheol is inherently incompatible with Yahwism. The OT provides no genesis for Sheol, nor does it embrace it within Yahweh's domain. Sheol is contrary to the fundamental notion of memory in Israelite worship: Yahweh does not remember the dead, nor can the dead memorialize Yahweh. When near to death, OT worshipers appeal to Yahweh's "faithfulness," a divine attribute that death (esp. premature) puts in jeopardy. The best way to account for the presence of these notions particularly, in earlier OT passages, is to regard Sheol as an inheritance of the cultural memories that the Israelites shared with their Semitic neighbors.

Tradition history criticism studies, in the words of Michael Fishbane, the *traditum* (the content of the tradition) and the *traditio* (the transmission process of the tradition).[32] This form of biblical criticism has made considerable contributions to our understanding of the OT and Israelite religion, but practitioners may construe tradition as an object and its transmission as an objective process whereby received traditions are consciously analyzed, sifted, reconfigured, and authorized.

The process of memory, I believe, is a more apt, nuanced, and sophisticated conceptualization of Israel's beliefs. It includes the content of what is remembered—the objective/external objects, events, and data. And it includes the subjective/internal complexities of how humans remember and conceptualize what they have learned. Memory studies are more cognizant that what we learn individually and collectively is often simply received from our forebears. Memories are often appropriated unconsciously and not scrutinized for logical consistency and coherence.[33] What each generation learns may be

32 Michael Fishbane, *Biblical Interpretation in Ancient Israel* (Oxford: Clarendon Press, 1985), 6.

33 Aleida Assmann maintains that "stored memory" includes "the cultural forms of the unconscious." Jan Assmann goes as far to say, "This is why the concept of tradition, as usually understood, is completely inadequate as a description of this phenomenon. 'Tradition' refers to the business of handing down and receiving, as well as the continued existence of what has been received. The only dynamics conceivable in terms of this concept are those which are released in cultural work in a controlled and conscious fashion;

passively received and go unprocessed. As we learn our "native" language, we do not scrutinize its grammar for logical consistency or its vocabulary for foreign loanwords. Language is a subset of culture. As the Canaanite and Ugaritic languages are cognate to Hebrew, so West Semitic culture formed part of Israel's cultural memory. For some memories there may be no evaluation whether or not they are Israelite or Canaanite. The distinction that we make may be artificial. There are indeed ethnic traditions that help construct ethnic identity, but we should not assume that all inherited memories are sifted like ethnic and religious traditions. The Bible's early affirmations of Sheol serve as an example. These images of death and Sheol may be considered part of Semitic speech and vocabulary, not as traditions that are distinctively Israelite.

Pre-exilic and Exilic Counter-Memories: Oral Publication and Sound Bites

Table 2.5 Beliefs of death and afterlife in the OT

Counter-Memories: Terms, Images	**Public Source**[34]
Yahweh puts to death, brings to life (Deut 32:39; 1 Sam 2:5–6; echoed in Hos 6:1–2)	Archaic poems
Yahweh = my portion/inheritance (Pss 16:5–6, 10–11; 73:24–26)	Levites and psalms
Righteous awake, see God (Pss 11:7; 17:2–3, 15)	Psalms and temple trial ritual
Yahweh can redeem, take (Amos 9:2; Hos 13:14; echoed in Ps 49:15)	Historical memories in Amos, Hosea
Yahweh brings flesh and breath to bones, raises from graves (Ezek 37: 1–14)	Ezekiel (priest)
Suffering Servant (52:13–53:12)	Second Isaiah

every interaction with the dynamics of identity and memory is cut off. The concept of tradition leaves no space for the unconscious" (*Religion and Cultural Memory*, trans. Rodney Livingstone [Stanford: Stanford University Press, 2006], 25). On "mnemohistory," as a new branch of historiography, which is interested in tracing "the involuntary paths of memory," which can become "an unconscious burden," see Aleida Assmann, "Transformations between History and Memory," *Social Research* 75 (2008): 62.

34 "Source" here denotes not a literary source from which scribes drew, but a literary witness where a memory/tradition, known to the wider public, is embedded and happens to surface.

An assessment of Israel's developing beliefs in death and afterlife reveals some intriguing observations. There are hints and glimpses peppered throughout the OT, but none conclusively claims an afterlife for humans. Archaic poems hymn Yahweh's capacity to bring one to life after death, but they make no general claim that afterlife is promised to the people of God. A few psalms hint of a rescue from Sheol (whatever that entails), but they are phrased as individual claims. Other psalms hint of seeing God after awaking, but likely refer to the legal vindication of the falsely accused. Amos and Hosea both affirm Yahweh's reach into Sheol, but lack any wide-ranging claims for human existence. In the Babylonian exile the prophets Ezekiel and Second Isaiah offered unique conceptualizations of hope, but this hope was likely for corporate Israel's restoration after the exile.

Hope in an afterlife is not an issue central to early Yahwism. Most of these verses predicate interventions of Yahweh: Yahweh heals and brings to life (Deut 32:39; 1 Sam 2:6), and Yahweh takes and redeems (Amos 9:2; Hos 13:14; Pss 49:15; 73:24). Attention is focused on Yahweh's portfolio, not the human condition.

Moreover, these hints surface in various images across various social circles with no hints of direct contact with each other: rituals in the Psalms, Levitical privileges, historical memories in the Prophets, and mythological figures. Their tradents show no evidence of interaction on the level of "communicative/social memory."[35] Psalm 49 makes the same predications of God found in the pre-exilic prophets Hosea and Amos, who appeal to memories of the exodus. But this psalm, likely from the wisdom tradition, exhibits no genetic links with prophetic material.

These passages all reflect an original mode of oral publication: archaic songs, psalms, and prophetic oracles.[36] We must recognize their *Sitz im Text/Schrift* is secondary. These hints of afterlife first circulated orally in Israelite society and so operated in the memories and imaginations of the ancient Israelites.

Form and tradition history criticism began in part as a healthy reaction to *literary* criticism and thus draw our attention to *oral* tradition. Hermann Gunkel proposed form criticism in response to Julius Wellhausen's literary/source criticism because the literary documents, JEDP, presupposed an earlier phase of oral transmission and publication. In practice, however, the historical-critical

35 See Jan Assmann, "Communicative and Cultural Memory," in *Cultural Memories: The Geographical Point of View*, ed. Peter Meusburger, Michael Heffernan, and Edgar Wunder (Dordrecht: Springer, 2011), 15–27.

36 Indeed, even in Deuteronomy, a written law code and covenant, the operative imperatives are "hear" and "remember."

methods—using the tools of form, tradition history, literary/source, and redaction criticism—ultimately focus on the formation of texts. As scholars who are centuries removed from ancient Israel, we have no choice but to study their religion and society through the texts they left behind. But while they must be our primary means of studying their memories and beliefs, our limitation does not entail that their beliefs were constructed solely within a canonical envelope bounded by scrolls and scribes.

Walter Ong likewise observes that biblical studies tends to give primacy to texts and "literate memory" over "oral memory."[37] He remarks how difficult it is for literate people to imagine how an oral culture operates. If we cannot recall something from memory, we "look it up." But in an oral culture "you know what you can recall" via "mnemonics and formulas": "you have to do your thinking in mnemonic patterns, shaped for ready oral recurrence… . Formulas help implement rhythmic discourse and also act as mnemonic aids in their own right, as set expressions circulating through the mouths and ears of all."[38]

In the chart above, the key vocabulary and imagery of Yahwism's counter-memories to Sheol are relatively simple: Yahweh brings to life, Yahweh is my portion, Yahweh redeems/takes, Yahweh raises and I awake, bones and servants. These are formulas, stock images, and sound bites that can lodge in the popular memory. Their access is not restricted to libraries and literates. Thus, glimpses of hope for an afterlife could be fostered in the imaginations of ancient Israel's wider listening public.

The discipline of biblical studies is like archaeology. Archaeologists discover architecture, artifacts, and texts by accident and by what happens to survive. But their study is not limited to stratigraphy and pottery. It includes reconstructing the lives of the people who lived there, contributing to the fields of Israelite history, society, and religion. They can study their beliefs only insofar as they can be inferred from material remains.

Similarly, biblical scholars study a landscape of texts that happen to have found their way into the sacred scrolls of the Jews. They are the monuments and artifacts that survived among the many inscriptions, psalms, oracles, and speeches that circulated in Israelite cities and villages but are now lost to us. Biblical scholars can study Israelite beliefs only insofar as they can be inferred from this sampling of selected scrolls. So, they need to move beyond the exegesis of texts and extrapolate how the beliefs embedded in these texts circulated and operated in ancient Israel's oral culture (e.g., in their symbols and rituals).

37 Ong and Hartley, *Orality and Literacy*, 170.

38 Ong and Hartley, *Orality and Literacy*, 31–35.

Biblical passages are not merely frozen, authoritative texts, but *testimonies* of religious and societal beliefs. The crucible where biblical beliefs were forged was broader than the scribe's study.[39] While these sacred texts may have been inscribed by literate elites, they bear witness to the ideas and beliefs that gained traction in wider Israelite society. These beliefs were written down, not simply because they were deemed authoritative by scribal elites, but because they were recognized as having already achieved a sacred status through their oral publication and circulation. Israel's scriptures were not owned by scribes under copyright; they bear witness to public memories that had some measure of popular consent.

These various counter-memories are manifest not as texts connected exegetically, but as key phrases and metaphoric images associated imaginatively (mental links). There is no exegetical argument presented. The process is best understood as an imaginative one than an analytical one. It is more right brain than left brain. In short, it is best described as a function of memory, not as an assessment of written traditions.

Postexilic Counter-Memories: Apocalyptic, Written Scriptures

Table 2.6 Assertations of afterlife

Death → ritual impurity (Lev, Num) God takes (Gen 5:24)	Aaronic priests (P)
Yahweh swallows Death (Isa 25:8) Earth births Rephaim (Isa 26:19) Dead live and rise, sleep and awake (Isa 26:19; Dan 12:2)	Mythological memories Temple trial ritual?
Enlighteners lead the many to righteousness (Dan 12:3)	Apocalyptic (re-)interpretation of Second Isaiah's Servant

39 I have benefited greatly from John Day's two articles, "The Development of Belief in Life after Death in Ancient Israel" and "Resurrection Imagery from Baal to the Book of Daniel," but as a philologist skilled in historical-critical research he argues that scribes developed these ideas by exegesis of preceding authoritative texts. He writes, "I hope to demonstrate that the first clear reference to the literal resurrection of the dead in the Old Testament in Dan. xii 2 is *a reinterpretation of the verse* in Isa. xxvi 19 about resurrection… . Isa. xxvi 19 in turn, I shall argue, *is dependent on* the death and resurrection imagery in the book of Hosea, especially on *a reinterpretation of* Hos. xiii 14. Finally, the imagery of death and resurrection in Hosea … is *directly taken over by the prophet from* the imagery of the dying and rising fertility god, Baal" (emphasis mine, "Resurrection Imagery from Baal to the Book of Daniel," in *Congress Volume Cambridge 1995*, ed. J. A. Emerton, VTSup 66 (Leiden: Brill, 1997), 125.

The clearest assertions of afterlife appear in the later passages that are predominantly apocalyptic (Isaiah 24–27; Daniel) and were published in written sources (P source, Daniel 12). They exhibit few echoes of the earlier suggestive passages in the archaic poems, the pre-exilic prophets, and the Psalms (which are difficult to date). When we think to ask, "what is remembered in these passages?" it is striking to observe that the earlier passages foreground Yahweh's capacity to bring to life and to redeem from Sheol. But the later passages predicate little of God (taking Enoch, swallowing Death) and instead highlight natural lifecycles (sleeping and waking, birthing) and mythological images (the Rephaim, the dead as "sleeping in the ground of the dust," Isa 26:19; Dan 12:2). The earlier and later passages share the root חיה, but have different subjects and verbal stems: Yahweh "brings to life" (Piel) versus humans "live" (Qal). This shift may be because afterlife becomes a universal claim for humanity, not a specific claim of God's intervention on behalf of individuals. But this change certainly signifies a shift in memories: from Yahweh and his interventions to mythological images grounded in Israel's Semitic memory and imagination. Given that Yahwism was often at odds with Canaanite beliefs, the persistence of these mythological artifacts from the Late Bronze period to the Hellenistic period is better explained as cultural memories, than as traditions passed from generation to generation of Israelite scribes trying to maintain an exclusive identity.

Prior to Daniel 12, none of the passages exhibits a clear intertextual flag, pointing to an earlier text to support its authority and significance. The echoes of Semitic mythology (esp. Death swallowed, the Rephaim, Leviathan) in Isaiah's postexilic apocalypse are best explained as cultural memory, not as literary dependence. The parallels of "sleeping and waking" found in the Psalms and the apocalypses of Isaiah and Daniel are best explained as shared imagery, not as social communication between psalmists interested in ritual trials and apocalyptic writers. These associations emerged, not by exegesis of texts, but by images and "sound bites" stored in memory.

Dan 12:2 is the first to promise a general resurrection for individuals. Unlike the others, it was exegetically derived from previous authoritative texts. Nevertheless, each of the preceding passages becomes more compelling for individual resurrection once a canon is formed and becomes authoritative. These diverse passages can then be read in association with each other. Read individually, they are ambiguous, but once these glimpses of afterlife are stitched into a wider panorama of the Scriptures a clearer picture emerges.

But even after all these passages are compiled in an authoritative written canon of Scripture, the processes by which readers appropriate and apply them is not limited to exegesis of texts. The processes of (oral) memory are still operative. While literates may "look something up" in the Bible, their interpretations are still influenced by their "recall" of mnemonic formulas and images (echoing Ong's comments above).

Let us imagine ancient Jews interring the bones of a loved one in an ossuary, and they recall the Lord's voice, "Can these bones live?" (Ezek 37:3). Should we imagine them insisting, "Of course not, Ezekiel's vision applies only metaphorically to Israel's corporate resurrection from the Babylonian exile"? Biblical exegetes insist on interpreting texts according to context, which limits their meaning. But for Jewish and Christian readers these texts are not merely artifacts from ancient Israel's singular past. They are "torah," enduring teaching, for the people of God living in their present. As Augustine noted, "memory" is "the present of things past."[40] Biblical torah transports Israel's past into the reader's present memory. Reading involves not simply objective exegesis of tradition, but also the exercise of memory and imagination, which embrace the subjective hopes of the readers themselves and maximize meaning.

In sum, the phenomena and processes operating in both the Bible's formation and its subsequent reading as Scripture are best conceived and studied as memories, not simply as objective traditions.

Bibliography

Assmann, Aleida. "Collective Memory and Cultural Identity." *New German Critique* 65 (1995): 128–133.

———. *Religion and Cultural Memory*. Translated by Rodney Livingstone. Stanford: Stanford University Press, 2006.

———. "Transformations between History and Memory." *Social Research* 75 (2008): 49–72.

———. "Communicative and Cultural Memory." Pages 15–27 in *Cultural Memories: The Geographical Point of View*. Edited by Peter Meusburger, Michael Heffernan, and Edgar Wunder. Dordrecht: Springer, 2011.

———. "Memory and Culture." Pages 330–42 in *Memory: A History*. Edited by Dmitri Nikulin. Oxford: Oxford University Press, 2015.

Broyles, Craig C. *Psalms*. Grand Rapids: Baker Books, 2012.

Collins, John J. *The Apocalyptic Imagination: An Introduction to Jewish Apocalyptic Literature*. 2nd ed. Grand Rapids: Eerdmans, 1998.

40 *Confessions* 9.20, cited in Ronald Hendel, "Culture, Memory, and History: Reflections on Method in Biblical Studies," in *Historical Biblical Archaeology and the Future: The New Pragmatism*, ed. Thomas E. Levy (London: Equinox, 2010), 254.

Day, John. "The Development of Belief in Life after Death in Ancient Israel." Pages 231–57 in *After the Exile: Essays in Honour of Rex Mason*. Edited by John Barton and David J. Reimer. Macon: Mercer University, 1996.

———. "Resurrection Imagery from Baal to the Book of Daniel." Pages 125–33 in *Congress Volume Cambridge 1995*. Edited by J. A. Emerton. VTSup 66. Leiden: Brill, 1997.

Fishbane, Michael. *Biblical Interpretation in Ancient Israel*. Oxford: Clarendon Press, 1985.

Hallo, William W., and K. Lawson Younger. *The Context of Scripture*. Leiden: Brill, 1997–.

Hendel, Ronald. "Culture, Memory, and History: Reflections on Method in Biblical Studies." Pages 250–261 in *Historical Biblical Archaeology and the Future: The New Pragmatism*. Edited by Thomas E. Levy. London: Equinox, 2010.

Huebenthal, Sandra. "Social and Cultural Memory in Biblical Exegesis: The Quest for an Adequate Application." Pages 175–199 in *Cultural Memory in Biblical Exegesis*. Edited by Pernille Carstens, Trine B. Hasselbalch, and Niels Peter Lemche. PHSC 17. Piscataway: Gorgias, 2012.

Johnston, Philip. *Shades of Sheol: Death and Afterlife in the Old Testament*. Downers Grove: InterVarsity Press, 2002.

Levenson, Jon D. *Resurrection and the Restoration of Israel: The Ultimate Victory of the God of Life*. New Haven: Yale University Press, 2006.

Milgrom, Jacob. *Leviticus*. CC. Minneapolis: Fortress Press, 2004.

Mosca, Paul G. "Ugarit and Daniel 7: A Missing Link." *Bib* 67.4 (1986): 496–517.

Ong, Walter J., and John Hartley. *Orality and Literacy: The Technologizing of the Word*. 3rd ed. New York: Routledge, 2012.

Pardee, Dennis. *Ritual and Cult at Ugarit*. Edited by Theodore J. Lewis. Writings from the Ancient World 10. Atlanta: Society of Biblical Literature, 2002.

Roberts, J. J. M. *First Isaiah: A Commentary*. Edited by Peter Machinist. Hermeneia. Minneapolis: Fortress Press, 2015.

Smith, Mark S. *The Early History of God: Yahweh and the Other Deities in Ancient Israel*. 2nd ed. Grand Rapids: Eerdmans, 2002.

Smith, Mark S. and Wayne T. Pitard. *Ancient Texts for the Study of the Hebrew Bible: A Guide to the Background Literature*. Peabody: Hendrickson Publishers, 2005.

———. *God's Word in Human Words*. Grand Rapids: Baker Academic, 2008.

———. *The Ugaritic Baal Cycle: Introduction with Text, Translation and Commentary of* KTU/CAT *1.3–1.4*. Vol. 2. Leiden: Brill, 2009.

Wyatt, Nicolas. *Space and Time in the Religious Life of the Near East*. BibSem 85. Sheffield: Sheffield Academic Press, 2001.

Ancient Egyptian Judgment of the Dead in Visual Memory of Jewish Apocalyptic Literature

Jiří Janák and Michael Sommer

The scene of the judgement of the dead before Osiris is one of the most iconic images of ancient Egypt. It does not only hold this position currently, but it did so from ancient times into late antiquity. Moreover, it partly coheres with Jewish, Christian, and Muslim cultural traditions and their respective concepts of eschatology.[1] The ancient Egyptian notion of the judgement of the dead may have even influenced the notion of the judgment in Hellenism, Judaism, Gnosticism, and Christianity. Although the topic of the so-called judgment of the dead has been analysed and interpreted by many scholars of Egyptology and other related fields of research, some important aspects of the concept are still veiled in mystery. It is precisely this fact that makes our understanding of the concept's possible influence in later religious traditions even more difficult. Thus, the aim of the present study[2] is to present the latest Egyptological summary of the ancient Egyptian notion of the judgement of the dead together with the notions of the judgement in Jewish apocalyptic tradition, in order to analyse their possible interactions.

Two Modes of Judgment

When dealing with the ancient Egyptian religious tradition, one has to be aware that there were two very different, though partly interconnected, concepts of a judgment that was believed to take place in the afterlife. The first is a trial concerning a specific misdeed of a deceased person *in* the afterlife. The second is a more general trial that was also undertaken individually, but awaited all the dead *before* their acceptance into afterlife.

---

1 John G. Griffith, *The Divine Verdict. A Study of Divine Judgment in the Ancient Religions*, Numen Book Series 52 (Leiden: Brill, 1991); Jerry L. Walls, ed., *The Oxford Handbook of Eschatology* (Oxford: Oxford University Press, 2007).

2 This study was supported by the Charles University Research Program Q11, "*Complexity and Resilience. Ancient Egyptian Civilisation: A Multidisciplinary and Multicultural Approach*" and by the European Regional Development Fund-Project, "*Creativity and Adaptability as Conditions of the Success of Europe in an Interrelated World*" (*KREAS*, No. CZ.02.1.01/0.0/0.0/16_019/0000734).

 | DOI:10.30965/9783657796212_004

The first of the two variants presents a judgment or a trial focussing on a specific (both earthly or posthumous) misconduct of a deceased individual. This hearing takes place before the highest authority presiding over the afterlife (the ruler of the dead) and could occur any time during the posthumous period. Tomb inscriptions mentioning, or at least pointing towards this concept (mainly the so-called Appeals to the Living), are attested already in the time of the Old Kingdom.[3] In these texts, the tomb owners (usually referred to as the *akhu*, i.e., the mighty and blessed dead[4]) speak about a violent revenge upon the evil-doers (i.e., tomb violators) and about a posthumous divine judgment before the Great God. The effects of such trials are anticipated to occur either in the world of the living, maybe causing a premature death of wrongdoers, or later in the hereafter, after their natural death. The idea that justice did not cease with death and that a judgment could take place even in the afterlife, is attested also in the so-called Letters to the Dead, which the living address to the *akhu* (usually their ancestors) with pleas for urgent help.[5] The writers of these letters often asked a benevolent spirit to take action in their name, including legal actions at the divine court of the afterlife.

The second mode of an Egyptian posthumous judgment is best known as the judgment of the dead before Osiris, the ruler of the dead, and a tribunal of forty-two deities. Unlike the first variant, this one conceives of a divine

3 Elmar Edel, "Untersuchungen zur Phraseologie der ägyptischen Inschriften des Alten Reiches," *MDAI* 13 (1944): 1–90, here 10–11; Jean Sainte-Fare Garnot, *L'Appel aux vivants dans les textes funéraires égyptiens des origines à la fin de l'ancien empire* (Cairo: l'Institut français d'archéologie orientale, 1938); Scott Morschauser, *Threat-Formulae in Ancient Egypt: A Study of the History, Structure and Use of Threats and Curses in Ancient Egypt* (Baltimore: Johns Hopkins University Press, 1991); Martin A. Stadler, "Judgment after Death (Negative Confession)," in *UCLA Encyclopedia of Egyptology*, ed. Jacco Dieleman and Willeke Wendrich (Los Angeles: University of California, 2008), 1–4, here 1–2, https://escholarship.org/uc/item/07s1t6kj.pdf.

4 Jiří Janák, "Akh," in *UCLA Encyclopedia of Egyptology*, ed. Jacco Dieleman and Willeke Wendrich (Los Angeles: University of California, 2013), 1–9, https://escholarship.org/uc/item/7255p86v.

5 Edward F. Wente, *Letters from Ancient Egypt*, SBL Writings from the Ancient World 1 (Atlanta: Scholars Press, 1990); John Baines, "Society, Morality, and Religious Practice," in *Religion in Ancient Egypt: Gods, Myths, and Personal Practice*, ed. Byron E. Shafer (Ithaca: Cornell University Press, 1991), 123–200, here 151–61; Michael O'Donogue, "The 'Letters to the Dead' and Ancient Egyptian Religion," *Bulletin of the Australian Centre for Egyptology* 10 (1999): 87–104; Stephen G. J. Quirke, "Judgment of the Dead," in *The Oxford Encyclopedia of Ancient Egypt*, ed. Donald B. Redford (Oxford: Oxford University Press, 2001), 2.211–14; Ursula Verhoeven, "Post ins Jenseits—Formular und Funktion altägyptischer Briefe an Tote," in *Bote und Brief: Sprachliche Systeme der Informationsübermittlung im Spannungsfeld von Mündlichkeit und Schriftlichkeit*. ed. Andreas Wagner (Frankfurt am Main: Peter Lang, 2003), 31–51.

trial that takes place immediately *after* the person's death and *before* being accepted into the afterlife. Such a trial or hearing includes an assessment of the deceased's character and values before entering the blessed state of the afterlife rather than a judgment concerning specific misdeeds or accusations. Hence, it probably may not have even been conceived of as a judgment in the true sense, but rather as an interrogation at the divine bureau of immigration. Although some aspects of this concept are traceable in texts dated to the final phase of the Old Kingdom and First Intermediate Period, the notion of the posthumous assessment of character (i.e., heart) before Osiris is, in its developed form, attested from the early New Kingdom when it forms part of the *Book of the Dead* spells 30B and 125.[6] Since this second variant of the judgment of the dead has become iconic and survived ancient Egyptian civilisation within the (social) memory of other cultures, we shall limit our attention to it in this article.

The Judgment of the Dead and the Negative Confession

As both pictorially and verbally described in the *Book of the Dead* spell 125, the judgment of the dead was believed to take place in the Hall of Two Maats. The name of the place explicitly refers to the concept of universal order, justice and divine status quo that was called *maat* in Egyptian[7] and it had to be protected against *isfet* (chaos). Although the name of the hall itself (especially the duality of Maats) has not satisfactorily been explained yet,[8] it is clearly indicated as the place of justification of the worthy and damnation of the unrighteous. The *Book of the Dead* illustrations (the so-called vignettes) describe the hall as a broad court where the deceased appear before the supreme authority of the afterlife and a tribunal of forty-two other gods.[9] The vignettes sometimes show the deceased accompanied by a divine entity, usually Horus, Anubis, Thoth or the goddess Maat, when entering the court hall. Spell 125 equips him with secret knowledge which enables him both to enter the hall, where he stands in the presence of the divine court of justice, namely the Great God and the tribunal of forty-two deities. There, the deceased is expected to greet the deities and proclaim his innocence, fidelity and justice in a series of negative statements

6 Christine Seeber, *Untersuchungen zur Darstellung des Totengerichts im alten Ägypten*, Münchner Ägyptologische Studien 35 (München: Deutscher Kunstverlag, 1976).

7 Jan Assmann, *Ma'at. Gerechtigkeit und Unsterblichkeit im Alten Ägypten* (München: C. H. Beck, 1990).

8 Seeber, *Untersuchungen zur Darstellung des Totengerichts*, 36–67.

9 Seeber, *Untersuchungen zur Darstellung des Totengerichts*, 120–36.

(e.g., "I have done no evil; I have not robbed; I have not been greedy"). This denial of crimes, sins, or acts against ritual purity is usually divided into two sets in the *Book of the Dead* spell 125 and is often denoted as the "protestation/declaration of innocence" or the "negative confession" by scholars.[10] The concept proves that at least from the beginning of the New Kingdom, though most probably earlier, the acceptance into the afterlife was closely bound to a person's past conduct and his correct behaviour during the span of earthly life.[11]

The first set of proclamations covers thirty-six declarations of innocence spoken before the Great God and concludes with a repeated affirmation of the deceased's purity.[12] The second set consists of forty-two negative statements (often tabulated graphically) that encompass denials of forbidden, sinful, impure, or blasphemous actions, which were to be recited before a tribunal of forty-two gods. The deceased addressed each member of the tribunal in turn by their names and local affiliations (e.g., "O Broad of step who comes from Iunu; O Flame embracer who comes from Kheraha; O Beaked god who comes from Khemenu"). These divine names have the form of unusual epithets or mysterious names (for instance, the "Beaked god" instead of Thoth) that hint at the secret knowledge of the deceased and indicate his elevated, or even initiated, status. The number "forty-two" most probably refers to the total number of Lower and Upper Egyptian districts (the so-called nomes). Thus, the "judgment" was seen as an assessment of purity before the country as a whole.[13] Other scholars, however, have proposed another suggestion which regards the number as a symbolic sum of the multiplication of the sacred number "seven," the symbolic plural of "three," and the number "two" which represents the two lands of Egypt.[14]

The content of the negative confession stays consistent throughout different historical periods and varying only in sequence.[15] The range of the wrongdoings (or "sins") assessed by the Great God and the tribunal of forty-two deities is very wide. The statements of innocence cover topics that span from general

10 Stadler, "Judgment after Death," 1–4.

11 John H. Taylor, ed., *Journey through the Afterlife: Ancient Egyptian Book of the Dead* (Cambridge: Harvard University Press, 2010), 204.

12 Jan Assmann and Andrea Kucharek, *Ägyptische Religion. Totenliteratur* (Frankfurt am Main: Verlag der Weltreligionen, 2008), 835–37.

13 Jan Assmann, *Tod und Jenseits im alten Ägypten* (München: C. H. Beck, 2001), 111.

14 Seeber, *Untersuchungen zur Darstellung des Totengerichts*, 137; Stephen G. J. Quirke, *Going Out in Daylight—prt m hrw. The Ancient Egyptian Book of the Dead: Translation, Sources, Meanings*, GHP Egyptology 20 (London: GHP, 2013), 276.

15 Quirke, "Judgment of the Dead," 175; Günther Lapp, *Synoptische Textausgabe nach Quellen des Neuen Reiches*, Totenbuchtexte 3 (Basel: Orientverlag, 2008); Stadler, "Judgment after Death," 2.

ethical norms and moral maxims (e.g., instructions against doing evil, stealing, killing, lying, adultery, etc.) to more specific crimes against social order and peace (e.g., causing hunger, pain or tears, gossiping, holding back waters of the inundation and sexual offences) and personal or ritual purity (reducing or stealing offerings or temple property, killing sacred animals and blaspheming). Some scholars consider the negative confession to be a summary of ancient Egyptian ethical standards.[16] Some even link the origin of the negative confession with priestly oaths.[17]

All the above-mentioned aspects of the negative confession deal both with ethical norms together with religious observances or piety and with practical issues concerning posthumous transfiguration and initiation into divine secrets. The confession and this form of the judgment of the dead as a whole represents neither an ultimate (apocalyptic) judgment, nor a final separation of the blessed and the damned. It rather resembles an assessment of purity before initiation (or acceptance into a sacred office, as proposed by some scholars) or a migration interview before being accepted as an eternal resident of the afterlife.

The Weighing of the Heart

In the process of the judgment or the assessment of purity, the arrival of the deceased into the Hall of Two Maats, his proclamation of innocence and his acceptance by the divine tribunal was followed by another very important aspect of the trial. From the New Kingdom's *Book of the Dead* (spells 30A/B and 125) to the *Documents for Breathing* of the Roman Period, the trial was visually represented as the weighing of the deceased's consciousness or deeds, manifested by the heart, against the order of *maat*.[18] Ancient Egyptians considered the heart to be the seat of the mind, emotions and consciousness. Thus, they connected it closely with the earthly deeds of the deceased. However, the text

16 Assmann, *Tod und Jenseits im alten Ägypten*, 110–15.

17 Reinhold Merkelbach, "Ein griechisch-ägyptischer Priestereid und das Totenbuch," in *Religions en Égypte hellénistique et romaine*, ed. Philippe Derchain (Paris: Presses universitaires du France, 1969): 69–73; Joachim F. Quack, "Ein ägyptisches Handbuch des Tempels und seine griechische Übersetzung," *ZPE* 119 (1997): 297–300; John L. Gee, "The Requirements of Ritual Purity in Ancient Egypt," Ph.D. Diss., (New Haven: Yale University, 1998), 114; Assmann, *Tod und Jenseits im alten Ägypten*, 110–12; Martin A. Stadler, *Der Totenpapyrus des Pa-Month (P. Bibl. Nat. 149)*, Studien zum Altägyptischen Totenbuch 6 (Wiesbaden: Harrassowitz Verlag, 2003), 23–24; *Judgment after Death*, 2; Taylor, *Journey through the Afterlife*, 208–9.

18 Seeber, *Untersuchungen zur Darstellung des Totengerichts.*

of *Book of the Dead* spell 125, which bears the negative confession, surprisingly only refers to the weighing of the heart in hints. Only vignettes to spell 125, their captions, and spells 30A and 30B, shed light upon the motif of weighing the deceased's heart.

The weighing itself was also believed to take place in the Hall of Two Maats before the throne of Osiris. On the *Book of the Dead* vignettes, one can usually observe massive scales operated by the god Anubis and supervised by Thoth. The most common depiction of the judgment of the dead scene shows the deceased's heart on one pan of the scales being weighed against a manifestation of *maat* on the other. The cosmic order of *maat* might have been represented either by its hieroglyph (an ostrich feather) or personified by a figure of the goddess Maat. Although this image (that in the process of time has become iconic for both domestic and foreign understanding of the Egyptian concept of the afterlife) occurs on the majority of vignettes to the *Book of the Dead* spells 125 and 30B, it had many variants and significant modifications. Some *Book of the Dead* versions present the scene with a depiction of the deceased himself being weighed against his own heart. Other interesting variants show the weighing of the head or the eyes of the deceased against the order of *maat*. Such examples may indicate that the return of the person's corporeal integrity, bodily functions and ability to be revived represented the main outcome of a successful weighing.[19]

As is almost always the case in ancient Egyptian iconography, even the vignettes to the *Book of the Dead* spells 30B and 125 do not present us with any hint of a possible negative result. On the contrary, all the known attestations of the judgment scene recorded in the *Book of the Dead*, on coffins or tomb walls, present the ideal, that is positive, result of the trial. The vignettes, thus, depict the deceased or his heart as righteous, literally resting in balance with *maat* without shaking the arms of the scales. But one, of course, must ask a question on the negative result as well. What would happen if an unjust heart was placed on the scale? Would it rise, being too light, or drop, being too heavy?

Although depictions do not provide much information about the two possible results of weighing, textual comments on the scene reveal a very significant detail. They describe the pure heart of the righteous deceased person as "full," "complete" and "intact" or "sound."[20] This coheres with the idea that the heart

19 Jiří Janák, "The Judgment," in *The Oxford Handbook of the Book of the Dead*, ed. Martin J. Stadler and Rita Lucarelli (Oxford: Oxford University Press, forthcoming).

20 Seeber, *Untersuchungen zur Darstellung des Totengerichts*, 79–80, 111; Heike C. Schmidt, "Gewogen und zu leicht befunden," in *Pharaos Staat. Festschrift für Rolf Gundlach zum*

of a just and faithful person should be *filled* with *maat*, wisdom, duties or gods and be free of all things that make the heart light, as found in Egyptian wisdom literature, stories, autobiographic inscriptions and hymns.[21] So, if a just heart was viewed as full and complete, the "sinful" heart had to be considered imperfect and, thus, lighter both than *maat* and the just heart. Unrighteousness, impurity and violation of *maat* did not represent a burden, but rather an insufficiency of *maat* or damage to the heart.[22]

After passing through the obstacles of the judgment of the dead and being justified before by the divine tribunal (literally, being declared "true of voice"), the deceased could enter the afterlife. The acceptance among the blessed spirits of the afterlife (the *akhu*) was also linked to the permission to leave the netherworld and come back again as the deceased pleased, which was the main theme of the *Book of the Dead*.[23]

The final victory over death was, however, dependent on the return of vital organs and senses to the deceased. The return of the heart, eyes or mouth represents the main topic of the *Book of the Dead* spells 21–29.[24] And it is also sometimes depicted or mentioned in vignettes to spell 125. Thus, the deceased was physically equipped for entering the afterlife. Such corporeal redemption metaphysically supplements similar actions undertaken physically during the embalming process or ritually prescribed by the *Opening of the Mouth*.[25]

---

75. Geburtstag, ed. Dirk Bröckelmann and Andrea Klug (Wiesbaden: Harrassowitz, 2006), 251–58; Janák, "The Judgment."

21 Jan Assmann, *Ägyptische Hymnen und Gebete* (München and Zürich: Artemis Verlag, 1975), 188, 191; R. B. Parkinson, *The Tale of Sinuhe and Other Ancient Egyptian Poems 1940–1640 B.C.* (Oxford: Oxford University Press, 1997), 54–88, 246–72; Renata Landgráfová, *It is My Good Name That You Should Remember. Egyptian Biographical Texts on Middle Kingdom Stelae* (Prague: Czech Institute of Egyptology, 2011); Hans W. Fischer-Elfert, "Papyrus Northumberland Nr. III: Zeugnis einer Entsakralisierung der Herzenswägung von Totenbuch 125 unter Sethos I," in *Es werde niedergelegt als Schriftstück. Festschrift für Hartwig Altenmüller zum 65. Geburtstag*, ed. Nicole Kloth, Karl Martin and Eva Pardey (Hamburg: Helmut Buske, 2003), 109–115; Schmidt, *Gewogen und zu leicht befunden*, 254.

22 Schmidt, *Gewogen und zu leicht befunden*; Janák, "The Judgment."

23 Burkhard Backes, "Was zu sagen ist—zum Gesamttitel des Totenbuchs," in *Ausgestattet mit den Schriften des Thot. Festschrift für Irmtraut Munro zu ihrem 65. Geburtstag*, ed. Burkhard Backes, Marcus Müller, and Simone Stöhr, Studien zum Altägyptischen Totenbuch 14 (Wiesbaden: Harrassowitz, 2009), 5–27; Quirke, *Going Out in Daylight*, viii.

24 Seeber, *Untersuchungen zur Darstellung des Totengerichts*, 93–8.

25 Jiří Janák, "From Dusk till Dawn," *Archiv Orientální* 71 (2003), 9–10.

Late Developments

A different variant of both the judgment and the weighing process is attested in the *Story of Setne Khamwas* which is dated to the Roman Period.[26] One part of the story, similarly to the New Testament parable of the rich man and Lazarus (Luke 16:19–31), explains how a poor man shall be rewarded with blessings in the hereafter, whereas a rich man shall suffer eternal torments. The main message of the story is that the reversal of fortunes in the afterlife stems directly from assessments of earthly deeds undertaken in the underworld. Unlike the above-mentioned *Book of the Dead* spells 30B and 125 of the earlier periods, which refer to the counterbalancing of the heart and the order of the world, the trial process described in the *Story of Setne Khamwas* examines the difference between the good and the bad deeds of the deceased person. Such an assessment had three possible outcomes:

> He who would be found to have more bad deeds than the good deeds is handed over to the Devourer belonging to the Lord of the West. His *ba* (i.e. soul) and body is destroyed, and thus she (i.e. the Devourer) does not allow him to breathe ever again. He who would be found to have more good deeds than the bad deeds is taken in among the gods (and/of?) the Entourage of the Lord of the West, while his *ba* goes to the sky together with the prominent spirits. He who would be found to have good deeds equal to his bad is taken among the excellent spirits who serve Sokar-Osiris.[27]

The *Setne* story is, of course, dated much later and may reflect late (even Hellenistic) ideas or other religious, philosophic and apocalyptic influences of the time.[28] According to some scholars, however, the story is still deeply rooted in traditional Egyptian religious and cultural concepts and does not represent a novelty shaped by external influences.[29] This textual description of the judgment coheres with a few pictorial representations of the weighing scene recorded on a coffin and a mummy shroud dated to the Roman Period.[30] These images show a person being balanced against an oval stone weight. The scale pan bearing the deceased is depicted in a much lower position than the

26 Friedhelm Hoffmann and Joachim F. Quack, *Anthologie der demotischen Literatur*, Einführungen und Quellentexte zur Ägyptologie 4 (Münster: Lit Verlag, 2007), 118–37.

27 Miriam Lichtheim, *Ancient Egyptian Literature, Volume III: The Late Period* (Berkeley: University of California Press, 1980), 140; Hoffmann and Quack, *Anthologie der demotischen Literatur*, 121.

28 Taylor, *Journey through the Afterlife*, 215.

29 Stadler, *Judgment after Death*.

30 Seeber, *Untersuchungen zur Darstellung des Totengerichts*, 77.

other scale pan, which implies that the deceased, just person must have been much heavier than his counterweight. Such depiction might have referred to the idea of balancing the good deeds (represented by the deceased) against the misdeeds as in the second *Story of Setne Khamwas*.

In Ptolemaic and Roman Egypt, the late Hellenistic cultural narratives on the underworld journey of the deceased to the state of the blessed afterlife has been adopted to a new multicultural milieu and created new concepts, images and stories using ancient motifs and current ideas.[31] Tombs dated to that period of Egyptian history excavated in the Dakhla oasis, in Tuna el-Gebel, Akhmin, Western Thebes and at other places throughout Egypt[32] bear witness to how cultural memories were shaped by religious images taken from very different backgrounds.[33] The craftsmen embellished the tomb chambers, re-used artful illustrations of the *Book of the Dead* vignettes and intermingled them with Roman-Hellenistic cultural heritage in order to portray the deceased's way through the underworld. Various cultural, social, religious and iconographic discourses merged and new narratives about the otherworld came to life from old Egyptian traditions. Among the rock-cut tombs of the el-Muzawwaqa cemetery in the Dakhla oasis, one finds a tomb of a certain Petubastis, where the owner's journey to the afterlife is well represented on the walls, often using imagery known from the *Book of the Dead*.[34] Among the depictions is a variation on the judgment scene, which stands out. The artisans interweaved these remembrances of the *Book of the Dead* with Greco-Roman motifs and iconography. Both the style of the decorations of the tomb and the images of Petubastis himself seem to be Hellenistic.[35] Moreover, a Greek zodiac adorns the ceiling of the tomb. The tomb of Petosiris, also found in Dakhla, reveals very similar style and features, including the Greek zodiac.[36]

Similar iconographic structures and motifs are also found, for instance, on several coffins from the Tune el-Gebel area.[37] The wooden sarcophagus of

31 For further information, see Seeber, *Untersuchungen zur Darstellung des Totengerichts*.

32 Marjorie S. Venit, *Visualizing the Afterlife in the Tombs of Graeco-Roman Egypt* (Cambridge: Cambridge University Press, 2016), 182–95.

33 See Venit, *Visualizing the Afterlife*, 194–95.

34 Venit, *Visualizing the Afterlife*, 157.

35 Jürgen Osing, "Qāret el-Muzawwaqa. Die Gräber des Petubastis und Petosiris," in *Denkmäler aus der Oase Dachla: aus dem Nachlass von Ahmed Fakhry*, ed. Jürgen Osing et al. (Mainz: von Zabern, 1982), 71–95; Venit, *Visualizing the Afterlife*, 158–65.

36 See *Totenbuchprojekt Bonn, TM 135165*, (*totenbuch.awk.nrw.de/objekt/tm135165*).

37 Katja Lembke, Cäcilia Fluck and Günter Vittmann, *Ägyptens späte Blüte: Die Römer am Nil, Sonderbände der Antiken Welt* (Mainz: von Zabern, 2004), 59–60.

Teuris from the Hermopolitan necropolis[38] and the coffin of a certain Didyme from Zawyet el-Meytin do not share only the motifs, but also the structure of the underworld journey. Although both were of very different origins and cultural background (Teuris was Egyptian and Didyme was Greek), they share the same cultural memories and the same hope of the afterlife. Both hoped to enter the hall of justice after a successful burial. Then, they hoped to travel together with the sun on the solar barque to the place of the justified.[39]

In the family tomb of Pollius Soter, people of different cultural backgrounds were buried. The father of Pollius was Roman, his mother was Egyptian and his wife was probably of Nubian origin. Again, the imagery and the narrative on the sarcophagus of Pollius Soter follow the same pattern as the tomb decoration from Dakhla and Akhmim and the coffins from Tuna el-Gebel.[40]

Within the Egyptian *chora*, the Egyptians, the Greeks, the Romans as well as people of other cultural and religious origin used similar cultural narratives and visual imagery. Hence, images originally belonging to vignettes of the *Book of the Dead* remained in use in funerary contexts until the first and second centuries CE, when people of the *chora* transformed them into narratives *sui generis*. Individual motifs and iconographical details of the *Book of the Dead* were still present, but in many instances they expressed different, or at least altered ideas. Similarly, even ancient Egyptian religious concepts (mainly that of the afterlife) were partly open to new interpretations and were allowed to integrate non-Egyptian thoughts. Some Hellenistic, Roman and even Jewish ideas have, thus, become incorporated into the ancient narratives about life after death representing memories of the *Book of the Dead*.

Visual Memory

When approaching ancient Egyptian religious ideas and concepts from the perspective of cultural[41] or social memory theory,[42] we enter into a process

38 *Totenbuchprojekt Bonn, TM 112099*, (*totenbuch.awk.nrw.de/objekt/tm112099*); Willem van Haarlem, "De sarcofaag van Teuris," *APm: Allard Pierson mededelingen* 101/102 (2010): 8–11.

39 For more information, see Dieter Kurth, *Der Sarg der Teüris. Eine Studie zum Totenglauben im römerzeitlichen Ägypten*, Aegyptiaca Treverensia 6 (Mainz: von Zabern, 1990).

40 Lembke, Fluck, and Vittmann, *Ägyptens späte Blüte*, 62–65.

41 See Jan Assmann, *Das kulturelle Gedächtnis: Schrift, Erinnerung und politische Identität in frühen Hochkulturen* (Munich: C. H. Beck, 1992); *Moses der Ägypter: Entzifferung einer Gedächtnisspur* (Munich: Carl Hanser, 1998); *Religion und kulturelles Gedächtnis: Zehn Studien* (Munich: C. H. Beck, 2000).

42 For a fuller description of social memory, see the introduction to this book.

where the survival and transmission of ideas in the Egyptian context faced more obstacles then elsewhere in the Eastern Mediterranean. First, we should always be aware that no more than five percent of Egyptians were literate. Usually, it is assumed by scholars that only two percent of the society could read and write.[43] Not surprisingly, members of the society's elite guarded the secret and sacred privilege of literacy. The Egyptians called their script *medu netjer* ("divine words"). The Greeks understood the Egyptian concept well and referred to the script as the *hiero-glyphs* ("sacred carvings").

The concept of sacred image writing has also strongly influenced ancient Egyptian iconography, which has adapted hieroglyphic imagery into a highly developed system of representing the unrepresentable in a way that even illiterate people would understand. For instance, the depictions of ancient Egyptian gods and goddesses, who seemed so strange to Hellenistic foreigners, were not presented in their true forms, but as pictorial descriptions of their main characteristics, roles and functions. The representations of gods were complex hieroglyphic images built with smaller hieroglyphs using the grammar of iconography. Such descriptive images could then well represent the otherwise unseen and undepictable deities.[44]

In later periods of Egyptian history, when the country was dominated by foreign rulers and its society was permeated with soldiers, merchants, officials and foreign travellers, ancient concepts as well as iconographical features and styles mingled with new ones. During the Ptolemaic and Roman Periods, Egypt witnessed on the one hand a tendency to accumulate and to protect traditional sacred knowledge and the secret divine writings attributed to Egyptian priests; and on the other hand, it saw a demand for the very same kind of knowledge from an ever-increasing multicultural audience. It was, thus, a period when temple walls were decorated with ritual and liturgical texts (or excerpts) that were very old. Yet, it was also a period when tombs of private individuals bore representations of seemingly traditional concepts that were altered to take on a new look. This alteration is attested in the above-mentioned cases from Dakhla, Akhmin and Tune el-Gebel, not to mention the multicultural melting pot of Alexandria, which was the New York City of that time.

The complexity of the Egyptian script and the sacred writings not only made them difficult to comprehend, but allowed them to be protected by

43 John Baines, "Literacy and Ancient Egyptian Society," in *Visual and Written Culture in Ancient Egypt*, ed. John Baines (Oxford: Oxford University Press, 2007), 33–62.

44 Jiří Janák, *Staroegyptská náboženství I. Bohové na zemi a v nebesích* (Praha: Oikoymenh, 2009), 180; Jiří Janák, "Akhenaten: Monotheism or Monopoly?" in *Civilisations: Collapse and Regeneration Addressing the Nature of Change and Transformation in History*, ed. Miroslav Bárta and Martin Kovář (Prague: Academia, 2019), 187–211, here 193–95.

the Egyptian priesthood. For others in Ptolemaic and Roman Egypt, access to "secret" ideas was gained through iconographical features, well-known iconic images and popular religious concepts (as well as new ideas), visual motifs and foreign influences. The repository of religious ideas available to the public was filled with visual motifs, often repeated images and iconic scenes rather than with complex and fully interpreted theological concepts. As a result, ancient Egyptian traditions were transmitted in the remembrance process more through visual images than through written narratives. Moreover, the transmission drew on the repository of popular (often multicultural) motifs rather than on the traditional priestly sources. Not only were the traditional religious concepts and iconographical motifs altered, shifted in their meanings and supplemented with additional features, but they were also subjected to cultural "translations" or "transfers" (*interpretatio Graeca* and *interpretatio Romana*). The Hellenistic goddess Isis,[45] for instance, who was venerated in Alexandria, did not totally overlap in her characteristics, roles and iconography with the "original" Egyptian goddess Eset. Even more, the cult of Hermes in Egypt in Late Antiquity did not encompass all of the facets of Thoth's characteristics and cult.

The alteration of traditional Egyptian concepts affected also the judgment of the dead in several ways. The first and the most apparent was represented by a slow change of key iconographic features of the judgment scene.[46] This alteration of form was followed by the above-mentioned change in content. The character of the deceased was no longer measured against the cosmic order of *maat*, which was a concept that could not be transmitted into other cultures, and instead the good and the bad deeds of the person were examined on the scales in the underworld (see above).

As always, there were some misunderstandings by foreign interpreters of the judgment in Egyptian tradition, as is evident in the accounts of Diodorus Siculus. In his work *Bibliotheca Historica* (1.91–3),[47] the author indicates that the judgment of the dead might have originally been performed as a drama, or as a ritual trial during burial ceremonies.[48] This view of the judgment appears to follow Hellenistic ideas and it may have also stemmed from misinterpretation of the contemporary depictions of the judgment of the dead that

45 See Reinhold Merkelbach, *Isis Regina—Zeus Sarapis: Die griechisch-ägyptische Religion nach den Quellen dargestellt* (Stuttgart and Leipzig: Vieweg and Teubner, 1995).

46 Seeber, *Untersuchungen zur Darstellung des Totengerichts*.

47 Edwin Murphy, trans., *Diodorus "On Egypt,"* Book 1 of Diodorus Siculus' Historical Library (Jefferson: McFarland, 1985).

48 Reinhold Merkelbach, "Diodor über das Totengericht der Ägypter," *ZÄS* 120 (1993): 71–84; Assmann, *Tod und Jenseits im alten Ägypten*, 114.

placed the scene of the judgment into a direct connection with the image of the burial rites.

Egyptian Motifs in Apocalyptic Literature

The remembrance of iconic features rooted deep in ancient Egyptian religious tradition was widespread in Late Antiquity, particularly in the Eastern Mediterranean, including the Levant. The topic of possible Egyptian and other foreign influences in Jewish literature has received considerable attention.[49] The analysis, however, has offered no definitive conclusions. In the present article, we focus on two case-studies from the attested material to show how Egyptian motifs might have entered Jewish apocalyptic tradition through the process of trans-cultural memory which first altered and then appropriated iconographic features and visual images.

The *Apocalypse of Sophonias*, and the *Testament of Abraham* show striking similarities with the narratives of decorative programs of the afore-mentioned tombs, sarcophagi and coffins of Ptolemaic and Roman Egypt. These texts, however, do not mix Hellenistic ideas with remembrances of ancient Egyptian tradition directly, since the Egyptian concepts present in these works of apocalyptic literature stem from the already altered notions and imagery of the multicultural melting pot of Hellenistic Egypt. They retell the Hellenistic cultural memories of ancient Egyptian ideas in a Jewish way.

The Apocalypse of Sophonias

Several fragments of an Akhminic Codex which is dated approximately to the fourth or fifth century, today stored in the Nation Library in Paris (Inv. Nr. Copte 135) and the Egyptian Museum in Berlin (Inv. Nr. P. 1862), contains a translation of an anonymous Apocalypse.[50] Bernd Diebner believes that these

---

49 Jan N. Bremmer, "Orphic, Roman, Jewish and Christian Tours of Hell: Observations on the *Apocalypse of Peter*," in *Other Worlds and Their Relation to This World: Early Jewish and Ancient Christian Traditions*, eds. Tobias Nicklas, Jospeh Verheyden, Erik M. M. Eynikel and Florentino García Martínez, JSJSup 143 (Leiden: Brill, 2010), 305–21; David Frankfurter, *Christianizing Egypt: Syncretism and Local Worlds in Late Antiquity* (Princeton: Princeton University Press, 2017).

50 Georg Steindorff, *Die Apokalypse des Elias. Eine unbekannte Apokalypse und Bruchstücke der Sophonias-Apokalypse*, TUGAL 17 (Leipzig: J. C. Hinrich's Buchhandlung, 1899) 1–4; Albrecht Dieterich, *Nekyia. Beiträge zur Erklärung der neuentdeckten Petrusapokalypse*

nine leaves of the codex belong to the tradition of the *Apocalypse of Sophonias*, to which he also adds a fragment of a Sahidic codex and a short quotation in the writings of Clement of Alexandria (*Strom.* 5.11.77).[51] The text of the Apocalypse does not only contain leitmotifs and iconographic features of Egyptian religious tradition (mainly that of the *Book of the Dead*), but the whole narrative structure of this work shows many parallels with the *Book of the Dead* imagery from Late Antiquity.

The *Apocalypse of Sophonias* begins with a scene of funerary rites and it also includes the burial of the narrator. A description of a procession accompanying the rites shows people singing psalms while his body is being put into the tomb, which begins the journey of the deceased seer to the afterlife. He leaves this life and travels to another world accompanied by an advising angel called Eremiel. The main character then descends into the underworld and passes through several rooms, each protected by fiery gates and demonic guardians in the form feline beings with sharp teeth and flaming swords. These protective measures, both the gates and the demons, keep the impure human beings out of the sacred realm. After the deceased is found pure, he is allowed to enter the Hall of Judgement, called Amente.

The central part of the *Apocalypse of Sophonias*, narrated in the first-person, portrays the seer's trial which is organized by Eremiel and supervised by a great god called Adonai Sebaoth, though he is not involved in the juridical process. Instead, an angelic prosecutor is called upon to assess the guilt of the deceased, who opens the process by reading from two scrolls a series of good and bad deeds performed by the deceased during his life. Then, both scrolls are placed on a scale. The prosecutor, who is described as a snake-like being with feminine features, a lion's mane and sharp teeth, was believed to devour the humans who were found guilty of committing more evil deeds than good deeds. This, however, is not the fate of the main protagonist of the Apocalypse. On the contrary, when the result of the weighing is logged and announced, he is found righteous. As a justified human he can board a barque with an angelic crew who navigates him safely over the waters of the underworld. At the very end, the seer reveals that the living who participate on funerary rites can also intercede for him and aid his successful passage through the obstacles of the underworld.

(Leipzig: B. G. Teubner, 1893); Orval S. Wintermute, "Apocalypse of Zephaniah (First Century BC-First Century AD): A New Translation and Introduction," in *Old Testament Pseudepigrapha. Volume 1*, ed. James H. Charlesworth (Garden City: Doubleday, 1983), 497–501.

51 Bernd J. Diebner, "Zephanjas Apokalypse," *JSHRZ* 9 (2003): 55–60.

The structure and key features of the *Apocalypse of Sophonias* bears striking similarities with the Egyptian concept of the Judgement of the Dead as attested in copies of the *Book of the Dead*, tomb decoration and coffins of the Ptolemaic and Roman Periods. The most iconic scenes represented on *Book of the Dead* vignettes of that time (as was noted above) show the burial ceremonies located at the tomb (including a procession of priests, mourners and offering bearers). The scene is of the trial in the Hall of Judgment and a depiction of a solar barque with its divine crew and the deceased who, during the sun's nightly journey, travel through the underworld towards the place of resurrection at the eastern horizon. Not only are all these scenes present in the narrative in a correct sequence, but they play a significant role, as they did in Egyptian tradition.

Moreover, even the individual motifs and persons in the narrative correspond to their Egyptian precedents. The fiery gates of the underworld and the demons with animal heads and knives in their hands are often found on coffins, sarcophagi and tomb walls, as well as in the *Book of the Dead* scrolls from the second millennium BCE until the period when Egypt was ruled by the Romans. The notion of a deity who accompanies the deceased on his way towards resurrection in the afterlife was also present in ancient Egypt. Usually, this role was played by Horus or Thoth, as depicted on the vignettes of the *Book of the Dead*, including the judgement scene (spell 125). One may even speculate whether the angel's name (Eremiel) might have been influenced by the Greek version of Thoth's name, Hermes. The name of the Hall of Judgment (Amente) attested in the *Apocalypse of Sophonias* fits nicely with this perspective, as it is derived from an ancient Egyptian word *Imenti* or *Amentet*, which refers to "the West." From the time of the Old Kingdom until the Roman period, the West in Egypt was considered to be the realm of the dead. One of the earliest Egyptian gods of the dead was called Khenti-imentiu, meaning "the Foremost of the Westerners" (i.e. the ruler of the dead). The physical description and the role of the prosecutor are similar to those of the famous feminine demonic being called Amemait or Ammut, the "Devourer of the Dead," whose figure in traditional Egyptian iconography was a combination of a lion, hippopotamus and crocodile. In the Ptolemaic and Roman periods, however, the Devourer was sometimes depicted as an infernal dog or a combination of other animals (maybe due to Hellenistic influence). And last but not least, the trial itself, which was supposed to consist of the assessment (literally, weighing) of good and bad deeds, was one of the typical variants of judgement in Roman Egypt (in light of the aforementioned evidence).

But, of course, the *Apocalypse of Sophonias* combines the originally Egyptian motifs with Jewish tradition. Thus, the seer prays to Adonai Sebaoth several times during his underworld journey, praising God, for instance, by referring to the stories of the Exodus and the prophet Daniel. Moreover, Eremiel, who might resemble Thoth or Hermes, is portrayed using motifs found in other apocalyptic writings, such as 4 Ezra and the Revelation of John.

The Testament of Abraham

The narrative of the *Testament of Abraham*, which probably dates to the second century CE,[52] proves that the *Apocalypse of Sophonias* was not an isolated case.[53] Remembrances of Egyptian tradition, mainly based on iconic images and other visual features, circulated among the Jewish communities (similarly to other non-Egyptian social groups) in Egypt during the first two centuries of the Common Era. Their conceptions of afterlife existence and that of the underworld are at this stage of the reception history neither completely Jewish, nor typically Egyptian.

The connections between the *Testament of Abraham* and the *Book of the Dead* are not as strong and as explicitly pronounced in the *Apocalypse of Sophonias*. However, one can clearly see how the Jewish author of the work re-enacted the ideas and images within the cultural memory of the time by preserving several well-known and certainly popular ancient Egyptian thought patterns. The *Testament of Abraham* does not refer to the sun bark or the funeral, but the text uses several motifs that recall the scene of the judgment of the dead as attested in the *Book of the Dead* spell 125. For instance, it contains the idea that the good and evil deeds of the deceased are weighed on a scale and recorded (T. Ab. 10–11). It is the archangel Michael who guides Abraham to the underworld's Hall of Judgment, where Abraham notices a judge evaluating the sins of the deceased (T. Ab. 10,8–12).[54] Similar to the *Apocalypse of Sophonias*, the judge compares the two scrolls in which the good and evil deeds of the accused are recorded. The narrative continues with the description of the lawsuit (T. Ab. 11). Archangel Michael interprets individual aspects and features of the trial to Abraham while Abel serves as a judge in the court hall. Later, the text introduces Enoch as a clerk and a scribe at the trial whom Abel instructs to ascertain the guilt of the deceased. Enoch oversees the books

52 Dale C. Allison, Jr., *Testament of Abraham*, CEJL (Berlin: de Gruyter, 2003), 34–40.

53 Allison, *Testament of Abraham*, 32–33.

54 Allison, *Testament of Abraham*, 3.

of the underworld and reports to the Lord. The guilt or innocence of a person (as indicated in T. Ab. 11,5) is determined by the weighing process.[55]

The *Testament of Abraham* uses Enoch in a role played by Thoth in the *Book of the Dead*.[56] The figure of Abel strongly resembles Osiris who not only was the ruler of the dead, but also the first resurrected person originally killed by his own brother. It is apparent that the apocalyptic narrative of the *Testament of Abraham* appropriates the imagery of the *Book of the Dead*. However, it is difficult to ascertain whether it was borrowed directly from the late Egyptian tradition or whether its inspiration comes from the repository of motifs accumulated in the cultural memory of the Jewish communities in Roman Egypt.

Conclusion

After carefully analysing both the ancient Egyptian concept of judgment in the afterlife and the textual and iconographical evidence concerning the judgment of the dead in the *Book of the Dead* and its developments, it is hard to escape the probability of ancient Egyptian influences on the rise and form of Jewish and early Christian apocalypses. Two selected case studies show that, at least in the cases of the *Apocalypse of Sophonias* and the *Testament of Abraham*, Jewish apocalyptic tradition was strongly influenced by Egyptian religious concepts. Yet, caution is required with respect to two important issues.

First, Jewish as well as the Gnostic and later Christian traditions did not draw directly from ancient Egyptian sources and conceptions, but rather from their receptions as altered, partly mixed-up or even Hellenised concepts of Egyptian religious tradition of late antiquity. Thus, possible influences are not to be found in the pyramids of the Old Kingdom or in the Valley of the Kings of the New Kingdom, but in the intellectual milieu of Alexandria around the time of the turn of the Common Era.

And second, since the sages and scribes were not familiar with Egyptian script and language, the inspiration was transferred mainly through well-known, iconic images as attested on sarcophagi and tomb and temple walls. The process explains how the iconographic form of the older tradition was endowed with new meanings or contents and recorded textually. In this respect, we must ascribe significance to the importance of the visual aspects of cultural or social memory.

55 Allison, *Testament of Abraham*, 257.
56 Allison, *Testament of Abraham*, 266.

Bibliography

Allison, Dale C. Jr. *Testament of Abraham*. CEJL. Berlin: de Gruyter, 2003.

Assmann, Jan. *Ägyptische Hymnen und Gebete*. München and Zürich: Artemis Verlag, 1975.

———. *Ma'at: Gerechtigkeit und Unsterblichkeit im Alten Ägypten*. München: Beck, 1990.

———. *Das kulturelle Gedächtnis: Schrift, Erinnerung und politische Identität in frühen Hochkulturen*. Munich: C. H. Beck, 1992.

———. *Moses der Ägypter: Entzifferung einer Gedächtnisspur*. Munich: Carl Hanser, 1998.

———. *Religion und kulturelles Gedächtnis: Zehn Studien*. Munich: C. H. Beck, 2000.

———. *Tod und Jenseits im alten Ägypten*. München: C. H. Beck, 2001.

Assmann, Jan, and Andrea Kucharek. *Ägyptische Religion. Totenliteratur*. Frankfurt am Main: Verlag der Weltreligionen, 2008.

Backes, Burkhard. "Was zu sagen ist—zum Gesamttitel des Totenbuchs." Pages 5–27 in *Ausgestattet mit den Schriften des Thot. Festschrift für Irmtraut Munro zu ihrem 65. Geburtstag*. Edited by Burkhard Backes, Marcus Müller and Simone Stöhr. Studien zum Altägyptischen Totenbuch 14. Wiesbaden: Harrassowitz, 2009.

Baines, John. "Literacy and Ancient Egyptian Society." Pages 33–62 in *Visual and Written Culture in Ancient Egypt*. Edited by John Baines. Oxford: Oxford University Press, 2007.

———. "Society, Morality, and Religious Practice." Pages 123–200 in *Religion in Ancient Egypt: Gods, Myths, and Personal Practice*. Edited by Byron E. Shafer. Ithaca: Cornell University Press, 1991.

Bremmer, Jan N. "Orphic, Roman, Jewish and Christian Tours of Hell: Observations on the Apocalypse of Peter." Pages 305–21 in *Other Worlds and Their Relation to This World: Early Jewish and Ancient Christian Traditions*. Edited by Tobias Nicklas, Jospeh Verheyden, Erik M. M. Eynikel, and Florentino García Martínez. JSJSup 143. Leiden: Brill, 2010.

Diebner, Bernd J. "Zephanjas Apokalypse." JSHRZ 9 (2003): 55–60.

Dieterich, Albrecht. *Nekyia: Beiträge zur Erklärung der neuentdeckten Petrusapokalypse*. Leipzig: B. G. Teubner, 1893.

Edel, Elmar. "Untersuchungen zur Phraseologie der ägyptischen Inschriften des Alten Reiches." MDAI 13 (1944): 1–90.

Fischer-Elfert, Hans W. "Papyrus Northumberland Nr. III: Zeugnis einer Entsakralisierung der Herzenswägung von Totenbuch 125 unter Sethos I." Pages 109–115 in *Es werde niedergelegt als Schriftstück. Festschrift für Hartwig Altenmüller zum 65. Geburtstag*. Edited by Nicole Kloth, Karl Martin and Eva Pardey. Hamburg: Helmut Buske, 2003.

Frankfurter, David. *Christianizing Egypt: Syncretism and Local Worlds in Late Antiquity*. Princeton: Princeton University Press, 2017.

Garnot, Jean Sainte-Fare. *L'Appel aux vivants dans les textes funéraires égyptiens des origines à la fin de l'ancien empire*. Cairo: l'Institut français d'archéologie orientale, 1938.

Gee, John L. "The Requirements of Ritual Purity in Ancient Egypt." Ph.D. Diss. New Haven: Yale University, 1998.

Griffith, John G. *The Divine Verdict. A Study of Divine Judgment in the Ancient Religions*. Numen Book Series 52. Leiden: Brill, 1991.

Hoffmann, Friedhelm, and Joachim F. Quack. *Anthologie der demotischen Literatur*. Einführungen und Quellentexte zur Ägyptologie 4. Münster: Lit Verlag, 2007.

Janák, Jiří. *Staroegyptská náboženství I. Bohové na zemi a v nebesích*. Praha: Oikoymenh, 2009.

———. "Akh." Pages 1–9 in UCLA *Encyclopedia of Egyptology*. Edited by Jacco Dieleman and Willeke Wendrich. Los Angeles: University of California, 2013. https://escholarship.org/uc/item/7255p86v.

———. "Akhenaten: Monotheism or Monopoly?" Pages 187–211 in *Civilisations: Collapse and Regeneration Addressing the Nature of Change and Transformation in History*. Edited by Miroslav Bárta and Martin Kovář. Prague: Academia, 2019.

———. "The Judgment." in *The Oxford Handbook of the Book of the Dead*. Edited by Martin J. Stadler and Rita Lucarelli. Oxford: Oxford University Press, forthcoming.

Kurth, Dieter. *Der Sarg der Teüris. Eine Studie zum Totenglauben im römerzeitlichen Ägypten*. Aegyptiaca Treverensia 6. Mainz: von Zabern, 1990.

Landgráfová, Renata. *It is My Good Name That You Should Remember. Egyptian Biographical Texts on Middle Kingdom Stelae*. Prague: Czech Institute of Egyptology, 2011.

Lapp, Günther. *Synoptische Textausgabe nach Quellen des Neuen Reiches*. Totenbuchtexte 3. Basel: Orientverlag, 2008.

Lembke, Katja, Cäcilia Fluck and Günter Vittmann. *Ägyptens späte Blüte: Die Römer am Nil, Sonderbände der Antiken Welt*. Mainz: von Zabern, 2004.

Lichtheim, Miriam. *Ancient Egyptian Literature, Volume* III*: The Late Period*. Berkeley: University of California Press, 1980.

Merkelbach, Reinhold. "Ein griechisch-ägyptischer Priestereid und das Totenbuch." Pages 69–73 in *Religions en Égypte hellénistique et romaine*. Edited by Philippe Derchain. Paris: Presses universitaires du France, 1969.

———. "Diodor über das Totengericht der Ägypter." ZÄS 120 (1993): 71–84.

———. *Isis Regina—Zeus Sarapis: Die griechisch-ägyptische Religion nach den Quellen dargestellt*. Stuttgart and Leipzig: Vieweg and Teubner, 1995.

Morschauser, Scott. *Threat-Formulae in Ancient Egypt: A Study of the History, Structure and Use of Threats and Curses in Ancient Egypt*. Baltimore: Johns Hopkins University Press, 1991.

Murphy, Edwin, trans. *Diodorus "On Egypt."* Book 1 of Diodorus Siculus' Historical Library. Jefferson: McFarland, 1985.

O'Donogue, Michael. "The 'Letters to the Dead' and Ancient Egyptian Religion." *Bulletin of the Australian Centre for Egyptology* 10 (1999): 87–104.

Osing, Jürgen. "Qāret el-Muzawwaqa. Die Gräber des Petubastis und Petosiris." Pages 71–95 in *Denkmäler aus der Oase Dachla: aus dem Nachlass von Ahmed Fakhry*. Edited by Jürgen Osing et al. Mainz: von Zabern, 1982.

Parkinson, R. B. *The Tale of Sinuhe and Other Ancient Egyptian Poems 1940–1640* B.C. Oxford: Oxford University Press, 1997.

Quack. Joachim F. "Ein ägyptisches Handbuch des Tempels und seine griechische Übersetzung." ZPE 119 (1997): 297–300.

Quirke, Stephen G. J. "Judgment of the Dead." Pages 2.211–14 in *The Oxford Encyclopedia of Ancient Egypt*. Edited by Donald B. Redford. Oxford: Oxford University Press, 2001.

———. *Going Out in Daylight—prt m hrw. The Ancient Egyptian Book of the Dead: Translation, Sources, Meanings*. GHP Egyptology 20. London: GHP, 2013.

Schmidt, Heike C. "Gewogen und zu leicht befunden." Pages 251–58 in *Pharaos Staat. Festschrift für Rolf Gundlach zum 75. Geburtstag*. Edited by Dirk Bröckelmann and Andrea Klug. Wiesbaden: Harrassowitz, 2006.

Seeber, Christine. *Untersuchungen zur Darstellung des Totengerichts im alten Ägypten*. Münchner Ägyptologische Studien 35. München: Deutscher Kunstverlag, 1976.

Stadler, Martin A. *Der Totenpapyrus des Pa-Month (P. Bibl. Nat. 149)*. Studien zum Altägyptischen Totenbuch 6. Wiesbaden: Harrassowitz Verlag, 2003.

———. "Judgment after Death (Negative Confession)." Pages 1–4 in UCLA *Encyclopedia of Egyptology*. Edited by Jacco Dieleman and Willeke Wendrich. Los Angeles: University of California, 2008. https://escholarship.org/uc/item/07s1t6kj.pdf.

Steindorff, Georg. *Die Apokalypse des Elias. Eine unbekannte Apokalypse und Bruchstücke der Sophonias-Apokalypse*. TUGAL 17. Leipzig: J. C. Hinrich's Buchhandlung, 1899.

Taylor, John H. ed. *Journey through the Afterlife: Ancient Egyptian Book of the Dead*. Cambridge: Harvard University Press, 2010.

van Haarlem, Willem. "De sarcofaag van Teuris." *APm: Allard Pierson mededelingen* 101/102 (2010): 8–11.

Venit, Marjorie S. *Visualizing the Afterlife in the Tombs of Graeco-Roman Egypt*. Cambridge: Cambridge University Press, 2016.

Verhoeven, Ursula. "Post ins Jenseits—Formular und Funktion altägyptischer Briefe an Tote." Pages 31–51 in *Bote und Brief: Sprachliche Systeme der Informationsübermittlung im Spannungsfeld von Mündlichkeit und Schriftlichkeit*. Edited by Andreas Wagner. Frankfurt am Main: Peter Lang, 2003.

Walls, Jerry L., ed. *The Oxford Handbook of Eschatology*. Oxford: Oxford University Press, 2007.

Wente, Edward F. *Letters from Ancient Egypt.* Society of Biblical Literature Writings from the Ancient World 1. Atlanta: Scholars Press, 1990.

Wintermute, Orval S. "Apocalypse of Zephaniah (First Century BC–First Century AD): A New Translation and Introduction." Pages 497–501 in *Old Testament Pseudepigrapha. Volume 1.* Edited by James H. Charlesworth. Garden City: Doubleday, 1983.

Remembering the Martyrs in 2 and 4 Maccabees

David Cielontko

Introduction

No one is born a martyr. Martyrs are called "martyrs" only retrospectively when their stories are retold through the lens of their heroic deaths from the perspective of someone for whom those deaths are heroic. As Paul Ricoeur noted, it is only from the vantage point of the end that the story can be seen as an intelligible whole.[1] Those who cherish the memories of martyrs usually emphasise their bravery in defending values and truths that they hold in high esteem. There can be no martyrs without the retelling of their stories. It should not come as a surprise that remembering heroes of the past is always connected to their importance within a community's present. If there is no one that reveres them, they are not heroes anymore. Martyrs are remembered because they were willing to die for particular values and truths that resonate with the identities of those who remember them. Present values are usually projected back onto the narrative of the past so that, on the one hand, their sacrifices are still honoured with the same insistency, and, on the other hand, the values inseparably linked to them are emphasised in the present. Throughout time, some details are added to these stories while others are omitted or forgotten. Still others are accentuated. This is done either unconsciously or by a deliberate interpretation of memories for various ideological interests among those who formulate, establish and represent them. As Maurice Halbwachs stressed, the decisive factor for viability of memories is their relevance.[2] Remembrances and re-interpretations of the stories about martyrs are especially appealing since their heroic dedications and unjust deaths cause an emotional impact that can often lead the recipients of those stories to action in the face of an ethical demand.[3] In the words of Elizabeth Castelli, "Martyrdom is not simply an action. Martyrdom requires audience (whether real or fictive), retelling, interpretation, and world- and meaning-making activity. Suffering violence in

---

1 Paul Ricoeur, *Time and Narrative. Volume 1* (Chicago: University of Chicago Press, 1984), 65.

2 See especially the seminal study on social frameworks of memory in Maurice Halbwachs' *On Collective Memory*, ed. and trans. Lewis A. Coser (Chicago: University of Chicago Press, 1992).

3 For Halbwachs, events that arouse deep emotions for groups are more likely to generate creative reinterpretations (*On Collective Memory*, 194).

 | DOI:10.30965/9783657796212_005

and of itself is not enough. In order for martyrdom to emerge, both the violence and its suffering must be infused with particular meanings."[4]

In this study[5], I focus on this meaning-making activity in relation to 2 Maccabees and 4 Maccabees. Both accounts reframe the story of the Maccabean martyrs (i.e., Eleazar, the seven sons, and their mother) in their own cultural contexts, resulting in different collective memories that reflect and affect the respective identities of two audiences.[6] Since most martyrs are believed to receive a blessed reward for their bravery, stories about them also offer insights into afterlife conceptions.

I approach these texts as literary compositions written by creative authors who used rhetorical strategies to present their particular purposes and theological agendas. As such, these texts are viewed as creative products of a process that includes historical memory, ideology and construction of social identity. To understand these discourses in their historical context, the diachronic probing into historical and social location of the compositions is necessary as an integral accompaniment to the literary analysis.

Eleazar and the Martyrs in 2 Maccabees

2 Maccabees provides a selective history of the Maccabean revolt from the period of 175–161 BCE.[7] The author, who presents himself as an abridger of the five-volume history of Jason of Cyrene, states in the prologue (2 Macc 2:19–32) that his purpose is to prepare the book for the entertainment of a reader and for easier memorisation.[8] This book was later prefixed with two letters from

4 Elizabeth Castelli, *Martyrdom and Memory: Early Christian Culture Making* (New York: Columbia University Press, 2004), 34.

5 This study was funded by the Charles University programs PRIMUS/20/HUM/010 and UNCE HUM/012 n. 204052.

6 On the connection of social memory and social identity, see, for example, Raimo Hakola, Samuel Byrskog, and Jutta Jokiranta, "Introduction," in *Social Memory and Social Identity in the Study of Early Judaism and Early Christianity*, eds., Samuel Byrskog, Raimo Hakola, and Jutta Jokiranta (Göttingen: Vandenhoeck & Ruprecht, 2016), 7–13; James Fentress and Chris Wickham, *Social Memory* (Oxford: Blackwell, 1992), 87–91.

7 The date of composition is debated, ranging between 150 to 63 BCE. See the survey in David A. deSilva, *Introducing the Apocrypha: Message, Context, and Significance*, 2nd ed. (Grand Rapids: Baker Academic, 2018), 292–95. Although it is not crucial for this study, I incline toward a date in the first decades of the 1st century BCE.

8 As is standard practice, I refer to the author of 2 Maccabees as "the abridger." On the practice of abbreviating a longer historical work in the context of 2 Maccabees, see Luke Neubert, "Inventing Jason of Cyrene? 2 Maccabees and the Epitome," in *Die Makkabäer*, eds., Friedrich Avemarie, Predrag Bukovec, Stefan Krauter, and Michael Tilly, WUNT 382 (Tübingen: Mohr

Jews in Jerusalem to those in Egypt (1:1–2:18).[9] This abridger was a Hellenised Jew skilled in Greek and rhetorical techniques.[10] His theological agenda is embedded into the overall plot of the narrated history.[11] The story arc is presented in the form of a cosine curve and reflects the Deuteronomistic theology of history.[12] It starts during the reign of Seleucus IV when Onias III is serving as the high priest in Jerusalem, ensuring peace and stability through his piety and careful observance of the Law (3:1–3). This peace is disrupted when a certain Simon convinces Seleucus to rob the temple treasury. However, because of the faithfulness of Onias and his fellow Jews, this attempt fails, which is credited to God's protection of his Holy place. This episode intends to demonstrate the general mechanism of God's protection of his temple and people, which accords with the traditional Deuteronomistic theological scheme. The next episode begins with the description of apostasy started by Jason, the brother of Onias, who usurped the high priesthood from his faithful brother and lead his fellow Jews astray. He initiated intensive Hellenistic enculturation of Jerusalem (4:7–17). After this, the course of events escalated quickly—Jason was replaced in the high priest office by Menelaus who was not fit for it; Menelaus murdered the faithful Onias, which led to the corruption of everything and everyone. The apostasy resulted in the conquest of Antiochus IV Epiphanes, who is depicted as an agent of God's punishment (6:12–17). The description of severe persecutions by Antiochus is presented as the climax of the despair that came upon Jews for their infidelity and straying away into a Hellenistic way of life (5:11–6:11). All of the catastrophes he causes—the desecration of the Temple, persecutions and murders—are regarded as didactic events that express God's discipline (6:16; 10:6).

The story of Eleazar and the seven sons with their mother is placed into this climactic moment of the narrative plot in which it functions as the turning point. As the sin of the people has been initiated through representational individuals (high priests Jason and Menelaus), the repentance and restoration of the obedience of the Law will also be mediated through representational

Siebeck, 2017), 187–208. See also Francis Bochardt, "Reading Aid: 2 Maccabees and the History of Jason of Cyrene Reconsidered," *JSJ* 47 (2016): 71–87.

9 For a critical discussion of the relationship between the letters and the work of the abridger see Bertram Herr, "Der Standpunkt des Epitomators. Perspektivenwechsel in der Forschung am Zweiten Makkabäerbuch," *Bib* 90 (2009), 1–31.

10 Robert Doran, *Temple Propaganda: The Purpose and Character of 2 Maccabees*, CBQMS 12 (Washington: The Catholic Biblical Association, 1981), 24–46.

11 DeSilva, *Introducing the Apocrypha*, 298–302.

12 Doran, *Temple Propaganda*, 110; deSilva, *Introducing the Apocrypha*, 288–89, 296; On the Deuteronomistic theology of history, see Erich Zenger and Christian Frevel, eds., *Einleitung in das Alte Testament*, 9th ed. (Stuttgart: Kohlhammer, 2016), 252–54.

individuals, namely the martyrs. Their heroism is seen as an expiatory sacrifice for the nation (7:31–38) through which the covenant is renewed. Hence, for their righteousness, God is willing, once again, to protect his people and bless the Jewish cause. Only after this moment of the story, Judas the Maccabee is introduced as God's agent for restoring what has been destroyed by Antiochus, and consequently reclaiming, purifying, and rededicating the temple (8:1–10:9). After this, the narrative continues with a series of successful battles (10:10–13:26) that share common features such as boasting of a pagan ruler, pious devotion of Jewish warriors and the subsequent triumphant victory of God.[13] Finally, the last episode describes the attempt to attack the temple, in which the Seleucid general Nicanor is sent to Judea to regain control over Jerusalem and the temple (14–15). In this powerful scene, pervaded with prayers, Judas's armies successfully destroy Nicanor's forces. The scene ends with a graphic report of Nicanor's death (15:25–36).

This story is narrated as a theological interpretation of history from a particular perspective. Although the story culminates in a happy ending, claiming that "from that time the city has been in possession of the Hebrews" (15:37), this was not the case historically.[14] In response to Nicanor's defeat, the Seleucid Ruler Demetrius I Soter sent his general Bacchides to battle Judas's forces, which he defeated at the Battle of Elasa. In addition to the killing of Judas, Bacchides recaptured Jerusalem and reinstalled Alcimus as high priest (1 Maccabees 9). The narrated events in 2 Maccabees end just prior to a tragedy. Nonetheless, without these subsequent events, the narrative serves the abridger's aim to demonstrate that God punishes the sinners and rewards the faithful.

Within this traditional theological scheme, the threat to prosperity and peace is seen as a by-product of the conflict between Jewish (Ἰουδαϊσμός) and Hellenistic ways of life (Ἑλληνισμός/Ἑλληνικός/ἀλλοφυλισμός),[15] which probably reflects the historical and social setting of the intended audience.[16] It seems that the issue of what constitutes true Jewish identity within the Hellenized world was of paramount importance for the abridger. The abridger's rhetorical strategy, using cultural values of honour and shame,[17] aims to depict the

13 The abridger places strong emphasis on the fact that it is God who is responsible for the victories in battles (3:34–40; 8:27–29, 36; 9:12–18; 11:12–13; 12:28–31; 15:27–29; 15:34).

14 The quotations are taken from the NRSV.

15 See "Ἰουδαϊσμός" in 2:21; 8:1; 14:38; "ἀλλοφυλισμός" in 4:13; 6:24; "Ἑλληνισμός" in 4:13; and the adjective "Ἑλληνικός" in 4:10, 15; 6:9; 11:24; 13:2.

16 DeSilva, *Introducing the Apocrypha*, 296–297; Doran, *Temple Propaganda*, 13–14.

17 DeSilva, *Introducing the Apocrypha*, 302–303. On these values, see Bruce J. Malina, *The New Testament World: Insights from Cultural Anthropology*, 3rd ed. (Louisville: Westminster

Hellenistic way of life in association with despicable characters (such as Jason, Menelaus, Antiochus Epiphanes, Nicanor), whose actions are presented as corrupt, unjust and wicked.[18] This is particularly noticeable in the way that these antiheroes die. Jason dies in a foreign land and is left unburied (5:10), Menelaus remains unburied (13:7), Antiochus dies outside of his homeland in a pitiful way (10:28–29), and, finally, Nicanor is cut into pieces and displayed publicly (15:32–25).

An exact and complete reconstruction of the polemics that identified the Hellenistic/foreign way of life is impossible. We have some features preserved in the spread of Hellenism instituted by Jason (4:7–22) and in the forced incorporation of Greek gods in Jerusalem by Antiochus (6:1–7). However, identifying specifically new contributions is difficult because Jewish culture at this time was already thoroughly Hellenized in Palestine and in the Diaspora. Nevertheless, even within such a multicultural society, certain cultural identity markers always stand out to delineate boundaries between different ethnic identities. The identity is not fixed and stable but is constantly changing within the social dynamic. Different aspects of identity take priority in different contexts since social identity is always an outcome of variegated interactions both inside and outside of a group.[19] Therefore, while some aspects of what constitutes the ideal Jewish identity in 2 Maccabees are rather traditional, such as the observance of circumcision and Sabbath, others represent more current issues, such as not wearing of a broad-brimmed hat (πέτασος; 4:12) or not attending a gymnasium.[20]

By contrast, a representation of the Jewish way of life (Ἰουδαισμός) is presented in the narrative through the centrality of the Maccabean martyrs.[21] In

John Knox Press, 2001), 27–57. For the recent discussion, see Zeba Crook, "Honor, Shame, and Social Status Revisited," *JBL* 128 (2009): 591–611.

18 However, for the abridger, foreigners were not enemies (e.g., 4:35). Only the enforcing of their way of life, in contrast to Judaism, is regarded as sinful. See Jan W. van Henten, *Maccabean Martyrs as Saviours of the Jewish People: A Study of 2 and 4 Maccabees*, JSJSup 57 (Leiden: Brill, 1997), 168.

19 See Richard Jenkins, *Social Identity*, 4th ed. (New York: Routledge, 2014); Jutta Jokiranta, *Social Identity and Sectarianism in the Qumran Movement* (Leiden: Brill, 2013), 77–89.

20 Martha Himmelfarb considers new values represented by the gymnasium as the major threat in 2 Maccabees. See her "Judaism and Hellenism in 2 Maccabees," *Poetics Today* 19 (1998): 19–40.

21 In 2 Maccabees, Ἰουδαισμός does not denote the modern notion of Judaism as a religion or ethnic identification, but rather it denotes a description of adherence to Jewish causes, Jewish manners and a way of life *in contrast* to that of the Greek. For a discussion of the meaning of Ἰουδαισμός, see Markus Öhler, "Judäer oder Juden? Die Debatte 'Ethnos vs. Religion' im Blick auf das 2. Makkabäerbuch," in *Die Makkabäer*, eds., Friedrich Avemarie,

the literary context, Antiochus Epiphanes, orchestrating policies of persecution, is determined to eradicate Jewish ancestral customs so as to expunge Jewish identity. The traumatic events are stated clearly in 2 Macc. 6:6: "People could neither keep the Sabbath, nor observe the festivals of their ancestors, *nor so much as confess themselves to be Jews* (οὔτε ἁπλῶς Ἰουδαῖον ὁμολογεῖν εἶναι)." Earlier in the episode we are told Antiochus targets fundamental Jewish identity markers, notably Sabbath observance, circumcision, and dietary regulations. The story of Eleazar begins with him being forced to eat unclean swine's flesh in the company of other Jews. Portrayed as a noble-looking old scribe who is well-respected in his community, he steps onto a podium and spits out the unclean meat as an expression of his willingness to die with honour rather than to live in shame.[22] His resistance provides inspiration and instils courage among those who are similarly struggling to be brave and true to their beliefs. Overseeing this disgraceful incident were Jewish collaborators who were former acquaintances of Eleazar. They advise him to eat the clean meat and make it appear as if he is eating the pork. Eleazar vigorously refuses their advice, regarding it as both hypocritical because it could lead many youths astray when adapting "foreign customs" (ἀλλοφυλισμός) and insincere since it would bring him shame. Through this answer, the abridger shows that the collaborators, while born as Jews, do not participate in Ἰουδαισμός, but rather in Ἑλληνισμός. Eleazar condemns their actions, saying that while one can avoid punishment from people, one cannot avoid the same from God. Thus, this distinction is not only cultural, but also ethical as the abridger turns the situation around by showing that Eleazar, although mocked and tortured, is in fact acting with honour in contrast to his Jewish acquaintances whose adaptation of foreign customs leads to dishonour. Eleazar's judgement on the collaborators results in his torture. Just before he dies, he confesses his conviction that he will be saved by God, who is the only rightful judge. Eleazar's heroism sets a noble example for the whole nation, especially to its youth. Through this story, the abridger artfully demonstrates the value and integrity of the Jewish way of life, in contrast to the deceitful and shameful "foreign customs." His acknowledgement of the true authority of God, to whom belongs absolute loyalty and visible faithfulness (in contrast to hypocrisy and compromising oneself), is highlighted as

---

Predrag Bukovec, Stefan Krauter, and Michael Tilly, WUNT 382 (Tübingen: Mohr Siebeck, 2017), 157–85.

22 The honourable character of Eleazar is highlighted by his physical appearance, his virtuous acts, and his thoughts. Jonathan Goldstein also notes that the resemblance of Eleazar to Socrates in Plato's *Apologia* must have been clear to everyone with a Greek education. Jonathan A. Goldstein, *II Maccabees. A New Translation with Introduction and Commentary*, AB 41A (Garden City: Doubleday, 1983), 285.

exemplary behaviour worthy of imitation and remembrance. The abridger's contrast between the shameful behaviour of the antagonists and the honourable actions of Eleazar serves as a foundation for what it means to be part of the Ἰουδαισμός.

This story is supplemented with the martyrdom account of the seven brothers and their mother, which probably existed as a separate legend prior to its inclusion in 2 Maccabees.[23] In the wake of Eleazar's example to the youth, this story further recounts what ideal "discipleship" required. The account about the seven sons and their mother brings two new important expansions to conceptions of martyrdom. The first can be viewed on an individual level, which is the hope of the resurrection as the reward for faithfulness. The second can be viewed on a collective level, which regards the suffering of the righteous as a means to reconciliation (καταλλάσσω; 7:6, 33) between God and his nation (7:33, 37–38). This conception is instrumental in the eventual defeat of Antiochus and the victory to the Jews in 2 Maccabees.[24] These two expanded conceptions about the afterlife highlight God's vindication of the faithfulness of the martyrs. These conceptions are natural expressions of the Deuteronomistic theological scheme. The collective concept is the most important for the whole plot of the narration as it offers the turning point for the reversal of the fate of the Jewish people. The individual concept demonstrates the individual level of retribution, but also allows us a unique insight into the perception of the afterlife in 2 Maccabees. As I stated in the introduction, the martyrs' stories include promises of a reward in the afterlife for those who die nobly, which serve as an important window into its imaginative constructs in various contexts. In 2 Maccabees, the seven sons express their hope in the post-mortem vindication. While Antiochus, as an earthly king, might have power over them in the earthly conditions, the "king of the universe" (7:9) is the one who possesses the power over eternity and the pending judgment. The seven sons relentlessly express that they would rather die than break the laws of their ancestors.[25] The cruel king can sever their body parts, but God will give them back in the resurrection (7:9, 11, 14). For this, there is no hope in the resurrection for Antiochus, but only torture and punishment (7:14, 17, 19, 31–36). Human existence is, therefore, viewed from a cosmological and eschatological perspective. The conflict

23 Christian Habicht, 2. *Makkabäerbuch*, JSHRZ 1.3 (Gütersloh: Gerd Mohn, 1976), 233; Goldstein, *II Maccabees*, 283. It is also notable that this story is never paired with Eleazar's account in the rabbinic tradition. See Robert Doran, "The Martyr: A Synoptic View of the Mother and Her Seven Sons," in *Ideal Figures in Ancient Judaism: Profiles and Paradigms*, ed. George W. E. Nickelsburg and John J. Collins (Chico: Scholars Press, 1980), 189–221.

24 Daniel R. Schwartz, *2 Maccabees*, CEJL (Berlin: de Gruyter, 2008), 299.

25 "The (holy) law (of ancestors)" is a repeatedly mentioned (6:23, 28; 7:2, 9, 11, 23, 24, 30, 37).

between Antiochus and the martyrs (and by extension, the conflict between different identities represented by these two parties) would have been presented very differently if it did not include this post-mortem component. The intended perspective guaranteed by God is presented through the final vindication of their lives.

Afterlife for the righteous is famously conceived as a bodily resurrection.[26] The afterlife bodies of the righteous are imagined as perfect re-creations and not as representations of the mutilated tortured bodies. In this description, the author combines the creation motif (7:22–23, 27–28; cf. 14:46) with the emphasis on suffering and vindication (e.g., 7:36). These motifs are intertextually adopted from several images of Isaiah, notably from the servant poems (esp. Isa 52:13–53:12) and the eschatological imagery of the anticipated new creation and restoration (Isa 65:17–25). The Genesis creation account may have also played an influential role.[27] The creation motif is especially important, as it is used as an analogy to the resurrection: "Therefore the Creator of the world, who shaped the beginning of humankind and devised the origin of all things, will in his mercy give life and breath back to you again" (2 Macc 7:23). In 2 Macc 7:29, the mother begs her last son to accept death in the same way as his brothers, hoping, "so that, in God's mercy, I may get you back again along with your brothers". However, this fate is extended to all the righteous as, in 7:36, everlasting life is promised to all those keeping the covenant.[28] The future resurrection is, therefore, envisioned as the reward for the righteous, and righteous *only*, while the wicked can expect punishment (7:14).

This conception is not that common in early Judaism as it is usually expected. For example, in Dan 12:2–3, the resurrection is seen as a precondition for the last judgment. That means that even (some) sinners will be raised, but to "everlasting contempt" (12:2)—in contrast to an angelic existence of the

26 This emphasis on the *bodily* resurrection is surprisingly scarce in early Jewish literature. It is explicit only in 4QPseudo-Ezekiel (which is partly a midrash on Ezekiel 37), Apocryphon of Ezekiel and 2 Baruch 49–51 (where it serves to accentuate that the personal identity is preserved only in the interconnection of the body and soul), 4 Ezra and in two texts from Diaspora: Ps.-Phoc. 103–104 and Sib. Or 4:170–190. See Casey D. Elledge, *Resurrection of the Dead in Early Judaism, 200 BCE–CE 200* (Oxford: Oxford University Press, 2017), 20–31.

27 See George W. E. Nickelsburg, *Resurrection, Immortality, and Eternal Life in Intertestamental Judaism* (Cambridge: Harvard University Press, 1972), 102–108, 130–37.

28 Some commentators translate and interpret 2 Macc 7:36 as a reference to some form of interim afterlife existence. However, Doran convincingly shows the problems with this interpretation (*Temple Propaganda*, 163).

righteous.[29] The afterlife transformation to blessedness promised only to the righteous is found, for example, in the *Epistle of Enoch* (1 En. 92–105), where great joy (as experienced by angels) is promised to the righteous (103:3–4; 104:1–4) and, by contrast, judgment is promised to the sinners. The emphasis on the restoration of the body, which in this case reflects the dire reality of torture and mutilation of bodies, betrays a more traditional Jewish anthropology of 2 Maccabees.

Nevertheless, while 2 Maccabees 7 is a classical text for those interested in the afterlife beliefs of early Judaism, the lack of attention to details in 2 Maccabees suggests that this was not the intention of the abridger. The text also avoids any spatial descriptions of afterlife existence of the righteous. Rather, the abridger appears to be more interested in conveying his eschatological perspective in order to highlight the value of Jewish identity.

While the setting of 2 Maccabees is often disputed, its attention to matters that do not appear to concern Judean Jews, along with the appended letters at the beginning, suggest that the target audience was Diaspora Jews, probably those living in Egypt.[30] For the abridger, it is important to identify what constitutes the true Jewish way of life since many in the Diaspora were highly influenced by various aspects of Hellenistic culture, which in his perspective jeopardizes their inclusion within God's covenant. The author is not opposed to Hellenistic culture as such. After all, his high level of competence in Greek and rhetoric indicate that he was thoroughly Hellenised. The opposition was theological in the sense that he maintained his devotion to his ancestral Jewish beliefs, or more precisely, what he believed to be the true articulation of those beliefs in a changing world.[31]

The entire book can be read as an identity-construction. This seems to be a plausible assessment in light of the abridger's description of his own work in comparison to that of Jason in the prologue (2:19–32). He complains about the length and difficulty of the original text and thus attempts to shorten it and present it in a more amusing fashion. This has the benefit of enhancing its memorization which makes it accessible beyond the scope of those who simply wanted it read. Therefore, the author presents only an outline (υπογραμμός) of Jason's history which is suitable for his purpose (2:28–31).

29 For details, see John J. Collins, *Daniel*, Hermeneia (Minneapolis: Fortress Press, 1993), 393. This scenario seems to be close to that of the Book of the Watchers (1 Enoch 1–36), in which only the worst sinners will not rise up from Sheol (22:13). Implicitly, all the others—righteous and sinners—will rise up for the last judgment.

30 Doran, *2 Maccabees*, 15; Schwartz, *2 Maccabees*, 45–56; Malka Z. Simkovich, "Greek Influence on the Composition of 2 Maccabees," *JSJ* 42 (2011): 293–310.

31 Habicht, *2. Makkabäerbuch*, 185; Himmelfarb, "Judaism and Hellenism," 28–31.

In the abridger's story, the nobility of martyrdom, strategically placed in the climax of the narrative, imposes its rhetorical argumentation and also emotional quality to stimulate the ideal Jewish identity.[32] The argumentation for the ideal Jewish way of life appeals to both cultural and religious values. On the one hand, righteous and wicked behaviour is deeply interwoven with strands of key cultural values of honour and shame. On the other hand, the decisive motivation for their bravery is expressed through theological (eschatological) perspectives in at least two ways. First, it conveys that the true power lays in the hands of "Almighty God" who rewards faithfulness with resurrection and salvation from punishment. Second, it conveys that the blessing of the nation is contingent on the faithfulness of the Jewish people who await the eschatological ingathering of Israel (1:27; 2:7, 18). These two aspects generate an ethical demand for responsibility on both individual and collective levels. The identity-construction is further accentuated in the first of the appended letters which invites the readers to participate in the commemoration of the narrated events through annual festivals (1:1–9; 10:8). This retelling of the story about the Maccabean martyrs serves as a medium for developing an ideal Jewish identity construction within its particular cultural and historical setting.

Eleazar and the Maccabean Martyrs in 4 Maccabees

4 Maccabees is a very different piece of literature. The author expands the narrative of the martyrdoms in 2 Maccabees in the form of a philosophical discourse. The topic of the discourse is conveyed in the initial thesis that, "pious reason is the absolute master of the passions (αὐτοδέσποτός ἐστιν τῶν παθῶν ὁ εὐσεβὴς λογισμός)" (1:1).[33] It is a work of epideictic rhetoric which promotes a set of values and a certain way of life as praiseworthy and therefore ideal for imitation.[34] The author displays extensive cultural literacy, high competence in the Greek language, and his broad use of rhetoric suggests a formal education.[35] He contributes to an important theme in Greco-Roman philosophical ethics, which concerns the question of how one can achieve a life of virtue through the mastery of the passions. In doing so, he uses a common scenario that was applied by various ancient writers. The scene is of a tyrant who

32 Van Henten, *Maccabean Martyrs*, 25.

33 All the quotations from 4 Maccabees are taken from David A. deSilva, *4 Maccabees. Introduction and Commentary on the Greek Text in Codex Sinaiticus* (Leiden: Brill, 2006).

34 Hans-Josef Klauck, *4 Makkabäerbuch*, JSHRZ 3.6 (Gütersloh: Gerd Mohn, 1989), 659–60.

35 See the extensive discussion in Urs Breitenstein, *Beobachtungen zu Sprache, Stil und Gedankengut des Vierten Makkabäerbuchs* (Basel: Schwabe, 1976).

confronts a philosopher with arguments, threats, and tortures for the purpose of bending his will. The philosopher, however, proves the value of his philosophy by remaining steadfast.[36] Although this work is entirely immersed in the Hellenistic world, it remains solely focused on presenting the Jewish way of life as the best way to achieve perfection in virtue.

The story of Eleazar and other Maccabean martyrs serves to demonstrate (ἐπιδείκνυμι) to his audience the proposed thesis as well as to praise (ἐπαινέω) the martyrs for their willingness to die for the sake of nobility and goodness (καλοκἀγαθία) and moral excellence (ἀρετή)—which sum up the Greek ideals of an admirable person.[37] This composition presents the martyrs as contestants who, one by one, triumph over the tyrant for the sake of their piety (cf. esp. 17:11–20).[38] In contrast to 2 Maccabees, the text is expanded mainly by the insertion of several dialogues between Antiochus and the martyrs. These dialogues allow the author to present arguments that convey the superiority of the Jewish way of life as the best philosophy.

The scene about Eleazar is cleverly crafted. Antiochus is presented as an arrogant tyrant possessing no credibility and ethos. In his opening speech, Antiochus urges Eleazar to give up his foolish philosophy (φλυάρος φιλοσοφία; 5:10) for the sake of his old age. Antiochus ridicules Eleazar by pointing out that though his elderly appearance might suggest a proficiency in philosophy, it is quite to the contrary. Eleazar is told that his philosophy is nothing more than the religion of the Jews. Antiochus advises him to do what is natural and beneficial by promoting nature (φύσις) as the primary source of knowledge of the truth, which at the same time requires devaluation of inferior laws of a particular ethnic group since it is a human-made construct.[39] Antiochus infers that even if the god that Eleazar worships exists, that god would be willing to pardon a trivial sin such as eating pork. Eleazar's response is predictable. He vehemently claims that he will not violate the Torah that was given by God, who himself is the creator of nature. He also refuses to trivialize sin, because the law does not distinguish among offenses against God. He argues that Jewish philosophy is the best instructor of four cardinal virtues: moderation (σωφροσύνη), courage (ἀνδρεία), justice (δικαιοσύνη), and piety (εὐσέβεια).[40] Eleazar

---

36 DeSilva, *Introducing the Apocrypha*, 394.

37 DeSilva, *4 Maccabees*, 79–80.

38 Van Henten, *Maccabean Martyrs*, 119–22.

39 To live κατὰ φύσιν was the Stoic goal of living. On the presentation of Antiochus's philosophy in 4 Maccabees, see Reinhard Weber, "Eusebeia und Logismos. Zum philosophischen Hintergrund von 4. Makkabäer," *JSJ* 22 (1991): 212–34.

40 See deSilva, *4 Maccabees*, 135–36. The four cardinal virtues, initially recognized by Socrates (Plato, *Republic* 4.426–35), were the basis of Stoic ethics. The fourth virtue

emphasizes that Jewish philosophy is in full accordance with nature because God, who gave the law, is the creator of nature (κατὰ φύσιν; 5:25). The intended result of the exchange is to reinforce that the philosophy of Eleazar is based on better arguments than those of his opponent.[41]

The story continues with Eleazar being subjected to tortures in an effort to force his obedience to Antiochus. However, he remains steadfast and does not change his mind. At this moment, the author interestingly notes that this act of heroism defines Eleazar "as a true Eleazar" (ὡς ἀληθῶς Ελεαζάρος, 6:5). Some commentators explain this note as a reference to the etymology of his Hebrew name, i.e. אל עזר ("God helps").[42] It is, however, questionable whether the author wanted to convey this association or whether the audience would have picked up on it. I would argue to view the note as a reference to a Jewish cultural memory in which Eleazar already functioned as the symbol of the faithful, steadfast and brave martyr, who was an emblem of resistance against an oppressive power. As Shmuel Shepkaru notes, by the Early Roman Period, Eleazar became "father of all martyrs" for Jews.[43] Thus, the author, while describing the torture of this old scribe paused in this confrontation for a moment to say, that right now, in this situation, with this attitude, this Eleazar acted as *the true* Eleazar.

In the torturing scene, his noble attitude is linked with a youthful stamina. He outlasts his much younger torturers, who get tired of beating him, and is even able to urge his fellow Jews to "Die nobly for the sake of piety!" (6:22). Finally, immediately before he dies, Eleazar prays that God would accept his life as a ransom for his people. At his death Eleazar is convinced in the power of God's righteousness and that he dies "on account of the law by means of reason" (6:30).

In the author's reflection of this scene, he harks back to his opening thesis by stating that it is "undeniably then, that pious reason is the master of the passions" (6:31). Eleazar not only argued for the superiority of Jewish philosophy, but also proved it practically in his supreme example. Pious reason, which

according to Socrates was wisdom (σοφία), which is in 4 Maccabees associated with education in Torah. It is interesting to notice that holiness (ὁσιότης) is mentioned as the fifth virtue in Plato's *Protagoras* (330b), and similarly piety (εὐσέβεια) is among the virtues in Xenophon's *Memorabilia* (4.6).

41 Tessa Rajak, "Paideia in the Fourth Book of Maccabees," in *Jewish Education from Antiquity to the Middle Ages. Studies in Honour of Philip S. Alexander*, ed. George J. Brooke and Renate Smithuis (Leiden: Brill, 2017), 67–69.

42 E.g., deSilva, *4 Maccabees*, 143.

43 Shmuel Shepkaru, *Jewish Martyrs in the Pagan and Christian Worlds* (Cambridge: Cambridge University Press, 2006), 34.

stems from an education in the Torah, overrides not only physical pain and pleasures, but leads to a truly courageous and virtuous life. Though mocked by his opponents, he is portrayed as the example of piety and honour, much like a noble athlete, irrespective of his old age. His endurance and ultimate victory over his torturers, which served as an example of piety to the youth, was viewed as a ransom for the sake of his nation and endured as a remembrance of a holy man.

The author's case is further developed by the inclusion of the tortures and eventual martyrdom of the seven sons (8:1–12:19) and their mother (14:11–17:6). Antiochus tries to convince the sons to accept the Greek way of life (Ἑλληνικός βίος; 8:8) as he offers them friendship and great political and economic reward if they renounce their ancestral laws and eat the unclean meat. If they reject, he threatens them with terrifying tortures. But the sons are neither swayed by his intimidations and threats of using terrifying instruments of torture nor by his offers of wealth and power. They hold firm to their philosophy "through right reasoning," which eventually undermines Antiochus' power (8:15). Antiochus proceeds with the tortures during which the brothers repeatedly encourage each other and assure themselves of God's righteousness. As the brothers are tortured, they express their unshaken courage, mutual encouragement, and devotion to the law.[44] Through these examples, the author once more proves that it is pious reason, learned from the law, which is the best way to achieve mastery of one's virtues. Neither great personal gain nor physical tortures can dissuade their spirit from the path to virtue.

Finally, the author presents their mother as the purest example of the superiority of pious reason by comparing her actions to the natural order. He explains that when one observes the animals, it is obvious that nature tells us that all parents have a deep affection and love for their offspring. Above all, a mother, who is considered the weaker parent, has strong instincts toward her children. Yet, she chooses piety over the temporary deliverance of her seven sons (15:2). While there is no stronger passion than the inclination of a mother to save her children, her pious commitment to the Law drives her to encourage each one of her sons to be pious in the face of death (15:23–24).[45]

Through these vivid examples the author proves that pious reason, conveyed in the Torah, is a better guide to virtue than nature because where nature

44 See Hans-Josef Klauck, "Brotherly Love in Plutarch and in 4 Maccabees," in *Greeks, Romans, Christians: Essays in Honor of Abraham J. Malherbe*, eds. David L. Balch, Everett Ferguson, and Wayne A. Meeks (Minneapolis: Fortress Press, 1990), 144–56.

45 See David A. deSilva, "The Perfection of 'Love for Offspring': Greek Representations of Maternal Affection and the Achievement of the Heroine of 4 Maccabees," *NTS* 52 (2006): 251–68.

fails to empower the virtuous course (i.e., in the instinct to save one's life, gain a political and economic good, and above all, rescue one's children), knowledge of piety in the Torah enables victory over the passions and consequently over the tyrant.

As in 2 Maccabees, also here the reward for the steadfast faithfulness to the Law by the martyrs is envisaged in the blessed afterlife. However, in 4 Maccabees we can see interactions with Hellenistic philosophical versions of immortality where afterlife conceptions are understood within a model of dualistic anthropology which separates the body from the soul.[46] Though, the separation does not devalue the body as in Platonism.[47] The details of post-mortem existence are lacking since the author is primarily interested in the classical conflict between reason and the passions. In the philosophical exchange, he claims that reason cannot fully eliminate the passions; it can only provide the means to avoid enslavement to them (3:2).[48] The soul, which is affected by both reason and the passions (1:20–32), is the bearer of future afterlife existence (18:23). Also, the language and form of afterlife existence are expressed in light of Greek concepts wherein the soul is promised incorruptibility (ἀφθαρσία, 9:22; 17:12) and immortality (ἀθανασία, 14:5; 16:13). These are terms that have no counterparts in the Hebrew Bible, but are typical qualities of Greek gods and souls of individuals.[49] It is, therefore, not surprising that this immortal existence is seen in the form of some kind of astral immortality that is hinted in 17:5 and 18:3. Further, the author repeatedly emphasizes that the heroic death of the martyrs brings benefits to others. This is an essential part of a laudatory speech that has a decisive impact on the perception of death as a noble event.[50]

---

46 Predrag Bukovec, "Per aspera ad astra. Leben nach dem Tod im 4. Makkabäerbuch," in *Die Makkabäer*, eds. Friedrich Avemarie, Predrag Bukovec, Stefan Krauter, and Michael Tilly, WUNT 382 (Tübingen: Mohr Siebeck, 2017), 275–303, here 281.

47 Klauck, *4 Makkabäerbuch*, 672.

48 Here the author agrees with, e.g., Seneca (*Ep.* 11.1; 116.1) and Plutarch (*Mor.* 442D; 443D) who also claimed that reason can only *master* the passions, not *eliminate* them (as expressed, for example, by Cicero (*Tusc.* 3.22; 4.38).

49 This terminology is already present in a "Hellenistic" sense in the Book of Wisdom (ἀφθαρσία [2:23' 6:13]; ἀθανασία [3:4; 4:1; 8:13, 17; 15:3]), and also in Philo. See Dieter Zeller, "The Life and Death of the Soul in Philo of Alexandria: The Use and Origin of Metaphor," SPhiloA 7 (1995): 19–55. In 1 Cor 15:52–54, these terms denote the mode of existence in the resurrected state. In 1 Tim 6:16, ἀφθαρσία is a quality of God. On the meaning of these terms in Greek literature, see Dag Øistein Endsjø, *Greek Resurrection Beliefs and the Success of Christianity* (New York: Palgrave Macmillan, 2009), 21–120. On the use of the terms in Greek and Christian literature, see Rudolf Bultmann, "ἀφθαρσία," *TDNT* 3.22–25 and Günther Harder, "φθείρω," *TDNT* 9.93–106.

50 See *Rhet. Her.* 3.7.14, Quintilian, *Inst.* 3.7.10–18; deSilva, *4 Maccabees*, 249.

Not all the terms and concepts derive from a Greco-Roman origin. Many aspects of the afterlife in 4 Maccabees are undoubtedly derived from Jewish tradition. The dead are welcomed into communion with their ancestors. In death, they share in the company of Abraham, Isaac, Jacob, and the patriarchs, who stand out as examples of those who now live with God (5:37; 7:19; 13:17; 16:25). Within the "heavenly topography", the martyrs are located in close proximity to the divine throne (17:18). A theologically rooted approach to justice affects the conceptualization of entrance. Those who live righteously according to the Law are promised to live eternally in blessedness, while those who break the law are promised only divine punishment (10:15; 13:15).[51] This evaluative process is aligned with the examples of the righteous martyrs who are contrasted with the wicked tyrant. Though in 13:15, the author makes it clear that the decision to live a righteous life is open to everyone.[52] Throughout 4 Maccabees, the author promotes the importance of living according to the laws of the Torah for the sake of righteousness.[53]

Returning to the mother's concluding speech (18:6–19), the author includes several references to scripture that are usually associated with resurrection in the Second Temple Period, such as Deut 30:20; 32:39 and Ezekiel 37. These accounts may have been part of a broader pool of afterlife texts that might have been applied to the conception of both resurrection and immortality.[54] If the author used 2 Maccabees as his source alongside common afterlife scriptural texts, it may suggest that he regarded the resurrection concept in 2 Maccabees by itself as insufficient for his argumentation. Casey Elledge suggests that the reason for this might have been that there was no desire to restore bodily existence, especially as the perfection in virtues is achieved by defeating the bodily passions.[55] The problem with this suggestion is that the passions in 4 Maccabees are not only concerned with the body, but also with the soul (esp. 1:20). Rather, as Hans-Josef Klauck argues, the author attempts to enculturate old eschatological Jewish concepts into contemporary Hellenistic discourse in order to underscore their relevance.[56] The general theological aim is to maintain a conception of afterlife as a blessed reward for a righteous life

51 Bukovec, "Per aspera ad astra," 282.

52 Klauck, *4 Makkabäerbuch*, 673.

53 In his analysis of the concept of the law in 4 Maccabees, Paul Redditt concludes that "the term *nomos* refers to the Pentateuch in the Hebrew Bible, which the author of 4 Maccabees considers divinely promulgated." Paul L. Redditt, "The Concept of *Nomos* in Fourth Maccabees," *CBQ* 45 (1983): 249–70, here 249.

54 Elledge, *Resurrection of the Dead*, 123; deSilva, *4 Maccabees*, 264–65.

55 Elledge, *Resurrection of the Dead*, 123.

56 Klauck, *4 Makkabäerbuch*, 674.

that is in accordance with a more appropriate anthropology. It is not surprising that within this process some of the aspects of the Jewish heritage were reinterpreted.

The location of 4 Maccabees, which impacted its conceptions of afterlife, is also a matter of debate. Most likely, it originated in an urban context in Asia Minor or Syria during the time of so-called Second Sophistic period in which philosophical ideas of various schools became available through their popular public presentations.[57] This would coincide with a description of the philosophical opinions that the author of 4 Maccabees challenges as part of a "philosophical koine" which Robert Renehen defines as a general eclectic tendency that was widespread from the first century BCE onwards.[58] Consequently, 4 Maccabees does not interact with any specific philosophical school, but rather with the widespread philosophical ideas that might have been popular also among urban Jews—notably those that the author saw as incompatible with the Jewish way of life. The author does not aim to convince the outsiders about the Jewish way of life, but rather to encourage his fellow Jews to persevere in their ancestral identity and practices (18:1–2) in the face of increasing pressures to assimilate to the dominant culture.[59] For example, the author addresses temptations for personal gain through assimilation. Jews in the Roman urban setting were tolerated, though they were viewed with suspicion.[60] The suspicion is exemplified in Antiochus's amazement that the Jews would want to follow supposed unreasonable and obscure ethnic philosophy instead of enjoying all the advantages of Hellenistic pluralism and the benefits of a cosmopolitan world. The author of 4 Maccabees speaks into this context of an intense social and cultural situation which, through compromises,

---

57 André Dupont-Sommer, *Le Quatrième Livre des Machabées* (Paris: Librairie Ancienne Honoré Champion, 1939), 75–85. See especially Tessa Rajak, "The Fourth Book of Maccabees in a Multi-Cultural City," in *Jewish and Christian Communal Identities in the Roman World*, ed. Yair Furstenberg (Brill: Leiden, 2016), 134–50. Rajak locates the origin of 4 Maccabees in the late 1st or early 2nd century CE in Antioch. On the dating and provenance, see also van Henten, *Maccabean Martyrs*, 73–81; Klauck, *4 Makkabäerbuch*, 665–69. On the Second Sophistic, see Barbara E. Borg, ed., *Paideia: The World of the Second Sophistic* (Berlin: de Gruyter, 2007).

58 Robert Renehan, "The Greek Philosophical Background of Fourth Maccabees," *Rheinisches Museum für Philologie* 115 (1972): 223–38. In his influential study, Renehan convincingly refutes the often-repeated thesis that the author of 4 Maccabees was a kind of Jewish Stoic.

59 John J. Collins, *Between Athens and Jerusalem*, 2nd ed. (Grand Rapids: Eerdmans, 2000), 207–208.

60 Rajak notes that the late 1st and early 2nd century CE was a very troubled period for Jews everywhere in the Roman Empire because of the three Jewish revolts. Rajak, "The Fourth Book of Maccabees," 145–48.

threatened the existence of what he perceived as ideal Jewish identity.[61] To achieve his goal, the author attempts to show the value of the Jewish way of life by using philosophical (ethical), cultural (language related to honour and shame), and religious (eschatological) discourses.[62] The composition, through praising of exemplary heroes Eleazar, the seven sons and their mother, promotes supremacy of the Jewish way of life that needs to be defended.[63]

Conclusion

Martyrdom is inextricably linked on the one hand to social identity and memory, and on the other hand to cultural conceptions of afterlife. Social perceptions of someone as a terrorist and a murderer as opposed to a hero and a martyr are determined by a given group's self-identity construction within its frames of meaning. Since martyrdom is a product of discourse, its relevance is always embedded into interpretation and retelling. As Castelli points out: "Martyrdom is … rhetorically constituted and discursively sustained."[64] The impact on identity change for those who look to their martyrs with awe and reverence always requires a respective change in how the past is remembered, which includes creative retelling and reinterpretation of the stories about their heroism. I have attempted to show how the story of a certain Jewish elder Eleazar and a mother with her seven sons in the second century BCE were creatively narrated in two different texts that both express and create respective memories of the one event. In these stories, their torture and death were transformed into heroic resistance against agents of an oppressive foreign power that attacked the foundations of Jewish identity.

Both texts seek a similar purpose, but in a different form, in a different way and in a different context. 2 Maccabees is a typical narrative that fits the style of biblical history. It is conservative in the sense that it is set within a traditional theological scheme. It is a retelling of the history of Hellenistic reforms in Palestine, but from a specific Jewish perspective. This perspective is extrapolated retrospectively, probably from another historical and social context, and responds to a new situation. The martyrdom contributes to the plot

61 DeSilva, *Introducing the Apocrypha*, 406–407.

62 For an analysis of honour and shame language in 4 Maccabees, see David A. deSilva, "The Noble Contest: Honor, Shame, and the Rhetorical Strategy of 4 Maccabees," *JSP* 13 (1995): 31–57.

63 Van Henten, *Maccabean Martyrs*, 237–38.

64 Castelli, *Martyrdom and Memory*, 173.

by portraying an ideal Jewish identity in contrast to the undesirable traits of Hellenistic culture.

By contrast, 4 Maccabees focuses almost exclusively on the description of the martyrdom by keeping the tangential historical descriptions of the era to a minimum. The author of 4 Maccabees, writing some two centuries later within a different geographical context, reflects a different social condition when Jewish inculturation and assimilation was more prominent and complex. He adapts his style by presenting the account within a philosophical discourse of epideictic rhetoric, and interacts more closely with popular values and beliefs of the so-called "philosophical koine." Nevertheless, the overall aims of 4 Maccabees are similar to those of 2 Maccabees.

Afterlife conceptions reflected in these recollections were not immune to the processes of change that one commonly finds when tradition collides with new cultural ideals. This observation might be especially intriguing in the case of 2 Maccabees 7, which is a standard text to which scholars often appeal when advancing the view that bodily resurrection in Second Temple Judaism was prevalent. It is important to note, however, that the physicality of the resurrection is discursively linked with the narration of martyrdom. Since the abridger neither provides details of his afterlife conceptions nor descriptions of widespread constructs, extensive claims about common beliefs and their specific content require caution.

Finally, the urgency of martyrdom, which carries with it an emotional impact, is very productive for upholding certain values that are revered by remembering communities. This is obvious also from the further trajectories of the story of the Maccabean martyrs in later sources. Conspicuously, after 4 Maccabees, we have no clear literary evidence of this story in subsequent Jewish literature in Antiquity.[65] One of the reasons for this disappearance might be the vast appropriation of this story by early Christian martyrologies, which served their own theological purposes. Christian bishops and clergy continued the process of retelling the story in new contexts, defining new social identities that distinguished Christians from rival groups, which ironically included Jews.[66] One fascinating exception to this silence in the

65 Though, there are a few rabbinic sources that retell the story of the mother and her seven sons (Lam. Rab. 1.16; b. Giṭ 57b; Pesiq. Rab. 43). See Daniel Joslyn-Siemiatkoski, "The Mother and Seven Sons in Late Antique and Medieval Ashkenazi Judaism: Narrative Transformations and Communal Identity," in *Dying for the Faith, Killing for the Faith. Old-Testament Faith-Warriors (1 and 2 Maccabees) in Historical Perspective*, ed. Gabriela Signori, BSIH 206 (Leiden: Brill, 2012), 127–46.

66 Daniel Joslyn-Siemiatkoski, *Christian Memories of the Maccabean Martyrs* (New York: Palgrave-Macmillan 2009), 1–2, 29–77.

Jewish milieu is the so-called Elephant Mosaic from a late fourth or early fifth century CE Galilean Synagogue in Huqoq. This beautiful mosaic probably depicts the heroism of the Maccabean martyrs who, through their resistance, caused the downfall of Antiochus and his army. The strife between the martyrs and the Seleucid king, which is portrayed at the top of the mosaic, has a surprising outcome portrayed in the bottom section which shows the Seleucid army underfoot of the glorified martyrs (most likely in their afterlife existence) who are ultimately the victors.[67] Once again, this portrayal might have played a role in defining the self-identity of the minority community that regularly gathered inside the walls of the synagogue as they were pressured by the dominant culture. According to Matthew Grey, who attempted to reconstruct the socio-religious context of Lower Galilee around Tiberias and Mt. Arbel, there was a strong need for Jewish self-determination within the region. As result, nationalistic, apocalyptic and messianic expectations flourished within Jewish circles as a reaction to increasingly Christian-imperial culture that was omnipresent in the Roman Galilee during that period.[68] Remembering this story might have been one of the answers to the growing need for heroes who could stand up against foreign oppressors.

The memory of the Maccabean martyrs is, therefore, an open-ended story. Heroes are needed in every generation and it is not surprising that in oppressed societies, martyrs take the role of the most admired heroes who function as cultural examples that can be imitated as expressions of an "ideal" identity.

Bibliography

Bochardt, Francis. "Reading Aid: 2 Maccabees and the History of Jason of Cyrene Reconsidered." JSJ 47 (2016): 71–87.

Borg, Barbara E., ed. *Paideia: The World of the Second Sophistic*. Berlin: de Gruyter, 2007.

Breitenstein, Urs. *Beobachtungen zu Sprache, Stil und Gedankengut des Vierten Makkabäerbuchs*. Basel: Schwabe, 1976.

Britt, Karen, and Ra'anan Boustan. *The Elephant Mosaic Panel in the Synagogue at Huqoq: First Publication and Initial Interpretations*. *JRA* Supplement Series 106. Portsmouth: Journal of Roman Archaeology, 2017.

---

67 See Karen Britt and Ra'anan Boustan, *The Elephant Mosaic Panel in the Synagogue at Huqoq: First Publication and Initial Interpretations*, *JRA* Supplement Series 106 (Portsmouth: Journal of Roman Archaeology, 2017); David Cielontko, "The Elephant Mosaic Panel in the Huqoq Synagogue: A Reappraisal of the Maccabean Interpretation," (forthcoming).

68 Matthew J. Grey, "'The Redeemer to Arise from the House of Dan': Samson, Apocalypticism, and Messianic Hopes in Late Antique Galilee," *JSJ* 44 (2013): 553–89.

Bukovec, Predrag. "Per aspera ad astra. Leben nach dem Tod im 4. Makkabäerbuch." Pages 275–303 in *Die Makkabäer*. Edited by Friedrich Avemarie, Predrag Bukovec, Stefan Krauter, and Michael Tilly. WUNT 382. Tübingen: Mohr Siebeck, 2017.

Castelli, Elizabeth. *Martyrdom and Memory. Early Christian Culture Making*. New York: Columbia University Press, 2004.

Cielontko, David. "The Elephant Mosaic Panel in the Huqoq Synagogue: A Reappraisal of the Maccabean Interpretation." In *Hellenism, Early Judaism, and Early Christianity. Transmission and Transformation of Ideas*. Edited by Radka Fialová, Jiří Hoblík and Petr Kitzler. Berlin: de Gruyter (forthcoming).

Collins, John J. *Daniel*. Hermeneia. Minneapolis: Fortress Press, 1993.

———. *Between Athens and Jerusalem*. 2nd ed. Grand Rapids: Eerdmans, 2000.

Crook, Zeba. "Honor, Shame, and Social Status Revisited." *JBL* 128 (2009): 591–611.

DeSilva, David A. "The Noble Contest: Honor, Shame, and the Rhetorical Strategy of 4 Maccabees." *JSP* 13 (1995): 31–57.

—. "The Perfection of 'Love for Offspring': Greek Representations of Maternal Affection and the Achievement of the Heroine of 4 Maccabees." *NTS* 52 (2006): 251–68.

———. *4 Maccabees: Introduction and Commentary on the Greek Text in Codex Sinaiticus*. Leiden: Brill, 2006.

———. *Introducing the Apocrypha: Message, Context, and Significance*. 2nd ed. Grand Rapids: Baker Academic, 2018.

Doran, Robert. "The Martyr: A Synoptic View of the Mother and Her Seven Sons." Pages 189–221 in *Ideal Figures in Ancient Judaism: Profiles and Paradigms*. Edited by George W. E. Nickelsburg and John J. Collins. Chico: Scholars Press, 1980.

———. *Temple Propaganda: The Purpose and Character of 2 Maccabees*. CBQMS 12. Washington: The Catholic Biblical Association, 1981.

———. *2 Maccabees*. Hermeneia. Minneapolis: Fortress Press, 2012.

Dupont-Sommer, André. *Le Quatrième Livre des Machabées*. Paris: Librairie Ancienne Honoré Champion, 1939.

Elledge, Casey D. *Resurrection of the Dead in Early Judaism, 200 BCE–CE 200*. Oxford: Oxford University Press, 2017.

Endsjø, Dag Øistein. *Greek Resurrection Beliefs and the Success of Christianity*. New York: Palgrave Macmillan, 2009.

Fentress, James, and Chris Wickham. *Social Memory*. Oxford: Blackwell, 1992.

Goldstein, Jonathan A. II *Maccabees: A New Translation with Introduction and Commentary*. AB 41A. Garden City: Doubleday, 1983.

Grey, Matthew J. "'The Redeemer to Arise from the House of Dan': Samson, Apocalypticism, and Messianic Hopes in Late Antique Galilee." *JSJ* 44 (2013): 553–89.

Habicht, Christian. *2. Makkabäerbuch*. JSHRZ 1.3. Gütersloh: Gerd Mohn, 1976.

Hakola, Raimo, Samuel Byrskog, and Jutta Jokiranta. "Introduction." Pages in 7–13 in *Social Memory and Social Identity in the Study of Early Judaism and Early Christianity*. Edited by Samuel Byrskog, Raimo Hakola, and Jutta Jokiranta. Göttingen: Vandenhoeck & Ruprecht, 2016.

Halbwachs, Maurice. *On Collective Memory*. Edited and translated by Lewis A. Coser. Chicago: University of Chicago Press, 1992.

Herr, Bertram. "Der Standpunkt des Epitomators. Perspektivenwechsel in der Forschung am Zweiten Makkabäerbuch." *Bib* 90 (2009): 1–31.

Himmelfarb, Martha. "Judaism and Hellenism in 2 Maccabees." *Poetics Today* 19 (1998): 19–40.

Jenkins, Richard. *Social Identity*. 4th ed. New York: Routledge, 2014.

Jokiranta, Jutta. *Social Identity and Sectarianism in the Qumran Movement*. Leiden: Brill, 2013.

Joslyn-Siemiatkoski, Daniel. *Christian Memories of the Maccabean Martyrs*. New York: Pagrave-Macmillan, 2009.

Joslyn-Siemiatkoski, Daniel. "The Mother and Seven Sons in Late Antique and Medieval Ashkenazi Judaism: Narrative Transformations and Communal Identity." Pages 127–46 in *Dying for the Faith, Killing for the Faith. Old-Testament Faith-Warriors (1 and 2 Maccabees) in Historical Perspective*. Edited by Gabriela Signori. BSIH 206. Leiden: Brill, 2012.

Klauck, Hans-Josef. *4 Makkabäerbuch*. JSHRZ 3.6. Gütersloh: Gerd Mohn, 1989.

Klauck, Hans-Josef. "Brotherly Love in Plutarch and in 4 Maccabees." Pages 144–56 in *Greeks, Romans, Christians: Essays in Honor of Abraham J. Malherbe*. Edited by David L. Balch, Everett Ferguson, and Wayne A. Meeks. Minneapolis: Fortress Press, 1990.

Malina, Bruce J. *The New Testament World: Insights from Cultural Anthropology*. 3rd ed. Louisville: Westminster John Knox Press, 2001.

Neubert, Luke. "Inventing Jason of Cyrene? 2 Maccabees and the Epitome." Pages 187–208 in *Die Makkabäer*. Edited by Friedrich Avemarie, Predrag Bukovec, Stefan Krauter, and Michael Tilly. WUNT 382. Tübingen: Mohr Siebeck, 2017.

Nickelsburg, George W. E. *Resurrection, Immortality, and Eternal Life in Intertestamental Judaism*. Cambridge: Harvard University Press, 1972.

Öhler, Markus. "Judäer oder Juden? Die Debatte "Ethnos vs. Religion" im Blick auf das 2. Makkabäerbuch." Pages 157–85 in *Die Makkabäer*. Edited by Friedrich Avemarie, Predrag Bukovec, Stefan Krauter, and Michael Tilly. WUNT 382. Tübingen: Mohr Siebeck, 2017.

Rajak, Tessa. "The Fourth Book of Maccabees in a Multi-Cultural City." Pages 134–50 in *Jewish and Christian Communal Identities in the Roman World*. Edited by Yair Furstenberg. Brill: Leiden, 2016.

———. “Paideia in the Fourth Book of Maccabees.” Pages 63–84 in *Jewish Education from Antiquity to the Middle Ages. Studies in Honour of Philip S. Alexander*. Edited by George J. Brooke and Renate Smithuis. Leiden: Brill, 2017.

Redditt, Paul L. “The Concept of Nomos in Fourth Maccabees.” *CBQ* 45 (1983): 249–70.

Renehan, Robert. “The Greek Philosophical Background of Fourth Maccabees.” *Rheinisches Museum für Philologie* 115 (1972): 223–38.

Ricoeur, Paul. *Time and Narrative. Volume* I. Chicago: University of Chicago Press, 1984.

Shepkaru, Shmuel. *Jewish Martyrs in the Pagan and Christian Worlds*. Cambridge: Cambridge University Press, 2006.

Simkovich, Malka Z. “Greek Influence on the Composition of 2 Maccabees.” *JSJ* 42 (2011): 293–310.

Van Henten, Jan W. *Maccabean Martyrs as Saviours of the Jewish People. A Study of 2 and 4 Maccabees*. JSJSup 57. Leiden: Brill, 1997.

Weber, Reinhard. “Eusebeia und Logismos. Zum philosophischen Hintergrund von 4. Makkabäer.” *JSJ* 22 (1991): 212–34.

Zeller, Dieter. “The Life and Death of the Soul in Philo of Alexandria: The Use and Origin of Metaphor.” SPhiloA 7 (1995): 19–55.

Zenger, Erich, and Christian Frevel, eds. *Einleitung in das Alte Testament*. 9th ed. Stuttgart: Kohlhammer, 2016.

Isaac's Death and Resurrection Remembered: Reception History, Cultural Memory, and the Aqedah in Jewish Tradition

Bradford A. Anderson

Introduction

In his commentary on Genesis, the medieval rabbi Abraham Ibn Ezra offers a curious statement concerning Gen 22:19, a verse which mentions Abraham, but not Isaac, returning to Beersheba after the traumatic events recounted at Moriah. "Those who say," Ibn Ezra notes, "that Abraham slaughtered Isaac and left him on the altar and following this Isaac came to life are contradicting Scripture."[1] Ibn Ezra's cryptic comment refers to a tradition that was well known in his time—namely, the idea that Isaac actually died and was resurrected on Moriah. This is an interesting aspect of the tradition, not least because, as Ibn Ezra pointedly observes, Isaac very clearly does *not* die in the broader account of the ancestors in Genesis. In spite of this apparent dissonance, this interpretive tradition, in various forms, would go on to have an extensive afterlife in the traditions of Judaism.

How might we account for the emergence, development, and longevity of such a tradition? In what follows I trace a number of key elements in the Jewish reception of the Aqedah that point to Isaac's death and resurrection in the account of Genesis 22—from traditions concerning Isaac's blood and ashes, to those focusing on the merits of the fathers. Drawing on these examples as well as the work of Jan and Aleida Assmann, I offer some reflections on what Isaac's death and resurrection might contribute to our understanding of the relationship between cultural memory and reception history.

Death and Resurrection of Isaac in Jewish Tradition

The story of the Aqedah, the "Binding of Isaac" as recounted in Genesis 22, is one of the most famous and commented on narratives in the Hebrew Bible. God calls Abraham to take his son to the mountain that he will show him, and

1 Abraham Ibn Ezra, *Ibn Ezra's Commentary on the Pentateuch: Genesis* (*Bereshit*), trans. H. Norman Strickman and Arthur B. Silver (New York: Menorah, 1988), 226–27.

 | DOI:10.30965/9783657796212_006

to offer Isaac as a sacrifice. Abraham and Isaac make the journey, and Abraham binds Isaac to the altar. Just before the fateful act, Abraham is commanded to stop by an angel of the Lord—Abraham is told that this has been a test. God now knows that Abraham truly fears him, and a ram is provided for the sacrifice instead of the beloved son.

The place of privilege which this story has in the traditions is due in large part to the role of Abraham, whose determined obedience in this story would become a foundational example in both Judaism and Christianity.[2] The role of Isaac—the other patriarch in this narrative—is less clear. Indeed, the place and fate of Isaac in the Aqedah has been taken up in diverse ways, particularly in Jewish tradition.[3] Many of these readings stem from gaps, ambiguities, or small details in the story, or alternatively are based on intertextual links with other biblical texts and traditions. A number of these are worth noting and are relevant for the present study, as they point to or note explicitly the idea that Isaac did indeed die and was raised from the dead.

Ritual Sacrifice and Suitable Offerings

To begin, the connection of Moriah with the site of the Temple, seen already in 2 Chr 3:1, would lead to associations related to ritual sacrifice, many of which are quite ancient. While the Aqedah is read liturgically on Rosh Ha-Shanah (where the ram's horn is blown), the story also has ancient connections to Passover. This can be seen in Jubilees 18, where the story becomes associated with the paschal lamb, the lamb as substitute, with Isaac foreshadowing the actual sacrifice.[4] Meanwhile, Genesis Rabbah observes that while Abraham

---

2 See, e.g., the discussion in R.W.L. Moberly, *The Bible, Theology, and Faith: A Study of Abraham and Jesus* (Cambridge: Cambridge University Press, 2000).

3 Helpful studies on Jewish and rabbinic engagement with the Aqedah include Shalom Spiegel, *The Last Trial: On the Legends and Lore of the Command to Abraham to Offer Isaac as a Sacrifice: The Akedah*, trans. Judah Goldin (Woodstock: Jewish Lights, 1967); Isaac Kalimi, "'Go, I beg you, take your beloved son and slay him!' The Binding of Isaac in Rabbinic Literature and Thought," *Review of Rabbinic Judaism* 13 (2010): 1–29; Jon D. Levenson, *The Death and Resurrection of the Beloved Son: The Transformation of Child Sacrifice in Judaism and Christianity* (New Haven: Yale University Press, 1993); Jon D. Levenson, *Resurrection and the Restoration of Israel: The Ultimate Victory of the God of Life* (New Haven: Yale University Press, 2006); David Jay Derovan, "The Resurrection Motif in the Midrash on the Akedat Yitzchak," in *The Lookstein Centre for Jewish Education*, URL: http://www.lookstein.org/articles/resurrection.pdf; Yvonne Sherwood, *"Textual Carcasses and Isaac's Scar, or What Jewish Interpretation Makes of the Violence that Almost Takes Place on Mount Moriah,"* in *Sanctified Aggression: Legacies of Biblical and Post-Biblical Vocabularies of Viole*nce, ed. Yvonne Sherwood and Jonneke Bekkenkamp (London: T&T Clark, 2004), 22–43.

4 *Jubilees* 18; Cf. *Lev. Rab.* 29:9ff, which notes that the Aqedah took place on the day of atonement, with Abraham depicted as a high priest. Cf. Levenson, *Death and Resurrection*, 175–77.

and Jacob spent time outside the land of promise, Isaac never leaves. Why is this the case? Isaac was to be unblemished, suitable as a burnt offering.[5] There are, then, ancient traditions that extrapolated on the theme of sacrifice as seen in the Aqedah, including the notion of Isaac as an unblemished offering.[6]

Isaac's Absence

Another stream of this tradition draws on the absence of Isaac following the events on Mount Moriah. Why is only Abraham mentioned returning to his servants in 22:19? A common interpretation, seen for example in *Genesis Rabbah* and *Targum Pseudo-Jonathan*, is that Isaac went directly to the schoolhouse of Shem, where he studied for three years.[7] However, an alternative tradition states that Isaac was taken to the Garden of Eden for three years.[8] Other texts expand on this latter notion, stating the reason that Isaac was in paradise so long was that he was being healed of the wounds received at the Aqedah.[9] A more specific account (from Isaac ben Asher ha-Levi) states that the wound in question was a cut which Abraham had made when he began to offer Isaac as a sacrifice.[10] These readings move from Isaac's absence at the end of the story, to his being transported to paradise, to his needing to stay in paradise

---

5 *Gen. Rab.* 64:3.

6 Further issues related to the sacrificial ram would appear in other parts of the tradition, and it too became associated with death and resurrection. R. Hanina ben Dosa says, "That ram, not a part of it went to waste: its tendons became the ten strings of the harp that David used to play on: its skin became the leather girdle around the loins of Elijah; as to its horns, with the left one the Holy One, blessed be He, sounded the alarm at Mount Sinai; and with the right one, which is larger than the left, He will in the future sound the alarm at the Ingathering of the Exiles in the Age to Come" (*Pirqe R. El.* 31; see *Pirke de Rabbi Eliezer*, trans. G. Friedlander). Later tradition would expand on this, saying that this ram's horn is blown to herald the coming of the Messiah (*Midr. HaGadol* at Gen 22:13; cf. Rashi at Exod 19:13). On the connection of the ram's horn and Rosh ha-Shanah and the Aqedah, see *b. Roš Haš.* 26. Some suggested that this ram was fashioned anew from the ashes; it too was resurrected (*Midr. HaGadol* at 22:13).

7 *Tg. Ps.-J.* 22:19, where the heavenly beings take him; cf. *Gen. Rab.* 56:11, where Abraham sends him.

8 *Midr. HaGadol* at 22:19. Cf. Ginzberg: "After the sacrifice on Mount Moriah, Abraham returned to Beer-Sheba, the scene of so many of his joys. Isaac was carried to Paradise by angels, and there he sojourned for three years. Thus Abraham returned home alone" (Louis Ginzberg, *The Legends of the Jews, Volume 1: From the Creation to the Exodus* [Philadelphia: Jewish Publication Society, 1937], 282–83).

9 *Paaneah Raza* 29a (R. Isaac bar Juda ha-Levi); cf. Spiegel, *The Last Trial*, 6.

10 *Hadar Zekenim* 10b; cf. Spiegel, *The Last Trial*, 7.

to recover from the wounds which he received when Abraham had begun to sacrifice him.

Isaac's Ashes

As noted above, aspects of the tradition focus on Abraham's appropriate observance of ritual sacrifice. One stream of interpretation points out how Abraham followed sacrificial procedure as laid out in Lev 1:7, putting the fire on the altar, and arranging the wood on the fire. However, according to *Pirke de Rabbi Eliezer*, Abraham can be exonerated from Isaac's death, as it was all an accident: the wood caught fire and Isaac was reduced to ashes.[11] This idea of Isaac's ashes would be taken up in other contexts. In the Babylonian Talmud, tractate *Ta'anit*, we read, "And why do they place ashes upon the head of each and every individual? Rabbi Levi bar Ḥama and Rabbi Ḥanina disagree with regard to this matter. One said that this is as though to say: We are considered like ashes before You. And one said that these ashes are placed in order to remind God of the ashes of our forefather Isaac, on our behalf."[12] The Targum to 1 Chronicles 21, meanwhile, states that when God sent an angel to destroy Jerusalem in the time of David, God changes his mind. Why? God saw Isaac's ashes in the foundation of the altar.[13] This relates to another tradition found in the Talmud: when the exiles returned from Babylon, how did they know where to put the altar? They saw Isaac's ashes on the very spot.[14]

Isaac's Blood

Along with readings that focused on Isaac's ashes, a number of traditions would comment in different ways around the notion of Isaac's blood.[15] In *Genesis Rabbah*, after the angel of the Lord has stopped Abraham from harming Isaac, Abraham states, "I will take a drop of blood from him."[16] In another early midrash, Isaac himself says "maybe it be His will that a quarter of my blood serve as an atonement for Israel." In the *Mekilta de-R. Simeon ben Yohai*,

---

11 *Pirqe R. El.* 31.

12 *B. Ta'anit* 16a (William Davidson edition); cf. *b. Ber.* 62b.

13 Targum to 1 Chr 21:15.

14 *b. Zebaḥ.* 62a; cf. *Pirqe R. El.* 31. This theme of Isaac's ashes has a long history; it goes back at least to the Amoraim, and is found in the Targum, the Babylonian Talmud, and Rashi.

15 For more on this trope, see Spiegel, *The Last Trial*, 58–9.

16 *Gen. Rab.* 56:7. Spiegel (*The Last Trial*, 64) suggests this might reflect the shift from human to animal sacrifice, with Abraham wanting to retain in symbolic fashion an aspect of the old system.

"R. Joshua says, 'And God spoke to Moses and said to him, I am the Lord (Exod 6:2)—said the Holy One, blessed be He, to Moses, I can be trusted to reward Isaac son of Abraham, for he left a quarter of his blood on top of the altar.'"[17] Rabbi Ishmael, meanwhile, notes that Abraham names the place "the Lord sees." What did he see? The blood of Isaac's Aqedah—an interpretation that implies more than a token shedding of blood.[18] Jon Levenson brings together these traditions:

> The possible interpretations of the midrashic allusions to the blood of Isaac are three. The first is the minimalist view: no blood was spilled, but God graciously reckoned Abraham's and Isaac's devout *intention* as the equivalent of bloody *deed*. Next comes the intermediate position: Abraham drew a fraction of Isaac's lifeblood as a token of the sacrifice he was prepared to carry out. The third view is maximalist: the father slew his son, and the son gave up his life, in obedience to the command of God.[19]

Isaac's Self-Giving and Merit

The idea that Isaac gave of his own blood resonates with other parts of the tradition that emphasize Isaac's self-giving in this episode. *Genesis Rabbah* states that, at the time of the Aqedah, Isaac was 37 years old, and a willing sacrifice, an idea that is echoed in a number of other ancient traditions.[20] This self-giving became the basis for understanding Isaac's act as a merit for Israel in the future. In *Midrash Tanḥuma*, God says to Abraham: "In the future Isaac's descendants will sin against Me, and I will judge them on Rosh Hashanah. If they want Me to discover something to their credit, and to recall for their advantage the binding of Isaac, let them blow upon this shofar ... Let them

---

17 Translation from Spiegel, *The Last Trial*, 46. Cf. Midr. Tanḥ. Vaera 1 (trans. Berman). There is some disagreement on the amount of blood denoted here; see Levenson, *Death and Resurrection*, 193–95.

18 *Mek. de-Rabbi Ishmael* 12a (ed. Friedman). Levenson also points out a rabbinic tradition that connects the Passover in Egypt with the Aqedah: in this tradition, the blood that God sees when passing over Egypt is the blood of Isaac—through the connection of the word "seeing" found in Exod 12, Gen 22, and 1 Chr 21. "According to this text [*Mek. de-Rabbi Ishmael*], a line runs from Abraham's great act of obedience to the deliverance of Jerusalem from pestilence in the days of King David. It must not be overlooked that this line runs through the tenth plague upon the Egyptians and the corollary sparing of the Israelite first-born. For, as the midrash would have it, where the text of Exodus speaks of the blood of the lamb, God saw the blood of Isaac." Levenson, *Death and Resurrection*, 182.

19 Levenson, *Death and Resurrection*, 194.

20 On Isaac's willingness to go to his death in ancient Jewish sources, see Leroy A. Huizenga, "*Obedience unto Death*: The Matthean Gethsemane and Arrest Sequence and the Aqedah," *CBQ* 71 (2009): 507–26. Ibn Ezra also comments on this at length in his commentary on Genesis.

blow upon the ram's horn to Me, and I will save them and redeem them from their sins."[21]

What is interesting is the shift from merits to resurrection in several of the traditions that comment on this theme. *Pesiqta Rab Kahanah*, for example, notes that "By virtue of Isaac who offered himself as a sacrifice on top of the altar, the Holy One blessed be He, will resurrect the dead in the future, as it is said, 'To hear the groaning of him who is bound [to open up release for the offspring appointed to death]' (Psalm 102:21)."[22] Shalom Spiegel unpacks the connection with Ps 102:21: "'Him who is bound' is interpreted as Isaac bound on top of the altar. 'To open up release for the offspring appointed to death' [is interpreted] as the dead whose graves the Holy One ... will open up so that He may set them on their feet in the Age to Come."[23] Thus, the merit of Isaac's self-giving sacrifice leads to the resurrection of the dead in the future.

Ritual and Liturgical Use

Finally, the Aqedah became associated with resurrection in a number of ritual and liturgical contexts. This is seen, for example, in the second benediction of the Shemoneh 'Esreh (or Amidah), which blesses the Lord who raises the dead.[24] Several interpretive traditions highlight this connection and, interestingly, put these words on Isaac's (rather than Abraham's) lips. Thus, R. Judah is quoted in *Pirke de Rabbi Eliezer* 31 as saying:

> When the blade touched his neck, the soul of Isaac fled and departed, (but) when he heard His voice from between the two Cherubim, saying (to Abraham), "Lay not thine hand upon the lad", his soul returned to his body, and (Abraham) set him free, and Isaac stood upon his feet. And Isaac knew that in this manner the dead in the future will be quickened. He opened (his mouth), and said: "Blessed art thou, O Lord, who quickeneth the dead."[25]

Shibboleth ha-Leket, meanwhile, notes that,

---

21 *Tanḥ. Vayera* 23 (trans. Berman); cf. *Pesiq. Rab.* 171b.

22 *Pesiq. Rab Kah.* 200b; Spiegel, *The Last Trial*, 111.

23 Spiegel, *The Last Trial*, 111. On the question of whether or not Judaism received the idea of a meritorious death from (or developed it as a response to) Christianity, see Philip R. Davies and Bruce D. Chilton, "The Aqedah: A Revised Tradition History," *CBQ* 40 (1978): 514–46; C. T. R. Hayward, "The Sacrifice of Isaac and Jewish Polemic Against Christianity," *CBQ* 52 (1990): 292–306.

24 On this aspect of the Shemoneh 'Esreh, see Levenson's remarks in *Resurrection and the Restoration*, 3–4, where he dates this connection with resurrection to the early Mishnaic era.

25 *Pirqe R. El.* 31, trans. Friedlander. Cf. comment in Spiegel, *The Last Trial*, 31–2.

> When Father Isaac was bound on the altar and reduced to ashes and his sacrificial dust was cast on to Mount Moriah, the Holy One, blessed be He, immediately brought upon him dew and revived him. That is why David, may he rest in peace, said: "Like the dew of Hermon that cometh down from the mountains of Zion" etc (Ps 133:3)—for he is referring to that dew with which [the Holy One, blessed be he] revived Father Isaac. Forthwith the ministering angels began to recite, Blessed art Thou, O Lord, who quickens the dead.[26]

In these readings, Abraham is almost entirely absent—and in this sense, he is absolved from what happens to Isaac, as Isaac takes on a more central role in the story.

Along with being read on Rosh Ha-Shanah, as noted above, another interesting liturgical connection is the fact that the Haftarah reading for Genesis 18–22 is the story of Elisha and the raising of the Shunnamite's son in 2 Kgs 4:1–37. It is unclear how early this haftarah reading might be, though it would go on to become the paired reading for the Aqedah in the Sephardic, Ashkenazi, and Yemeni liturgical rites. This pairing is suggestive—a story that clearly relates a son being brought back to life is read alongside the story of Abraham and Isaac.[27]

Summary: Isaac's Death and Resurrection

We have, then, traditions which speak of Isaac's ashes, his blood, his self-giving sacrifice, and his resurrection. Bringing these various tropes together, Levenson helpfully summarizes this stream of interpretation:

> The Aqedah had, by early in the second century B.C.E., emerged as a supreme moment in the life of Abraham. Soon thereafter it had already become a foundation story for the festival of Passover, with the near-sacrifice of Isaac foreshadowing the literal slaughter of the lamb. The association of Abraham's beloved son with the paschal lamb continued to grow in the rabbinic period, and eventually the Aqedah became an etiology even of lamb offerings that were not paschal. At the same time, Isaac's role in the drama was becoming increasingly active. He was reconceived as a willing participant, freely and gladly choosing, like a martyr, to give up his life in obedience to the heavenly decree, and, again like a martyr, his choice was seen as effecting atonement for the many. This transformation, already in evidence in the first century C.E., gathered force in the rabbinic period. Eventually it became possible to allude to the Aqedah without

26 *Shibboleth ha-Leket* 9a-b; trans. Spiegel, *The Last Trial*, 33.

27 On the haftarah of Genesis 22 and 2 Kings 4, see Michael Fishbane, *Haftarot: The Traditional Hebrew Text with the New JPS Translation* (Philadelphia: Jewish Publication Society, 2002), 16–20, who notes a connection between resurrection and reward for acts of charity in the two accounts. Cf. the discussion in Levenson, *Resurrection and the Restoration* 126–27.

> mention of the hero of the biblical story, Abraham: Isaac bound himself and offered himself upon the altar. Moreover, the sacrifice to which he had given joyful assent was imagined, in contradiction to the biblical report, to have in some sense taken place—in the reckoning of God, through a token shedding of blood, or even literally, with Isaac reduced to ashes and then raised to life anew.[28]

The late medieval midrash *Yalkut Reubeni* makes explicit this connection between the Aqedah and resurrection: "If Abraham had not subjected his son Isaac to Aqedah, there would be no resurrection of the dead."[29]

Reception History and Cultural Memory

These interpretations of the Aqedah can—with little disagreement, I think—be labeled as examples of Jewish tradition, or part of the reception history of the Aqedah.[30] But how, if at all, might they relate to memory?

The Ancestral Narratives and Memory Studies

First, it is worth noting some work that has been done on the ancestral narratives of Genesis in light of memory theory. Recent decades have witnessed a dramatic change in our understanding of Israel's ancestors in the book of Genesis. While a previous generation of scholars was happy to situate these characters in the second millennium BCE, works by Thomas Thompson, John Van Seters, and others made clear that this association is much less sure footed

---

28 Levenson, *Death and Resurrection*, 198–99.

29 *Yalkut Reubeni*, Vayera; trans. Spiegel, *The Last Trial*, 111, n. 131. It is worth noting one further text in early Judaism that brings together the Aqedah and resurrection, and that is found in Hebrews 11:17–19: "By faith Abraham, when put to the test, offered up Isaac. He who had received the promises was ready to offer up his only son, of whom he had been told, 'It is through Isaac that descendants shall be named after you.' He considered the fact that God is able even to raise someone from the dead—and figuratively speaking (καὶ ἐν παραβολῇ), he did receive him back." This text is often assumed to be about Abraham's faith, and the patriarch's belief in resurrection. However, some have suggested that this might be the earliest witness we have to the Jewish idea that Isaac died and was resurrected. See, e.g., Halvor Moxnes, *Theology in Conflict: Studies in Paul's Understanding of God in Romans*, NovTSup 53 (Leiden: Brill, 1980), 187. Cf. discussion in James Swetnam, *Jesus and Isaac: A Study of the Epistle to the Hebrews in the Light of the Aqedah* (Rome: Biblical Institute Press, 1981).

30 For further insightful examples related to the reception of Genesis 22, see Edward Noort and Eibert J. C. Tigchelaar, eds., *The Sacrifice of Isaac: The Aqedah (Genesis 22) and Its Interpretations* (Leiden: Brill, 2002); Devorah Schoenfeld, *Isaac on Jewish and Christian Altars: Polemic and Exegesis in Rashi and the Glossa Ordinaria* (New York: Fordham University Press, 2012).

than was often assumed.[31] Indeed, there is no direct historical evidence at all for any of the ancestral characters, and so establishing any historical record of the biblical patriarchs is an impossible task.

However, studies in recent years have suggested that memory may offer a helpful way forward—both in terms of understanding the origins of texts and traditions, as well as their later use.[32] Ron Hendel, for example, understands these narratives as composites of "historical memory, traditional folklore, cultural self-definition, and narrative brilliance."[33] He makes clear that there is no historical evidence regarding Abraham, Isaac, or Jacob as historical figures. What can be explored, however, are traditions that grew up around these figures, and such traditions can be situated historically. Looking at examples of geographical locations and other historical markers from Israel's history, Hendel posits that aspects of "the patriarchal traditions have ancient roots. From these roots the stories grew and changed, adapted and embellished by storytellers of each age, until they came to be written down."[34]

This, for Hendel, points again to the collective and cultural aspects of such remembering: "Such stories of an epic past function as a symbolic shaper of community, joining people together around a common ethnic, cultural, and religious identity."[35]

31 Thomas L. Thompson, *The Historicity of the Patriarchal Narratives,* BZAW 133 (Berlin: de Gruyter, 1974); John Van Seters, *Abraham in History and Tradition* (New Haven: Yale University Press, 1975). This idea, of course, was not a new discovery at this time; see, e.g., Julius Wellhausen, *Prolegomena zur Geschichte Israels,* 6th ed. (Berlin: de Gruyter, 1927).

32 In relation to Abraham, see, e.g., the essays collected in Pernille Carstens and Niels Peter Lemche, eds., *The Reception and Remembrance of Abraham* (Piscataway: Gorgias, 2011). An important study which impacted historical, religious, and biblical studies was Jan Assmann, *Moses the Egyptian: The Memory of Egypt in Western Monotheism* (Cambridge: Cambridge University Press, 1997). Further uses of memory in Hebrew Bible scholarship include Joseph Blenkinsopp, "Memory, Tradition, and the Construction of the Past in Ancient Israel," *BTB* 27 (1997): 76–82; Philip R. Davies, *Memories of Ancient Israel: An Introduction to Biblical History—Ancient and Modern* (Louisville: Westminster John Knox, 2008); Daniel Pioske, "Retracing a Remembered Past: Methodological Remarks on Memory, History, and the Hebrew Bible," *BibInt* 23 (2015): 291–315; Ian Wilson, *Kingship and Memory in Ancient Judah* (Oxford: Oxford University Press, 2017). On the broader field of memory studies (including collective, social, and cultural), see Maurice Halbwachs, *On Collective Memory* [1952], trans. Lewis A. Coser (Chicago: University of Chicago Press, 1992); James J. Fentress and Chris Wickham, *Social Memory* (Oxford: Blackwell, 1992); Astrid Erll and Ansgar Nünning, eds., *A Companion to Cultural Memory Studies* (Berlin: de Gruyter, 2010).

33 Ronald Hendel, *Remembering Abraham: Culture, History, and Memory in the Hebrew Bible* (Oxford: Oxford University Press, 2005), 46.

34 Hendel, *Remembering Abraham,* 55.

35 Hendel, *Remembering Abraham,* 8.

Ehud Ben Zvi, meanwhile, traces the cultural memory of Abraham in the other direction, pointing out how the patriarch served as an important "site of memory" in the Judaism of late Persian and early Hellenistic period as reflected in the biblical texts. He notes the various ways in which Abraham was taken up in the material of what would become the Hebrew Bible, commenting that "Social memory is about the past that is constantly present within the community and about the present of the community that is legitimized by that past."[36]

In different ways, then, Hendel and Ben Zvi are both interested in how the biblical texts as passed down reflect the ways in which Abraham (and the ancestors more generally) were remembered in Genesis and beyond. However, an issue that is left underdeveloped in these studies is how exactly we might understand the relationship of memory, tradition, and reception history. In an introduction to an edited volume on memory, Diana Edelman addresses this very issue:

> The current interest in reception history in Hebrew Bible studies could raise confusion over how it differs from social memory studies, since both involve an investigation of how the collections of books of what now form, on the one hand, Jewish Tanak and, on the other, denominational versions of the Christian Old Testament, was understood in subsequent time periods. As practiced, reception history has tended to focus on a single biblical book and has examined the writings and sermons of individuals in or more time periods relating to that book, paying various degrees of attention to the individuals' historical contextualization. It has not concentrated on how groups have continued to perpetuate views they received of biblical meanings across the full range of texts while, at the same time, changing some aspects of the inherited meanings to address their current circumstances.[37]

Although reception history has developed and matured in the years since Edelman penned these reflections, there is still some truth in the larger observation that there are differing concerns and foci in reception history and memory studies. Nevertheless, I would suggest that the gap is not as large as

---

36 Ehud Ben Zvi, "The Memory of Abraham in Late Persian/Early Hellenistic Yehud/Judah," in *Remembering Biblical Figures in the Late Persian & Early Hellenistic Periods: Social Memory and Imagination*, ed. Diana V. Edelman and Ehud Ben Zvi (Oxford: Oxford University Press, 2013), 4. From the perspective of New Testament studies, see, e.g., Chris Keith, who explains, "The primary task of social memory theory is to conceptualize and explain the various manners in which cultures (and individuals as culture-members) appropriate the past in light of … the present." Chris Keith, "Memory and Authenticity: Jesus Tradition and What Really Happened," *ZNW* 102 (2011): 168.

37 Diana V. Edelman, "Introduction," in *Remembering Biblical Figures in the Late Persian & Early Hellenistic Periods: Social Memory and Imagination*, ed. Diana V. Edelman and Ehud Ben Zvi (Oxford: Oxford University Press, 2013), xxi.

Edelman suggests, and there are potentially fruitful avenues for collaboration between reception and memory studies, particularly in the area of cultural memory.

Cultural Memory

Of particular importance here is the work of Jan and Aleida Assmann, who in numerous publications have advocated for giving further attention to the *cultural* dimensions of memory.[38] In a study tracing the lineage of cultural memory, Jan Assmann notes the work of the art historian Aby Warburg, who

> coined the term "social memory" with regard to ... the cultural level; he seems to have been the first one who treated images, that is, cultural objectivations, as carriers of memory. His main project was to study the "afterlife" (*Nachleben*) of classical antiquity in Western culture and he termed this project "Mnemosyne," the ancient Greek term for memory and the mother of the nine Muses. As an art historian, Warburg specialized in what he called *Bildgedächtnis* (iconic memory), but the general approach to reception history as a form of (cultural) memory could be applied to every other domain of symbolic forms as well.[39]

Arguing that collective memory as put forward by Maurice Halbwachs does not give sufficient attention to cultural dimensions, the Assmanns suggest that the notion of collective memory is better represented as two categories, which they call communicative and cultural memory. Jan Assmann explains,

> Cultural memory is a form of collective memory, in the sense that it is shared by a number of people and that it conveys to these people a collective, that is, cultural, identity. Halbwachs, however, the inventor of the term "collective memory" was careful to keep his concept of collective memory apart from the realm of traditions, transmissions, and transferences which we propose to subsume under the term "cultural memory." We preserve Halbwachs's distinction by breaking up his concept of collective memory into "communicative" and "cultural memory," but we insist on including the cultural sphere, which he excluded, in the study of memory.[40]

---

38 Jan Assmann, "Das kulturelle Gedachtnis," *Erwagen, Wissen, Ethik* 13 (2002): 239–47; Aleida Assmann, "Memory, Individual and Collective," in *The Oxford Handbook of Contextual Political Analysis*, ed. Robert E. Goodin and Charles Tilly (Oxford: Oxford University Press, 2006), 210–24; Jan Assmann, "Communicative and Cultural Memory," in *Cultural Memory Studies: An International and Interdisciplinary Handbook*, ed. Astrid Erll and Ansgar Nünning (Berlin: de Gruyter, 2008), 109–18; Jan Assmann, *Religion and Cultural Memory: Ten Studies*, trans. Rodney Livingstone (Stanford: Stanford University Press, 2006).

39 Assmann, "Communicative and Cultural Memory," 110.

40 Assmann, "Communicative and Cultural Memory," 110.

Assmann continues:

> External objects as carriers of memory play a role already on the level of personal memory. Our memory, which we possess as beings equipped with a human mind, exists only in constant interaction not only with other human memories but also with "things," outward symbols. With respect to things such as Marcel Proust's famous madeleine, or artifacts, objects, anniversaries, feasts, icons, symbols, or landscapes, the term "memory" is not a metaphor but a metonym based on material contact between a remembering mind and a reminding object. Things do not "have" a memory of their own, but they may remind us, may trigger our memory, because they carry memories which we have invested into them, things such as dishes, feasts, rites, images, stories and other texts, landscapes, and other "lieux de memoire." On the social level, with respect to groups and societies, the role of external symbols becomes even more important, because groups which, of course, do not "have" a memory tend to "make" themselves one by means of things meant as reminders such as monuments, museums, libraries, archives, and other mnemonic institutions. This is what we call cultural memory ... This institutional character does not apply to what Halbwachs called collective memory and what we propose to rename communicative memory.[41]

Several further aspects of this focus on the cultural dimensions of memory are worth noting. First, cultural memory is not concerned with memory as transmitted among the living community; rather, it deals with the distant past. If communicative memory deals with interacting generations, cultural memory is concerned with memory across generations, down through the ages. Consequently, cultural history is not concerned with the past "as it really happened," but with the past as it has been remembered. This does not discount the role of the past in shaping the present; rather, as Jan Assmann outlines in his study on *Moses the Egyptian*, the present is "haunted by the past and the past is modelled, invented, reinvented, and reconstructed by the present."[42]

Second, because of the distance of the transmission, the modes of remembering in cultural memory are different from communicative memory. While communicative memory tends to be informal, cultural memory is institutionalized in writing and other formal modes of remembrance. "Cultural memory," Assmann notes, "is a kind of institution. It is exteriorized, objectified, and stored away in symbolic forms ... with respect to groups and societies, the role of external symbols becomes even more important, because groups which, of course, do not 'have' a memory tend to 'make' themselves one by means of things meant as reminders such as monuments, museums, libraries, archives,

41 Assmann, "Communicative and Cultural Memory," 111.

42 Assmann, *Moses the Egyptian*, 9.

and other mnemonic institutions. This is what we call cultural memory."[43] As Jan Assmann pithily summarises elsewhere, "What communication is for communicative memory, tradition is for cultural memory."[44]

A third key feature of cultural memory is the relationship between canon and archive. In another study, Jan Assmann notes that,

> Whereas the social or "collective" memory comprises knowledge commonly shared by a given society in a given epoch, cultural memory in literate societies includes not only a "canon" of normative knowledge but also an "archive" of apocryphal material that may be rediscovered and brought to the fore in later epochs. The formation of a canon of "classical" or sacred texts requires techniques of interpretation to keep accessible the meaning of the texts that may no longer be altered or multiplied.[45]

Assmann refers to this generative process as "a form of intracultural diglossia, corresponding to the distinction between one 'great tradition' and several 'little traditions.'"[46] Thus, "transitions and transformations account for the dynamics … within cultural memory, the move from the rear stage to the forefront, from the periphery into the center, from latency or potentiality to manifestation or actualization and vice versa. These shifts presuppose structural boundaries which are to be crossed: … the boundary between … 'canon' and 'archive.'"[47]

Finally, cultural memory is still ultimately concerned with how the present shapes our understanding of the past, particularly in terms of identity. Jan Assmann writes,

> Cultural memory reaches back into the past only so far as the past can be reclaimed as "ours." This is why we refer to this form of historical consciousness as "memory" and not just as knowledge about the past. Knowledge about the past acquires the properties and functions of memory if it is related to a concept of identity…. Whereas knowledge has a universalist perspective, a tendency towards generalization and standardization, … cultural memory, is local, egocentric, and specific to a group and its values… . Memory is knowledge with an identity-index."[48]

---

43 Assmann, "Communicative and Cultural Memory," 110–11.

44 Assmann, *Religion and Cultural Memory*, 8.

45 Jan Assmann, "Communicative and Cultural Memory [2]," in *Cultural Memories. The Geographical Point of View*, ed. Peter Meusburger, Michael Heffernan, and Edgar Wunder (Dordrecht: Springer, 2011), 15.

46 Assmann, "Communicative and Cultural Memory," 116.

47 Assmann, "Communicative and Cultural Memory," 117–18.

48 Assmann, "Communicative and Cultural Memory," 113–14.

As Sandra Huebenthal has pointed out, in distinguishing between communicative and cultural memory, the Assmanns have brought memory and tradition back into conversation with one another.[49]

Reflections on the Reception of the Aqedah and the Memory of Isaac's Death and Resurrection

Returning to the traditions surrounding Genesis 22 outlined above, what might be the implications of reading these interpretive traditions in light of the Assmanns' work on cultural memory? Using the disciplinary frameworks that I am accustomed to, my instinct would be to think of these traditions concerning Genesis 22 as examples of reception history. And yet, drawing on the theoretical construction offered by the Assmanns, one can clearly see how such interpretive traditions could fit into a scheme of cultural memory. They are concerned with the ancient past, embodied in cultural artefacts/written texts (both canonical and apocryphal), and are concerned with notions of identity. Let me turn briefly to reflections on Isaac's death and resurrection by Jon Levenson, David Derovan, and Shalom Spiegel that highlight these issues, particularly the interplay of canon and archive, as well as the notion that the present informs these understandings of the past.

Revelation and Resurrection

In his volume *Resurrection and the Restoration of Israel*, Jon Levenson explores the theme of Isaac's death and resurrection, and focuses on the way in which this story would become intertwined with the Sinaitic and the eschatological. To begin with, Levenson notes that there was a sense in which it was important to find resurrection in the Torah. He explains, "The high status of the Written Torah is the major reason that the rabbis expended so much

49 Sandra Huebenthal, "Social and Cultural Memory in Biblical Exegesis: The Question for an Adequate Application," in *Cultural Memory in Biblical Exegesis*, ed. Pernille Carstens, Trine Hasselbalch, and Niels Peter Lemche (Piscataway: Gorgias Press, 2012), 184–85. Huebenthal offers here a very helpful discussion of how the Assmanns' ideas concerning communicative and cultural memory have developed over time. Several of these issues are clearly modeled in Jan Assmann's *Moses the Egyptian*, where he more explicitly makes the connection between reception and memory. This is not about recovering the past as it actually happened, but investigating the past as it has been remembered. He comments that "Mnemohistory is reception theory applied to history. But 'reception' is not to be understood here merely in the narrow sense of transmitting and receiving. The past is not simply 'received' by the present… . the past is modeled, invented, reinvented, and reconstructed by the present." Assmann, *Moses the Egyptian*, 9.

effort to root the resurrection of the dead therein. To them it was inconceivable that something as central to the relationship of God to humanity as resurrection would have been unknown to Moses or unanticipated at Sinai."[50] Secondly, Levenson highlights a number of places where the rabbis bring together what Levenson calls "the Sinaitic and the eschatological, or, if you will, revelation and resurrection"—and the Aqedah is one such example.[51] Drawing on *Pirke de Rabbi Eliezer* 31, Levenson shows how this is particularly clear with the ram's two horns which are blown respectively at Sinai and the end of days with the resurrection of the dead.[52] He writes,

> Given the multiple associations of the aqedah with resurrection, it was perhaps inevitable that these two horns would be associated not only with each other but eventually with the sacrifice on Mount Moriah as well. For the aqedah had long been interpreted as the act by the grace of which the people Israel had come into being and had been rescued from death, and the expectation of resurrection in Judaism had likewise always been inseparable from the restoration of the ever-dying, ever-reviving people who are the Jews. That those three great moments—the binding of Isaac, the giving of the Torah, and the resurrection of the dead—came to be interfused is itself powerful evidence for the centrality of resurrection in the Judaism that the rabbis bequeathed later generations of Jews.[53]

The Merits of the Fathers

David Derovan discusses the tradition of Isaac's death and resurrection and highlights the importance of the Zekhut Avot (merits of the fathers), as well as the Zekhut ha-Akedah (merit of the Aqedah).[54] He writes, "To recall the Akedah is to invoke the merit of Isaac, of the Akedah—'Zekhut HaAkedah is a process whereby God allows His Midah of Chesed, of loving kindness, to overcome and limit the functioning of the Din, his Midah of judgement and discipline. Therefore, to recall the Akedah is to invoke this merit."[55] Derovan continues: "In general, say the Rabbis in numerous sources, Zekhut HaAkedah becomes the basis for the deliverance by God from any and every kind of threat or problem."[56] As we see in *Pesiqta Rab Kahanah*, "In the future, God

50 Levenson, *Resurrection and the Restoration*, 219.
51 Levenson, *Resurrection and the Restoration*, 227.
52 Levenson, *Resurrection and the Restoration*, 227.
53 Levenson, *Resurrection and the Restoration*, 229.
54 Derovan, "The Resurrection Motif," 5–6, 7–9.
55 Derovan, "The Resurrection Motif," 6.
56 Derovan, "The Resurrection Motif," 8.

will resurrect the dead because of the merit of Yitzchak, who sanctified himself on the altar."[57]

Persecution and Martyrdom

Perhaps the most well-known and intriguing exploration of the trope of Isaac's death and resurrection is found in Shalom Spiegel's *The Last Trial.* Spiegel notes a number of the issues outlined above, but focuses in particular on the issue of persecution and martyrdom.[58]

He concludes his volume with reference to the Jewish martyrs in Mainz in the twelfth century, and in particular Ephraim of Bonn's retelling of the Aqedah, which he presents in a new (and moving) translation. In this retelling, the merits of the fathers and martyrdom are both on full display, as Abraham takes Isaac's life not once but twice, and this sacrifice becomes the pattern for future martyrs. Part of this reads as follows:

> He made haste, he pinned him down with his knees, he made his two arms strong. With steady hands he slaughtered him according to the rite, Full right was the slaughter.
>
> Down upon him fell the resurrecting dew, and he revived. (The father) seized him (then) to slaughter him once more. Scripture, bear witness! Well-grounded is the fact: And the Lord called Abraham, even a second time from heaven. [...]
>
> Thus prayed the binder and the bound, That when their descendants commit a wrong This act be recalled to save them from disaster, from all their transgressions and sins.
>
> O righteous One, do us this grace! You promised our fathers mercy to Abraham. Let then their merit stand as our witness, And pardon our iniquity and our sin, and take us for Thine inheritance.
>
> Recall to our credit the many Akedahs, The saints, men and women, slain for Thy sake. Remember the righteous martyrs of Judah, Those that were bound of Jacob.[59]

---

57 Derovan, "The Resurrection Motif," 10.

58 During times of severe persecution (e.g., Rome in antiquity, or Worms in the eleventh century), Spiegel notes that Abraham's sacrifice was deemed to be not actually that bad. One Kabbalistic texts has a parent stating, "Go tell Father Abraham not to puff up his heart; if he made an Akedah of one son, I made an Akedah of seven" (*Tiferet Hayyim* 42; Spiegel, *The Last Trial*, 16). See Spiegel, *The Last Trial*, 121–38, on the medieval retrieval of the martyrdom motif.

59 The retelling of the Aqedah by Rabbi Ephraim ben Jacob of Bonn, from Spiegel, *The Last Trial*, 148–52; cf discussion in Levenson, *Death and Resurrection*, 198. For a penetrating discussion of how Spiegel's own context of writing during the second World War may have impacted Spiegel's own focus on Isaac's death and resurrection, see Arnold J. Band, "Scholarship as Lamentation: Shalom Spiegel on 'The Binding of Isaac'," *Jewish Social Studies* 5 (1998): 80–90.

As Isaac Kalimi notes, the legends of Ephraim of Bonn and others "showed that martyrdom for the oneness of God occurred already in patriarchal times and that the resurrection of the dead is from Torah, exemplified by Isaac's resurrection." In other words, "Rhineland Jews who preferred death over denying their religion considered their death as a new Aqedah. They trusted that there is hope and life after the horrible massacres. All who die for being a Jew, for being loyal to the God of Israel and his commandments, would be resurrected even from ashes."[60] Speaking of Ibn Ezra's concern over this reading, Levenson remarks, "the retort is tragically simple: which better captures the reality of the Jewish martyrs of the twelfth or any other century, the plain sense of Gen 22 beloved of Ibn Ezra, or the rewritten Aqedah of Jewish tradition?"[61]

The analyses of Levenson, Derovan, and Spiegel map quite clearly onto the framework of cultural memory noted above: these ancient and medieval retellings of the Aqedah engage with both canon and archive, in order to allow the story to be re-appropriated in new settings and contexts, in the service of the needs of the present. It is the need to find resurrection in the Torah, to connect revelation and resurrection; it is the merits of the fathers that points to God's ongoing deliverance for his people; it is the pressure of martyrdom from ancient Rome to medieval Europe that leads to this re-appropriation of Isaac as a willing self-sacrifice for whom death is not the end. In various ways, the story is brought to bear on the needs of the present.

Conclusion

From Isaac's blood and ashes, to the self-giving sacrifice and indeed resurrection of Abraham's son, the interpretive traditions surrounding the Aqedah have been intimately linked with death and resurrection. Even though it is clear in the larger biblical story that Isaac does not die in this episode, his death and resurrection on Moriah have been remembered in diverse ways in Jewish tradition—not for the sake of embellishing an already fascinating story, but to bring the story and its significant to bear in ever-changing contexts.

These trajectories are clearly part of the reception history of Genesis 22. Can we also speak about these traditions as cultural memory? The theoretical work

60 Kalimi, "'Go, I beg you'," 25.

61 Levenson, *Death and Resurrection*, 198. Levenson discusses the traditions concerning Isaac's death and resurrection elsewhere in this volume and, like Spiegel, focuses in particular on the idea of Isaac as self-giving sacrifice—that is, his status as a martyr. See Levenson, *Death and Resurrection*, 190–92.

done by the Assmanns might encourage us to reflect further on such a possibility. As we have seen, along with employing ancient traditions from the distant past, these traditions draw out numerous neglected elements in the text along with apocryphal traditions, in order to allow the story to be re-appropriated in new settings and contexts—all in the service of meaning-making and identity formation for the larger community.[62]

I wonder, then, if there is room for greater dialogue within and between the academic frameworks of those investigating tradition, reception history, and memory as we continue to explore not only how these texts and traditions originally took shape, but how and why they have been used throughout history. In the case of the Aqedah, such analysis that draws on both reception history and cultural memory might help us better understanding why the tradition remembers Isaac's death and resurrection even where, as Ibn Ezra reminds us, it contradicts the very words of Scripture.

Bibliography

Assmann, Aleida. "Memory, Individual and Collective." Pages 210–24 in *The Oxford Handbook of Contextual Political Analysis*. Edited by Robert E. Goodin and Charles Tilly. Oxford: Oxford University Press, 2006.

Assmann, Jan. *Moses the Egyptian: The Memory of Egypt in Western Monotheism*. Cambridge: Cambridge University Press, 1997.

———. "Das kulturelle Gedachtnis." *Erwagen, Wissen, Ethik* 13 (2002): 239–47.

———. *Religion and Cultural Memory: Ten Studies*. Translated by Rodney Livingstone. Stanford: Stanford University Press, 2006.

———. "Communicative and Cultural Memory." Pages 109–18 in *Cultural Memory Studies: An International and Interdisciplinary Handbook*. Edited by Astrid Erll and Ansgar Nünning. Berlin: de Gruyter, 2008.

———. "Communicative and Cultural Memory [2]." Pages 15–27 in *Cultural Memories. The Geographical Point of View*. Edited by Peter Meusburger, Michael Heffernan, and Edgar Wunder. Dordrecht: Springer, 2011.

Band, Arnold J. "Scholarship as Lamentation: Shalom Spiegel on 'The Binding of Isaac'." *Jewish Social Studies* 5 (1998): 80–90.

Blenkinsopp, Joseph. "Memory, Tradition, and the Construction of the Past in Ancient Israel." *BTB* 27 (1997): 76–82.

62 For more on these elements, see Sandra Huebenthal, "Cultural Memory," in *The Dictionary of the Bible and Ancient Media*, ed. Tom Thatcher, Chris Keith, Raymond F. Person, Jr., and Elsie R. Stern (London: Bloomsbury, 2017), 69–71.

Ben Zvi, Ehud. "The Memory of Abraham in Late Persian/Early Hellenistic Yehud/Judah." Pages 3–37 in *Remembering Biblical Figures in the Late Persian & Early Hellenistic Periods: Social Memory and Imagination*. Edited by Diana V. Edelman and Ehud Ben Zvi. Oxford: Oxford University Press, 2013.

Carstens, Pernille, and Niels Peter Lemche, eds. *The Reception and Remembrance of Abraham*. Piscataway: Gorgias, 2011.

Davies, Philip R. *Memories of Ancient Israel: An Introduction to Biblical History—Ancient and Modern*. Louisville: Westminster John Knox, 2008.

Davies, Philip R., and Bruce D. Chilton. "The Aqedah: A Revised Tradition History." *CBQ* 40 (1978): 514–46.

Derovan, David Jay. "The Resurrection Motif in the Midrash on the Akedat Yitzchak." The Lookstein Centre for Jewish Education. URL http://www.lookstein.org/articles/resurrection.pdf

Edelman, Diana V. "Introduction." Page xxi in *Remembering Biblical Figures in the Late Persian & Early Hellenistic Periods: Social Memory and Imagination*. Edited by Diana V. Edelman and Ehud Ben Zvi. Oxford: Oxford University Press, 2013.

Erll, Astrid, and Ansgar Nünning, eds. *A Companion to Cultural Memory Studies*. Berlin: de Gruyter, 2010.

Fentress, James J. and Chris Wickham, *Social Memory*. Oxford: Blackwell, 1992.

Fishbane, Michael. *Haftarot: The Traditional Hebrew Text with the New JPS Translation*. Philadelphia: Jewish Publication Society, 2002.

Ginzberg, Louis. *The Legends of the Jews, Volume 1: From the Creation to the Exodus*. Philadelphia: Jewish Publication Society, 1937.

Halbwachs, Maurice. *On Collective Memory*. Edited and translated by Lewis A. Coser. Chicago: University of Chicago Press, 1992.

Hayward, C. T. R. "The Sacrifice of Isaac and Jewish Polemic Against Christianity." *CBQ* 52 (1990): 292–306.

Hendel, Ronald. *Remembering Abraham: Culture, History, and Memory in the Hebrew Bible*. Oxford: Oxford University Press, 2005.

Huebenthal, Sandra. "Social and Cultural Memory in Biblical Exegesis: The Question for an Adequate Application." Pages 175–99 in *Cultural Memory in Biblical Exegesis*. Edited by Pernille Carstens, Trine Hasselbalch, and Niels Peter Lemche. Piscataway: Gorgias Press, 2012.

———. "Cultural Memory." Pages 69–71 in *The Dictionary of the Bible and Ancient Media*. Edited by Tom Thatcher, Chris Keith, Raymond F. Person, Jr., and Elsie R. Stern. London: Bloomsbury, 2017.

Huizenga, Leroy A. "Obedience unto Death: The Matthean Gethsemane and Arrest Sequence and the Aqedah." *CBQ* 71 (2009): 507–26.

Ibn Ezra, Abraham. *Ibn Ezra's Commentary on the Pentateuch: Genesis (Bereshit)*. Translated by H. Norman Strickman and Arthur B. Silver. New York, Menorah, 1988.

Kalimi, Isaac. "'Go, I beg you, take your beloved son and slay him!' The Binding of Isaac in Rabbinic Literature and Thought." *Review of Rabbinic Judaism* 13 (2010): 1–29.

Keith, Chris. "Memory and Authenticity: Jesus Tradition and What Really Happened." *ZNW* 102 (2011): 155–77.

Levenson, Jon D. *The Death and Resurrection of the Beloved Son: The Transformation of Child Sacrifice in Judaism and Christianity*. New Haven: Yale University Press, 1993.

———. *Resurrection and the Restoration of Israel: The Ultimate Victory of the God of Life*. New Haven: Yale University Press, 2006.

Moberly, R. W. L. *The Bible, Theology, and Faith: A Study of Abraham and Jesus*. Cambridge: Cambridge University Press, 2000.

Moxnes, Halvor. *Theology in Conflict: Studies in Paul's Understanding of God in Romans*. NovTSup 53. Leiden: Brill, 1980.

Noort, Edward, and Eibert J. C. Tigchelaar, eds. *The Sacrifice of Isaac: The Aqedah (Genesis 22) and Its Interpretations*. Leiden: Brill, 2002.

Pioske, Daniel. "Retracing a Remembered Past: Methodological Remarks on Memory, History, and the Hebrew Bible." *BibInt* 23 (2015): 291–315.

Schoenfeld, Devorah. *Isaac on Jewish and Christian Altars: Polemic and Exegesis in Rashi and the Glossa Ordinaria*. New York: Fordham University Press, 2012.

Seters, John Van. *Abraham in History and Tradition*. New Haven: Yale University Press, 1975.

Sherwood, Yvonne. "Textual Carcasses and Isaac's Scar, or What Jewish Interpretation Makes of the Violence that Almost Takes Place on Mount Moriah." Pages 22–43 in *Sanctified Aggression: Legacies of Biblical and Post-Biblical Vocabularies of Viole*nce. Edited by Yvonne Sherwood and Jonneke Bekkenkamp. London: T&T Clark, 2004.

Spiegel, Shalom. *The Last Trial: On the Legends and Lore of the Command to Abraham to Offer Isaac as a Sacrifice: The Akedah*. Translated by Judah Goldin. Woodstock: Jewish Lights, 1967.

Swetnam, James. *Jesus and Isaac: A Study of the Epistle to the Hebrews in the Light of the Aqedah*. Rome: Biblical Institute Press, 1981.

Thompson, Thomas L. *The Historicity of the Patriarchal Narratives*, BZAW 133 (Berlin: de Gruyter, 1974).

Wellhausen, Julius. *Prolegomena zur Geschichte Israels*, 6th ed. Berlin: de Gruyter, 1927.

Wilson, Ian. *Kingship and Memory in Ancient Judah*. Oxford: Oxford University Press, 2017.

II.

Afterlife in Early Christianity

Mnemonic Cross-pollination: Water Symbolism and the Fluidity of Resurrection Memory

Anthony Le Donne

The first Christians carried forward the idea of resurrection in a number of ways. It was a symbol codified within a creed (Rom. 1:4). It was embedded in narratives that shaped particular sayings of Jesus (Mark 8:31). The idea of resurrection is carried by eschatological catechism (*Didache* 16:6) and apocalyptic vision (Rev 20:5–6). Not only was resurrection a highly potent symbol in the early stages of Christianity, it was also highly flexible. This illustrates a key element of social memory theory: the more significant a memory is for collective identity, the more subject to interpretation it will become. This paper explores the ways that resurrection became saturated with water symbolism in Christian commemorative activity and thereby contributed to its multivalent impact. Touchstones will include discussions of ritual, symbol, and myth. I will introduce a concept that I call "mnemonic cross-pollination" and illustrate its applicability to several New Testament texts about resurrection.

Ritual as Memory Event

Memory events (both autobiographical and collective) are never pure. This is to say that new perceptions are always colored by preconceptions. Expectations color memory events from the start. So, every memory event is both an interpretive act and an act of reinterpreting prior mnemonic patterns. Such is the case with rituals. Indeed, we could say that a ritual is a classic example of a memory event that builds from a previously established mnemonic pattern.

A memory event, in its most simple terms, is an experiential act or an act of perception. A memory event could be a few moments (e.g., the experience of falling from a pine tree) or it could last hours (e.g. the experience of first watching *The Royal Tenenbaums*). Over time, it is possible for several memory events to collapse together without specific reference to a single event (e.g. the vague experience of participating in several Christmas tree lightings). Whatever the case, a memory event is in some way contained as a unit of mental content.[1]

1 "Memory event" is my own terminology. It should not be confused with studies of "event memory" which seeks to distinguish episodic memory from other kinds of memory. See

 | DOI:10.30965/9783657796212_007

Note that I am not distinguishing between perceptions and memories as if the former comes first and the latter happens at some later time. While it may sometimes be necessary to distinguish between the initial act of perception and subsequent recollections, it is important to remember that even the initial experiential act occupies a (or multiple) mnemonic frame(s). Even if experiencing something for the first time, the human participant is projecting thought categories upon their sensory data in an attempt to interpret it. Doing so requires prior mnemonic frameworks.

This is especially true of ritual whereby the ceremony presupposes memory of cultural symbols and collective identity. For example, witnessing a baptism may provide a different sort of memory event to differing parties. One person may have witnessed hundreds of like ceremonies; another may have only seen the ritual performed in *The Godfather*. In either case, in order to understand such an event—*in order for it to be a memory event*—the perception must incorporate social memory. Categories of language, symbol, ideology, etc., are at work within the mnemonic framework. All of these are examples of *social* memory.

Memory events can sometimes present as private events without social frames. The example of falling from a tree may seem to require no language, symbol, or collective expression of any kind. In such cases, it may be worth distinguishing the initial experience from later narrativizations.[2] But when analyzing ritual, the social memory frames within the memory event are most pronounced.

At the risk of stating the obvious, baptismal rites are experienced variously depending on the cultural environment. Modern participants informed only by *The Godfather* will experience the memory event of baptism differently than participants in first-century Judea. While the primary experience of water (what it is, what it does, how humans relate to it) may be shared across cultural boundaries, the symbolic value of water will differ. Moreover, the meaning that the ceremony communicates will differ depending on social memory frameworks.

David C. Rubin and Sharda Umanath, "Event Memory: A Theory of Memory for Laboratory, Autobiographical, and Fictional Events," *Psychological Review* 122 (2015): 1–23. Although both this study and the present essay are interested in memory that presents as a unit of mental content. My work builds from sociology and historiography. See Anthony Le Donne, *The Historiographical Jesus: Memory, Typology, and the Son of David* (Waco: Baylor University Press, 2009).

2 Putting the experience into words would exemplify several key elements of social memory. See James Fentress and Chris Wickham, *Social Memory: New Perspectives on the Past* (Oxford: Blackwell, 1992), 72–74.

As is well known, first-century Jews experienced baptism most commonly as repeated ablution for ritual purification. This ritual was not, however, unique to Jewish experience. In the wider Mediterranean context, we observe a range of purification rites involving water.[3] Most often, these rituals were for the purpose of ongoing purification rather than a single act of initiation. We can safely say that baptism was especially important for Jews of the Second Temple period. Textual and material evidence suggests that symbolic bathing was common. This ritual was a part of Jewish life in Galilee, the Golan, Samaria, and Judea with special emphasis on Jerusalem. Examples of textual evidence include the *Letter of Aristeas*, 1QS, and several other Qumran texts that discuss the parameters and regulations of baptism.[4] At least two ascetic figures known by Josephus feature ritual bathing in regular practice. Josephus claims that he was once a disciple of a hermit named Bannus, a man who frequently baptized himself in "cold water, by day and night, for purity's sake" (*Vita* 11).[5] Josephus recalls John the Baptist in similar terms. Accordingly, John's baptism was "a consecration of the body" for the soul that had been purified already through "right behavior" (*Ant.* 18.117).[6] Material evidence includes the remains of several *mikva'ot* at Qumran and those in closer orbit of the Jerusalem Temple.[7] This brief survey demonstrates that ritual bathing functioned as a ritual within cultural memory in first-century Jewish life. As such, Jesus' baptism by John (whatever sort of memory event it was) would have stood in some relationship to these rituals.

Turning now to first-century Christian baptism, it is a ritual that can be thought of as autobiographical, collective, or (more likely) a combination of both. If, for example, Jesus' baptism by John was a memory event pushed forward by a particular storyteller who first perceived it as punctiliar act, it must also be an act of *social memory* because the memory event required prior

---

3 Andres Klostergaard Petersen, "Rituals of Purification, Rituals of Initiation: Phenomenological, Taxonomical and Culturally Evolutionary Reflections," in *Ablution, Initiation, and Baptism: Late Antiquity, Early Judaism, and Early Christianity*, ed. David Hellholm, Tor Vegge, Oyvind Norderval, and Christer Hellholm (Berlin: de Gruyter, 2011), 3–40.

4 Petersen, "Rituals," 43–154. For a treatment of John the Baptist's ablution juxtaposed with 4Q414 and 4Q512, see Eyal Regev, "Washing, Repentance, and Atonement in Early Christian Baptism and Qumranic Purification Liturgies," *Journal of the Jesus Movement in His Jewish Setting* 3 (2016): 33–60.

5 LCL 186.7. Cf. Petersen, "Rituals of Purification," 10.

6 Both John and Bannus are described as men who forage food in the wilderness and dress in rustic fashion.

7 Johnathan D. Lawrence (*Washing in Water: Trajectories of Ritual Bathing in the Hebrew Bible and Second Temple Literature* [Atlanta: SBL, 2006]) provides two helpful appendices. Appendix B: Textual References (221–250) and Appendix C: *Miqva'ot* (251–268).

mnemonic frames (e.g. purity, ordering chaos, group membership) in order to understand it. Conversely, if Jesus' baptism was invented in a collective storytelling experience to illustrate doctrine, it still requires autobiographical experiences to make sense of the story. Jesus' baptism is an example of a memory event that exists at the intersection of communicative memory (an autobiographical subset) and cultural memory (a collective subset).[8]

Rituals are symbolic enactments that carry meaning. But they do not communicate in a simple, unidirectional fashion. A ritual like baptism will draw from the distant past, underlying mythologies, broader social constructs, and personal experiences to create a memory event.

Baptism as Mnemonic Cross-pollination

The Christian ritual of baptism certainly evinces the DNA of Jewish semiotics. But its symbolic value was perhaps more flexible, able to draw from a wider world of meaning. Not only was the ritual repurposed as a ceremony of initiation, Christians exploited the symbolic value of water in creative exegesis. 1 Peter suggests that at times mnemonic cross-pollination was warranted to explain the significance of the rite.

> For Christ also suffered for sins once for all, the righteous for the unrighteous, in order to bring you to God. He was put to death in the flesh, but made alive in the spirit, in which also he went and made a proclamation to the spirits in prison, who in former times did not obey, when God waited patiently in the days of Noah, during the building of the ark, in which a few, that is, eight people, were saved through water. And baptism, which this prefigured, now saves you—not as a removal of dirt from the body, but as an appeal to God for a good conscience, through the resurrection of Jesus Christ, who has gone into heaven and is at the right hand of God, with angels, authorities, and powers made subject to him. (1 Pet 3:18–22)

Here we see a conflation of references to the Myth of the Watchers, baptism, resurrection, and Jesus' cosmic authority. The claim that the myth somehow prefigured the salvific waters of baptism suggests a type-antitype relationship. Yet this claim is made without diminishing its symbolic enactment of the death and resurrection of Jesus. As a category of memory, the ritual seems to have attracted a wide range of myths, doctrines, and symbols. I have called this mnemonic cross-pollination.

---

8 Aleida Assmann, *Zeit und Tradition: Kulturelle Strategien der Dauer*, Beiträge zur Geschichtskultur 15 (Köln: Böhlau, 1999), 64.

In anthropology, this is called "condensation." In his classic work, *Symbols: Public and Private*, Raymond Firth explains:

> Symbols as stores of meaning help to cope with problems of communication over time, aiding recall and obviating to some extent a need for reformulation of ideas. As such they are a cultural asset. Condensation, the encapsulation of many forms, or many meanings, is
> one symbol by processes of contraction, suppression, transformation, can also facilitate communication by giving a common reference point for a variety of originally disparate ideas. If a symbol is to be an effective instrument of communication, it is essential that it should convey much the same thing to people involved—or that the range of variation in their interpretations should not inhibit the action desired.[9]

Firth did not, I think, intend to explain any particular concept within social memory theory. He does, however, capture something crucial about the way that symbols carry and distort communicative content over time, (as he puts it) "aiding in recall." Memory theorists sometimes call this sort of carrier a "mnemotechnique" (a vehicle for memory).[10] But mnemonic vehicles are not necessarily ritualized or utilize symbols. So Firth strikes closer to the heart of the topic of baptism, which is both ritualized and traffics in symbols. Conversely, condensation means to explain symbolic values; whereas mnemonic cross-pollination would include symbols, it is a feature of memory that is not limited to symbols. When it comes to a ritualized memory event, we might say that a commemorative act has cross-pollinated as personal experience (thereby becoming mutually interpretive).

Returning to Aleida Assmann's language, there are different kinds of memory. Cultural memory (e.g., identity-forming myth) functions differently and serves a different purpose than communicative memory (e.g. shared personal experience). But memory is a fluid process and the more significant a personal experience is, the more it will draw from archetypes, mythologies, etc. So we must talk about the intersection of cultural and communicative memory. And with specific focus on baptism, we must talk about the communicative value of symbols as Firth does.

When memory events are cross-pollinated they become mutually interpretive and mutually distortative. The above example of 1 Peter illustrates the

---

9 Raymond Firth, *Symbols: Public and Private* (1973; repr., New York: Routledge, 2011), 175. Firth borrows from Victor Turner, *The Forest of Symbols: Aspects of Ndembu Ritual* (Ithaca: Cornell, 1967), esp. 28–29.

10 For examples of how ancient Greeks and Romans used mnemotechniques, see Fentress and Wickham, *Social Memory*, 12.

relationship. Therein, a well-known myth in Israel's scripture is reframed as a prefiguration of baptism. One could claim that this interpretation of Noah and the Myth of the Watchers stretches credulity. At the very least, this reading of the Myth of the Watchers might have seemed bizarre to those outside the Jesus-venerating *ekklesia*. In mnemonic cross-pollination, we expect two or more memory events to become mutually informative. But we should not be surprised to find that their capacity to distort prior meanings is asymmetrical. One of these will usually have the greater force of gravity.[11]

Before moving on, an example of a modern ritual is relevant. The 2000–2015 iteration of the "prayer over the water" in the Church of England shows just as much flexibility in scriptural reference as 1 Peter. This baptismal prayer reads:

> Loving Father,
> we thank you for your servant Moses,
> who led your people through the waters of the Red Sea
> to freedom in the Promised Land.
> We thank you for your Son Jesus,
> who has passed through the deep waters of death
> and opened for all the way of salvation.
> Now send your Spirit,
> that those who are washed in this water
> may die with Christ and rise with him,
> to find true freedom as your children,
> alive in Christ for ever.

This prayer is attached to the ancient ritual of baptism, but with a new combination of mnemonic cross-pollination. Douglas Davies explains:

> In the rite itself many more motifs are brought to bear in the special "prayer over the water." This is a classic example of what Turner describes as the process of "condensation," in which many meanings come to be associated with a single phenomenon. Here a wide variety of biblical references to water focus on the water in the font around which priests, family and congregation are gathered. Accordingly, the multivocal water is spoken of as a gift that sustains, refreshes and cleanses. It reflects that water existing at the beginning of creation, when the Holy Spirit, echoing the Book of Genesis, moved over it. This is an interesting item, devoid of any explicit signification, but available for exegesis as the beginning of divine activity in the formation of order out of chaos. It also has the virtue of a reference to the "beginning" of things.[12]

11 It should also be noted here that distortative acts will often propel the memory event forward, rendering it intelligible in the next mnemonic framework or social environment.

12 Douglas J. Davies, *Anthropology and Theology* (Oxford: Berg, 2002), 175.

Somewhat reminiscent of Gezera Shawa in ancient Jewish exegesis, the scriptural references useful in baptismal rites are sometimes set in parallel simply because water was a key element of the passage. "In baptism water is the dominant symbol: it bears a multiplicity of meanings and controls the meaning available through the other symbols used."[13] Something very similar could be said of 1 Peter's mnemonic cross-pollination.

Water Symbolism and Resurrection

Water is a potent symbol in several mythologies and in many times and places. Water features prominently in several ancient myths. Water can evoke the amniotic fluid that accompanies birth, a life-giving river like the Nile, or passage to the afterlife over the River Styx. Several myths link water to magical creatures like dragons. In the Tang, Qing, and Han dynasties, dragons functioned as rain deities that governed the weather. During droughts, farmers performed rites to coax sleeping dragons to fly into the clouds, thus restoring balance. In northern China, regular prayers to dragons were spoken before the rainy season.[14] In ancient Egypt, there was also an association between divine creatures and water, although the symbols involved conceptions of chaos and order. Apep was a giant serpent of chaos (*isfet*) that brought and attacked the divine order (*ma'at*) mediated through the pharaoh. Ancient Israel seems to have drawn from Egypt's chaos monsters (cf. Job 40:15–24). Indeed, much of Israelite mythology assumes that the sea is a place of profound chaos.

While the water ritual of baptism in first-century Judea cannot borrow from all of the above, it may be valuable to note that something as fundamental as water may bring an undercurrent of cultural meaning beneath the intended communicative value of the ritual. This is not surprising as water is a fundamental element of the human experience.

So too is death. By extension, the use of death as a metaphor is common. While the point of departure is difficult to locate, these two metaphors were linked in certain circles of nascent Christianity. Take for example, Paul's logic concerning baptism:

---

13 Davies, *Anthropology*, 178.

14 See John Thorbjarnarson and Xiaoming Wang, *The Chinese Alligator: Ecology, Behavior, Conservation, and Culture* (Baltimore: Johns Hopkins University Press, 2010).

> Do you not know that all of us who have been baptized into Christ Jesus were baptized into his death? Therefore, we have been buried with him by baptism into death, so that, just as Christ was raised from the dead by the glory of the Father, so we too might walk in newness of life. For if we have been united with him in a death like his, we will certainly be united with him in a resurrection like his. (Rom. 6:3–5)

In context, Paul argues that the Christian initiation ritual ends the initiate's life in slavery under sin. In a way, then, being baptized is a death to an old way of life (or outmoded epoch). The initiate enacts the ritual to participate in the death and rising of Jesus.

Paul's association between the water ritual and the burial and resurrection of Jesus is awkward on the face of it. Simply put, "Baptism is hardly like Jesus' death."[15] To evoke the image of burial and resurrection, no water symbolism is required and introducing the ritual of baptism may well confuse the image. Moreover, Jesus was not drowned to death, nor did his resurrection involve water. At this point in Romans (unlike 1 Cor. 1:23 and Phil. 2:8) the reader of this letter has been given no indication about how Jesus was executed. In what follows the reader does, however, hear a reference to crucifixion: "We know that our old self was crucified with him …" (Rom. 6:6). So in some sense, the reader is meant to imagine immersion as a type of burial that recalls also Jesus' death on the cross.

In Romans 6, we hear several metaphors. The readers are to imagine (1) being baptized—not into water—but into Christ Jesus; (2) being buried (united) with Christ; (3) being baptized into death (and/or new life); (4) walking; (5) crucifying oneself (the old self) with Christ; (6) slavery and freedom. It's a barrage of imagery that fails to explain how baptism relates to crucifixion. But, without any doubt, Paul assumes some kind of symbolic relationship. At the risk of conjecture, we might ask if this association impacted the frequency of baptism in Christian practice: *if Jesus' death and resurrection only occurred once*—as a singular event—*shouldn't baptism only occur once in the life of the believer?*

The association between Jesus' resurrection and the believer's ascent from baptismal water is seemingly more natural. In the ancient Mediterranean, being under water was perilous. As pulmonary resuscitation did not yet exist, almost every known case of drowning was fatal.[16] So ascending to the surface would evoke notions of near death or new life.

---

15 James D. G. Dunn, *Romans 1–8*, WBC 38A (Waco: Thomas Nelson, 1988), 317. Dunn surveys a number of various interpretations springing from Paul's awkward grammar.

16 Stathis Avramidis, "Drowning in Ancient Greek History and Mythology," *International Journal of Aquatic Research and Education* 3.4 (2009): 422–31; Most incidences of survival are found in mythology rather than in historical memory.

What the reader witnesses from Paul is the haphazard unfolding of a complex symbol. If what Turner and Firth say is correct—that symbols sometimes condense a wide range of previously unrelated meanings—trying to unpack such a symbol in such a short space will be messy. It is then understandable that Paul's logic bleeds out several mixed metaphors.

In terms of memory, we might say that mnemonic cross-pollination is mutually distortative to memory events. Therefore, trying to untangle such a mnemonic framework is difficult. Notice that Paul is not simply condensing symbols; he is cross-pollinating symbols, rituals, and communicative memories (assuming that the readers have experienced the ritual themselves). In an attempt to make sense of this mess, Richard Longenecker writes:

> Jesus is recorded in Mark 10:38–39 and Luke 12:50 as referring to his approaching death as his "baptism," thereby bringing into association ideas of "baptism" and "death"—and, by extension, the correspondence of "resurrection" and "new life." Paul evidently picked up on this imagery in urging the Christians at Rome to view their Christian baptism as representing their union with Jesus in both his death and his resurrection …[17]

The pericope in question indeed shows that some Christians considered baptism a legitimate metaphor for Jesus' death:

> James and John, the sons of Zebedee, came forward to him and said to him, "Teacher, we want you to do for us whatever we ask of you." And he said to them, "What is it you want me to do for you?" And they said to him, "Grant us to sit, one at your right hand and one at your left, in your glory." But Jesus said to them, "You do not know what you are asking. Are you able to drink the cup that I drink, or be baptized with the baptism that I am baptized with?" They replied, "We are able." Then Jesus said to them, "The cup that I drink you will drink; and with the baptism with which I am baptized, you will be baptized; but to sit at my right hand or at my left is not mine to grant, but it is for those for whom it has been prepared."

But is Longenecker justified in thinking that Paul has some knowledge of this saying? It is possible. It is also possible that both Jesus and Paul draw from the same cultural memory. This is to say, perhaps the metaphoric relationship between death and baptism was known in first-century Jewish culture. If indeed the symbol of baptism was able to condense multiple and varied ideas into a single expression,[18] the peril of aquatic abyss may well recall death. And the "water" that accompanies birth may well occupy the same symbol. But these suggestions must remain speculative.

---

17 Richard N. Longenecker, *The Epistle to the Romans*, NIGTC (Grand Rapids: Eerdmans, 2016), 613.

18 Cf. Turner, *Forest of Symbols*, 28–29.

What we can say with confidence is that the symbolic values of baptism and (temporary) death have been cross-pollinated in Christian commemoration.[19]

The Sign of Jonah

Moving beyond the discussion of any specific symbol, it may be helpful to recall that water submersion can be a key stage of the hero's journey. For example, in the Gilgamesh epic, the hero quests for characters who might give him the secret of eternal life. After a sojourn under and then through a mountain, the hero boards a ferryman's boat to cross the waters of death. Gilgamesh hears that Uta-napishti (his forefather) once obtained eternal life after building a large ship to survive a world-wide flood. Gilgamesh then learns of the "heartbeat plant" which is also called the "old-man-grows-young" plant. He dives deep and takes the plant to obtain eternal life. On his journey home, Gilgamesh stops to wash in a pool. While bathing, a serpent steals his boon, and by inference, eternal life.

While this myth betrays no simple one-to-one correlation with any biblical myth, several key elements suggest mythological symbols in the Mediterranean at large. Readers of the Bible will recognize loose parallels to secret knowledge, eternal life, sages, waters of death, a world-wide flood, and a serpent.[20]

While the Hebrew imagination did not borrow the ferry over Stygian Lake or the River Styx, several texts from the Hebrew Bible remind us that the sea is a place of great peril. Indeed, the sea almost functions as an archetype in this cultural memory. The sea itself is as much of a chaos monster as any great beasts that roam the deeps.

The biblical myth of Jonah illustrates the point. The story features many non-human characters that do God's bidding. These include a wind, a fish, a plant, a worm, and cattle. In Jonah's hymn of repentance, he describes his plight:

> The waters closed in over me; the deep surrounded me;
> weeds were wrapped around my head at the roots of the mountains.
> I went down to the land whose bars closed upon me forever;
> yet you brought up my life from the Pit, O Lord my God. (Jonah 2:5–6)

---

19 We might hear another echo of this in 1 John 5:6 which claims that Jesus is "the one who came by water and blood." The referent of the "testimony of blood" is debatable, but the standard interpretation by commentators is that "water" is a reference to Jesus' baptism. See e.g., Raymond E. Brown, *The Epistles of John*, AB 30 (New York: Doubleday, 1982), 67.

20 This is perhaps not the place to detail every parallel evinced in the epic.

This symbolic description of the watery depths suggests finality, almost as if the sea is a kind of underworld. In this story, Jonah literally comes back from "the belly of sheol" (2:2). Judging from this story, we might say that the sea is more than deadly; *it is death*.

If we widen the scope to Greek influence, we see how the story of Jonah might relate to other stories of near drowning. In his exhaustive survey of drowning in classical Greek literature, Stathis Avramidis writes that,

> Drowning in mythology was attributed less often to a human accidental submersion ... and more often was perceived as an act of God or act of demigod (e.g., in the Great Flood that was caused by Jupiter and Neptune all the inhabitants on Earth drowned except Deucalion and Pyrrha; Hekatonkheires, three gargantuan figures from the archaic stage of Greek mythology drowned many inhabitants on Earth during the War of the Titans, etc.).[21]

Avramidis also explains that the few episodes wherein the drowning man is saved in Greek mythology, it is a god or demigod who is the savior.[22] Audiences familiar with myths like Jonah would thus expect an act of divine intervention. When reading Jonah, one could conclude that the act of throwing the main character into the water was caused by the sailors, Israel's God, or perhaps Jonah himself was personally responsible. But the fact that God sends the storm (1:4) and the fish (1:17) clearly indicates "acts of God." Moreover, Jonah survives these acts of God after three days by another act of divine intervention. Against this backdrop, consider Jesus' saying about the so-called "sign of Jonah."

Matthew interpolates a saying concerning Jonah in the Jesus tradition, construing it to be about Jesus' death and resurrection. The passage reads:

> Then some of the scribes and Pharisees said to him, "Teacher, we want to see a sign from you." But he answered and said to them, "An evil and adulterous generation craves for a sign; and yet no sign will be given to it but the sign of Jonah the prophet; for just as Jonah was three days and three nights in the belly of the sea monster, so will the son of man be three days and three nights in the heart of the earth. The men of Nineveh will stand up with this generation at the judgment, and will condemn it because they repented at the preaching of Jonah; and behold, something greater than Jonah is here. (Matt. 12:38–41)

21 Avramidis, "Drowning in Ancient Greek History and Mythology," 426.

22 He notes that there are only two episodes from historical memory wherein the drowning person is saved from death. One involves another man reaching in and pulling the victim out. The other episode involves being saved by a dolphin ("Drowning," 426–27).

By contrast, Luke includes no reference to "three days" or the "sea monster" or the "heart of the earth." Luke's interpretation of Jonah's significance is simply, "For just as Jonah became a sign to the Ninevites, so will the Son of Man be to this generation" (Luke 11:30).

Seemingly, Luke (and/or Q[23]) saw the association between Jesus and Jonah in terms of gentile repentance.[24] Both Jesus and Jonah are preachers. Both feature sermons about repentance. And both are associated in some way with a gentile audience (a key theme in Luke). Matthew, like other Jewish interpreters, seems to have been attracted to Jonah's perilous—and ultimately miraculous—encounter with the sea monster.[25] If we couple this point with the comparative mythology above, we can safely posit that Matthew's exegetical creativity is almost predictable. After all, stories about heroes who are saved from death often involve acts of God.

To underscore the point, the story of Jonah is memorable because it involves something miraculous: *God is a key actor in the narrative*. Whether the audience was listening to Jesus, or a performance of Q, Luke, or Matthew, the language of "sign" signals some revelation from heaven. And anyone familiar with stories like Jonah would be interested in what the deity does in the story. In drawing from this episode of cultural memory, the mnemonic framework is already positioned to exploit the story in the way that Matthew does.

The author of Matthew might have read this story as one that prefigures Jesus' death and resurrection in the same way that 1 Pet 3:18–22 uses the Myth of the Watchers to prefigure Christian baptism. In the case of Matthew's interpolation, there is no overt association with baptism.

In sum, we might say that Luke was most interested in gentile repentance whereas Matthew was more interested in resurrection.[26] Matthew used the

---

23 Adolf von Harnack, *The Sayings of Jesus* (London: Williams and Norgate, 1908), 23–4; Ever since Harnack's reconstruction of Q, Luke's version been considered closer to Q than Matthew's. Harnack argued that Matthew's interpretation of the sign was secondary. Moreover, the original interpretation lay not in the "three days" parallel, but in the "preaching of repentance" that is common to both Jonah and Jesus.

24 See Anthony Le Donne, "Greater than Solomon: Orality, Mnemonics, and Scriptural Narrativization in Luke," in *Biblical Interpretation in Early Christian Gospels. Volume 3: The Gospel of Luke*, ed. Thomas R. Hatina; LNTS 376; SSEJC 16 (London: T & T Clark, 2010), 96–112.

25 Cf. 3 Macc 6:8; *b. Ta'an.* 2.4; *b. Sanh.* 89ab.

26 R. A. Edwards took a both/and solution. He argued that the Q tradition encapsulated two meanings: (1) both Jonah and Jesus are considered preachers of repentance preceding a divine judgment; (2) both Jonah and Jesus overcame death. According to Edwards, the overcoming of death proves the worth of the preacher.
See his *The Sign of Jonah in the Theology of the Evangelists and Q*, SBT 18 (Naperville: Allenson, 1971), 86.

opportunity to foreshadow Jesus' death and resurrection. Matthew's interpretation, of course, is only intelligible within the mnemonic framework of post-Easter doctrine. Matthew's narrative has the ability to reach forward to Jesus' ultimate outcome and backward to the cultural memory of Jonah. This suggests that the "sign" is understood via mnemonic fluidity.

Conclusion

Human memory pushes memory events together. In my brief survey, we have seen this feature at work within cultural memory including myth, symbol, and ritual. Sometimes these commemorative categories are informally appended to communicative memories (e.g., 1 Peter and Romans). Because we are dealing in a world of symbolic value, we might borrow a term from cultural anthropology: condensation. Somewhere along the way in nascent Christianity, the symbolic values of resurrection and water immersion were *condensed*. This would explain why baptism seems to have attracted multiple and varied myths and images.

It is also important to note that pushing together memory events acts to interpret, distort, and propel forward both mnemonic frames. In other words, we must underscore the *mutuality* involved in such a marriage. I have called this mnemonic cross-pollination. This element of memory framing is broader than the study of symbols and therefore cross-pollination is wider in scope than the anthropological category of condensation (different though not mutually exclusive). Mnemonic cross-pollination has the capacity to frame communicative memories and cultural memories together.

Bibliography

Assmann, Aleida. *Zeit und Tradition: Kulturelle Strategien der Dauer*. Beiträge zur Geschichtskultur 15. Köln: Böhlau, 1999.

Avramidis, Stathis. "Drowning in Ancient Greek History and Mythology." *International Journal of Aquatic Research and Education* 3.4 (2009): 422–31.

Brown, Raymond E. *The Epistles of John*. The Anchor Yale Bible Commentaries. New York: Double Day, 1982.

Davies, Douglas J. *Anthropology and Theology*. Oxford: Berg, 2002.

Dunn, James D. G. *Romans 1–8*. WBC 38A. Waco: Thomas Nelson, 1988.

Edwards, Richard A. *The Sign of Jonah in the Theology of the Evangelists and Q*. SBT 18. Naperville: Allenson, 1971.

Fentress, James and Chris Wickham. *Social Memory*. Oxford: Blackwell, 1992.

Firth, Raymond. *Symbols: Public and Private*. New York: Routledge, 2011.

Harnack, Adolf von. *The Sayings of Jesus*. London: Williams and Norgate, 1908.

Klostergaard Petersen, Andres. "Rituals of Purification, Rituals of Initiation: Phenomenological, Taxonomical and Culturally Evolutionary Reflections." Pages 3–40 in *Ablution, Initiation, and Baptism: Late Antiquity, Early Judaism, and Early Christianity*. Edited by David Hellholm, Tor Vegge, Oyvind Norderval, and Christer Hellholm. Berlin: de Gruyter, 2011.

Lawrence, Johnathan D. *Washing in Water: Trajectories of Ritual Bathing in the Hebrew Bible and Second Temple Literature*. Atlanta: Society of Biblical Literature, 2006.

Le Donne, Anthony. *The Historiographical Jesus: Memory, Typology, and the Son of David*. Waco: Baylor University Press, 2009.

———. "Greater than Solomon: Orality, Mnemonics, and Scriptural Narrativization in Luke." Pages 96–112 in *Biblical Interpretation in Early Christian Gospels. Volume 3: The Gospel of Luke*. LNTS 376. SSEJC 16. Edited by Thomas R. Hatina. London: T & T Clark, 2010.

Longenecker, Richard N. *The Epistle to the Romans*. NIGTC. Grand Rapids: Eerdmans, 2016.

Regev, Eyal. "Washing, Repentance, and Atonement in Early Christian Baptism and Qumranic Purification Liturgies." *Journal of the Jesus Movement in His Jewish Setting* 3 (2016): 33–60.

Rubin, David C., and Sharda Umanath. "Event Memory: A Theory of Memory for Laboratory, Autobiographical, and Fictional Events." *Psychological Review* 122 (2015): 1–23.

Thorbjarnarson, John and Xiaoming Wang. *The Chinese Alligator: Ecology, Behavior, Conservation, and Culture*. Baltimore: Johns Hopkins University Press, 2010.

Turner, Victor. *The Forest of Symbols: Aspects of Ndembu Ritual*. Ithaca: Cornell University Press, 1967.

From Romans to Colossians: Making Sense of Competing Conceptions of Resurrection

Kyle R. L. Parsons

Pauline scholars have long observed theological differences between Colossians and Paul's undisputed letters. For example, Colossians contains a higher Christology, a more developed ecclesiology, and a more realized eschatology. These unparalleled differences have led many scholars, though certainly not all, to view Colossians as a pseudepigraphal writing.[1]

Presuming that Colossians is pseudepigraphal, the goal of this study[2] is to understand how it contributed to (1) the formation of the (actual) audience's collective identity, and (2) the emergent historical reputation of Paul.[3] Using social memory theory as a hermeneutic, I argue that Colossians was a counter-memory, produced by a reputational entrepreneur (the actual author) who reconstructed an image of Paul in order to legitimize a new Pauline conception of resurrection that would satisfy the (actual) audience's present identity needs. The paper is divided into two parts. The first part explains the memory approach that I am using. The second part focusses on the letter as a counter-memory, with particular attention given to Colossians 2.

Memory and Identity

In the last few years, social memory theory has been appropriated by a handful of Pauline scholars. For example, Benjamin White's innovative study demonstrates

1 I use the adjective "pseudepigraphal" since it is used more broadly than "pseudonymous" in relation to Colossians. On authorship, see the discussion by Nijay Gupta, "What Is in a Name? The Hermeneutics of Authorship Analysis Concerning Colossians," *CurBR* 11 (2013): 196–217. For example, those who argue that Colossians is pseudepigraphal include F. C. Baur, Eduard Lohse, Joachim Gnilka, Eduard Schweizer, Petr Pokorný, James D. G. Dunn, Andrew T. Lincoln, Robert M. Wilson, and Margaret Y. MacDonald. Those who argue that Colossians is an authentic Pauline letter include Werner Kümmel, Peter T. O'Brien, George E. Cannon, F. F. Bruce, Marcus Barth and Helmut Blanke.

2 This study was supported by the Protestant Theological Faculty of Charles University, project GA UK no. 1576219. All translations are my own unless otherwise noted.

3 Historical reputation refers to a specific area of memory research. "Historical" here does not mean the historicity of the reputation of a figure or event, but the socially mediated perception of that reputation.

 | DOI:10.30965/9783657796212_008

the explanatory power that social memory has in describing the competing images of Paul primarily in second-century memories *of* him.[4] Rafael Rodríguez applies social memory to memories *for* Paul, specifically in how circumcision was remembered and altered by Paul himself in light of his encounter with Christ. Where Rodríguez emphasizes the "obduracy of the past," I will emphasize its malleability.[5]

Most applications of social memory begin with Maurice Halbwachs' observation that memory is a social phenomenon.[6] Collectively shared memories "define a group, giving it a sense of its past and defining its aspirations for the future."[7] These memories are embedded in an individual's consciousness through acts of commemoration, creating what Eviatar Zerubavel calls an "existential fusion" of one's identity with the shared collective identity of the group to which one belongs.[8] Therefore, collective memories shape and sustain collective identities.

In the act of remembering, the past is not passively *retrieved* but actively *reconstructed* according to the needs of the present.[9] Memory is not static.

---

4 Benjamin L. White, *Remembering Paul: Ancient and Modern Contests over the Image of the Apostle* (Oxford: Oxford University Press, 2014).

5 Rafael Rodríguez, "Paul and Social Memory," in *Paul in the Greco-Roman World: A Handbook, Volume 2*, ed. J. Paul Sampley, 2nd ed. (London: Bloomsbury T&T Clark, 2016), 348–52. As Rodríguez puts it, "Despite the popularity of images of Paul as a radical innovator vis-á-vis his native Judaism and its view of Gentiles, Paul shows evidence of the 'obduracy of the past' in his indebtedness to established symbolic frameworks that foster traditional meanings even in the face of new experiences" (361).

6 Maurice Halbwachs, *On Collective Memory, The Heritage of Sociology*, trans. Lewis A. Coser, The Heritage of Society (Chicago: University of Chicago Press, 1992). Halbwachs' original works were published as *Les cadres sociaux de la mémoire* (Paris: Alcan, 1925), *La topographie légendaire des Évangiles en Terre Sainte: étude de mémoire collective* (1941), and *La mémoire collective* (Paris: Presses Universitaire 1950). The introduction by Lewis Coser provides a helpful entry for understanding Halbwachs' ideas and how they relate to his teachers on "collective representations" and "pure time"—respectively Émile Durkheim and Henri Bergson.

7 James Fentress and Chris Wickham, *Social Memory*, New Perspectives on the Past (Cambridge: Blackwell, 1992), 25.

8 Eviatar Zerubavel, "Social Memories: Steps to a Sociology of the Past," *Qualitative Sociology* 19.3 (1996): 290. He further observes that, "The extent to which our social environment affects the way we remember the past becomes even clearer when we realize that much of what we 'remember' is actually filtered (and therefore inevitably distorted) through a process of interpretation that usually takes place within particular social surroundings" (285).

9 Halbwachs, *On Collective Memory*, 40. argues that memories "reconstruct an image of the past which is in accord, in each epoch, with the predominant thoughts of the society." Thus, individuals remember collectively, influenced by the concerns and interests generated by the various communities in which they simultaneously exist (e.g. family, gender, nationhood, vocation, political camp, economic class).

Instead, memory is a dynamic process, ever-changing "because it is wired into the ever-shifting present."[10] Therefore, collective memories (1) define the collective identity of a group, and (2) are reconstructed *through* and *for* present needs.

The Past in Identity Formation

In addition to the influence of Halbwachs, most scholars today who appropriate social memory theory to the study of historical Jesus and early Christianity have leaned on the work of Barry Schwartz.[11] Although it could be argued that Schwartz's (perhaps overly) *traditionalist* approach to memory has its shortcomings, when it is taken in moderation, it offers a necessary corrective to what Jeffrey Olick terms a "purely presentist" approach.[12] Such extreme approaches fail "to explain where present interests come from in the first place," or exactly what "the past does for us?"[13] Olick asserts that a group's sense of the past, their history and tradition—their collective memory—"all function to establish identities and give them moral purposes."[14] The past provides vital resources

---

10 Alan Kirk, "Social and Cultural Memory," in *Memory, Tradition, and Text: Uses of the Past in Early Christianity*, ed. Alan Kirk and Tom Thatcher, Semeia Studies 52 (Atlanta: SBL Press, 2005), 10. Or as Jan Assmann puts it, "Das Gedächtnis verfährt also rekonstruktiv. Die Vergangenheit vermag sich in ihm nict als solche zu bewahren. Sie wird fortwährend von den sich wandelnden Bezugsrahmen der fortschreitenden Gegenwart her reorganisiert." See Jan Assmann, *Das Kulturelle Gedächtnis: Schrift, Erinnerung Und Politische Identität in Frühen Hochkulturen* (Munich: Beck, 1992), 41–42.

11 E.g., Barry Schwartz, "Where There's Smoke, There's Fire: Memory and History," in *Memory and Identity in Ancient Judaism and Early Christianity: A Conversation with Barry Schwartz*, ed. Tom Thatcher, SemeiaSt 78 (Atlanta: SBL Press, 2014), 7–37.

12 Many within New Testament studies follow Schwartz as the champion of the "continuity perspective" (synonymous with "essentialist" and "traditionalist"). Followers of this perspective place it in opposition to the "presentist perspective" (or "constructivist"). Both positions tend to perceive the other as extreme, neither of which reflect the field accurately. Nevertheless, it cannot be overstated that social memory theory is as much *presentist* as it is *social*. Schwartz does not deny the presentist qualities of memory, but he narrowly engages the mnemonic process with the present as the destination, not the starting point. Often, what gets smuggled in with Schwartz's theory is his epistemological optimism, which is peripheral to his robust memory theory. See Jeffrey K. Olick, "From Usable Pasts to the Return of the Repressed," *The Hedgehog Review* 9.2 (2007): 19–31.

13 Olick, "From Usable Pasts to the Return of the Repressed," 20. See also: Idem., "Products, Processes, and Practices: A Non-Reificatory Approach to Collective Memory," *BTB* 36 (2006): 5–14; Jeffrey K. Olick and Joyce Robbins, "Social Memory Studies: From 'Collective Memory' to the Historical Sociology of Mnemonic Practices," *Annual Review of Sociology* 24.1 (1998): 105–40.

14 Olick, "From Usable Pasts to the Return of the Repressed," 20. Olick also claims that the past is "not just a tool in the arsenal of power but the very wellspring of identity."

for defining collective identity in the present, as well as influencing its norms, behaviours, and actions. Therefore, identity formation compels different groups to compete for control of the past, especially any culturally salient event, location, ritual, holiday, or figure.[15]

But what precisely is the *past* that is remembered? Is it the actual past or a mediated one? I understand the (mnemonic) past to be collectively *shared*, collectively *perceived*, and therefore always mediated through the present. It may not be the actual past, but it functions as the real past for the remembering group.[16] Therefore, "[t]he past exists *virtually* in contrast to the present which always exists actually."[17] George Herbert Mead explains it this way: "The actual passage of reality is in the passage of one present into another, where alone is reality, and a present which has merged in another is not a past. Its reality is always that of a present. The past as it appears is in terms of representations of various sorts, typically in memory images, which are themselves present."[18] Therefore, the past never exists apart from the remembering present.[19] The collectively shared past is always mediated through the present.

Since members of a community perceive the past, and remembering this past provides those members with their identity, Jan Assmann perceptively

15 See Thomas R. Hatina, "The Social Memory Theory and Competing Identity Constructions: The Function of Genesis 15:6 in Romans and James," in *500 Jahre der Reformation in der Slowakei*, ed. M. Nicák and M. Tamcke (Münster: Lit Verlag, 2019), 38–9. Eviatar Zerubavel ("Social Memories," 295) notes that, "The most common mnemonic battles are the ones fought over the 'correct' way to interpret the past." Benjamin White (*Remembering Paul*, 74) quips that "Traditions confront traditions."

16 Thomas R. Hatina cautions that, "While the present can be affected by the actual past, it can also be affected by a stable image or tradition that did not originate in the actual past, but was simply accepted over time as true." See his "The Provenance of Jesus' Quotations of Scripture from a Social Memory Perspective," in *The Earliest Perceptions of Jesus in Context: Essays in Honour of John Nolland on His 70th Birthday*, ed. Aaron W. White, Craig A. Evans, and David Wenham, LNTS 566 (London: Bloomsbury T&T Clark, 2018), 67.

17 See the article in this volume by Thomas R. Hatina, "When the Saints Go Marching In: Remembering Vengeance and Vindication in Matthew 27:52–53."

18 George Herbert Mead, "The Nature of the Past," in *Essays in Honor of John Dewey*, ed. John Coss (New York: Henry Holt & Co., 1929), 235.

19 Note the helpful reliance on Gilles Deleuze in Thomas R. Hatina, "Scripture, Memory, and Time: Matthew's Fulfilment Quotations as Historiographical Devices" in *The Gospel of Matthew in its Historical and Theological Context*, ed. Mikhail Seleznev, William R. G. Loader, and Karl-Wilhelm Niebuhr, WUNT 459 (Tübingen: Mohr Siebeck, 2021), 75–97. Gilles Deleuze (*Bergsonism*, trans. Hugh Tomlinson and Barbara Habberjam [New York: Zone Books, 1988], 59) argues: "The past and the present do not denote two successive moments, but two elements which coexist: one is the present, which does not cease to pass, and the other is the past, which does not cease to be but through which all presents pass."

concludes that all communities are imagined.[20] He writes, "It is not 'blood' or 'descent' as such that keeps a group together but the shared *consciousness* of it, the idea of common descent … Identity, on all its levels, from the individual person to large groups such as nations and religious communities, is a product of imagination and of mental representation."[21]

Viewing the Colossian community as imagined carries two implications for the mnemonic past. First, a community's very existence relies on its actively perceived and shared past. This collective past operates as a tradition.[22] Second, since a group's collective identity is a product of mental representations, traditions are malleable. Ironically, this malleability renders traditions, and the resulting identities, both fragile and obdurate. Traditions are repeated, reaffirmed, and—perhaps unknowingly—altered by the group *ad libitum*.[23] Traditions that are consistently updated remain relevant and are more likely to remain culturally active. In this way, they become obdurate. However, if a group does not actively and continuously remember a tradition, it may be left behind in an amnesic void.[24] In this sense, traditions are fragile.[25]

---

20 Benedict Anderson provides the concept of "imagined communities" but applies it to nations as opposed to smaller groups like families or tribes. See Benedict Anderson, *Imagined Communities: Reflections on the Origin and Spread of Nationalism* (London: Verso, 1983).

21 Jan Assmann, "Form as a Mnemonic Device: Cultural Texts and Cultural Memory," in *Performing the Gospel. Orality, Memory, and Mark. Essays Dedicated to Werner Kelber*, ed. Richard A. Horsley, Jonathan A. Draper, and John Miles Foley (Minneapolis: Fortress Press, 2006), 67.

22 I use the term "tradition" to refer to a specialized "collective memory" that is actively remembered, as opposed to forgotten, and is thus influential for the group's present identity formation and resulting normative behaviours. As such, a tradition is a shared, perceived, salient, and binding past. This working definition relies on Jan Assmann's development of Halbwachs' idea of *collective memory* by distinguishing *cultural memory* and *communicative memory*. Note also Aleida Assmann's distinction between actively remembered pasts and actively forgotten ones.

23 Change in one's traditions is more visible and easily seen by outsiders. Edward Shils explains that "tradition might undergo very great changes but its recipients might regard it as significantly unchanged." See Edward Shils, *Tradition* (Chicago: University of Chicago Press, 1981), 14.

24 Consider Aleida Assmann's concepts of cultural memory as either *canon* or *archive*. As canon, the tradition is actively informing collective identity in the present; as archive, it is somewhere between inactive and forgotten. See Aleida Assmann, "Canon and Archive," in *Cultural Memory Studies: An International and Interdisciplinary Handbook*, ed. Astrid Erll and Ansgar Nünning (Berlin: Walter de Gruyter, 2008), 97–108.

25 Note the segment of memory studies called "memory distortion," which investigates how memories change via their transmission into communicable forms and symbols. See Michael Schudson, "Dynamics of Distortion in Collective Memory," in *Memory Distortion: How Minds, Brains, and Societies Reconstruct the Past*, ed. Daniel L. Schachter

Reputational Entrepreneurs

Traditions, like reputations, do not make themselves. They are constructed by people motivated by societal forces. These people are called *reputational entrepreneurs*.[26] Their role is both to construct historically perceived reputations of specific figures or events and to make those reputations collective knowledge in order to traditionalize them. Benjamin White describes their social influence. He writes,

> Reputational entrepreneurs ... are members of communities and experience the force of tradition. In a canon as variegated as was the earliest layer of the Pauline tradition, however, entrepreneurs can easily shift pieces of the tradition forward and backward, bringing into conscious view particular elements, eliminating others from public memory, and introducing new bits that must cohere with those that already have currency.[27]

Therefore, historical reputations are mnemonic resources, created and implemented by entrepreneurs in the strategic construction of the collective past.[28]

Counter-memory and Pseudepigraphy

A counter-memory is a deliberate recasting of memories in order to refute, revise, or replace a previously accepted memory of the past.[29] In short, it is the act of inventing a tradition. Defining counter-memory as inventing a tradition

---

(Cambridge: Harvard University Press, 1995), 348. Schudson provides four categories of distortion, which become increasingly reliant on human creativity, as opposed to natural forces. (1) Distanciation: over time the details and intensity of memories fade. (2) Conventionalization: memories conform to present socio-typical expectations. (3) Instrumentalization: the past is reinterpreted based on the needs of the present to achieve relevance. (4) Narrativization: the past is not reported but represented through the constraints of storytelling.

26 This term is coined by Gary Alan Fine, *Difficult Reputations: Collective Memories of the Evil, Inept, and Controversial* (Chicago: University of Chicago Press, 2002).

27 White, *Remembering Paul*, 168.

28 Fine, *Difficult Reputations*, 17. The processes used by reputation entrepreneurs offer explanations for how traditions are transmitted, altered, shaped, forgotten, or even invented. These processes are not natural, mechanical, involuntary, or evolutionary. They are intentional, deliberate, and importantly, they require agency.

29 Ronald S. Hendel, *Remembering Abraham: Culture, Memory, and History in the Hebrew Bible* (Oxford: Oxford University Press, 2005), 41. The term originates from Michel Foucault (*Language, Counter-Memory, Practice: Selected Essays and Interviews*, ed. Donald F. Bouchard (Ithaca: Cornell University Press, 1980), 160.), where he describes his own writing as a counter-memory against traditional historiography.

may appear extreme to some.[30] However, all traditions are, in a fundamental sense, *invented* rather than *discovered*. Traditions do not establish or remember themselves. Moreover, natural forces do not place specific traditions alongside previous ones. Traditions are deliberate attempts to shape a community's view of the past.

The reputational entrepreneur does not necessarily invent the past event or figure. Instead, the entrepreneur (or tradition-maker) invents a *pastness* (or antiquity) so the event or figure can be perceived as rediscovered. A countermemory is implemented by creating a continuity with a suitable past. What better way to do this than through the act of pseudepigraphy? Pseudepigraphy is an effective strategy, when successful, in producing a pastness through which a community can orientate itself and its future. Pseudepigraphy is "oppositional and reform literature," where "[w]hat is new legitimates itself as the old that has been forgotten."[31]

Traditions undergo alterations "more frequently" when the social patterns are weakened or destroyed by a "rapid transformation of society."[32] This claim is related to Jan Assmann's concept of *Traditionsbruch*, which posits that traditions fracture consistently after each generational passing, especially after the death of the first generation with its living memory of the event.[33] Therefore, a rapid transformation of society can be any change to present circumstances (or life as is), which, in turn, pressures a group's attachment to its current traditions. This pressure opens the door for new traditions to compete in satisfying the group's present identity needs. Again, I repeat: traditions and identities are fragile and obdurate.

However, there are some limits or constraints on what can be successfully invented. An "invented tradition can be successful only as long as it passes as

30 Eric J. Hobsbawm, "Introduction: Inventing Traditions," in *The Invention of Tradition*, ed. Eric J. Hobsbawm and Terence Ranger (Cambridge: Cambridge University Press, 1983), 1–14. Scholars who prefer to detect the authentic past in transmissions of traditions tend to see Hobsbawm's work as advocating egregious presentism. Regardless, Hobsbawm's thesis is more nuanced than such caricatures suggest. At issue is how one interprets and understands the term *invention*, which Hobsbawm uses to refers to the creative efforts individuals exercise in reconstructing the past on behalf of their community. See also Jan Assmann, *Cultural Memory and Early Civilization: Writing, Remembrance, and Political Imagination* (Cambridge: Cambridge University Press, 2011), 33.

31 Jan Assmann, *Religion and Cultural Memory: Ten Studies* (Stanford: Stanford University Press, 2006), 99–100.

32 Hobsbawm, "Introduction: Inventing Traditions," 4.

33 Assmann, *Das Kulturelle Gedächtnis*, 100–01, 216–17, 294–95.

tradition."[34] In other words, a counter-memory can only become an established collective memory if the community accepts it. Therefore, the more a new tradition aligns with present needs, social conventions and expectations, then the more likely it is to find a legitimizing audience.

In summary, traditions, reputations, and collective memories all share similar functions. They are actively shared representations of the past. They are generated *for* and *by* the needs of the present. And they compete with other representations of the past to contribute to present identity constructions.

The Colossian Counter-memory of Resurrection

Turning to the construction of the Colossian counter-memory on the resurrection, I first discuss the rhetorical strategies used by the reputational entrepreneur to legitimize Colossians as a genuine Pauline letter. Second, I examine the social role that concepts of resurrection played in early Christian identity constructions. Third, I compare the Pauline conception of resurrection in Romans 6 with Colossians 2.[35] Fourth, I propose possible social factors that motivated this particular counter-memory. And Fifth, I evaluate what the pseudepigraphal letter achieved for the actual audience and the reputation of Paul.

---

34 Yael Zerubavel, *Recovered Roots: Collective Memory and the Making of Israeli National Tradition* (Chicago: University of Chicago Press, 1995), 232. Roy Baumeister and Stephen Hastings similarly claim: "by and large outright fabrication of collective memory is rare. The implication may be that collective memories are to some extent constrained by the facts. Facts may be deleted, altered, shaded, reinterpreted, exaggerated, and placed in favorable contexts, but wholesale fabrications seem to lie beyond what most groups can accomplish." See their "Distortions of Collective Memory: How Groups Flatter and Deceive Themselves," in *Collective Memory of Political Events: Social Psychological Perspectives*, ed. James W. Pennebaker, Darío Páez, and Bernard Rimé (Mahwah: Erlbaum, 1997), 282. Although wholesale invention might be rare, it is still possible and cannot be dismissed as impossible.

35 Romans 6 serves as a general representation of the eschatology of the undisputed Pauline corpus. I realize that this has its shortcomings. A reader's perception of the Roman Paul is distinguishable from the perception of the Philippian Paul, which can be distinguished from the Corinthian Paul, etc. Each perception of Paul (and even his own self-perception) exists in a different temporal (present) context that influences Paul's identity and sense of the past. A similar idea is presented from the perspective of "death of the author" theory (influenced by the works of Barthes, Foucault, and Derrida) by Gregory P. Fewster, "'Can I Have Your Autograph?' On Thinking about Pauline Authorship and Pseudepigraphy," *Bulletin for the Study of Religion* 43.3 (2014): 30–39. What follows is a future-oriented Pauline conception of resurrection as compared to a realized one.

The Rhetorical Strategy of Creating a Reality Effect

A pseudepigraphal letter cannot merely be mirror-read to reconstruct the author, audience, or the occasion behind it. As David Lincicum contends, there are interpretive implications. One must take seriously the fact that "a pseudepigrapher poses as the apostle Paul" to write a letter to the Colossians, who are "fictional addressees masking an unknown actual group of recipients" about a fictional situation (such as the Colossian opponents spewing erroneous teachings).[36] Simply put, a pseudepigrapher aims to create a "reality effect."[37] The letter's enclosed fictional world achieves this reality effect, outside of which exists an actual author attempting to reach an actual audience through that fictitious world.[38] The communication model in *Figure 7.1* illustrates this process.

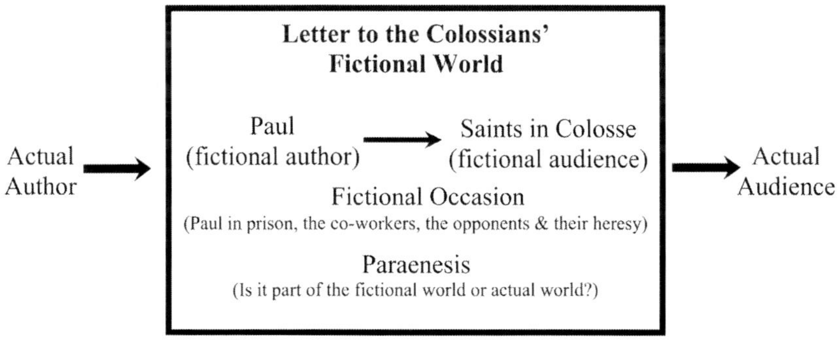

Figure 7.1 Adapted from Sandra Huebenthal, "Pseudepigraphie als Strategie in frühchristlichen Identitätsdiskursen? Überlegungen am Beispiel des Kolosserbriefs," *SNTU.A* 5.36 (2011): 68[39]

36 David Lincicum, "Mirror-Reading a Pseudepigraphal Letter," *NovT* 59.2 (2017): 172.

37 Lincicum, "Mirror-Reading a Pseudepigraphal Letter," 172.

38 Sandra Huebenthal, "Pseudepigraphie Als Strategie in Frühchristlichen Identitätsdiskursen? Überlegungen Am Beispiel Des Kolosserbriefs," *SNTU.A* 5.36 (2011): 67. Huebenthal reflects, "dass kein Text die Realität einfach abbildet, sondern die Textwelt immer eine Realität erschafft." This is even more the case with pseudepigraphy.

39 This figure is adapted from Huebenthal's structure, which is based on Ansgar Nünning's communication model. See Huebenthal, "Pseudepigraphie Als Strategie in Frühchristlichen Identitätsdiskursen?" 68 and Ansgar Nünning, *Grundzüge eines kommunikationstheoretischen Modells der erzählerischen Vermittlung: Die Funktion der Erzählinstanz in den Romanen George Eliots*, Horizonte, Studien zu Texten und Ideen der europäischen Moderne 2 (Trier, 1989), 22–124.

In this communication model, the fictional (or narrative[40]) world elements, such as the author, audience, and occasion for writing, functioned as rhetorical strategies of legitimization.[41] Thus, statements about Paul and his co-workers (Col 4:7–17) were "legitimizing fictions," which utilized Paul's reputation and provided "verisimilitude to the letter."[42] This perspective is contrary to those who interpret Pauline pseudepigraphy as benignly updating Pauline teaching in order to honour him.[43] This "updating" view is especially problematic since the author of Colossians exerted quite an effort to convince the readers of the letter's authorial authenticity.[44] As a result, the evidence does not allow the letter to have been both pseudonymous and non-deceptive.

The rhetorical strategies of the author of Colossians are noteworthy. Statements about Paul and his co-workers reveal a strategy of *imitation*. The closing of the letter offers a further example of this strategy, where, whether by

40 The notion of a fictional world draws on the insights of narratological approaches, such as the one utilized in Norman Petersen's *Rediscovering Paul: Philemon and the Sociology of Paul's Narrative World* (Eugene: Wipf & Stock, 2008).

41 Eckart Reinmuth, "Exkurs: Zur Neutestamentlichen Paulus-Pseudepigraphie," in *Die Briefe an die Philipper, Thessalonicher und an Philemon*, ed. Nikolaus Walter, Eckart Reinmuth, and Peter Lampe, NTD 8/2 (Göttingen: Vandenhoeck & Ruprecht, 1998), 200. Reinmuth states, "Der Text, der sich durch seine Pseudonymität scheinbar zu einem Element vergangener Geschichte macht, tut dies, um die aktuelle Botschaft dieser Geschichte, ihre Bedeutung zu umreißen und so zu einem Element der Identität der Adressaten zu werden."

42 Lincicum, "Mirror-Reading a Pseudepigraphal Letter," 181. Lincicum also draws on Petersen's work.

43 While many Pauline scholars recognize the pseudepigraphal nature of Colossians, they ignore the negative impact this has on determining the historical Paul or interpreting Pauline thought. For example, the literary and theological differences are explained as resulting from (1) the freedom of an amanuensis, and/or (2) an eager contemporary student or follower of Paul. In both cases the author is believed to be gently updating Pauline thought on his behalf in a non-deceptive manner. Representatives of this non-deceptive view include David G. Meade, *Pseudonymity and Canon: An Investigation into the Relationship of Authorship and Authority in Jewish and Early Christian Tradition*, WUNT 39 (Tübingen: Mohr Siebeck, 1986); James D.G. Dunn, *The Epistle to the Colossians and to Philemon*, NIGTC (Grand Rapids: Eerdmans, 1996). For a contrasting view that argues against Dunn, see Lincicum's discussion, "Mirror-Reading a Pseudepigraphal Letter," 179–81. See also the discussion on the divergent approaches that scholars use for analysis of canonical and non-canonical writings in Bart Ehrman, *Forgery and Counterforgery: The Use of Literary Deceit in Early Christian Polemics* (Oxford: Oxford University Press, 2014), 128–32.

44 Paul does not merely open the letter with his name (Col 1:1) and then add his signature at the end (Col 4:18). He also reminds the reader that he is the author in 1:23–25, 29; 2:1, 5; 4:3–4, 7–8, and v. 18. See Lincicum, "Mirror-Reading a Pseudepigraphal Letter," 181.

literary or oral dependence,[45] the author imitated 1 Cor 16:21–24, Gal 6:11–18, and Philemon 19.[46]

Another rhetorical strategy is used in the letter's description of opponents who are portrayed as propagating false teachings. Scholarly attempts to identify these opponents and their heresies differ from one another and, though they continue offering new proposals, there is no consensus in sight.[47] This difficulty in identifying the Colossian opponents hints at the rhetorical function the opponents and their heresies have. The lack of specificity indicates a rhetorical strategy of *ambiguity*.[48] The opponents and their heresies functioned as "empty signifiers," perhaps freeing the actual audience to consider the signified as their opponents.[49] This strategy coincides with a third rhetorical strategy, which Angela Standhartinger calls the Colossian emphasis on "the universal."[50] Through imitation, the letter achieves verisimilitude. Through ambiguity and universals, the letter can be relevant to the actual audience, even if they did not think it was primarily addressed to them.

What this means for understanding the author, audience, and occasion is that they were not descriptions of actual people and events, but rhetorical means to a legitimizing end. But, to what end? If all these elements of the letter were fictionalized, how does the letter address the needs of the actual audience?

---

45 See, for example, the literary dependence of Colossians on the authentic letters in Outi Leppä, *The Making of Colossians: A Study on the Formation and Purpose of a Deutero-Pauline Letter*, Publications of the Finnish Exegetical Society 86 (Helsinki: The Finnish Exegetical Society, 2003).

46 See Col 4:18, which states, "I Paul write this greeting in my own hand."

47 Lincicum ("Mirror-Reading a Pseudepigraphal Letter," 175) notes forty-two different scholarly reconstructions of the Colossian opponents and their teachings since 1970. Many more have been proposed since then. Scholarly reconstructions of the Colossian opponents include, but are not limited to: Gnostic groups, Jewish mystics, Essenes, Pythagoreans, Middle Platonists, Cynic philosophers, and even Christian apocalypticists.

48 See Morna D. Hooker, "Were There False Teachers in Colossae?" in *Christ and Spirit in the New Testament: Essays in Honour of C.F.D. Moule*, ed. Barnabas Lindars and Stephen S. Smalley (Cambridge: Cambridge University Press, 1973), 315–31. While Hooker believes that Paul wrote Colossians, she argues that its "false teaching" was not a specific problem the community faced, but rather a more general address to combat potential pressures from both Jewish and pagan neighbours.

49 See Angela Standhartinger, "Colossians and the Pauline School," *NTS* 50.4 (2004): 585; Lincicum, "Mirror-Reading a Pseudepigraphal Letter," 191–92.

50 Standhartinger, "Colossians and the Pauline School," 585. Standhartinger notes how in Col 1:6 the phrase "as in the whole world" supersedes the salutation "to those in Colossae." In 1:28, the author claims that Paul's work is for "all people," even those who "have not seen" Paul "in the flesh." The instruction at the end of the letter (4:16) to share it with the other churches indicates its universal aim.

The intended message is primarily expressed in the letter's paraenetic content. Since a large portion of the instructional material parallels other (undisputed) Pauline letters, it is likely that this imitation strategy was intended to reaffirm Paul's past instructions as being morally relevant and to give the impression that the new material is from Paul as well. But it is the new paraenetic material, presented in a convincing and legitimizing way, that is most likely the locus of the intended message.[51]

The resurrection teaching in Col 2:12–13 holds the most divergent content of the letter. Not only is this material unique among the undisputed letters, but its importance is also further conveyed by its position at the letter's epicentre.[52] It urged the (actual) audience to accept this particular view of resurrection so they could successfully resist the false teachings and persist in virtuous living (which is explicated in the moral prohibitions in 3:5–11, the moral exhortations in 3:12–17, and finally in the *Haustafel* in 3:18–4:1). So why was one's view of resurrection so crucial?

Resurrection in Early Christianity and Paul

Outi Lehtipuu convincingly demonstrates that conceptions of resurrection formed collective identities.[53] In collective memory terms, resurrection beliefs were "bonding" memories.[54] One's understanding of resurrection encapsulated an entire worldview and drew boundaries demarcating those who belonged from those who did not.[55] How one viewed resurrection directly affected other core beliefs, "such as the power of God, the meaning of Christ, the way of salvation,

51 Eduard Lohse explains the divergent and unparalleled content. He states, "Pauline theology has undergone a profound change in Col, which is evident in every section of the letter and has produced new formulations in Christology, ecclesiology, the concept of the apostle, eschatology, and the understanding of baptism." See Eduard Lohse, *Colossians and Philemon*, trans. W.R. Poehlmann and R.J. Karris, Hermeneia (Philadelphia: Fortress Press, 1971), 180–81.

52 Petr Pokorný, *Colossians: A Commentary* (Peabody: Hendrickson, 1991), 126. He states that Col 2:12–13 "contain the argument of the entire epistle."

53 Outi Lehtipuu, *Debates over the Resurrection of the Dead: Constructing Early Christian Identity* (Oxford: Oxford University Press, 2015).

54 Assmann, *Religion and Cultural Memory*, 5–11, 81–100. He underscores the "bonding" potency of collective memory in powerfully creating a sense of belonging. Assmann builds on the work of Halbwachs, along with Nietzsche and Abby Warburg. Nietzsche saw memory's bonding nature as oppressive due to the obligations (and thus restrictions to one's freedoms) it forces upon individuals. Warburg saw it as emancipatory. For Halbwachs, memory ends when tradition begins.

55 Claudia Setzer, "Resurrection of the Dead as Symbol and Strategy," *AAR* 69.1 (2001): 65; and Lehtipuu, *Debates over the Resurrection*, 13.

anthropological ideas, ritual practices, and lifestyle issues."[56] Therefore, to implement a new conception of resurrection was tantamount to forming a new community.

Though some argue that resurrection beliefs unified Christian or Jewish communities against outsiders, the opposite was, in fact, the case.[57] Resurrection beliefs were divisive within early Judaism, early Christianity, and even within the Pauline tradition.[58]

Jesus' resurrection was central to Paul's identity formation,[59] becoming the primary bonding memory for the people of God, where "the God of the Exodus" shifted to "the God of the resurrection."[60] In Paul's post-Easter context, everything changed (see Gal 1:11–12). This new present experience pressured his Jewish past resulting in both continuities and discontinuities. Paul's conception of resurrection was an ongoing process, and it did not yield a static belief system. As A. J. M. Wedderburn concludes: "Paul left behind a somewhat ambiguous legacy regarding resurrection."[61] Paul is especially unclear about

---

56 See Lehtipuu, *Debates over the Resurrection*, 15; and Setzer, "Resurrection of the Dead as Symbol and Strategy," 87.

57 See Claudia Setzer, *Resurrection of the Body in Early Judaism and Early Christianity: Doctrine, Community, and Self-Definition* (Boston: Brill Academic Publishers, 2004). Lehtipuu (*Debates over the Resurrection*, 15) concludes, "I find it hard to agree with the conclusion that belief in resurrection was useful as a unifying symbol for the small Christian communities that absorbed new members at a rapid rate."

58 See C.D. Elledge, *Resurrection of the Dead in Early Judaism: 200 BCE–CE 200* (Oxford: Oxford University Press, 2017), 43. He concludes, "The diversity of conceptions, across the span of historical development in the Hellenistic and Roman eras and in a variety of different literary genres, thus resists standardization in many points of detail."

59 E.g., Rom 4:24; 8:11; 10:9; 2 Cor 4:14; 5:12–19; Gal 1:1.

60 George W.E. Nickelsburg, *Resurrection, Immortality, and Eternal Life in Intertestamental Judaism and Early Christianity: Expanded Edition*, HTS 56 (Cambridge: Harvard University Press, 2006), 229. "The God who brought up Israel from the land of Egypt" shifted to "the God who raised Jesus from the dead." Mnemonically, this is a matter of the present (God who raised Christ from the dead) being *keyed* to the past frame (God who brought them up out of Egypt), producing a new frame by which individuals will access meaning. On keying, see Barry Schwartz, *Abraham Lincoln and the Forge of National Memory* (Chicago: University of Chicago Press, 2000), 18. Schwartz argues that keying is an intentional act of connecting a present event or figure to a past one. This act of keying then activates culturally accessible and shared frames within which members locate and find meaning for their present experiences.

61 See A. J. M. Wedderburn, *Beyond Resurrection* (London: SCM Press, 1999), 119. This ambiguity concerning resurrection surfaces in questions about the nature of the resurrected body. Will it be transformed back into an earthly (flesh) body, or into a heavenly (spiritual) body? See 1 Cor 15:50. This question was prominent following Paul's death, which can imply that he left the issue in an ambiguous state that allowed for a vast range of interpretive options.

the state of the believer between death and the Parousia. However, Paul is clear about *when* the resurrection would take place. He always places it in the future (with a couple of minor caveats).[62] It was the issue of temporality that divided the author of Colossians from Paul as represented particularly in Romans 6.

From Romans to Colossians

The author of Colossians found much of Paul's conception of resurrection relevant and therefore worth retaining. For the sake of brevity, five examples suffice. First, both understand the concept of resurrection to have implications for moral behaviour.[63] Second, both understand the resurrection of Christ to be indicative of God's power and justice. Third, both believe that only those baptized ἐν Χριστῷ ("in Christ") will experience the resurrection. Fourth, both link the initiation ritual of baptism to Christ's burial and resurrection. And fifth, both focus on the transformation of the believer from a lowly or earthly state to a spiritual or heavenly state. Paul temporally links this transformation with the resurrection of the dead in the immediate future; whereas the author of Colossians does not. In Colossians, the resurrected state is reached before one's death, once one is identified as being in Christ through baptism, but the glory of that state will be ultimately revealed when Christ returns (Col 3:4). While both had an "already but not yet" view of eschatology, they differed about the timing of the resurrection within their eschatological timelines.

Before comparing Romans 6 and Colossians 2, it is necessary to address whether the author of Colossians was familiar with Romans 6. Scholars are divided over whether the author of Colossians read Romans or whether he was simply familiar with it and the Pauline tradition on a more oral level. For example, Angela Standhartinger cautiously concludes that the author of Colossians knew only Philemon as a literary document and the ideas contained in Paul's other writings were known orally.[64] Conversely, Outi Leppä argues that the

62 Lehtipuu, (*Debates over the Resurrection*, 159) summarizes the variety of expectations early Christians would have had regarding the question of when: "in an indefinable future when Christ would return to gather his own, or immediately after the death of each individual, or even before death, as a spiritual experience in this life?" The third option is found in Colossians. Paul believed mostly in the first option (but with a solid dose of immediacy). However, in Phil 1:23, Paul appears to lean toward the second option, although he may be allowing himself a martyr's death.

63 Col 1:11, 21–24; 2:6, 20; 3:1–4:6.

64 Standhartinger, "Colossians and the Pauline School," 581. She states that "Colossians is the product of a circle familiar with the oral teaching of Paul" (582). On the literary dependence on both Philippians and Philemon, see Mark Christopher Kiley, *Colossians as Pseudepigraphy*, The Biblical Seminar 4 (Sheffield: JSTOT, 1986).

author of Colossians was aware of all the undisputed Pauline letters.[65] In relation to Romans 6 specifically, Leppä maintains that there is sufficient evidence that the author of Colossians read it.[66] Although certainty is not attainable here, at minimum there is evidence that the author of Colossians knew Paul's teaching in Romans 6 enough to imitate it and alter it.

Now for the comparison of Romans 6:4–8 and Colossians 2:12–13. The former reads,

> Therefore, we have been buried with him (συνθάπτω) through baptism (βάπτισμα) into death, so that, just as Christ was raised (ἐγείρω) from the dead (νεκρός) by the glory of the Father, so we too might walk (subjunctive of περιπατέω) in a new life. For if we have been united with him in a death like his, certainly we will be (future of εἰμί) in a resurrection like his … and if we have died (aorist) with Christ, we believe (present) also that we will live with (future of συζάω) him.

Paul's discussion of the resurrection of believers features verbs in the future tense, which is not uncommon (e.g. 1 Cor 15:52; 1 Thess 4:13–18; Phil 3:10–12). In Rom 6:8, Paul reasons that since believers "have died with Christ," then they "will also live with him." Sequentially, Christ's death was in the past, and the resurrection of believers is in the future.

In Rom 6:4, the purpose of being baptized and buried with Christ is not only the eventual attainment of resurrection, but also one's "walk in the newness of life." The subjunctive use of περιπατέω can imply that this "newness of life" is not yet experienced. If this is the case, then the "newness of life" concerns the moral transformation of the believer coterminous with the resurrection. Paul's ambiguity continues in vv. 10–11. Since Christ is believed to be alive at the present, Paul tells his audience to consider themselves both dead to sin and "alive" (present use of ζάω) to God in Christ Jesus. Paul's "already not yet" structure provides considerable flexibility in how the believer might understand his or her identity in Christ.[67]

---

65 Leppä, *The Making of Colossians*. Also, E. P. Sanders argues that the author of Colossians was dependent on all of the undisputed Pauline letters, but he does not distinguish between knowing undisputed Pauline quotations from (oral) memory and knowing them literarily. See E.P. Sanders, "Literary Dependence in Colossians," *JBL* 85 (1966): 28–45.

66 Leppä, *The Making of Colossians*, 136–38. There are four words that are shared in the two passages: the verbs συνθάπτω and ἐγείρω, and the nouns βάπτισμα and νεκρός.

67 Lehtipuu, (*Debates over the Resurrection*, 61) recognizes that Paul's conception of resurrection "creates a special kind of hermeneutical potential that develops in different directions in the writings of subsequent Christian generations."

Three beliefs comprise Paul's eschatological conception of resurrection in Romans and the other undisputed Pauline letters.[68] First, Paul believed in an imminent Parousia. The future return and moral/mortal transformation of those in Christ was at hand. Paul, as an apocalyptic Jew, understood himself and his communities as living in the last days. Second, although Christ was absent in body, Paul believed his risen spirit remained within the community, spurring them toward their moral and mortal transformation, which would come at the impending Parousia.[69] And third, Paul believed that Christ's resurrection meant that all believers would be resurrected as well.[70]

Of these beliefs, Colossians only appears to reject the first one. Col 2:12–13 reads,

> When you were buried with (συνθάπτω) him in baptism (βαπτισμός), you were also raised (aorist of συν + ἐγείρω) with him through faith in the action of God, who raised him from the dead (νεκρός). And when you were dead (νεκρός) in trespasses and the uncircumcision of your flesh, God made you alive together (aorist of συζωοποιέω [συν + ζάω + ποιέω]) with him, having forgiven us all our trespasses.

The author of Colossians, at the epicentre of the letter, altered Paul's conception of resurrection from what is described in Romans 6.[71] Where Romans 6 attested only to the present resurrected state of Christ and places the resurrection event in the (near) future, the author of Colossians instead declares that believers were already raised with Christ when they were baptized. The subtle change of the future (and subjunctive) to the aorist achieves this transition. The author of Colossians presents Paul teaching the church that, through baptism, they have not only been buried with Christ but also have been raised with him.[72]

The terms used in both Romans 6 and Colossians 2, namely συνθάπτω, ἐγείρω, βάπτισμα, and νεκρός, are not merely copied over.[73] Apart from νεκρός,

68 Nickelsburg, *Resurrection, Immortality, and Eternal Life*, 232–35.

69 Nickelsburg posits that the literary form of the "two ways" and "two spirits" exemplifies this most clearly (see Gal 5–6; and Rom 6–8; cf. Colossians 3). Those who walk according to the flesh, do wrong; whereas those who walk according to the spirit, do right. The reward for living in the spirit is eternal life, and the punishment for not living in the spirit is corruption or death. See Nickelsburg, *Resurrection, Immortality, and Eternal Life*, 232.

70 The notion that Christ's resurrection was a foreshadow of what awaited believers was not always effectively argued. Jesus' resurrection was unique from more general (Jewish) expectations since it (1) occurred within "history," and not at its end, and (2) was realized in an individual instead of the larger community.

71 Leppä, *The Making of Colossians*, 136. Leppä notes, "Although Col 2:12–13 follows the language of Rom 6, the texts reflect different opinions about eschatology."

72 Standhartinger, "Colossians and the Pauline School," 589.

73 There is another alteration of the term χαρίζομαι in v.13. It does not occur in Romans 6, but it does in Romans 8. In Colossians 2 it means "to remit, or to forgive," whereas in

the author of Colossians made subtle alterations to forms and functions, which disclosed a "new development of the Pauline heritage."[74] First, apart from changing the verb ἐγείρω to an aorist, the author of Colossians also added the prefix συν (συνεγείρω), which is unique within early Christianity only occurring in Col 2, 3:1, Eph 2:6,[75] and in Ign. *Pol.* 6:1.[76] This use of ἐγείρω reinforces the idea that the baptized believer was raised at the same moment as Christ. Second, where Rom 6:4 uses βάπτισμα, the author of Colossians uses βαπτισμός, which tends to be used in relation to Jewish ceremonial washing.[77] This use does not appear in Paul's writings nor in the LXX. Moreover, the author of Colossians omits "εἰς τὸν θάνατον" (into death) in contrast to Romans 6, which reads, "συνετάφημεν οὖν αὐτῷ διὰ τοῦ βαπτίσματος εἰς τὸν θάνατον" (therefore we have been buried with him through baptism into death). Why might this be?[78] Did the author of Colossians believe that one's experience of the resurrection did not require experiencing death first (θάνατος)?[79]

The Colossian counter-memory aims to redefine the important ritual of baptism. Romans 6 presents the baptized initiate as buried with Christ, and at present, in death, awaiting both mortal and moral transformation. Whereas the author of Colossians presents the baptized initiate as buried with Christ and, at present, raised with him. Death is conspicuously absent. Thus, the Colossian initiate already lives the resurrected life, pursuing moral transformation by seeking "the things that are above" until one day in the (distant?) future, he would be in glory with Christ (3:1–4).

But why alter the understanding of baptism? Jan Assmann provides an answer, asserting that the most potent medium of bonding memory is ritual.[80] Rituals "dramatize the interplay of the symbolic with the corporeal"

Romans 8 it means "to bestow." This is all the more striking since, as Leppä (*The Making of Colossians*, 139) states, "Paul never [said] that God forgives trespasses," See also Col 1:14.

74 Pokorný, *Colossians: A Commentary*, 126.

75 Many scholars believe that Ephesians is dependent on Colossians. See the discussion in Andrew T. Lincoln, *Ephesians*, WBC 42 (Waco: Word Books, 2005), xlvii–lviii. On the relationship between Romans, Colossians and Ephesians, see A. J. M. Wedderburn, *Baptism and Resurrection: Studies in Pauline Theology against Its Graeco-Roman Background*, WUNT 44 (Tübingen: Mohr Siebeck, 1987), 70–84.

76 Leppä, *The Making of Colossians*, 137.

77 See Leppä, *The Making of Colossians*, 137; Lohse, *Colossians and Philemon*, 104. Some manuscripts read βαπτίσματι (preferred by Lohse). However, Leppä correctly notes that "it is more probable that βαπτισμός has been changed to the more usual βάπτισμα than vice versa." See Leppä, *The Making of Colossians*, 137, n. 570; Lohse, *Colossians and Philemon*, 104, n. 71.

78 Lohse (*Colossians and Philemon*, 104) argues that this was done to shift the focus emphatically to the clause: "you have been raised."

79 The only use of θάνατος is in Col 1:22 used in reference to Jesus' death which has brought reconciliation. This is contrasted with its frequent use in the undisputed letters.

80 Assmann, *Religion and Cultural Memory*, 11.

and thereby reintegrate individual members so that they continue to share a common point of view.[81] In this light, *remembering* through ritual is literally an act of *re-membering* individuals to the group. Thus, the implication of altering an initiation ritual like baptism indicates the author's desire to redefine Paul's reputation to suit the actual audience's identity needs. Paul's reputation, including his teachings on the resurrection, was no longer viable in its new reception. The Colossian letter expressed a new historical reputation of Paul and the rhetorical strategy by which the actual audience could connect to it. The letter created continuity with a suitable Pauline past while breaking from a previously held past. Both aspects are important for explaining the new reception which gives us a glimpse at the distinct identity of a Pauline community. What was the impetus for such a break and the new reception?

Motivations for the Colossian Counter-memory

Why was the author of Colossians no longer satisfied with the view of resurrection and the broader eschatological perspective in Romans? I propose two motives for the Colossian counter-memory. The first concerns the delayed Parousia,[82] and the second concerns the death of Paul. These together comprise what Hobsbawm calls a rapid transformation of society, or what Assmann labels as *Traditionsbruch*, which necessitated a break with Paul's imminent eschatology and the need for a new Pauline conception of resurrection.

Paul expected the Parousia within his lifetime (cf. 1 Thess 4:15–5:8; Rom 13:11). The Parousia, however, did not occur. As such, the Pauline church(es) faced a *Traditionsbruch*, perhaps even threatening, as Standhartinger avers, "to give up and collapse."[83] The choices were limited. Either the Parousia was not going to happen, or it was delayed. If delayed, then it was delayed either briefly or indefinitely.

In Colossians, the Parousia is completely absent. An eschatological judgment was thought to have already happened since God has triumphed over the "rulers and authorities" (2:15). The actual audience is concerned about how to live and remain "in Christ" until Christ is revealed, and they with him in glory (3:4). This expectation appears to have been extended to a distant future. The inclusion of the *Haustafel* (household code) in Col 3:18–4:1 reflects the actual audience's desire to live within the world indefinitely.[84]

81 Assmann, *Religion and Cultural Memory*, 10–11.

82 Standhartinger ("Colossians and the Pauline School," 585) calls the delayed Parousia "the true purpose of Colossians."

83 Standhartinger, "Colossians and the Pauline School," 585.

84 Pokorný, *Colossians: A Commentary*, 177. Household codes were (1) paraenetic instructions that reflected the broader social norms within the Greco-Roman world as well as

The social impact that the failed Parousia had on identity constructions for post-Pauline communities can be further understood by comparing their conceptions of resurrection. Petr Pokorný provides a useful illustration of this impact (*Figure 7.2* below). *Figure 7.2* demonstrates that there is substantial *continuity* when comparing the undisputed letters of Paul with Colossians (and Ephesians), or the Pastoral letters. The differences are minor and sometimes challenging to detect. However, there is substantial *discontinuity* when comparing Colossians (and Ephesians) with the Pastorals (and 2 Thessalonians). Pokorný argues that "the theological divergences of the two groups of letters can easily be explained as different interpretations of the Pauline heritage by two groups of disciples."[85] These divergences are especially visible when comparing each letter's conception of resurrection. While Colossians posits a resurrection that had already happened, the Pastoral letters (and 2 Thessalonians) warn that this view is false. 2 Tim 2:17–18 reads, "Among them are Hymenaeus and Philētus, who have swerved from the truth by saying the resurrection has happened already, and they are overturning the faith of some."

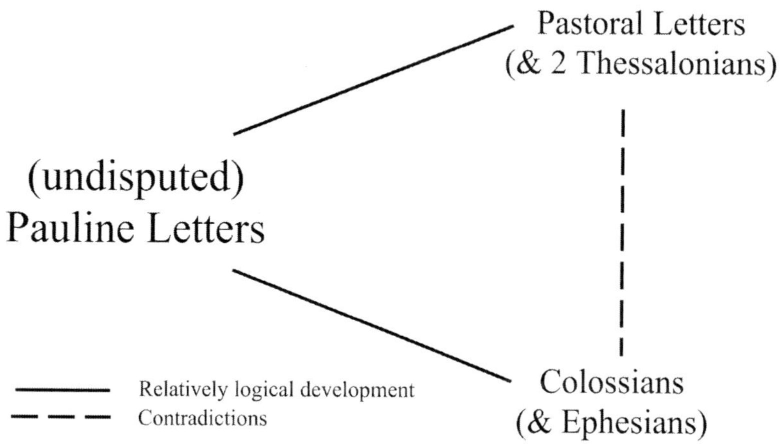

Figure 7.2 Adapted from Petr Pokorný, *Colossians: A Commentary* (Peabody: Hendrickson, 1991), 6–7

within Hellenistic Judaism; (2) intended for sustaining daily, and family life over multiple generations; and (3) provided instructions for how to "wisely" act toward outsiders to not come into conflict with them (see Col 4:5–6). Moreover, Pokorný observes that the "adoption of the household codes could not yet have taken place in the era of the apocalyptic expectation of an imminent return during which the main letters of Paul were written."

85 Pokorný, *Colossians: A Commentary*, 6–7.

The author of 2 Timothy specifically names two culprits who postulate an eschatology that sounds very similar to the one found in Colossians. The Pastorals clearly endorse a resurrection that will occur in the near future (2 Tim 2:11: "if we have died with him, we will also live with (συζάω) him"). Currently, however, the author of 2 Timothy understands his community to be living at the precipice of the last days, but not quite in them yet (2 Tim 3:1). The other Pastorals are concerned with paraenesis, instructing their audiences to employ household codes (1 Tim 2:1ff; Titus 2:1–10), as though they need to consider their lives on this side of the Parousia. Similarly, in 2 Thess 2:1–2, the author pleads with his audience that they not be swayed by teachings that the resurrection has already taken place, writing, "But we beg you, brothers, for the coming (παρουσία) of our Lord Jesus Christ and our meeting with him, do not become quickly shaken from mind or be alarmed either through a spirit or through a word or through a letter, as though from us, that the day of the Lord has come."

As in the Pastorals, the author of 2 Thessalonians too endorses an imminent eschatology that looks forward to a future resurrection.[86] However, for both 2 Thessalonians and 2 Timothy, the delayed Parousia and the death of Paul did not bring about the same changes that Colossians endorses. The Pastorals and 2 Thessalonians advocate an eschatological imminence which is vacant in Colossians (and Ephesians). The same *Traditionsbruch* occurred in each of these communities, but produced different eschatological traditions and different reconstructions of the past.

The Purpose of a Pseudepigraphal Paul

Again, the death of Paul served as one of the factors that motivated the creation of this pseudepigraphal letter. Two questions follow: (1) why was Paul selected to be the author of the pseudepigraphon? And (2) how does this impact the purpose of the Colossian pseudepigraphy?

Interpreting Colossians as a letter that presupposes the death of Paul is well attested by scholars.[87] The letter hints at its post-Paul setting in 2:1, which

86 Another point of difference is Col 2:8 where the audience is warned to not be taken captive by "human tradition," whereas in 2 Thess 3:6, they are told to keep away from those not keeping the tradition (see also 2 Thess 2:15, which commands the reader to "hold fast to traditions that were taught to us").

87 Standhartinger, "Colossians and the Pauline School"; Leppä, *The Making of Colossians*; Hans Dieter Betz, "Paul's 'Second Presence' in Colossians," in *Texts and Contexts: Biblical Texts in Their Textual and Situational Contexts: Essays in Honor of Lars Hartman*, ed. Tord Fornberg and David Hellholm (Oslo: Scandinavian University Press, 1995), 507–18; Pokorný, *Colossians: A Commentary*; and Lohse, *Colossians and Philemon*.

indicates that the actual audience never knew Paul in the flesh, and in 2:5, where Paul described himself as "absent in body (σάρξ)" but present with them "in spirit (πνεύματι)."[88] Based on these hints, some conclude that the purpose of the pseudepigraphon was "to convey the spiritual presence of Paul or to replace the (bodily) presence of Paul."[89] However, if a grieving community longed for Paul's presence through a letter, why did its members not simply copy one of the authentic letters? Why exert the effort to compose a forged letter that contains different teachings? The explanations could lie in the need to *re-present* who Paul was and what he taught, which a copy of an authentic letter or a *representation* of it could not achieve.

Sandra Huebenthal argues in a similar way, concluding that the Colossian pseudepigraphon did not rely on a past authority, but instead sought to establish it.[90] The Colossian pseudepigraphon was more about whom Paul needed to be than about retrieving who he was.[91] Huebenthal's argument is a needed counterpoint to those that view Paul's authority as *only* borrowed for purposes of legitimization.[92]

While Huebenthal's argument adds a deeper layer to the explanation, it does not account for why the author of Colossians selected Paul instead of someone else. If Paul held no previous position of authority among the Colossians, what was gained by writing the letter in his name? It may be that Paul's authority was not the issue, but a means to an end. It is quite possible that the author elevated Paul's authority to a higher status in the process, which coincides with the well-established goal of pseudepigraphy in achieving "normativity and authority."[93] That *telos* was the letter's normative content. Prior to its construction, Paul may not have held enough authority for the letter's paraenetic content to be accepted or even compelling. If this is the case, then the author elevated the reputation of Paul so that his teachings would be compelling and appear as authoritative.

---

88 Betz, "Paul's 'Second Presence' in Colossians," 513.

89 Standhartinger, "Colossians and the Pauline School," 583.

90 Huebenthal, "Pseudepigraphie als Strategie in frühchristlichen Identitätsdiskursen?" 61, writes, "Nicht mehr der Schrift wird durch den Namen einer Autorität aus der Vergangenheit Geltung verschafft, sondern durch die Schrift wird einer Person oder Tradition aus der Vergangenheit Autorität und Geltung verschafft."

91 Charles Horton Cooley, *Human Nature and the Social Order* (New York: Schocken Books, 1964), 342. Reputation may not represent who individuals are, "but it always represents what humanity needs for them to have been."

92 Cf. Betz, "Paul's 'Second Presence' in Colossians," 513; Pokorný, *Colossians: A Commentary*, 14.

93 Huebenthal, "Pseudepigraphie als Strategie in frühchristlichen Identitätsdiskursen?" 86. "Normativität und Autorität sind dabei nicht Voraussetzung, sondern Ziel der Autorfiktion."

The author of Colossians demonstrates Paul's reputational elevation in two ways. First, he presents Paul as the one who suffers on behalf of the church (Col 4:18, "remember my chains"). Paul's sufferings are even described as "filling up" what was lacking in Christ's afflictions (Col 1:24). Second, the author presents Paul as the servant (διάκονος) of the church, commissioned by God, "to fulfill the Word of God" (Col 1:23, 25; cf. Rom 8:4; 13:8–10). Together, these two examples demonstrate that the author of Colossians elevated Paul's reputation by *keying* him to Christ's reputation.[94] Keying Paul to Christ did not elevate Paul's authority for its own sake; instead, it elevated the new conception of resurrection through Paul's elevated authority.

Conclusion

After Paul's death, his views on resurrection took on an afterlife of their own. Among successive generations, which were pressured by different interests, concerns, and hopes, Pauline images and his theological conceptions were produced and received and reproduced as often as the needs of the present demanded. Relevance demanded that the process of transmission allowed for both continuity and discontinuity. Colossians is but one example of the production of new Pauline images and ideas among the earliest receivers after his death.

In early Christianity and Judaism, conceptions of resurrection condensed entire worldviews and formed collective identities. As such, divergent conceptions of resurrection fractured Pauline followers into distinct communities. The audience to whom Colossians was written was one such community. After the failed Parousia and the death of Paul, a reputational entrepreneur produced a pseudepigraphal letter, which achieved two goals. First, it provided a counter-memory of Paul's reputation, which elevated Paul's authority and presented a new memory of Paul as one who taught a realized view of resurrection within a non-apocalyptic eschatological context. Second, it provided a continuity between the community's identity needs in the present, and this new memory of Paul from the past.

The present needs of a community are always in tension with the legacies of its past. As such, all memories of the past are socially created. Regardless of whether a community produces a history of its people, a biography of its founder, or an *apologia* of its beliefs, they are all strategies for reconstructing

94 Schwartz, *Abraham Lincoln and the Forge of National Memory*, 18. Also see my previous note on Schwartz's use of keying (n. 60).

the past for the needs of the present. Among the strategies available to the reputational entrepreneur then, pseudepigraphy is another "legitimate strategy in the battle of memories."[95]

Bibliography

Anderson, Benedict. *Imagined Communities: Reflections on the Origin and Spread of Nationalism*. London: Verso, 1983.

Assmann, Aleida. "Canon and Archive." Pages 97–108 in *Cultural Memory Studies: An International and Interdisciplinary Handbook*. Edited by Astrid Erll and Ansgar Nünning. Berlin: Walter de Gruyter, 2008.

Assmann, Jan. *Das kulturelle Gedächtnis: Schrift, Erinnerung und Politische Identität in frühen Hochkulturen*. Munich: Beck, 1992.

———. "Form as a Mnemonic Device: Cultural Texts and Cultural Memory." Pages 67–82 in *Performing the Gospel. Orality, Memory, and Mark. Essays Dedicated to Werner Kelber*. Edited by Richard A. Horsley, Jonathan A. Draper, and John Miles Foley. Minneapolis: Fortress Press, 2006.

———. *Religion and Cultural Memory: Ten Studies*. Stanford: Stanford University Press, 2006.

———. *Cultural Memory and Early Civilization: Writing, Remembrance, and Political Imagination*. Cambridge: Cambridge University Press, 2011.

Baumeister, Roy F., and Stephen Hastings. "Distortions of Collective Memory: How Groups Flatter and Deceive Themselves." Pages 277–93 in *Collective Memory of Political Events: Social Psychological Perspectives*. Edited by James W. Pennebaker, Darío Páez, and Bernard Rimé. Mahwah: Erlbaum, 1997.

Betz, Hans Dieter. "Paul's 'Second Presence' in Colossians." Pages 507–18 in *Texts and Contexts: Biblical Texts in Their Textual and Situational Contexts: Essays in Honor of Lars Hartman*. Edited by Tord Fornberg and David Hellholm. Oslo: Scandinavian University Press, 1995.

Cooley, Charles Horton. *Human Nature and the Social Order*. New York: Schocken Books, 1964.

Dunn, James D. G. *The Epistle to the Colossians and to Philemon*. NIGTC. Grand Rapids: Eerdmans, 1996.

Ehrman, Bart D. *Forgery and Counterforgery: The Use of Literary Deceit in Early Christian Polemics*. Oxford: Oxford University Press, 2014.

Elledge, C. D. *Resurrection of the Dead in Early Judaism: 200 BCE–CE 200*. Oxford: Oxford University Press, 2017.

95 Assmann, *Religion and Cultural Memory*, 99.

Fentress, James, and Chris Wickham. *Social Memory*. New Perspectives on the Past. Cambridge: Blackwell, 1992.

Fewster, Gregory P. "'Can I Have Your Autograph?' On Thinking about Pauline Authorship and Pseudepigraphy." *Bulletin for the Study of Religion* 43.3 (2014): 30–39.

Fine, Gary Alan. *Difficult Reputations: Collective Memories of the Evil, Inept, and Controversial*. Chicago: University of Chicago Press, 2002.

Foucault, Michel. *Language, Counter-Memory, Practice: Selected Essays and Interviews*. Edited by Donald F. Bouchard. Ithaca: Cornell University Press, 1980.

Gupta, Nijay. "What Is in a Name? The Hermeneutics of Authorship Analysis Concerning Colossians." *CurBR* 11 (2013): 196–217.

Halbwachs, Maurice. *On Collective Memory*. Translated by Lewis A. Coser. *The Heritage of Sociology*. The Heritage of Society. Chicago: University of Chicago Press, 1992.

Hatina, Thomas R. "The Provenance of Jesus' Quotations of Scripture from a Social Memory Perspective." Pages 59–76 in *The Earliest Perceptions of Jesus in Context: Essays in Honour of John Nolland on His 70th Birthday*. Edited by Aaron W. White, Craig A. Evans, and David Wenham. LNTS 566. London: Bloomsbury T&T Clark, 2018.

———. "The Social Memory Theory and Competing Identity Constructions: The Function of Genesis 15:6 in Romans and James." Pages 35–56 in *500 Jahre der Reformation in der Slowakei*. Edited by M. Nicák and M. Tamcke. Münster: Lit Verlag, 2019.

Hendel, Ronald S. *Remembering Abraham: Culture, Memory, and History in the Hebrew Bible*. Oxford: Oxford University Press, 2005.

Hobsbawm, Eric J. "Introduction: Inventing Traditions." Pages 1–14 in *The Invention of Tradition*. Edited by Eric J. Hobsbawm and Terence Ranger. Cambridge: Cambridge University Press, 1983.

Hooker, Morna D. "Were There False Teachers in Colossae?" Pages 315–31 in *Christ and Spirit in the New Testament: Essays in Honour of C.F.D. Moule*. Edited by Barnabas Lindars and Stephen S. Smalley. Cambridge: Cambridge University Press, 1973.

Huebenthal, Sandra. "Pseudepigraphie als Strategie in frühchristlichen Identitätsdiskursen? Überlegungen am Beispiel des Kolosserbriefs." *SNTU.A* 5.36 (2011): 61–92.

Kiley, Mark Christopher. *Colossians as Pseudepigraphy*. The Biblical Seminar 4. Sheffield: JSTOT, 1986.

Kirk, Alan. "Social and Cultural Memory." Pages 1–24 in *Memory, Tradition, and Text: Uses of the Past in Early Christianity*. Edited by Alan Kirk and Tom Thatcher. Semeia Studies 52. Atlanta: SBL Press, 2005.

Lehtipuu, Outi. *Debates over the Resurrection of the Dead: Constructing Early Christian Identity*. Oxford: Oxford University Press, 2015.

Leppä, Outi. *The Making of Colossians: A Study on the Formation and Purpose of a Deutero-Pauline Letter*. Publications of the Finnish Exegetical Society 86. Helsinki: The Finnish Exegetical Society, 2003.

Lincicum, David. "Mirror-Reading a Pseudepigraphal Letter." *NovT* 59.2 (2017): 171–93.

Lincoln, Andrew T. *Ephesians*. WBC 42. Waco: Word Books, 2005.

Lohse, Eduard. *Colossians and Philemon*. Translated by W. R. Poehlmann and R. J. Karris. Hermeneia. Philadelphia: Fortress Press, 1971.

Mead, George Herbert. "The Nature of the Past." Pages 235–42 in *Essays in Honor of John Dewey*. Edited by John Coss. New York: Henry Holt & Co., 1929.

Meade, David G. *Pseudonymity and Canon: An Investigation into the Relationship of Authorship and Authority in Jewish and Early Christian Tradition*. WUNT 39. Tübingen: Mohr Siebeck, 1986.

Nickelsburg, George W. E. *Resurrection, Immortality, and Eternal Life in Intertestamental Judaism and Early Christianity: Expanded Edition*. HTS 56. Cambridge: Harvard University Press, 2006.

Nünning, Ansgar. *Grundzüge eines kommunikationstheoretischen Modells der erzählerischen Vermittlung: Die Funktion der Erzählinstanz in den Romanen George Eliots*. Horizonte, Studien zu Texten und Ideen der europäischen Moderne 2. Trier, 1989.

Olick, Jeffrey K. "Products, Processes, and Practices: A Non-Reificatory Approach to Collective Memory." BTB 36 (2006): 5–14.

———. "From Usable Pasts to the Return of the Repressed." *The Hedgehog Review* 9.2 (2007): 19–31.

Olick, Jeffrey K., and Joyce Robbins. "Social Memory Studies: From 'Collective Memory' to the Historical Sociology of Mnemonic Practices." *Annual Review of Sociology* 24.1 (1998): 105–40.

Petersen, Norman R. *Rediscovering Paul: Philemon and the Sociology of Paul's Narrative World*. Eugene: Wipf & Stock, 2008.

Pokorný, Petr. *Colossians: A Commentary*. Peabody: Hendrickson, 1991.

Reinmuth, Eckart. "Exkurs: Zur Neutestamentlichen Paulus-Pseudepigraphie." Pages 190–226 in *Die Briefe an die Philipper, Thessalonicher und an Philemon*. Edited by Nikolaus Walter, Eckart Reinmuth, and Peter Lampe. NTD 8/2. Göttingen: Vandenhoeck & Ruprecht, 1998.

Rodríguez, Rafael. "Paul and Social Memory." Pages 346–68 in *Paul in the Greco-Roman World: A Handbook, Volume 2*. Edited by J. Paul Sampley. 2nd ed. London: Bloomsbury T & T Clark, 2016.

Sanders, E. P. "Literary Dependence in Colossians." *JBL* 85 (1966): 28–45.

Schudson, Michael. "Dynamics of Distortion in Collective Memory." Pages 346–64 in *Memory Distortion: How Minds, Brains, and Societies Reconstruct the Past*. Edited by Daniel L. Schachter. Cambridge: Harvard University Press, 1995.

Schwartz, Barry. *Abraham Lincoln and the Forge of National Memory*. Chicago: University of Chicago Press, 2000.

———. "Where There's Smoke, There's Fire: Memory and History." Pages 7–37 in *Memory and Identity in Ancient Judaism and Early Christianity: A Conversation with Barry Schwartz*. Edited by Tom Thatcher. SemeiaSt 78. Atlanta: SBL Press, 2014.

Setzer, Claudia. "Resurrection of the Dead as Symbol and Strategy." *AAR* 69.1 (2001): 65–102.

———. *Resurrection of the Body in Early Judaism and Early Christianity: Doctrine, Community, and Self-Definition*. Boston: Brill Academic Publishers, 2004.

Shils, Edward. *Tradition*. Chicago: University of Chicago Press, 1981.

Standhartinger, Angela. "Colossians and the Pauline School." *NTS* 50.4 (2004): 572–93.

Wedderburn, A. J. M. *Baptism and Resurrection: Studies in Pauline Theology against Its Graeco-Roman Background*. WUNT 44. Tübingen: Mohr Siebeck, 1987.

———. *Beyond Resurrection*. London: SCM Press, 1999.

White, Benjamin L. *Remembering Paul: Ancient and Modern Contests over the Image of the Apostle*. Oxford: Oxford University Press, 2014.

Zerubavel, Eviatar. "Social Memories: Steps to a Sociology of the Past." *Qualitative Sociology* 19.3 (1996): 283–99.

Zerubavel, Yael. *Recovered Roots: Collective Memory and the Making of Israeli National Tradition*. Chicago: University of Chicago Press, 1995.

Re-membering Life after Death: Constructing, Receiving, and Contesting the Pauline Body

Frederick S. Tappenden

Introduction

Since 1917, the theological college at which I teach and research has annually conferred honorary doctorates upon individuals who have made exceptional contributions of leadership, ministry, or scholarship. At the 2018 convocation, we honoured Lyle Keewatin Richards and Donald Hepburn of Red Deer, Alberta for their work with the "Remembering the Children Society." This Society is a joint Indigenous/Church partnership that paid tribute in culturally appropriate ways to the many aboriginal children who died at the Red Deer Industrial School in the late-nineteenth and early-twentieth century. Some historical knowledge of the Canadian context will help situate the importance of their work. From the 1880s through to 1996, the Canadian government and a number of Christian churches jointly established a nationwide school system—known as the Indian Residential Schools—with the mandate of assimilating Indigenous children into the various western/European cultural heritages of Canada. The long-term impact of these schools upon Canada's many first peoples is profound, as youth were removed from their families, indigenous communities were disrupted, and indigenous cultures were systematically devalued, dissolved, and subjected to acts of genocide. In the case of the Red Dear Industrial School, though this institution had been in operation only for some 26 years (1893–1919), at the turn of the twentieth century it nevertheless held the dubious distinction of possessing the highest child mortality rate of any residential school in Canada.[1] Many of the children who

1 As reported in Augustine S. J. Park, "Remembering the Children: Decolonizing Community-Based Restorative Justice for Indian Residential Schools," *CJR* 19.4 (2016): 424–44, doi: 10.1080/10282580.2016.1226818. It is noteworthy that, in May and June of 2021, unmarked graves of some 215 and 751 anonymous indigenous children were discovered at the sites of the former Indian Residential Schools in both Kamloops, British Columbia and Marieval, Saskatchewan, respectively. See Courtney Dickson and Bridgette Watson, "Remains of 215 Children Found Buried at Former B.C. Residential School," *CBC News*, May 27, 2021, https://www.cbc.ca/news/canada/british-columbia/tk-emlúps-te-secwépemc-215-children-former-kamloops-indian-residential-school-1.6043778, and Bryan Eneas, "Sask. First Nation

 DOI:10.30965/9783657796212_009

died at this school had not been given proper burials, their families and communities had not been engaged or contacted regarding their deaths, and their roots and family histories had been forgotten. In an effort to bring restorative justice to this atrocity, Keewatin Richards and Hepburn did the hard work of identifying where many of the children had come from, engaging the elders of those children's ancestral communities, and facilitating gatherings of elders and indigenous representatives who conducted ceremonies and feasts in honour of the children who had passed. At our 2018 convocation, many attendees were brought to tears by the description of how the children, whose bodies and identities had long been forgotten, were again remembered. By recalling not just the names of these children, but also by attending to the transition of their bodies from life to death, the act of remembering served to restore and thus to grant some measure of dignity to those who had previously been forgotten.

How are the bodies of the deceased remembered by those who commemorate them? This is one of the central questions I want to consider in this paper[2], particularly as this question is explored within ancient Judean and Christ-believing communities. It goes without saying that, when it comes to scholarship on resurrected bodies in ancient Judaism and Christianity, the academic community has bought ink by the barrel (to use an old newspaper adage).[3] While much interpretive attention has been given to topics such

Announces Discovery of 751 Unmarked Graves near Former Residential School," *CBC News*, June 24, 2021, https://www.cbc.ca/news/canada/saskatchewan/cowessess-marieval-indian-residential-school-news-1.6078375. These more recent discoveries in Kamloops and Marieval speak to the horrific magnitude of the Residential School crisis, and they have led to renewed local and national action to identify similarly unmarked gravesites across Canada.

2 Earlier versions of this paper or portions thereof were presented at the Lautenschläger Colloquium at the Forschungszentrum Internationale und Interdisziplinäre Theologie, Universität Heidelberg (2017), the Annual Meeting of the Society of Biblical Literature (2018), and the Annual Meeting of the Studiorum Novi Testamenti Societas (2019). The author extends profound thanks to the many colleagues who have engaged and offered insightful comments to these earlier drafts.

3 The list of recent scholarly monographs and edited volumes, not including journal articles and book chapters, on resurrection since the turn of the century is substantial: Friedrich Avemarie and Hermann Lichtenberger, eds., *Auferstehung = Resurrection: The Fourth Durham—Tübingen Research Symposium: Resurrection, Transformation, and Exaltation in the Old Testament, Ancient Judaism, and Early Christianity*, WUNT 135 (Tübingen: Mohn Siebeck, 2001); Reimund Bieringer, Veronica Koperski, and Bianca Lataire, eds., *Resurrection in the New Testament*, BETL 165 (Leuven: Peeters, 2002); Philip S. Johnston, *Shades of Sheol: Death and Afterlife in the Old Testament* (Downers Grove: Intervarsity Press, 2002); N. T. Wright, *The Resurrection of the Son of God* (Minneapolis: Fortress Press, 2003); Alan F. Segal, *Life after Death: A History of the Afterlife in the Religions of the West* (New York: Doubleday, 2004); Claudia Setzer, *Resurrection of the Body in Early Judaism and Early Christianity: Doctrine, Community, and Self-Definition* (Leiden: Brill, 2004); James H. Charlesworth, ed., *Resurrection:*

as, "*how ancient peoples conceive of the body that is to come*," my focus in this paper is oriented toward, "*how ancient peoples remember the body that was*." I am interested in how the lifeless bodies of the deceased are remembered, and what significances those bodies continue to take for those who commemorate them. While my analysis in this paper will touch briefly on a variety of Second Temple Judean texts, my interests rest squarely on the traditions associated with one Second Temple Judean in particular: Saul or Paul of Tarsus.

Paul takes centre stage for three reasons: (1) the dual themes of resurrection and the body are pervasive across the Pauline tradition, both in the undisputed and disputed texts. (2) In the undisputed Paulines, the body of the deceased takes a particular meaning, one whereby death and resurrection is viewed as a process that is simultaneously embodied in Christ-devotees themselves (both individually and collectively).[4] Extending from this, we will see that (3) the

The Origin and Future of a Biblical Doctrine (London: T&T Clark, 2006); J. R. Daniel Kirk, *Unlocking Romans: Resurrection and the Justification of God* (Grand Rapids: Eerdmans, 2008); Geza Vermes, *The Resurrection* (London: Penguin, 2008); Turid Karlsen Seim, and Jorunn Økland, eds., *Metamorphoses: Resurrection, Body, and Transformative Practices in Early Christianity*, Ekstasis 1 (Berlin: de Gruyter, 2009); Tobias Nicklas, Friedrich V. Reiterer, and Joseph Verheyden, eds., *The Human Body in Death and Resurrection* (Berlin: de Gruyter, 2009); Dag Øistein Endsjø, *Greek Resurrection Beliefs and the Success of Christianity* (New York: Palgrave Macmillan, 2009); Hugo Lundhaug, *Images of Rebirth: Cognitive Poetics and Transformational Soteriology in the Gospel of Philip and the Exegesis on the Soul*, NHMS 73 (Leiden: Brill, 2010); Tobias Nicklas, Joseph Verheyden, Erik M. M. Eynickel, and Florentino García Martinez, eds., *Other Worlds and their Relation to this World: Early Jewish and Ancient Christian Traditions*, JSJSup 143 (Leiden: Brill, 2010); Markus Vinzent, *Christ's Resurrection in Early Christianity and the Making of the New Testament* (Franham: Ashgate, 2011); Geert Van Oyen and Tom Shepherd, eds., *Resurrection of the Dead: Biblical Traditions in Dialogue*, BETL 249 (Leuven: Peeters, 2012); Outi Lehtipuu, *Debates over the Resurrection of the Dead: Constructing Christian Identity*, OECS (Oxford: Oxford University Press, 2015); Taylor Petrey, *Resurrecting Parts: Early Christians on Desire, Reproduction, and Sexual Difference* (London: Routledge, 2015); Frederick S. Tappenden, *Resurrection in Paul: Cognition, Metaphor, and Transformation*, ECL 19 (Atlanta: SBL Press, 2016); Katharina Waldner, Richard Gordon, and Wolfgang Spickermann, eds., *Burial Rituals, Ideas of Afterlife, and the Individual in the Hellenistic World and the Roman Empire*, PAWB 57 (Stuttgart: Franz Steiner Verlag, 2016); Andrew Boakye, *Death and Life: Resurrection, Restoration, and Rectification in Paul's Letter to the Galatians* (Eugene: Pickwick, 2017); C. D. Elledge, *Resurrection of the Dead in Early Judaism: 200 BCE–CE 200* (Oxford: Oxford University Press, 2017); Frederick S. Tappenden and C. Daniel-Hughes, eds., *Coming Back to Life: The Permeability of Past and Present, Mortality and Immortality, Death and Life in the Ancient Mediterranean* (Montreal: McGill University Library, 2017; http://comingbacktolife.mcgill.ca); Thomas D. McGlothlin, *Resurrection as Salvation: Development and Conflict in Pre-Nicene Paulinism* (Cambridge: Cambridge University Press, 2018); Candida R. Moss, *Divine Bodies: Resurrecting Perfection in the New Testament and Early Christianity* (New Haven: Yale University Press, 2019); and Kai-Hsuan Chang, *The Impact of Bodily Experience on Paul's Resurrection Theology*, LNTS 655 (London: T&T Clark, 2022).

4 See Tappenden, *Resurrection in Paul*, esp. chapters 4–5.

commemoration of Paul in the late-first and second centuries utilizes death and resurrection as a mnemonic frame that simultaneously defines the memory of the apostle's body, and so also the reputation of his person.

In considering these commemorative threads, my analysis proceeds from the recognition that texts function in the ancient Mediterranean as oral-/aural-performative reading events.[5] William David Shiell, for instance, draws on ancient literary and artistic evidence to re-imagine the ways in which early Christian texts were delivered within ecclesial banquet settings.[6] Central to Shiell's treatment is the recognition that lectors/readers served as the intermediary through whom audiences encountered texts, and further that lectors would gesture and vocally inflect the texts while audiences would likewise respond in characteristic ways. Reading, in this context, is active and dynamic, and it presumes that both the lector/reader and the audience have performative roles to play. Accordingly, the *lector/reader* functions as an *oral-performer* such that the very act of *reading/performing* a Pauline text—say, the Epistle to the Colossians, or the book of Acts—serves to embody Paul and the Pauline voice to the hearers/readers.[7] To an extent, then, "Paul" very much remains present before the reading communities that commemorate him; his person and authority *come back to life* through the performance of writings both in his name and about him.[8]

---

5 See Frederick S. Tappenden, "Aural-Performance, Conceptual Blending, and Intertextuality: The (Non-)Use of Scripture in Luke 24:45–48," in *The Gospel of Luke, Volume 3 of Biblical Interpretation in Early Christian Gospels*, ed. Thomas R. Hatina, LNTS 376 (London: T&T Clark, 2010), 180–200.

6 William David Shiell, *Reading Acts: The Lector and the Early Christian Audience*, BibInt 70 (Boston: Brill, 2004).

7 Though this oral-/aural-performative dynamic has been less explored with respect to the Pauline tradition, it has been examined in the context of eucharistic traditions and ancient performances of Jesus's death within ecclesial banquet settings (see esp. Ellen Bradshaw Aitken, *Jesus' Death in Early Christian Memory: The Poetics of Passion*, NTOA 53 [Göttingen: Vandenhoeck & Ruprecht, 2004] and Angela Standhartinger, "Bringing Back to Life: Laments and the Origin of the So-Called Words of Institution," in *Coming Back to Life: The Permeability of Past and Present, Mortality and Immortality, Death and Life in the Ancient Mediterranean*, ed. Frederick S. Tappenden and Carly Daniel-Hughes, with the assistance of Bradley N. Rice [Montreal: McGill University Library, 2017, Online: https://comingbacktolife.mcgill.ca], 71–101).

8 An argument can certainly be made that this oral-performative dynamic is most true of epistolary texts, where the reader/lector embodies the Pauline voice and thus directly addresses the reading community *as if* s/he (that is, the reader/lector) is Paul. If such is true, then it follows that this oral-performative dynamic is less significant in the performances

Within this oral-/aural-performative matrix, I am struck by the crisscrossing dissonance that is present in the commemoration of Paul. On the one hand, Paul remains *living* and *alive* to his communities through the reading/performance of Pauline writings (either texts in his name or texts about him). And yet, on the other hand, the precise content of Paul's ongoing existence finds definition within images of an apostolic body perpetually given to suffering and death. For example, texts such as Acts, Ephesians, the Pastoral Epistles, *3 Corinthians*, and *Epistle to the Laodiceans* all remember Paul as one in prison and at times on the verge of death. Similar themes are found in both Philippians and 2 Corinthians, two ostensibly authentic Pauline texts that, in their present form, are nevertheless post-Pauline redactions.[9] And, in one of the more enigmatic descriptions in this tradition, Colossians recounts an image of Paul as one who is "filling up in my own flesh that which is lacking of Christ's afflictions for the sake of his body" (Col 1:24). Many of these texts will be discussed below, and when they are taken together, we see that Paul's

of narratives about Paul (such as Acts, or the *Acts of Thecla*), since in such cases the reader/lector embodies Paul as a character in the narrative, not Paul as an epistolary addresser. But given the dynamism of oral-performance as a reading event, such a distinction seems overly restrictive, especially in light of the globalizing tendency of the Pauline tradition. Indeed, as soon as epistolary texts are shared beyond their intended reading communities, the reading experience becomes expressly dependent upon an element of imagination. For example, Christ-believing communities in Ephesus receive and read Paul's Letter to the Romans *as if* Paul had something to say to them in Asia Minor; through the engagement of their imaginations, these Ephesians transcend the locality of the epistle's address to instead hear Paul speaking in ways that are relevant to their context. As an extension of this leveraging of imagination, the performance of narratives about Paul function in similar ways. Regardless of the difference in genre between an epistle and a narrative, the character of Paul is performed and thus embodied by the reader/lector in the midst of the reading community, not so much addressing the audience directly, but rather fostering an imaginative space in which narratives about Paul come to shape and inform the meaning-making systems of the hearers. Indeed, narratives about Paul may well involve story elements that elicit more concrete interactions between lectors/readers and audiences, thus enabling Paul's person to be more directly present to the reading community.

9 Here it is worth noting that we constantly encounter a constructed image of Paul in the sense that all the surviving writings of Paul—both the undisputed and disputed writings—are filtered for us through the tradition, and thus our vision of Paul is not indifferent. See further Benjamin L. White, *Remembering Paul: Ancient and Modern Contests over the Image of the Apostle* (Oxford: Oxford University Press, 2014).

body not only becomes a recurrent theme within the emerging Pauline tradition, but it also is commemorated as a body that is simultaneously dying and living.[10]

Over the past several decades, the "body" as a thematic and analytical category has become a mainstay within the study of Paul's writings. Several monographs have explored just how forthcoming Paul is regarding the body and its place in his broader Christ-believing ideals.[11] A little more than a decade ago, Troels Engberg-Pedersen recounted a comment by Wayne Meeks: "I cannot think of anybody in antiquity who spoke so much about the body as Paul did."[12] Nevertheless, despite this ubiquity, relatively little has been done on the development and reception of the body thematic within Paul's earliest interpreters. Richard Pervo's, *The Making of Paul*, for instance, has virtually no discussion of the body thematic,[13] while other book-length studies that are devoted specifically to early Paulinism are similarly silent on this matter.[14] Even body-specific studies such as Jennifer Glancy's *Corporeal Knowledge* or Judith Newman's *Before the Bible: The Liturgical Body and the Formation of Scriptures in Early Judaism* are focused much more broadly than the Pauline tradition alone.[15] Most commonly, analyses of somatic themes in Paulinism

10 See further Philip F. Esler, "'Remember my Fetters': Memorialisation of Paul's Imprisonment," in *Explaining Christian Origins and Early Judaism: Contributions from the Cognitive and Social Sciences*, ed. Petri Luomanen, Ilkka Pyysiäinen, and Risto Uro, BibInt 89 (Leiden: Brill, 2007), 231–258. Esler examines the mnemonic framework of the suffering and imprisoned apostle and links that to the forming of communal identity and individual autobiographical memory in the late-first century CE. For Esler: "The authors of Colossians, Ephesians, and 2 Timothy all present Paul as an exemplar of the Christ-movement, that is, as a real person characteristic of its identity" (p. 239).

11 See, for example, Dale B. Martin, *The Corinthian Body* (New Haven: Yale University Press, 1995); Tappenden, *Resurrection in Paul*; and Chang, *The Impact of Bodily Experience on Paul's Resurrection Theology*.

12 Troels Engberg-Pedersen, *Cosmology and Self in the Apostle Paul: The Material Spirit* (Oxford: Oxford University Press, 2010), 3.

13 Richard Pervo, *The Making of Paul: Constructions of the Apostle in Early Christianity* (Minneapolis: Fortress Press, 2010).

14 See, for example, Isaac W. Oliver and Gabriele Boccaccini, eds., *The Early Reception of Paul the Second Temple Jew: Text, Narrative, and Reception History*, LSTS 92 (London, T&T Clark, 2019); Peter Lampe, *From Paul to Valentinus: Christians at Rome in the First Two Centuries* (Minneapolis: Fortress Press, 2003); and William S. Babcock, ed., *Paul and the Legacies of Paul* (Dallas: Southern Methodist University Press, 1990).

15 See Jennifer A. Glancy, *Corporeal Knowledge: Early Christian Bodies* (Oxford: Oxford University Press, 2010) and Judith H. Newman, *Before the Bible: The Liturgical Body and the Formation of Scriptures in Early Judaism* (Oxford: Oxford University Press, 2019).

are relegated to individual chapters, and thus the body is seen as a smaller part of a larger thematic whole.[16]

My analysis in this article examines the body thematic within the Pauline tradition. I focus specifically on some of the ways that Paul's reputation develops within a mnemonic framework of perpetual death and coming-back-to-life.[17] First, I begin by examining the theme of Paul's "body" in the undisputed letters.[18] Here I give attention to the ways death and life are dynamically mapped to the apostle's body, and the resulting visions of death and life that emerge within Paul's somatic self-presentation. Second, I examine the many ways Paul's "body" is remembered within the late-first and second centuries. Here I examine the memory of Paul's "body"—his presence, his absence, his reputation, and his (living) voice—in Colossians, Acts, and the *Acts of Thecla*, noting particularly that these later texts draw upon a mnemonic framework that Paul himself helped construct: namely, the framework of perpetual death and coming-back-to-life. Paul's image is constructed within a rhetoric of death and decay, while the performance of that very rhetoric enables the apostle to be revivified constantly within the commemorative community. What results is a mnemonic reputation of the perpetually suffering Paul, simultaneously absent-from yet present-to those who remember him.

---

16 For example, several seminal studies of early Christian interpretations of Paul devote individual chapters to somatic issues; see in particular Margaret M. Mitchell, *Paul, the Corinthians, and the Birth of Christian Hermeneutics* (Cambridge: Cambridge University Press, 2010); Laura Salah Nasrallah, *Christian Responses to Roman Art and Architecture: The Second-Century Church Amid the Spaces of Empire* (Cambridge: Cambridge University Press, 2010); and Michael Allen Williams, *Rethinking "Gnosticism": An Argument for Dismantling a Dubious Category* (Princeton: Princeton University Press, 1996).

17 Here and throughout this paper, the construction and negotiation of reputations is understood to be an activity and process of social and cultural memory. This approach is rooted in the work of Barry Schwartz and esp. Gary Alan Fine (respectively, see esp. Barry Schwartz, *Abraham Lincoln and the Forge of National Memory* [Chicago: University of Chicago Press, 2000] and Gary Allen Fine, *Difficult Reputations: Collective Memories of the Evil, Inept, and Controversial* [Chicago: University of Chicago Press, 2001]).

18 A brief word on method: my analysis will stretch from the Second Temple period through to the second century CE. My choice in doing so relates to the nature of the Pauline writings. Though the undisputed letters of Paul date to the late Second Temple period, these texts are not unbiased second temple writings. Yes, Paul's letters were written prior to 70 CE, but their selection for and presence within the New Testament canon reflects the thoughts and concerns of Christ-believing communities well after the events of 70 CE. In light of social memory theory, it is very difficult to disentangle Paul the Second Temple Judean from Paul the constructed Early Christian Apostle (see further, White, *Remembering Paul*; also, Eric W. Scherbenske, *Canonizing Paul: Ancient Editorial Practice and the Corpus Paulinum* [Oxford: Oxford University Press, 2013]). Such a mnemonic reality permits—indeed, necessitates—that we map mnemonic trajectories that span the late Second Temple Period through the second century CE.

Paul's Body: The Undisputed Letters and Broader Second Temple Jewish Sources

While there is a good deal of conceptual diversity in Second Temple Jewish literature regarding the afterlife and *how* bodies come back to life,[19] the mnemonic configurations of deceased bodies themselves tends to follow a descriptive pattern set out in Judean scriptural texts. Most texts speak of a return to the *ground* (e.g., Gen 3:19; Job 34:15; Ps 22:30), which leads many resurrection-oriented texts to speak of bodies either *sleeping in* or *returning to* the *dust of the earth* (e.g., Dan 12:1–3; 2 Macc 12:44–45; *1 En.* 92:3, 100:5–6; *Pss. Sol.* 3:1–2). One noteworthy strand of tradition relates to the narrative depiction of martyrs' bodies; the story of the mother and her seven sons in 2 Maccabees 7, with its graphic descriptions of dismemberment and other forms of torture, serves to underscore the conviction and importance of resurrection as a process of *gaining-back* that which was taken (see also 2 Macc 14:43–46). The promise of reconstituted flesh serves as a just sign that the martyrs have not been forgotten. Complementing this, other resurrection texts offer a more beatific promise of somatic transformation toward a celestial and otherworldly ideal (Dan 12:3; *1 En.* 104:2, 4, 6; *T. Mos.* 10:9). Despite the diversity across these texts, the deceased body is remembered not so much for its own sake, but rather for the sake of remembering injustice and punctuating the hope of restoration and even transformation.

The undisputed letters of Paul contain many of these same mnemonic constructions of deceased bodies. In 1 Thessalonians, for example, those who have died are described as having "fallen asleep" in the Lord (1 Thess 4:13–18). But elsewhere in the undisputed letters, the memory of deceased bodies takes a much more dynamic and even individualized focus. In many cases, Paul personalizes the language of death and resurrection, thus constructing a vision of the living, still breathing body as something that is perpetually in a state of death and revivification. In Galatians 2, for instance, Paul perceives himself as being continually in a state of co-crucifixion with Christ: "I have been crucified

---

19 See Elledge, *Resurrection of the Dead in Early Judaism*, for a recent overview of the period literature. To cite only a few examples: the Epistle of Enoch speaks of the re-embodiment of souls (*1 En.* 103:4). The Book of *Jubilees*, by contrast, prefers that the "bones [of the deceased remain] … rest[ing] in the earth," while the righteous nevertheless continue to exist (*Jub.* 23:29–31). More often than not, however, the deceased undergo some form of restorative transformation into a luminous, angelic glory-body (Dan 12:1–3; *1 En.* 62:15–16; *Pss. Sol.* 3:12; *T. Mos.* 10:9; see also *1 En.* 58:2–6).

with Christ [and I am still hanging there] (συνεσταύρωμαι) …" (2:19–20).[20] Similarly, in Philippians 3 Paul personalizes the resurrection experience by insisting that he has a share in Christ's death and so also in Christ's resurrection: "I want to know Christ and the power of his resurrection and the sharing of his sufferings by becoming like him in his death, if somehow I may attain the resurrection from the dead" (3:10–11). And most pointedly, in the ostensibly authentic 2 Corinthians 4, Paul writes: "[we apostles are] always carrying in the body the death of Jesus, so that the life of Jesus may also be made visible in our bodies. For while we live, we are always being given up to death for Jesus' sake, so that the life of Jesus may be made visible in our mortal flesh" (4:10–11).[21] Each of these texts contributes to a mnemonic framework in which the personalized, apostolic body is remembered as a site in which death and resurrection are actualized.

Importantly, while Paul is in part asking his readers to think of their own bodies as corpses that are being brought back to life (e.g., Gal 5:22–24; Romans 6–8, 12:1–3), he also (and perhaps with more punctuation) is constructing a vision in which the bodies of the apostles are continually undergoing suffering and death so as to impart life to the communities with which they are associated. This is particularly seen in 2 Cor 4:12: "death is at work in us [apostles], but life in you [Corinthians]." What results from this is a particular mnemonic framework, one that Paul himself has helped construct, and which sets a pattern for how Paul will be remembered after his death. In the posthumous Pauline pseudepigrapha and narratives, Paul's body itself is mnemonically inscribed through this framework of perpetual death and coming-back-to-life. Paul's own body is remembered as a site in which death and resurrection are enacted.

Remembering Paul's Body: The Post-Pauline Writings

Few figures in the early Christian movement were so variously understood and vigorously interpreted as the apostle Paul. In his masterful treatment of Paul in the second century, Ben White rightly notes that, "within a century and a half after his death, Paul had become '*the* Apostle' for an entire range of ideological adversaries."[22] Within this vast array of ideological stances, Paul's reputation is

---

20 Here noting the force of the perfect tense, συνεσταύρωμαι (cf., James D. G. Dunn, *The Theology of Paul the Apostle* [Grand Rapids: Michigan, 1998], 485).

21 In addition to these statements found in Galatians, Philippians, and 2 Corinthians, similar conceptions can also be found in Romans 6 and 12, as well as 1 Thessalonians 5.

22 White, *Remembering Paul*, 7.

often constructed through the framework of the perpetually dying and rising-again apostolic body. I draw our attention to three specific depictions of the apostle's body in the Pauline pseudepigrapha and narratives. The first comes from the canonical Acts of the Apostles (early second century), the second from the Epistle to the Colossians (late-first century), and the third from the *Acts of Thecla* (mid-second century). In their own way, each text commemorates a vision of Paul's body that simultaneously keys into the pattern set out in the undisputed letters: that is, the pattern of the perpetually dying and rising-again apostolic body.

Acts of the Apostles

While certain aspects of the Pauline body in Acts are well known, others are less so. The more infamous elements concern the narrative happenings of Acts 9, where Saul's eyes are blinded for three days, at which time his sight is restored through the laying-on of Ananias' hands (Acts 9:8–19). Through this temporary somatic infliction, transformation is born. As the Acts narrative unfolds, Paul's body makes many other appearances. In more than one instance, Paul's body is presented as a channel of divine power for healing and miracles (Acts 14:9–10; 15:12; 19:11–12; 20:7–12), and on two occasions Paul's bodily presence is mistaken for that of a deity.[23] In other instances, Paul's body is presented as a sacred space, one that is subject to vows and on which Jewish piety is inscribed (Acts 18:18; 21:20–26).[24]

For the implied author and readers of Acts, Paul clearly is a figure worthy of remembrance, yet the raw reputational details of his life are not the stuff that one would normally use to construct an honorific image. For example, the Pauline body is a suffering and persecuted body; it is a somatic space inflicted with beatings, sexual humiliations such as forceable undressing, and imprisonments (Acts 14:19–20; 16:19–40; 21:27–36; 24:27; 27:1; 28:16). On the whole, Paul's somatic image is difficult to negotiate, yet the author of Acts is able to create a favorable reputation for Paul by keying[25] these somatic features into the epis-

---

23 (I) In Acts 14:11–18, Paul is taken for Hermes, to which he rends his clothing to expose *his naked body* as proof of his humanity, and (II) in Acts 28:3–6, *Paul's hand* is impervious to a snakebite, to which the locals of Malta presume him to be a god of some kind.

24 Indeed, for the Paul of Acts it is not unreasonable to ask Gentiles to mark their bodies with circumcision (see Acts 16:3, where Paul has Timothy "circumcised because of the Jews"), even though such a request enrages the Paul of the epistles (see esp. Gal 5:2–6).

25 My use of the term "keying" draws upon the work of Barry Schwartz, who explains, "keying transforms the meaning of activities understood in terms of one reference frame by comparing them with activities understood in terms of another… . Keying defines social memory's function, matching the past to the present as (1) a model *of* society, reflecting its needs, interests, fears, and aspirations; (2) a model *for* society, a template for thought,

tolary notion of the body that perpetually dies and rises again.[26] For instance, the value of Paul's body is self-described in Acts 20:23–24 in relation to its suffering for the good news of Jesus. Similarly, not only is Paul able to bring the dead back to life (Acts 20:7–12), but Paul's body itself is also permitted to come-back-to-life after being stoned to (the point of) death (Acts 14:19–20). Most noteworthy of all is the ending of Acts. After a long set of trials and imprisonments (Acts 21–28), the Lukan Paul is a suffering apostle who does not die but rather ends his life in a state of ongoing imprisonment (see esp. 21:10–14; Acts 28:16, 30–31). On this point, the somatic display that prophetically accompanies Paul's farewell speech in Acts 21:10–14 is particularly noteworthy: the prophet Agabus takes Paul's belt and binds his (Agabus') hands and feet with it, indicating that such will be the fate of the belt's owner. Here the Pauline body takes centre stage, albeit indirectly through the somatic enactment of the prophet Agabus. Paul's body is to be subjected to suffering, and in response to this prophetic dramatization, the apostle responds: "I am ready not only to be bound but also to die" (Acts 21:13). By giving voice and somatic agency to the long-deceased Paul, the Lukan author constructs a reputation for the apostle that keys into the notion of the body that perpetually dies and rises again.[27]

---

sentiment, morality, and conduct; and (3) a *frame* within which people find meaning for their experience… . In these senses, social memory is preserved by and for the function it performs" (Barry Schwartz, "Where There's Smoke, There's Fire: Memory and History," in *Memory and Identity in Ancient Judaism and Early Christianity: A Conversation with Barry Schwartz*, ed. Tom Thatcher, SemeiaSt 78 [Atlanta: SBL Press, 2014], 7–37 [15–16, emphasis original]).

26 My argument at this point presumes that the author of Acts was aware of (at least some of) the Pauline epistles and further that s/he framed the portrayal of Paul in Acts in light of those epistles; in defense of this presumption, see Frederick S. Tappenden, "Luke and Paul in Dialogue: Ritual Meals and Risen Bodies as Instances of Conceptual Blending," in *Resurrection of the Dead: Biblical Traditions in Dialogue*, ed. Geert Van Oyen and Tom Shepherd, BETL 249 (Leuven: Peeters, 2012), 203–28; and "On the Difficulty of Molding a Rock: The Negotiation of Peter's Reputation in Early Christian Memory," in *Memory and Identity in Ancient Judaism and Early Christianity: A Conversation with Barry Schwartz*, ed. Tom Thatcher, SemeiaSt 78 (Atlanta: SBL Press, 2014), 263–87.

27 Framed in this way, Paul's image in Acts comes into clearer relief. Though the Pauline body is an incarcerated body, it is not a defamed or dishonored body. Rather, Paul is one who is innocent of the charges brought against him (Acts 26:30–32); his body is not that of a criminal but rather that of a Roman citizen (Acts 16:37–38; 22:25–28). Thus, when Paul is imprisoned and the shackles are miraculously opened by an earthquake (Acts 16:25–36), there is no need for Paul to escape, for his innocent sufferings bring about the proclamation of the gospel to the prison guards. And, as already noted, the author concludes the Acts narrative by fashioning an image of Paul as one in ongoing imprisonment with the promise of ongoing proclamation. Note that Paul's imprisonment in Rome is a comparably comfortable imprisonment, one that is funded at his own expense (Acts 28:30). On

Colossians

Like Acts, much of the Pauline pseudepigraphal literature constructs an image of the apostle as one perpetually suffering for the sake of the gospel. Among the canonical and non-canonical pseudepigraphal letters, Colossians, Ephesians, the Pastorals, *Epistle to the Laodiceans*, and *3 Corinthians* all present an image of Paul as one imprisoned.[28] In each of these texts, Paul is remembered as the suffering and imprisoned apostle who nevertheless remains present before his communities through the oral-performance of texts that bear his name. This is particularly found in Colossians, where Paul's suffering body takes an acute and peculiar focus.

The key passage I draw our attention to is the ever-enigmatic Col 1:24, which reads: "I am now rejoicing in my sufferings for your sake, and in my flesh I am completing what is lacking in Christ's afflictions for the sake of his body, that is, the church" (NRSV). The interpretive spectrum for this text is unusually broad, and with good reason. The Pauline voice ostensibly suggests that Christ's sufferings were in some sense deficient and in need of Paul's supplement. But when this passage is seen in the light of broader Pauline traditions, the enigmatic statements of 1:24 suggest a developing reputation in which Paul's somatic activities possess positive benefit for those who remember him. At one level, this passage echoes 2 Cor 4:10–12, where the apostle's sufferings play a beneficial role for the Corinthians ("always carrying in the body the death of Jesus, so the life of Jesus may also be made visible in our bodies… . death is at work in us, but life in you" [2 Cor 4:10, 12]). To this we can note that elsewhere in Colossians Paul is presented as struggling for those who have not seen him face-to-face (2:1), and as one who is present in spirit even while absent in body (2:5).

Nevertheless, Col 1:24 has a more commemorative—perhaps, hagiographic—sense than what we see in 2 Corinthians. In the post-Pauline period of the late-first century, where the Pauline communities are making sense of the death of their founder, the audience now looks back on and commemorates an image of Paul as one who had a role in the salvific process. Angela Standhartinger has argued that Colossians is written as a response to two interrelated crises in the Pauline communities: the death of Paul, on the one hand, and the

---

this point, Acts is both mitigating the dishonor that comes with imprisonment (by suggesting that Paul is able to move around freely) while also presenting Paul as one who is affluent enough to be able to fund his own house arrest (Acts 28:30).

28 To this we can also note that both Philippians and 2 Corinthians—two undisputed letters that bear the marks of later Christian redaction—betray strong themes of suffering and imprisonment.

delayed eschaton, on the other.[29] To some extent, all of Paul's communities were founded as eschatological communities that expected the end immediately (e.g., 1 Thess 4:13–5:11; 1 Cor 1:7–8; 7:29; Rom. 13:11–12). When Paul died, and the eschaton continued to delay, suspicions and questions undoubtedly arose as to the veracity of Paul's message. Colossians provides a solution to these questions, specifically by keying an understanding of Paul's body into Paul's own self-presentation of perpetually dying and rising-again. The conclusion of the author of Colossians is that Paul had to die because the sufferings of his body had a role to play in the eschatological achievement. Now that he has died (been martyred?), his role is fulfilled and the precise time of the end is relativized (hence Col 3:1–4, which asserts a realized eschatological vision and thus dismisses a more teleological eschatology).

In Colossians, Paul's body is remembered not for its own sake, but rather because it embodies suffering in a way that contributes to the salvific process. Accordingly, through the cumulative sufferings of not only Christ but also Paul, the implied readers of Colossians are compelled to embody in their somatic selves Christ's resurrection.[30] A common theme emerges. Paul's body is subject to perpetual death and life, to ongoing absence and presence. Though he has long since passed and thus is absent, his body nevertheless continues to hold relevance and importance for the post-Pauline reader. In ways different though not totally incongruent with Acts, Colossians fixes mnemonic significance to the suffering of the apostle's body.

The Acts of Thecla

The final text I draw attention to is perhaps one of the most famous depictions of Paul's body. The passage comes from the mid-second century *Acts of Thecla*, where in chapter 3 we find the following description of the apostle:

---

29 Angela Standhartinger, *Studien zur Entstehungsgeschichte und Intention des Kolosserbriefs*, NovTSup 94 (Leiden: Brill, 1999).

30 Thus Col 2:12 and 3:1: "you were buried with him in baptism, you were also raised with (συνηγέρθητε) him through faith in the power of God … so if you have been raised with Christ (συνηγέρθητε τῷ Χριστῷ), seek the things that are above, where Christ is, seated at the right hand of God." As subjects in the salvific drama, the participatory dimension is diminished for Christ-devotees. The transformation from death to life takes place not on the coordinates of the human body but rather in Christ himself (see esp. 1:22). This is seen explicitly in Col 1:21–23, which describes the salvific drama in terms entirely external to the Christ-believing subject; so v. 22: "he has now reconciled in his fleshly body through death, so as to present you holy and blameless and irreproachable before him." While it is true that v. 23 includes a kind of moral requirement of ongoing obedience, the entire salvific process is already complete and only awaits revelation.

> Then [Onesiphorus] saw Paul coming: a man short in stature, with a bald head, bowed legs, in good condition, eyebrows that met, a fairly large nose, and full of grace. At times he seemed human, at other times he looked like an angel.

The image of Paul's body in this text is curious on several levels. While this description does not indicate that Paul's body underwent perpetual death and life, this physiognomic depiction nevertheless engages in a related process of integrating contrasting opposites. Viewed through the lens of ancient Mediterranean physiognomy—that is, the process by which bodily traits/features are seen to depict aspects of an individual's character—the image of Paul presented in this passage is, for the most part, quite negative. (1) Paul's "short stature" is a sign of weakness and unimportance; (2) while his "bald head" could be a sign of intelligence, it also is a sign of sensuality; (3) his "bowed legs" are a sign of cowardice and weakness; (4) his state of being "in a good condition" (lit. well fed, or plump) indicates foolishness, laziness, and sleepiness; (5) his "eye-brows that meet" are a sign of crudeness and a lack of intelligence; and (6) his "fairly large nose" (lit. a crooked nose) indicates slyness, combativeness, cunning, and even cowardice. And yet, in the midst of all these negative traits, Paul is described as one who is "full of grace" and, though human, "looked like an angel." These latter descriptions betray an air of physiognomic esteem—even sublimity, as seen in the reference to looking "like an angel"—which is further reiterated in *Acts of Thecla* 21. In this later passage, Thecla looks out into a crowd of people to catch a glimpse of Paul, whose body had recently been flogged by the governor, and in doing so "she saw the Lord sitting there, in the appearance of Paul." Again, the narrative betrays a dizzying configuration of both negative and positive somatic descriptions, which simultaneously dishonour and honour the apostle.

János Bollók has outlined the physiognomy of Paul's body in *Acts of Thecla* 3, noting in particular many intertextual connections between the *Acts of Thecla* and 2 Corinthians.[31] According to Bollók, connections with 2 Corinthians are as follows: (1) Paul is described by those in Corinth as powerless (2 Cor 10:10; 11:29–30; 12:5, 9–10); this matches his shortness in *Acts of Thecla* 3; (2) Paul is described as one who "acts according to the flesh" (2 Cor 10:2) which implies sensuality and laziness; this matches his baldness and bowed legs in *Acts of Thecla* 3; (3) Paul is described as humble and timid (2 Cor 10:1); this matches his bowed leg in *Acts of Thecla* 3; (4) Paul is described as a fool (2 Cor 12:11); this matches his "good condition" (or plumpness) in *Acts of Thecla* 3; (5) Paul

31 János Bollók, "The Description of Paul in the Acta Pauli," in *The Apocryphal Acts of Paul and Thecla*, ed. Jan N. Bremmer, SAAA 2 (Kampen: Kok Pharos, 1996), 1–15.

is described as merciless (2 Cor 13:2); this matches his meeting eyebrows in *Acts of Thecla* 3; and (6) Paul is described as cunning or tricky (2 Cor 12:16); this matches his crooked nose in *Acts of Thecla* 3. Taken together, Bollók notes that in both texts, Paul embodies a diverse array of personal characteristics, some honouring and others dishonouring. In 2 Corinthians, Paul uses these diverse depictions to his advantage, leveraging the notion of perpetual death and coming-back-to-life as a way of circumventing the dishonour being hurled upon him by the so-called "super apostles" (2 Cor 11:21–12:10; see also 4:7–12).[32] *Acts of Thecla* does not employ the same rhetoric of death and coming-back-to-life—the closest it comes is the Jesus-esque vision of Paul's flogged body in *Acts of Thecla* 21—though it does promote an image of Paul whereby the apostle's somatic character simultaneously embodies dissonant reputational features.

Noteworthy here is the work of Callie Callon, who examines physiognomy as a strategy of persuasion in early Christian discourses.[33] Callon recognizes that, despite a tendency among early Christian authors to utilize common physiognomic depictions to further their rhetorical ends (either by elevating Christ-believers or denigrating outsiders), not all physiognomic depictions were exclusively positive. For example, some ancient Christian texts were content with an "ugly" Jesus. Despite the fact that such descriptions likely threatened claims to Jesus' divinity, the authors who promoted such images likely had larger rhetorical goals in mind, such as "proving" the corporeal humanity of Jesus (to name only one).[34] As a correlate, something similar may well be happening with the depictions of Paul's body—and so also, Paul's reputation—in the *Acts of Thecla*. Here as in Acts and in Colossians, with respect to Paul, one of the larger rhetorical goals to address is: how ought one to negotiate the apostle's favourable reputation (on the one hand) with the otherwise difficult and unflattering accounts of Paul that are enshrined within the oral and written traditions passed down within early Christ-believing communities? To this end, the *Acts of Thecla* asks its readers to recognize that a distance or a space

32 See also J. Albert Harrill, "Invective Against Paul (2 Cor 10:10), the Physiognomics of the Ancient Slave Body, and the Greco-Roman Rhetoric of Manhood," in *Antiquity and Humanity: Essays on Ancient Religion and Philosophy Presented to Hans Dieter Betz on his 70th Birthday*, ed. Adela Yarbro Collins and Margaret M. Mitchell (Tubingen: Mohr Siebeck, 2001), 189–213. Harrill sees Paul's opponents in 2 Corinthians 10–13 as taking advantage of common physiognomic conceptions as a way of discrediting the apostle's masculinity (and thus also his character).

33 Callie Callon, *Reading Bodies: Physiognomy as a Strategy of Persuasion in Early Christian Discourse*, LNTS 597; (London: T&T Clark, 2019).

34 See further, Callon, *Reading Bodies*, 158.

exists between Paul's appearance and Paul's character; between what Paul is thought to have said and done, on the one hand, and his significance and meaning, on the other. Perhaps this is partly what the *Acts of Thecla* is getting at when it notes that, prior to encountering Paul on the Royal Road in *Acts of Thecla* 3, Onesiphorus "had never seen [Paul] in the flesh, but only in the spirit" (*Acts of Thecla* 2). On one level, the text invites its reader not to be duped by what they see, for this slothful, well-fed, lazy, unintelligent fool actually is full of grace and comparable to an angel. Or, in the language of *Acts of Thecla* 21, though Paul's body is flogged and dishonoured, to those who view him properly (as Thecla does) the apostle looks like the Lord.

Similar to Acts and Colossians, the *Acts of Thecla* fixes mnemonic significance to the shamed and suffering apostolic body, and it does so in ways that key into Paul's own self-presentation in the undisputed letters of perpetual suffering, death, and resurrection.

Conclusion: Resurrection and the Memory of Paul's Body

The focus of this paper has been an examination of how the bodies of the deceased are remembered by those who commemorate them. My primary focus has been upon the letters of Paul, a Second Temple Judean whose writings simultaneously inherit an array of broader Jewish tradition while also shaping the activities and thought-worlds of emerging Christ-believing communities. As we have seen, Paul himself constructs notions of the apostolic body as one that perpetually dies-and-rises-again. In turn, this mnemonic framework is taken up by later commemorators who use it to shape the apostle's image in various ways. To these ends, through the performance of texts that commemorate an image of Paul as the constantly suffering apostle, the memory of Paul's body is the memory of one who is perpetually dying and coming back to life. Within the emerging movement of Christ-devotees, though Paul had long since passed, the memory of his suffering and dying body found lasting significance.

At one level, the authors of each of the texts examined above function as reputational entrepreneurs who utilize death and resurrection as a mnemonic framework to define the apostle's image through the memory of his body. Why? What is at stake in remembering Paul as a figure whose somatic presence embodied both suffering and death? One obvious answer relates to the rhetoric of suffering and martyrdom that emerges among Christ-believing communities from the late-first century onward.[35] Another answer may be found in the developing eschatology and asceticism of these Pauline communities, such that their remembered founder is seen to emblemize a pattern of living that is somatically disciplined and socially marginalized. Still another answer may be found in the recognition that Paul's was a difficult reputation in the early Christian movement, one that was subject to much contestation and dispute in the first and second centuries. By keying Paul and his body into notions of death and resurrection, Paul's commemorators are able to leverage a presumed tension between death and life as a way of negotiating many tensions within Paul's reputational image. In the *Acts of Thecla*, for instance, the reader is invited to see this slothful, unintelligent fool as one who is full of grace and like an angel. Similarly, in Acts Paul's reputation is more than once contested by the characters within the narrative (e.g., Acts 14:11–18; 21:27–36; 28:3–6), and the overall tenor of Acts seeks to convey Paul's innocence and civic status in the face of misunderstanding and false accusations (Acts 26:30–32). We see a related dynamic in Colossians, where the shame associated with Paul's suffering and imprisonment is transformed to possess a salvific purpose (Col 1:24).[36]

By keying the memory of Paul's body into a resurrection frame, those who remember him are able to better negotiate the difficulty of his reputation. This is particularly punctuated by the fact that the logic of resurrection is a logic of reversal,[37] and so just as life can flow from death, so too can a favourable reputation flow from otherwise difficult reputational elements. All of this underscores that Paul is a figure of early Christian memory and culture making.[38] In considering the depictions of Paul's body, we do better to trace the many different and interlocking reputational paths that Paul's image takes, each of which cross over with one another, intersect, diverge, meet again, and even double back in early Christian traditions.

---

35 See, for example, Candida R. Moss, *The Other Christs: Imitating Jesus in Ancient Christian Ideologies of Martyrdom* (Oxford: Oxford University Press, 2010) and *Ancient Christian Martyrdom: Diverse Practices, Theologies, and Traditions* (New Haven: Yale University Press, 2012). See also Esler, "'Remember my Fetters.'"

36 Note: the canonical Pauline pseudepigrapha also include elements in which Paul's reputation is being contested, specifically around the authenticity of his writings (2 Thess 2:2).

37 See Tappenden, *Resurrection in Paul*, 57–58 and 190–192 for discussions of how the notion of reversal is inherent in conceptions of resurrection. Accordingly, conceptions of resurrection provide useful tools with which to think about reversals.

38 See further, White, *Remembering Paul.*

Bibliography

Aitken, Ellen Bradshaw. *Jesus' Death in Early Christian Memory: The Poetics of Passion.* NTOA 53. Göttingen: Vandenhoeck & Ruprecht, 2004.

Avemarie, Friedrich, and Hermann Lichtenberger, eds. *Auferstehung = Resurrection: The Fourth Durham—Tübingen Research Symposium: Resurrection, Transformation, and Exaltation in the Old Testament, Ancient Judaism, and Early Christianity.* WUNT 135. Tübingen: Mohn Siebeck, 2001.

Babcock, William S., ed. *Paul and the Legacies of Paul.* Dallas: Southern Methodist University Press, 1990.

Bieringer, Reimund, Veronica Koperski, and Bianca Lataire, eds. *Resurrection in the New Testament.* BETL 165. Leuven: Peeters, 2002.

Boakye, Andrew. *Death and Life: Resurrection, Restoration, and Rectification in Paul's Letter to the Galatians.* Eugene, OR: Pickwick, 2017.

Bollók, János. "The Description of Paul in the Acta Pauli." Pages 1–15 in *The Apocryphal Acts of Paul and Thecla.* Edited by Jan N. Bremmer. SAAA 2. Kampen: Kok Pharos, 1996.

Callon, Callie. *Reading Bodies: Physiognomy as a Strategy of Persuasion in Early Christian Discourse.* LNTS 597. London: T & T Clark, 2019.

Chang, Kai-Hsuan. *The Impact of Bodily Experience on Paul's Resurrection Theology.* LNTS 655. London: T & T Clark, 2022.

Charlesworth, James H., ed. *Resurrection: The Origin and Future of a Biblical Doctrine.* London: T & T Clark, 2006.

Dickson, Courtney, and Bridgette Watson. "Remains of 215 Children Found Buried at Former B.C. Residential School." *CBC* News, May 27, 2021. https://www.cbc.ca/news/canada/british-columbia/tk-emlúps-te-secwépemc-215-children-former-kamloops-indian-residential-school-1.6043778.

Dunn, James. D. G. *The Theology of Paul the Apostle.* Grand Rapids: Michigan, 1998.

Elledge, C. D. *Resurrection of the Dead in Early Judaism: 200 BCE–CE 200.* Oxford: Oxford University Press, 2017.

Eneas, Bryan. "Sask. First Nation Announces Discovery of 751 Unmarked Graves near Former Residential School." *CBC* News, June 24, 2021. https://www.cbc.ca/news/canada/saskatchewan/cowessess-marieval-indian-residential-school-news-1.6078375.

Engberg-Pedersen, Troels. *Cosmology and Self in the Apostle Paul: The Material Spirit.* Oxford: Oxford University Press, 2010.

Esler, Philip F. "'Remember my Fetters': Memorialisation of Paul's Imprisonment." Pages 231–258 in *Explaining Christian Origins and Early Judaism: Contributions from the Cognitive and Social Sciences.* Edited by Petri Luomanen, Ilkka Pyysiäinen, and Risto Uro. BibInt 89. Leiden: Brill, 2007.

Fine, Gary Alan. *Difficult Reputations: Collective Memories of the Evil, Inept, and Controversial*. Chicago: University of Chicago Press, 2001.

Glancy, Jennifer A. *Corporeal Knowledge: Early Christian Bodies*. Oxford: Oxford University Press, 2010.

Harrill, J. Albert. "Invective Against Paul (2 Cor 10:10), the Physiognomics of the Ancient Slave Body, and the Greco-Roman Rhetoric of Manhood." Pages 189–213 in *Antiquity and Humanity: Essays on Ancient Religion and Philosophy Presented to Hans Dieter Betz on his 70th Birthday*. Edited by Adela Yarbro Collins and Margaret M. Mitchell. Tubingen: Mohr Siebeck, 2001.

Johnston, Philip S. *Shades of Sheol: Death and Afterlife in the Old Testament*. Downers Grove: Intervarsity Press, 2002.

Karlsen Seim, Turid, and Jorunn Økland, eds. *Metamorphoses: Resurrection, Body, and Transformative Practices in Early Christianity*. Ekstasis 1. Berlin: de Gruyter, 2009.

Kirk, J. R. Daniel. *Unlocking Romans: Resurrection and the Justification of God*. Grand Rapids: Eerdmans, 2008.

Lampe, Peter. *From Paul to Valentinus: Christians at Rome in the First Two Centuries*. Minneapolis: Fortress Press, 2003.

Lehtipuu, Outi. *Debates over the Resurrection of the Dead: Constructing Christian Identity*. OECS. Oxford: Oxford University Press, 2015.

Lundhaug, Hugo. *Images of Rebirth: Cognitive Poetics and Transformational Soteriology in the Gospel of Philip and the Exegesis on the Soul*. NHMS 73. Leiden: Brill, 2010.

Martin, Dale B. *The Corinthian Body*. New Haven: Yale University Press, 1995.

McGlothlin, Thomas D. *Resurrection as Salvation: Development and Conflict in Pre-Nicene Paulinism*. Cambridge: Cambridge University Press, 2018.

Mitchell, Margaret M. *Paul, the Corinthians, and the Birth of Christian Hermeneutics*. Cambridge: Cambridge University Press, 2010.

Moss, Candida R. *The Other Christs: Imitating Jesus in Ancient Christian Ideologies of Martyrdom*. Oxford: Oxford University Press, 2010.

———. *Ancient Christian Martyrdom: Diverse Practices, Theologies, and Traditions*. New Haven: Yale University Press, 2012.

———. *Divine Bodies: Resurrecting Perfection in the New Testament and Early Christianity*. New Haven: Yale University Press, 2019.

Nasrallah, Laura Salah. *Christian Responses to Roman Art and Architecture: The Second-Century Church Amid the Spaces of Empire*. Cambridge: Cambridge University Press, 2010.

Newman, Judith H. *Before the Bible: The Liturgical Body and the Formation of Scriptures in Early Judaism*. Oxford: Oxford University Press, 2019.

Nicklas, Tobias, Friedrich V. Reiterer, and Joseph Verheyden, eds. *The Human Body in Death and Resurrection*. Berlin: de Gruyter, 2009.

Nicklas, Tobias, Joseph Verheyden, Erik M. M. Eynickel, and Florentino García Martinez, eds. *Other Worlds and their Relation to this World: Early Jewish and Ancient Christian Traditions*. JSJSup 143. Leiden: Brill, 2010.
Øistein Endsjø, Dag. *Greek Resurrection Beliefs and the Success of Christianity*. New York: Palgrave Macmillan, 2009.
Oliver, Isaac W., and Gabriele Boccaccini, eds. *The Early Reception of Paul the Second Temple Jew: Text, Narrative, and Reception History*. LSTS 92. London, T&T Clark, 2019.
Park, Augustine S. J. "Remembering the Children: Decolonizing Community-Based Restorative Justice for Indian Residential Schools." *Contemporary Justice Review* 19.4 (2016): 424–444. https://doi.org/10.1080/10282580.2016.1226818.
Pervo, Richard. *The Making of Paul: Constructions of the Apostle in Early Christianity*. Minneapolis: Fortress Press, 2010.
Petrey, Taylor. *Resurrecting Parts: Early Christians on Desire, Reproduction, and Sexual Difference*. London: Routledge, 2015.
Scherbenske, Eric W. *Canonizing Paul: Ancient Editorial Practice and the* Corpus Paulinum. Oxford: Oxford University Press, 2013.
Schwartz, Barry. *Abraham Lincoln and the Forge of National Memory*. Chicago: University of Chicago Press, 2000.
———. "Where There's Smoke, There's Fire: Memory and History." Pages 7–37 in *Memory and Identity in Ancient Judaism and Early Christianity: A Conversation with Barry Schwartz*. Edited by Tom Thatcher. SemeiaSt 78. Atlanta: SBL Press, 2014.
Segal, Alan F. *Life after Death: A History of the Afterlife in the Religions of the West*. New York: Doubleday, 2004.
Setzer, Claudia. *Resurrection of the Body in Early Judaism and Early Christianity: Doctrine, Community, and Self-Definition*. Leiden: Brill, 2004.
Shiell, William David. *Reading Acts: The Lector and the Early Christian Audience*. BibIntS 70. Boston: Brill, 2004.
Standhartinger, Angela. *Studien zur Entstehungsgeschichte und Intention des Kolosserbriefs*. NovTSup 94. Leiden: Brill, 1999.
———. "Bringing Back to Life: Laments and the Origin of the So-Called Words of Institution." Pages 71–101 in *Coming Back to Life: The Permeability of Past and Present, Mortality and Immortality, Death and Life in the Ancient Mediterranean*. Edited by Frederick S. Tappenden and Carly Daniel-Hughes, with the assistance of Bradley N. Rice. Montreal: McGill University Library, 2017. Online: https://comingbacktolife.mcgill.ca.
Tappenden, Frederick S. "Aural-Performance, Conceptual Blending, and Intertextuality: The (Non-)Use of Scripture in Luke 24.45–48." Pages 180–200 in *The Gospel of Luke, Volume 3 of Biblical Interpretation in Early Christian Gospels*. Edited by Thomas R. Hatina. LNTS 376. London: T&T Clark, 2010.

———. "Luke and Paul in Dialogue: Ritual Meals and Risen Bodies as Instances of Conceptual Blending." Pages 203–228 in *Resurrection of the Dead: Biblical Traditions in Dialogue*. Edited by Geert Van Oyen and Tom Shepherd. BETL 249. Leuven: Peeters, 2012.

———. "On the Difficulty of Molding a Rock: The Negotiation of Peter's Reputation in Early Christian Memory." Pages 263–87 in *Memory and Identity in Ancient Judaism and Early Christianity: A Conversation with Barry Schwartz*. Edited by Tom Thatcher. SemeiaSt 78. Atlanta: SBL Press, 2014.

———. *Resurrection in Paul: Cognition, Metaphor, and Transformation*. ECL 19. Atlanta: SBL Press, 2016.

Tappenden, Frederick S., and Carly Daniel-Hughes, eds. *Coming Back to Life: The Permeability of Past and Present, Mortality and Immortality, Death and Life in the Ancient Mediterranean*. Editorial assistance from Bradley N. Rice. Montreal: McGill University Library, 2017. Online: http://comingbacktolife.mcgill.ca.

Van Oyen, Geert, and Tom Shepherd, eds. *Resurrection of the Dead: Biblical Traditions in Dialogue*. BETL 249. Leuven: Peeters, 2012.

Vermes, Geza. *The Resurrection*. London: Penguin, 2008.

Vinzent. Markus. *Christ's Resurrection in Early Christianity and the Making of the New Testament*. Franham: Ashgate, 2011.

Waldner, Katharina, Richard Gordon, and Wolfgang Spickermann, eds. *Burial Rituals, Ideas of Afterlife, and the Individual in the Hellensitic World and the Roman Empire*. PAWB 57. Stuttgart: Franz Steiner Verlag, 2016.

White, Benjamin L. *Remembering Paul: Ancient and Modern Contests over the Image of the Apostle*. Oxford: Oxford University Press, 2014.

Williams, Michael Allen. *Rethinking "Gnosticism": An Argument for Dismantling a Dubious Category*. Princeton: Princeton University Press, 1996.

Wright, N. T. *The Resurrection of the Son of God*. Minneapolis: Fortress Press, 2003.

Additional Notes to an Unfinished Symphony: Resurrection and Afterlife According to Mark

Sandra Huebenthal

Mark as a Symphony

Let us imagine the Gospel according to Mark is a symphony.[1] Its name is "Ἀρχή" and it consists of three movements, an overture and a coda. As it is habitually the case in a symphony, Ἀρχή also introduces the main theme, which is found in 1:15: "the kingdom of God has come close, change your mind and trust the good news."[2] The author subsequently executes it, whilst continually varying it, making it audible in a different way every time it is used.

The first movement of Mark's Ἀρχή is in a cheerful C Major, *allegro* and mostly in *forte*. It is powerful, colorful and varied. Already in this first movement there are, however, undertones, modest accounts and dissonances, a development that will become more intense in the following movements. In the beginning, the key changes repeatedly to an A minor. The execution of the motif becomes more and more disharmonic and subject to syncopation, until the mood has finally completely changed at the end of the third movement. The *tempo* is still rather high, but the theme is mainly used in an inverse way and in the subdominant parallel D minor, which is known to be one of the keys of death.

In 15:39, the centurion's acknowledgment, "Indeed, this man was a Son of God," can be understood as the final chord, followed by a brief *coda*. Interestingly enough, this final chord is again in C major, while the following *coda* changes once more between a major and minor and closes unfinished on the leading tone in 16:8 with "they did initially not tell anything to anyone because they were scared." It is obvious that the end is hanging in the air and that something has to follow.

This unfinished state of the work was already noted in Antiquity when varied solutions were proposed to deal with it. Canonical readers of the New

1 The idea to read Mark as a symphony was first presented in Sandra Huebenthal, "Das Evangelium nach Markus. Eine Hörerfahrung," in *73 Ouvertüren. Die Buchanfänge der Bibel und ihre Botschaft*, ed. Egbert Ballhorn, Georg Steins, Regina Wildgruber and Uta Zwingenberger (Gütersloh: Gütersloher Verlagshaus, 2018), 461–70.

2 All translations are mine.

© BRILL SCHÖNINGH, 2023 | DOI:10.30965/9783657796212_010

Testament for more than 1500 years have listened to the version of the "Longer Ending" (16:9–20). In this version, it takes the disciples several attempts to arrive at Easter faith. They only do so after a personal encounter with the risen Jesus, who rebukes them for not believing those who had seen him before. It further needs a special commission for the eleven to eventually begin to proclaim the Gospel of Jesus Christ, after he has ascended into heaven and seated himself at the right hand of God. The narrator uses the last verse, 16:20b, as a consoling evaluation: The proclamation of the disciples is supported (τοῦ κυρίου συνεργοῦντος) by the Lord who confirms the message by accompanying signs (ἐπακολουθούντων σημείων). This makes for an interesting extension of the *coda*, which now closes in the dominant key of G Major.

All's well that ends well, it seems. The disciples in the end overcome their doubts, arrive at Easter faith and embark on a fruitful mission. The canonical reader recognizes allusions to the other canonical Gospels and their afterlife-stories, just as a good piece of music alludes to other works. The allusions include the encounter with Mary Magdalene (John 20:11–18), the disciples at Emmaus (Luke 24:13–35), the encounter at the table (Luke 24:36–49) and a slight rebuke (Luke 24:37–40; John 21:24–29; the element of doubt is also present in Matt 28:17), the commission to proclaim and baptize (Matt 20:19–20; Luke 24:28 and Acts 1:4–8) and the ascension into heaven (Luke 24:50–51; Acts 1:9–11). The preview of what their mission will look like further alludes to Acts, and the use of πίστις and σημεία echo Johannine language. Jesus' rebuke about the hardness of their hearts on the other hand closes a Markan theme. It links up with the narrator's evaluation of the disciples' faith in 6:52 (and Jesus' question about it in 8:17–18). The message seems to be that even the disciples needed some time to arrive at Easter faith. Just hearing about it was not enough. They needed a direct encounter with the risen Jesus. Their own proclamation after Jesus' ascension is a lot stronger and more convincing because Jesus works with them and the accompanying signs confirm the truth of their proclamation. This stabilizing[3] way to end the narrative solves a few problems connected with Jesus's resurrection and *afterlife*: it explains (a) the disciples' initial failure to belief and how they managed to overcome it in the course of time; (b) where Jesus is now; and (c) how encounter and communion with the risen Lord are possible.

3 The concept of progressive, regressive, and stabilizing narratives comes from Kenneth Gergen, "Erzählung, Moralische Identität und historisches Bewusstsein," in *Erzählung, Identität, Historisches Bewusstsein*, ed. Jürgen Straub, trans. Alexander Kochinka and Jürgen Straub (Frankfurt: Suhrkamp, 1998), 170–202. For an application to the Gospel narratives, especially their endings, see Sandra Huebenthal, *Reading the Mark's Gospel as a Text from Collective Memory* (Grand Rapids: Eerdmans, 2020), 251–53.

Even though it can be considered canonical, the stabilizing end is not how the storyline is presented at the beginning. Textual critics have made the compelling case that (a) the Markan text originally ended in 16:8 and (b) the Gospel's ending changed more in the first 150 years than at any other time.[4] Both insights cohere with each other as the somewhat abrupt end in Mark 16:8 leaves the reader dissatisfied both with the story and its theological message. The afterlife conception in Mark's text raises difficult questions, specifically: What does resurrection mean and how does one arrive at Easter faith? Where is Jesus—and especially his σῶμα—now? And how is encounter and community with the risen Lord possible?

When we return to the idea of Mark as a symphony, resurrection is the *clef* to the whole work. The different endings of Mark's Gospel have a lot to do with afterlife or the question about what should come after the *leading tone*. There are different answers, which have all been tried in the afterlife or reception history of the text.

As we will see in this essay, there are basically two ways to deal with the problem. One is to add further notes and finish the work, and the other is to perform the symphony in its current state as a meaningful piece of music. We will briefly explore both options in their chronological order. The first part will present two ways to finish the symphony: by rewriting it (section 2) and by adding a new end (section 3). The second part will consider different ways to read and understand the text as it originally ended (section 4). The focus will be on the question about how the different readings deal with the aforementioned theological questions. The conclusion and hermeneutical *coda* (section 5) will also address the latest development in textual research that Mark was not intended to be published as a book, but was considered a collection of unfinished notes (ὑπομνήματα).[5]

First Movement: Rewriting the Symphony in Matthew and Luke

The point of departure seems to be an initial dissatisfaction with the end of Mark on the part of its earliest readers. Two of these readers are the authors of Matthew and Luke. Somewhat surprising, their way of addressing this problem was not by simply providing a satisfactory end, but by re-writing the entire

4 David C. Parker, *The Living Text of the Gospel* (Cambridge: Cambridge University Press, 1997), 131.

5 Matthew Larsen, *Gospels before the Book* (New York: Oxford University Press, 2018).

work. In other words, they did not only add more notes to the symphony, but also changed the motifs, the keys and the outline of the work.

Matthew

According to a general consensus in New Testament scholarship, the Gospel of Matthew is the first attempt to deal with Mark and its dissatisfying ending. As Matthew Larsen has correctly observed, "Meeting readers' expectations in a pleasing way is important for book writing,"[6] but this is only half of the truth. When we read the New Testament texts as externalizations from collective memory and thus serving the identity construction of the groups behind them, the requirement is not only that the texts meet the readers' expectations in a satisfying way, but also meet the theological needs of the group.[7] We will concentrate on the last chapter of Matthew in order to see what has changed compared to the Markan text and how it provides answers to the theological questions.

Matthew both has closed (logical) gaps of Mark's story and added explanations. When Mary Magdalene and the other Mary reach the tomb,[8] the reader learns how it comes about that the stone has been lifted and why the guards do not interact with the women. The words and actions of the young man are basically the same as in Mark, but he is introduced as a messenger of the Lord (ἄγγελος γὰρ κυρίου), which gives the scene a different twist from the beginning. After his message is delivered, the women flee from the tomb in fear and with great joy (μετὰ φόβου καὶ χαρᾶς μεγάλης) rather than in fear alone. Matt 28:8–9 have a nice chiastic pattern to underline that the correct reaction to Jesus' resurrection should be joy and not fear. After the women have departed from the tomb in fear and great joy, they meet Jesus who tells them to rejoice[9] (χαίρετε) and not to fear (μὴ φοβεῖσθε). He repeats the command to tell the brothers to go to Galilee where they will see him.

Matthew does not inform the reader about the disciples' reaction, but instead directs the reader's attention to the guards and the high priests, who decide to spread the rumor that Jesus' body was stolen at night by the disciples.

---

6 Larsen, *Gospels before the Book*, 107.

7 For a comprehensive introduction into the underlying theory and general hermeneutical reflections about reading New Testament texts as externalizations of collective memory, see Sandra Huebenthal, "Frozen Moments. Early Christianity through the Lens of Social Memory Theory," in *Memory and Memories in Early Christianity*, ed. Simon Butticaz and Enrico Norelli, WUNT 398 (Tübingen: Mohr Siebeck, 2018), 17–43; *Reading Mark's Gospel*, 179–262, 523–29.

8 The otherwise unknown Salome does not appear in Matthew.

9 This detail escapes the attention of most commentators and translators who (mis)take χαίρετε for the standard greeting of the time instead of catching its double meaning.

Their action provides an explanation why contemporaries of those behind Matthew's Gospel do not accept the gospel. Even though the reader does not learn about the disciples' reaction to the women's message, the theme of disbelief is introduced. It is continued in the Gospel's last episode when the eleven meet Jesus on the mount in Galilee. Even though they see Jesus and kneel down, they are in doubt (ἰδόντες αὐτὸν προσεκύνησαν, οἱ δὲ ἐδίστασαν). The Gospel closes with Jesus' instruction and his confirmation that he will be with them until the end of the age. The disciples' reaction is not narrated. This is not by chance as the readers (a) know that they obeyed Jesus' command and (b) such a sentence would ruin the Gospel's powerful end. Jesus' final words can be read as transgressing the borders of the text and addressing everyone who hears them, not only the disciples on the mountain, *but* every audience of the text at every point in time.

As regards the theological questions, Matthew confirms the impression that a Markan reader might have, namely that it needs an encounter with the risen Lord as a prerequisite to arrive at Easter faith. Like Mark, Matthew does not include details about the nature of Jesus' afterlife or the location of his body. The fact that the women take hold of Jesus' feet suggests that some physicality of the resurrected state is implied. Intriguingly, Jesus speaks to both the women and the disciples, but receives no answer. It suggests that encountering the risen Jesus was a one-way-street. While meeting the risen Lord seems entirely possible, a communion with him remains difficult to envision if the faithful are reduced to a passive role. The question as to *how* exactly will Jesus, including his resurrected body, be with his disciples until the end of the age remains unsolved.

Luke

In 24:1–12, Luke also gives a summary of what happened to the women at the tomb and how they process the events. Apart from the addition of two men in shining garments talking to them, the scenery is more reminiscent of Mark than of Matthew. The women clearly can't make much of the men's words, so the men remind them of Jesus' own words that the Son of Man would be handed over to sinners, be crucified and rise on the third day. After the women remember Jesus' own words, in connection with their own experiences with Jesus, they return to the disciples and deliver the message. In the circle of the disciples, the already known reaction is disbelief. The message of the women, even connected with Jesus's own prediction, is not enough for them to arrive at Easter faith.

The story of the disciples at Emmaus (24:13–35) settles the matter: in order to arrive at Easter faith, it is not enough just to encounter the risen Lord. This encounter needs to connect to their previous experiences with Jesus and requires preparation insofar as the disciples need to be ready and willing to accept a different interpretation of the events than the semi-stable identity-construct they develop as they leave Jerusalem behind. Once they are receptive for a different interpretation, they are ready not only to see, but also to recognize the risen Lord with whom they have just experienced communion in sharing the word and breaking bread.[10]

When they return to Jerusalem, they encounter the eleven and the others who also have arrived at Easter faith through Peter's encounter with the risen Jesus. Once they all agree that Jesus is alive, he appears in their midst and wishes them peace. This third apparition functions to explain that the risen Lord is neither a ghost nor another form of a vision, but is alive and even eating. He reminds them once more of his predictions and Israel's scriptures as the foundation of faith in Christ. Once this is settled, Jesus entrusts them with their mission: to bear witness for the proclamation of repentance and the forgiveness of sins for all people. Before he is carried up to heaven (ἀνεφέρετο εἰς τὸν οὐρανόν), Jesus promises to send them down the promise of his father (τὴν ἐπαγγελίαν τοῦ πατρός μου) and blesses them.

Luke thus solves the first theological question very much the same way as Mark and Matthew. In order to arrive at Easter faith, one needs an encounter with the risen Lord. This encounter, however, needs to connect to previous experiences with Jesus and/or requires preparation by closely listening to Jesus' words and Israel's scriptures. Otherwise, it is impossible to recognize the risen Jesus. Luke's new twist to the first question nicely connects the disciples with the new and non-Jewish target audiences of the Gospel. Luke makes a clear point that faith in Jesus means faith in Israel's Messiah, even for non-Jews. Once this prerequisite is accepted, an encounter with the risen Lord or his witnesses paves the way to Easter faith, which is habitually enjoyed in community—only Peter encounters Jesus on his own—and in commensality around Israel's Scriptures.

Luke's risen Jesus is even more physical than the one of Matthew. In his encounter with the eleven and the others in Jerusalem (24:36–43), he distinguishes himself from a πνεῦμα, claiming that he has flesh and bones. He invites

10 For a more thorough treatment of the Emmaus story, see Sandra Huebenthal, "Luke 24:13–35 and Social Memory in Luke," in *Biblical Interpretation in Early Christian Gospels. Volume 3: The Gospel of Luke*, ed. Thomas R. Hatina, LNTS 376 (London: T & T Clark, 2010), 85–95. For a novel reading of the entire Gospel as a text from the perspective of collective memory, see Sandra Huebenthal, "Another Frozen Moment. Reading Luke in a Social Memory Theoretical Framework," PIBA 41/42 (2019): 23–43.

them to see, but still they do not believe, though this time it is because of joy.[11] Whether his meal of fish settles the matter remains unclear. However, the reader learns that the risen Lord has flesh and bones (and can be touched) and can eat. As regards the question about where Jesus' body is now, Luke provides a plausible scenario in a world that is familiar with apotheosis: the body of the risen Lord is offered up and ascends to heaven.

Encounter and communion with the risen Lord are possible and the encounter on the road to Emmaus shows that it does not have to be in the form of a one-way communication, as it could be construed in Matthew. The encounter with Jesus in Jerusalem, however, displays a similar picture as in Matthew: only Jesus talks and acts while the disciples and the others are glad, but remain silent and have their doubts. They are never portrayed as interacting with him. Jesus' assurance to send them what the father has promised him along with his ascension to heaven indicate that communion with Jesus will be different in the future. It will not be a continuation of what they have experienced during their time with him.

The exact character of this new type of communion remains opaque in Luke, just as it is not clear what the ἐπαγγελία of the father is. These gaps are closed in Acts where Luke extends the time with the risen Lord from one day to forty days and includes his teaching about the kingdom of God (Acts 1:3). He is also more specific about the ἐπαγγελία of the father: the disciples will be baptized in the Holy Spirit (1:5) and will receive δύναμις when the Holy Spirit comes down on them (1:8). In the course of Acts, it will become gradually clear that the Holy Spirit is the basis of community with Jesus after his resurrection and ascension. It is through the Spirit that the disciples will teach, heal, work miracles and experience community. The sending of the Spirit on the baptized will eventually become an identity marker for the Χριστιανοί. As we learn from Paul's vocation, direct encounters with the risen Jesus are still possible, but they appear in the form of visions and as encounters with the Spirit within groups rather than among specific individuals.

John, whom we will not consider here as a reader of Mark who attempts to finish the symphony, conveys the same ideas as in Luke-Acts, namely that arriving at Easter faith requires a personal encounter with Jesus in connection with previous experiences, and it might even require physical contact with him. None of the post-Easter encounters with Jesus is one-way: Mary Magdalene, Thomas, and Peter interact with Jesus. As in Luke-Acts, this physical phase does not last forever since Jesus inevitably returns to his father (20:17). Subsequent communion with Jesus will be possible in the spirit and in truth. To prepare

11 A similar reaction is expressed by Rhoda (Acts 12:12–15) who, out of joy, fails to open the gate for Peter.

for that, the risen Jesus wishes them peace, breathes on them and asks them to receive the Holy Spirit. In John, too, receiving the Holy Spirit is tied to mission: As the father has sent him, Jesus now sends the disciples. After they have received the Holy Spirit, Jesus further discloses that whomsoever they forgive sins, the sins are indeed forgiven, indicating that from now on the disciples will through the Holy Spirit be in community with Jesus and the father.

Second Movement: Finishing the Symphony in Different Endings of Mark

A second way of dealing with the problem posed by the ending of Mark is to "repair" the text itself. The manuscript tradition provides ample evidence that this happened in different ways. David Parker explains that, "The text changed more in the first century and a half than at any subsequent time. A high proportion of all variant readings are thus very early, irrespective of the text types supporting them."[12] Obviously, readers were not satisfied with the original end of Mark and developed the text in different directions, trying to fill its gaps and provide theological answers.

Building on the work of David Parker and Matthew Larsen, the following chart visualizes the different possible endings of Mark and how they at times they were even combined in the manuscripts.[13] It is striking that some manuscripts even seem to offer a choice as to which ending could be used for a liturgical reading.[14] The variety of versions demonstrates that the ending of Mark was still "fluid" or open to negotiation for a long time. This also indicates

12 Parker, *The Living Text*, 131.

13 Parker, *The Living Text*, 124–47; Larsen, *Gospels before the Book*, 114–120. I follow Parker's terminology calling 16:1–8 the "Shorter Ending," 16:9–20 the "Longer Ending" and the brief sentence between 16:8 and 16:9 the "Intermediate Ending."

14 Larsen (*Gospels before the Book*, 119) writes, "Several manuscripts contain multiple, different endings. For instance, Codex Regius (L; eighth century) and Codex Athous Laurae (Ψ, ninth or tenth century) offer both shorter and longer endings. In such manuscripts, readers find themselves in a choose-your-own-adventure approach to the ending of the textual tradition we now call the Gospel according to Mark. Readers have the opportunity to collapse the divide between themselves and the textual tradition and to insert themselves into the production of the story. That the resurrected Jesus appeared to his disciples is clear in these manuscripts. How the resurrection appearances occurred is a question open to readers, who are left with more than one option, and therefore must choose for themselves. Moreover, many manuscripts provide readers' notes with information about how to negotiate textual plurality." In the notes, Larsen mentions L, Ψ, 083, 099, the margins of 274, l^{1602} and some Syriac, Coptic and Ethiopic manuscripts as examples. For further examples, he refers to Bruce Metzger and Bart D. Ehrman, *Text of the New Testament: Its Transmission, Corruption and Restoration*, 4th edn. (New York: Oxford University Press, 2005), 77, 84–5.

that there was no final agreement about underlying theological questions. If we take into account that the manuscripts originate from different locations, they provide evidence that these questions were still subject to negotiation and might have been answered differently in different locations.

Table 9.1 Different Endings in Mark's Gospel

Type	Known since	Greek witnesses/ manuscripts	Church Fathers
Shorter Ending (16:1–8)	(early) 2nd century	– Codex Sinaiticus (א) – Codex Vaticanus (B) – 304 (12th century, Mark/ Matt Comm.)	Clement of Alexandria Origen Eusebius Jerome
Longer Ending (16:9–20)	(late) 2nd century	– A, C, D, W, Θ, fam^{13} – Majority of the Greek manuscripts	Irenaeus Hippolytus Apostolic Constitution (Justin)
Intermediate Ending	4th century		
Intermediate Ending with insertion after v. 3	4th century	– Codex Bobiensis	
Longer Ending (16,9–20) with text critical note after V.8	[4th century]	– I 209^{mg}, 1582 – 22 – 20 – 137, 137	
Longer Ending + Freer-Logion	[4th century]	– Codex Washingtonianus (W)	Jerome
All Endings [+ text critical note after v. 8]	[4th century]	– Alexandrinian text – Ψ 0112 (and variants) – 274mg, 579 syrh ^{mg}	
Intermediate and Longer Ending	6th/7th century	– 0112	

For our purposes, it is not necessary to analyze all the different versions. We will leave aside the versions combining different endings and those with a text-critical note and concentrate on the Longer Ending (3.1 below), the Intermediate Ending (3.2 below), the Intermediate Ending with an additional insertion after verses 3–4 in Codex Bobiensis (3.3 below) and the Longer Ending with the Freer-Logion (3.4 below). When we examine these versions, it will become obvious that they address the same theological questions we have already encountered in Matthew and Luke, but provide different answers.

The Longer Ending **(*16:9–20*)**

According to the manuscript tradition, the Longer Ending has been known at least since the late second century. It consists of motifs already known from the other canonical Gospels and uses them for its own ends. With respect to the theological questions, this version links up with the idea that was first developed in Luke-Acts and also appears in John, namely that Jesus ascends into heaven. The longer ending even goes a step further as Jesus does not only ascend into heaven, but seats himself at the right hand of God, which provides a larger cosmological order and thus an even more stable religious framework.

Arriving at Easter faith requires a personal encounter with the risen Jesus. Hearing about his resurrection and about encounters with him is not enough. This, of course, raises the problem for future generations about how a personal encounter with Jesus is possible after he has ascended into heaven and is seated at the right hand of the Father. The longer ending provides the following solution. It connects the commissioning of the disciples to the proclamation of the gospel and to the baptized believers, who take on the role of authorized witnesses (16:17–18). With a nod to Matt 7:20, the longer ending mentions the signs that will occur through the faithful followers. They will be able to cast out demons in Jesus' name, speak in new languages, avoid harm when they touch venomous snakes or drink poison, and when they lay their hands on the sick, they will be healed—events which are recorded in Acts. As seen above, the last sentence about the disciples going out and proclaiming the gospel, while the Lord works with them and confirms the word by accompanying signs, is both an authorial comment and an evaluation, conveying that what Jesus has promised happens indeed.

Looking at this ending through the lens of social memory theory, the question is not only about which traditions and frames are used to narrate the story, but also about what experiences lie behind it and which needs are to be met. The focus on disbelief, despite the witnessed apparitions and the special authorization given to the faithful to carry out the general commission, suggest that there were issues in this area. Unbelief is still framed in the Isaian appeal of obduracy (Mark 4:10–12; 6:52; 8:17–18; cf. Isa 6:9–11), which might either reflect a reliance on Jewish tradition or an emerging Christian theme.[15] What catches the eye is that the question about how the next generation can arrive at Easter faith is much more important than the question about how encounter and community with the risen Lord are to be envisioned. The risen Lord is much more remote, and a direct encounter seems out of the picture. He is as remote as God. The disciples as intermediaries now pass on the gospel. Thus, the focus of attention is on the second generation, their authority and the issues they face during their mission. The authorial comment at the end aims to provide a stabilizing closure to the story, indicating that the Lord is a co-worker in the mission and confirms the proclamation with signs.[16]

Intermediate Ending

The Intermediate Ending is found in the manuscript tradition of the fourth century, but it might be earlier. It consists of two sentences,[17] expressing that the women reported everything to those accompanying Peter and that subsequently Jesus himself sent the holy and everlasting *kerygma* of eternal salvation through them, which they preach from the East to the West. The Intermediate Ending closes with a liturgical *Amen*.

This brief addition is almost like the final chord which is demanded by the leading note, and thus it represents the briefest possible way to end the Markan symphony. Understanding this complex chord requires additional assumptions and the closure of narrative gaps: After the women overcome the first shock, they deliver the message to Peter and the others. This group in turn sees Jesus in Galilee as he has promised and is commissioned to proclaim the message, as Jesus also had promised (13:10; 14:9). It is only implicitly hinted

---

15 Sandra Huebenthal, "Framing Jesus and Understanding Ourselves. Isaiah in Mark's Gospel and Beyond," in *Creative Fidelity, Faithful Creativity: The Reception of Jewish Scripture in Early Judaism & Christianity*, ed. Michael A. Daise and Dorota Hartmann, JSJSup (Leiden: Brill, 2021 forthcoming); "What's Form Got to Do with It? Preliminaries on the Impact of Social Memory Theory for the Study of Biblical Intertextuality," in *The Gospels and Ancient Literary Criticism: Continuing the Debate on Gospel Genre(s)*, ed. David P. Moessner, Matthew Calhoun, and Tobias Nicklas; WUNT 451 (Tübingen: Mohr Siebeck, 2020), 145–76.

16 Since it does not say anything about the success of this mission, one might conclude that its current missionary activity is less important to the group than the authority of the intermediaries, which provides the security to have chosen the right path and to be in the right group.

17 Πάντα δὲ τὰ παρηγγελμένα τοῖς περὶ τὸν Πέτρον συντόμως ἐξήγγειλαν. Μετὰ δὲ ταῦτα καὶ αὐτὸς ὁ Ἰησοῦς ἀπὸ ἀνατολῆς καὶ ἄχρι δύσεως ἐξαπέστειλεν δι᾽ αὐτῶν τὸ ἱερὸν καὶ ἄφθαρτον κήρυγμα τῆς αἰωνίου σωτηρίας. ἀμήν.

at that the disciples arrived at Easter faith through an encounter with Jesus, which was made possible because they believed the women's message.

The identity and the number of those who accompany Peter remains unclear. It simply may not have been that important to the author. All the disciples left Jesus at Gethsemane and only Peter, who regrets his betrayal (14:66–72), is now mentioned by name. Jesus' appearance to those accompanying Peter may have represented the only apparition and it remains unclear how large the group around Peter really is. It may well be less than the eleven and the composition of the group seems to be of no importance. It is likewise unclear whether the mission of Peter and those with him is already accomplished or still under way. In this ending, it finally remains unclear where Jesus is and how the disciples and the faithful are to relate to him. No ascension is provided. The focus is on the message of eternal salvation, which is proclaimed to the entire world, just as Jesus promised.

Codex Bobiensis (Intermediate Ending with an Insertion After 16:3)

It almost seems as if the Codex Bobiensis, a manuscript from the fourth century, aims at closing at least one further gap of the Intermediate Ending by disclosing where Jesus is. This manuscript adds one sentence after the women wonder who will roll away the stone.[18] The insertion gives an account of the events connected with Jesus' resurrection, which contains darkness, angels descending from heaven, Jesus rising in the brightness of the living God, and the angels ascending with him.

The additional sentence achieves two things. On the one hand, it gives an explanation of what happened to Jesus and his body and discloses that he is in heaven. On the other hand, it prepares the women's encounter with the young man in the tomb. It is hinted that the angels rolled away the stone and that the young man is one of them. With Jesus in heaven and angels taking care of the events on earth, the cosmological and theological order is restored. It seems as if this sentence states explicitly what was already known or assumed, namely that Jesus is in heaven. The insertion in the Codex Bobiensis thus has relatively little new to add. Its function rather seems to be one of consolidation and stabilization by conveying that Jesus has safely arrived in heaven and will continue to operate from there. The cosmological order is restored. Angels are messengers and intermediaries between both worlds.

---

18 *Subito autem ad horam tertiam tenebrae diei factae sund per totum orbem terrae et descenderunt de caelis angeli et surgent in claritate vivi Die; simus ascenderunt cum eo et contunuo lux facta est.*

Longer Ending with the Freer-Logion

According to the manuscript tradition, the longer ending with the Freer-Logion is also first traceable to the fourth century. This version of the ending of Mark uses the longer ending and inserts additional sentences between vv. 14 and 15.[19] At first glance, the Freer-Logion does not add much to the three theological issues, as it addresses the disciples' lack of understanding. They defend themselves and explain their failure by baling Satan who still being in control of this age. Their request is that Jesus reveals his righteousness right away. Obviously, they deem it necessary to deal with the issues of faith that they still have and their consequential failure to come to terms with the unclean spirits. Jesus' response does not target Satan himself since his time is up. Even though the cosmic battle is over, the world is not saved yet and there are still sinners. Jesus' death is explained as being beneficial for sinners who are able to repent and participate in eternal salvation by inheriting the spiritual and uncorrupted heavenly glory of righteousness.

The focus of this addition is not about resurrection and afterlife, but provides a further explanation for Jesus' death and what it achieved. It also provides an explanation for the disciples' failure and envisions a difficult time ahead. The "terrible things" might point to the experiences of the readers and be directed to console them that what they experience is on a different level than what they deem it to be. There enemy is not Satan, but sinful people. This does not make more pleasant what lies ahead, but the worst is over. Through Jesus's death and resurrection, they can now, under these circumstances, be saved eternally. For those who continue to sin and do not believe, the Longer Ending continues, there is no hope in the final judgement. This links up nicely with Jesus seating himself at the right hand of the father, from where he will return to judge the living and the dead. This construct is found in both the Old Roman and the Nicene Creeds, which were in existence at that time. The addition of the Freer-logion also aims at stability through the cosmological order and clear authoritative connection between Jesus' resurrection and his Parousia.

The driving question is not concerned with how one arrives at Easter faith or with what follows from it for Jesus, but rather it is about what happens if one

19 Κακεινοι απελογουντο λεγοντες οτι ο αιων ουτος της ανομιας και της απιστιας υπο τον σαταναν εστιν, ο μη εων τα υπο των πνευματων ακαρθαρτα την αληθειαν του θεου κατακλαβεσθαι δυναμιν· δια τουτο αποκαλυψον σου την δικαιοσυνην ηδη, εκεινοι ελεγον τω χριστω. και ο χριστος εκεινοις προσελεγεν οτι πεπλερωται ὅρος των ετων της εξουσιας του σατανα, ἀλλὰ εγγιζει ἄλλα δεινα· και υπερ ων εγω αμαρτησαντων παρεδοθην εις θανατον ινα υποστρεψωσιν εις την αληθειαν και μηκετι αμαρτνσωσιν ιν α την εν τω ουρανω πνευματικην και αφθαρτον της δικαιοσυνης δοξαν κληρονομησωσιν.

does not. Being lured by Satan or the evil world is no longer an excuse. Jesus' death and resurrection have settled salvation once and for all. The mandate is to take up the challenge and live it accordingly. The ending also provides a stable cosmology and a frame for formulating a genuinely "Christian" identity which is expressed in the current life of the faithful with its challenges as well as in the expectations of an afterlife.

Third Movement: Performing the Symphony as It Is with the Shorter Ending

After listening to the different suggestions for additional notes, it is time to consider the remaining option: Reading the text as it is. With respect to the manuscript evidence, the initial solution is to read Mark with the Shorter Ending. With respect to the exegetical treatment, however, reading the Shorter Ending is rather a late and recent development, building on the work of textual critics. Parker puts it this way, "Textual criticism has, by patient and generally unspectacular work, managed in the course of the last 150 years to recover the Short and original Ending of Mark. To read the Gospel with this ending is to read a new book. This new book offers radical theological interpretations which had been wholly stifled by the ecclesiastical pieties of the Intermediate and Long Endings."[20] When textual critics deem the Short Ending as original, we are left with what appears to be an unfinished symphony that at first glance raises questions about Jesus' location and the nature of Easter faith. What happened to his body? How can one arrive at Easter faith? How does one encounter Jesus and have communion with him? Questions like these are difficult to solve without additional notes.

One of the classics in a list of humorous insurance claims is the assertion that "an invisible car came out of nowhere, hit me, and then disappeared." In some regards, Mark's Gospel in its original form (1:1–16:8) is a similar experience. Without prologue, infancy narratives, and apparition stories, it almost seems as if Jesus came out of nowhere, hit the people and disappeared. The Gospel consequently opens with the words Ἀρχὴ τοῦ εὐαγγελίου Ἰησοῦ Χριστοῦ [υἱοῦ θεοῦ], which already indicate that what follows is only the beginning of a partial story.[21] There is a lot more to the story of the beginning of the gospel of Jesus, the anointed Son of God, than what is told in Mark's text. Consequently, the story must continue somewhere else.

20 Parker, *The Living Text*, 147.

21 Huebenthal, *Reading Mark's Gospel*, 189–192.

One plausible scenario is that the story is told in a more expansive way within the lives of its readers. As such, the story's future retellings link up with the audiences' own pasts. In Parker's words: "They flee in trembling and astonishment, and tell nobody anything, out of fear. End. They are told that Jesus is risen, and they receive a promise that they will see him. But no encounter is narrated. Instead, the story opens out into the present experience of the Gospel's first audience."[22] The story's future is the readers' present and they themselves have to decide how to continue it. The regressive closing, designed to stimulate the motivation and strength of the addressees in order to pursue the goal of a living community of followers in the face of the βασιλεία τοῦ θεοῦ can help with that.[23]

Another possibility is reading the redirection to Galilee in 16:7 as a signal to return to, and re-read, the reference to Galilee in 1:14, where Jesus begins his ministry. The resumption of the beginning, to where the end leads, is indeed a harmonic and logical continuation. Reading and listening this way encourages the audience to listen more carefully the second time around. In the *reprise* or *relecture*, the Markan Gospel about the beginning of the gospel of God turns into the beginning of the Gospel that is proclaimed *about* Jesus, the messenger of the gospel of God. Listening to the story a second time, the messenger is integrated into the message and the gospel now proclaims Jesus who has proclaimed the Kingdom of God, which is at hand.[24] The textualized proclamation becomes the founding story of faith in Christ and the personal account of those who have set out to follow this Jesus and orient their lives in accordance with his message.

How does such a reading deal with the theological issues? The Shorter Ending also hints that Easter faith can only be achieved through a personal encounter with the risen Lord based on previous experiences. This is why the disciples are redirected back to their daily life in Galilee. The key questions concern the location of Jesus, the lack of encounters with him, and the viability of a community in his absence. There are three possible answers. First, Jesus continues to live in the lives of the community members where he can be encountered. Second, Jesus can be encountered in the broken bread that

22 Parker, *The Living Text*, 144.

23 Huebenthal, *Reading Mark's Gospel*, 251.

24 Huebenthal, *Reading Mark's Gospel*, 189–192. Karl Matthias Schmidt, *Wege des Heils: Erzählstrukturen und Rezeptionskontexte des Markusevangeliums*, NTOA 74 (Göttingen: Vandenhoeck & Ruprecht, 2010), also assumes a relecture model. He distinguishes between "foundational reading" (*Grundlektüre*) and "completion reading" (*Komplettierungslektüre*) and recognizes 1:35–8:26 as the continuation of 16:8 and thus the ending of the Gospel.

the community shares.[25] And third, Jesus continues to live in the text of the Gospel and can be encountered through communal (liturgical) readings.[26] It is, of course, also possible to combine the different options and envision Jesus as living within the community, present in the word of the gospel and the broken bread that the group shares in memory of him. This requires us to imagine a "Mark group" that enjoys a vivid communal life of shared faith and experiences, willing to explore the will of God and their mission together, which is based on their common foundation of Christ's example. We encounter a glimpse of such groups in the Pauline letters and in Acts. Such a reading brings us also surprisingly close to the *presence* of Christ as it is envisioned in the Roman Catholic Church today, where Jesus can be encountered in the community, in the Scriptures, and in the Eucharist. Read this way, the Shorter Ending likewise answers the theological issues, though in a somewhat unexpected way. It makes a case for a communal life that is different from the remote Christ in the readings of the second movement. When the risen Lord is not in heaven, but in the community, we have to assume a horizontal Christology instead of a vertical hierarchy.

Conclusion and Hermeneutical Coda

Determining which of these *afterlives* of Mark is historically and theologically "correct" is difficult. The Shorter Ending is currently the most widely accepted version in New Testament scholarship. The rationale is that it most closely represents the original text and reflects the earliest stage of theological interpretation. This is well justified, as long as the notion of an "earliest stage" does not imply that it was the "only possible understanding" of a Gospel was meant to be the first book reflecting the events and encounters with Jesus and what followed from them.

The notion that Mark was meant to be published as a book has recently been challenged by the work of Matthew Larsen. Arguing on the basis of a profound knowledge of text production and reception in antiquity, especially the first century, Larsen confirms what textual criticism has been suspecting for quite some time, namely that oral and written texts can be understood in

---

25 Stefan Alkier, "Auferweckung denken, Oder: wie das Markusevangelium mit seinen Wundergeschichten seine Leser theologisch bildet," *BL* 84 (2011): 258–67.

26 David S. du Toit, *Der abwesende Herr: Strategien im Markusevangelium zur Bewältigung. der Abwesenheit des Auferstandenen*, WMANT 111 (Neukirchen-Vluyn: Neukirchener Verlag, 2006), 298–302.

much broader ways than the standard historical-critical position would tolerate. His focus on *hypomnemata* as a rather fluid genre within the transitional process from oral to written indicates that the characteristics of the former are more prevalent than the latter.[27] Based on the textual evidence, Larsen suggests an understanding of Mark's Gospel along with the patristic descriptions resembles *hypomneuma* instead of a book planned for publication. In other words, what we know as Mark's Gospel could be nothing more than a collection of stories, ideas, interpretations and *aide-mémoire* circulating and waiting to be reworked and published as a real book.

If Larsen is correct, what does it mean for our readings and the afterlives of Mark's Gospel? Does it render reading Mark with the Shorter Ending historically and theologically wrong? Does it mean that when we read Mark anything goes and that we can "pick our own adventure" from the options that the manuscripts allow? Are there still clear rules for historically and theologically correct readings or does reading the Bible allow for more openness as long as it enhances one's personal faith?

As is so often the case, there is no one correct answer. A helpful way to proceed is to consider the different answers to the underlying theological questions in light of the different movements that I have addressed. Each can be evaluated in their respective contexts as expressions of the needs experienced by the groups for whom these were clearly important. Thus, each Markan version of Jesus' afterlife provides answers to the questions that are raised in their respective historical and theological situations. The contextualization, interpretation, and evaluation of these different endings is one of the primary tasks of the New Testament scholar. Making visible the different moments in Early Christian identity formation is a huge service that adds to a broader and more balanced picture of the development of Early Christianity.

The Christian reader, who is guided by the canon can and should benefit from the variety of answers found in the New Testament. More specifically, for the Christian reader in the tradition of the Nicene Creed, resurrection, ascension, the gift of the Holy Spirit, the Parousia and the final judgement are indispensable articles of Christian faith based on the devotees' experience of Jesus and his message as it is presented in the New Testament. That does not imply, however, that every text has to represent every part of the Creed. Neither does

27 On *hypomnemata* as a particular textual form, see Larsen (*Gospels before the Book*, 107) who writes, "*Hypomnēmata* lack 'order' (*taxis*) and are unfinished, unpolished and uncorrected. It is one of their characteristics, and not a flaw. Adding order to notes is an integral part of turning them into polished pieces of writing." Further, Larsen (112) writes, "*Hypomnēmata* were textual objects with a specific purpose. At their root, they are about remembering the already known, not informing about the not yet known."

it imply that Christianity prescribes a reading model where "one-size-fits-all." The theological impact of the different endings shows that they imply different understandings of Christ's presence in the world, the Church, and community life, which must not be played off against each other.

Personal encounter and communion with Christ seem to be less important in the Intermediary and Longer Endings, which might point to a later generation with different needs. The hierarchical order of the Church, which evolved in consequence, might be logical explanation for the shift, but certainly is not the only one. Christianity can indeed be much more variegated as the retrieval of the Shorter Ending shows. Textual criticism has brought back the Shorter Ending from the archive or *storage memory* to the *functional memory* of Christianity,[28] and it fits the requirements for a good and interesting story of the post-modern and post-structuralist reader like a glove. The question of how Jesus can be encountered first-hand is also an important question for modern Christians who are sometimes more interested in identifying with the first generation of Jesus followers rather than subsequent ones. Thus, the third movement is highly appealing to today's Christian readers, especially to the newly converted and to those who have returned back to the practice of their faith. The difference is that the first generation is guided by an inherited religious tradition and experiences, namely a Christian cultural memory, that is not accessible to modern readers in the same way.

The deeper understanding of the Christ event and its theological interpretation—including questions about the afterlife of Jesus—have developed gradually over time. It can be very consoling for the faithful to realize neither that the disciples were born to be exemplars of faith nor that every aspect of Christian faith was unambiguously present from the beginning. It is, therefore, important to convey Mark's unfinished symphony, Ἀρχή, to contemporary Christian audiences so they can listen to it and discuss its different possible afterlives in later traditions. They might even provide unexpected moments of encounter with the living Lord.

Bibliography

Alkier, Stefan. "Auferweckung denken, Oder: wie das Markusevangelium mit seinen Wundergeschichten seine Leser theologisch bildet." *BL* 84 (2011): 258–267.

28 Aleida Assmann, *Erinnerungsräume: Formen und Wandlungen des kulturellen Gedächtnisses* (München: Beck, 1999), 137.

Assmann, Aleida. *Erinnerungsräume: Formen und Wandlungen des kulturellen Gedächtnisses*. München: Beck, 1999.

Gergen, Kenneth. "Erzählung, Moralische Identität und historisches Bewusstsein." Pages 170–202 in *Erzählung, Identität, Historisches Bewusstsein*. Edited by Jürgen Straub. Translated by Alexander Kochinka and Jürgen Straub. Frankfurt: Suhrkamp, 1998.

Huebenthal, Sandra. "Luke 24:13–35 and Social Memory in Luke." Pages 85–95 in *Biblical Interpretation in Early Christian Gospels. Volume 3: The Gospel of Luke*. LNTS 376. Edited by Thomas R. Hatina. London: T & T Clark, 2010.

———. "Das Evangelium nach Markus. Eine Hörerfahrung." Pages 461–470 in *73 Ouvertüren. Die Buchanfänge der Bibel und ihre Botschaft*. Edited by Egbert Ballhorn, Georg Steins, Regina Wildgruber and Uta Zwingenberger. Gütersloh: Gütersloher Verlagshaus, 2018.

———. "Frozen Moments. Early Christianity through the Lens of Social Memory Theory." Pages 17–43 in *Memory and Memories in Early Christianity*. Edited by Simon Butticaz and Enrico Norelli. WUNT 398. Tübingen: Mohr Siebeck, 2018.

"Another Frozen Moment. Reading Luke in a Social Memory Theoretical Framework." PIBA 41/42 (2019): 23–43.

———. *Reading the Mark's Gospel as a Text from Collective Memory*. Grand Rapids: Eerdmans, 2020.

———. "What's Form Got to Do with It? Preliminaries on the Impact of Social Memory Theory for the Study of Biblical Intertextuality." Pages 145–76 in *The Gospels and Ancient Literary Criticism: Continuing the Debate on Gospel Genre(s)*. Edited by David P. Moessner, Matthew Calhoun, and Tobias Nicklas. WUNT 451. Tübingen: Mohr Siebeck, 2020.

———. "Framing Jesus and Understanding Ourselves. Isaiah in Mark's Gospel and Beyond." Forthcoming in *Creative Fidelity, Faithful Creativity: The Reception of Jewish Scripture in Early Judaism & Christianity*. Edited by Michael A. Daise and Dorota Hartmann. JSJSup. Leiden: Brill, 2021.

Larsen, Matthew. *Gospels before the Book*. New York: Oxford University Press, 2018.

Metzger, Bruce, and Bart D. Ehrman. *Text of the New Testament: Its Transmission, Corruption and Restoration*, 4th edn. New York: Oxford University Press, 2005.

Parker, David C. *The Living Text of the Gospel*. Cambridge: Cambridge University Press, 1997.

Schmidt, Karl Matthias. *Wege des Heils: Erzählstrukturen und Rezeptionskontexte des Markusevangeliums*. NTOA 74. Göttingen: Vandenhoeck & Ruprecht, 2010.

Du Toit, David S. *Der abwesende Herr: Strategien im Markusevangelium zur Bewältigung. der Abwesenheit des Auferstandenen*. WMANT 111. Neukirchen–Vluyn: Neukirchener Verlag, 2006.

Sexual Asceticism and Eternal Life in the *Acts of Paul and Thecla*: A Collective and Cultural Memory Perspective

Jiří Lukeš

This study focuses on the theme of restraint and purity in connection with the resurrection in the apocryphal *Acts of Paul and Thecla*. After briefly defining collective and cultural memory, the study compares the image of the apostle Paul in the canonical Acts of the Apostles, which appears to be influenced by Cicero, with the one presented in the *Acts of Paul and Thecla*. The shift in both Paul's image and his soteriology are explained within cultural frameworks of the second century which saw a developing interest in the genre of fiction. The theme of the resurrection does not deviate from that of Paul's letters, but in the *Acts of Paul and Thecla* it is accompanied by dramatic-humorous scenes that frequently incorporate miracles. Thecla's social protest is an important underlying theme which offers Christianity a connection between defiance against the powerful men of the Roman Empire and sexual austerities that are important for eternal life. Attention is also given to the role of the Acts genre in relation to the Pastoral Epistles since Paul's image shifts within the collective memory which is affected by contemporary ideals, competes with popular literary genres, and is even overshadowed by the female heroine.

Collective and Cultural Memory as a Hermeneutical Lens

Memory is a broader concept than a set of individual remembrances. If we examine its form or development through literary records, then social, collective, or cultural processes of memory are inescapable. Remembrances never capture only the memories of an individual, despite their potential accuracy in reconstructing the past, but they are always constructed in relation to a broader lived reality within the present. Within the process, memories can be forgotten due to changing circumstances. Surviving memories are often incorporated into, and shaped by, a variety of social, political, religious, linguistic and geographical frameworks with which individuals within a society identify. Conceptions of the past are, therefore, products of reconstruction. They result from new interpretations of the past, which are always selective, and they are always placed in new contexts. The remembrances of an Indivudual is

 | DOI:10.30965/9783657796212_011

affected by the group to which he or she belongs. As Émile Durkheim observed long ago, a group acts and thinks in a completely different way than an isolated individual who is theoretically not concerned with the interests of the group.[1] Remembrances within a community undergo a different process from that of the individual who is more concerned about his or her own past. While Durkheim captured this distinction, Maurice Halbwachs developed it in relation to the concept of collective memory, which he distinguished from what he called the historical sciences.[2] The process of collective memory concerns a community's self-identity, which is never the product of the mere sum of individual experiences. However, the remembrances of the individual and those of the collective are related. The personalities of individual members can significantly influence the history and structure of the group through their memories and activities, but the group is never just a cluster of its members. Collective memory from the community's perspective completes the identity of its individual members and helps to incorporate fragmentary memories into a coherent narrative, which is expressed at certain times and within a social framework. Collective memory is thus the work of an ongoing process that reassembles the image of the past through the pressures of current stimuli and the group's identity.[3]

The meaning of collective memories, and the resulting pictures of the past, is thus determined by the interaction between the individual and the community. This process is influenced by a number of variable factors and backward projections onto past events, resulting in some memories (intentionally) being out of date, while for others, are recreated to meet the needs of the community as it pertains to its self-identity. The accepted memories which are pressured by the community's present are only part of the reality being created. Although it may consist of a set of testimonies from a number of witnesses, it expresses only a particular slice of possible constructs of reality, which is constantly affected by new circumstances. While social groups possess traditions

1 Jiří Šubrt, Nicolas Maslowski, and Štěpánka Lehmann, "Maurice Halwachs, koncept rámců paměti a kolektivní paměti," in *Kolektivní paměť: k teoretickým otázkám*, ed. Nicolas Maslowski and Jiří Šubrt (Praha: Karolinum, 2014), 15–30, esp. 17.

2 Historical memory does not ensure identity, but provides an integrative framework for a multitude of stories. Collective memory dampens changes, and historical memory specializes in them. Collective memory constantly exists in the plural and is responsible for the distinctive character of the group. In contrast, historical memory establishes a singular integrative framework for a multitude of stories. See Šubrt, Maslowski, and Lehmann, "Maurice Halwachs, koncept rámců paměti a kolektivní paměti," 17. Aleida Assmann, *Erinnerungsräume. Formen und Wandlungen des kulturellen Gedächtnisses* (München: C. H. Beck, 1999), 131–3.

3 Šubrt, Maslowski, Lehmann, "Maurice Halwachs, koncept rámců paměti a kolektivní paměti," 18–19.

and rituals, they still create their own historical narratives. Some images of the past are stored as part of consciously created *memoria*. Their preservation, or tradition, is governed by rules and specific interpretations, which are binding for members of the community.[4] Suppose the product of the community is a text. In that case, it is not just a projection of the author's ideals, memories and thought constructions, but embodies the demands and identity of the whole community, which then listens to the text and spreads it further.[5] Cultural memory preserves components of knowledge with which a certain group identifies. It is a concretization of its identity that contains fixed points, and its horizon does not shift with time.[6] Cultural memory is passed down from generation to generation through repeated appropriation.

When we refer to social memory, we are concerned with how individual memory acquires its shape within social and cultural frameworks that act as structures.[7] The process of social memory reveals filters that separate the official from the unofficial remembrances. In this sense, it reveals why and how traditions can at times be preserved and at other times be changed when present circumstances pressure interpretation.[8] This process also applies to the apocryphal *Acts of Paul and Thecla* (*APThl*) which shift Paul's soteriological claims and the image of his character to suit the ideals of the second century. Therefore, the study of social memory reveals not only the individual's conceptions of the past, but also those of the community, society, and culture, thereby exposing both continuity and discontinuity in relation to, for example, power interests and perceptions of self and the other.[9] The resulting reception

4 Stefan Rieger, "Memoria und Oblivio. Die Aufzeichnung des Menschen," in *Einführung in die Literaturwissenschaft*, ed. Miltos Pechlivanos, Stefan Rieger, Wolfgang Struck, and Michael Weitz (Stuttgart: J. B. Metzler Verlag, 1995), 378–82, esp. 392.

5 On collective memory, see Sandra Huebenthal, *Reading Mark's Gospel as a Text from Collective Memory* (Grand Rapids: Eerdmans, 2020), 133–50. Maurice Halbwachs was not concerned with how texts were read by groups, but rather his interest lay in how groups share in a common identity in relation to a common, hence cohesive, memory. He argues that common memories strengthen groups and in turn result in those memories having a unified form. Halbwachs concludes that the stability of group memories depends on the composition and character of the group. Maurice Halbwachs, *Kolektivní paměť* (Praha: Sociologické nakladatelství, 2009). Originally publishes as *La mémoire collective. Édition critique établie par Gérard Namer* (Paris: A. Michel, 1997).

6 Jan Assmann, "Collective Memory and Cultural Identity," *New German Critique* 65 (1995): 125–33, esp. 129.

7 Harald Welzer, "Co je to komunikativní paměť a z čeho se skládá," in *Paměť a trauma pohledem humanitních věd*, ed. Alexander Kratochvíl (Praha: Akropolis, 2015), 73–89, esp. 74, 77.

8 Rieger, "Memoria und Oblivio," 378, 380–82.

9 Aleida Assmann and Jan Assmann, "Exkurs: Archäologie der literarischen Kommunikation," in *Einführung in die Literaturwiessenschaft*, ed. Miltos Pechlivanos, Stefan Rieger, Wolfgang

is an interplay of factors that include shocking ideals and antagonists that play on the emotions as they are constructed to contrast between those who are accepted and those who are rejected.

According to Renate Lachmann, the aim of cultural memory is not to accumulate historical data, but to re-create symbols.[10] Old images are copied, altered and appropriated to meet the needs of new social conditions and conversations within a process of change that addresses relevance. In this way, information is not accumulated, but rather certain remembrances are strengthened in the reception of tradition. These remembrances aid in the constructs of symbols that connect the past and the present. The commonality of the symbols allows the individual to participate in a common memory of the ideals and identity of the group. Of course, a literary persona who is essential for the community and lives in tradition or is the subject of legend or mythologization can also become a symbol. Impressions of what is fictional or the fictitious is determined by the social pressure guiding the memory. The fictitious is not without cultural value and can exist parallel to what is considered to be the real or non-fictitious. When it comes to matters of faith, these are inextricably linked, resulting in genres that can smoothly accommodate the fictitious and non-fictitious. The reader perceives the real world as well as the fictional world and relies on the authenticity of the confluence on the basis of accepted authorities. This is a complex reception process and numerous factors can affect it, especially the relationship between hegemonic culture and counterculture.[11]

The content of the text is thus assembled and unified through the reader's sense of identity and pre-understanding, which are factors that influence the choices made by the reader within his or her participation in the social and cultural memory. These factors affect historicity, literary genres, rhetoric, circulation of stories, memories, typology of characters and social patterns, virtues, and ideological milieu. In addition, with reference to my focus, these factors are integrated with the gender of listeners and their social positions in society.

Struck, and Michael Weitz (Stuttgart: J. B. Metzler Verlag, 1995), 200–206, esp. 202. Rieger, "Memoria und Oblivio," 383. Halbwachs refers to four levels of social memory: family, social classes, global society, and religious societies. See Šubrt, Maslowski, Lehmann, "Maurice Halwachs, koncept rámců paměti a kolektivní paměti," 19–20.

10 Wolfgang Struck, "Soziale Funktion und kultureller Status literarischer Texte oder: Autonomie als Heteronomie," in *Einführung in die Literaturwiessenschaft*, ed. Miltos Pechlivanos, Stefan Rieger, Wolfgang Struck, and Michael Weitz (Stuttgart: J. B. Metzler Verlag, 1995), 182–99, esp. 197. See also Renate Lachmann, *Gedächtnis und Literatur. Intertextualität in der russischen Moderne* (Frankfurt: Suhrkamp, 1990).

11 Struck, "Soziale Funktion," 197–8.

Paul's Image in Collective Memory

The image of the Apostle Paul in antiquity is multi-dimensional. It is initially expressed in his own epistles written in the 50s. Soon after, it is conveyed in the Acts of the Apostles by Luke probably in the 80s or 90s. It is also found in the deutero-Pauline epistles, which are dated between 70 and 130,[12] and in the apocryphal *Acts of Paul* and *Acts of Paul and Thecla*, which were probably composed shortly before the year 200.[13] These writings represent various literary genres, express different intentions, and target diverse groups of Christian readers.

On the basis of his own writings, Paul conveys that he was well educated. He was able to dictate his letters to a scribe while maintaining rhetorical rules and masterfully handling a number of argumentation techniques, including the appropriation of scripture. His erudite writing skills contributed to his letters being copied and widely read after his death. He was early regarded the most important theologian in the first Christian generation, who conveyed the significance of Christ's crucifixion and resurrection to urban non-Jewish groups. In Asia Minor, by the end of the second century, Paul was portrayed as the preacher-rhetorician, which is represented by the author of canonical Acts. This portrayal differs in the *Acts of Paul and Thecla* where he threatens an established urban social order. He is no longer opposed by the Jews, as in the Acts of the Apostles, but rather by outraged upper-class men whose wives (represented as children without choice)[14] favour his ascetic teachings, even though he is regarded as a foreigner with whom they had no physical contact.

Comparing Paul and Cicero in the Acts of the Apostles

The community of Luke's readers/listeners, who were probably from a higher educated class, demanded a hero figure with which they could identify. Paul's dramatic experiences are presented as those of a virtuous Roman citizen, an

12 Petr Pokorný and Ulrich Heckel, *Einleitung in das Neue Testament. Seine Literatur und Theologie im Überblick* (Tübingen: Mohr Siebeck, 2007), 181–94, 189, 533, 642, 648, 653–4. David E. Aune, *The Westminster Dictionary of New Testament and Early Christian Literature and Rhetoric* (Louisville: Westminster John Knox Press, 2003), 339. Eva Ebel, "The Life of Paul," in *Paul: Life, Setting, Work, Letters*, ed. Oda Wischmeyer (London: T & T Clark, 2012), 97–109.

13 Aune, *The Westminster Dictionary*, 10. Wilhelm Schneemelcher and Rodolphe Kasser, "The Acts of Paul," in *New Testament Apocrypha. Volume 2: Writings Relating to the Apostles; Apocalypses and Related Subjects*, ed. Wilhelm Schneemelcher (Louisville: Westminster/John Knox Press, 1992), 234–5.

14 Aline Rousselle, *Porneia: On Desire and the Body in Antiquity* (Eugene: Wipf and Stock, 2013), 93–106, esp. 93.

orator-apostle, whose life was devoted to the salvation of the Gentile nations, to which he was sent by God. His portrayal represents his contemporaries' ideals, pathos, symbols and memories of ancient heroes. Within this character framework, Luke seamlessly presents Paul as a rhetorician (Acts 13:6; 17:22–31; 20:18–35; 22:1–21; 24:10–21; 26:29–29; 28:17–20) who represents the ethical ideal of that time.[15] For Luke's Paul, the world and its forum is opened up (Acts 17:19; 19:9–10). He can interact with not only the common people, but also with philosophers, warlords, kings, their wives and proconsuls. Luke's portrayal is undoubtedly influenced by the rhetorical quality that he appreciated in Paul's own letters. From this perspective, Paul as the ideal Roman citizen in the Acts can be viewed as the "new Cicero," whose image of the "orator-martyr" would have been well preserved in the broader collective memory. This portrayal is probable given that rhetoric was a field that combined all kinds of education with the moral qualities and commitments of the citizen (Quintilian, *Institutio Oratoria* 12.8–10).[16]

Paul's speeches portray him as not only an expert in rhetorical theory and practice, but also in the Law (Acts 22:3; 23:6), which again is similar to Cicero, who was also a legal expert. Like Paul, who writes in *koine* Greek, Cicero writes his letters (which he did not intend to publish) in a way that reflected the speech of the average Roman (*sermo cottidianus*). In *De Officiis*, Cicero deals with what was considered to be socially appropriate, namely *decorum*. In particular, he addresses social behaviours, gestures and practices of self-control which were expected to be dutifully applied by every Roman. In a similar way, Paul attempts to instill a *decorum* at Corinth, where he teaches a disrupted Christian community how to properly behave as followers of Christ. In 1 Cor 6:12–20 and 10:23–33, where he begins with the words, "All things are lawful for me, but not all things are helpful" (RSV), he addresses what constitutes a good and conscientious person, much like Cicero's attention to the *vir bonus* which conveyed through the form of a *diatribe*, which can be very briefly described as a tool suitable for *decorum*. Both the Lukan Paul and Cicero argue that individuals have obligations to the whole, be it to the *polis*, nations, or empire.

---

15 George A. Kennedy, *New Testament Interpretation through Rhetorical Criticism* (Chapel Hill: The University of North Carolina Press, 1984). He writes, "Greek historians also use speeches as ways of dramatically setting forth conflicting policies in debate, as Luke does in Acts 15, and Thucydides, followed to some extent by the Roman historians Sallust, Livy, and Tacitus, uses them as ways of indicating how events may be interpreted" (115).

16 Jiří Kraus, *Rhetoric in European Culture and Beyond* (Prague: Karolinum, 2014), 65–70, 72–3.

Cicero wanted the foundations of morality, which he found in moderate Stoicism (Panaitius), to guide daily life. Paul also focussed on the foundations of morality for daily life, but he found them in his conceptions of participating in Christ. Though on occasion, he appears to overlap with Stoic virtues, such justice, wisdom, firmness of principles, and restraint, which he interprets. For example, he replaces stoutness with magnanimousness (*magnitudo animi*) since for Paul a good-hearted person can gain control over his desires.

Within Stoicism, the task of reason is to control instincts, transform them into virtues, and rid them of selfishness and delusion. The importance of reason is conveyed in both the Corinthian community with which Paul interacted as well as the community that is associated with the apocryphal *Acts of Paul* wherein powerful men and elite egoists are presented as being full of delusion and bodily desires. Cicero recognized that Stoicism provided the strongest moral basis for a citizen's participation in society. Luke appears to be well aware of this and harmonizes his work with Stoic philosophy to a certain extent.

Cicero held friendship (*amicitia*) in high esteem. He argued that friendship should be based on values such as *virtus* (variously nuanced as bravery or honour) and *probitas* (integrity), which were recognized by the population as valued character traits. As a Roman citizen Paul is portrayed by Luke in precisely this way. In *Pro Sestio*, Cicero draws attention to the need for sincere relationships. *Amicitia* includes brotherly love and mutual demonstration of the good among those who support the social order. Paul's letters also correspond to this (Philem 8–20). As a lawyer, orator, rhetorician, Cicero was concerned with religious, social, philosophical issues, free speech, and the building of the state. Defense of his values eventually led to his martyrdom. As a Pharisee and Hellenized Jewish scholar, Paul similarly concerned himself with religious, social, and philosophical issues, built churches, and was martyrdom for his conviction. Cicero, trying to save Rome, ended up murdered by order of Antony (in 43 BC). Paul, who was concerned with the eternal salvation of the peoples of the Roman Empire, ended up being executed by Nero (between the years 62 and 66; *MP* [*Martyrium Pauli*] 115–116/5).[17] Cicero dealt with issues concerning good and evil, the subject of pain, death, sadness, mental restlessness, happiness and often showed deep emotional participation. Paul likewise concerned himself with similar topic in his letters (e.g., Rom 9:1–3), such as the masterful treatment of pathos or emotional appeal. (Gal 4:8–20). According to Cicero, the law is not a personal conviction, but is based on motives that

17 The numbering reflects the translations in Schneemelcher, *New Testament Apocrypha. Volume* 2, 239–46, 260–3 and Jan A. Dus, ed. *Příběhy apoštolů. Novozákonní apokryfy II* (Praha: Vyšehrad, 2003), 185–97, 228–31.

can benefit all people. Likewise, Paul argues (Rom 8:5–13) that the law is not rooted in human constructs, but is given by God and revealed in scripture.[18] Cicero is, therefore, a universalist, which can also be said of Paul in both Acts and the Epistles. For the Greeks, Paul may be typologically considered as the new Socrates or Demosthenes, which were well maintained image-figures in Hellenistic tradition. He debates with philosophers (Epicureans and Stoics as in Acts 17:18) in Athens and delivers a speech on the Areopagus, where he quotes Greek poets.[19] His oratory would have been enormously appealing to an educated listener.[20]

If Luke intended to portray Paul as the new Cicero, he would not have to look far for his cultural influence. Cicero as a representational figure was widespread in the collective and cultural memory, especially with respect to the practice of rhetoric and in relation to the political historical events of the recent past. These would have played a symbolic role in Luke's day and social context. Luke did not directly address all of the issues found in Cicero's writings, such as sexuality or attitudes toward it. But then again, Luke did not write a novel or romance, but rather a rhetorical historiography of a mixed Ciceronian type[21] in which salvation is not conditioned by sexual asceticism. According to Richard Pervo, who considers apocryphal acts to be historical novels,[22] it is possible

18 See Gian B. Conte, *Dějiny římské literatury* (Praha: KLP, 2003. Originally published as *Letteratura latina. Manuale storico dalle origini alla fine dell'impero romano* (Firenze: Le Monnier, 1996), 174–203. Marcus Tullius Cicero, *Tusculanarum disputationum*, ed. C. F. W. Müller (Leipzig: B. G. Teubner, 1913); *Laelius de amicitia, Cato Maior de senectute*, ed. C. Meissner (Leipzig: B. G. Teubner, 1917); *De oratore*, ed. Kazimierz F. Kumanicki, (Leipzig: B. G. Teubner, 1969); *On Life and Death*, ed. John Davie and Miriam T. Griffin, Oxford World's Classics (New York: Oxford University Press, 2017); *Výbor z korespondence*, I. Díl, ed. Václav Marek (Praha: Argo, 2019); *Řečník. Řeči proti Catilinovi. Filipiky a iné*, ed. Peter Kuklica and Daniel Škoviera (Bratislava: Tatran, 1982).

19 Dennis R. MacDonald, "Paul's Farewell to the Ephesian Elders and Hector's Farewell to Andromache: A Strategic Imitation of Homer's *Iliad*," in *Contextualizing Acts: Lukan Narrative and Greco-Roman Discourse*, ed. Todd Penner and Caroline Vander Stichele, SBLSymS 20 (Atlanta: SBL Press, 2003), 189–203.

20 More Daniel Marguerat, *The First Christian Historian: Writing the 'Acts of the Apostles'* (Cambridge: Cambridge University Press, 2002), 91–6. Bruce J. Malina and Jerome H. Neyrey, *Portraits of Paul: An Archeology of Ancient Personality* (Louisville: Westminster John Knox Press, 1996), 67–76.

21 Kota Yamada, "A Rhetorical History: The Literary Genre of the Acts of the Apostles," in *Rhetoric, Scripture and Theology. Essays from the 1994 Pretoria Conference*, ed. Stanley E. Porter and Thomas H. Olbricht, JSNTSup 131 (Sheffield: Sheffield Academic Press, 1996), 230–50, esp. 242, 249.

22 Richard Pervo, *Profit with Delight. The Literary Genre of the Acts of the Apostles* (Philadelphia: Fortress Press, 1987), 90–102, 121–31, esp. 122. Tomas Hägg, *The Novel in Antiquity* (Oxford: Basil Blackwell 1983), 88–9, 161–62.

that the canonical author did not wish to portray Christianity as a destabilizing factor in social life. Luke may have known some of the stories that are found in the apocryphal acts, but he kept them hidden because Christianity was accused of sexual indecency when the Acts of the Apostles was written. He did not use celibacy for promotional purposes.[23] As is discussed below, when the apocryphal acts were composed, the climate in society changed, and culture as a whole admired chastity (and a certain moderation), as conveyed in the development of novels. And yet, the apocryphal acts try to protect the "radical spirituality" of early Christianity.

Acts of Paul and Thecla: Comparison of Character Portrayals, Sexuality and Resurrection

When we look at the apocryphal acts through the lens of contemporary literary theory with the aim of analyzing genre or portrayal of heroes, there is a variety of contemporary theorists to whom we can turn.[24] I rely in particular on the insights of Northrop Frye who isolates the modes of fiction (deliberately differing from Aristotle, but in connection with him; *Poetics* 15.15–30) and argues that the plot of literary fiction is propelled by the actions of a specific character. If by nature the hero is superior to the people and the environment, then according to Frye, he is a divine being and the story can be identified as a myth.[25] If he is superior in his role or position, then the story can be identified as a romance. This type of hero, who is only human, performs wonderful deeds, has miraculous courage, and can even talk to the animals around him. The portrayal comes close to the ones found in legends and fairy tales.[26] He is a leader figure whose feelings and abilities are more advanced than those of other people, but he is still subject to social criticism and the forces of nature. In the ancient world, this type of hero is found in epics and tragedies in a mimetic way. The hero is one of us, presented in a low mimetic mode, especially in comedy and realistic prose.[27] When the hero's power or intelligence is below

23 Pervo, *Profit with Delight*, 122–3, 128.

24 Umberto Eco, Tzvetan Todorov, Norman Friedman, Paul Ricoeur, Algirdas J. Greimas, Antoine Compagnon, Stanley Fish, Frank Kermode, Wolfgang Iser, Hans R. Jauss, and more.

25 Northrop Frye, *Anatomy of Criticism: Four Essays* (Princeton: Princeton University Press, 1973), 33–67, esp. 33.

26 Frye, *Anatomy of Criticism*, 34. Tzvetan Todorov, *Introduction à la littérature fantastique* (Paris: Seuil, 1970). Todorov writes, "On lit généralement le genre du merveilleux à celui du conte de fées; en fait, le conte de fées n'est qu'une des variétés du merveilleux et les événements surnaturels n'y provoquent aucune surprise …" (citation is taken from EPUB version, 2013, chap. 3).

27 Frye, *Anatomy of Criticism*, 34.

that of the common person, the plot conveys absurdity and disappointment. The hero takes on an ironic mode, and the reader often judges his situation by how much freedom he exercises.[28] This categorization especially suits the narratives in which the characters are classified as "good" and "evil", which is ideal for analyzing the Acts of the Apostles and the *Acts of Paul and Thecla*.[29] In these writings, Paul is portrayed as a hero figure who oscillates between romance and epic, presented in a high mimetic mode. But he is also portrayed as the hero of legend and even comedy. It depends on which Acts, and which part therein, we read. In the *Acts of Paul*, the section about his martyrdom, for example, can be viewed as a depiction of a legendary or romantic hero. However, in *Acts of Paul and Thecla*, Paul sometimes appears as a comical figure within the Roman context when he is surpassed by a woman whom he denies, like Abraham denied Sarah (Gen 12: 11–14). Like the other men in the story, Paul is the target of situational irony. Thecla, however, is platonically in love with him (*APThl* 248/19). She is fascinated with his teaching (*APThl* 240/7) and does everything she can to be in his presence (*APThl* 247/18, 253/25, 266/40). The image of Paul as an impressive orator, who mediates eternal life to the peoples of the Roman Empire, continues in the apocryphal *Acts of Paul and Thecla*, but with a focus on women and sexual asceticism.[30]

The pivotal statement about the gospel of Paul's asceticism is expressed in the *Acts of Paul and Thecla* in the context of the sermon after the Eucharist in the house of Onesiphorus, where Paul presents a series of beatitudes. It reads, "The word of God concerning abstinence and resurrection" (*APThl* 238/5).[31]

---

28 Hayden White, *Metahistory: The Historical Imagination in Nineteenth-Century Europe* (Baltimore: Johns Hopkins University Press, 1975), 7–11; Seymour Chatman, *Story and Discourse: Narrative Structure in Fiction and Film* (Ithaca, New York: Cornell University Press, 1980), 85–7.

29 Texts of the apocryphal acts are found in Richard A. Lipsius and Maximillien Bonnet, eds., *Acta Apostolorum Apocrypha* (Lipsiae, APVD Hermannum Mendelssohn, 1891). Wilhelm Schubart and Carl Schmidt, *ΠΡΑΞΕΙΣ ΠΑΥΛΟΥ* (Glückstadt: J. J. Augustin, 1936).

30 Helen Rhee, (*Early Christian Literature: Christ and Culture in the Second and Third Centuries. The Apologies, Apocryphal Acts and Martyr Acts* [New York: Routledge, 2005]) writes, "In the imperial period, these issues of sexuality and marriage became matters of public concern and were intertwined with the traditional and social conventions and more. For the Apologists, Christian chastity validates the 'new but really ancient' religion's harmony with the Stoic ethical ideals and establishes its moral and social respectability in the dominant society. For the writers of the Apocryphal Acts, categorical denial and renunciation of sexuality are essentially linked to the fundamental Christian identity and calling, which reject the conventional social ethos and undermine the established patriarchal structure" (109).

31 All English translations are taken from Wilhelm Schneemelcher and Rodolphe Kasser, "Acts of Paul," in *New Testament Apocrypha. Volume 2: Writings Related to the Apostles,*

The whole series of Beatitudes ("M" refers to macarism) presented in Paul's sermon is focused on the restraint that is practiced by those who are saved. The Beatitudes are a programmatic manifestation and a key to interpreting other episodes in the story. Particularly significant are the appeals in Beatitudes M2, M3, M4, M5, M11, M13, which illuminate the conduct of Thecla.

Moving from a general description to the theology of the Beatitudes and their themes, it can be said that the author of the *Acts of Paul and Thecla* (perhaps a presbyter from Asia Minor) interprets Paul's teaching on "abstemiousness" (ἐγκράτεια) in relation to the concept of "purity" (ἁγνεία). The understanding of purity as presented in the Beatitudes and the story that follows is different from the canonical biblical writings. The "pure" (οἱ ἁγνὴν τὴν σάρκα in M2) are those for whom abstemiousness means a life of celibacy or virginity. For those who are married, abstemiousness is sexual abstinence (M5). It does not, therefore, refer to the forbidding of illegal or extramarital sexual activities, but to abstention from all sexual life. It can be assumed that the author was influenced by the temperate way of thinking that was propagated by Ebionites, Gnostics, Montanists, Therapeutae and the Essenes.[32] Abstemiousness (ἐγκράτεια) as "perseverance" or "strength" was understood as a manifestation of the inner strength that ascetic life brought and was also considered a means of achieving God's favour.[33]

The author interprets Paul's teaching on the "resurrection" (ἀνάστασις) in relation to sexual asceticism. The resurrection is presented as a reward for those who have lived "cleanly" (M5, 6, 9, 11). By contrast, opponents of Paul, like Demas and Hermogenes (*APThl* 245/14), will not experience it.[34] Resurrection,

Apocalypses and Related Subjects, ed. W. Schneemelcher (Louisville: Westminster John Knox Press, 1992).

32 E. Margaret Howe, "Interpretations of Paul in the Acts of Paul and Thecla," in *Pauline Studies. Essays Presented to Professor F. F. Bruce on his 70th Birthday*, ed. Donald A. Hagner and Murray J. Harris (Devon: The Paternoster Press, 1980), 33–49, esp. 36. Sheila E. McGinn, "The Acts of Thecla," in *Searching the Scripture. Volume 2: A Feminist Commentary*, ed. Elisabeth Schüssler Fiorenza (New York: Crossroad, 1994), 800–28, esp. 809.

33 Howe, "Interpretations of Paul," 36; J. Massingberd Ford, "The Meaning of 'Virgin,'" *NTS* 12 (1966): 293–99. Ford believes that virginity was more widespread in early Christianity than is generally thought. Similarly, see, E. R. Dodds, *Pagan and Christian in an Age of Anxiety* (Cambridge: Cambridge University Press, 1994), 32–5. The use of Ἐγκράτεια in the *Acts of Paul and Thecla* is completely different from the use of ἄσκησις in Plato and Aristotle, where it refers to "training." Even the asceticism in pagan religious and moral aphorisms is mild and self-control is perceived as the basis of virtue (e.g., eating only when we are hungry, not getting drunk, sexual intercourse only for procreation).

34 For further discussion, see Benjamin A. Edsall, "Hermogenes the Smith and Narrative Characterization in the Acts of Paul: A Note on the Reception of 2 Timothy," *NTS* 64 (2018): 108–21.

then, is a lived reality for these two negative characters.[35] Life (and therefore resurrection) continues in future generations. When one has children, one cannot live ascetically. These two characters mask their passions and sexual activity. They live for this world. Thus, both Demas and Hermogenes are initially called "hypocrites" (ὑποκριτής in *APThl* 235/1 and 238/4), who illustrate the false concept of resurrection, which is the opposite of Paul's futural vision. The connection between abstinence and resurrection is a fundamental theme in Paul's crucial sermon which is composed exclusively of beatitudes. This sermon is the key to the whole story.[36]

Statements about the resurrection permeate the narrative and are most pronounced through the voice of Queen Tryphaena (Thecla's patroness, whose daughter Falconilla died) who in *APThl* 265/39, confesses, "Now I believe my child lives." The deceased Falconilla asks her mother Tryphaena in a dream for Thecla to pray for her, and she wants Tryphaena to adopt Thecla as a daughter. Thecla's prayer is a request that Falconilla will live forever (*APThl* 256/29). However, Thecla herself goes to the arena to fight the beasts and is in danger of death. Thecla asks God to reward Tryphaena for keeping her "immaculate" (*APThl* 258/31). Because of this, she can gain eternal life. However, she does not die in the arena and Tryphaena asks God keep her alive (*APThl* 257/30). It is a women's story in which the widow and the virgin receive God's salvation. Falconilla, through Thecla's prayer, hopes to take the place of the righteous (*APThl* 256/28). Thecla is portrayed as a saint during her lifetime due to her sexual austerities and her trials (by fire) in the arena.

From the beginning of the narrative, Paul's conception of eternal life has been associated with abstemiousness and resurrection (*APThl* 238/5), which is in tension with the views of Paul's opponents Demas and Hermogenes (*APThl* 235/1). In dialogue with a certain Thamyris, an objection is raised concerning Paul's view of the resurrection, stating, "But he [Paul] deprives young men of wives and maidens of husbands, saying 'Otherwise there is no resurrection for you, except ye remain chaste and do not defile the flesh, but keep it pure'" (*APThl* 244/12). They advise Thamyris to bring Paul to the governor, Castellius, with accusations that "he is seducing the crowds to the new doctrine of Christians." They teach Thamyris that Paul's anticipated resurrection has already come, saying, "It has already taken place in the children whom we

35 In addition, in PHeid (Heidelberg Coptic Papyrus) 13:24–25, καὶ ἀνιστάμεθα θεὸν ἐπεγνωκότες ἀληθῆ, which would suggest that they may be Gnostics in the case of Demas and Hermogenes.

36 The resurrection plays an important role in all of the Acts about Paul. See Eugene V. Gallagher, "Conversion and Salvation in the Apocryphal Acts of the Apostles," *SecCent* 8 (1991): 13–29, esp. 23.

have and that we are risen again in that we have come to know the true God" (*APThl* 245/14).

There is an interesting link here with 2 Tim 2:18, where Hymenaeus and Philetus likewise hold the view that children are in a resurrected state—to which the author of 2 Timothy objects. Hermogenes (and Phygelus) is mentioned specifically in 2 Tim 1:15 as one of several persons who turned away from Paul, in contrast to the household of Onesiphorus which is given mercy by God because of their support of Paul (2 Tim 1:16–18). The main point is that there was a competing conception of resurrection in circulation, which is already expressed in 2 Timothy, and continued in the *Acts of Paul and Thecla.* The author of the Acts most likely knew the Pastoral Epistles and capitalized on their references to both Paul's opponents and supporters in his presentation of the resurrection. What is clearly missing in 2 Timothy is the advocation that Christians should live in sexual abstinence and should not have children. The primary similarity between the two writings is the condemnation of the "heretical" conception of the resurrection taught by Paul's opponents, particularly Hermogenes (2 Tim 2:21). In this sense, the theological continuity between 2 Timothy and the *Acts of Paul and Thecla* is preserved. Though, again, Paul's gospel of sexual abstemiousness, which is used to counter false doctrines in the *Acts of Paul and Thecla*, turns Paul's conception in a more radical direction compared to 2 Timothy. Paul's shift in the *Acts of Paul and Thecla* can partly be explained by the shift in genre. Unlike a letter, the narrative about Paul and Thecla takes on a fictional tone that attempts to amuse its readers, particularly in relation to sexual abstinence which was a common theme in folk tales and novels. What cannot be lost, however, is its clear presentation of Christian eschatological hope which remains consistent apart from the conditions for achieving it. What is missing in the *Acts of Paul and Thecla* is the expectation of a *parousia* (cf. 1 Thess 2:19), though it is implied. The main concern is that resurrection is achieved through abstemiousness, but only after physical death. The reader encounters Christ in this life in existential confessions and through miracles, as exemplified by Thecla and Paul (*APThl* 263/37, 265/39, 269/43).

The use of ἐγκράτεια ("abstinence"), which is common in the beatitudes of the *Acts of Paul and Thecla*, is only occasionally found in the New Testament.[37] In Acts 24:24–25, Paul speaks before Felix and his Jewish wife Drusilla, about justice, abstemiousness (ἐγκράτεια), and God's judgment, which causes Felix to be anxious. In Gal 5:23, abstemiousness is listed among the fruits of the Spirit

37 Acts 24:25; Gal 5:23; 2 Pet 1:6; 1 Cor 7:9; 9:25; Titus 1:8. See also Alfred Schmoller, *Handkonkordanz zum griechischen Neuen Testament* (Stuttgart: Deutsche Bibelgesellschaft, 1994).

of God (πραΰτης ἐγκράτεια). In 1 Cor 9:25, the one who exercises "abstinence" or "self-control" like an athlete will be rewarded with a victory wreath (πᾶς δὲ ὁ ἀγωνιζόμενος πάντα ἐγκρατεύεται,). Paul's self-practice is presented in even more radical terms in v. 27 (ἀλλὰ ὑπωπιάζω μου τὸ σῶμα). The closest text relating to the motif in the *Acts of Paul and Thecla* is found in 1 Cor 7:9, where Paul advises all those who are unable to live with restraint to enter into marriage, which can alleviate worry (εἰ δὲ οὐκ ἐγκρατεύονται, γαμησάτωσαν κρεῖττον γάρ ἐστιν γαμῆσαι ἢ πυροῦσθαι). Later in vv. 29–35, Paul urges the Corinthians that since the "the time is short," the married are to live as though they have no wives, which is similar to the *Acts of Paul and Thecla* where the term μακάριος is applied to a widow who does not remarry. In 1 Cor 7:40, the term is likewise applied to widows. Paul writes, μακαριωτέρα δέ ἐστιν ἐὰν οὕτως μείνῃ, κατὰ τὴν ἐμὴν γνώμην ("But in my judgement, she is happier if she remains as she is," RSV).[38]

As the previous examples show, Paul does not shy away from abstemiousness in his epistles. Even Luke's Paul does not hesitate to present his theology before Felix with a message of restraint linked with an eschatological (or apocalyptic) emphasis. Nevertheless, it is clear in contrast to these texts that the apocryphal Paul tightens his concept of moderation. Whereas marriage and marital relations are permitted by the canonical Paul, they are not permitted by the apocryphal Paul. The shift may be the due to the apocalyptic orientation of the "Asia Minor presbyter" who was responsible for the composition of the *Acts of Paul and Thecla*, but it may have also functioned as a tool for women's social defiance. At the same time, what cannot be forgotten is that the story was meant to convey exaggeration for the sake of entertaining its audience, as is seen in popular novels in Roman society that relied on parody and romance.

Despite the overlap of Pauline themes and the influence of the Pauline epistles, especially 1 Corinthians 15,[39] the problems addressed in the *Acts of Paul and Thecla* are different. One of the main issues that Paul confronts when corresponding with the Corinthians is the denial of a resurrection. He asks, "How can some among you say that there is no resurrection?" (1 Cor 15:12). In 1 Corinthians 15, the continuation of life for children is not a topic of discussion as it is the *Acts of Paul and Thecla*. Rather, Paul interacts with radical deniers of a bodily resurrection of the body and in the process urges them

38 Peter Dunn writes, "In Clement of Alexandria (*Strom.* 3.80.1) and P 46, the absolute μακάρια stands in the place of the relative μακαριωτέρα, illustrating a tendency to intensify Paul's position on ἐγκράτεια in a way not unlike the *APl.*" See Peter W. Dunn, "The Influence of 1 Corinthians on the Acts of Paul," *SBLSP* 35 (1996): 448. See also McGinn, "The Acts of Thecla," 808.

39 Dunn, "The Influence of 1 Corinthians," 438–54.

not to sin. To support his case, he even quotes from Menander's lost comedy *Thais* (1 Cor 15:33). According to the canonical Paul, attaining resurrection is hindered by immorality, which is harmful not only for Christians, but also for the broader society. In the *Acts of Paul and Thecla*, the main hindrance is sexual intercourse, which implies that Christianity's survival would be severely limited (e.g., the beatitudes M2, M3, M4, M5, M11, M13 in *APThl* 238/5; 239). This implication interestingly overlaps with Paul's eschatology in 1 Cor 7:29 (and 10:11), where he forecasts, "I mean, brethren, the appointed time has grown very short; from now on, let those who have wives live as though they had none." The short time-frame in Paul's eschatological scenario points toward an imminent future age. His conception of a post-mortem existence that is linked with abstinence is found elsewhere in early Christian literature. For example, sexual abstinence is viewed as a foretaste of the heavenly life in Matt 22.30 where the resurrected state is likened to the heavenly angels who do not marry. In the *Acts of Paul and Thecla*, Paul's opponents, Demas and Hermogenes, do not share this perspective, and thus are condemned since they do not have the knowledge of the true God (*APThl* 245/14).

The central theological theme in the *Acts of Paul and Thecla* can be reduced to a contrast between two conceptions of resurrection. The first is Paul's conception which allows for a post-mortem existence. And the second is that of Demas and Hermogenes, which does not consider a post-mortem existence in the future. This second conception is only concerned with the present life and its continued existence in future generations. It is possible that this view may have been influenced by Old Testament texts that refer to the blessings bestowed on the surviving sons of Patriarchs (Gen 48:21). However, in the end, it is difficult to account for this. Even the reference in 2 Tim 2:18 ("our resurrection has already taken place") offers little help in reconstructing this conception.[40]

Pieter Lalleman points out that the *Acts of Paul* would have participated in the vibrant debate about the resurrection in the second century, which affected competing views of Christian identity.[41] Lalleman, who leans on Hippolytus and the work of W. C. van Unnik, suggests that within the context of the larger debate, the views of Demas and Hermogenes could have been based on select Jewish (namely Sadducean) views stemming from Sir 11:28 (LXX). The problem

40 For a complete exegetical analysis of the *Acts of Paul and Thecla*, see Jiří Lukeš, *Raně křesťanská rétorika. Vybrané apokryfní skutky a řeči ve světle rétorických analýz* (Praha: CBS/SGS, 2009), 110–253, esp. 153–253.

41 Pieter J. Lalleman, "The Resurrection in the Acts of Paul," in *The Apocryphal Acts of Paul and Thecla*. ed. Jan N. Bremmer (Kampen: Pharos, 1996), 126–141, esp. 127–8.

is that this text does not refer to resurrection.[42] It may be more closely connected with Pauline texts where Demas is presented as Paul's collaborator in Phil 24 and Col 4:14, but later 2 Tim 4:10 is portrayed as a betrayer of Paul who was "in love with this present world." Demas' position is not unusual among those who rejected Paul's gospel of abstemiousness in favour of prioritizing the joys of the present world over a future resurrection. Hermogenes is also portrayed as a traitor in 2 Tim 1:15. It is, therefore, quite likely for someone in the second century who was familiar with Paul's letters, and involved in the resurrection debate, to create a pair of resurrection deniers from these earlier texts. It is also likely that if Paul's letters were well known in the second century, the names of his opponents in those letters could have functioned as stereotypes, much like "Judas." If this indeed was the case, then there is no need to point to the influence of Jewish or Gentile groups who may have posed a threat to Christianity. The opponents stem from Christian circles.

Remembered Soteriology in the Acts of Paul and Thecla: Women as Bearers of Values

According to Richard Bauckham, the story of Thecla deserves special attention because it is the only section in the *Acts of Paul* where Paul is not the central character.[43] The focus on Thecla resembles Greek novels, which often focus attention on both lovers in a relationship (e.g., the novels of Chariton and Xenophon).[44]

42 Lalleman, "The Resurrection in the Acts of Paul," 136–7.

43 Richard Bauckham, "The Acts of Paul as a Sequel to Acts," in *The Book of Acts in Its First Century Setting. Volume 1: Ancient Literary Setting*, eds. Bruce W. Winter and Andrew D. Clarke (Carlisle: The Paternoster Press 1993), 105–52, here 144, 151. On Theclas' nudity, see Margaret R. Miles, *Carnal Knowing: Female Nakedness and Religious Meaning in the Christian West* (Boston: Beacon, 1989). Miles writes, "Thecla reinterprets her nakedness away from its traditional significance, removing it from the governor's power and aligning it with her strength as a confessor of Christ" (58).

44 The category of ancient novel is used to refer to fictional prose in which the themes of love, journey, and violence are emphasized (often in the lives of two lovers separated and then reunited after numerous trials). They appear more in the late Hellenistic or early Roman period (first century BCE to the first century CE). The "golden age" of these writings is the second and third centuries CE. Five of the most influential "love-and-adventure" novels were written between the first century BCE and the fourth century CE. See Bořivoj Borecký, Karel Hrdina, Rudolf Mertlík, and Ferdinand Stiebitz, *Antické novely* (Praha: KLU, 1965), 197–204, here. 200. Graham Anderson, *Ancient Fiction. The Novel in the Graeco-Roman World* (London: Croom Helm, 1984), 1–6, 25–40, 160–171, 217–20. The Greeks did not have a generic term for novels, but referred to them as *ainos, diégéma,*

The conscious playing with eroticism, though as overtones, is reminiscent of Greek novels, which attracted the attention of female readers.[45] Thecla's commitment to abstinence, as a product of her understanding of the gospel, appealed strongly to readers. In the story, Thecla's devotion to Paul is presented as an example of absolute fidelity to God. The characterisation of Thecla and the other characters who engage the topic of sexual abstinence (in conversion) lead Bauckham to conclude that the story of Thecla was influenced by Greek *erotic novels*.[46]

Dennis McDonald presents an elaborate hypothesis that the *Acts of Paul/ Acts of Paul and Thecla* and the Pastoral Epistles represent a clash of Christian traditions.[47] MacDonald argues that Pastoral Epistles clash with oral legends about Paul which existed long before their incorporation into the *Acts of Paul*

---

logos, historia, akousma. They have been classified as "fictional stories" (*plasmatika*) or "dramatic stories" (*dramatika*) by David E. Aune, *The New Testament in Its Literary Environment* (Philadelphia: The Westminster Press, 1987), 83–4, esp. 150–51. The aim of novels (romances and short stories) was to entertain and please its listeners. Along with peripatetic biography and rhetorical historiography, the novels are close to fiction, but they do not have the same interest in *encomium*. See Pervo, *Profit with Delight*, 120–3. Yamada, "A Rhetorical History," 232. Wilhelm Schneemelcher, "Introduction," in *New Testament Apocrypha. Volume 2: Writings Related to the Apostles, Apocalypses and Related Subjects*, ed. W. Schneemelcher (Louisville: Westminster John Knox Press, 1992), 78–83.

45 According to Virginia Burrus (*Chastity as Autonomy. Women in the Stories of Apocryphal Acts* [Lewiston: The Edwin Mellen Press, 1987], 33–44, 49, 60, 113, 117), the narrators in these stories are Christian women who longed for autonomy and rebelled against male–dominated social structures. There are similarities of motifs and narrative structure in stories of chastity and Hellenistic novels about love, but stories of chastity must not simply be reduced to "Christian novels." For Burrus, stories of chastity are historical experiences which attempt to connect social realities with religious ideals and represent the Christian female heritage. She writes, "These references to women's story–telling in Greco-Roman society suggest the high likelihood that the woman of the Hellenistic communities of the eastern Mediterranean would have produced and transmitted sex-specific women's folk–stories" (71). See also Lynne C. Boughton, "From Pious Legend to Feminist Fantasy. Distinguishing Hagiographical License from Apostolic Practice in the Acts of Paul/Acts of Thecla," *JR* 71 (1991): 362–83, here 375.

46 Bauckham, "The Acts of Paul as a Sequel to Acts," 135–7, 142–5.

47 Dennis R. McDonald, *The Legend and The Apostle: The Battle for Paul in Story and Canon* (Philadelphia: Westminster Press, 1983); Burrus, *Chastity as Autonomy*, 105.

and Thecla, whose narrators were women.[48] The root of the clash, according to MacDonald, lies in disagreements about the role and function of women in the second-century Church. The Pastoral Epistles portray a socially *conservative* Paul which differs from a more socially *radical* portrayal in later legends. The broader context that accounts for this shift, according to MacDonald, is the dispute between the "great church" and the followers of the "new prophecy" advocated within the Montanist movement. Whereas 1 Tim 2:12 forbids women to teach, the *Acts of Paul* has no problem with Thecla taking on the role of Paul's prophetess who teaches the word of God (*APThl* 41). In 1 Tim 5:14, Paul exhorts younger widows to marry and have children, but in the *Acts of Paul and Thecla*, Paul is opposed to Thecla marrying (*APThl* 242/9). In Titus 2:5, women are advised to submit to their husbands and to be chaste, whereas the *Acts of Paul and Thecla* unequivocally rejects cohabitation with a man (*APThl* 238–240/5–6). Other differences concern dietary practices, usually in relation to false teachers who advocate restrictions. For example, moderate practices in relation to drinking in 1 Tim 5:23 and Titus 2:2–3 are forbidden in *APThl* 253/25, which also advocates vegetarianism and the substitution of wine for water in the Eucharist (PH 4 /Hamburg Papyrus).[49] MacDonald views the admonition against entertaining "old wives' tales" in 1 Tim 4:7 as a response to groups of Christian women who were supporters of the Montanist movement and its apocalyptic Christianity. According to MacDonald, the accompanying feature of radical apocalypticism was the rejection of marital cohabitation and rebellion against male dominance.[50]

MacDonald's position is shared by others. For example, Kate Cooper concludes that the importance of "chastity" is rooted in the desire for self-determination.[51]

---

48 MacDonald, *The Legend and The Apostle*, 17–33.

49 MacDonald (*The Legend and The Apostle*, 85, 89) dates the *Acts of Paul* between 160 and 190 when the conflict between the bishops and Montanism was most intense. According to MacDonald, the Pastoral Epistles "became domesticated" in the church only at the end of the second century.

50 MacDonald, *The Legend and The Apostle*, 17–89, here 62. Margaret Y. MacDonald, *Early Christian Women and Pagan Opinion* (Cambridge: Cambridge University Press, 1996), 165–82; Stevan L. Davies, "Women in the Third Gospel and the New Testament Apocrypha," in *Women Like This. New Perspectives on Jewish Women in the Greco-Roman World*, SBLEJL 1, ed. Amy-Jill Levine (Atlanta: Scholars Press, 1991), 185–97, esp. 194–97. On the social and political context of the *Acts of Paul and Thecla*, see Korinna Zamfir, "The Acts of Paul and Thecla: Ecclesial, Social and Political Context," *ETL* 92 (2016): 355–80.

51 Kate Cooper, "Apostles, Ascetic Women, and Questions of Audience: New Reflections on the Rhetoric of Gender in the Apocryphal Acts," *SBLSP* 31 (1992): 147–53, here 152. Kate Cooper, *The Virgin and the Bride. Idealized Womanhood in Late Antiquity* (Cambridge: Harvard University Press, 1996), 28–36.

However, it can also be argued that the stipulations in the apocryphal acts are not directed against injustices in pre-existing unions, but rather they are directed toward promoting sexual abstinence, so that men who cohabitate with women might live as if they are single (*APThl* 5; 1 Cor 7:27–29). The problem, then, is not the patriarchal model of marriage, but the unconverted husband or fiancé, who does not respect the sexual abstinence that was to be the result of conversion.[52] According to MacDonald, the author(s) of the Pastoral Epistles supports marriage, the household, the traditional role of women, so that the church can be embraced socially. However, this is achieved through the dominant role of male leadership structures, which relies on Paul's legacy. In the *Acts of Paul and Thecla* the emphasis is on the ideal of virginity, which represented a social value of that day. While the author(s) of the Pastoral Epistles does not forbid virginity, he recommends marriage as a defence against immorality (1 Tim 5:11–15; 2 Tim 3:6–7), which is consistent with Paul's teaching in 1 Corinthians 7. These Pauline statements, however, can also be interpreted as agreeing with the *Acts of Paul* (1 Cor 7:7, 8, 17, 20). In the Pastoral Epistles and the legends that preceded the *Acts of Paul*, it is possible to find discontinuity with Paul (as MacDonald does), but it is also possible to find continuity. In each case, inspiration from Paul's primary writings can used in support.[53] At stake is the metaphysical quality of life in the future age that salvation will bring in relation to the specific social conflict and identity formation of the readers. The community represented in the *Acts of Paul and Thecla* could have even read the story in a way where metaphysical questions are secondary. The narrative can be taken as a model for action in an entirely earthly context.

To today's reader, the *Acts of Paul and Thecla* sounds comical. The characters are straightforward, predictable, perhaps even black and white, and the plot addresses bizarre topics, especially sexual abstinence. In the story, Paul competes for Thecla with her fiancé Thamyris. Paul's teaching is so intoxicating that he triumphs over the young and high-ranking fiancé. Despite the mother's insistence (*APThl* 242/243–10) and Paul's unappealing appearance

52 Gallagher, "Conversion and Salvation," 13–29.

53 Peter W. Dunn, "Women's Liberation, the Acts of Paul, and Other Apocryphal Acts of the Apostles," *Apocrypha* 4 (1993): 245–61, here 253. Yue L. Ng, "Acts of Paul and Thecla. Women's Stories and Precedent?" *JTS* 55 (2004): 1–29, esp. 24–8. For a critique of MacDonald's theory, see Richard Valantasis, "Narrative Strategies and Synoptic Quandaries: A Response to Dennis MacDonald's Reading of Acts of Paul and Acts of Peter," *SBLSP* 31 (1992): 234–39. Margaret P. Aymer ("Hailstorms and Fireballs: Redaction, World Creation and Resistance in the Acts of Paul and Thecla," *Semeia* 79 [1997], 45–62) suggests that the story of Paul and Thecla is the product of editing and the merging of two folk legends, which is indicated by a rhetoric of "resistance and identity formation."

(*APThl* 273/3), the alure is too strong. Undoubtedly, the ancient reader would have drawn comparisons between the *Acts of Paul and Thecla* and contemporary romances (e.g., Achilles Tatius, *Clitophon and Leucippe*) and shorter, more frivolous, stories (e.g., by Livius, Plutarch, and Apuleius) which describe love in a variety of ways. However, Thecla stands out because she is the heroine expressed in a highly mimetic mode. She achieves her goals by strictly adhering to the demands of Paul's beatitudes and by redirecting her focus away from a conventional feminine role. Like other heroines in romance stories (e.g., Antheia from the *Ephesian Tale* /*Ephesiaca* by Xenophon of Ephesus), she is portrayed as being beautiful (*APThl* 250/22; 253/25; 257/29).[54]

There are many other similarities that the educated ancient reader would have observed as the following comparisons indicate. First, God's role in the process is similar to that of Zeus in comparable stories. For example, in the work of the orator Libanius (ca. 314–393), Zeus sends thunder and lightning, obscuring the sun behind thick clouds. Second, the roles of young people in the *Acts of Paul and Thecla* correspond to contemporary stories, such as their comparable portrayals in, again, the work of Libanius and *APThl* 250/22 where the young people loyally carry wood to the place where Thecla is to be burned.[55] And third, the narrative about Thecla resembles the works of the rhetoricians of Hellenism and more broadly late antiquity. Where the story about Thecla differs from these is that she is not associated with the conventional heroines who are portrayed as being frivolous and unfaithful to their husbands. The sexual abstemiousness in the apocryphal acts composed supposedly by Leucius Charinus is a new feature that is linked to a Christian community's ethos, which ultimately is concerned with salvation. While the heroine's portrayal makes sense within some Christian contexts, it is not clear how it would have been received in other Christian contexts, let alone within the broader culture. We do know that certain bishops censored the apocryphal acts because they supposedly did not cohere with the authoritative teaching of the "great church."

It is hard to say how much of an influence Thecla's character had on the readers. Within the narrative, Thecla's attitude inspires the sympathy of female spectators in the arena (*APThl* 255/27; 264/38), and thereby threatens the disintegration of household structures and the city as a whole. The tone of the whole story is comedic, but has a pathetic conclusion. Nevertheless, the

54 Anderson, *Ancient Fiction*, 2–6, 17–19, 30–40, 160–71. *Libanius' Autobiography* (*Oration I*), ed. A. F. Norman (Oxford: Oxford University Press, 1965), par. 9; compare with *APThl* 250/22.

55 *Libanius' Autobiography*, par. 25.

narrative contains authentic confessions, prayers and teachings about the resurrection, which would have impacted the Christian reader/hearer's identity as a member of a faith community. The ideal of abstemiousness, however, in the *Acts of Paul and Thecla*, as well as in other apocryphal acts of the apostles, is a requirement that has no flexibility, which again differs from Greek romances where it is limited to the duration of time that lovers are separated. These differences reflect the variations in the narrative-rhetorical structure (*dispositio*) of apocryphal acts and romances. While *eros* is privileged in romances and short stories when describing the relationship between lovers, the apocryphal acts devalue *eros* and replace it with fidelity to the faith associated with one or several apostles.[56] Whereas romances end with an enthusiastic celebration of marriage, the apocryphal acts end with the martyrdoms of the apostles. Specifically, in the *Acts of Paul and Thecla*, the story ends with the death of Thamyris and Thecla in Seleucia (*APThl* 269/43). From the vantage point of what is achieved, it can be said that both romances and the *Acts of Paul and Thecla* end happily since both sets of characters achieve their aspiration, even though the conclusions are completely different.

It is noteworthy that Thecla's passion for Paul is as intense as that of the heroines in romances. Thecla's intensity explains why Thamyris is so jealous (*APThl* 245/15). Her gestures, eyes, speech, and other expressions (*APThl* 241–243/8–10) suggest that the relationship transcends the spiritual plane (*APThl* 247–248/18–19). Thecla is willing to get her hair cut and accompany Paul wherever he goes (*APThl* 253/25). Throughout her accompaniment, she experiences suffering and loss, which can be seen as an expression of devotion to Paul and his teaching. She loses her mother who turns against Thecla and wants to burn her (*APThl* 249/20). She loses her fiancé. She gives away her jewellery (*APThl* /18) and completely detaches from the structures of the οἶκος (household, family, home, background). Her beauty leads to further trials when she rejects a suitor's proposal. She becomes the victim of the "conspiracy" launched by her fiancé Thamyris along with Demas and Hermogenes (*APThl* 245/14–16). She tries to suppress her femininity by wearing a *chiton*, which was a male garment, so that she could join Paul with the other men (*APThl* 260/34; 266/40). The veiling of beauty and defeminization give Thecla a special status that separates and protects her from Alexander's interests. When Thecla meets up with Paul, who marvels at her character, she attracts the attention of the crowds (*APThl* 266/40) and is sent clothing and gold from Queen Tryfaina, which she leaves for the poor (*APThl* 267/41). In all these incidents,

56 David Konstan, "Acts of Love: A Narrative Pattern in the Apocryphal Acts," *JECS* 6 (1998): 15–36, here 15.

Thecla conveys happiness because she achieves her goals. She is portrayed as a pagan girl who becomes a model of the ideal Christian in the second century, for both men and women. She is a symbol for those who will be resurrected. Her personality, like that of the Apostle Paul, is legendary.

The collective memory expressed through the story describes Paul's image very well. However, that image takes on several nuances, as we have seen, in his letters, Acts of the Apostles, the Pastoral Epistles, and even in the *Acts of Paul*. The character Paul remains in them all, but takes on different portrayals. Paul's image remains influential long after his death, but his portrayal is affected by the communities, genres, and cultural frameworks which receive and express it. The written texts temporally suspend the memories of the person, but they also suspended receptions of Paul's conceptions of the resurrection, which appear to have been been more stable perhaps due to the broader conception found in Judaism. Alongside these memories, the reader is confronted with the motif of sexual abstinence and purity, sometimes with humour, which places the *Acts of Paul* and the *Acts of Paul and Thecla* within a category of entertaining works that still appeal to modern readers, some eighteen centuries later.

The apostle, who was apparently unmarried since his "conversion" (1 Cor 7: 8), becomes the "seducer" of all the women in Iconium in the *Acts of Paul and Thecla* (245/15) through his gospel of restraint and purity (*APThl* 241/7). Although this comment can be taken in jest, the image of Paul as an influential Christian orator is preserved in the collective memory of a group that was fixated on propagating a specific ethical ideal. As a preacher, Paul conquers the world for Christ and brings hope to the women of the Roman Empire. As a literary figure, he enters new possible worlds, and his image becomes another variation of reality, which corresponds to the genre and ideals of (ascetic) communities. The hope and conception of a metaphysical future life in the resurrection which is initiated by Christian women can be understood as a "social revolution" aimed against the prevailing social order.[57]

---

57 Stevan L. Davies (*The Revolt of the Widows. The Social World of the Apocryphal Acts* [Carbondale: Southern Illinois University Press, 1980], 70–94, esp. 86, 107) also focuses on identifying dissatisfied Christian women behind the apocryphal deeds of the apostles, who remember women from the group of widows who supposedly played a significant role in the writings of the early church. Davies believes that these women also wrote apocryphal acts, and that their stories are an expression of the desire for freedom and emancipation. These were women who held authoritative and perhaps prophetic positions. According to Davies, apocryphal acts are similar to ancient romances, and they were probably written primarily for female audiences, which is the opinion of Nicola Denzey, *The Bone Gatherers: The Lost Worlds of Early Christian Women* (Boston: Beacon Press, 2007), 106–108. See also Judith Perkins (*The Suffering Self: Pain and Narrative Representation in the Early Christian Era* (Routledge, London 1995, 44–5) who argues that "the stories precisely do *not* celebrate chastity (*sophrosyne*), the virtue proper to a

Conclusion

When the portrayals of Paul are viewed from the perspective of collective memory, we notice how the image of a revered figure is not only shaped by what he has actually accomplished in the past, but we also notice how the image is shaped to conform to new environments which necessarily remove, select and add to the received image. At the same time, it is clear that each community assumed that it was preserving the "true" and applying it in support of its values. In the second century, the canonical Paul in the NT expressions co-exists with the Paul of apocryphal literature and they intensely interact with one another in relation to conceptions of the "great church." Paul lives in a world of literature and orality. Together with Thecla,[58] his image is appropriated by women in their narrated stories and by authors of propagandistic literature. His image is not diminished in any way. On the contrary, Paul and Thecla are at home in the world of fictional and canonical compositions, which are further orally translated and received. It is even possible that received images at times merged. In addition, the censorship of the apocryphal acts by bishops suggests that they sought to protect the canonical Paul from the popular Paul of legends and unauthorized traditions. One is reminded of Christine Thomas' observation about "stories without authors and without texts," which were "stories that belonged to the world."[59]

---

devoted, and fertile, wife. Rather, they celebrate heroines who substitute for chastity the (potentially antithetical) virtue of continence (*enkrateia*)." Note also, Cooper, "Apostles, Ascetic Women, and Questions of Audience," 151. Contra Dunn, "Women's Liberation," 257; Jean-Daniel Kaestli, "Fiction littéraire et réalité sociale. Que peut-on savoir de la place des femmes dans le milieu de production des Actes apocryphes des Apôtres?" *Apocrypha/ Le champ des apocryphes 1* (1990): 279–302; Christine M. Thomas, "The Scriptures and the New Prophecy: Montanism as Exegetical Crisis," in *Early Christian Voices in Texts, Traditions and Symbols: Essays in Honor of François Bovon*, ed. David H. Warren, Ann Graham Brock, and David W. Pao, BIS 66 (Leiden: Brill, 2003), 155–65. Current feminist research, as represented for example by Kate Cooper and Melissa Aubin, does not classify the apocryphal acts of the apostles as romance stories. Still, this view admits that the similarity is not accidental. I argue that romance seeks to preserve the idea of social stability by elevating the role of marriage and the approval of the curial class. See Melissa Aubin, "Reversing Romance? The Acts of Thecla and the Ancient Novel," in *Ancient Fiction and Early Christian Narrative*, ed. Ronald F. Hock, J. Bradley Chance, and Judith Perkins (Atlanta: Scholars Press, 1998), 257–72. esp. 257, 260.

58 Stephen J. Davis, *The Cult of Saint Thecla: A Tradition of Women's Piety in Late Antiquity* (Oxford: Oxford University Press, 2001).

59 Christine M. Thomas, "Stories Without Texts and Without Authors: The Problem of Fluidity in Ancient Novelistic Texts and Early Christian Literature," in *Ancient Fiction and Early Christian Narrative*, ed. Ronald F. Hock, J. Bradley Chance, and Judith Perkins (Atlanta: Scholars Press, 1998), 273–91, esp. 289.

Bibliography

Anderson, Graham. *Ancient Fiction. The Novel in the Graeco-Roman World.* London: Croom Helm, 1984.

Assmann, Aleida. *Erinnerungsräume. Formen und Wandlungen des kulturellen Gedächtnisses.* München: C. H. Beck, 1999.

Assmann, Aleida and Jan Assmann. "Exkurs: Archäologie der literarischen Kommunikation." Pages 200–206 in *Einführung in die Literaturwiessenschaft.* Edited by Miltos Pechlivanos, Stefan Rieger, Wolfgang Struck, and Michael Weitz. Stuttgart: J. B. Metzler Verlag, 1995.

Assmann, Jan. "Collective Memory and Cultural Identity." *New German Critique* 65 (1995): 125–33.

Aubin, Melissa. "Reversing Romance? The Acts of Thecla and the Ancient Novel." Pages 257–72 in *Ancient Fiction and Early Christian Narrative.* Edited by Ronald F. Hock, J. Bradley Chance, and Judith Perkins. Atlanta: Scholars Press, 1998.

Aune, David E. *The New Testament in Its Literary Environment.* Philadelphia: The Westminster Press, 1987.

——. *The Westminster Dictionary of New Testament and Early Christian Literature and Rhetoric.* Louisville: Westminster John Knox Press, 2003.

Aymer, Margaret P. "Hailstorms and Fireballs: Redaction, World Creation and Resistance in the Acts of Paul and Thecla." *Semeia* 79 (1997), 45–62.

Bauckham, Richard. "The Acts of Paul as a Sequel to Acts." Pages 105–52 in *The Book of Acts in Its First Century Setting. Volume 1: Ancient Literary Setting.* Edited by Bruce W. Winter and Andrew D. Clarke. Carlisle: The Paternoster Press 1993.

Borecký, Bořivoj, Karel Hrdina, Rudolf Mertlík, and Ferdinand Stiebitz. *Antické novely.* Praha: KLU, 1965.

Boughton, Lynne C. "From Pious Legend to Feminist Fantasy. Distinguishing Hagiographical License from Apostolic Practice in the Acts of Paul/Acts of Thecla." *JR* 71 (1991): 362–83.

Burrus, Virginia. *Chastity as Autonomy. Women in the Stories of Apocryphal Acts.* Lewiston: The Edwin Mellen Press, 1987.

Cicero, Marcus Tullius. *Tusculanarum disputationum.* Edited by C. F. W. Müller. Leipzig: B. G. Teubner, 1913.

——. *Laelius de amicitia, Cato Maior de senectute.* Edited by C. Meissner. Leipzig: B. G. Teubner, 1917.

——. *De oratore.* Edited by Kazimierz F. Kumanicki. Leipzig: B. G. Teubner, 1969.

——. *Řečník. Řeči proti Catilinovi. Filipiky a iné.* Edited by Peter Kuklica and Daniel Škoviera. Bratislava: Tatran, 1982.

——. *On Life and Death.* Edited by John Davie and Miriam T. Griffin. Oxford World's Classics. New York: Oxford University Press 2017.

———. *Výbor z korespondence*, I. Díl. Edited by Václav Marek. Praha: Argo, 2019.

Chatman, Seymour. *Story and Discourse: Narrative Structure in Fiction and Film*. Ithaca, New York: Cornell University Press, 1980.

Conte, Gian B. *Dějiny římské literatury*. Praha: KLP, 2003.

Cooper, Kate. "Apostles, Ascetic Women, and Questions of Audience: New Reflections on the Rhetoric of Gender in the Apocryphal Acts." *SBLSP* 31 (1992): 147–53.

———. *The Virgin and the Bride. Idealized Womanhood in Late Antiquity*. Cambridge: Harvard University Press, 1996.

Davis, Stephen J. *The Cult of Saint Thecla: A Tradition of Women's Piety in Late Antiquity*. Oxford: Oxford University Press, 2001.

Davies Stevan L. *The Revolt of the Widows. The Social World of the Apocryphal Acts*. Carbondale: Southern Illinois University Press, 1980.

———. "Women in the Third Gospel and the New Testament Apocrypha." Pages 185–97 in *Women Like This. New Perspectives on Jewish Women in the Greco-Roman World*, SBLEJL 1. Edited by Amy-Jill Levine. Atlanta: Scholars Press, 1991.

Denzey, Nicola. *The Bone Gatherers: The Lost Worlds of Early Christian Women*. Boston: Beacon Press, 2007.

Dodds, E. R. *Pagan and Christian in an Age of Anxiety*. Cambridge: Cambridge University Press, 1994.

Dunn, Peter W. "Women's Liberation, the Acts of Paul, and Other Apocryphal Acts of the Apostles." *Apocrypha* 4 (1993): 245–61.

———. "The Influence of 1 Corinthians on the Acts of Paul." *SBLSP* 35 (1996): 438–54.

Dus, Jan A., ed. *Příběhy apoštolů. Novozákonní apokryfy II*. Praha: Vyšehrad, 2003.

Ebel, Eva. "The Life of Paul." Pages 97–109 in *Paul: Life, Setting, Work, Letters*. Edited by Oda Wischmeyer. London: T & T Clark, 2012.

Edsall, Benjamin A. "Hermogenes the Smith and Narrative Characterization in the Acts of Paul: A Note on the Reception of 2 Timothy." *NTS* 64 (2018): 108–21.

Ford, J. Massingberd. "The Meaning of Virgin." *NTS* 12 (1966): 293–99.

Frye, Northrop. *Anatomy of Criticism: Four Essays*. Princeton: Princeton University Press, 1973.

Halbwachs, Maurice. *Kolektivní paměť*. Translated by Yasar Abu Ghosh, et al. Praha: Sociologické nakladatelství, 2009.

Hägg, Tomas. *The Novel in Antiquity*. Oxford: Basil Blackwell 1983.

Howe, E. Margaret. "Interpretations of Paul in the Acts of Paul and Thecla." Pages 33–49 in *Pauline Studies. Essays Presented to Professor F.F. Bruce on his 70th Birthday*. Edited by Donald A. Hagner and Murray J. Harris. Devon: The Paternoster Press, 1980.

Huebenthal, Sandra. *Reading Mark's Gospel as a Text from Collective Memory*. Grand Rapids: Eerdmans, 2020.

Kaestli, Jean–Daniel. "Fiction littéraire et réalité sociale. Que peut-on savoir de la place des femmes dans le milieu de production des Actes apocryphes des Apôtres?" *Apocrypha/Le champ des apocryphes 1* (1990): 279–302.

Kennedy, George A. *New Testament Interpretation through Rhetorical Criticism*. Chapel Hill: The University of North Carolina Press, 1984.

Konstan, David. "Acts of Love: A Narrative Pattern in the Apocryphal Acts." *JECS* 6 (1998): 15–36.

Kraus, Jiří. *Rhetoric in European Culture and Beyond*. Prague: Karolinum, 2014.

Lachmann, Renate. *Gedächtnis und Literatur. Intertextualität in der russischen Moderne*. Frankfurt/M.: Suhrkamp, 1990.

Lalleman, Pieter J. "The Resurrection in the Acts of Paul." Pages 126–41 in *The Apocryphal Acts of Paul and Thecla*. Edited by Jan N. Bremmer. Kampen: Pharos, 1996.

Lukeš, Jiří. *Raně křesťanská rétorika. Vybrané apokryfní skutky a řeči ve světle rétorických analýz*. Praha: CBS/SGS, 2009.

MacDonald, Dennis R. "Paul's Farewell to the Ephesian Elders and Hector's Farewell to Andromache: A Strategic Imitation of Homer's Iliad." Pages 189–203 in *Contextualizing Acts: Lukan Narrative and Greco-Roman Discourse*, SBLSymS 20. Edited by Todd Penner and Caroline Vander Stichele. Atlanta: SBL Press, 2003.

Malina, Bruce J. and Jerome H. Neyrey. *Portraits of Paul: An Archeology of Ancient Personality*. Louisville: Westminster John Knox Press, 1996.

Marguerat, Daniel. *The First Christian Historian: Writing the 'Acts of the Apostles.'* Cambridge: Cambridge University Press, 2002.

MacDonald, Margaret Y. *Early Christian Women and Pagan Opinion*. Cambridge: Cambridge University Press, 1996.

McDonald, Dennis R. *The Legend and The Apostle: The Battle for Paul in Story and Canon*. Philadelphia: Westminster Press, 1983.

McGinn, Sheila E. "The Acts of Thecla." Pages 800–28 in *Searching the Scripture. Volume 2: A Feminist Commentary*. Edited by Elisabeth Schüssler Fiorenza. New York: Crossroad, 1994.

Miles, Margaret R. *Carnal Knowing: Female Nakedness and Religious Meaning in the Christian West*. Boston: Beacon, 1989.

Ng, Yue L. "Acts of Paul and Thecla. Women's Stories and Precedent?" *JTS* 55 (2004): 1–29.

Perkins, Judith. *The Suffering Self: Pain and Narrative Representation in the Early Christian Era*. Routledge, London, 1995.

Pervo, Richard. *Profit with Delight. The Literary Genre of the Acts of the Apostles*. Philadelphia: Fortress Press, 1987.

Pokorný, Petr and Ulrich Heckel. *Einleitung in das Neue Testament. Seine Literatur und Theologie im Überblick*. Tübingen: Mohr Siebeck, 2007.

Rieger, Stefan. "Memoria und Oblivio. Die Aufzeichnung des Menschen." Pages 378–82 in *Einführung in die Literaturwissenschaft*. Edited by Miltos Pechlivanos, Stefan Rieger, Wolfgang Struck, and Michael Weitz. Stuttgart: J. B. Metzler Verlag, 1995.

Rhee, Helen. *Early Christian Literature: Christ and Culture in the Second and Third Centuries. The Apologies, Apocryphal Acts and Martyr Acts.* New York: Routledge, 2005.

Rousselle, Aline. *Porneia: On Desire and the Body in Antiquity.* Eugene: Wipf and Stock, 2013.

Schneemelcher, Wilhelm. "Introduction." Pages 78–83 in *New Testament Apocrypha. Volume 2: Writings Related to the Apostles, Apocalypses and Related Subjects.* Edited by W. Schneemelcher. Louisville: Westminster John Knox Press, 1992.

Schneemelcher, Wilhelm and Rodolphe Kasser. "The Acts of Paul." Pages 234–35 in *New Testament Apocrypha. Volume 2: Writings Relating to the Apostles; Apocalypses and Related Subjects.* Edited by Wilhelm Schneemelcher. Louisville: Westminster/John Knox Press 1992.

Schubart, Wilhelm and Carl Schmidt. *ΠΡΑΞΕΙΣ ΠΑΥΛΟΥ.* Glückstadt: J. J. Augustin, 1936.

Struck, Wolfgang. "Soziale Funktion und kultureller Status literarischer Texte oder: Autonomie als Heteronomie." Pages 182–99, in *Einführung in die Literaturwiessenschaft.* Edited by Miltos Pechlivanos, Stefan Rieger, Wolfgang Struck, and Michael Weitz. Stuttgart: J. B. Metzler Verlag, 1995.

Šubrt, Jiří, Nicolas Maslowski, and Štěpánka Lehmann. "Maurice Halwachs, koncept rámců paměti a kolektivní paměti." Pages 15–30 in *Kolektivní paměť: k teoretickým otázkám.* Edited by Nicolas Maslowski and Jiří Šubrt. Praha: Karolinum, 2014.

Thomas, Christine M. "Stories without Texts and Without Authors: The Problem of Fluidity in Ancient Novelistic Texts and Early Christian Literature." Pages 273–91 in *Ancient Fiction and Early Christian Narrative.* Edited by Ronald F. Hock, J. Bradley Chance, and Judith Perkins. Atlanta: Scholars Press, 1998.

———. "The Scriptures and the New Prophecy: Montanism as Exegetical Crisis." Pages 155–65 in *Early Christian Voices in Texts, Traditions and Symbols: Essays in Honor of François Bovon*, BIS 66. Edited by David H. Warren, Ann Graham Brock, and David W. Pao. Leiden: Brill, 2003.

Todorov, Tzvetan. *Introduction à la littérature fantastique.* Paris: Seuil, 1970.

Valantasis, Richard. "Narrative Strategies and Synoptic Quandaries: A Response to Dennis MacDonald's Reading of Acts of Paul and Acts of Peter." *SBLSP* 31 (1992): 234–39.

Welzer, Harald. "Co je to komunikativní paměť a z čeho se skládá." Pages 73–89 in *Paměť a trauma pohledem humanitních věd.* Edited by Alexander Kratochvíl. Praha: Akropolis, 2015.

White, Hayden. *Metahistory: The Historical Imagination in Nineteenth-Century Europe.* Baltimore: Johns Hopkins University Press, 1975.

Yamada, Kota. "A Rhetorical History: The Literary Genre of the Acts of the Apostles." Pages 230–50 in *Rhetoric, Scripture and Theology. Essays from the 1994 Pretoria Conference*. Edited by Stanley E. Porter, Thomas H. Olbricht. JSNTSup 131. Sheffield: Sheffield Academic Press, 1996.
Zamfir, Korinna. "The Acts of Paul and Thecla: Ecclesial, Social and Political Context." *ETL* 92 (2016): 355–80.

“And I saw another place …” (*ApcPet* 21): The Greek *Apocalypse of Peter* and its Otherworldly Landscape of Memories

Tobias Nicklas

Introduction

Texts and stories influence our perception of the world. What could be seen as a small country in the East of the Mediterranean, consisting of a mixture of desert, coastline, a few cities and the Dead Sea plus some fertile regions around Lake Tiberias has been perceived as the “Holy Land” for centuries.[1] In its historical capital, Jerusalem, we find a place of the size of a soccer field, which is perceived as “holy” by the members of three different world religions. Battles were fought and people died for this space—and a big part of today’s conflicts in the Near East cannot be understood without the idea that Jerusalem’s Temple Mount is the holiest place in the world. The world we construct, however, does not only consist of places, which can be located on a map—it is full of imagined spaces whose role and function can change in different times and contexts. The connection of space,[2] story, plus in many cases aspects of different media like rituals, art, music or material culture, can construct “landscapes of memories.”[3] It is these landscapes which help us to make sense of the world wherein we live.

1 Regarding the origins of this idea see, for example, Joan E. Taylor, *Christians and the Holy Places: The Myth of Jewish-Christian Origins* (Oxford: Clarendon Press, 1993). For a new, interreligious approach to this idea that focuses on the role of apocryphal material, see the collection of essays in Harald Buchinger, Andreas Merkt and Tobias Nicklas, eds., *Extracanonical Traditions and the Holy Land: Texts, Rituals and Material Culture*, STAC (Tübingen: Mohr Siebeck, forthcoming 2021).

2 Regarding the idea of space created by narrative, see Albrecht Koschorke, *Wahrheit und Erfindung. Grundzüge einer Allgemeinen Erzähltheorie* (Frankfurt am Main: S. Fischer, 2012), 111–5.

3 For this term and the ideas connected to it see Pierre Nora, *Les lieux de mémoire*, Volumes 1–3 (Paris: Gallimard, 1984–1992). See also the German translation, *Erinnerungsorte Frankreichs* (Munich: C. H. Beck, 2005). I appropriate this concept in Tobias Nicklas, “New Testament Canon and Ancient Landscapes of Memory,” *Early Christianity* 7 (2016): 5–23; “Neutestamentlicher Kanon, christliche Apokryphen und christliche ‘Erinnerungskulturen,’” *NTS* 62 (2016): 588–609; “Die Akten des Titus: Rezeption ‘apostolischer’ Schriften und Entwicklung antik-christlicher ‘Erinnerungslandschaften,’” *Early Christianity* 8 (2017): 458–80.

 | doi:10.30965/9783657796212_012

In the following study, I would like to have a look at a widely neglected text. Despite its neglect, it played a decisive role in the development of ideas about an imagined space which—even if nobody knows the extent of its portrayal of the "real"—influenced Christianized societies (as well as others) for centuries. I will draw our attention to the *Apocalypse of Peter*, an extracanonical writing which contains probably the earliest detailed Christian description of "hell" (but also refers to additional "otherworldly" places like paradise and the kingdom of Christ).[4] Within its special description of hell the *Apocalypse of Peter* both creates (and/or reshapes) a "landscape of memories" that constructs an image of the world by which it wants to reframe and influence its readers' perceptions. At the same time, the text can be understood as the textual expression of a "frozen moment"[5] in the addressed community's *collective memory*.[6] Even if this memory is related to past events, that is, a series of revelations given by Jesus to Peter,[7] its main focus is not on the past alone. Instead, Jesus' predictions about the end of the world and the world(s) to come relate to (imagined) future events which are decisive for the addressed group's

4 Of course, we find comparable ideas already in the New Testament like the fiery furnace in Matt 13:42 and "hades" in Luke 16:23, which is separated from Abraham's side by an unbreachable abyss (Luke 16:26).

5 I adopt this expression from Sandra Huebenthal, "'Frozen Moments'—Early Christianity through the Lens of Social Memory Theory," in *Memory and Memories in Early Christianity. Proceedings of the International Conference held at the Universities of Geneva and Lausanne (June, 2–3, 2016)*, eds. Simon Butticaz and Enrico Norelli, WUNT 398 (Tübingen: Mohr Siebeck, 2018), 17–44. I approach the same phenomenon in relation to ancient Christian Gospels which can be understood as "re-enactments" of a story which made it into the collective (and after some time) cultural memories of early Christian groups. See, for example, Tobias Nicklas, "Zwischen Redaktion und 'Neuinszenierung.' Vom Umgang erzählender Evangelien des 2. Jahrhunderts mit ihren Vorlagen," in *Gospels and Gospel Traditions in the Second Century: Experiments in Reception*, eds. Jens Schröter, Tobias Nicklas and Joseph Verheyden, BZNW 235 (Berlin: de Gruyter, 2019), 311–30.

6 As is generally known, this term goes back to Maurice Halbwachs, *La mémoire collective*, Bibliothèque de l'Évolution de l'Humanité 28 (Paris: Les Presses universitaires de France, 1950). An important example of its use in New Testament exegesis is offered by Sandra Huebenthal, *Das Markusevangelium als kollektives* Gedächtnis, FRLANT 253 (Göttingen: Vandenhoeck & Ruprecht, 2014).

7 Of course, one could see the text also as an expression of a "remembered Jesus" (and thus even relate it to questions about the historical Jesus and his reception) or a remembered Peter. On this approach to the text (influenced by Jens Schröter, "Der 'erinnerte Jesus': Erinnerung als geschichtshermeneutisches Paradigma der Jesusforschung," in *Jesus Handbuch*, eds. Jens Schröter and Christine Jacobi [Tübingen: Mohr Siebeck, 2017], 112–24) see Tobias Nicklas, "Apocalypse of Peter," in *From Thomas to Tertullian: Christian Literary Receptions of Jesus in the Second and Third Centuries*, eds. Jens Schröter and Christine Jacobi (London: T&T Clark, 2019), 331–40.

construction of its present. This leads to my main questions: (1) To what extent does the *Apocalypse of Peter*'s description of hell construct and/or reshape a landscape of memories? (2) To what extent can this expression of collective memory relate to decisive questions for the addressed group's construction of "identity"?[8]

Before I take a closer look at the text, a few introductory issues are necessary: The Greek/Ethiopic *Apocalypse of Peter* (which should not be confused with the Coptic *Revelation of Peter* from Nag Hammadi [NHC VII,3]) is transmitted in several versions. Besides two small fragments in Greek (plus a few quotations by ancient Christian authors) there is a long Greek fragment preserved in the six/seventh century (so-called) Akhmim-Codex which also contains the *Gospel of Peter*.[9] This fragment, however, is in many ways different from the only full version of the text, which is, however, extant only in Ethiopic.[10] All this makes any scholarly treatment of the text quite difficult. At the same time the (presumed) original version of the *Apocalypse of Peter* is certainly much older than the available fragments. The text is quoted explicitly in the early works of Clement of Alexandria (who even seems to have commented on it in his *Hypotyposes*) and other ancient authors.[11] Since Wolfgang Grünstäudl

8 I am aware of the problems related to the term "identity" (even "social identity" or "group identity"). That is why I try to avoid the idea of something like a stable, given "identity" and try to speak only of "constructions of identity" which implement dynamic processes that never come to an end. On this issue, see Jürgen Straub, "Identität," in *Handbuch der Kulturwissenschaften 1: Grundlagen und Schlüsselbegriffe*, eds. Friedrich Jaeger and Burkhard Liebsch (Stuttgart: J. B. Metzler, 2011), 277–303. See also Straub's informative bibliography.

9 On the Greek fragments, see Thomas J. Kraus and Tobias Nicklas, eds., *Das Petrusevangelium und die Petrusapokalypse. Die griechischen Fragmente mit deutscher und englischer Übersetzung*, Neutestamentliche Apokryphen 1, GCS Neue Folge 11 (Berlin: Walter de Gruyter, 2004), 81–138. All quotations of the Greek text come from this edition. The English translations are adapted from pages 118–20 of this edition. For an overview of the text's transmission, see Wolfgang Grünstäudl, "Enthüllung im Fragment—Notizen zu Überlieferungsgestalt und Figureninventar der Offenbarung des Petrus," in *Shadowy Characters and Fragmentary Evidence. The Search for Early Christian Groups and Movements*, eds. Joseph Verheyden, Tobias Nicklas and Elisabeth Hernitscheck, WUNT 388 (Tübingen: Mohr Siebeck, 2017), 109–23, esp. 110–15.

10 A full critical edition of the Ethiopic text is currently being prepared by Alessandro Bausi. Currently, I use Paolo Marrassini, "L'Apocalisse di Pietro," in *Etiopia e oltre. Studi in onore di Lanfranco Ricci*, eds. Yaqob Beyene, Rodolfo Fattovich, Paolo Marrassini and Alessandro Triulzi, Studi Africanisti, Series Etiopica 1 (Naples: Istituto Universitario Orientale, 1994), 171–232. The best translation (which also includes a good grammatical discussion) is by Eric J. Beck, *Justice and Mercy in the Apocalypse of Peter*, WUNT 427 (Tübingen: Mohr Siebeck, 2019), 54–96.

11 For an overview, see Kraus and Nicklas, *Petrusevangelium und Petrusapokalypse*, 87–99.

has shown that 2 Peter (quite probably) makes use of the *Apocalypse of Peter* as one of its sources[12]—the other being the Epistle of Jude[13]—a date in the not too late second century CE is quite probable.[14] There is still some ongoing discussion regarding the more exact date and provenance. While some authors point to Palestine or Syria during the Bar-Kokhba War, I make a case elsewhere for Alexandria (perhaps though not necessarily around the times of the 115–117 Diaspora War).[15] For our purpose, however, it is not necessary to decide this matter. Though, it is interesting that the *Apocalypse of Peter* gained some importance in the East—with both Egypt and Syria being the centers of its reception[16]—since it was read during Good Friday liturgies in some Palestinian communities until the fifth century CE.[17] After the fourth century it seems to have been increasingly replaced by the *Apocalypse of Paul* which (through its Latin translation, the *Visio Pauli*) gained enormous influence on Medieval Western Christianity's perception of the other world and the end of times.[18] This difficult situation—with its textual fluidity—makes it quite dif-

12 Wolfgang Grünstäudl, *Petrus Alexandrinus. Studien zum historischen und theologischen Ort des zweiten* Petrusbriefes, WUNT II.353 (Tübingen: Mohr Siebeck, 2013), 97–143. Grünstäudl's ideas have been appropriated by Jörg Frey, *The Letter of Jude and the Second Letter of Peter. A Theological Commentary* (Waco: Baylor University Press, 2018), 201–6, and have more recently been critically discussed in Jörg Frey, Matthijs den Dulk and Jan van der Watt, *2 Peter and the Apocalypse of Peter: Towards a New Perspective*, BibInt 174 (Leiden: Brill, 2019). I regard them as still very convincing.

13 On the literary relationship between 2 Peter and Jude, see, for example, Frey, *The Letter of Jude*, 182–92.

14 The main counter-argument is found in Jan N. Bremmer's analysis of the text's martyrdom terminology. See his, "The *Apocalypse of Peter* as the First Christian Martyr Text: Its Date, Provenance and Relationship with 2 Peter," in *2 Peter and the Apocalypse of Peter: Towards a New Perspective*, ed. Jörg Frey, Matthijs den Dulk and Jan van der Watt, BibInt 174 (Leiden: Brill, 2019), 75–98.

15 See Tobias Nicklas, "Jewish, Christian, Greek? The Apocalypse of Peter as a Witness of Early 2nd Cent. Christianity in Alexandria," in *Beyond Conflicts. Cultural and Religions Cohabitations in Alexandria and Egypt between the 1st and the 6th Century CE*, ed. Luca Arcari, STAC 103 (Tübingen: Mohr Siebeck, 2017), 1–24. Note also his discussion of the relevant secondary literature.

16 For a (not always fully reliable) overview see Attila Jakab, "The Reception of the Apocalypse of Peter," in *The Apocalypse of Peter*, ed. Jan N. Bremmer and Istvan Czachesz, Studies on Early Christian Apocrypha 7 (Leuven: Peeters, 2003), 174–86.

17 See the evidence by Sozomenos, *Historia Ecclesiastica* VII 19,9 (also discussed by Kraus and Nicklas, *Petrusevangelium und Petrusapokalypse*, 97).

18 Regarding the relationship between the *Apocalypse of Peter* and the *Apocalypse of Paul*, see Jan N. Bremmer, "Christian Hell: From the *Apocalypse of Peter* to the *Apocalypse of Paul*," in *Magic and Martyrs in Early Christianity*, ed. Jan N. Bremmer, WUNT 379 (Tübingen: Mohr Siebeck, 2017), 295–312. On the broader impact of the *Visio* Pauli, see, for example, the evidence offered by Lenka Jiroušková, *Die Visio Pauli. Wege und Wandlungen einer*

ficult to speak about an original text of the *Apocalypse of Peter*. That is why I prefer to treat the (often under-studied) Greek *Apocalypse* in the form transmitted by the Akhmim fragment as a text in its own right and concentrate only on its description of hell.

The Greek Apocalypse of Peter and its Otherworldly Landscape

The extant text starts with a few sayings of Jesus, which obviously form the end of an otherwise lost eschatological speech (vv. 1–3). After this, Jesus, who is called "the Lord" throughout the fragment, invites his disciples to go to "the mountain[19] and pray." This leads "the twelve disciples"[20] to approach him with a fascinating request:

> ᾿Απερχόμενοι δὲ μετ᾿ αὐτοῦ ἡμεῖς οἱ δώδεκα μαθηταὶ ἐδεήθημεν ὅπως δείξῃ ἡμῖν ἕνα τῶν ἀδελφῶν ἡμῶν δικαίων τῶν ἐξελθόντων ἀπὸ τοῦ κόσμου, ἵνα ἴδωμεν ποταποί εἰσι τὴν μορφὴν καὶ θαρσήσαντες παραθαρσύνωμεν καὶ τοὺς ἀκούοντας ἡμῶν ἀνθρώπους.
>
> When we went with him, we, the twelve disciples, begged (him) that he would show us one of our righteous brothers, who had gone forth out of the world, in order that we might see of what manner of form they are, and having taken courage, might encourage the people who hear us (v. 5).

The passage does not just introduce a new topic, it opens the door for the readers' perspective on several levels. Even if the term "righteous brothers" could denote righteous ones of the Old Covenant, the term "brothers" (and "sisters") is so closely connected to the language of early Christian communities[21] that one is at least reminded of possible righteous Christ followers and their post-mortem fate as well. Although the extant text does not indicate whether the

orientalischen Apokryphe im lateinischen Mittelalter (Leiden: Brill, 2006). The question of whether Dante's *Divina Comoedia* draws from this text is still a matter of dispute. See, for example, Gerhard Regn, *Die Apokalypse im Irdischen Paradies. Offenbarung, Allegorie und Dichtung in Dantes Comoedia*, in *Autorschaft und Autoritisierungsstrategien in apokalyptischen Texten*, ed. Jörg Frey, Michael R. Jost and Franz Tóth, WUNT 426 (Tübingen: Mohr Siebeck, 2019), 391–412.

19 In the extant fragment it is not clear which mountain is meant. One option is the Mount of Olives where Jesus' eschatological speech, according to the Ethiopic version, is given. Another option is Mount Horeb since the text seems to be influenced by some of the features found in the Synoptic transfiguration stories. It is also possible that the text conveys no specific location.

20 The text does not seem to presuppose Jesus' betrayal by Judas Iscariot.

21 For important evidence see Peter Arzt-Grabner, "'Brothers' and 'Sisters' in Documentary Papyri and in Early Christianity," *RivB* 50 (2002): 185–204.

scene is pre- or post-Easter, the above question is in any case anachronistic. Speaking about "righteous brothers" who already died (and at the same time thinking of "Christ believers"[22]) does not fit into the time of Jesus's life (or even within the earliest post-Easter period). This corresponds with a second aspect of the text: The disciples do not ask out of simple interest or even because they only want to know something about *their* future fate. Their request is set into the horizon of their own preaching. If they see what will happen to the righteous ones after their death, they will take courage, but can also encourage "the people who hear us" (v. 5). Of course, none of the second century and later readers of the *Apocalypse of Peter* had direct access to the apostles' kerygma. The text thus relates a question which could have been of interest to everyone in Apostolic times: What will *my* post-mortem fate will look like *if I am considered a righteous one*? The answer is connected with the authority of Jesus, the "Lord," but transmitted through the witness of Peter.[23] The text thus connects a present question (and its answer) with imagined origins of what we could call the "Christian movement" by putting it into the mouth of some decisive authorities related to these origins. In this way, it bridges the gap between past and present by framing an important aspect of the addressed group's collective memory.

The answer is even more interesting. In a certain sense, the whole extant text can be related to v. 5,[24] which leads to the first reference about a vision of two of these righteous brothers (vv. 6–13).[25] This leads Peter to ask a second question: "And where are all the righteous ones (πάντες οἱ δίκαιοι) or what is

---

22 I hesitate to use the term "Christians" in relation to a text that does not apply it (but obviously uses another term for the community of followers of the "Lord." For a (very helpful) approach that first tries to understand the emic terms used by individual texts, see Stefan Alkier, "Terminologien kollektiver Identitäten in der Apostelgeschichte des Lukas," in *Juden—Heiden—Christen. Religiöse Inklusion und Exklusion in Kleinasien bis Decius*, ed. Stefan Alkier and Hartmut Leppin, WUNT 400 (Tübingen: Mohr Siebeck, 2018), 301–32.

23 Regarding the construction of authority (and especially Petrine authority) in the *Apocalypse of Peter* (with a focus on the Ethiopic text), see Tobias Nicklas, "Petrusoffenbarung, Christusoffenbarung und ihre Funktion: Autoritätskonstruktion in der *Offenbarung des Petrus*," in *2 Peter and the Apocalypse of Peter: Towards a New Perspective*, ed. Jörg Frey, Matthijs den Dulk and Jan van der Watt, BibInt 174 (Leiden: Brill, 2019). 319–35.

24 For a more detailed discussion of the text's structure, see Tobias Nicklas, "'Our Righteous Brethren': Reflections on the Description of the Righteous Ones according to the Greek *Revelation of Peter* (Akhm. 2)," in *Empsychoi Logoi. Religious Innovations in Antiquity. Studies in Honour of Pieter Willem van der Horst*, ed. Alberdina Houtman, Albert de Jong and Magda Misset-Van de Weg, AGJU 73 (Leiden: Brill, 2008), 319–46, esp. 331–34.

25 In the Ethiopic version a kind of mixture between transfiguration and ascension story is offered.

the aeon (αἰών)[26] in which they are who have this glory?" (v. 14). This, again, leads to a second vision of a "very large country outside of this world" which is a kind of paradise (vv. 15–20).[27] The text, however, does not end here. Even if Peter had not asked about it, we are not only exposed to paradise, but also to a kind of hell which is subsequently described *in extenso* (vv. 22–34). After this, the fragment ends abruptly.

Of course, it is always problematic to interpret a fragmentary writing. But even in its present state the text creates an image of the past wherein questions are handled which remain decisive until both the first and later readers' present (in relation to their hope for the future). In addition, the readers reinterpret this world by adding outside spaces to it, namely a paradise and a "hell"[28] in direct opposition to it.

A closer look at a few passages will reveal a bit more about the concrete functions of this construction. First, our text is not only interested in the possible future fate of its readers. It also wants to encourage them to be and remain "righteous" in a situation which is obviously understood as dangerous where they probably feel hard-pressed and even persecuted.

First, everything that is said about the future fate of the righteous ones is related to ideas of glory (v. 14), beauty (vv. 7, 9 and 11; but see also 10 in relation to the use of εὐπρέπεια) and light.[29] We read about "a ray as of the sun" coming from their countenance and shining garments (v. 7) and bodies "whiter than any snow and redder than any rose" (v. 8) The disciples are "shocked" (v. 11) about this epiphany. When Peter asks "who are these?" (v. 12), the "Lord" identifies them as "your righteous brothers whose forms you desired to see" (v. 13). But not only is the first vision concerned with the righteous ones. The second one is framed in similar terms: Peter asks about the *aeon* wherein the all the righteous ones are (v. 14) He envisions the paradisiacal country and is taught: "This is the place of your high priests,[30] the righteous men" (v. 20).

All this leads to a third vision, which is probably the most revealing. While the paradise had been described as a "big country outside of this world" (v. 15: μέγιστον χῶρον ἐκτὸς τούτου τοῦ κόσμου), hell is introduced as "another place

26 Interestingly, this term conveys both a temporal and a spatial dimension of meaning.

27 For a detailed discussion see Tamás Adamik, "The Description of Paradise in the *Apocalypse of Peter*," in *The Apocalypse of Peter*, ed. Jan N. Bremmer and Istvan Czachesz, Studies on Early Christian Apocrypha 7 (Leuven: Peeters, 2003), 78–90.

28 The extant text never gives a concrete name, like Hades, Sheol, etc. to this place.

29 For a detailed discussion of the motifs used in this passage, see Nicklas, "Brethren," 334–45.

30 The actual manuscript offers the reading αρχερω, which is usually transcribed as ἀρχιερέων. See Kraus and Nicklas, *Petrusevangelium und Petrusapokalypse*, 109.

opposite to that one" (v. 21: εἶδον δὲ καὶ ἕτερον τόπον καταντικρὺς ἐκείνου) and called the "place of punishment" (τόπος κολάσεως). While paradise is a garden-like place full of light with the fragrance of flowers, the "other place" consists of darkness (σκοτεινόν).[31] The first group of sinners we encounter is described in the following words:

> Καί τινες ἦσαν ἐκεῖ ἐκ τῆς γλώσσης κρεμάμενοι. Οὗτοι δὲ ἦσαν οἱ βλασφημοῦντες τὴν ὁδὸν τῆς δικαιοσύνης.
>
> And some there were hanging by the tongue. And these were those who had blasphemed the way of righteousness … (v. 22).

This is followed by the vision of a "great lake full of flaming mire" which is inhabited by "some who had turned away from righteousness" (v. 23: ἀποστρέφοντες τὴν δικαιοσύνην). Of course, the author of the *Apocalypse of Peter* did not invent the idea of "hellish" places of punishment. We do not know whether the author reshaped it from (what are now lost) written sources and/or took it from the "cultural memories" of his society[32] where it must have been present through the influence of both Orphics and Jews.[33] This is, however, not crucial for our interest. Rather, these first verses of *this* presentation of hell are instructive on different levels. They show again, in how "righteousness" is a key issue for the construction of the world in the *Apocalypse of Peter*. This construct is an important term for understanding the addressed group's self-identification. Like many other early Christian writings, the *Apocalypse of Peter* does not use the term "Christians." Instead, it belongs to a group of (perhaps literarily unrelated) writings that referred to early Christ believers (see v. 3: τοὺς πιστούς μου [in the mouth of Jesus!]) as "the righteous ones."[34] We can point to the

31 The idea that the devil/Satan and everything which has to be related to him must be described in a dark or even black color can be found in several early Christian texts like *Barn.* 4.10, the *Acts of Peter* (Actus Vercellenses) § 22 and *Pass. Perp.* 10.6.

32 This term is taken from Jan Assmann, *Das kulturelle Gedächtnis. Schrift, Erinnerung und politische Identität in frühen Hochkulturen* (Munich: Beck, 1992).

33 The religious background of this (and comparable) descriptions of hell is controversial. For a good overview, see Jan N. Bremmer, "Orphic, Roman, Jewish and Christian Tours of Hell: Observations on the *Apocalypse of Peter*," in *Other Worlds and their Relation to This World. Early Jewish and Ancient Christian Traditions*, ed. Tobias Nicklas, Joseph Verheyden, Erik M. M. Eynikel and Florentino Garcia Martinez, JSJSup 143 (Leiden: Brill, 2010), 305–22; Jan N. Bremmer, "Tours of Hell: Greek, Jewish, Roman and Early Christian," in his *Maidens, Magic and Martyrs in Early* Christianity, WUNT 379 (Tübingen: Mohr Siebeck, 2017), 313–28.

34 If we follow the terminology of v. 3, then they are in opposition to the "sons of lawlessness" (see 2 Thess 2:3 where we read of only one "son of lawlessness").

Gospel of Matthew according to which "righteousness must surpass that of the Pharisees and Scribes" (Matt 5:20) or the *Ascension of Isaiah* whose "we"-group seems to have understood itself as the righteous and the holy ones. The reference to the "way of righteousness" (v. 22 and 28: ὁδὸς τῆς δικαιοσύνης) in the Greek *Apocalypse of Peter* resembles the canonical Book of Acts which speaks about the "way" or the "followers of the way" (Acts 9:2; 19:9–23; 22:4; 24:14–22; see also 16:17; 18:25–26). In any case, this term is so important that (more or less) the same group of sinners is mentioned a second time and then punished in another way. Verse 28 reads, "And near those were again women and men gnawing their lips and being punished and having heated iron in their eyes. These were the ones who blasphemed and spoke evil of the way of righteousness (τὴν ὁδὸν τῆς δικαιοσύνης)."

I do not see this as a sign of a somewhat clumsy redaction of an older source, but as the expression of a special emphasis. This is made even clearer by the two other passages that frame v. 28. Verse 27 addresses the fate of those "who had persecuted the righteous and delivered them up" (οἱ διώξαντες τοὺς δικαίους καὶ παραδόντες αὐτούς). Verse 29 speaks about "false witnesses" (ψευδομάρτυρες), a term which is reminiscent of Matt 26:59–60 (see also Mark 15:19) and 1 Cor 15:15. Does it refer to witnesses who are against Christ followers or to people who do not give the kind of witness that was expected from righteous ones?[35] We have to take into account that any description of hell has to be selective. It also cannot be interested in the fate of actual human beings (who never commit only *one* special sin). Instead, the texts create combinations of sinners who represent special sins. These combinations are either inherited from older written sources, or "tradition," or are inserted because the text shows special interest in them. This text's emphasis seems clear and makes sense only where persecution is so much of a reality or at least a real possibility that it has to be included into the addressed group's construction of identity.[36] But this is not the only point. The main point is expressed in the final part of the vision (v. 34), which refers to "other women and men [who] were burned and turned and roasted." It concludes by stating, "These were the ones who forsook the way of God (οὗτοι δὲ ἦσαν οἱ ἀφέντες τὴν ὁδὸν τοῦ θεοῦ)." The text thus constructs two doublets. The first is vv. 22 and 28 (surrounded by 27 and 29) which are

35 For the impact of martyrdom terminology in the *Apocalypse of Peter*, see Bremmer, "The *Apocalypse of Peter* as the First Christian Martyr Text," 75–98.

36 On the importance of the idea of being persecuted in the "constructions of identity" for different early Christian groups, see James A. Kelhoffer, *Persecution, Persuasion and Power. Readiness to Withstand hardship as a Corroboration of Legitimacy in the New* Testament, WUNT 270 (Tübingen: Mohr Siebeck, 2010). Kelhoffer, however, does not deal with the *Apocalypse of Peter*.

interested in the blasphemers and persecutors; and the second is vv. 23 and 32 which focus on the ones who leave "the way of God" (v. 32). In other words, the hell described here is "another place" (v. 21) far away from God's glory. It is a place that is reserved for both the "others" who have always been outside and the "ones" who leave the righteous ones and become "others." It looks like the text's pedagogical impetus is mainly directed towards this second group (or better, to people who are in danger of becoming part of this group).

All of this corresponds to the observation that the text is not focused on a concrete or even sophisticated idea of "justice." Instead, the term "justice" is used as an identity marker to create a "border line"[37] directed at outsiders who can be labelled "sons of lawlessness" (v. 3). This is confirmed by the passages which describe other sins. Interestingly, most of these are not very specific in relation to a certain group. We read about adultery (v. 24), murder (v. 25), abortion (v. 26), the lending of money and taking usury (v. 31) and same-sex relations (v. 32). All of these can both be found within the horizon of Torah reception[38] and be accepted by "Christians" who had no Jewish heritage. Wolfgang Grünstäudl hits the nail on the head when he writes, "Salopp gesprochen könnte man hier die Umrisse einer etwas biederen Hölle erkennen, deren pädagogischer Nutzen für das Diesseits wohl am ehesten in der Bewahrung eines mit der Mehrheitsgesellschaft konformen Sozialgefüges besteht."[39] One could also point to the words of Jan N. Bremmer: "Most decent Jews, Christians, and, probably, even some pagans would hardly have had a problem with the great majority of these implicit commandments."[40]

In other words, this vision of hell does not construct a special ethos distinct from outside groups. It does not introduce the special sins of insiders like clerical sinners (as we find them reflected in the *Apocalypse of Paul* or the *Apocalypse of the Virgin*) or even transgressions against a developing Christian "dogma."[41] Instead, it serves to distinguish the in-group which pursues the "way

---

37 I borrow this term from Daniel Boyarin, *Border Lines: The Partition of Judaeo-Christianity* (Philadelphia: University of Pennsylvania, 2006).

38 See the observations by Michael Sommer, "Von Monstern und Männern. Eine Auseinandersetzung mit E. Reinmuths 'Parodien der Macht,'" in *Neutestamentliche Wissenschaft in gesellschaftlicher Verantwortung. Studien im Anschluss an Eckart Reinmuth*, ed. Stefan Alkier and Christfried Böttrich (Leipzig: Evangelische Verlagsanstalt, 2017) 353–76, esp. 366–9.

39 Grünstäudl, "Enthüllung im Fragment" 120.

40 Bremmer, "Tours of Hell," 314.

41 Among the very few exceptions in late antiquity of otherworldly journeys that reflect the development of Christian doctrine is a passage in the *Visio Pauli* (§ 41) where the Sankt Gallen manuscript contains the (probably) secondary reading *quia genuit eum Mariam uerum deum*. The text thus speaks about sinners who do not believe that Mary should be

of righteousness" in relation to God from the unjust who lack a knowledge of God (and his just judgment in v. 25). This latter group includes the sinners mentioned in v. 33 who "made carved images" of God, which is perhaps the most Torah-like aspect of this portrayal of hell (see Exod 20:3; Deut 5:7; 6:14; 7:14; 8:19; 11:16.28; 13:14; 28:14,36; 30:17).[42] The "way of righteousness" is so closely connected to God that speaking in evil ways about it is necessarily "blasphemy" (see vv. 22 and 28).[43] Leaving it means leaving the way of God. Following it will lead to paradise whose inhabitants "have glory" (v. 14: ταύτην ἔχοντες τὴν δόξαν; cf. v. 19), praise God, and are so closely connected to Him that they can be called "high priests" (v. 20). It thus becomes clear that the author of our text wants to construct an idea of "identity" that is distinct from the "others" who are equated with the "unjust." It both closes the doors for anybody who wants to leave the "way of righteousness" and at the same time seems to leave them open for the outsider to whom salvation can be offered via an ethos, which is not too demanding.[44]

This, again, is related to the text's creation of a "landscape of memories." In the readers' present world, it is not easy to follow "the way of righteousness"—and some of its followers are about to leave (or have already done so). The ones who understand themselves as righteous and the ones who speak evil about them or even persecute and give false witness against them are still intermingled. They share the same space and the same time, even if they are opposite to each other. But the Greek *Apocalypse of Peter* wants its readers to remember that this is not the only world. After death people will have to leave this world (see v. 5) and live in another place which is either in the paradisiacal "big country outside of this world" (v. 15), or in "another place opposite to that one" (v. 21), which is characterized by darkness, pain and punishment (v. 21). These two worlds are both distinguished from each other and connected.[45] There is no chance for the sinners to leave hell. We read, for example, about the

called the Mother of God. On the relative lack of doctrinal discussion in even Byzantine apocalypses, see Jane Baun, *Tales from Another Byzantium. Celestial Journey and Local Community in the Medieval Greek Apocrypha* (Cambridge: Cambridge University Press, 2007) 176–7.

42 See Sommer, "Von Monstern und Männern," 367.

43 Even if Acts is concerned with comparable cases, it does not speak about "blaspheming" (βλασφημέω) the "way," but uses the word κακολογέω (Acts 19:9).

44 This does not mean that the *Apocalypse of Peter* has to be read by outsiders to function in this way. The text simply supports a group ethos which considers itself as being very elitist and at the same time follows an ethos which is not very demanding.

45 This is an interesting parallel to what we find in Luke 16:19–31.

"souls"[46] of those who were murdered watching their murderers' punishment and praising God for his justice (v. 25; but see also v. 26).

Conclusion

Even if the *Apocalypse of Peter* may be the oldest Christian writing to offer a detailed description of hell, its author certainly did not invent this idea. He may have used source material and/or taken it from already existing "cultural memory." This idea of "hell" as "another space," a "place of punishment," was transmitted through various media into the "cultural memory" of Christians, which continues to endure today. At the same time the text's *precise* description of hell (vs. paradise) can be understood as an expression of a particular form of collective memory, which wants to lead its readers to a special perception of this world. Even if the present is perceived as dominated by injustice and even if the "we"-group is under pressure from outsiders, the world that the "we"-group sees *during its present* is only part of a deeper reality. In addition to this world, there are two "other places"[47] that can be clearly distinguished from each other, namely paradise and hell. When the present unjust period of time is over, there will be a future when both the righteous ones, the "believers in the Lord" (v. 3), and their enemies, the "sons of lawlessness," will receive justice which—in the truest sense of the word—is described in the most contrasting colors possible. This memory is authorized by a narrative that is related to the addressed group's origins. Together with Peter (and the Twelve), the text's readers witness visions and revelations offered by Jesus (the "Lord") himself. These must be remembered so that they themselves can "take courage" and "encourage the ones who will listen to them" (v. 5). The concrete shape of this

46 As far as I can see, the term ψυχαί here does not denote a soul in the classical sense of the word, but is used in a way that is comparable to what we find in Rev 6:9–11. For a more detailed discussion, see Tobias Nicklas, "'Die Seelen der Geschlachteten' (Offb 6,9)? Zum Problem leiblicher Auferstehung in der Offenbarung des Johannes," in *The Human Body in Death and Resurrection*, ed. Tobias Nicklas, Friedrich V. Reiterer, and Joseph Verheyden, DCL, Yearbook 2009 (Berlin: de Gruyter, 2009), 329–50. On the development of ideas about the soul in antiquity, see Jan N. Bremmer, *The Early Greek Concept of the Soul* (Princeton: Princeton University Press, 1983).

47 The (related) idea that hell can be understood as a *heterotopia* in Foucault's sense has been formulated by Meghan Henning, "Hell as 'Heterotopia': Edification and Interpretation from Enoch to the Apocalypses of Peter and Paul," in *Between Canonical and Apocryphal Texts. Processes of Reception, Rewriting, and Interpretation in Early Judaism and Early Christianity*, ed. Jörg Frey, Claire Clivaz and Tobias Nicklas (WUNT 419; Tübingen: Mohr Siebeck, 2019), 309–32.

memory—its use of the term "justice" as an identity marker and its widely acceptable ethos—is important for keeping the doors open for outsiders who want to become followers of the "way of righteousness" and at the same time it warns everyone about the danger of leaving it.

Bibliography

Adamik, Tamás. "The Description of Paradise in the Apocalypse of Peter." Pages in 78–90. *The Apocalypse of Peter*. Edited by Jan N. Bremmer and Istvan Czachesz. Studies on Early Christian Apocrypha 7. Leuven: Peeters, 2003.

Alkier, Stefan. "Terminologien kollektiver Identitäten in der Apostelgeschichte des Lukas." Pages 301–32 in *Juden—Heiden—Christen. Religiöse Inklusion und Exklusion in Kleinasien bis* Decius. Edited by Stefan Alkier and Hartmut Leppin. WUNT 400. Tübingen: Mohr Siebeck, 2018.

Arzt-Grabner, Peter. "'Brothers' and 'Sisters' in Documentary Papyri and in Early Christianity." *RivB* 50 (2002): 185–204.

Assmann, Jan. *Das kulturelle Gedächtnis. Schrift, Erinnerung und politische Identität in frühen Hochkulturen*. Munich: Beck, 1992.

Baun, Jane. *Tales from Another Byzantium. Celestial Journey and Local Community in the Medieval Greek Apocrypha*. Cambridge: Cambridge University Press, 2007.

Beck, Eric J. *Justice and Mercy in the Apocalypse of Peter*. WUNT 427. Tübingen: Mohr Siebeck, 2019.

Boyarin, Daniel. *Border Lines: The Partition of Judaeo-Christianity*. Philadelphia: University of Pennsylvania, 2006.

Bremmer, Jan N. *The Early Greek Concept of the Soul*. Princeton: Princeton University Press, 1983.

———. "Orphic, Roman, Jewish and Christian Tours of Hell: Observations on the Apocalypse of Peter." Pages 305–22 in *Other Worlds and Their Relation to This World. Early Jewish and Ancient Christian Traditions*. Edited by Tobias Nicklas, Joseph Verheyden, Erik M. M. Eynikel and Florentino Garcia Martinez. JSJSup 143. Leiden: Brill, 2010.

———. "Christian Hell: From the Apocalypse of Peter to the Apocalypse of Paul." Pages 295–312 in *Magic and Martyrs in Early Christianity*. Edited by Jan N. Bremmer. WUNT 379. Tübingen: Mohr Siebeck, 2017.

———. "Tours of Hell: Greek, Jewish, Roman and Early Christian." Pages 313–28 in *Maidens, Magic and Martyrs in Early Christianity*. WUNT 379. Tübingen: Mohr Siebeck, 2017.

———. "The Apocalypse of Peter as the First Christian Martyr Text: Its Date, Provenance and Relationship with 2 Peter." Pages 75–98 in *2 Peter and the Apocalypse of Peter:*

Towards a New Perspective. Edited by Jörg Frey, Matthijs den Dulk and Jan van der Watt. BibInt 174. Leiden: Brill, 2019.

Buchinger, Harald, Andreas Merkt and Tobias Nicklas, eds. *Extracanonical Traditions and the Holy Land: Texts, Rituals and Material Culture*. STAC. Tübingen: Mohr Siebeck, forthcoming 2021.

Frey, Jörg. *The Letter of Jude and the Second Letter of Peter. A Theological Commentary*. Waco: Baylor University Press, 2018.

Frey, Jörg, Matthijs den Dulk and Jan van der Watt. *2 Peter and the Apocalypse of Peter: Towards a New Perspective*. BibInt 174. Leiden: Brill, 2019.

Grünstäudl, Wolfgang. *Petrus Alexandrinus. Studien zum historischen und theologischen Ort des zweiten Petrusbriefes*. WUNT II.353. Tübingen: Mohr Siebeck, 2013.

———. "Enthüllung im Fragment—Notizen zu Überlieferungsgestalt und Figureninventar der Offenbarung des Petrus." Pages 109–23 in *Shadowy Characters and Fragmentary Evidence. The Search for Early Christian Groups and Movements*. Edited by Joseph Verheyden, Tobias Nicklas and Elisabeth Hernitscheck. WUNT 388. Tübingen: Mohr Siebeck, 2017.

Halbwachs, Maurice. *La mémoire collective*. Bibliothèque de l'Évolution de l'Humanité 28. Paris: Les Presses universitaires de France, 1950.

Henning, Meghan. "Hell as 'Heterotopia': Edification and Interpretation from Enoch to the Apocalypses of Peter and Paul." Pages 309–32 in *Between Canonical and Apocryphal Texts. Processes of Reception, Rewriting, and Interpretation in Early Judaism and Early Christianity*. Edited by Jörg Frey, Claire Clivaz and Tobias Nicklas. WUNT 419. Tübingen: Mohr Siebeck, 2019.

Huebenthal, Sandra. *Das Markusevangelium als kollektives Gedächtnis*. FRLANT 253. Göttingen: Vandenhoeck & Ruprecht, 2014.

———. "'Frozen Moments'—Early Christianity through the Lens of Social Memory Theory." Pages 17–44 in *Memory and Memories in Early Christianity. Proceedings of the International Conference held at the Universities of Geneva and Lausanne (June, 2–3, 2016)*. Edited by Simon Butticaz and Enrico Norelli. WUNT 398. Tübingen: Mohr Siebeck, 2018.

Jakab, Attila. "The Reception of the Apocalypse of Peter." Pages 174–86 in *The Apocalypse of Peter*. Edited by Jan N. Bremmer and Istvan Czachesz. Studies on Early Christian Apocrypha 7. Leuven: Peeters, 2003.

Jiroušková, Lenka. *Die Visio Pauli. Wege und Wandlungen einer orientalischen Apokryphe im lateinischen Mittelalter*. Leiden: Brill, 2006.

Kelhoffer, James A. *Persecution, Persuasion and Power. Readiness to Withstand hardship as a Corroboration of Legitimacy in the New Testament*. WUNT 270. Tübingen: Mohr Siebeck, 2010.

Koschorke, Albrecht. *Wahrheit und Erfindung. Grundzüge einer Allgemeinen Erzähltheorie*. Frankfurt am Main: S. Fischer, 2012.

Kraus, Thomas J., and Tobias Nicklas, eds. *Das Petrusevangelium und die Petrusapokalypse. Die griechischen Fragmente mit deutscher und englischer Übersetzung*. Neutestamentliche Apokryphen 1. GCS Neue Folge 11. Berlin: Walter de Gruyter, 2004.

Marrassini, Paolo. "L'Apocalisse di Pietro." Pages 171–232 in *Etiopia e oltre. Studi in onore di Lanfranco Ricci*. Edited by Yaqob Beyene, Rodolfo Fattovich, Paolo Marrassini and Alessandro Triulzi. Studi Africanisti, Series Etiopica 1. Naples: Istituto Universitario Orientale, 1994.

Nicklas, Tobias. "'Our Righteous Brethren': Reflections on the Description of the Righteous Ones according to the Greek Revelation of Peter (Akhm. 2)." Pages 319–46 in *Empsychoi Logoi. Religious Innovations in Antiquity. Studies in Honour of Pieter Willem van der Horst*. Edited by Alberdina Houtman, Albert de Jong and Magda Misset–Van de Weg. AGJU 73. Leiden: Brill, 2008.

———. "'Die Seelen der Geschlachteten' (Offb 6,9)? Zum Problem leiblicher Auferstehung in der Offenbarung des Johannes." Pages 329–50 in *The Human Body in Death and Resurrection*. Edited by Tobias Nicklas, Friedrich V. Reiterer, and Joseph Verheyden. DCL, Yearbook 2009. Berlin: de Gruyter, 2009.

———. "Neutestamentlicher Kanon, christliche Apokryphen und christliche 'Erinnerungskulturen." *NTS* 62 (2016): 588–609.

———. "New Testament Canon and Ancient Landscapes of Memory." *Early Christianity* 7 (2016): 5–23.

———. "Die Akten des Titus: Rezeption 'apostolischer' Schriften und Entwicklung antik–christlicher 'Erinnerungslandschaften.'" *Early Christianity* 8 (2017): 458–80.

———. "Jewish, Christian, Greek? The Apocalypse of Peter as a Witness of Early 2nd Cent. Christianity in Alexandria." Pages 1–24 in *Beyond Conflicts. Cultural and Religions Cohabitations in Alexandria and Egypt between the 1st and the 6th Century* CE. Edited by Luca Arcari. STAC 103. Tübingen: Mohr Siebeck, 2017.

———. "Apocalypse of Peter." Pages 331–40 in *From Thomas to Tertullian: Christian Literary Receptions of Jesus in the Second and Third Centuries*. Edited by Jens Schröter and Christine Jacobi. London: T&T Clark, 2019.

———. "Petrusoffenbarung, Christusoffenbarung und ihre Funktion: Autoritätskonstruktion in der Offenbarung des Petrus." Pages 319–35 in *2 Peter and the Apocalypse of Peter: Towards a New Perspective*. Edited by Jörg Frey, Matthijs den Dulk and Jan van der Watt. BibInt 174. Leiden: Brill, 2019.

———. "Zwischen Redaktion und 'Neuinszenierung'." Vom Umgang erzählender Evangelien des 2. Jahrhunderts mit ihren Vorlagen." Pages 311–30 in *Gospels and Gospel Traditions in the Second Century: Experiments in Reception*. Edited by Jens Schröter, Tobias Nicklas and Joseph Verheyden. BZNW 235. Berlin: de Gruyter, 2019.

Nora, Pierre. *Les lieux de mémoire, Volumes 1–3*. Paris: Gallimard, 1984–1992.

Regn, Gerhard. "Die Apokalypse im Irdischen Paradies. Offenbarung, Allegorie und Dichtung in Dantes Comoedia," in *Autorschaft und Autoritisierungsstrategien in apokalyptischen Texten*. Edited by Jörg Frey, Michael R. Jost and Franz Tóth. WUNT 426. Tübingen: Mohr Siebeck, 2019.

Schröter, Jens. "Der 'erinnerte Jesus': Erinnerung als geschichtshermeneutisches Paradigma der Jesusforschung." Pages 112–24 in *Jesus Handbuch*. Edited by Jens Schröter and Christine Jacobi. Tübingen: Mohr Siebeck, 2017.

Sommer, Michael. "Von Monstern und Männern. Eine Auseinandersetzung mit E. Reinmuths 'Parodien der Macht.'" Pages 353–76 in *Neutestamentliche Wissenschaft in gesellschaftlicher Verantwortung. Studien im Anschluss an Eckart Reinmuth*. Edited by Stefan Alkier and Christfried Böttrich. Leipzig: Evangelische Verlagsanstalt, 2017.

Straub, Jürgen. "Identität." Pages 277–303 in *Handbuch der Kulturwissenschaften 1: Grundlagen und Schlüsselbegriffe*. Edited by Friedrich Jaeger and Burkhard Liebsch. Stuttgart: J. B. Metzler, 2011.

Taylor, Joan E. *Christians and the Holy Places: The Myth of Jewish–Christian Origins*. Oxford: Clarendon Press, 1993.

Advanced Knowledge of Afterlife: Reading the *Passion of Perpetua and Felicity* as a Memory Text

Christian Handschuh

> The day of their victory dawned, and they marched from the prison to the amphitheatre, joyously, as if going to heaven, their faces radiant; and if by chance they trembled, it was from joy and not from fear. Perpetua followed, with a shining face and a calm step, as a wife of Christ and darling of God, and the intensity of her stare caused the spectators to look away.[1]

One of the most impressive passages from the *Passio Perpetuae et Felicitatis* (hereafter *Passio*) introduces Perpetua and her companions as exemplary martyrs in Carthage in 202 CE. Perpetua and her companions are on their way to suffer martyrdom in the amphitheatre, but with reversed roles. The victims are on their way to victory and their conquering gaze puts the spectators to shame. The reader, along with the eyewitness of the martyrdoms, is invited to understand the reversal of the roles. Centuries later, this text becomes part of Christian cultural memory and influences how martyrs were to behave.

In this paper, I address two aspects of the story. First, I survey the landscape of current research on *Passio*. Understanding how this text is interpreted in historical and culture-scientific contexts is an important first step toward proposing my own perspective. Second, I interpret *Passio* as a whole from the perspective of the text as an artefact of collective memory. I ask what can be achieved by assuming that this is a popular[2] memory text that was written for a special reception group that I call the "memory group," namely the Christians living in and around Carthage in approximately 200 CE. Moreover, I undertake to explain why this group was especially interested in the afterlife as it can be found in the famous visions of Perpetua and Saturus.

---

1 *Passio Perpetuae et Felicitatis* 18.1–2: "Illuxit dies victoriae illorum, et processerung de carcere in amphitheatrum, quasi in caelum, hilares, vultu decori, si forte gaudio paventes non timore. Sequebatur Perpetua lucido vultu et placido incessu, ut matrona Christi, ut Dei delicata vogore oxulorum deiciens omnium conspectum." Translation is taken from Thomas J. Heffernan, *The Passion of Perpetua and Felicity* (Oxford: University Press, 2012), 133.

2 Eliezer Gonzalez, *The Fate of the Dead in Early Third Century North African Christianity* (Tübingen: Mohr Siebeck, 2014), 8–10.

 | DOI:10.30965/9783657796212_013

The Field of Research: Between longue durée and antique laboratory[3]

Passio has attracted considerable attention in both history and Church history over the last five decades. This "avalanche of studies"[4] has significantly changed our perspective on early Christian martyrdom.[5] Undoubtedly, this semi-biographical narrative offers one of the earliest and most singular insights into ancient martyrdom. The possibility that this is a "unique record"[6] written (at least in part) by a literate woman further increases the interest of modern scholars.

Recent studies clearly reflect a shift in interpretation patterns and suggest how those patterns can change when looking at the same text from different angles. By far the majority of scholars who study *Passio* adopt the position of classical (Church) historians and interpret the text as part of the Christian discourse about martyrdom.[7] By "situating this text in the tradition of literature of martyrdom"[8] within the context of the early church development has been one of the central aims of scholars over the last fifty years. In the process, scholars have followed their own cultural memory of how the early church developed.

3 Christoph Markschies, "Alte Kirche," in *Religion in Geschichte und Gegenwart 1*, ed. H. D. Betz (Tübingen: Mohr Siebeck, 1998), 344–60, 353.

4 Heffernan, *The Passion*, xi.

5 Candida R. Moss, *Ancient Christian Martyrdom: Diverse Practices, Theologies, and Traditions* (New Haven: Yale University Press, 2012); Claude Lepelley, "Die Christen und das Römische Reich," in *Die Zeit des Anfangs (bis 250). Die Geschichte des Christentums I*, ed. Luce Pietri (Freiburg: Herder, 2003), 229–68, 257–59.

6 Heffernan, *The Passion*, x.

7 Hans Reinhard Seeliger and Wolfgang Wischmeyer, eds., *Märtyrerliteratur*, TU 172 (Berlin: De Gruyter, 2015), 1–46.

8 Heffernan, *The Passion*, xi.

Read in this way, the text offers important insights into significant topics, such as the afterlife[9], martyrdom[10], prophecy[11] and Montanism.[12]

---

9 Juliette Harrison, ed., *Imagining the Afterlife in the Ancient World* (New York: Routledge, 2019); Andreas Merkt, "Hindernisse, Feuerflüsse und andere Straforte: das Jenseits außerhalb des Kanons," *TPQ* 167.2 (2019): 167–75; Mark T. Finney, *Resurrection, Hell, and the Afterlife* (New York: Routledge, 2016); Gonzalez, *The Fate of The Dead*; Jutta Dresken-Weiland, Andreas Angerstorfer, Andreas Merkt, eds., *Himmel, Paradies, Schalom: Tod und Jenseits in christlichen und jüdischen Grabinschriften der Antike* (Regensburg: Schnell und Steine, 2012); Walter, Ameling, ed., *Topographie des Jenseits: Studien zur Geschichte des Todes in Kaiserzeit und Spätantike* (Stuttgart: Steiner, 2011); Andreas Merkt, *Das Fegefeuer: Entstehung und Funktion einer Idee* (Darmstadt: Wissenschaftliche Buchgesellschaft, 2005).

10 Éric Rebillard, ed., *Greek and Latin Narratives about the Ancient Martyrs* (Oxford University Press: Oxford, 2017), 1–27; Jan N. Bremmer, *Maidens, Magic and Martyrs in Early Christianity* (Tübingen: Mohr Siebeck, 2017), 349–467; Silke–Petra Bergjan and Beat Näf, eds., *Märtyrerverehrung im frühen Christentum. Zeugnisse und Wirkungsweisen* (Stuttgart: Kohlhammer, 2014); Jakob Engberg, ed., *Contextualizing Early Christian Martyrdom* (Frankfurt: Lang, 2011); Johan Leemans and Boudewijn Dehandschutter, eds., *Martyrdom and Persecution in Late Antique Christianity* (Leuven: Peeters, 2010); Jan N. Bremmer, "'Christianus sum:' The Early Martyrs and Christ," in *Evlogia, Mélanges offerts à Antoon A. R. Bastiaensen à l'occasion de son soixante-cinquième anniversaire*, ed. G. J. M. Bartelink *et al.* (Steenbrugge: Abbatia S. Petri, 1991), 11–20.

11 Katharina Waldner, "Visions, Prophecy, and Authority in the *Passio Perpetuae*," in *Perpetua's Passions: Multidisciplinary Approaches to the Passio Perpetuae et Felicitatis*, ed. Jan N. Bremmer and Marco Formisano (Oxford: University Press, 2012), 201–19; Rex D. Butler, *The New Prophecy and "New Visions": Evidence of Montanism in the Passion of Perpetua and Felicitas* (Washington: Catholic University of America Press, 2006); Cecil M. Robeck, *Prophecy in Carthage: Perpetua, Tertullian, and Cyprian* (Cleveland: The Pilgrim Press, 1992); Elaine C. Huber, *Women and the Authority of Inspiration: A Reexamination of Two Prophetic Movements from a Contemporary Feminist Perspective* (London: University Press, 1985).

12 Victor Saxer, "Das christliche Afrika (180–260)," in *Die Zeit des Anfangs (bis 250). Die Geschichte des Christentums I*, ed. Luce Pietri (Freiburg: Herder, 2003), 622–65; Christoph Markschies, "The Passio Perpetuae et Felicitatis and Montanism?" in *Perpetua's Passions: Multidisciplinary Approaches to the Passio Perpetuae et Felicitatis*, ed. Jan N. Bremmer and Marco Formisano (Oxford: Oxford University Press, 2012), 277–90; William Tabbernee, "Perpetua, Montanism and Christian Ministry in Carthage c. 203 C.E.," *PRSt* 32.4 (2005): 421–41; Maureen A. Tilley, *The Bible in Christian North Africa. The Donatist World* (Minneapolis: Fortress Press, 1996); Maureen A. Tilley, ed., *Donatist Martyr Stories. The Church in Conflict in Roman North Africa* (Liverpool: University Press, 1996); Christine Trevett, *Montanism: Gender, Authority and the New Prophecy* (Cambridge; University Press, 1996). On the importance of the background, see William Tabbernee, *Fake Prophecy and Polluted Sacraments: Ecclesiastical and Imperial Reactions to Montanism* (Leiden: Brill, 2007).

Nevertheless, a deeper look at the scholarship in recent years reveals an underlying discontent with what has become the common perspective. Numerous scholars have sought new and alternate ways of understanding this text, which continues to foster questions about its meaning on several levels. There is still much to explore. Our way of perceiving ancient Christian texts has fundamentally changed in recent years, and *Passio* is no exception. As Katharina Waldner points out, *Passio* is representative of second- and early third-century Christian literature. It serves an outstanding example of the contemporary Christian "laboratory"[13] in which "a great number of eager intellectuals sought to make sense of their fascination by using a peculiar kind of new philosophy and its scriptures."[14] As "laboratory", they need to be read as legitimisations of religious authority, developing organisational structures, and attempts to solve religious problems experienced by specific groups. With regard to *Passio*, Waldner stresses that its use of prophecy and prophetic speech is not unique to Christianity since these features were widespread in ancient discourse throughout the Mediterranean basin.[15] With this in mind, it is not surprising that *Passio* has become a medium of experimentation among readers who employ new hermeneutical and methodological approaches, especially cultural-historical and cultural-scientific ones.

Scholars are mainly interested in the field of cultural history tend to read the text as an important source for the Christian perspective on the different cultures of antiquity,[16] which significantly aims to extend our knowledge about

---

13 Christoph Markschies (*Das antike Christentum. Frömmigkeit, Lebensformen, Institutionen* [München: C. H. Beck, 2016], 44) writes,"Eine kurze Charakterisierung des Christentums könnte so aussehen: Die Christenheit des zweiten Jahrhunderts unterscheidet sich von der des ersten schon allein durch die verschiedenen hochgebildeten Theologen, die sich um das wissenschaftliche Verständnis der neuen Religion bemühen. Auf breitester Front werden in den Großstädten Menschen verschiedenster Schichten gewonnen, und die Kirche wirkt wie ein 'Laboratorium', in dem verschiedene Gestalten von Theologie, Ämterhierarchie und Ethik ausprobiert werden. Nur sehr allmählich ist eine 'Mehrheitskirche' erkennbar, die abweichende Positionen als 'häretisch' ausscheidet."

14 Waldner, "Visions," 202.

15 Waldner, "Visions," 203.

16 See especially Robert Paul Seesengood, *Competing identities: The Athlete and the Gladiator in Early Christianity* (London: T & T Clark, 2006); Sigrid Weigel, "Exemplum und Opfer, Blutzeugnis und Schriftzeugnis: Lucretia und Perpetua als Übergangsfiguren in der Kulturgeschichte der Märtyrer," in *Grenzgänger der Religionskulturen. Kulturwissenschaftliche Beiträge zu Gegenwart und Geschichte der Märtyrer*, ed. Silvia Horsch and Martin Treml (München: Wilhelm Fink, 2011), 25–45. See also the very innovative and intellectually entertaining contribution by Sheldon Stehen, "The Blair Martyr Project: The Passion of Perpetua and Fount Footage Horror," *Journal of Religion and Popular Culture* 31.3 (2019): 183–95.

Carthage[17] around 200 CE and its perception of Christianity.[18] In addition, the field of reception history has contributed important insights on the *longue durée* of this representative text. Recent studies emphasize on the one hand both its importance and its broad reception, expressed in transformations and adaptive constructions, and on the other hand the processes that integrated this text into the cultural memory.[19] Most of all, *Passio* has become an important text for those interested in gender studies, which raises far-reaching perspectival issues in current scholarship. From this perspective, *Passio* can be regarded as a "work which resonates to this day with the urgency of the voice of the young Christian wife, mother and martyr with a power that belies the almost two millennia between her times and the present day."[20] Within this wide range of approaches, Perpetua as the person in the writing can be seen as an exceptional female personality who extends our understanding of her in relation to "women's spiritual empowerment,"[21] the typical prophet[22], a Montanist[23] and a gladiator fighting for her own identity.[24]

---

17 L. Stephanie Cobb, "Suicide by Gladiator? The Acts of Perpetua and Felicitas in its North African Context," *CH* 88.2 (2019): 597–628; Saxer, "Das christliche Afrika," 622–65; Eva Baumkamp, *Kommunikation in der Kirche des 3. Jahrhunderts* (Tübingen: Mohr Siebeck, 2014); Alexander Evers, *Church, Cities, and People: A Study of the Plebs in the Church and Cities of Roman Africa in Late Antiquity* (Leuven: Peeters, 2010); Allen Brent, *Cyprian and Roman Carthage* (Cambridge: University Press, 2010); Andreas Hoffmann, *Kirchliche Strukturen und römisches Recht bei Cyprian von Karthago* (Paderborn: Schöningh, 2000); Georg Schöllgen, *Ecclesia sordida? Zur Frage der sozialen Schichtung frühchristlicher Gemeinden am Beispiel Karthagos zur Zeit Tertullians* (Münster: Aschendorff, 1984).

18 Note the recent rise of new translations: Heffernan, *The Passion*; Peter Habermehl, *Perpetua und der Ägypter oder Bildes des Bösen im frühen afrikanischen Christentum. Ein Versuch zur Passio sanctorum Perpetua et Felicitatis* (Berlin: Walter de Gruyter, 2004); Jacqueline Amat, *Passion de Perpétue et de Félicité: Introduction, Texte critique, Traduction, Commentaire et index* (Paris: Les Éditions du CERF, 1996).

19 Margaret Cotter-Lynch, *Saint Perpetua across the Middle Ages: Mother, Gladiator, Saint* (New York: Palgrave Macmillan, 2016).

20 Petr Kitzler, *From Passio Perpetuae to Acta Perpetuae: Recontextualisizing a Martyr Story in the Literature of the Early Church* (Berlin: de Gruyter, 2015), ix. On gender-oriented interpretation, see 35–55. See also Gail P. C. Streete, *Redeemed Bodies: Women Martyrs in Early Christianity* (Louisville: Westminster John Knox Press, 1989); Barbara K. Gold, *Perpetua: Athlete of God* (New York: Oxford University Press, 2018); William Farina, *Perpetua of Carthage: Portrait of a Third-Century Martyr* (Jefferson: McFarland, 2009). For a feminist approach, see Huber, *Women and the Authority of inspiration.*

21 Streete, *Redeemed Bodies*, 1.

22 Robeck, *Prophecy in Carthage*, 11–86; Ferdinand Hahn and Hans Klein, *Die frühchristliche Prophetie. Ihre Voraussetzungen, ihre Anfänge und ihre Entwicklung bis zum Montanismus. Eine Einführung* (Neukirchen-Vluyn: Neukirchener Verlagsgesellschaft, 2011).

23 Butler, *The New Prophecy*, 88–96. For a more cautious approach, see Tabbernee, *Fake Prophecy*, 64–66.

24 Seesengood, *Competing Identities*, 97–105.

In addition to these different approaches, I suggest adding a new cultural-scientific one that reads *Passio* primarily as a construct of memory shared within a fledgling Christian group in North Africa. As such, the text takes on the metaphor of a laboratory, as mentioned earlier. It functions to distinguish a group of Christian believers from the populace and reacts to the new reality of persecution and martyrdom. It does so by presenting a narrative that contains a number of visions that function to guarantee the truth of the narrative as a divinely ordained product through the authorship of Perpetua and Saturus. Both the narrative and the visions it contains are approached as products of memory, especially in relation to conceptions of the afterlife as they were imagined by this group of Christians. In and around Carthage, *Passio* expressed a remembrance of the martyrs and their practice of the Christian faith. The visions in the narrative, which were biblically influenced and contextually shaped, provided a new kind of knowledge that was integrated into this group's conception of Christian identity.

Memory and Identity as Key Aspects of Understanding Passio

There are distinct indications that martyr texts in general should be considered and analysed in the context of memory formation of early Christian identity. One of the strongest indications is that these texts were used for only 200 years. In 393 CE, the Council of Hippo declared these texts to be an important element of *memoria* and decided that they should be part of liturgical contexts and preaching.[25] At this point, martyr texts gained a new function. According to Reinhard Seeliger, up to that point they had delivered important memory and identity markers for groups of Christian believers all around the Roman Empire. Now, they also additionally contributed to social control and the individual preparation for the Christian way of dying.[26] *Passio* provides a good example of this highly successful agenda. Both the martyrs' names and the visions had spread from North Africa to Rome (350 CE), Spain (360 CE) and the Greek East (360 CE) within 60 years, indicating that the narrative in its original form was widely known in Christian contexts.[27] Several later revised versions (*Acta Perpetuae* A and B) and three of Augustinus' sermons (280–282 CE) additionally verify the enormous importance of the text in antiquity.[28]

25 Seeliger, *Märtyrerliteratur*, 4–5.
26 Seeliger, *Märtyrerliteratur*, 9–10.
27 Kitzler, *From Passio Perpetuae*, 123–24.
28 Kitzler, *From Passio Perpetuae*, 80–116.

Around 500 CE, there seems to have been a cult in Carthage that was represented in pictorial forms of Perpetua and Felicitas that can still be seen in the mosaics in Ravenna.[29]

All of these later developments strongly indicate that *Passio* was much more than a narrative about Carthaginian martyrs. It was a narrative that influenced widespread remembrance of an event in a peculiar way. From the very beginning, it was a narrative that was intended to deliver a common memory structure, along with an interpretation of narrated events, to a particular group that outlived the martyrs. If one takes this perspective, then martyr texts like *Passio* can be examined in light of group memory processes that were products of the current conditions. Hermeneutically, *Passio* becomes a text of "artefacts of group memory."[30] Since both the redactor and the author of *Passio* are eyewitnesses, these events recorded in the writing are part of their recent past. For them, this text is a way of structuring the events so as to give them meaning within collective group memory. Since the process of remembrance does not "preserve the past as such, but parts of it in particular perspective,"[31] it is the present circumstance that shapes how the group remembers the past. Overall, *Passio* is both an important source of narrated events, yet at the same time those events are presented and shaped within contexts of the remembering groups—in this case Carthaginian and North African Latin-speaking Christians. Thus, *Passio* is best viewed as an artefact that is a product of collective memory formation.

From a (historical) hermeneutical point of view, an analysis of the memory process within social groups is an important contribution to historical inquiry into how early Christians understood their own past. However, it should not be viewed as a replacement of other approaches that likewise aim to understand the past and its interpretation.[32] Nevertheless, the concepts of memory cul-

29 Kitzler, *From Passio Perpetuae*, 124.

30 Sandra Huebenthal, "Frozen Moments—Early Christianity through the Lens of Social Memory Theory," in *Memory and Memories in Early Christianity. Proceedings of the International Conference held at the Universities of Geneva and Lausanne (June 2–3, 2016)*, ed. Simon Butticaz and Enrico Norelli (Tübingen: Mohr Siebeck, 2016), 17–43, here 17. While Huebenthal's approach focusses on the New Testament, it is applicable here as well.

31 Huebenthal, "Frozen Moments," 17.

32 Stefan Jordan, *Theorien und Methoden der Geschichtswissenschaft* (Paderborn: Ferdinand Schöningh, 2016), 170–176; Lothar Kolmer, *Geschichtstheorien* (Paderborn: Ferdinand Schöningh GmbH, 2008), 70–71, 80–81. Thomas Wünsch, "Erinnerungskultur," in *Online-Lexikon zur Kultur und Geschichte der Deutschen im östlichen Europa, 2013* in https://ome-lexikon.uni-oldenburg.de/begriffe/erinnerungskultur/. Accessed Aug. 1, 2020.

ture[33] and public history[34] are widely accepted methods of analysis,[35] despite current debates about the viability of constructing history in a collective way.[36] Memory theory has shown great relevance for inter- and trans-disciplinary research over the last twenty years. Usually housed in the cultural sciences, memory theory provides a platform for discussion and research that can bring diverse academic fields together.[37]

The interaction between historical and cultural inquiry, which is possible through conceptions of memory, is credited especially to the work of Maurice Halbwachs[38] and Aleida and Jan Assmann.[39] From their general perspective, the concept of collective memory can be differentiated in two ways.[40] First, *social memory* is a category that refers to the "recent past," typically targeting the initial 30–50 years of remembrance while potential eye witnesses are still available to be questioned about the event that are remembered. The past event is non-intentionally localised within given frames by means of a communicative process (*Vergemeinschaftung*).[41] This "recent past" extends

33 Astrid Erll, *Memory in Culture* (Basingstoke: Palgrave Macmillan, 2011), 49–53.

34 Martin Lücke and Irmgard Zündorf, *Einführung in die Public History* (Göttingen: Vandenhoeck & Ruprecht, 2018).

35 Lücke and Zündorf, *Einführung*, 28–35.

36 Aleida Assmann, *Das neue Unbehagen an der Erinnerungskultur. Eine Intervention* (München: C. H. Beck, 2013). For an example of an open concept, see Christoph Corneließen, "Erinnerungskulturen 2.0," in *Docupedia-Zeitgeschichte* in https://docupedia.de/zg/Erinnerungskulturen_Version_2.0_Christoph_Corneli%C3%9Fen. Accessed May 28, 2020.

37 Astrid Erll, *Kollektives Gedächtnis und Erinnerungskulturen. Eine Einführung* (Stuttgart: Metzler, 2017), ix, 1–10.

38 Maurice Halbwachs, *La mémoire collective* (Paris: Presses Universitaires de France, 1950; repr., Paris: Albin Michel, 2005); *Les cadres sociaux de la mémoire* (Paris: F. Alcan, 1925; repr., Paris: Albin Michel 2004); Gerald Echterhoff, ed., *Kontexte und Kulturen des Erinnerns. Maurice Halbwachs und das Paradigma des kollektiven Gedächtnisses* (Konstanz: UVK, 2002).

39 Jan Assmann, *Das kulturelle Gedächtnis. Schrift, Erinnerung und politische Identität in frühen Hochkulturen* (München: C. H. Beck, 2018); *Religion und kulturelles Gedächtnis* (München: C. H. Beck, 2007); Aleida Assmann, *Formen des Vergessens* (Göttingen: Wallstein, 2018); *Ist die Zeit aus den Fugen? Aufstieg und Fall des Zeitregimes der Moderne* (München: Hanser, 2013); *Das neue Unbehagen an der Erinnerungskultur*.

40 Sandra Huebenthal, "Collective Memory, Communicative Memory, Cultural Memory, Social Memory," in *The Dictionary of the Bible and Ancient Media*, ed. Tom Thatcher, Chris Keith, Raymond F. Person, Jr., and Elsie R. Stern (London: Bloomsbury, 2017), 66, 69–70, 368–69.

41 Angela Keppler, *Tischgespräche. Über Formen kommunikativer Vergemeinschaftung am Beispiel der Konversation in Familien* (Frankfurt: Suhrkamp, 1994); Harald Welzer, Sabine Moller, and Karoline Tschuggnall, *"Opa war kein Nazi." Nationalsozialismus und Holocaust im Familiengedächtnis* (Frankfurt am Main: Fischer, 2012).

to the *Generational Gap*, which represents a period of time when the eyewitnesses start to die. In Halbwach's theory, *social memory* "refers to the influence of the social framework on the individual's memory processes" which is distinguished from *collective memory* which "denotes the process of the group establishing a framework to semanticize and actualize events as memories."[42] Collective memory refers to the recent past as well, but includes the last 40–80 years in which the event is consciously recalled (or forgotten) and embedded in new, often multiple and varying frames.[43] In this process, there is quite often a change in the medium of communication. This is when the first texts are produced. In these texts, different constructions of memory can exist at the same time.[44]

The second category of memory is so-called *cultural memory*, which refers to a period that begins about 80–100 years after the original event. At this stage of memory construction, what remains are the re-shaped memories of the past that continue to be relevant for each community's present.[45] Memories of the past tend to take the form of mythical constructs that are detached from the earliest groups that initiated the process. The past is no longer directly negotiable or accessible through eyewitness. The remembered past nevertheless exists as an established objectification, akin to a canonization.[46] The canon, mostly in the form of formalised narratives, is interpreted and appropriated in the receivers' present life situations.[47]

Passio as a Text of Memory and Identity Formation

The written text, the *Passio* is a "hybrid of different narrative forms—prison narrative, *hypomnema*, oral reportage, and the epistolary tradition."[48] In short, the central parts of its content tell the story of a group of Carthaginian Christians around 200 CE—in part *adolescentes catechumeni, young catechumens*[49]—

42 Huebenthal, "Collective Memory," 368.

43 Sandra Huebenthal, *Reading Mark's Gospel as a Text from Collective Memory* (Grand Rapids: Eerdmans, 2020), 529–544.

44 Sandra Huebenthal, *Das Markusevangelium als kollektives Gedächtnis* (Göttingen: Vandenhoeck und Ruprecht, 2014), 148.

45 Erll, *Memory in Culture*, 28–37.

46 Erll, *Memory in Culture*, 29.

47 Erll, *Memory in Culture*, 29; Huebenthal, *Markusevangelium*, 146.

48 Heffernan, *The Passion*, 7; Sönke Finnern, *Narratologie und biblische Exegese* (Tübingen: Mohr Siebeck, 2010), 40–43 (frames and scripts).

49 Heffernan, *The Passion*, 28–43, 46–50.

who confess their faith in front of a Roman Proconsul, named Hilarianus,[50] in 202 or 203 CE.[51]

Table 12.1 Structure of *Passio* (genres)

Frame (redactor[52])	**Narrative**	**Visions**
1–2: theological classification and introduction		
	3–6: martyr narrative (Perpetua)	
		7–8: visions: Dinocrates
	9: martyr narrative (Perpetua)	
		10: visions: Pomponius
		11–13: visions: Saturus
	14–21: Martyrium (Redactor)	
21: Doxology and interpretation		

The preceding Table 12.1 presents three dominant genres within *Passio*, which is primarily a martyr story consisting of parts 3–6, 9, and 14–21. The members of the victim group experience considerable suffering during their custody,[53] trial, and eventual imprisonment.[54] Two of them, Perpetua and Saturus, are often viewed as the authors of at least part of the ordeal.[55] Additionally, they both experience visions, whose recounting played an influential role for subsequent generations of Christians.[56] These are inserted into the text in 7–8 and 10–13. In the end, the members of the victim group pay the ultimate price for their unwavering faith when they are fed to the wild animals.[57]

---

50 Heffernan, *The Passion*, 50–52.

51 Heffernan, *The Passion*, 60–78.

52 "Redactor" is a technical term used by Heffernan for the author of the introduction and the conclusion. See Heffernan, *The Passion*, 8–9. On the redactor's biography, see 15–17.

53 Jens-Uwe Krause, *Gewalt und Kriminalität in der Spätantike* (München: C. H. Beck, 2014); *Gefängnisse im Römischen Reich* (Stuttgart: Franz Steiner, 1996).

54 *Passio* 6. All references to *Passio* are from Heffernan, *The Passion*.

55 Heffernan, *The Passion*, 5.

56 *Passio* 7, 10, 11–13.

57 *Passio* 18–21.

Additionally, the text comprises of a redactorial frame consisting of a theological classification and an introduction in 1–2 and a doxology and interpretation in 21. These parts clearly differ from the narrative character of the text, and were highly disputed because of their Montanist tendencies. What can be said for sure is that the redactor exhibits significant training in classical rhetoric and theological argumentation.[58]

Hermeneutically, this text cannot be anything other than a text that expresses collective memory. The structure of the text reveals two ways of defining the collective identity of Christians in Carthage. Primarily, it functions as a concept of how martyrdom in Carthage should be remembered and interpreted. The martyrs were exemplars of victory, serving as patterns for how Christians should behave when their faith was radically challenged. Christians could look to Perpetua who learned to accept her faith as a process of development initiated by God. As a reward, Christians could be sure of God's goodwill and their place in heaven. The memory of Perpetua, Felicity, and their companions served as an integral part of the group's identity. The story became part of the group's self-image and worldview.

Secondarily, identity construction is also conveyed by the redactor who extends the narrative by adding his own theological perspective. For him, the visions of Perpetua and Saturus were important as they directly revealed the will of the Holy Spirit.[59] For the redactor, the "newer events" and visions were direct proofs of God's grace and a special gift for the Carthaginian Christians.[60] Consequently, both the introduction and the doxology at the end point to a liturgical use of the text.[61]

The Historical and Cultural Context of Passio: Christians in Carthage Around 200 CE

At the beginning of the third century, Carthage (along with the surrounding region) was one of the most important and prosperous cities in the Roman Empire.[62] Although ethnologically diverse,[63] Carthage was one of the largest cities in the Roman Empire with more than 100,000 residents who were exposed to an array of rich cultural amenities, including thermal baths, theatres, and

58 *Passio* 8–17.
59 *Passio* 10.
60 *Passio* 1.
61 Seeliger, *Märtyrerliteratur*, 1–10.
62 Saxer, "Das christliche Afrika," 622–26.
63 Saxer, "Das christliche Afrika," 622.

leading philosophical schools.[64] Its elevated status was a relatively new development. When the Romans finally conquered the region around Carthage in the middle of the first century, they started to develop it agriculturally and economically. Northern Africa was colonised by systematically irrigating the landscape, thereby settling the nomadic populace, which was one of the main aims of this long-term investment.[65] The result was a society that was diverse in its origin—simultaneously Punic, nomadic, and Roman. Society as a whole was in the process of transformation, and the Christians in North Africa were part of this radical change.[66]

Socially, the Christian residents were a heterogenous group. Although most Christians were part of the lower, self-sustaining class, the Christian parishes also had their share of highly specialised craftsmen, slave owners and even members of the establishment (*senatores, equestres*).[67] Culturally, we can conclude from Tertullian that at least the higher classes were able to speak and write Latin and Greek. Perpetua herself serves as a prominent example when she speaks with a bishop and a presbyter in Greek.[68]

The number of Christians was quite considerable. Georg Schöllgen estimates that there were several thousand Christians living in and around Carthage.[69] It is also estimated that there were approximately thirty cathedral cities[70] in the province of *Africa Consularis* around 250 CE. Regular church services, with Eucharist and fellowship meals, structured everyday Christian life.[71] Assemblies took place mainly in houses.[72] Apart from these customs, North African Christianity was as diverse as the culture in which it was situated. In particular, Carthage was a melting pot of different Christian sects and expressions—Gnosticism, Montanism, Marcionism. Eventually, Donatism also played an influential role in the parishes.[73]

Christians living in North Africa during this period experienced difficult social situations. In addition to the daily pressures brought about by societal and internal heterogeneity, the political pressure started to become increasingly

64 Habermehl, *Perpetua und der Ägypter*, 37.
65 Saxer, "Das christliche Afrika," 624–26.
66 Schöllgen, *Ecclesia sordida?* 17–98; Saxer, "Das christliche Afrika," 626–63.
67 Saxer, "Das christliche Afrika," 635 (Tertullian, *Idol.* 7.1.1106).
68 Saxer, "Das christliche Afrika," 629–31.
69 Schöllgen, *Ecclesia sordida?* 295.
70 Saxer, "Das christliche Afrika," 642–43.
71 Saxer, "Das christliche Afrika," 632–38.
72 Saxer, "Das christliche Afrika," 635–37.
73 Saxer, "Das christliche Afrika," 638–41.

serious. Between 180 and 200 CE, we know of at least two persecutions in the province of *Africa Proconsularis*. The first occurred in Scilli, which claimed at least 12 victims.[74] The second occurred around 200 CE in Carthage, which is included in the *Passio*. Due to these events, the question regarding the different internal theological positions gained additional weight. One of the central problems was the question of the Christian conception of time in relation to life and death. While the Christians had clear ideas about resurrection and the afterlife,[75] their concept of time and the importance placed on every human life differed significantly from the norms of Roman society.

Passio was written when Christians were experiencing cultural and political pressures, which created a crisis of hope. While the martyrs were a source of pride for Christians, their example did not eliminate the intense pressure that elevated the reflections and dialogue about Christian identity. In response to the crisis, *Passio* attempts to offer its audience a sense of group identity by means of a common memory.

The Passio as a Memory Text

Perpetua and her fellow martyrs gained enormous significance, which is indicated in the text. From a memory perspective, there are three different levels within the text that serve different purposes. On a first level, the martyrs' narrative (3–6, 9, 14–21) itself serves to establish the martyrs' authority. At the same time, it is a narrative that mirrors Perpetua's inner development and her becoming a martyr. She leaves the bindings of her earthly life by incrementally seeing herself as existing in the face of God. The diverse prophecies and visions (7–8, 10–13) gain plausibility because of the grounding narrative. From the perspective of memory construction, the theological and liturgical frames delivered by the redactor in 1–2 and 21 are secondary, as these parts do not contribute to the argumentation and the contents, but give an additional interpretation of the significance of the text and its events.

The first level primarily deals with the fate of Perpetua and her companions, chiefly narrated from Perpetua's perspective.[76] The narrator/redactor begins

---

74 Saxer, "Das christliche Afrika," 626–28.

75 Gonzalez, *The Fate of The Dead*; Habermehl, *Perpetua und der Ägypter*, 109–208; Jan N. Bremmer, "The Passion of Perpetua and the Development of Early Christian Afterlife," *NedTT* 54 (2000): 97–111.

76 *Passio* 2, 3: "haec ordinem totum martyrii sui iam hinc ipsa narravit sicut conscriptum man sua et suo sensu reliquit." Heffernan (*The Passion*, 126) translates it as: "From this

and finishes the story line. From a memory perspective, this narration is a story of legitimation. For the memory group reading the text, it was largely irrelevant whether Perpetua herself had written the text or not. The argumentation gained persuasive power because of the change of perspective from the narrator to the martyr herself. Ego documents contain condensed information and personal interpreted experiences that become part of social memory through narration and—in this case—by being written down.

Table 12.2 Narrative Structure of Passio

Phases (narrative intentions)	**Events/development**
Leaving the world	2: Imprisonment as a catechumen Social background 3: Leaving social background (father) Confession I: "I am a Christ" Baptism
Greatly esteemed	4: Brother: "ask for a vision" Acceptance of *Passio* (Perpetua, brother, mother) 5: Parting of father 6: Public hearing Confession II: "I am a Christian" Condemnation Parting of the / a child 9: Support of military adjutant Pudens
Greatly esteemed Martyrdom as mercy	13: Secundus' Death 15: Felicity and her birth 16–21: Exemplary martyrdom

On a second level, we encounter a highly dynamic inner development when Perpetua and her group of martyrs begin leaving the world to face God. As Table 12.2 shows, the narrative develops as a story of leaving the world (2–3), whose participants are greatly esteemed by God (4–9) and experience martyrdom as his mercy (13–21). In 2 and 3, Perpetua describes the time directly after her imprisonment. In the sequences dealing with her father (3, 5, 6), she leaves

point there follows a complete account of her martyrdom, as she left it, written in her own hand and in accordance with her understanding."

her life and its social bindings behind and refuses to obey her father who tries to convince her to save herself. Instead, she gives a statement with the utmost significance for whatever time she has left by saying, "I am a Christian."[77] With this confession, she confirms her religion as the core of her identity.[78] Significantly, baptism in prison becomes the next step. This is a decision with strong connections to the North African understanding of the sacrament of baptism, which thus connects Perpetua with the memory group.[79]

From this point onward, she and her companions are in a state of grace or, as her brother formulates it in 4.1, they are "greatly esteemed." From a memory perspective, the climax of the narrative is reached in 4. Following her brother's suggestion, Perpetua asks God for a "*visio*", thus indicating to the memory group that her visions are directly given by God because of her status as a martyr. Both she and Saturus have visions that they record personally. Consequently, for the memory group of Carthaginian Christians, these visions were highly relevant for those who accepted this narrative as a worthwhile guide to how they are to live life. It conveys the importance of remembrance within an argumentative process. By accepting Perpetua's paradigmatic martyrdom as a role model for their own lives, Perpetua and Saturus' visions had to be accepted and taken into account as well. The martyrs' memory was not possible without accepting the memory of their visions.

The remaining parts of this founding narrative conclude the process of martyrdom in several steps. Remaining in God's esteem without stumbling, Perpetua departs from both her father and her child, giving up the last bonds to mundane life. The public hearing *in foro* (6), the martyrs' confession in front of Hilarianus, and even the sudden support of the military adjutant in prison (9) and the triumphal and perfect martyrdom in the arena (14) are well known elements of other martyr narratives that serve to accentuate the exemplary and holy behaviour of the martyrs.

---

77 *Passio* 3.2: "sic et ego aliud me dicere non possum nisi quod sum, Christiana." Heffernan (*The Passion* 126) translates it as, "In the same way, I am unable to call myself other than what I am, a Christian."

78 Heffernan, *The Passion*, 154–55.

79 *Passio* 3.5: "in ipso spatio paucorum dierum baptizati sumus, et mihi Spiritus dictavit non aliud petendum ab aqua nisi sufferentiam carnis." Heffernan (*The Passion*, 126) translates it as, "In the space of a few days we were baptized. The Spirit told me that nothing else should else should be sought from the water other than the endurance of the body." On the practice of baptism in the North African context, see Heffernan, *The Passion*, 154–55, who writes, "The African church saw this initiatory sacrament as crucial to salvation. It conveyed a passage from the world of idolatry to that of the blessed elect."

Table 12.3 Narrative Structure of Perpetua

Phases	Events/development	Visions
Leaving the world	2: Imprisonment as a catechumen Social background 3: Leaving social background (father) Confession I: "I am a Christ" Baptism	
Greatly esteemed	4: Brother: "ask for a vision" Acceptance of *Passio* (Perpetua, brother, mother) 5: Parting of father 6: Public hearing Confession II: "I am a Christian" Condemnation Parting of the child	4: Ladder to Paradise
		7: Dinocrates I 8: Dinocrates II
	9: Support of military adjutant Pudens	
		10: Transformation and Leave-Taking (Fight against the Egyptian) 11: Saturus' vision
Greatly esteemed martyrdom as mercy	13: Secundus' death 15: Felicity and her birth 16–21: Exemplary martyrdom	

On a third level, the visions play an important part in memory construction. Table 12.3 shows how the visions are integrated into the story line and convey information about the conceptions of afterlife. Two of the visions (4 and 10) are directly linked to the narrated events, as they are included in the process of becoming esteemed martyrs. In 4, the *Ladder to Paradise* predicts the future martyrdom, which is strongly linked to biblical and, at the same time, cultural frames (e.g., Jacob's ladder in Gen 28:10–22; and the dragon in Revelation 12).[80] In 10, the pending martyrdom in the arena is interpreted as a contest between good and evil, where Perpetua represents the good and an Egyptian represents evil.[81]

The other three visions, however, have a completely different quality if they are interpreted from the perspective of memory construction. They attempt to deliver additional information about the afterlife that is relevant for the memory group. Interpreted in this way, Perpetua's visions are more than they seem to be at first sight. From a memory perspective, these visions have to be viewed in light of the authority of two martyrs who near to God as they awaited their martyrdom. From the perspective of the memory group, they are important sources for conveying what God wanted them to know as a basis for living the Christian life on a daily basis.

In her second and third visions, Perpetua recollects her brother Dinocrates dying of cancer at the age of seven. In her vision, she encounters Dinocrates, who is trying to drink from a pool but is not successful because the rim is too high.[82] The whole scenario shares similarities with the ancient underworld (Hades), which would have been familiar to the memory group since it was part of their common cultural memory.[83] After envisioning her brother, Perpetua prays him day and night. In her next vision, Dinocrates is able to drink from the pool.[84] It is not quite clear why her brother was punished in the underworld

80 Habermehl, *Perpetua und der Ägypter*, 84–103.

81 Habermehl, *Perpetua und der Ägypter*, 109–15.

82 *Passio* 7.7–8: "Erat deinde in illo loco, ubi Dinocrates erat, piscina plena aqua, altiorem marginem habens quam erat statura pueri; et expendebat se Dinocrates quasi bibiturus. Ego dolebam, quod piscina illa aquam habebat, et tamen probper altitudinem marginis bibiturus non esset." Heffernan (*The Passion*, 129) translates it as, "Moreover, in that place where Dinocrates was, there was a pool full of water with a rim that was higher than the height of the boy. I was saddened because, although the pool had water in it, he was not able to drink because of the height of the rim."

83 Heffernan (*The Passion*, 53) writes, "She sees him in a type of hades or proto-purgatory." For the Roman context see Gonzalez, *The Fate of The Dead*, 129–162.

84 *Passio* 7.9–10: "Et experta sum, et cognovit fratrem meum laborare; sed fedebam me profuturam labori eius. Et orabam pro eo omnibus diebus quousque trasivimus in carcerem castrensem; munere enim castrensi eramus pugnaturi; natale tunc Getae Caesaris. Et feci pro illo orationem die et nocte gemens et lacrimans, ut mihi donaretur." Heffernan (*The Passion*, 129) translates it as, "And I awakened, and I knew that my brother was suffering. But I trusted that I could help him in his suffering. And I prayed for him every day until we were transferred to the military games; it was on the birthday of Geta Caesar. And I prayed day and night for my brother with groans and tears so that this gift might be given to me."

in the first place, but for the memory group another message was more important. I conveyed that it was possible to get out of trouble in the underworld through prayer.

Saturus' vision, by contrast, describes another element of the afterlife, namely heaven itself. Although narrowly connected to existing conceptions, the picture outlined is quite innovative. Carried to paradise by four angels, Saturus experiences a "magical palace, whose walls of light gleam radiantly,"[85] where the martyrs are escorted to God's throne. They meet Him as a "hoary old man"[86] and are afterwards dismissed. This vision is special because, in the end, Saturus and Perpetua meet their bishop Optatus and a presbyter named Aspasius in front of the gates to heaven. Both throw themselves at the martyrs' feet and ask them to mediate between them.[87] The answer is delivered by the angels who explain that it is not the martyrs' task, but rather that of the bishop who has to rebuke his people "because they are gathering around you [bishop]."[88]

Both of Perpetua's visions about Dinocrates and Saturus' vision about paradise can be read as an attempt to transfer new knowledge to their fellow Christians, conveying certainty about the afterlife by delivering an offer as part of the *memoria martyrum*. These ideas were at least partly known within the memory group on the basis of their familiarity with religious (biblical and apocryphal) texts whose motifs were extended and illustrated by means of these visions and integrated into the collective knowledge that influenced the group's identity formation. For the members of this group, the underlying Christian ideas from contemporary texts were clearly visible.[89] At the same time, the broader cultural context would have allowed for influences from Jewish apocalyptic literature and broader Greek and Roman conceptions of afterlife.[90] Already existing ways of imagining the interim and the afterlife amalgamated in the vision and enabled the memory group to adapt new ideas and pictures. This simultaneously meant that the "new" contents needed to be compatible with the knowledge already familiar to the memory group. Overall,

85 Heffernan, *The Passion*, 284.

86 Heffernan, *The Passion*, 285.

87 Heffernan, *The Passion*, 131.

88 *Passio* 13.6: "Et conturbaverunt eos, et dixerunt Optato: 'Corrige plebem tuam, quia sic ad te convenient quasi de circo redeuntes et de factionibus certantes.'" Heffernan (*The Passion*, 131) translates it as, "And the angels admonished them and said to Optatus: 'Rebuke your people, because they are gathering around you, just as if they were returning from the chariot races, arguing about the different teams.'"

89 Especially in *visio* 1 and *visio* 4. Habermehl, *Perpetua und der Ägypter*, 85–86, 90–103 (*visio* 1), 189–96 (*visio* 4). Cf. Gonzalez, *The Fate of The Dead*, 82–89 (*visio* 1), 139–61.

90 Gonzalez, *The Fate of The Dead*, 89–103 (*visio* 1), 130–39 (*visio* 2 and 3).

the narrative seems to argue along already-existing lines, but it adds significant points and paints complete pictures endorsing the authority of the martyrs.

This way of reading *Passio* makes it possible to develop a new perspective on the redactor and his frequently discussed *exordium*. One gets the impression that he exaggerates, as the argumentation of the narrative does not necessarily support his theologically marked position. The redactor's intent is to create a permanent, rhetorically developed frame around the narratives and to set them in a context in which they can become a permanent part of the group's collective memory. For that purpose, he establishes an additional frame that is otherwise not existent in the text, but is probably intended to strengthen remembrance. Arguing eschatologically, the redactor proposes, on the one hand, Christian tradition and scripture as sources of actual Christian belief. Yet, on the other hand, he drafts a—possibly Montanist[91]—interpretation that gives actual prophecies even greater importance than the revered texts. From his point of view, the "one spirit" is far more present in "newer events" since they "are necessarily greater because they are more recent, because of the overflow of grace promised for the end of time."[92]

Conclusion

The analysis of *Passio* from a memory perspective yields four conclusions. First, *Passio* is a text that was written to address a specific situation in the North African context. The persecutions that occurred between 180 and 200 CE, in combination with the spread of heterogeneous Christian ideas such as Montanism, created a condition in which Christians had strong reasons to discuss their own identity because of external pressure and internal diversity. Additionally, North African society was in the midst of transformation, which may have contributed to the persecutions. Further developments in North Africa (e.g., the social problems emerging some decades later in the context

91 Robeck, *Prophecy in Carthage*, 11–94.

92 *Passio* 1.3: "Sed viderint qui unam virtutem Spiritus unius Sancti pro aetativus iudicent temporum, cum maiora reputanda sunt novitiora quaeque, ut novissimiora, secundum exuperationem gratiae in ultima saeculi spatia decretam." Heffernan (*The Passion*, 125) translates it as, "But let those who would restrict the singular power of the one spirit to certain times understand this: that newer events are necessarily grater because they are more recent, because of the overflow of grace promised for the end of time."

of the *circumcircelliones*)[93] indicate at least some regional long-term social problems.

Second, *Passio* can be read as a memory story that attempts to provide solutions to the problems experienced by the Christian memory group. This is a typical example of a process that results in the construction of social memory. In the face of persecution and martyrdom, the text focuses on central contents of faith and gives Christians certainty during a time of instability and danger.

Third, the story serves to establish the authority of the group of martyrs that suffered persecution and execution in 202/3 CE. Primarily, it is a story of development. The martyrs in general, and Perpetua as an extraordinary example, dissociate themselves from their lives and their social contexts and gain a new perspective. They live their last days from a perspective of being in the face of God. In this way, they gain authority within the memory group. Being "greatly esteemed," their visions can be read as messages that aimed at the memory group.

Finally, through the authority of the martyrs, the Christian memory group receives the central message—or perhaps the distinct reminder—that there is life after death (4, "ladder to paradise") They are presented with clear portrayals and ideas about what the afterlife was like (11, Saturus). Escaping Hades is possible (7/8, Dinocrates), but achieving a Christian afterlife requires a hard fight against evil (10, Leave-Taking and Fight against the Egyptian).

In this way, the text of *Passio* was an offer to remember both the martyrs as persons who lived their Christian lives in an extraordinary way. Their visions provided their fellow contemporaries the security to follow the right path and have a clear picture of the eschatological goal. As the *longue durée* has shown, this attempt was extremely successful. The text was not only accepted as part of the collective memory of North Africa, it also found a place in the cultural memory of Christendom that has persisted until today.

Bibliography

Amat, Jacqueline. *Passion de Perpétue et de Félicité: Introduction, Texte critique, Traduction, Commentaire et index*. Paris: Les Éditions du CERF, 1996.

93 Remo Cacitti, *Furiosa turba. I fundamenti religiose delléversione sociale, della dissidenza politica e della contestazione ecclesiale dei Ciconcellione d' Africa* (Milano: Biblioteca francescana, 2006); Paulus G. Schulten, *De circumcillionen. Een sociaal-religieuze beweging in de late oudheid* (Scheveningen: Edauw and Johannissen, 1984).

Assmann, Aleida. *Das neue Unbehagen an der Erinnerungskultur. Eine Intervention.* München: C. H. Beck, 2013.

——. *Ist die Zeit aus den Fugen? Aufstieg und Fall des Zeitregimes der Moderne.* München: Hanser, 2013.

——. *Formen des Vergessens.* Göttingen: Wallstein, 2018.

Assmann, Jan. *Religion und kulturelles Gedächtnis.* München: C. H. Beck, 2007.

——. *Das kulturelle Gedächtnis. Schrift, Erinnerung und politische Identität in frühen Hochkulturen.* München: C. H. Beck, 2018.

Baumkamp, Eva. *Kommunikation in der Kirche des 3. Jahrhunderts.* Tübingen: Mohr Siebeck, 2014.

Bergjan, Silke–Petra, and Beat Näf, eds. *Märtyrerverehrung im frühen Christentum. Zeugnisse und Wirkungsweisen.* Stuttgart: Kohlhammer, 2014.

Bremmer, Jan N. "'Christianus sum:' The Early Martyrs and Christ." Pages 11–20 in *Evlogia, Mélanges offerts à Antoon A. R. Bastiaensen à l'occasion de son soixante-cinquième anniversaire.* Edited by G. J. M. Bartelink *et al.* Steenbrugge: Abbatia S. Petri, 1991.

——. "The Passion of Perpetua and the Development of Early Christian Afterlife." *NedTT* 54 (2000): 97–111.

——. *Maidens, Magic and Martyrs in Early Christianity.* Tübingen: Mohr Siebeck, 2017.

Brent, Allen. *Cyprian and Roman Carthage.* Cambridge: University Press, 2010.

Butler, Rex D. *The New Prophecy and "New Visions": Evidence of Montanism in the Passion of Perpetua and Felicitas.* Washington: Catholic University of America Press, 2006.

Cacitti, Remo. *Furiosa turba. I fundamenti religiose delléversione sociale, della dissidenza politica e della contestazione ecclesiale dei Ciconcellione d' Africa.* Milano: Biblioteca francescana, 2006.

Cobb, L. Stephanie. "Suicide by Gladiator? The Acts of Perpetua and Felicitas in its North African Context." *CH* 88.2 (2019): 597–628.

Cornelißen, Christoph. "Erinnerungskulturen 2.0." In Docupedia-Zeitgeschichte in https://docupedia.de/zg/Erinnerungskulturen_Version_2.0_Christoph_Corneli%C3%9Fen. Accessed May 28, 2020.

Cotter-Lynch, Margaret. *Saint Perpetua across the Middle Ages: Mother, Gladiator, Saint.* New York: Palgrave Macmillan, 2016.

Dresken-Weiland, Jutta Andreas Angerstorfer, Andreas Merkt, eds. *Himmel, Paradies, Schalom: Tod und Jenseits in christlichen und jüdischen Grabinschriften der Antike.* Regensburg: Schnell und Steine, 2012.

Echterhoff, Gerald, ed. *Kontexte und Kulturen des Erinnerns. Maurice Halbwachs und das Paradigma des kollektiven Gedächtnisses.* Konstanz: UVK, 2002.

Engberg, Jakob, ed. *Contextualizing Early Christian Martyrdom.* Frankfurt: Lang, 2011.

Erll, Astrid. *Memory in Culture.* Basingstoke: Palgrave Macmillan, 2011.

——. *Kollektives Gedächtnis und Erinnerungskulturen. Eine Einführung.* Stuttgart: Metzler, 2017.

Evers, Alexander. *Church, Cities, and People: A Study of the Plebs in the Church and Cities of Roman Africa in Late Antiquity*. Leuven: Peeters, 2010.

Farina, William. *Perpetua of Carthage: Portrait of a Third-Century Martyr*. Jefferson, NC: McFarland, 2009.

Finnern, Sönke. *Narratologie und biblische Exegese*. Tübingen: Mohr Siebeck, 2010.

Finney, Mark T. *Resurrection, Hell, and the Afterlife*. New York: Routledge, 2016.

Gold, Barbara K. *Perpetua: Athlete of God*. New York: Oxford University Press, 2018.

Gonzalez, Eliezer. *The Fate of the Dead in Early Third Century North African Christianity*. Tübingen: Mohr Siebeck, 2014.

Habermehl, Peter. *Perpetua und der Ägypter oder Bildes des Bösen im frühen afrikanischen Christentum. Ein Versuch zur Passio sanctorum Perpetua et Felicitatis*. Berlin: Walter de Gruyter, 2004.

Halbwachs, Maurice. *Les cadres sociaux de la mémoire*. Paris: F. Alcan, 1925.

——. *La mémoire collective*. Paris: Presses Universitaires de France, 1950.

Harrison, Juliette, ed. *Imagining the Afterlife in the Ancient World*. New York: Routledge, 2019.

Heffernan, Thomas J. *The Passion of Perpetua and Felicity*. Oxford: University Press, 2012.

Hoffmann, Andreas. *Kirchliche Strukturen und römisches Recht bei Cyprian von Karthago*. Paderborn: Schöningh, 2000.

Huebenthal, Sandra. *Das Markusevangelium als kollektives Gedächtnis*. Göttingen: Vandenhoeck und Ruprecht, 2014.

——. "Frozen Moments—Early Christianity through the Lens of Social Memory Theory." Pages 17–43 in *Memory and Memories in Early Christianity. Proceedings of the International Conference held at the Universities of Geneva and Lausanne (June 2–3, 2016)*. Edited by Simon Butticaz and Enrico Norelli. Tübingen: Mohr Siebeck, 2016.

——. "Collective Memory, Communicative Memory, Cultural Memory, Social Memory." Pages 66; 69–70; 368–369 in *The Dictionary of the Bible and Ancient Media*. Edited by Tom Thatcher, Chris Keith, Raymond F. Person, Jr., and Elsie R. Stern. London: Bloomsbury, 2017.

——. *Reading Mark's Gospel as a Text from Collective Memory*. Grand Rapids: Eerdmans, 2020.

Huber, Elaine C. *Women and the Authority of Inspiration: A Reexamination of Two Prophetic Movements from a Contemporary Feminist Perspective*. London: University Press, 1985.

Keppler, Angela. *Tischgespräche. Über Formen kommunikativer Vergemeinschaftung am Beispiel der Konversation in Familien*. Frankfurt: Suhrkamp, 1994.

Kitzler, Petr. *From Passio Perpetuae to Acta Perpetuae: Recontextualisizing a Martyr Story in the Literature of the Early Church*. Berlin: de Gruyter, 2015.

Jordan, Stefan. *Theorien und Methoden der Geschichtswissenschaft*. Paderborn: Ferdinand Schöningh, 2016.

Kolmer, Lothar. *Geschichtstheorien*. Paderborn: Ferdinand Schöningh GmbH, 2008.

Krause, Jens-Uwe. *Gefängnisse im Römischen Reich*. Stuttgart: Franz Steiner, 1996.

———. *Gewalt und Kriminalität in der Spätantike*. München: C. H. Beck, 2014.

Leemans, Johan, and Boudewijn Dehandschutter, eds. *Martyrdom and Persecution in Late Antique Christianity*. Leuven: Peeters, 2010.

Lepelley, Claude. "Die Christen und das Römische Reich." Pages 229–268 in *Die Zeit des Anfangs (bis 250). Die Geschichte des Christentums* I. Edited by Luce Pietri. Freiburg: Herder, 2003.

Lücke, Martin, and Irmgard Zündorf. *Einführung in die Public History*. Göttingen: Vandenhoeck & Ruprecht, 2018.

Markschies, Christoph. "Alte Kirche." Pages 344–360 in *Religion in Geschichte und Gegenwart 1*. Edited by H. D. Betz. Tübingen: Mohr Siebeck, 1998.

———. "The Passio Perpetuae et Felicitatis and Montanism?" Pages 277–290 in *Perpetua's Passions: Multidisciplinary Approaches to the Passio Perpetuae et Felicitatis*. Edited by Jan N. Bremmer and Marco Formisano. Oxford: Oxford University Press, 2012.

———. *Das antike Christentum. Frömmigkeit, Lebensformen, Institutionen*. München: C. H. Beck, 2016.

Merkt, Andreas. *Das Fegefeuer: Entstehung und Funktion einer Idee*. Darmstadt: Wissenschaftliche Buchgesellschaft, 2005.

———. "Hindernisse, Feuerflüsse und andere Straforte: das Jenseits außerhalb des Kanons." *TPQ* 167.2 (2019): 167–75.

Moss, Candida R. *Ancient Christian Martyrdom: Diverse Practices, Theologies, and Traditions*. New Haven: Yale University Press, 2012.

Rebillard, Éric, ed. *Greek and Latin Narratives about the Ancient Martyrs*. Oxford University Press: Oxford, 2017.

Robeck, Cecil M. *Prophecy in Carthage: Perpetua, Tertullian, and Cyprian*. Cleveland: The Pilgrim Press, 1992.

Saxer, Victor. "Das christliche Afrika (180–260)." Pages 622–665 in *Die Zeit des Anfangs (bis 250). Die Geschichte des Christentums* I. Edited by Luce Pietri. Freiburg: Herder, 2003.

Schöllgen, Georg. *Ecclesia sordida? Zur Frage der sozialen Schichtung frühchristlicher Gemeinden am Beispiel Karthagos zur Zeit Tertullians*. Münster: Aschendorff, 1984.

Schulten, Paulus G. *De circumcillionen. Een sociaal-religieuze beweging in de late oudheid*. Scheveningen: Edauw and Johannissen, 1984.

Seeliger, Hans Reinhard, and Wolfgang Wischmeyer, eds. *Märtyrerliteratur*. TU 172. Berlin: De Gruyter, 2015.

Seesengood, Robert Paul. *Competing identities: The Athlete and the Gladiator in Early Christianity*. London: T & T Clark, 2006.

Stehen, Sheldon. "The Blair Martyr Project: The Passion of Perpetua and Fount Footage Horror." *Journal of Religion and Popular Culture* 31.3 (2019): 183–95.

Streete, Gail P. C. *Redeemed Bodies: Women Martyrs in Early Christianity*. Louisville: Westminster John Knox Press, 1989.

Tabbernee, William. "Perpetua, Montanism and Christian Ministry in Carthage c. 203 C.E." *PRSt* 32.4 (2005): 421–41.

———. *Fake Prophecy and Polluted Sacraments: Ecclesiastical and Imperial Reactions to Montanism*. Leiden: Brill, 2007.

Tilley, Maureen A. *The Bible in Christian North Africa: The Donatist World*. Minneapolis: Fortress Press, 1996.

———, ed. *Donatist Martyr Stories. The Church in Conflict in Roman North Africa* Liverpool: University Press, 1996.

Trevett, Christine. *Montanism: Gender, Authority and the New Prophecy*. Cambridge; University Press, 1996.

Waldner, Katharina. "Visions, Prophecy, and Authority in the Passio Perpetuae." Pages 201–19 in *Perpetua's Passions: Multidisciplinary Approaches to the Passio Perpetuae et Felicitatis*. Edited by Jan N. Bremmer and Marco Formisano. Oxford: University Press, 2012.

Walter, Ameling, ed., *Topographie des Jenseits: Studien zur Geschichte des Todes in Kaiserzeit und Spätantike*. Stuttgart: Steiner, 2011.

Weigel, Sigrid. "Exemplum und Opfer, Blutzeugnis und Schriftzeugnis: Lucretia und Perpetua als Übergangsfiguren in der Kulturgeschichte der Märtyrer." Pages 25–45 in *Grenzgänger der Religionskulturen. Kulturwissenschaftliche Beiträge zu Gegenwart und Geschichte der Märtyrer*. Edited by Silvia Horsch and Martin Treml. München: Wilhelm Fink, 2011.

Welzer, Harald, Sabine Moller, and Karoline Tschuggnall. *"Opa war kein Nazi." Nationalsozialismus und Holocaust im Familiengedächtnis*. Frankfurt am Main: Fischer, 2012.

Wünsch, Thomas. "Erinnerungskultur." In Online-Lexikon zur Kultur und Geschichte der Deutschen im östlichen Europa, 2013 in https://ome-lexikon.uni-oldenburg.de/begriffe/erinnerungskultur/. Accessed Aug. 1, 2020.

III.

Hermeneutics and Memory

Form Criticism vs. Memory Theory on the Resurrection Narratives

Zeba Crook

In 2012, Paul Foster made the argument that memory theory and orality (that is, interest in the period of pre-gospel oral transmission of Jesus material) do not offer any of the much-promised improved access to the historical Jesus. On the topic of memory theory in particular, he made three related observations with respect to form criticism. The first was that memory theory "has a striking similarity to the perspectives of the early form critics" in terms of how the past is constructed for the present needs of a community.[1] The second observation was that more often than not, the conclusions drawn by memory theorists about particular issues were no different than the conclusions one might have made on standard historical-critical grounds.[2] And finally, he observed that in many ways, memory theory is just form criticism "with differences in terminology."[3] Foster did not say much more than this about form criticism because he was more concerned with addressing the assumption that commonly appears in the work of those promoting memory theory: that memory theory confirms the general reliability of the gospels.[4]

The question of the relationship between form criticism and memory theory receives a more sustained treatment from Ernest van Eck, if also a rather idiosyncratic one.[5] Van Eck explains the logic of gospel composition by proposing three levels of literary interrelationship: textual, referential, and contextual.[6] The *textual world* refers to the perspective generated by the gospel narratives

1 Paul Foster, "Memory, Orality, and the Fourth Gospel: Three Dead-Ends in Historical Jesus Research," *JSHJ* 10 (2012): 197.
2 Foster, "Memory," 199.
3 Foster, "Memory," 202.
4 I issued a similar complaint, addressed to some of the same works. The emergence of works such as these might not represent an "emerging consensus" (a claim Le Donne rightly contested) but it does represent a problematic usage of memory theory that needs to be strenuously corrected, as Foster also says. See my "Collective Memory Distortion and the Quest for the Historical Jesus," *JSHJ* 11 (2013): 53–76, and Le Donne's spirited response in "The Problem of Selectivity in Memory Research: A Response to Zeba Crook," *JSHJ* 11 (2013): 77–97.
5 Ernest van Eck, "Memory and Historical Jesus Studies: *Formgeschichte* in a New Dress?" *HTS Teologiese Studies / Theological Studies* 71 (2015): 1–10, https://doi.org/10.4102/hts.v71i1.2837.
6 The categories appear to be borrowed from Norman R. Petersen, *Rediscovering Paul: Philemon and the Sociology of Paul's Narrative World* (Eugene: Wipf and Stock, 2008), 6–14.

 | DOI:10.30965/9783657796212_014

themselves. For instance, Mark portrays a suffering messiah, and the other synoptic gospels, though they take over much Markan material, have their own perspectives. That is, they create their own textual worlds. The *referential world* refers to material that could go back to the historical Jesus. This might be material that certainly derives from the ministry of Jesus, or it might simply be pre-Markan material. What matters most is that the material for the construction of the referential world precedes the author in one way or another, whether that source is Jesus, oral tradition, or another written gospel. Lastly, the *contextual world* refers to the social location of each Gospel's intended audience. Van Eck arrives at a sort of formula to illustrate the relationship among these three literary and historical levels: referential world + contextual world = textual world. In prose: tradition filtered through the context of the writer who is writing for a particular audience generates a particular narrative in textual form.

One might be forgiven for thinking that van Eck was describing the logic of gospel composition in general, and form criticism in particular, albeit with new terminology. However, in this article he makes the usual dual claim that the criteria approach owes nothing to form criticism and that the description above refers to the criteria approach.[7] I must respectfully disagree, not least because Bultmann was the first to articulate the criterion of dissimilarity.[8] In addition, the description van Eck offers of the three "worlds" above is a perfect description, in my opinion, of the logic of form criticism. Thus, I am forced into the unusual position of using van Eck to correct van Eck: when he concludes that "the social memory approach argues that the Gospels are narratives in which the past is reconstructed in light of the needs of the present, [while] the criteria approach argues that the Gospel narratives are textual worlds (the referential world filtered through respective contextual worlds,"[9] I think what he ought to be saying is that form criticism does these things (together with the criteria approach). This line of interpretation—or, if you will, correction—is necessary in order to make sense of van Eck's overall point in the article, namely that "Memory studies, when applied to the study of the historical Jesus, are nothing else than *Formgeschichte* in a new dress."[10]

7 Van Eck, "Memory and Historical Jesus Studies," 4–6.

8 Rudolf Bultmann, *The History of the Synoptic Tradition*, Revised (Oxford: Blackwell, 1972), 205.

9 Van Eck, "Memory and Historical Jesus Studies," 8.

10 Van Eck, "Memory and Historical Jesus Studies," 6. I am not alone in having had trouble following van Eck's argument in this article. See Chris Keith, "The Narratives of the Gospels and the Historical Jesus: Current Debates, Prior Debates and the Goal of Historical Jesus Research," *JSNT* 38 (2016): 430, 432.

When Foster and van Eck claim that memory studies and form criticism are more similar than they are different, it is important to note that these claims are, in fact, counter-claims. They are counter-claims because the conversation was started by the tendency of memory theorists to single out form criticism as the primary problem memory theory fixes in the study of Christian origins. Repeatedly, form criticism is the chief target of memory theorists in biblical studies. This is not surprising, given the continued influence of form-critical explanations and assumptions for the transmission, shaping, and invention of Jesus material. Nonetheless, it is worth noting the extent to which form criticism is the primary target of memory theorists. This is seen, not least, in the conference-turned-book on the demise of the quest for the historical Jesus criteria.[11] The project was spearheaded by two memory theorists, and scholars with a publication record that reveals serious engagement with memory theory comprise more than half of the contributors. Before that, targeting form criticism was the primary goal of a 2011 article by Chris Keith.[12]

According to Alan Kirk, memory theory "supplies the grounds for a comprehensively revised account of the history of the Jesus tradition, one capable of displacing the moribund form-critical model while incorporating—indeed, giving a better account of—the latter's enduring insights."[13] Thirteen years earlier he had written that "the continuing influence of classical form criticism" is what is responsible for the myopia of biblical scholars to social memory theory, unlike most other disciplines in the humanities which had already undertaken it.[14] In the interim, he wrote that the "form-critical approach that then came to dominate scholarship completely eliminated memory as a factor in the tradition."[15]

Kirk is not alone, of course. Rafael Rodríguez finds the wooden form-critical framing of historicity in terms of *ipsissima verba* lacking and unrealistic, preferring orality's interest in performance and articulating an experience.[16]

---

11 Chris Keith and Anthony Le Donne, eds., *Jesus, Criteria, and the Demise of Authenticity* (London: T & T Clark, 2012).

12 Chris Keith, "Memory and Authenticity: Jesus Tradition and What Really Happened," *ZNW* 102 (2011): 155–77.

13 Alan Kirk, *Memory and the Jesus Tradition* (New York: Bloomsbury, 2018), 1. Many of the chapters in Kirk's collection return to this point.

14 Alan Kirk, "Social and Cultural Memory," in *Memory, Tradition, and Text: Uses of the Past in Early Christianity*, ed. Alan Kirk and Tom Thatcher (Leiden: Brill, 2005), 1. In four of the essays in this book, form criticism is explicitly named and referred to critically.

15 Alan Kirk, *Q in Matthew: Ancient Media, Memory, and Early Scribal Transmission of the Jesus Tradition*, LNTS 564 (London: Bloomsbury, 2016), 171.

16 Rafael Rodríguez, *Structuring Early Christian Memory: Jesus in Tradition, Performance and Text* (London: T&T Clark, 2010), 5–6.

Before illustrating how memory theory explains the competing gospel images of Jesus' literacy, Chris Keith offers a several-page summary and critique of form criticism.[17] Keith's complaint, echoing the complaints of a growing number, relates to the putative historical positivism that inheres in the assumption that we can distinguish between authentic and inauthentic Jesus material.[18] Even Barry Schwartz, a sociologist befriended by biblical scholars, participates in the critique: "Bultmann's and Halbwachs's common failure is their refusal even to ask how pericopae, texts, and physical sites reflected what ordinary people of the first century believed."[19]

Form Criticism

These scholars are not wrong about the influence of form criticism on the study of Christian Origins and the composition of early Christian writings about Jesus. They are not even wrong in all of their negative assessments of the assumptions of form criticism (though none of the assessments originate with them, either). Form criticism has three key aspects, which though they relate, can all the same be helpfully separated, especially the second and third from the first. Some, though not all of them, have stood the test of time, in that they continue to prove themselves indispensable to the study of the New Testament. Most closely reflecting its own eponym, form criticism seeks to identify and distinguish among the different forms of material found in the Bible. At the most basic level in New Testament studies, this relates to sayings vs. narrative material. From there, sayings material can be divided into a number of forms (pronouncement stories, parables, and a variety of Jesus-sayings), as is the case also with narrative material (miracle stories, conflict stories, legends, the Passion, etc.).

The second and third aspects of form criticism are more controversial and have proven to be more fruitful. The second aspect is that the forms indicated above took shape and some degree of invention by virtue of being utilized by

17 Chris Keith, *Jesus against the Scribal Elite: The Origins of the Conflict* (Grand Rapids: Baker Academic, 2014), 73–81.

18 To point out that form criticism is the primary target of memory theorists is not to say that they are entirely and exclusively critical of it. See Chris Keith, "Social Memory Theory and Gospels Research: The First Decade (Part Two)," *Early Christianity* 6 (2015): 523–25. From here forward, this work will be referred to as "Social Memory Theory 2."

19 Barry Schwartz, "Christian Origins: Historical Truth and Social Memory," in *Memory, Tradition, and Text: Uses of the Past in Early Christianity*, ed. Alan Kirk and Tom Thatcher (Leiden: Brill, 2005), 49.

Christians before they came to be recorded in the gospels. The third aspect is that these changes occurred in reasonably predictable patterns, such that one could discern earlier more original versions of material from secondary versions and their later accretions. By extension, if one can discern earlier from later material, then one can reverse the process of shaping and invention in order to arrive at an original version of any piece of material. The latter two aspects are what have been most influential on historical Jesus studies, and are what is most in mind when scholars, including memory theorists, demur. At stake in their critique, and of keenest interest to me in this paper, is form criticism's ability to explain the shape (and sometimes the origin) of Jesus-material (i.e., sayings of and stories about Jesus of Nazareth).

It is perhaps not fair to start with Schwartz, since he is not a biblical scholar, but he is flatly wrong when he complains that Bultmann never considered what ordinary people in the first century believed (see n. 19). Every single argument Bultmann makes about how the stories about Jesus were changed as they were used, or how stories came to be invented, rests on the attempt to account for what the earliest Jesus followers believed about Jesus. It is these beliefs that have shaped the material we find in the gospels. Memory theorists generally make the opposite complaint: that Bultmann accorded early Christian faith too much influence in the shape of the tradition, rather than the memorial impact of Jesus' ministry. Nonetheless, what this shows is that explaining the shape and origin of gospel material is the heart of the challenge for *both* form critics and memory theorists.

For the form critics, the challenge was to explain what happened between the Palestinian, rural career of Jesus (and the things he said and did there) and the Hellenistic composition of the gospels. The fact is as acute as it is mammoth, and it needs to be seriously grappled with, regardless of one's method of explaining the history of the gospel materials. The form-critical explanation is that as the Jesus-movement spread and grew, whatever Jesus material they had needed to be put to use. That usage naturally shaped the material.[20] But the movement also required material it did not have, material it needed to have in order to make certain points, and so some material (sayings and stories) also came be invented.[21] These were composed in order to deal with specific issues as they arose. Finally, the key need of these Christ-followers was to defend and

---

20 Rudolf Bultmann, "The Study of the Synoptic Gospels," in *Form Criticism: Two Essays on New Testament Research*, ed. Rudolf Bultmann and Karl Kundsin, trans. Frederick C. Grant (New York: Harper Torchbooks, 1962), 41–44; Vincent Taylor, *The Formation of the Gospel Tradition* (London: Macmillan, 1935), 135.

21 Bultmann, *The History of the Synoptic Tradition*, 240, 244.

explain their belief in the resurrection of Jesus. And so, for the form critics, one of the strongest forces that shaped the material that was transmitted and invented was the need of Christ-followers to defend and explain their belief in the resurrection of Jesus.[22]

In this way, the general pattern was one of shaping material for present needs. That is, whether the material was invented outright or merely shaped, it was the needs of growing and spreading Christ-following communities that drove it. Therefore, while it was rarely said, it was frequently assumed: if there were two forces at work in the transmission of Jesus material—the forces of memory and the forces of communal expansion and proselytization—the latter were the stronger influence than the former. Thus, because of form criticism, it came to be accepted that the burden of proof ought to lay with those claiming historicity.[23] Nonetheless, it is critical to acknowledge that this is not the case for all the form critics. For instance, Dibelius and Taylor both had considerably greater confidence than Bultmann in the reliability of the gospel stories about Jesus.[24] In fact, what complaint could today's memory theorists possibly level at Taylor when he claims that "what Jesus said was remembered."[25] Even on the topic of the Fourth Evangelist's sayings, which he characterizes as "inventions pure and simple," Taylor frames that invention in the context of the writer's memory of Jesus.[26]

That form criticism has *some* virtues has been admitted by memory theorists. Primary among them is the agreement that form criticism "recognized the powerful effects of present community realities and concerns—the *Sitz im Leben*—upon the tradition and its representation of the past."[27] Kirk appreciates the position that maintains some degree of autonomy for tradition. That is, as tradition moves from community to community, each with its own sets of concerns, the tradition will continue to be shaped. Tradition could therefore take on a life of its own, untethered by whatever past event originally gave rise to it.

22 Bultmann, *The History of the Synoptic Tradition*, 368; Martin Dibelius, *From Tradition to Gospel*, trans. Bertram Lee Woolf (Cambridge: James Clarke & Co., 1971), 37–38.

23 Norman Perrin, *Rediscovering the Teaching of Jesus* (New York: Harper & Row, 1967), 39.

24 Dibelius, *From Tradition to Gospel*, 59–62, 204; Taylor, *The Formation of the Gospel Tradition*, 113.

25 Taylor, *The Formation of the Gospel Tradition*, 88.

26 Taylor, *The Formation of the Gospel Tradition*, 114–15.

27 Kirk, *Memory and the Jesus Tradition*, 1; Chris Keith, "The Indebtedness of the Criteria Approach to Form Criticism and Recent Attempts to Rehabilitate the Search for an Authentic Jesus," in *Jesus, Criteria, and the Demise of Authenticity*, ed. Chris Keith and Anthony Le Donne (London: T&T Clark, 2012), 37; Keith, "Memory and Authenticity," 177.

But, the memory theorists tend to complain, form criticism falters because the relationship between tradition and the past is *too* autonomous, too untethered from the salient past. Form criticism had it that only communal present concerns affected the shape of tradition. What was missing, Kirk argues, is any accounting of memory, or a way for the past to account for the shape of tradition.[28] When memory is accounted for, the autonomy of tradition must be—to some extent—tempered by the actual past. That is to say, tradition does not represent a mirror to the past, but neither does it represent a bicycle (that is, something wholly unrelated to the originating event).

As we have seen, however, this critique of form criticism is not always fair.[29] Memory may not have been the primary shaper of tradition as far as Bultmann was concerned, and all the form critics may have lacked the vocabulary of memory, but the function of memory (or assumption of it) is more present for other form critics. When Dibelius and Taylor expressed confidence in the historicity of many of the gospel stories, implied there is a strong role for memory. But even when Bultmann is more sceptical than accepting of material, it must be remembered that he did allow for some stories to go back to Jesus. Therefore, memory might not overpower communal usage for Bultmann, but one cannot say it is entirely absent from his thinking about the formation of the gospel material either.

In the end, I would suggest that the common complaint about form criticism's lack of attention to memory is really a deeper disagreement over the origin of the force that propelled the transmission of Jesus material: was Jesus material pushed or pulled? That is, did the primary force of motion stand *behind* the tradition, pushing it forward by the impact and memory of Jesus (in one way or another, even allowing for the nuanced way that good memory theorists put it), or did that primary force stand *in front of* the tradition, pulling it along as it was used in contemporary settings for the work of the expanding community of Christ-followers (as was articulated by the classical form critics)?

Though there is certainly a difference between these two positions, it seems to me that the difference is too overstated in memory theory complaints about form criticism.[30] At the very least, one must remember: it was not an ideological

28 Kirk, *Memory and the Jesus Tradition*, 2–3.

29 Kirk knows this is not entirely true, as well. He cites a footnote from Bultmann referring to the part played by memories of Jesus (see Kirk, 2.). But this simply makes it all the more difficult to explain his strident complaints about form criticism. In the end, the criticism seems to amount to a complaint that the form critics didn't have memory theory two generations of biblical scholarship sooner than the rest of biblical scholarship.

30 Kirk calls memory "completely marginalized in form criticism" (5).

position that had Bultmann start out from the position that the stories about and sayings of Jesus had been changed more than they had been maintained. It was the ample evidence provided by the synoptic data that led Bultmann to this conclusion.[31] One cannot balk at the form-critical conclusion—that the past is highly malleable—without accounting for the synoptic data, which provide no shortage of evidence that the memories of Jesus found in gospel stories and sayings were abundantly malleable.

Social Memory

Social Memory theorists contend that they offer a more nuanced, a more theorized, and a more comprehensive accounting for the formation and transmission of gospel material.[32] It is easy to allow that their accounting is more theorized. After all, social memory *theory* was not a wide-spread theoretical framework at the time of the form critics. Given that, it hardly seems fair to fault them for under-theorizing memory.[33]

Ritva Williams summarizes social memory as "the many ways that social groups—families, clans, tribes, societies and nations—are shaped consciously and unconsciously by the past."[34] Social memory refers to the memories people have of events they did not witness. Surely owing entirely to it social aspect, this form of memory is also contested, in that different groups will have their own memories—and their own versions of shared memories.[35] Memory is

31 Chris Keith consistently mischaracterizes the form-critical (common but not universal) lack of confidence in the historicity of much of the gospel material as if it was an opening *assumption* about the gospels. He claims that form criticism's "failure to consider seriously the ways in which the past could have contributed to early Christians' presents is a severe oversight; for the early Christian communities were not theologizing castles in the sky detached entirely from pasts that led to their presents" (see Keith, "Social Memory Theory 2," 520). Later, he writes that the form critics "*assumed* that the interpretations of the written Jesus tradition did not represent the earliest stages of the tradition" (Keith, "Memory and authenticity," 160; emphasis added). The form-critical position Keith objects to is not an opening assumption, but rather the reasoned conclusion arrived at by the careful analysis of the gospels, as surely evidenced by the attention to detail in Bultmann's *The History of the Synoptic Tradition*.

32 Keith, "Social Memory Theory 2," 521.

33 Kirk, *Memory and the Jesus Tradition*, 3.

34 Ritva Williams, "BTB Readers' Guide: Social Memory," *BTB* 41 (2011): 191. This is similar to the definition Zelizer offers: "recollections that are instantiated beyond the individual by and for the collective" (Barbie Zelizer, "Reading the Past Against the Grain: The Shape of Memory Studies," *Critical Studies in Mass Communication* 12 [1995]: 214).

35 Rodríguez, *Structuring Early Christian Memory*, 47–50.

not uncommonly, therefore, related to power, status, influence, and identity.[36] Recognizing this, social memory theory maintains, along with postmodern historiographical advances, that we have no access at all to the past.

All social memory theorists think about how the past is represented, how it is utilized, and to what ends.[37] When it comes to relating past and present, or past events and present memories, there are two approaches among memory theorists: presentism and continuitism. Those who take a presentist approach to social memory focus on how groups manipulate the representation of the past to suit the needs of the present.[38] In this way of seeing things, the needs and interests of the present are more pressing than the past as it may actually have happened. The continuitist approach, conversely, maintains that past events exert pressure on the construction of memory in the present. The creativity of the present is considerably limited by the past. In Schwartz's estimation, "reality counts more than bias in the remembering of most events most of the time."[39]

Everyone agrees that memory is not a thing we retain and pass on from person to person, generation to generation, but rather a process by which we construct, reconstruct, represent, and sometimes create the past. Social memory generally focuses on how groups remember, rather than on individual (or episodic) memory. Of course, individuals have a role in transmitting social memory, not least when *they* are the ones receiving and transmitting the stories, but also when memory is transmitted in monuments, literary and historical texts, rituals, and art, all of which are the production of individuals.[40] Nonetheless, social memory theory is a sociological area of study, not a cognitive scientific or psychological one.[41]

When most memory theorists contend—along with every other scholar, of course—that we have no direct access to the past, they do not generally intend

---

36 J. Fentress and C. Wickham, *Social Memory* (Oxford: Blackwell, 1992), 127–37; Williams, "Social Memory," 192.

37 Jan Assmann, *Moses the Egyptian* (Cambridge: Harvard University Press, 1997), 9.

38 Schwartz calls this approach "constructionist," but "presentist" is more common because of the influence of Jeffrey K. Olick and Joyce Robbins, "Social Memory Studies: From 'Collective Memory' to the Historical Sociology of Mnemonic Practices," *Annual Review of Sociology* 24 (1998): 105–40.

39 Barry Schwartz, "Where There's Smoke, There's Fire: Memory and History," in *Memory and Identity in Ancient Judaism and Early Christianity: A Conversation with Barry Schwartz*, ed. Tom Thatcher (Atlanta: SBL Press, 2014), 21, emphasis removed.

40 Samuel Byrskog, *Story as History—History as Story: The Gospel Tradition in the Context of Ancient Oral History* (Tübingen: Mohr Siebeck, 2000), 255.

41 Jeffrey K. Olick, "Products, Processes, and Practices: A Non-Reificatory Approach to Collective Memory," *BTB* 36 (2006): 11.

to say that nothing can be known about the past. Some things can be known, continuitist memory theorists widely maintain, because representations of the past are normally limited by past events themselves. That is to say, quite a lot of the past survives into the present. Le Donne writes, "Our memories demand a high degree of continuity in order to tie all of our shifting frames of meaning together."[42] The construction of memory might involve some creativity, and the past might be malleable, but creativity and malleability are generally limited by the past as it actually happened. There is only so much the past can be stretched and shaped.[43] Therefore, one can theorize about past events and offer observations about past figures with the use of social memory theories.

Our ability to know something about the past without having access to it might be likened to an explosion. Someone standing a mile away does not have access to the past event (the explosion), but there might well be many things she could know about it, based on the available evidence: the nature of the sound, its volume, direction, whether the environment has been affected, and so on. One might be able to ascertain whether the sound was produced by dynamite, lightening, or a volcano, how far away it happened, and its location. In the absence of fulsome evidence, there might be competing explanations, but despite this, quite a lot can be ascertained, or hypothesized with confidence, about the originating event without having direct access to it.

Despite this, reconstruction of the past is not the most pressing concern of many memory theorists. In many ways, social memory (especially in its continuitist approach) is a form of reception history. Rather than focusing only on the correlation between a memory and some originating event, in terms of accuracy, historicity, and facticity, continuitist memory theory tends to be interested in explaining the function of those memories. This approach to social memory searches for the meaning that memories are invested with, since that meaning is *not* dependent upon factors such as "factuality or veracity."[44] Memory theorists ask: Why do some memories of Jesus exist and not others? Why do some memories have traction but not others? Why is Jesus cast in certain categories (e.g., Son of David)? The depiction of Jesus, the keys, categories, or frames used, and the sources themselves must be explained because they are all we have.

42 Anthony Le Donne, *The Historiographical Jesus: Memory, Typology, and the Son of David* (Waco: Baylor University Press, 2009), 73.

43 Kirk, *Memory and the Jesus Tradition*, 34.

44 Jens Schröter, "Memory, Theories of History, and the Reception of Jesus," *JSHJ* 16.2–3 (2018): 93.

This last point is worth repeating. Schröter stresses the need for Jesus research to explain the "narrative configurations of the gospels," because an approach that dissects the gospels, or that attempts to get behind them, ignores "the relation between present horizon of interpretation and past event."[45] An approach to the gospels must be able to explain how their stories came to be. The continuitist approach to social memory theory when applied to Jesus maintains that the depictions, keys, categories, and frames most likely, in some way, go back to Jesus, though not in a way that allows us to reconstruct the historical Jesus.

It is even said that social memory theory does not allow us to distill authentic from inauthentic material. In fact, even inauthentic Jesus material might in some instances have originated with Jesus himself. This could happen in the event of a crowd witnessing an event but misunderstanding it or if different people within the crowd interpreted it differently. Of those competing interpretations, some will surely be closer to the original intention, but all of them point to an originating event.[46]

The common complaint about form-criticism is that it was wholly embedded in historical positivism, in that it assumed to be able to reconstruct the past as it actually happened. It is a reasonable complaint. Even when historical positivism was widely abandoned among people engaged in historical enterprises, the Jesus-book industry remained largely unaware. With every new installment, authors claimed to have discovered the *real* Jesus, *the* historical Jesus, what *really happened*, what Jesus *really* said, and so on.[47] Positivism, or

---

45 Jens Schröter, *From Jesus to the New Testament: Early Christian Theology and the Origin of the New Testament Canon*, trans. Wayne Coppins (Waco: Baylor University Press, 2013), 42. It is a point explicitly endorsed by Chris Keith as well (Keith, "Social Memory Theory 2," 532). and Le Donne (Anthony Le Donne, *Historical Jesus: What Can We Know and How Can We Know It?* [Grand Rapids: Eerdmans, 2011], 130).

46 Chris Keith, *Jesus' Literacy: Scribal Culture and the Teacher from Galilee* (London: Bloomsbury Academic, 2011).

47 Gerd Lüdemann and Alf Özen, *What Really Happened to Jesus: A Historical Approach to the Resurrection* (Louisville: Westminster John Knox Press, 1995); Troy A. Miller, ed., *Jesus, the Final Days: What Really Happened* (Louisville: Westminster John Knox Press, 2009); Brad Steuerwald, *Jesus: What Really Happened* (Enumclaw: Redemption Press, 2014); Michael J. Lowis, *The Gospel Miracles: What Really Happened?* (Eugene: Wipf and Stock Publishers, 2014); Carl E. Olson, *Did Jesus Really Rise from the Dead? Questions and Answers about the Life, Death, and Resurrection of Jesus* (San Francisco: Ignatius, 2016); Liz Theoharis, *Always with Us? What Jesus Really Said about the Poor* (Grand Rapids: Wm. B. Eerdmans Publishing, 2017); Addison H. Hart, *Taking Jesus at His Word: What Jesus Really Said in the Sermon on the Mount* (Grand Rapids: Wm. B. Eerdmans Publishing, 2012); David Hamshire, *When Was Jesus Really Born?* (Eugene: Wipf and Stock Publishers, 2019); Luke Timothy Johnson, *The Real Jesus: The Misguided Quest for the Historical Jesus*

confidence that the past could be reconstructed, was certainly a key feature of the form-critical historical Jesus scholarship. By contrast, "the new historiography" with which memory theory is thoroughly intertwined, "can theorize a historical Jesus behind the gospels," but it "does not assume that scholars can access an un-interpreted past reality behind the gospels."[48]

In the end, however, memory theory can be used to do historical work, as long as the "end product is a re-presentation of the past in light of the sources, not a reconstruction of the past built with snippets that scholars have supposedly excavated from the evidence that exists."[49] Nonetheless, one wonders how seriously memory theoretical studies are informed by the new historiography when while claiming that historians have no access to the past, the thoughts and motivations of ancient people are being described.[50] How is access to the interior states of ancient people not the essence of historical positivism?

Resurrection Belief

Form criticism shapes the structure of New Testament scholarship in general. For example, as soon as a scholar describes a story or saying being shaped in transmission, she does not need to cite Bultmann or use the explicit language of form-criticism. That is how deeply influential form criticism has been; it is simply there in how we think. And it persists because consideration of how the needs of a community and the simple act of transmission through material space shaped the Jesus stories carries considerable explanatory power. When it

and the Truth of the Traditional Gospels (San Francisco: HarperCollins, 1997); Geza Vermes, *The Real Jesus: Then and Now* (Minneapolis: Fortress Press, 2010); Bill Bright, *Discover the Real Jesus* (Wheaton: Tyndale House Publishers, Inc., 2004); Barbara Thiering, *Jesus the Man: Decoding the Real Story of Jesus and Mary Magdalen* (New York: Simon & Shuster, 2006); J. Ed Komoszewski, M. James Sawyer, and Daniel B. Wallace, *Reinventing Jesus: How Contemporary Skeptics Miss the Real Jesus and Mislead Popular Culture* (Grand Rapids: Kregel Publications, 2006); Gregory A. Boyd, *Cynic Sage or Son of God? Recovering the Real Jesus in an Age of Revisionist Replies* (Wheaton, Ill: Bridgepoint/Victor, 1995); F. F. Bruce, *The Real Jesus*, Jesus Library (London: Hodder & Stoughton, 1985); Matthew Richard, *Will the Real Jesus Please Stand Up? 12 False Christs* (Saint Louis: Concordia Publishing House, 2017); David Winter, *The Search for the Real Jesus* (London: Hodder & Stoughton, 1982).

48 Keith, "Social Memory Theory 2," 530.

49 Keith, "Social Memory Theory 2," 530–31.

50 Compare Le Donne's excellent and sobering description of the new historiography (*Historical Jesus*, 33–41, 72–81) with comments on the inner thoughts, feelings, motivations, and self-understanding of Mary (p. 51), Jesus (p. 52, 87, 88, 89, 90, 124), and the writer of the gospel of Luke (p. 91).

comes to accounting for the resurrection narratives specifically, Jesus scholarship shows the influence of form critical thinking in three ways.

First, form criticism was part of the positivistic enterprise of distilling the factual from the fictive in the gospels. In keeping with that goal, the first approach to the resurrection, and likely the most common, is to explain what *actually* happened, since the literal resuscitation of a corpse (the main theological definition of resurrection) is not an historical event. Historiography has come a long way in the last twenty years, but all this really amounts to is changing the *actually* (what *actually* happened) to something more subjunctive: What was the experience that may have been interpreted or articulated as resurrection? The crudest of these explanations (to borrow Raymond Brown's wording) are likely that Jesus' body was stolen (going back to Reimarus and reappearing most recently in James Tabor), or that the experience was one of hallucination (going back to Strauss and Renan and reappearing most recently in Gerd Lüdemann).[51]

A less polemical version of this approach can be found in accounting for the resurrection as a visionary religious experience. This type of explanation attempts to take seriously the datum that people have religious (e.g., ecstatic, mystical) experiences, and that the resurrection could well be one of them.[52] For example, Pheme Perkins suggests that resurrection belief was grounded in a real religious experience.[53] Bruce Chilton grounds the visionary experience in kabbalistic practices taught to the disciples by Jesus.[54] John Dominic

---

51 Raymond E. Brown, "The Resurrection and Biblical Criticism," *Commonweal* 87 (1967): 233. On Jesus's body having been taken by the disciples, see Hermann S. Reimarus, *Reimarus: Fragments*, ed. Charles H. Talbert (Philadelphia: Fortress Press, 1970); James D. Tabor, *The Jesus Dynasty: The Hidden History of Jesus, His Royal Family, and the Birth of Christianity* (New York: Simon and Schuster, 2007), chap. 14. On Hallucination, see David Friedrich Strauss, *The Life of Jesus Critically Examined*, trans. Marian Evans (New York: Calvin Blanchard, 1860); Ernest Renan, *Life of Jesus* (New York: Random House, originally published in 1863); Gerd Lüdemann, *The Resurrection of Christ: A Historical Inquiry* (Amherst: Prometheus Books, 2004), 166.

52 Simon Joseph lumps visions in together with hallucinations, but I think this is unfair. Those who posit hallucination generally imply something negative (as in pathological) while those who posit a vision generally try to take seriously that a religious experience was had ("Redescribing the Resurrection: Beyond the Methodological Impasse?" *BTB* 45 [2015]: 163–64). I would follow Allison here, who distinguishes hallucinations from "genuine visions" (Dale C. Allison, *Resurrecting Jesus: The Earliest Christian Tradition and Its Interpreters* [New York: T & T Clark, 2005], 204, 208).

53 Pheme Perkins, "The Resurrection of Jesus," in *Handbook for the Study of the Historical Jesus*, ed. Tom Holmén and Stanley E. Porter, The Historical Jesus 3 (Leiden: Brill, 2011), 2430.

54 Bruce Chilton, *Rabbi Jesus: An Intimate Biography* (New York: Doubleday, 2000), 272.

Crossan locates the original experience in one of female lament, which was then developed through a (male) process of exegesis.[55]

That the experience could be both real and non-literal is also the conclusion reached when the issue is approached from a cognitive-anthropological perspective (e.g., alternate states of consciousness, visions, etc).[56] The Jesus Seminar places a "visionary religious experience" (particularly Paul's) at the beginning of the resurrection narrative traditions, but they do not go further in defending that position.[57] Geza Vermes posits an experience, but it is more cognitive than visionary: they were transformed from fear to courage "by the inward experience of the Spirit."[58] E. P. Sanders is quite careful in his recommendation. He takes as "fact" that some kind of "resurrection experiences" were had, but will not speculate about their "reality" (which is to say whether they were visionary or not).[59] And finally, based on extensive studies of apparitions, Dale Allison finds nothing extraordinary or unique about the gospel resurrection reports.[60]

The influence of form criticism on these particular ways of explaining the origin of resurrection can be found in two inter-related features of scholarship: skepticism concerning the trust-worthiness of gospel testimony on the resurrection and the attempt to describe what might have happened instead.[61]

The second direction of influence from form critical thinking comes in the form of the well-known criteria. This is of course related to the enterprise of discerning what actually happened in the life of Jesus, but when it comes to the question of the resurrection, the criteria are not invoked to argue against them, but rather in their defense. For example, William Lane Craig relies on the criterion of Multiple Independent Attestation. Because reports of an empty tomb and resurrection appearances enjoy multiple independent attestation, we are

---

55 John Dominic Crossan, *Birth of Christianity* (San Francisco: Harper, 1998), 550–73.

56 Pieter F. Craffert, "What Actually Happened? Miracle Stories in Anthropological Historical Perspective," in *Hermeneutik der frühchristlichen Wundererzählungen: Geschichtliche, literarische und rezeptionsorientierte Perspektiven*, ed. Bernd Kollmann and Ruben Zimmermann (Tübingen: Mohr Siebeck, 2014), 263–82.

57 Robert W. Funk and The Jesus Seminar, *The Acts of Jesus: What Did Jesus Really Do?* (San Francisco: HarperSanFrancisco, 1998), 454.

58 Geza Vermes, *The Real Jesus: Then and Now* (Minneapolis: Fortress Press, 2010), 109.

59 E. P. Sanders, *The Historical Figure of Jesus* (London: Penguin, 1993), 280.

60 Allison, *Resurrecting Jesus*, 269–99.

61 One might reasonably object that these explanations are not so much form-critical as they are basically historical-critical. But arguably, many (if not all) of our historical-critical questions and methods were begun in earnest with form criticism. For other examples of the "vision" hypothesis, see Allison, *Resurrecting Jesus*, 208–9.

obligated to conclude (rationally!) that the resurrection literally happened.[62] The criterion of embarrassment also appears in this type of work. Here it is claimed that the claim of a resurrected body is so unbelievable that if people claimed it, it must truly have happened.[63] A second example can be found in N. T. Wright. Wright's argument uses the same rhetorical construction as any other historical argument: that the raw data themselves are best explained by the literal raising of Jesus from the dead. He writes, "That question which must be faced is whether the explanation of the data which the early Christians themselves gave, that Jesus really was risen from the dead, 'explains the aggregate' of the evidence better than these sophisticated scepticisms. My claim is that it does."[64] And finally Michael Licona combines all these approaches. His defense of the resurrection narratives as reliable according to the universal standards of rigorous historical investigation includes multiple appeals to the criteria of multiple independent attestation and embarrassment, and occasional appeals to the criteria of dissimilarity and plausibility.[65] He also, like Wright, claims that an actual resurrection is simply the best explanation for all the data. In this way, these defenses of the resurrection narratives operate within precisely the same historically positivistic form-critical framework as do those who seek alternative explanations.

These approaches are similar in that they both seek to establish what *actually* happened, and in this, the cases for and against equally betray their form critical framework. A third form critical approach is less interested in what actually might have happened and more interested in speculating on why the narratives came to be composed. This is the *Sitz im Leben* approach, namely the composition of material by early Christians because they needed the material

62 William Lane Craig does this repeatedly in his debate with James Crossley. See "Was Jesus Bodily Raised from The Dead—William Lane Criag (sic) vs Crossley," 2008, https://www.youtube.com/watch?time_continue=1&v=WJpeJJlCK-U.

63 Gary R. Habermas and Michael R. Licona, *The Case for the Resurrection of Jesus* (Grand Rapids: Kregel Publications, 2004), 38, 94, 169, 296, 289. It is worth noting that the logic of the criterion of embarrassment is sometimes applied to details within the resurrection narratives, such as when Jeremias claims that the women being the ones to discover the empty tomb would never have been invented by early Christians, so it must be true. See Joachim Jeremias, *New Testament Theology: The Proclamation of Jesus* (New York: C. Scribner's Sons, 1971), 306.

64 N. T. Wright, *The Resurrection of the Son of God: Christian Origins and the Question of God, Vol. 3* (Minneapolis: Fortress Press, 2003), 717. This is a claim Wright makes many times in this book, and elsewhere. See his debate with Crossan: Robert B. Stewart, ed., *The Resurrection of Jesus: John Dominic Crossan and N. T. Wright in Dialogue* (Minneapolis: Fortress, 2006).

65 Michael R. Licona, *The Resurrection of Jesus: A New Historiographical Approach* (Downers Grove: InterVarsity Press, 2010), 284–95.

for their missionary work. The best source here is its originator. When Rudolph Bultmann describes resurrection narratives as "apologetical legends," he implies that the stories derived from the communal need to defend a belief.[66] Surprisingly this is all he says in *The History of the Synoptic Tradition*. He says more later, when he argues that the crucifixion and resurrection cannot be separated. The crucifixion was an event; the resurrection was an expression of the significance of that event. As soon as one demands that the resurrection function as an "authenticating miracle," one separates the expression from the event, and turns the expression into an event. In addition, one shifts the focus away from the historical event (crucifixion), thereby stripping it of its significance. In short, then, for Bultmann the story of the resurrection is developed as an expression of faith.[67]

Surprisingly, the Jesus Seminar offers very little by way of an explanation for the origin of resurrection beliefs. Their comments on resurrection passages and sayings are nearly all made from the perspective of source or literary criticism. That is to say, they colour a saying of the resurrected Jesus black because Matthew draws it from Mark, or because it was created as part of literary chain of development.[68] However, the one sentence they do offer on origins reflects this aspect of form critical thinking: "The evangelists in both instances are inventing words for Jesus that express their own perspectives" (in Luke's case, that all that happened was divinely mandated).[69] In so doing, they locate the gospel stories and sayings in the time of the gospel writers, and their interests.

Does memory theory do a better job of explaining resurrection belief? In time for the writing of this paper, I could only find one example of a memory theorist who discusses the resurrection, namely Jens Schröter. However, he does so from a thoroughly "continuitist" perspective, in that he is interested in how the memories function, not in their origin. Schröter argues that early Christians held the conviction that God was active in Israelite history, and that Jesus was part of that history. Therefore, the "execution of Jesus placed his adherents before a fundamental alternative inasmuch as they either had to abandon the conviction of the action of God in him or integrate his death into

66 Bultmann, *Synoptic Tradition*, 287, 290.

67 Rudolf Bultmann and Schubert M. Ogden, *New Testament and Mythology and Other Basic Writings* (Philadelphia: Fortress Press, 1984), 36–38.

68 Robert W. Funk, Roy W. Hoover, and The Jesus Seminar, *The Five Gospels: The Search for the Authentic Words of Jesus* (New York: MacMillan and Co, 1993), 398. Consider also this sentence that very much adopts Bultmann's separation of the process into Palestinian/oral and Hellenistic/writing: "In sum, none of the words put on Jesus' lips can be isolated from the contexts and traced back to the oral period" (400).

69 Funk, Hoover, and The Jesus Seminar, *The Five Gospels*, 399.

this conviction."[70] That this integration was full and effective can be seen in ways resurrection belief informs the theology of Paul, the Gospel of John, and the Gospel of Thomas, as well as in the willingness of people to suffer defending their resurrection beliefs. Schröter does not argue for the historicity of the event, but for the historicity of the belief.[71]

How does this differ from a form-critical explanation? Of course, it depends on which aspect of form criticism one considers. Obviously, it is very different from the criteria approach, which focuses on the event, and argues for or against it. But what about form criticism more generally? Schröter's is an explanation that accepts that resurrection belief was an undisputable fact among early Christians, but it seeks to explain its origins elsewhere than in the actual event as narrated in the gospels. The implication in Schröter is that the belief originated out of a need to maintain coherence: abandoning the faith that God was active in Jesus' life was perhaps intolerable to them, so they found a way to articulate their faith, their conviction, in a way that maintained that faith, namely a resurrection narrative. In other words, the pressing needs of Christ followers in the wake of the death of Jesus manufacture a memory as an expression of their historical faith—historical in the sense that it was real and in the sense that God is active in their history. I am really not convinced that there is a difference between memory theory and form criticism here. Having said that, in other ways Schröter's approach is pointedly anti-form critical, such as when he problematizes the Palestinian sayings vs. Hellenistic narratives dichotomy.[72]

On the other hand, a subsequent discussion on this topic by Schröter makes me wonder whether he would in fact think that memory theory has any part in a conversation about the resurrection at all. In a brief discussion of the birth narratives, he describes them as "mythological and legendary narratives."[73] Because of that, he claims that they cannot be called "memories": "To establish 'memory' as a suitable category in Jesus research, it is therefore necessary to distinguish it from receptions that are not bound to traces of the past but are rather 'legends' or 'fiction.'" Presumably, he would classify resurrection narratives the same way and thus argue that they are not "memories." This sounds pointedly form-critical.

70 Schröter, *From Jesus to the New Testament*, 61.

71 When it comes to resurrection belief, the memory's "truth claim ... cannot ... be reduced to the 'facticity' of the reported events ... such an approach ... does not get to the reality behind the events" (Schröter, *From Jesus to the New Testament*, 69).

72 Schröter, *From Jesus to the New Testament*, 94.

73 Schröter, *From Jesus to the New Testament*, 101.

Schröter here appears to require that factuality be a component of memory (not accuracy *per se*, but actuality). This is an odd claim to make when in the same paper he has argued that the meaning of memory does not reside in its facticity. In this particular paper, Schröter appears to demand that there must be *some* relationship between memory and facticity. It is not that memory is a reliable reflection of a past event, transporting us back into the past, but it is the case that a representation of the past cannot be called a memory if it is not connected, like a fishing line to a flailing fish, to some originating event. Schröter's perspective here does not work either for individual (episodic) memory or for social, collective, and communal memory, and worse, it departs from the broader field of memory studies quite sharply. There, "legends, fictional novels, and movies" are in fact treated as instantiations of collective memory, and fabrications and delusions are part of the phenomenon of memory.[74] Accounting for the complex phenomenon of memory must include the human capacity for holding memories of events that did not happen.

This raises the one way in which I think memory theory might do a better job of explaining resurrection belief than form criticism, namely in the sub-topic of memory distortion. The study of memory distortion considers the ways in which the memories people hold can be distorted by forgetting or exaggerating details (both of which can change the perception of meaning as well as the issues of culpability and self-presentation). Sometimes these distortions are inconsequential to the story, but sometimes their consequences are considerable. This applies to individual, eye-witness, or episodic memory, but it also applies to social memory.[75] We are often given our memories by the group

74 Schröter, "Memory, Theories of History, and the Reception of Jesus," 106.

75 Jan Assmann, "Ancient Egyptian Antijudaism: A Case of Distorted Memory," in *Memory Distortion: How Minds, Brains, and Societies Reconstruct the Past*, ed. Daniel Schacter (Cambridge, MA: Harvard University Press, 1995), 365–76; Roy F. Baumeister and Stephen Hastings, "Distortions of Collective Memory: How Groups Flatter and Deceive Themselves," in *Collective Memory of Political Events: Social Psychological Perspectives*, ed. James W. Pennebaker, Dario Paez, and Bernard Rimé (Mahwah: Erlbaum, 1997), 277–93; Peter Burke, "History as Social Memory," in *Memory: History, Culture and the Mind*, ed. Thomas Butler (Oxford: Basil Blackwell, 1989), 97–113; Stephen J. Ceci, "False Beliefs: Some Developmental and Clinical Considerations," in *Memory Distortion: How Minds, Brains, and Societies Reconstruct the Past*, ed. Daniel L. Schacter (Cambridge, MA: Harvard University Press, 1995), 91–125; Michael Kammen, "Some Patterns and Meanings of Memory Distortion in American History," in *Memory Distortion: How Minds, Brains, and Societies Reconstruct the Past*, ed. Daniel L. Schacter (Cambridge, MA: Harvard University Press, 1995), 329–45; Elizabeth F. Loftus, "When A Lie Becomes Memory's Truth: Memory Distortion After Exposure to Misinformation," *Current Directions in Psychological Science* 1 (1992): 121–23; Elizabeth F. Loftus, "The Reality of Repressed Memories," *American Psychologist* 48 (1993): 518–37; Elizabeth F. Loftus and Larry Cahill, "Memory Distortion: From Misinformation to Rich False Memory," in *The Foundations of Remembering: Essays*

around us, wherein membership in that group means accepting the memories we are given.[76] In this way, we can inherit memories that become our own, and through ritual enactment and the communal belonging come to feel as real to us as our own (sometimes no less distorted) memories. The past is filled with examples of people holding beliefs relating to events that we know perfectly well never happened (see n. 75).

So many memory theorists talk about the relationship of the past to the present as mutual and interdependent. The past does not precede present, nor *vice versa*. The past bears some imprint on the present. This sentiment abounds in works using social memory theory.[77] But, where do these sentiments leave us when we are dealing with events that, to borrow Rodríguez's phrasing, bear "no significant relation to the actual past"?[78] Rodríguez's acknowledgement of "strong distortion" (as in wholly fabricated) is uncommon among

---

in Honor of Henry L. Roediger III, ed. James S. Nairne (New York: Psychology Press, 2007), 413–25; Elizabeth F. Loftus, Julie Feldman, and Richard Dashiell, "The Reality of Illusory Memories," in *Memory Distortion: How Minds, Brains, and Societies Reconstruct the Past*, ed. Daniel L. Schacter (Cambridge, MA: Harvard University Press, 1995), 47–68; Morris Moscovitch, "Confabulation," in *Memory Distortion: How Minds, Brains, and Societies Reconstruct the Past*, ed. Daniel L. Schacter (Cambridge, MA: Harvard University Press, 1995), 226–51; Henry L. Roediger and Kathleen B. McDermott, "Distortions of Memory," in *The Oxford Handbook of Memory*, ed. Endel Tulving and Fergus I. M. Craik (New York: Oxford University Press, 2000), 149–62; Daniel L. Schacter, "Memory Distortion: History and Current Status," in *Memory Distortion: How Minds, Brains, and Societies Reconstruct the Past*, ed. Daniel L. Schacter (Cambridge, MA: Harvard University Press, 1995), 1–43; Daniel L. Schacter, ed., *Memory Distortion: How Minds, Brains, and Societies Reconstruct the Past* (Cambridge, MA: Harvard University Press, 1995); Michael Schudson, "Dynamics of Distortion in Collective Memory," in *Memory Distortion: How Minds, Brains, and Societies Reconstruct the Past*, ed. Daniel L. Schacter (Cambridge, MA: Harvard University Press, 1995), 346–64.

76 Maurice Halbwachs, *On Collective Memory*, trans. Lewis A. Coser (Chicago: University of Chicago Press, 1992); Jan Assmann and John Czaplicka, "Collective Memory and Cultural Identity," *New German Critique* 65 (1995): 125–33; Giorgia Foscarini, "Collective Memory and Cultural Identity: A Comparative Study of the Politics of Memory and Identity Among Israelis of Polish and Tunisian Descent," *Ethnologies* 39 (2017): 81–98; Marco Cinnirella, "Exploring Temporal Aspects of Social Identity: The Concept of Possible Social Identities," *European Journal of Social Psychology* 28 (1998): 227–48.

77 James D. G. Dunn, *Christianity in the Making. Volume 1: Jesus Remembered* (Grand Rapids: Eerdmans, 2003), 385, 698, 882; Keith, "Memory and authenticity," 176; Michael Schudson, "The Present in the Past Versus the Past in the Present," *Communication* 11 (1989): 107; Le Donne, *Historiographical Jesus*, 71; Le Donne, *Historical Jesus*, 79; Kirk, *Memory and the Jesus Tradition*, 835; Rodríguez, *Structuring Early Christian Memory*, 59; Samuel Byrskog, "Memory and Narrative—and Time: Towards a Hermeneutics of Memory," *JSHJ* 16 (2018): 122.

78 Rodríguez, *Structuring Early Christian Memory*, 53.

New Testament memory theorists.[79] Either it is not addressed at all, or it is dismissed as overblown and methodologically suspect.[80] But the resurrection of Jesus is only the most extreme example of material (of many examples that are less extreme, such as miracles) that should force memory theorists to say more about memory distortion in Rodríguez's "strong" sense. This is the limitation of this approach to social memory, for it almost imagines no instances of wholly manufactured memory and, thus, leaves the many instances of this unaddressed.

Our understanding of the resurrection narratives is enriched by a theoretical approach to memory distortion. It cannot, I think, explain the origin of these narratives. For that, I think we need to side with Dale Allison and similar approaches that posit a real, visceral, and powerful experience at the point (or points) of origin. The resurrection narratives are memorialized articulations of that experience, likely inherited as opposed to composed by the writers. They are also an example of social memory, in that the writers relate memory that is not their own. And they are examples of distorted memory, in that they relate the *experience* by inventing an event. It is not at all a stretch to accept that the experience can have felt real and powerful without having happened in the way narrated. What is more, it is also consistent with the study of memory distortion to admit that one person's experience could have been relayed to others in such a way as to become the authentic experience of others we well (eventually reaching, say, 500 others in addition).

Perhaps this approach is not very different from the form critical approach, which sees in the resurrection narratives a creative fiction rather than a straight-forward report of an event. The form critical approach that concludes (based on the abundance of data) a separation between history and tradition, that attempts to account for the creative additions and adaptions of the early Christian tradents is not so far removed from the memory distortion approach.[81] For example, concerning miracle stories, Bultmann accepts that some of the stories might derive from historical events, but "their narrative form *has been the work of the Tradition*."[82] It might not be memory theory, but it is not that far off. And it must be stressed that it is neither the claim nor the

79 Rodríguez, 53–56.

80 Alan Kirk, "Cognition, Commemoration, and Tradition: Memory and the Historiography of Jesus Research," *Early Christianity* 6 (2015): 288–95.

81 "Tradents" is Alan Kirk's useful term for acknowledging that transmitters of material are never *merely* transmitters. They are *tradents* because they are fully invested in that which they pass on. See Kirk, *Q in Matthew*, 40–42.

82 Bultmann, *Synoptic Tradition*, 228 (emphasis added).

implication of memory distortion that all memory is inherently unreliable and never to be trusted. It is that memory distortion is common enough to warrant attention, and that it is often impossible for the rememberer to tell the difference between an "accurate" memory and a heavily "distorted" memory.

Conclusion

Many individual elements related to Darwin's theory of evolution by natural selection have not survived scientific scrutiny and advances. Nonetheless, the theory still stands generally because of its tremendous heuristic power. Similarly, not all of Bultmann's operating assumptions have survived. For instance, the early form-critical assumptions that the gospels are "a mix of earlier oral and later interpretive traditions of the early Christians," that the tradition developed in a predictable manner, and that the oral and written strands of tradition can be neatly separated have largely been abandoned.[83] Chris Keith calls these "central assumptions," but I think they are better understood as *secondary assumptions*. These assumptions are secondary because they were explanatory. They were part of the attempt to explain what must be called form criticism's *primary assumptions*, and these primary assumptions have stood the test of time.

These primary assumptions are as follows: that material emanating from Jesus *must* have been adapted as it moved from a Palestinian setting to a Hellenistic setting, that it *must* have been shaped by its transmitters as it was used in a variety of settings, and that it *must* have been shaped again by the literary and theological interests of the gospel writers, even to the point of creating new material that did not emanate from Jesus. The heuristic power of these assumptions is so strong that the assumptions still stand despite the fact that the secondary assumptions that helped to explain them were proved unworkable. For instance, when Jens Schröter concludes his excellent paper on memory theory and historiography as it applies to the study of the historical Jesus, the *primary assumptions* of form criticism are (rightly and reasonably, I contend) quite apparent.[84] Conversely, the idea that individual traditions must be removed "from their narrative contexts in written texts and [reorganized] under categories of forms" is absent from Schröter's approach because it is not

83 Keith, "Memory and authenticity," 158.

84 Schröter, "Memory, Theories of History, and the Reception of Jesus," 88, 105.

a *primary* form-critical assumption.[85] To this extent, I think memory theory is a (right and reasonable) extension, or correction, of what is essentially still a form-critical enterprise: the attempt to explain how material that might go back to Jesus was shaped by the process of transmission from an originally Palestinian mission through the establishment of Greek associations to the written gospels.

Bibliography

Allison Jr., Dale C. *Resurrecting Jesus: The Earliest Christian Tradition and Its Interpreters*. New York: T & T Clark, 2005.

Assmann, Jan. "Ancient Egyptian Antijudaism: A Case of Distorted Memory." Pages 365–76 in *Memory Distortion: How Minds, Brains, and Societies Reconstruct the Past*, ed. Daniel Schacter. Cambridge, MA: Harvard University Press, 1995.

———. *Moses the Egyptian*. Cambridge: Harvard University Press, 1997.

Baumeister, Roy F. and Stephen Hastings. "Distortions of Collective Memory: How Groups Flatter and Deceive Themselves." Pages 277–93 in *Collective Memory of Political Events: Social Psychological Perspectives*, ed. James W. Pennebaker, Dario Paez, and Bernard Rimé. Mahwah: Erlbaum, 1997.

Brown, Raymond E. "The Resurrection and Biblical Criticism." *Commonweal* 87 (1967): 232–36.

Bultmann, Rudolf. "The Study of the Synoptic Gospels." Pages 5–76 in *Form Criticism: Two Essays on New Testament Research*, ed. Rudolf Bultmann and Karl Kundsin. Translated by Frederick C. Grant. New York: Harper Torchbooks, 1962.

———. *The History of the Synoptic Tradition*, Revised. Oxford: Blackwell, 1972.

Bultmann, Rudolf and Schubert M. Ogden. *New Testament and Mythology and Other Basic Writings*. Philadelphia: Fortress Press, 1984.

Burke, Peter. "History as Social Memory." Pages 97–113 in *Memory: History, Culture and the Mind*. Edited by Thomas Butler. Oxford: Basil Blackwell, 1989.

Byrskog, Samuel. *Story as History—History as Story: The Gospel Tradition in the Context of Ancient Oral History*. Tübingen: Mohr Siebeck, 2000.

Ceci, Stephen J. "False Beliefs: Some Developmental and Clinical Considerations." Pages 91–125 in *Memory Distortion: How Minds, Brains, and Societies Reconstruct the Past*. Edited by Daniel L. Schacter. Cambridge, MA: Harvard University Press, 1995.

Chilton, Bruce. *Rabbi Jesus: An Intimate Biography*. New York: Doubleday, 2000.

85 The words are Keith's, and represent how he characterises the *modus operandi* of form criticism ("Memory and authenticity," 160).

Craffert, Pieter F. "What Actually Happened? Miracle Stories in Anthropological Historical Perspective." Pages 263–82 in *Hermeneutik der frühchristlichen Wundererzählungen: Geschichtliche, literarische und rezeptionsorientierte Perspektiven*. Edited by Bernd Kollmann and Ruben Zimmermann. Tübingen: Mohr Siebeck, 2014.

Crook, Zeba. "Collective Memory Distortion and the Quest for the Historical Jesus." *JSHJ* 11 (2013): 53–76.

Crossan, John Dominic. *Birth of Christianity*. San Francisco: Harper, 1998.

Dibelius, Martin. *From Tradition to Gospel*. Translated by Bertram Lee Woolf. Cambridge: James Clarke & Co., 1971.

Fentress J. and C. Wickham, *Social Memory*. Oxford: Blackwell, 1992.

Foster, Paul. "Memory, Orality, and the Fourth Gospel: Three Dead-Ends in Historical Jesus Research," *JSHJ* 10 (2012): 191–227.

Funk, Robert W. and The Jesus Seminar, *The Acts of Jesus: What Did Jesus Really Do?* San Francisco: HarperSanFrancisco, 1998.

Funk, Robert W., Roy W. Hoover, and The Jesus Seminar. *The Five Gospels: The Search for the Authentic Words of Jesus*. New York: MacMillan and Co, 1993.

Habermas, Gary R. and Michael R. Licona. *The Case for the Resurrection of Jesus*. Grand Rapids: Kregel Publications, 2004.

Jeremias, Joachim. *New Testament Theology: The Proclamation of Jesus*. New York: C. Scribner's Sons, 1971.

Joseph, Simon J. "Redescribing the Resurrection: Beyond the Methodological Impasse?" *BTB* 45 [2015]: 155–73.

Kammen, Michael. "Some Patterns and Meanings of Memory Distortion in American History." Pages 329–45 in *Memory Distortion: How Minds, Brains, and Societies Reconstruct the Past*. Edited by Daniel L. Schacter. Cambridge, MA: Harvard University Press, 1995.

Keith, Chris. "Memory and Authenticity: Jesus Tradition and What Really Happened." *ZNW* 102 (2011): 155–77.

———. *Jesus' Literacy: Scribal Culture and the Teacher from Galilee*. London: Bloomsbury Academic, 2011.

———. "The Indebtedness of the Criteria Approach to Form Criticism and Recent Attempts to Rehabilitate the Search for an Authentic Jesus." Pages 25–48 in *Jesus, Criteria, and the Demise of Authenticity*, Edited by Chris Keith and Anthony Le Donne. London: T&T Clark, 2012.

———. *Jesus against the Scribal Elite: The Origins of the Conflict*. Grand Rapids: Baker Academic, 2014.

———. "Social Memory Theory and Gospels Research: The First Decade (Part Two)." *Early Christianity* 6 (2015): 517–42.

——. "The Narratives of the Gospels and the Historical Jesus: Current Debates, Prior Debates and the Goal of Historical Jesus Research." *JSNT* 38 (2016): 426–55.

Keith, Chris and Anthony Le Donne, eds. *Jesus, Criteria, and the Demise of Authenticity*. London: T & T Clark, 2012.

Kirk, Alan. "Social and Cultural Memory." Pages 1–24 in *Memory, Tradition, and Text: Uses of the Past in Early Christianity*. Edited by Alan Kirk and Tom Thatcher. Leiden: Brill, 2005.

——. *Q in Matthew: Ancient Media, Memory, and Early Scribal Transmission of the Jesus Tradition*. LNTS 564. London: Bloomsbury, 2016.

——. *Memory and the Jesus Tradition*. New York: Bloomsbury, 2018.

Le Donne, Anthony. *The Historiographical Jesus: Memory, Typology, and the Son of David*. Waco: Baylor University Press, 2009.

——. *Historical Jesus: What Can We Know and How Can We Know It?* Grand Rapids: Eerdmans, 2011.

——. "The Problem of Selectivity in Memory Research: A Response to Zeba Crook." *JSHJ* 11 (2013): 77–97.

Licona, Michael R. *The Resurrection of Jesus: A New Historiographical Approach*. Downers Grove: InterVarsity Press, 2010.

Loftus, Elizabeth F. "When A Lie Becomes Memory's Truth: Memory Distortion After Exposure to Misinformation." *Current Directions in Psychological Science* 1 (1992): 121–23.

——. "The Reality of Repressed Memories." *American Psychologist* 48 (1993): 518–37

Loftus, Elizabeth F. and Larry Cahill. "Memory Distortion: From Misinformation to Rich False Memory." Pages 413–25 in *The Foundations of Remembering: Essays in Honor of Henry L. Roediger III*. Edited by James S. Nairne. New York: Psychology Press, 2007.

Loftus, Elizabeth F., Julie Feldman, and Richard Dashiell. "The Reality of Illusory Memories." Pages 47–68 in *Memory Distortion: How Minds, Brains, and Societies Reconstruct the Past*. Edited by Daniel L. Schacter. Cambridge, MA: Harvard University Press, 1995.

Lüdemann, Gerd. *The Resurrection of Christ: A Historical Inquiry*. Amherst: Prometheus Books, 2004.

Moscovitch, Morris. "Confabulation." Pages 226–51 in *Memory Distortion: How Minds, Brains, and Societies Reconstruct the Past*. Edited by Daniel L. Schacter. Cambridge, MA: Harvard University Press, 1995.

Olick, Jeffrey K. "Products, Processes, and Practices: A Non-Reificatory Approach to Collective Memory." *BTB* 36 (2006): 5–14.

Olick, Jeffrey K. and Joyce Robbins. "Social Memory Studies: From 'Collective Memory' to the Historical Sociology of Mnemonic Practices." *Annual Review of Sociology* 24 (1998): 105–40.

Perkins, Pheme, "The Resurrection of Jesus." Pages 2409–2433 in *Handbook for the Study of the Historical Jesus*. Edited by Tom Holmén and Stanley E. Porter. The Historical Jesus Volume 3. Leiden: Brill, 2011.

Perrin, Norman. *Rediscovering the Teaching of Jesus*. New York: Harper & Row, 1967.

Petersen, Norman R. *Rediscovering Paul: Philemon and the Sociology of Paul's Narrative World*. Eugene: Wipf and Stock Publishers, 2008.

Reimarus, Hermann S. *Reimarus: Fragments*. Edited by Charles H. Talbert. Philadelphia: Fortress Press, 1970.

Renan, Ernest. *Life of Jesus*. New York: Random House, 1863 orig.

Rodríguez, Rafael. *Structuring Early Christian Memory: Jesus in Tradition, Performance and Text*. London: T&T Clark, 2010.

Roediger, Henry L. and Kathleen B. McDermott. "Distortions of Memory." Pages 149–62 in *The Oxford Handbook of Memory*. Edited by Endel Tulving and Fergus I. M. Craik. New York: Oxford University Press, 2000.

Sanders, E. P. *The Historical Figure of Jesus*. London: Penguin, 1993.

Schacter, Daniel L. "Memory Distortion: History and Current Status." Pages 1–43 in *Memory Distortion: How Minds, Brains, and Societies Reconstruct the Past*. Edited by Daniel L. Schacter. Cambridge, MA: Harvard University Press, 1995.

Schröter, Jens. *From Jesus to the New Testament: Early Christian Theology and the Origin of the New Testament Canon*. Translated by Wayne Coppins. Waco: Baylor University Press, 2013.

———. "Memory, Theories of History, and the Reception of Jesus." *JSHJ* 16.2–3 (2018): 85–107.

Schudson, Michael. "Dynamics of Distortion in Collective Memory." Pages 346–64 in *Memory Distortion: How Minds, Brains, and Societies Reconstruct the Past*. Edited by Daniel L. Schacter. Cambridge, MA: Harvard University Press, 1995.

Schwartz, Barry. "Christian Origins: Historical Truth and Social Memory." Pages 43–56 in *Memory, Tradition, and Text: Uses of the Past in Early Christianity*. Edited by Alan Kirk and Tom Thatcher (Leiden: Brill, 2005).

———. "Where There's Smoke, There's Fire: Memory and History." Pages 7–37 in *Memory and Identity in Ancient Judaism and Early Christianity: A Conversation with Barry Schwartz*. Edited by Tom Thatcher. Atlanta: SBL Press, 2014.

Stewart, Robert B., ed. *The Resurrection of Jesus: John Dominic Crossan and N.T. Wright in Dialogue*. Minneapolis: Fortress, 2006.

Strauss, David Friedrich. *The Life of Jesus Critically Examined*. Translated by Marian Evans. New York: Calvin Blanchard, 1860.

Tabor, James D. *The Jesus Dynasty: The Hidden History of Jesus, His Royal Family, and the Birth of Christianity*. New York: Simon and Schuster, 2007.

Taylor, Vincent. *The Formation of the Gospel Tradition*. London: Macmillan, 1935.

Van Eck, Ernest. "Memory and Historical Jesus Studies: Formgeschichte in a New Dress?" *HTS Teologiese Studies / Theological Studies* 71 (2015): 1–10, https://doi.org/10.4102/hts.v71i1.2837.
Vermes, Geza. *The Real Jesus: Then and Now*. Minneapolis: Fortress Press, 2010.
Williams, Ritva. "BTB Readers' Guide: Social Memory." *BTB* 41 (2011): 189–200.
Wright, N. T. *The Resurrection of the Son of God: Christian Origins and the Question of God, Volume 3*. Minneapolis: Fortress Press, 2003.
Zelizer, Barbie. "Reading the Past Against the Grain: The Shape of Memory Studies." *Critical Studies in Mass Communication* 12 (1995): 214–39.

Explaining Competing Representations of the Afterlife in Luke-Acts: A Social Memory Approach

Stu Talené

Alexey Somov has provided a valuable monograph that examines the representations of the afterlife in Luke-Acts.[1] His contribution has many strengths as it extensively reviews not only the various representations of the afterlife in Luke-Acts, but also the multifarious Jewish and pagan representations in the eastern Mediterranean milieu within which the evangelist found himself. The important observation that Somov makes, in view here, is that Luke seems comfortable including differing, and even at times conflicting, representations of the afterlife. Somov addresses this by providing many helpful insights into the nature of metaphor via Cognitive Metaphor Theory, but in the course of his study he does not give enough attention to explaining *how* Luke received various representations of the afterlife from his milieu *and how* this process of received traditions contributed to novel concepts and new combinations that met the needs of his audience. I propose that an explanation of the process can be enhanced by appealing to the insights of social memory theory and in particular the underlying work of Henri Bergson. The aim of this study is to provide an explanation for how differing, and at times even contradictory, representations of afterlife function for purposes of addressing the needs of the author's community within a specific place and point in time.

This study is divided into four parts. I begin with a summary of select key ideas presented in Somov's monograph. In the second part, I discuss select scholars whose work in the field of social memory theory are helpful for understanding the process of transmission and reception. Here I highlight the influential work of Maurice Halbwachs, Jan and Aleida Assmann, and Sandra Huebenthal. In the third part, I attempt to locate mnemonic transmission processes within the philosophy of Henri Bergson who was influential in Halbwachs' conception of the malleability of memory. While Bergson's influence on Halbwachs is widely acknowledged, it is not always given the attention that it deserves in social memory studies. Following the discussion of Bergson, I turn my attention to two philosophical concepts presented in the more recent work of Gilles Deleuze and Félix Guattari, who are likewise indebted to Bergson. Their work,

1 Alexey Somov, *Representations of the Afterlife in Luke-Acts*, LNTS 556 (London: Bloomsbury, 2017).

 | DOI:10.30965/9783657796212_015

which is useful for understanding the process of transmission, are often used to analyze literature in relation to conceptions of difference alongside conceptions of continuity. In the final section, I return to the field of social memory in conjunction with the work of Werner Kelber, who effectively urges readers not to view the Gospels (the Synoptic in particular) as reservoirs of tradition, but as products of diversity and difference that uniquely contribute to the specific needs of their audiences.

Select Summary of Alexey Somov's Representations of the Afterlife in Luke-Acts

Differences, even contradictions, in the Synoptic Gospels have been well-attested since at least the time of Tatian's *Diatesseron* (ca. 170 CE). This is not unusual since differences and inconsistencies exist widely among the various Christian writings in and outside the New Testament canon.[2] It is thus essential for New Testament interpreters to acknowledge and deal honestly with such differences, inconsistencies and even contradictions. This is neither new information, nor an aspect of New Testament studies that is not part of regular practice for most scholars. The aspect of difference is particularly interesting when it is located within the writings of a single author—in particular the author of Luke-Acts.

The different views of the afterlife in the ancient Jewish and pagan Mediterranean milieu within which the evangelist wrote Luke-Acts is the focus of Somov's study. Among the many strengths of Somov's study, two take center stage. Somov correctly and persistently (1) insists on acknowledging and interacting with the various views of the afterlife in both Jewish and pagan ancient Mediterranean milieu and (2) highlights the different, and even contradictory, representations of the afterlife found in Luke-Acts. Somov explains that these representations are the products of both cultural influences and the need to address the demands of Luke's community.

Somov's most consistent conversation partner is Outi Lehtipuu who provides a comprehensive examination of the afterlife in both pagan and Jewish literature.[3] Lehtipuu challenges the "common scholarly view" that "Luke did

2 For an extensive examination of diversity within the New Testament, see; Thomas R. Hatina, *New Testament Theology and Its Quest for Relevance: Ancient Texts and Modern Readers* (London: Bloomsbury T & T Clark, 2013).

3 Outi Lehtipuu, *The Afterlife Imagery in Luke's Story of the Rich Man and Lazarus*, NovTSup 123 (Leiden: Brill, 2007).

not work out a systematic eschatological doctrine" because his use of eschatological expectations was primarily used to exhort his audience to practice repentance since it leads to a blessed life.[4] Lehtipuu provides a model of how one should interact with the various views of the afterlife in Luke-Acts, as well as the pagan and Jewish texts and traditions which would have impacted Luke. It is Lehtipuu's narrowed focus on Luke's story of the Rich Man and Lazarus, however, that Somov suggests is an entry into the study of afterlife representations in Luke-Acts *in toto*.

In his "Introduction," Somov provides a thorough and fair survey of important scholarly studies that have examined conceptions of afterlife in Luke-Acts. Somov recognizes that the various studies approach the topic of the afterlife in Luke-Acts from various points of view and intentional limitations of scope. He nonetheless rightly emphasizes the importance of examining both pagan and Jewish representations of the afterlife in the eastern Mediterranean milieu that served as Luke's contextual frame of reference, which led to different and even contradictory views in Luke-Acts.[5]

Somov makes extensive use of cognitive linguistics in general and Cognitive Metaphor Theory more specifically in order to understand the different and at times contradictory representations of the afterlife in the various sources that he examines. The most fitting application for, and successful results from, applying Cognitive Metaphor Theory is the ways in which it can account for the innate human ability to understand and categorize metaphorical language and imagery, particularly when spatial language is used to describe the various afterlife outcomes for the righteous and the wicked.[6] This can be seen in Somov's helpful explanation of how the positions of the rich man and Lazarus are juxtaposed in life. While the former is presented in a high position, the latter is presented in a lower position, yearning for the scraps that fall from the rich man's table. The positions are reversed in the afterlife, assuming that Lazarus moved "up" to Abraham's bosom where he is the honored guest at the banquet.[7] The strength of this aspect of Somov's study, and fitting application of Cognitive Metaphor Theory, can be seen in the extensive and detailed

4 Lehtipuu, *Afterlife Imagery*, 303.

5 Somov (*Afterlife*, 10) disagrees with A. J. Mattill Jr., *Luke and the Last Things: A Perspective for the Understanding of Lukan Thought* (Dillsboro: Western North Carolina Press, 1979), 38–39; 148–50, stating that, "It seems that the main purpose of his explanation of Lucan passages about the afterlife which are difficult to interpret is to harmonize them. This makes the results of his research oversimplified."

6 Somov, *Afterlife*, 192 n. 12.

7 Somov, *Afterlife*, 215–216.

sections that interact with the use of metaphor in various pagan, Jewish, early Christian and Lukan material.

While Somov discusses general ways in which representations of the afterlife were often shared in the ancient Mediterranean world, Luke's reception of these various traditions requires further explanation.[8] Somov adopts Lehtipuu's term "intertextual milieu" when discussing how these representations were shared.[9] He also relies most on the intrinsically understood use of metaphor via cognitive linguistics, and Cognitive Metaphor Theory more specifically. Somov's reference to texts and traditions from a wide range of cultures, ideological views and periods of time is most strikingly seen in his reference to Mario Liverani's research regarding the Assyrian empire.[10] While the representations of the afterlife in the ancient world is a primary strength of Somov's study, the Assyrian empire seems to be too far removed from Luke's time and culture to have been a direct contributor to his received afterlife traditions. This is an excellent example of how the use of reception theory could strengthen Somov's work.

There are several important insights from Somov's monograph that deserve discussion. However, I target two of these so as to provide an example of the ways in which Luke provides novel presentations of his received traditions. In section 1.4, Somov explains that Luke presents the various views of the afterlife, with all of the complexities and inconsistencies that one finds in his sources.[11] Somov further explains that Luke actually complicates the traditions in relation to eschatological destiny of the dead, in future *and* in the present. Somov explains that Luke, "refers to realized eschatology in the context of collective destiny and the fate of the individual ...[which is a] shift of the traditional understanding of temporal aspects of eschatology."[12] Somov explains that this

---

8 Somov (*Afterlife*, 38) states that "it is hardly possible to demonstrate Luke's literary or textual dependence on any particular Hellenistic text or tradition (apart from his use of the LXX). It is safer to speak about his acquaintance with certain ideas, images, and beliefs that were widespread in his cultural environment."

9 In agreement with Lehtipuu, Somov (*Afterlife*, 38–39) writes, "it is better to indicate the intertextual, linguistic, cultural, and sociological relations between Luke's double work and his pagan and Jewish sources. Lehtipuu, therefore, prefers to speak about 'the wider Greco-Roman intertextual milieu,' adopting the term 'intertextual milieu' in the sense of the overall Hellenistic environment. This intertextuality 'does not form a fixed or clearly defined category but refers to the complex and multiform set of beliefs that were current at the time.'"

10 Mario Liverani, "The Ideology of the Assyrian Empire," in *Power and Propaganda. A Symposium on Ancient Empires*, ed. Mogens Trolle Larsen (Copenhagen: Akademisk Forlag, 1979), 306. See, Somov, *Afterlife*, 217.

11 Somov, *Afterlife*, 71.

12 Somov, *Afterlife*, 72.

shift of the traditional views is, in ways that are similar to that of the rich man and Lazarus account, "connected with Luke's view of the Kingdom of God and salvation as already experienced in this world."[13] This example leads to the first question that I address in this study, namely, how can we explain Luke's reception of the various, complex and inconsistent traditions of the afterlife that Somov presents?

A second example shows another way in which Luke presents a novel view of eschatological judgement. In Acts 7:55–59, Luke presents Jesus as "standing" (ἑστῶτα) at the right hand of God in a new, judicial position to receive the souls of at least those who have died as martyrs. Here Stephen is in view.[14] Luke essentially combines presentations of the Messiah in a judicial role that was known in some traditions, but modifies these traditions to present Jesus in this new way.[15] Somov concludes this section by agreeing with the views of Arie Zwiep[16] and Lehtipuu, who maintain that Luke does not seem overly interested in presenting a systematic eschatological doctrine.[17] This example leads to my second, albeit related, question: Why did a skilled writer like Luke not present an orderly conception of afterlife existence? This question is answered in part by Lehtipuu and Somov who regard Luke's motivation to be guided by the practical needs of his community and not a systematic conceptualization of personal eschatology. While this motivation is true, it leaves the explanation of the process of his formulation unanswered—to which I now turn.

Social Memory Theory

As has been discussed throughout this volume, Maurice Halbwachs is often credited with the launch of what he called "collective memory."[18] While Halbwachs was not the only early contributor to memory studies, it was his

13 Somov, *Afterlife*, 72.
14 Somov, *Afterlife*, 72.
15 Somov, *Afterlife*, 72.
16 While Zwiep is correct in his assessment that Luke does not offer a systematic eschatological picture in Luke-Acts, he argues that one is left with more than what Somov (*Afterlife*, 72) describes in his assessment that Luke's representations of the afterlife are "scattered utterances and allusions," because Luke is intentionally utilizing new and surprising representations of the afterlife as part of his overall theology and development of community identity. This will be discussed below in more detail. See Arie W. Zwiep, *The Ascension of the Messiah in Lukan Christology*, NovTSup 87 (Leiden: Brill, 1997), 176.
17 Lehtipuu, *Afterlife Imagery*, 41–42, 303.
18 See Jeffrey Olick, Vered Vinitzky-Seroussi, and Daniel Levy, eds., "Introduction," in *The Collective Memory Reader*, ed. Jeffrey K. Olick, Vered Vinitzky-Seroussi, and Daniel Levy (Oxford: Oxford University Press, 2011), 16–22.

innovative reliance on the philosophy of Henri Bergson and sociology of Émile Durkheim, that cannot be overestimated. Bergson has been recognized for influencing Halbwachs' understanding of memory as being "fluid and changing" as opposed to the more prevailing view of his day that memory is "passive storage" which the mind can retrieve.[19]

What makes Halbwachs' work so important for social memory theory in general, and this study in particular, is how he combines Bergson's work on memory with Durkheim's insistence that recall is influenced by social environment influences. Halbwachs began his doctoral work under Henri Bergson, whose work was so influential to him that he declared philosophy as his focus of study. Halbwachs subsequently began to work with Émile Durkheim who advocated for the social sciences within circles that focus primarily on the individual and his/her psychē.[20]

It was Durkheim's unrelenting insistence on the importance of the social sciences that convinced Halbwachs to abandon aspects of Bergson's thoughts that emphasized only the individual and subjective aspects of memory.[21] Halbwachs changed his focus of study from philosophy to sociology after he began studying under Durkheim, and this led him to conclude that, "memory is a social phenomenon and grows into a person from the outside world … [thus, for Halbwachs]… every recollection is per se social."[22] Halbwachs' adaptation of Bergson's concept of memory along with Durkheim's focus on the influences of one's social world in the shaping of memory is important in this study for giving explanation to Luke's processes that resulted in his afterlife conceptions. While Halbwachs does not deny that a person expresses individual memory, his insistence on the impact of one's social environment brings a much-needed dimension to Bergson's work on memory. Halbwachs has two primary categories for memory. (1) Social memory explains the social frames that are necessary for establishing individual recollection. (2) Collective memory is the social frame in which social memories are (re)constructed to form events. The following discussion further explains Bergson's influence on

19 Olick, Vinitzky-Seroussi, and Levy, "Introduction," 17.

20 Maurice Halbwachs, *On Collective Memory*, trans. L. A. Coser (Chicago: University of Chicago Press, 1992).

21 Maurice Halbwachs, *The Collective Memory*, trans. Francis J. Ditter, Jr. and Vida Yazdi Ditter (New York: Harper & Row, 1980), 93–98.

22 Sandra Huebenthal, "'Frozen Moments'—Early Christianity through the Lens of Social Memory Theory," in *Memory and Memories in Early Christianity*, ed. Simon Butticaz and Enrico Morelli, WUNT 398; Tübingen: Mohr Siebeck, 2018), 17. See more recently, Sandra Huebenthal, *Reading Mark's Gospel as a Text from Collective Memory* (Grand Rapids: Eerdmans, 2020), 97–101.

Halbwachs and targets specific recent developments in social memory theory so as to establish a working hypothesis that can account for the process which resulted in Luke's varied afterlife conceptions. In short, my aim is to provide a clearer explanatory foundation for Somov's study.

Jan Assmann

Major advancements in social memory studies can be attributed to Jan and Aleida Assmann. One of Jan Assmann's most well-known and helpful contributions to memory studies is what he calls "mnemohistory," which refers to the history of cultural memory.[23] Mnemohistory consists of received traditions and remembrances of the past which are not separated from the mythical aspects of a memory. The practice of discerning mnemohistory attempts to uncover or reconstruct a cultural or social retelling of the past. Assmann insists that mnemohistory is not opposed to history, but is a branch of its discipline that "is concerned not with the past as such, but only with the past as it is remembered."[24] He also rightly points out that remembrance of the past, or reception, should not be understood as a passive or neutral process of transmitting and receiving oral or written tradition, because, "The past is not simply 'received' by the present. The present is 'haunted' by the past and the past is modeled, invented, reinvented, and reconstructed by the present."[25]

For Assmann, the reason why certain memories live on is that they are relevant to the community in their current situation. He thus develops two categories, or levels, within collective memory to explain how memories move from a state of fluidity to a (more) fixed state. The categories are (1) communicative memory and (2) cultural memory. Communicative memory is based on everyday communication and has a limited horizon (or timespan) because it relies on the living generation and does not have fixed points (i.e. texts or monuments, etc.).[26] Assmann explains that all studies of oral history suggest that this stage of memory lasts roughly eighty years (one hundred years at the most), which is approximately three or four generations.[27] Cultural memory, on the other hand, is distanced from everyday communication and does not change with the passing of time because it has fixed points, which "are fateful events of the past, whose memory is maintained through cultural formation (texts, rites, monuments) and institutional communication (recitation,

23 Jan Assmann, *Moses the Egyptian* (Cambridge: Harvard University Press, 1997), 15.

24 Assmann, *Moses the Egyptian*, 9.

25 Assmann, *Moses the Egyptian*, 9.

26 Jan Assmann, "Collective Memory and Cultural Identity," *New German Critique* 65 (1995), 126–27.

27 Assmann, "Collective Memory," 127.

practice, observance)."[28] Building on the work of Jan Vansina[29], Assmann also incorporates the "floating gap,"[30] which is explained below through the work of Aleida Assmann and Sandra Huebenthal.

Aleida Assmann and Sandra Huebenthal

Jan Assmann's work is further developed by Aleida Assmann within her social memory matrix, which is applied to New Testament studies by Sandra Huebenthal.[31] Aleida Assmann's social memory matrix consists of three successive stages: social memory, collective memory and cultural memory.[32] The first two terms are adopted from Halbwachs, and the third is adopted from Jan Assmann (leaving aside his "communicative memory").[33] Especially helpful is Huebenthal's amalgam of Assmann's social memory matrix within a table that explains the matrix within a section in which she clarifies terms that are often used inconsistently within social memory studies, particularly due to their translations from German to the English. Translations have often overlooked seemingly small, but crucial nuances of meaning. Huebenthal thus offers a more precise nomenclature.[34]

Aleida Assmann and Huebenthal clearly state that the timespans that divide the stages within the social memory matrix are not intended to present a rigid and static model of how social memory works since the process of remembrance is malleable at social and individual levels and at every stage in the matrix. Rather, the matrix is intended to represent typical stages of social remembrance and to show how remembrance is dependent on relevance on the part of the community which aims to preserve a specific identity.[35] Huebenthal further explains that, on a broader scale, "The strength of the model lies in the connection of the theories of both social and cultural sciences

28 Assmann, "Collective Memory," 129.

29 Jan M. Vansina, *Oral Tradition as History* (Madison: University of Wisconsin Press, 1985), 23–24.

30 Jan Assmann, *Cultural Memory and Early Civilization: Writing, Remembrance, and Political Imagination* (Cambridge: Cambridge University Press, 2011), 34–37.

31 See Huebenthal's (*Reading Mark's Gospel*, 165–172) explanation of Jan Assmann's development of his approach and integration with her own.

32 Huebenthal, "Frozen Moments," 20.

33 The chart provided by Huebenthal is extremely helpful when working with this matrix. Huebenthal, *Reading Mark's Gospel*, 170.

34 See Huebenthal, *Reading Mark's Gospel*, 85–178.

35 Huebenthal (*Reading Mark's Gospel*, 164, n. 244; 165) emphasizes that, "In this form, the model not only will be more accessible to English-speaking discourse but it also offers more points of contact for interdisciplinary discourse."

that concentrate the specific observations of their particular fields and thus allow addressing very different phenomena."[36]

Aleida Assmann's social memory matrix places the transmission of the earliest oral tradition that is limited to the life of the initial carrier(s) into the first stage of the matrix (i.e., social memory). Collective memory refers to the stage where memory "is no longer limited in time; mental images become icons, and narratives turn into myths."[37] What is important to emphasize is that, while collective memory represents a stage when memory is more fixed, this stage is still open to change if the remembrances are no longer relevant.[38] Within the third stage, termed cultural memory, one finds more stable and fixed memories that often serve as frameworks for a group reflecting on its past (i.e. myth, ritual, text, monument, etc.).

The stages that make up the social memory matrix are separated by two periods of time, or gaps, when the stability of memories are most vulnerable. The first is called the "generational gap," since it occurs approximately a generation (or 30–50 years) after the initial memory/memories begin to circulate during the stage of collective memory.[39] The second period of time is called the "floating gap," and it occurs approximately 80–100 years after the initial memory/memories. It can be viewed as the precursor interval to cultural memory.[40] Both the interval gaps and the stages of memory can serve as helpful underlying explanations for the various representations of the afterlife presented by Somov. The oral and written representations of the afterlife that circulated around the eastern Mediterranean would have been affected through the various stages of transmission, which would have accounted for the variances. As a caveat, it needs to be pointed out that even though the cultural memory stage represents more stability, it can still represent a state of potential flux if the relevance of those memories is in jeopardy. While Luke most likely wrote his two-volume work within the collective memory stage, Somov's study suggests that some of his received representations of the afterlife traditions belong within the cultural memory stage. One reason that the received afterlife traditions from the more stable cultural memory stage would be malleable is that

36 Huebenthal, *Reading Mark's Gospel*, 166.

37 Huebenthal, *Reading Mark's Gospel*, 167. On Assmann's progression from history to memory to myth as a "Sense of History," see his *Cultural Memory*, 37–50.

38 Huebenthal, *Reading Mark's Gospel*, 167.

39 Huebenthal (*Reading Mark's Gospel*, 172) explains that the 30–50 years is not intended by Assmann to be an exact number, but is meant to represent a lifetime.

40 Huebenthal, *Reading Mark's Gospel*, 168–72. Jan Assmann (*Cultural Memory*, 34) adopts the floating gap from ethnologist Jan Vansina and explains that "'the floating gap' is familiar to all historians who deal with oral traditions."

the members of the community that Luke may have targeted appear to have experienced different crises than previous generations.[41]

Luke would have received the representations of the afterlife that circulated around the eastern Mediterranean milieu if they were relevant to his community. What is important about this social memory matrix for the next section is that it allows us to see how social memory is affected by processes that explain fluidity and competing conceptions of the afterlife. At times it allows us to see how some conceptions even dissolve.[42] In assessing New Testament texts, Huebenthal states that social memory "is less relevant than collective and cultural memory as we can rarely trace it."[43]

Attention will now turn to select aspects of Henri Bergson's work on memory to help further explain the malleability of memory that has been discussed in the social memory matrix from a philosophical perspective. My aim is to provide insight into how an author of Luke's literary skill can produce differing and even contradictory representations of the afterlife in his two-volume work.

The Philosophical Component: Henri Bergson

It is difficult today to fully appreciate the level of celebrity that Henri Bergson experienced during his day.[44] The popular references to the "Bergson Boom" and "Bergsonism" represented his widespread popularity in and outside academic circles. Notable examples of his importance include his role as a French emissary sent to persuade President Woodrow Wilson to increase support for the French war, and his receiving of the Nobel Prize for literature in 1927.[45] Although Bergson's work was for a while relegated to being part of the history of philosophy, there has been a resurging interest in Bergson's work in the last two decades. In what follows, I target select aspects of Bergson's philosophy that shed light on the transmission and reception processes that eventually result in products of social memory. Again, my aim is to provide a process-oriented explanatory foundation for Somov's study.

---

41 Huebenthal, *Reading Mark's Gospel*, 168–69.

42 Huebenthal, *Reading Mark's Gospel*, 165.

43 Huebenthal, "Frozen Moments," 22.

44 At one point, his lectures were attended not only by students but by the "Parisian high-society, which would send its butlers, much to the displeasure of the students, hours in advance in order to reserve seats." See Mark Sinclair, *Bergson* (New York: Routledge, 2019), 1.

45 Sinclair, *Bergson*, 1–2. Bergson is only one of four philosophers to have received this award. See also Craig Lundy, *Deleuze's Bergsonism* (Edinburgh: Edinburgh University Press, 2018), 155, n. 4.

Memory, for Bergson, is always present in various degrees between two poles. The first pole of memory is at a state of dilation (memory) and the state of contraction (consciousness, actualized-present/memory). The more contracted a memory is, the closer it is to becoming actualized in response to perception or actions in the world.[46] For the following discussion of memory as it is experienced in relation to one's social experiences, it is enough to say that, "Unlike the appearing and disappearing present of materiality, the present of consciousness has some thickness because memory prolongs the past into the present."[47] And, as will be discussed below, this is how the past and present dynamically, and continually shape one another as memories are actualized in response to one's individual and communal present reality. For Bergson, perception (the outside present) enacts with one's memory (anchored in one's past that is carried with them) to actualize a memory to meet the needs of the situation or action of the present.[48] Bergson's inverted cone provides a helpful reference to further explain this process.

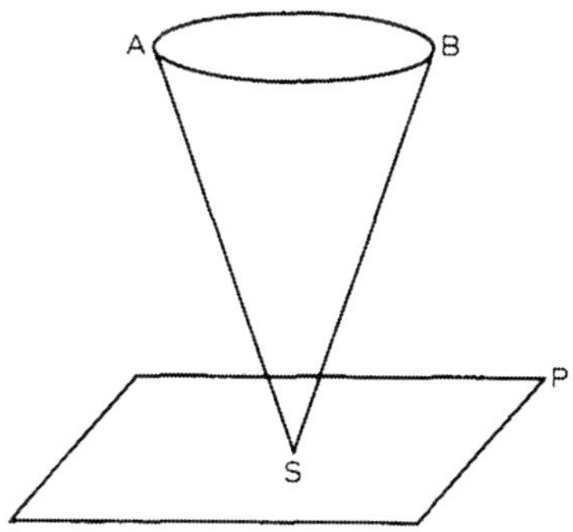

Figure 14.1
Taken from Henri Bergson, *Matter and Memory*, trans. N. M. Paul and W. S. Palmer (New York: Zone Books, 1991), 152.

46 The word "perception" is intentionally used here because Bergson distinguishes between two kinds of perception that eventually leads to his attempt to unite the mind and body that is too far afield to discuss here. Henri Bergson ambiguously closes *Matter and Memory*, trans. N. M. Paul and W. S. Palmer (New York: Zone Books, 1991) by leaving the mind-body duality separated. The issue is addressed in his later works. See Sinclair, *Bergson*, 126–31. See also Messay Kebede, *Bergson's Philosophy of Self-Overcoming: Thinking without Negativity or Time as Striving* (Cham: Palgrave Macmillan, 2019), 207–11.

47 Kebede, *Bergson's Philosophy*, 6–7.

48 Although Bergson discusses three types of memory throughout his works, I use the term "memory" in a simplified way that coheres with the concerns of social memory theory. For a discussion of wider approach to memory, see Keith Ansell-Pearson, *Bergson: Thinking Beyond the Human Condition*. (New York: Bloomsbury, 2018), 75–90.

Bergson introduces two cones in his *Matter and Memory* as illustrations of memory.[49] In the above cone, the actualized memory represented by S is a constantly moving present while AB represents the unconscious memory.[50] The entirety of the cone is made up of one's past-memory at different levels of dilation (AB) and contraction (S), which is closer to one's awareness in the present (and closer to actualization). As Bergson explains, one's perception is an action that actualizes in the present a memory that is located in one's entire past-memory that exists within their present experience (AB). The memories that are not relevant (i.e., practical and useful) remain in one's unconscious (AB), but can be brought back to consciousness (often in new ways) if they are relevant for one's present experience.[51]

In this model, perception is not representational as it is often assumed to be, but it is the present action of actualizing the past-memory. So how might this be applied to the varied representations of the afterlife in Luke-Acts? Once again, it must be emphasized that this study is adopting and adapting (that is, re-imagining) aspects of Bergson's terms in light of social memory research. Regarding remembrances of the afterlife in Luke-Acts, one can propose that Luke received remembrances and traditions of representations of the afterlife as memories that could have been transmitted in several ways (oral, written, etc.) by various people within the sphere of the communities with which he had contact. These would have been ready to be actualized when he wrote Luke-Acts. Understanding Bergson's references to actualization and perception in light of social memory theory, one can imagine the impact that a person's community had (its needs, crises, hopes, etc.) in the actualizing process of memory formation. This foreseeably led to the formation of new remembrances (expressed in oral, textual, ritualistic ways). For my purposes, the reference to actualizations are the various representations of the afterlife presented by Somov that he rightly claims would have been transmitted over time in various ways within Luke's eastern Mediterranean milieu. This model can help explain the dynamic transmission and reception processes over a period of

---

49 Bergson's cone is taken from his *Matter and Memory*, 152.

50 Suzanne Guerlac. *Thinking in Time: An Introduction to Henri Bergson* (Ithaca: Cornell University Press, 2006), 150–54; Bergson, *Matter and Memory*, 152–77.

51 See Paul Ricoeur's (*Memory, History, Forgetting*, trans. Kathleen Blamey and David Pellauer [Chicago: University of Chicago Press, 2004], 440) interaction with Bergson on useful and non-useful memories in relation to consciousness. Ricoeur explains that Bergson did not appear to think of "forgetting," but he does discuss "the powerlessness … [and] … the unconsciousness … [which is the] … forgetting in terms of a reserve or a resource. Forgetting then designates the *unperceived* character of the perseverance of memories, their removal from the vigilance of consciousness." Emphasis is Ricoeur's. See also Bergson, *Matter and Memory*, 141–46.

time as is proposed in Aleida Assmann's social memory matrix. Again, Somov's thorough historical research is important, but a theory of transmission and reception provides a process-oriented framework that is helpful for analyzing the data.

The second question that was raised earlier in this study also requires attention. How can a writer like Luke, who exhibits a high level of literary and rhetorical skill, present representations of afterlife that appear to differ among themselves? In his *Matter and Memory*, Bergson provides another illustration of an inverted cone that can provide a theoretical answer (see below). This illustration contains additional sections (shown below) that represent a "thousand repetitions of our psychical life, figured by as many sections *A′ B′*, *A″ B″*, etc., of the same cone."[52] The various levels within the cone do not represent different memories, but all of one's past-memory in various levels of contraction (close(r) to one's consciousness and/or actualization, *S*) and dilation (further from one's consciousness, *AB*) in their present. Suzanne Guerlac explains that *S* stands for a memory that is actualized for useful action in one's present, but emphasizes that that the multiple layers of memory in the base of the cone, "are free to circulate and to attract one another in the absence of any requirement for usefulness in relation to action."[53] The result is a process of memory production that allows for ongoing expressions of imagination that interact with one's experiences.

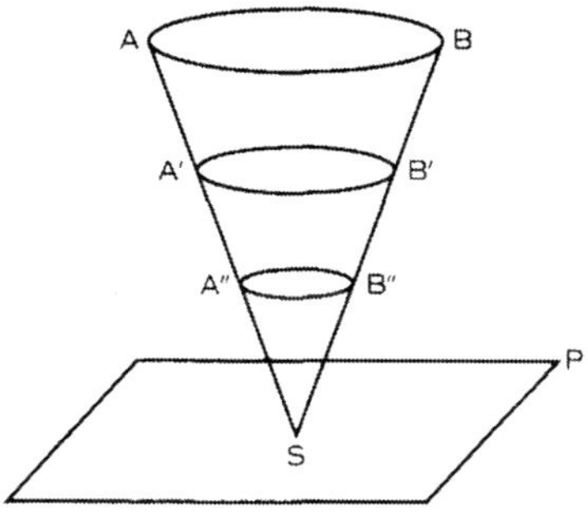

Figure 14.2
Taken from Henri Bergson, *Matter and Memory*, trans. N. M. Paul and W. S. Palmer (New York: Zone Books, 1991), 162.

The above cone represents one's remembered past constantly and dynamically existing in the present, which suggests that memories can be actualized in numerous ways in response to various experiences, needs and crises.[54] The

52 Bergson, *Matter and Memory*, 162.
53 Guerlac, *Thinking in Time*, 152.
54 Bergson's cone is taken from his *Matter and Memory*, 162.

different levels within the cone represent different levels of contraction and dilation of one's remembered past in each present. The base (*AB*) is the ultimate expansion that represents the unconscious and dreams, while *S* represents the ultimate contraction of the (past) memory pushing forward to meet the needs of one's (present) action(s) in the world. In the case of Luke, this represents the writing of Luke-Acts to meet the needs of his community's or communities' present. By mapping Bergson's work on to Aleida Assmann's social memory matrix, one can see how various practical and relevant needs and crises can ignite ongoing, ever-becoming and novel adaptations of received traditions. Moreover, this explanation of dynamic memory can explain how Luke could have received and adapted the many representations of the afterlife described by Somov.[55]

As mentioned above, Somov does not apply social memory. Instead, he follows Lehtipuu in acknowledging that the practical needs of Luke's community are the impetus that led to the different and even contradictory representations of the afterlife in Luke-Acts. The ways in which memory dynamically actualizes to serve practical needs is explained by Kebede as "the positive role of forgetting."[56] Memory dynamically actualizes to serve the practical needs in the present, and one's interaction with the world dynamically interacts with one's memory. Somov's study shows that historical research is a valuable means to better understand *that* Luke's novel adaptions of his received traditions both preserve and modify much of what he received to meet the needs of his own community, but it does not adequately explain *how* the process unfolded. What I am suggesting is that the dynamic quality of memory that is ready to be actualized in countless ways to meet one's present, is improved by, and successfully works with social memory theory to provide a hypothesis to explain how the phenomenon of novel, different and at times contradicting representations of the afterlife are presented in Luke-Acts.

The final section of this study incorporates selections from philosophers Gilles Deleuze and Félix Guattari that are often used to analyze diversity and fluidity in literature. These are applied to Gospel studies through Werner Kelber's conceptions of transmission. In other words, Kelber's foray into the processes of transmission opens the door widely for Deleuze and Guattari's

55 On the recent reception of Bergson's work on memory, see Ansell-Pearson, *Bergson*, 89.

56 Kebede, *Bergson's Philosophy*, 7; 128. Ricoeur (*Memory*, 417) explicitly mentions "a positive figure of forgetting" in relation to Bergson's work. In his third chapter (on forgetting), Ricoeur draws heavily from select portions of Bergson's *Matter and Memory*. Note also in Ricoeur's epilogue on the relationship between forgiveness and memory and forgetting.

understanding of what they call concept creation, which can provide a more robust explanation (alongside Kelber) of Luke's literary artistry.

Gilles Deleuze and Félix Guattari (*Rhizomic Minor Literature*)

Understanding literary divergence and inconsistency in the field of process philosophy further helps us to appreciate the activity of text production. In this section, I focus more specifically on the work of Gilles Deleuze and Félix Guattari. Gilles Deleuze, especially, is widely known as a philosopher who draws attention to the idea of difference in a way that is potentially beneficial for understanding competing conceptions of afterlife within the writings of a single author like Luke.[57] The link with Bergson is seamless. Bergson was one of the most influential thinkers with whom Deleuze interacted, as he adapted many of his concepts.[58] It is not, however, Deleuze's complex philosophy (or ontology) of difference in itself that is utilized here, but select concepts from his co-authored works with Félix Guattari.[59] Like others who have applied the insights of Deleuze and Guattari to literary analysis, I utilize them as part of my process-oriented framework for making sense of Luke's inconsistent conceptions of afterlife.[60]

According to Deleuze and Guattari, "philosophy is the art of forming, inventing, and fabricating concepts."[61] In addition, philosophical "concepts do not label or represent the world so much as produce a new way of thinking

57 For a helpful discussion of the philosophy of Deleuze in relation to traditional biblical theology, see Christopher Watkin, *Gilles Deleuze* (Phillipsburg: P & R Publishing, 2020); Brent Adkins and Paul R. Hinlicky, *Rethinking Philosophy and Theology with Deleuze: A New Cartography* (London: Bloomsbury, 2013). I want to thank Thomas Hatina for introducing me to the works of Gilles Deleuze and Félix Guattari and their potential benefit for appropriations of social memory theory in Gospels studies.

58 See Gilles Deleuze, *Bergsonism*, trans. Hugh Tomlinson and Barbara Habberjam (New York: Zone Books, 1988; orig. 1966), 7–8; Lundy, *Bergsonism*, 8–9; Kebede, *Bergson's Philosophy*, 192–99.

59 On the value of select concepts relating to the idea of difference, see Todd May, *Reconsidering Difference: Nancy, Derrida, Levinas, Deleuze* (University Park: Pennsylvania State University Press, 1997), 14, 165–201.

60 The appropriation of Deleuze (and Guattari) is far-reaching among various disciplines in ways that do not cohere with his intentions. Constantine V. Boundas (*Gilles Deleuze: The Intensive Reduction* [London: Continuum, 2009], 1) explains, "There are no Deleuzians; there are only people using Deleuze-blocs and Deleuze diagonal lines of transformation for the sake of creating concepts in philosophy, sensations in the arts, and modes of living in ethics and politics that are not necessarily (and sometimes not at all) Deleuze's."

61 Gilles Deleuze and Félix Guattari, *What Is Philosophy?* (New York: Columbia University Press, 1994), 2.

and responding to problems."[62] This is one of the reasons that Deleuzian concepts are often used to analyze literature from new angles. For my purposes, these insights that can help connect the phenomena of social memory, the transmission and reception of traditions with the creative process of writing literature that is relevant for, and even helps shape, the communal identities of the author's audience. There is fruitful material here for theoretically explaining the observations of Somov and Lehtipuu that Luke combines received afterlife traditions in unusual ways.[63] For Deleuze there is no radical difference between literature and philosophy.[64] Both fields, and their practitioners, use language to invoke new ways of experiencing the world. Claire Colebrook explains that, for Deleuze and Guattari, "The formation of a language responds to a way of approaching the world, so that language is an action, or a constant question and creation in response to experience."[65] In this way, Luke can be viewed as combining the skills of both a philosopher and a literary artisan.

Rhizome

One of the most helpful concepts proposed by Deleuze and Guattari for interpreting literature is the rhizome, especially when discussing the ways in which the malleable nature of social memory interacts with the creative process of writing literature. They explain that the arborescent growth of the tree, "is a system of derivation: first the roots, then the trunk, then the leaves. The roots are embedded here and not elsewhere. The branches are bound to the trunk, the leaves to the branches."[66] A rhizome (like a Kudzu), however, can sprout roots and stems from any point, as it only has a middle and is always in process of growing and making new connections.[67] Eugene Holland explains that "any point of a rhizome can be connected to any other."[68] Referring to felt as an example of a rhizome, Holland continues to explain that, "The strength of felt ... [as the result of a weaving process that] arises from the random overlapping of a myriad of fibers, not from the patterned regularity of a weave; in principle, any fiber in a piece of felt can overlap with any other."[69]

62 Claire Colebrook, *Gilles Deleuze* (New York: Routledge, 2002), 27.

63 For example, Somov, *Afterlife*, 17, 26; Lehtipuu, *Afterlife Imagery*, 303.

64 John Marks, *Gilles Deleuze: Vitalism and Multiplicity*. (London: Pluto Press, 1998), 123.

65 Colebrook, *Deleuze*, 20.

66 Todd May, *Gilles Deleuze: An Introduction* (Cambridge: Cambridge University Press, 2005), 133.

67 May, *Gilles Deleuze*, 133.

68 Eugene W. Holland, "Rhizome," in *Understanding Deleuze, Understanding Modernism*, ed. Paul Ardoin, S. E. Gontarski, and Laci Mattison (London: Bloomsbury, 2014), 271.

69 Holland, *Rhizome*, 271.

The various remembrances of the afterlife that Somov examines in his monograph can be viewed as a non-pattern of incoherent fibers that have been woven together through written and/or oral transmission which Luke received and wove together in new ways that were relevant for his community. To these fibers of tradition, Luke adds his own unique fibers to present to his audience a strengthened fabric of meaning woven together with disparate fibers that may seem, when unwound and examined individually, unconnected and incoherent. Read and heard together, however, Luke's combining of the received traditions due to the dynamic activity of memory and the creative writing process present new, meaningful and powerful images of afterlife that are part of his overall message.

Minor Literature

As a comparison with Luke, Franz Kafka represents for Deleuze and Guattari the essence of minor literature. As a Jew living in Prague and writing in German, he used deterritorialized language (explained below).[70] Kafka's works can be regarded as rhizomic.[71] Christopher Watkin explains that, "In *Kafka: Toward a Minor Literature*, Deleuze and Guattari define a 'minor' literature as one that deterritorializes language, destabilizing conventional grammar, rhythms, and stresses, and one that stresses social and political concerns."[72] Adrian Parr explains that, "Perhaps deterritorialisation can best be understood as a movement producing change. In so far as it operates as a line of flight, deterritorialisation indicates the creative potential of an assemblage."[73] Applying the concept of "assemblage" to the collection of images of the afterlife in Luke-Acts can help to explain how Luke has taken various traditions and combined them in new ways in which they were not often used (deterritorialized), and has reterritorialized those traditions to fit his presentation of Jesus, and the overall theological, social and political message in his two-volume work. Deterritorialization is thus used here in a positive sense, as it leads to the reterritorialization of images of the afterlife in Luke-Acts that positively serve Luke's overall message to his community. As Parr explains, "to deterritorialise

70 May, *Gilles Deleuze*, 150. See also, Ronald Bogue, "MINORITARIAN + LITERATURE," in *The Deleuze Dictionary*, ed. Adrian Parr (Edinburgh: Edinburgh University Press, 2010), 170–71.

71 Gilles Deleuze and Félix Guattari, *Kafka: Toward a Minor Literature*, (trans. Dana Polan; Minneapolis: University of Minnesota Press, 1986; first published 1975), 3.

72 Watkin, *Gilles Deleuze*, 146.

73 Adrian Parr, "DETERRITORIALISATION / RETERRITORIALISATION," in *The Deleuze Dictionary*, ed. Adrian Parr (Edinburgh: Edinburgh University Press, 2010), 69.

is to free up the fixed relations that contain a body all the while exposing it to new organisations."[74]

For Deleuze and Guattari minor literature refers to a high form of literature that takes well-known themes and images and presents them in new ways that change, and at times disrupt, their standard use.[75] This process is not necessarily negative or polemical, but seeks to create a new language, or set of concepts, that present new ways of thinking and is not a product so much as a process of establishing a communal identity. As Christopher Langlois summarizes, minor literature "is invented for a people who do not yet exist, or rather for a people who *will have existed*."[76] Because minor literature reimagines familiar language and images, it is "less a product than a process of becoming minor … immediately social and political issues are engaged, and a collective assemblage of enunciation makes possible the invention of a people to come."[77]

Luke is often thought to be a Gentile convert to Judaism who later became a Jesus-follower, had familiarity with Hellenistic traditions and the (Greek) Jewish Scriptures and wrote primarily to a Gentile audience whom he saw as participating in God's plan for Israel.[78] John Nolland persuasively argues that Luke's primary audience consisted of Gentile God-fearers who were at a crossroads. As new followers of Jesus, they were pressured by both Jewish and Gentile groups who were not willing to compromise their own traditions.[79] In light of the function of minor literature, Luke can be compared to Kafka, since both wrote from within and to a community of variance that affected social, political and religious tensions.

Luke begins his two-volume work by explicitly stating that others have set out to write an orderly account of the events that have been fulfilled, and that he too will provide an orderly account so that Theophilus "may know the truth" about the things he was told (Luke 1:1–4). Luke-Acts is an orderly account of a different kind. For example, Luke 4 presents a disrupted account of Jesus' visit to Capernaum where Jesus reads from a scroll in the synagogue that leads to amazement by the audience to which Jesus replies, "And you will say, 'Do here

74 Parr, "DETERRITORIALISATION / RETERRITORIALISATION," 69–72.

75 Christopher Langlois, "Minor Literature," in *Understanding Deleuze, Understanding Modernism*, ed. Paul Ardoin, S. E. Gontarski, and Laci Mattison (London: Bloomsbury, 2014), 266–67.

76 Langlois, *Minor Literature*, 267. Emphasis is his.

77 Bogue, "MINORITARIAN + LITERATURE," 170–71.

78 Joseph A. Fitzmyer, *The Gospel according to Luke I–IX*, AB 28 (New Haven: Yale University Press, 2008), 58–59 See also Somov, *Afterlife*, 2.

79 John Nolland, *Luke 1:1–9:20*, WBC 35A (Dallas: Word, Incorporated, 1989), xxxii–xxxiii. Note that Nolland also discusses (xxxiii) the likelihood that Luke also envisioned and hoped for a wider audience in addition to Gentile God-fearers.

also in your hometown the things that we have heard you did at Capernaum.'" (4:23b). A careful reader will note that the first time that Jesus is said to go down to Capernaum is in Luke 4:31. Luke relocates and significantly expands Mark's account (6:1–6), which provides further disruption. Jesus mentions Elijah and Elisha serving Gentiles when there were many widows in Israel who were in need, which leads to the expulsion of Jesus from the town (and almost leads to him being thrown off a cliff).[80] By "orderly account," Luke is thus not referring to correct chronology, or historical accuracy in the modern sense. Instead, Luke appears to be intentionally reconfiguring traditions that he has received, which include afterlife imagery, in ways that are relevant for his community.[81]

Werner Kelber and the Transmission Process

When discussing processes of transmission and reception in Gospel studies, interaction with the work of Werner Kelber is inescapable. His contributions provide valuable connections between social memory and fluidity in the shaping of traditions. In addition to his pioneering work on orality, Kelber provides a connecting point between the literary concepts discussed above and the uniquely creative aspects of the Gospels that can all-to-often get overshadowed in historically-based interpretive methods like form criticism. Kelber refers to the work of Birger Gerhardsson and Rainer Riesner as examples of scholars who work under the assumption that, "memory acts as the stalwart of stability, safeguarding an unchanging tradition and thus guaranteeing the historical reliability of the gospels."[82] Influential for their conceptions of transmission is in part Rudolf Bultmann's work on the transmission of tradition. Kelber notes that while Bultmann focuses a great deal of attention on establishing the original forms of the oral traditions behind the Synoptic Gospels, there is no mention of memory in his work. From our side of the memory boom, we can easily fault Bultmann for ignoring the creative abilities of the evangelists while engaging in a "project was informed by a trinity of theoretical principles: the original form of oral units, the dominance of directional growth processes, and the intrinsic causality of the tradition."[83]

80 On the disruptive role that Luke 4 plays within his narrative, see Dale B. Martin, *New Testament History and Literature* (New Haven: Yale University Press, 2012), 132–35.

81 See, for example, Martin's (*New Testament History*, 137, 149–151) discussion of Mark 13 in Luke 21.

82 Werner H. Kelber, "The Case of the Gospels: Memory's Desire and the Limits of Historical Criticism," *Oral Tradition* 17 (2002), 62.

83 Kelber, "The Case of the Gospels," 63.

What is important for the current discussion is that, while Gerhardsson and Riesner acknowledge the importance of memory in the process of transmitting and receiving traditions, they do not acknowledge the malleable nature of memory, or the impact that one's community has on memory. In the case of Bultmann, memory is not factored into his studies. Instead, he assumes a transmission of static oral traditions that are transmitted and received in ways that have been discussed above as arborescent rather than rhizomic in nature.[84] Put simply, memory is equated with tradition. This linear approach, according to Kelber, is not only untenable in light of our current understanding of the memory process, but does not allow for the literary creativity of skilled authors, like Luke, to establish new traditions and new collective identity.[85] Kelber describes Bultmann's view of the Synoptic Gospels as being, "nourished by, at least partially composed of, and above all intelligible as reservoirs of tradition."[86]

Kelber's description of transmission and reception, more finely tuned using social memory, allows for the Gospels to be viewed as products of creativity that operates in conjunction with new cultural identity formations. On this point, Kelber's thinking can be enhanced by the conceptions of difference proposed by Deleuze and Guattari. In particular, Deleuze and Guattari provide new concepts and nomenclature for understanding what scholars who work in the fields of orality and social memory call "traditioning (practices),"[87] which more closely resemble rhizomic rather than arborescent processes. With respect to process, Kelber explains that "memory is conceived less as a storage or archive, and more as a dynamic operation that reappropriates the past in the interest of communal identities." And, when this is acknowledged, it can be appreciated how "each gospel constructs a new representation of the sacred past in order to meet the demands of a changing present."[88]

Kelber points out that scribal technology does not necessarily eliminate the malleability of the past that one may assume only occurs in oral transmission.[89]

84 Kelber, "The Case of the Gospels," 63.

85 Kelber, "The Case of the Gospels," 62–65.

86 Building on Kelber's ("The Case of the Gospels," 62–65) insight regarding Bultmann's work on the Fourth Gospel, what is telling about the limitations of assuming arborescent transmission, is that Bultmann was not restricted by the same assumptions when reading the Gospel of John which was believed to have been shaped by theological creativity.

87 Werner H. Kelber, "The Works of Memory: Christian Origins as Mnemohistory—A Response," in *Memory, Tradition, and Text: Uses of the Past in Early* Christianity, ed. Alan Kirk and Tom Thatcher, SemeiaSt 52 (Atlanta: Society of Biblical Literature, 2005), 246.

88 Kelber, "The Case of the Gospels," 57.

89 Kelber ("The Case of the Gospels," 57–58) also adds an interesting note regarding the forgetfulness involved in oral (as opposed to scribal) transmission, claiming, "To be sure,

He refers to Walter Ong's phrase "the fictionalizing of the writer's audience" to discuss how written texts can meet the needs, and even (re)establish, a communal identity in ways that oral traditions cannot, especially during times of crises.[90] To be clear, what is being proposed here is not a simple reception of traditions that are merely re-arranged in the thousand layers of memory that meet social needs,[91] or merely a creative editing process. Rather, both of these processes are complex, fluid, and work together intrinsically in a way that allows received traditions to be creatively (re)collected and (re)shaped in the service of relevant identity formation.

This dynamic process, to which Bergson, Halbwachs, Deleuze, Guattari, and Kelber speak, allows for conceptions of difference and newness to be part of an ever-unfolding drive to give meaning to change as it affects identity. The medium is the constant expression of life, not a detached description of it. Deleuze and Guattari explain that, "the book is not an image of the world. It forms a rhizome with the world."[92] Eugene Holland describes rhizomic minor literature this way: "The rhizome-book enables us to think *with* the world, rather than thinking *about* the world."[93] In attempting to provide hope for his community, Luke does not allow his audience to passively read *about* Jesus or the early church, but expects it to read *with* Jesus and the early church. As such, he presents a rhizome of received traditions about the afterlife woven together in a novel way to exhort his community to repent and follow Jesus, through whom the Kingdom of God is present.[94] Luke creates a new eschatological time in which "repentance brings salvation, which is already in action in Luke-Acts and will continue to the age to come."[95]

---

scribality, due to its storing function, appears to have solved the problem of forgetting, but its scribally enforced distance from hearers may facilitate innovative thought and in a sense bring about an intensified form of forgetfulness."

90 Kelber ("The Case of the Gospels," 57–58) adds that, "scribality's disengagement from oral tradition may produce precisely the kind of alienation that will prove productive for creative reassessments of tradition in ways primary oral cultures cannot ordinarily tolerate … The textualization of a tradition is therefore by no means a guarantor of stability and continuity. In the case of the gospels one needs to take into account the medium of scribal technology and the potential it harbors for reshaping tradition."

91 Note the connection between the thousands of layers of memory in Bergson's work and the title of Gilles Deleuze and Felix Guattari, *Thousand Plateaus*, trans. Brian Massumi (Minneapolis: University of Minnesota Press, 1987; orig. 1980), where rhizome, minortorium (and thus minor literature) and becoming are central concepts. See also Guerlac, *Thinking in Time*, 152. 1–12.

92 Deleuze and Guattari, *Thousand Plateaus*, 11.

93 Holland, "Rhizome," 271. Emphasis is his.

94 Somov, *Afterlife*, 220.

95 Somov, *Afterlife*, 220.

Conclsion and Implications

Somov's monograph provides an invaluable study for those who want to better understand the complex and divergent representations of the afterlife in Luke-Acts. Somov is to be commended for his thorough study that emphasizes the divergent and even contradictory representations of the afterlife through the use of metaphorical language. Somov agrees with Lehtipuu's insistence that one must not attempt to unnecessarily force the inconsistent images of the afterlife in Luke (and Acts) that are largely based in "mechanical source critical work" that "is hopelessly circular … [and] … assumes that not only the evangelist is consistent in his thinking but also that the sources he uses are internally coherent."[96] What is surprising about Somov's monograph is that, while he emphasizes the different and at times even incoherent representations of the afterlife in Luke-Acts, he uses Cognitive Metaphor Theory to develop a way of reading the imagery of the afterlife in Luke-Acts that suggests the possibility of a coherent reading (even possibly intended by Luke).[97] On this point, I depart from Somov and side with Lehtipuu's insistence that, "it is not a coherent doctrine of the 'last things' Luke is after but eschatological images are in the service of paraenetic aims."[98] I have attempted to go a bit further than Lehtipuu by proposing that Luke intentionally utilizes differing, and even at times contradictory, representations of the afterlife to effectively, and positively, surprise his audience with eschatological images that would lead to correct behaviour in this life, with special emphasis placed on the Christian community caring for the poor and vulnerable. This is in keeping with Somov's summary of Luke's overall aim that "Those who entered the Christian community through repentance have already received salvation," and that, "their repentance and the proper social behavior, including charity and concern for their neighbors, affect their afterlife."[99]

In my attempt to provide an explanation for Luke's internally competing conceptions of afterlife, I have pointed to the insights from process-oriented approaches—particularly social memory theory in the works of Halbwachs and Bergson, the rhizomic view of literature in the works of Deleuze and Guattari, and finally the notions of transmission in the work of Kelber—as a heuristic explanation that can better inform Somov's descriptions of Luke's disparate afterlife imagery. When these images are viewed as expressions of

96 Lehtipuu, *Afterlife Imagery*, 239–240.
97 Somov, *Afterlife*, 227–30.
98 Lehtipuu, *Afterlife Imagery*, 241.
99 Somov, *Afterlife*, 220.

a process that is perpetually malleable, then the dissimilarities can be better understood without the need to make them cohere. Process thinking provides insights for contemporary readers allowing them to view Luke as being more than a mere passive recipient of malleable traditions, and as one who happens to recall memories in new ways, but as a literary architect who wrote to provide comfort, hope and a call to action with his novel and at times surprisingly divergent representations of the afterlife. On a theoretical level, this study proposes an approach to biblical literature that views differences, inconsistencies and even contradictions not only in positive terms, but as examples of a living tradition that is an expression of emerging communities that the Apostle Paul calls the body of Christ.

Bibliography

Adkins, Brent and Paul R. Hinlicky, *Rethinking Philosophy and Theology with Deleuze: A New Cartography*. London: Bloomsbury, 2013.

Ansell-Pearson, Keith. *Bergson: Thinking Beyond the Human Condition*. New York: Bloomsbury, 2018.

Assmann, Jan. "Collective Memory and Cultural Identity." *New German Critique* 65 (1995): 125–33.

———. *Moses the Egyptian*. Cambridge, Mass: Harvard University Press, 1997.

———. *Cultural Memory and Early Civilization: Writing, Remembrance, and Political Imagination*. Cambridge: Cambridge University Press, 2011.

Bergson, Henri. *Matter and Memory*. Translated by N. M. Paul and W. S. Palmer. New York: Zone Books, 1991.

Bogue, Ronald. *Deleuze and Guattari*. Critics of the Twentieth Century. London: Routledge, 1989.

———. "MINORITARIAN + LITERATURE." Pages 69–72 in *The Deleuze Dictionary*. Revised and edited by Adrian Parr. Edinburgh: Edinburgh University Press, 2010.

Boundas, Constantin V. *Gilles Deleuze: The Intensive Reduction*. Continuum Studies in Continental Philosophy. London: Continuum, 2009.

Colebrook, Claire. *Gilles Deleuze*. New York: Routledge, 2002.

Deleuze, Gilles. *Bergsonism*. Translated by Hugh Tomlinson and Barbara Habberjam. New York: Zone Books, 1988. Originally published in 1966.

Deleuze, Gilles and Félix Guattari. *Kafka: Toward a Minor Literature*, Translated by Dana Polan. Minneapolis: University of Minnesota Press, 1986 Originally published in 1975.

———. *Thousand Plateaus*, Translated by Brian Massumi. Minneapolis: University of Minnesota Press, 1987. Originally published in 1980.

——. *What Is Philosophy?* Translated by Hugh Tomlinson and Graham Burchell. European Perspectives. New York: Columbia University Press, 1994.

Fitzmyer, Joseph A. *The Gospel according to Luke I–IX*. AB 28. New Haven; London: Yale University Press, 2008.

Guerlac, Suzanne. *Thinking in Time: An Introduction to Henri Bergson*. Ithaca: Cornell University Press, 2006.

Halbwachs, Maurice. *The Collective Memory*. Translated by Francis J. Ditter, Jr. and Vida Yazdi Ditter. New York: Harper & Row, 1980.

——. *On Collective Memory*. Translated by Lewis A. Coser. Heritage of Sociology. University of Chicago Press, 1992.

Hatina, Thomas R. *New Testament Theology and Its Quest for Relevance: Ancient Texts and Modern Readers*. London: Bloomsbury T&T Clark, 2013.

Holland, Eugene W. "Rhizome." Pages 271–72 in *Understanding Deleuze, Understanding Modernism*. Edited by Paul Ardoin, S. E. Gontarski, and Laci Mattison. London: Bloomsbury, 2014.

Huebenthal, Sandra "'Frozen Moments'—Early Christianity through the Lens of Social Memory Theory." Pages 17–43 in *Memory and Memories in Early Christianity*. Edited by Simon Butticaz and Enrico Morelli. WUNT 398. Tübingen: Mohr Siebeck, 2018.

——. "Another Frozen Moment: Reading Luke in a Social Memory Theoretical Framework." *PIBA 41* (2020): 25–43.

——. *Reading Mark's Gospel as a Text from Collective Memory*. Grand Rapids: Eerdmans, 2020.

Kebede, Messay. *Bergson's Philosophy of Self-Overcoming: Thinking without Negativity or Time as Striving*. Cham: Palgrave Macmillan, 2019.

Kelber, Werner H. "The Case of the Gospels: Memory's Desire and the Limits of Historical Criticism." *Oral Tradition* 17 (2002): 55–86.

——. "The Works of Memory: Christian Origins as Mnemohistory—A Response," Pages 221–48 in *Memory, Tradition, and Text: Uses of the Past in Early Christianity*. Edited by Alan Kirk and Tom Thatcher. SemeiaSt 52. Atlanta: Society of Biblical Literature, 2005.

Kroeker, P Travis. "Rethinking Philosophy and Theology with Deleuze: A New Cartography." *Pro Ecclesia* 25 (2016): 496–498.

Langlois, Christopher. "Minor Literature." Pages 266–267 in *Understanding Deleuze, Understanding Modernism*. Edited by Paul Ardoin, S. E. Gontarski, and Laci Mattison. London: Bloomsbury, 2014.

Lehtipuu, Outi, *The Afterlife Imagery in Luke's Story of the Rich Man and Lazarus*. NovTSup 123. Leiden: Brill, 2007.

Liverani, Mario. "The Ideology of the Assyrian Empire." Pages 297–317 in *Power and Propaganda A Symposium on Ancient Empires*. Edited by Mogens Trolle Larsen. Copenhagen: Akademisk Forlag, 1979.

Lundy, Craig. *Deleuze's Bergsonism*. Edinburgh: Edinburgh University Press, 2018.

Marks, John. *Gilles Deleuze: Vitalism and Multiplicity*. London: Pluto Press, 1998.

Martin, Dale B. *New Testament History and Literature*. New Haven: Yale University Press, 2012.

Mattill, A. J., Jr. *Luke and the Last Things: A Perspective for the Understanding of Lukan Thought*. Dillsboro, NC: Western North Carolina Press, 1979.

May, Todd. *Reconsidering Difference: Nancy, Derrida, Levinas, Deleuze*. University Park: Pennsylvania State University Press, 1997

———. *Gilles Deleuze: An Introduction*. Cambridge: Cambridge University Press, 2005.

Nolland, John. *Luke 1:1–9:20*. WBC 35A. Dallas: Word, 1989.

Olick, Jeffrey, Vered Vinitzky-Seroussi and Daniel Levy. "Introduction." Pages 3–62 in *The Collective Memory Reader*. Edited by Jeffrey K. Olick, Vered Vinitzky-Seroussi, and Daniel Levy. Oxford: Oxford University Press, 2011.

Ricoeur, Paul. *Memory, History, Forgetting*. Translated by Kathleen Blamey and David Pellauer. Chicago: University of Chicago Press, 2004.

Sinclair, Mark. *Bergson*. New York: Routledge, 2019.

Somov, Alexy. *Representations of the Afterlife in Luke-Acts*. LNTS 556. London: Bloomsbury, 2017.

Vansina, Jan M. *Oral Tradition as History*. Madison: University of Wisconsin Press, 1985.

Watkin, Christopher. *Gilles Deleuze*. Phillipsburg: P & R Publishing, 2020.

William L. Petersen, "Diatessaron." *ABD* 2:189–90.

Young, Eugene B. "Minor Literature." Pages 196–97 in *The Deleuze and Guattari Dictionary: Bloomsbury Philosophy Dictionary*. London: Bloomsbury, 2013.

Zwiep, Arie W. *The Ascension of the Messiah in Lukan Christology*. NovTSup 87. Leiden: Brill, 1997.

When the Saints Go Marching In: Remembering Vengeance and Vindication in Matthew 27:52–53

Thomas R. Hatina

One of the strangest passages in early Christian literature is the account in Matt 27:52–53 where raised "saints" emerge out of their tombs and reveal themselves to many residents of Jerusalem *after* Jesus' resurrection. From the evangelist's perspective, the resurrection of the saints appears very similar to that of Jesus' resurrection. While there are a few differences such as the use of *sōma* for the saints, the omission of an angel, and the actual emergence from the tombs, which explains how the evangelist conceives of the resurrection process, this unusual episode is presented as a sensory event that is initiated by the sensory resurrection of Jesus.[1] In both cases, the raised forms could be experienced by others. This extraordinary set of events, which are only found in Matthew, have understandably given rise to much discussion over two millennia. Its eschatological significance, representation of death and the risen life, its timing, and its biblical allusions makes this one of the most densely packed theological texts in the New Testament. For convenience, I refer to this passage as the "zombie episode" since my cultural framework pressures me to think of resurrected saints walking around Jerusalem in this way. Apart from not being able to conceptualize the dead emerging from their tombs and walking around through any other framework, the attributed nomenclature is convenient and hopefully alluring.

In recent scholarship, much of the discussion about the zombie episode has been focussed on historical-critical inquiry that targets Matthew's sources, community, redactional activity, and/or the historicity of the events, all of which have stemmed from a hermeneutic that is rooted in a diachronic conception of texts. The aim of this study is to subject the zombie episode to an alternate analysis by conceiving of it as a memory text. This hermeneutic leads to an alternate set of questions and a re-prioritizing of exegetical methods. While this may not always lead to alternate readings, the results are based on a different set of exegetical priorities which particularly impinge on how we might understand Matthew's conception of the zombie episode in relation

1 That Matthew conveys a physical, instead of a metaphorical, resurrection is strongly acknowledged in Wim Weren, Huub van de Sandt, and Joseph Verheyden, eds., *Life beyond Death in Matthew's Gospel: Religious Metaphor or Bodily Reality?* BTS 13 (Leuven: Peeters, 2011).

 | DOI:10.30965/9783657796212_016

to competing conceptions of resurrection in early Christianity. This heuristic study contains three parts. In the first part, which functions as a contrasting point of departure, I compare the ontology of texts assumed in diachronic approaches with an ontology of texts that is more favourable to social memory theory. The second part focusses on the relationship between the past and present within the process of remembrance. In the final part, I address the exegetical method stemming from the hermeneutical construct and apply it to the zombie episode, concluding that the risen saints are Matthean missionaries who have come to make disciples in post-war Jerusalem.

Before proceeding to the first part of the study, consideration needs to be given to the structure of the passage, which has generated considerable debate. Since the delineation of the zombie episode is of preliminary importance, though not the aim of the study, I address it in this extended introduction. The main problem is that the zombie episode takes place *after* Jesus' resurrection (presumably Sunday, though no date is provided), but it is located in the context of Jesus' crucifixion on the Friday. Punctuation varies among translations.[2] Many English translations place a period at the end of v. 51, after the splitting of the rocks (e.g., NIV, NRSV); whereas a few translations place it at the end of v. 52, connecting the earthquake, rocks splitting, the tombs opening and the bodies rising as a subsequent portent to the tearing of the Temple curtain (e.g., NAB, TEV). Since the grammar cannot resolve the differences in punctuation, we are left with four events that need to be connected with two temporal referents: Jesus' death and his resurrection. I opt for the former proposal which connects the earthquake and the rocks splitting in v. 51 with the experience and confession of the Centurion in v. 54. Thus, the Centurion ("and those with him") is not privy to the opening of the tombs and the bodies rising since he is present only on the day of Jesus' death. Consequently, vv. 52–53 is a self-contained unit which functions like a mnemonic frame that provides meaning to Jesus' traumatic end. It explains how the evangelist, as a promoter of Jesus's memory, made sense of his death some sixty years later. As a literary device, the zombie episode resembles the narrator's emphasis in, for example, Mark 13:14 ("let the reader understand") and John 2:22 ("After he was raised from the dead, his disciples remembered that he had said this; and they believed the scripture and the word that Jesus had spoken") since both address the effect of a past event.[3]

---

2 See the discussion of punctuation in Charles L. Quarles, "Matthew 27:51–53: Meaning, Genre, Intertextuality, Theology, and Reception History," *JETS* 59 (2016): 271–86.

3 See also Jürgen K. Zangenberg, "Bodily Resurrection of Jesus in Matthew?" in *Life beyond Death in Matthew's Gospel: Religious Metaphor or Bodily Reality?* ed. Wim Weren, Huub van

Competing Ontologies and their Conceptions of Texts

Most Gospel scholars today have been trained in and continue to propagate what I would call a diachronic conception of the text. Within this conception, the Gospels are assumed to contain an archival character or quality which allows them to be dissected and anatomized into layers of tradition that can yield distinctions between the past and present, fact and fiction, continuity and discontinuity, memory and redaction, and even (for some) objectivity and subjectivity. Texts are viewed as products of prior influences whose layers can be excavated as opposed to media that capture or freeze existential realities in the author's present that may or may not preserve features from the past. Since conceptions of texts—what they are and what we can do with them— impinges on methods, diachronic conceptions have seamlessly led to historical-critical exegesis. Hermeneutics guides methods.

The plethora of historical questions posed to the zombie episode infer that reconstruction and/or comparison leads to a retrieval of Matthew's meaning. The primary influence to which everyone points is scripture. N. T. Wright summarizes the prevalent method, when he advocates that "the obvious starting-point for assessing Matthew's meaning is to examine the biblical echoes which, like the sleepers themselves, are awoken in this account."[4] In varying ways, David Strauss' conviction that the zombie episode is theologically derived from Ezek 37:12–13 is still influential after almost two centuries.[5] Most, however, have advanced his mythological approach in favour of midrashic one that situates the evangelist's exegetical practices among his Jewish and Christian contemporaries.[6] In addition, most scholars have argued that the scriptural influence should be expanded to include Zech 14:4–5.[7] Others, like

---

de Sandt, and Joseph Verheyden, BTS13 (Leuven: Peeters, 2011), 223 who sees it as a Matthean "purposeful commentary," and not a later gloss.

4 N. T. Wright, *The Resurrection of the Son of God* (Minneapolis: Fortress, 2003), 633.

5 David F. Strauss, *The Life of Jesus Critically Examined*, ed. and trans. Peter Hodgson (Philadelphia: Fortress, 1972), 694–96. Original German edition was published in 1840.

6 E.g., Charles H. Talbert, *Matthew* (Grand Rapids: Baker Academic, 2010), 306–307.

7 See the list of scholars in Timothy Wardle, "Resurrection and the Holy City: Matthew's Use of Isaiah in 27:51–53," *CBQ* 78 (2016): 667. Dale C. Allison Jr., "The Scriptural Background of a Matthean Legend: Ezekiel 37, Zechariah 14, and Matthew 27," in *Life beyond Death in Matthew's Gospel: Religious Metaphor or Bodily Reality?* ed. Wim Weren, Huub van de Sandt, and Joseph Verheyden, BTS 13 (Leuven: Peeters, 2011), 153–88, points to Matthew's customary practice of bringing two scripture texts together. Allison also points out that Matthew was not alone in bringing these texts together since they also appear in later sources, especially select Targumic traditions, the Dura Europos frescoes of Ezekiel's "valley of the dry bones," later Christian art, and isolated rabbinic texts, citing Codex Reuchlinianus' version of

Timothy Wardle, have argued that the evangelist's broader influence of LXX Isaiah 42–52 led him to develop the zombie episode specifically from the language of Isa 52:1–2.[8] Others still have seen traces of Isa 29:19 and Dan 12:1–3.[9]

In addition to scripture, some scholars have narrowed the influences to underlying Jewish exegetical and eschatological traditions. Here again, a variety of proposals are on offer. One example is *Tg. Isa.* 42:11 which replaces "let the inhabitants of *Sela* sing for joy" (MT, LXX, and lQIsa) with the intriguing phrase: "let the dead sing praise when they come forth from their tombs." While post-dating Matthew, Wardle claims that it represented a stream of tradition with which Matthew was familiar.[10] A second example is the Ezekiel panel of the Dura Europos Synagogue. While dating to the middle of the third century CE, its depiction of the resurrection of the dead after a presumed earthquake that split the tombs, is nevertheless vaguely associated with Matthew in the sense that both share a common tradition.[11] A third example is the exegetical derivation of Ezekiel 37 at Qumran in 4Q521, which shifts the prophetic hope from the nation to individual bodily resurrection of the deceased righteous as part of a newly developed theodicy.[12]

Finally, Paul's reference to Jesus' resurrection as the "first fruits of those who have fallen asleep" in 1 Cor 15:20 is sometimes connected with the zombie episode either as a proleptic and/or symbolic reference to the anticipated general resurrection. This is an indirect influence. For those who operate with a Pauline two-stage resurrection program, then the zombie episode cannot refer to the beginning of the general resurrection.[13] Wright, for example, argues that no one in the first century would have expected a few dozen raised saints at the most to be a fulfillment of Ezekiel, Isaiah, and Daniel, so there would have been no point in inventing this tradition as a signal for the general resurrection.[14]

Tg. Zech. 14:4 and *Tg. Cant.* 8:5, and Erwin R. Goodenough, *Jewish Symbols in the Greco-Roman Period* (New York: Pantheon, 1964), 10:179–96; ll: xxi.

8 Wardle, "Resurrection and the Holy City," 666–81.

9 Wim J. C. Weren, *Studies in Matthew's Gospel: Literary Design, Intertextuality, and Social Setting*, BIS 130 (Leiden: Brill, 2014), 213–14; Wright, *Resurrection*, 633.

10 Wardle, "Resurrection and the Holy City," 675–76.

11 Ulrich Luz, *Matthew 21–28* (Minneapolis: Fortress, 2005), 567–68; J. Grassi, "The Resurrection and the Ezechiel Panel of the DuraEuropos Synagogue," *TBT* 11 (1964): 721–26; Harald Riesenfeld, *The Resurrection in Ezekiel xxxvii and in the Dura- Europos Paintings* (Upsala: Lundaquistilca Bokhandeln, 1948), 37–48.

12 C. D. Elledge, *Resurrection of the Dead in Early Judaism 200 BCE–CE 200* (Oxford: Oxford University Press, 2017), 3–6.

13 Weren, *Studies in Matthew's* Gospel, 82.

14 Wright, *Resurrection*, 634; Ronald L. Troxel, "Matthew 27.51–4 Reconsidered: Its Role in the Passion Narrative, Meaning and Origin," *NTS* 48 (2002): 30–47.

Wright implies that the zombie episode represents some kind of phenomenon that occurred around the time of the crucifixion, with which the evangelist was familiar. He writes, "Some stories are so odd that they may have just happened. This may be one of them, but in historical terms there is no way of finding out."[15]

In response to the prevailing approaches, I draw attention to two assumptions of diachronic approaches in a way that is usually not discussed in Biblical Studies, but can provide a creative critique on the one hand and a link to conceptions of texts as products of memory on the other. The insights of the French philosopher Gilles Deleuze bring into sharper focus the diachronic assumptions of identity and time, which are operative in studies of the zombie episode. Theoretically, I want to link conceptions of texts with two prevailing ontological systems in the history of philosophy. These are what Deleuze calls the ontology of identity, which has dominated our conceptions of reality since Plato, and the ontology of difference which was first proposed by Spinoza. In brief, an ontology of identity or identification is a system that always begins with a transcendent reality functioning as a standard for all inquiry. Identification is the cohesive social element to which a group or society subscribes as reality, such as unity, justice, the world, the human, the divine, the free, "the good" in Aristotelian thought, forms in Platonic thought, or the afterlife. Emerging differences are viewed as stemming from these supposed stable concepts.

The notion of identification preceding difference is particularly well expressed in conceptions of resurrection by, for example, N.T. Wright and John Dominic Crossan, who otherwise have opposing views on the topic. Both presuppose that Jesus was "definitely dead" (as medical professionals understand death today) and was resurrected on the third day. Despite their different views on the nature of Jesus' resurrection, they both clearly distinguish it from other "resurrection" incidents in the Gospels that also use ἀνίστημι and ἐγείρω. A case in point is the raising of Lazarus whom Jesus "called out of the tomb" and raised (ἐγείρω) "from the dead" (John 12:1, 9, 17). While Lazarus is described as being definitely dead in the tomb for three days, his raising is understood as resuscitation, not resurrection.[16] This ontology of identification is carried into the zombie episode which supposedly should not be equated with the resurrection of Jesus. Jesus' resurrection, however it is conceived, functions as the identification for the emerging differences. While this is understandable, the problem is that it too is presented differently in early Christian literature.

15 Wright, *Resurrection*, 636.

16 Wright, *Resurrection*, 443–44; John Dominic Crossan, "The Resurrection of Jesus in Its Jewish Context," *Neot* 37 (2003): 46.

Deleuze provides an alternate approach which challenges the needless dualism and ontological hierarchy where the transcendent is always on top. He argues for an ontology of difference, which views reality as only being difference. It is a process of expression without the aid or intervention of an outside entity, force, or conception. What is particularly important for our understanding of texts as products of social memory is that unfolding expressions of reality can arrange themselves in an infinite number of combinations. These differences are like tiny dots in a long process of expression. Each expression leads to new identities or identifications, which are no longer prior, but subsequent. Gilles Deleuze and Felix Guattari's use of the metaphor of the rhizome within their political theory is a helpful way of conceiving the interconnecting process that makes sense of emerging identities. In contrast to a tree, which is a system of derivation in a specific location that embeds itself with one root that leads to a trunk and the branches, a rhizome (like the Kudzu) can sprout roots and stems from any point. It has no beginning, middle, or end. It has no shape and is not limited to any one space since it can connect itself to a tree, the ground, or a fence.[17] I would argue that the production of texts and their reception are like rhizomes. The text (say the zombie episode or Matthew's Gospel as a whole) mediates a single snapshot of one point in the unfolding rhizome of a society. The past could not have determined the text preserved in the snapshot and the future cannot determine how it will look because interconnections are limitless within an ontology of difference. Conceiving of texts as products of rhizomes instead of trees does not necessarily undermine more traditional diachronic conceptions and their related methods, but it certainly no longer tethers us, but provides for variegated perspectives that can lead to fuller understanding.

An ontology of difference and the process of expression is temporal, requiring an explanation of the relationship between the past, present, and future. Our conventional view of time, which is assumed in diachronic approaches, situates the present on a linear continuum between the past and the future, but it gives equal weight to each instant. This differs slightly from an existential view of time which privileges the future as the dominant dimension. Nevertheless, both views allow either the potential retrieval of the past in some form, even though the past does not really exist, or at least allows the past to have an effect on the present. In this sense, the sequence of events in time is perceived in spatial terms, which means that events in time can be divided into an infinite number of segments or epochs, each distinct from the other

17 Gilles Deleuze and Felix Guattari, *A Thousand Plateaus*, trans. Brian Massumi (Minneapolis: University of Minnesota Press, 1987).

like objects in space. The present can be influenced by the past, but it too is distinct and cannot occupy the same space.

When applied to texts, diachronic conceptions are epistemologically optimistic about reconstructing the text because the present is in principle distinguished from the past. In relation to the process of text production, the transmission principles tend to be linear whereby traditions build on one another like geological sediments. In many cases, practitioners of diachronic approaches fail to advance a theory of transmission or simply assume one that is consistent with their emic framework. The proverbial peeling back of the layers of the textual onion does not lead to an unmediated historical core of meaning. Every layer is also subject to the same problem because it too is never without mediation. As processes of recovery, diachronic approaches are well suited for data mining among the layers, akin to archaeology, but not for reconstructing their meanings or the internalization of the data by its varied recipients. Consequently, for diachronic exegetes, the meanings of texts tend to be determined by their underlying causes or influences. Methodologically, this understandably leads to prioritizing reconstructions of communities, their social conflicts, their opponents, and even authorial intentions. The aim is to retrieve a single meaning since the process is oriented toward a coherence between the text and a single point in time and space prior to the formation of the text. The derived meaning is often analyzed in relation to either preservations or distortions of a conceived "original" reality in the past or a continuity of a "static" tradition. The theological concepts in the Gospels have been particularly subjected to diachronic analysis.

The widespread pursuit of underlying sources for the zombie episode have been dependent on the linear conception of time which has led some to advocate that its meaning is in continuity with preceding ideas or parallel ideas. Others have drawn attention to the diversity of ideas, of which the zombie episode is one among many. Each set of conclusions, however, assumes that Matthew's meaning is distinct from a previous identification in another point in time, be it for example Ezekiel, Isaiah or Daniel. Comparisons and parallels are interesting, but how are they related and unrelated? What accounts for competing conceptions? How does the past of the sources relate to the present of the evangelist? Again, I am not advocating the diachronic approach is incorrect, but it is limited to only one perspective within an ontology of identity. I turn now to a social memory conception of the zombie episode which can be further linked theoretically to the ontology of difference.

While these views of time are practical, neither is consistent with an ontology of difference and the process of expression as theory of the real. If substance is expression, then whatever is being expressed needs to be within its expressions and not disconnected from them. As Todd May writes, "It is not as though at one moment there is one thing and at another there is something else."[18] By contrast, for Deleuze the concept of time—which was highly influenced by the philosophy of Henri Bergson who likewise was influential for Maurice Halbwachs—critiques spatial notions of time in favour of temporal notions whereby the past exists in the present.[19]

Enter Memory

For groups and individuals, memory is the link between the past and present.[20] Too often, however, in recent appropriations of social memory theory in New Testament studies, neither the notions of the past and the present, nor their ontological relationship, has been adequately explained. I suggest that when social memory theory, as Maurice Halbwachs conceived of it, is placed within an ontology of difference, it sheds more light on the process of their integration. Again, I turn to Deleuze, who explains it this way:

> The past and the present do not denote two successive moments, but two elements which coexist: One is the present, which does not cease to pass, and the other is the past, which does not cease to be but through which all presents pass.... The past does not follow the present, but on the contrary, is presupposed by it as the pure condition without which it would not pass.[21]

This understanding of the relationship between the past and present moves beyond a linear conception of time, which places points in time beside each other, to one that allows for the existence of the past to which the present passes. Thus, the present does not simply cease to be when it passes. It passes to a past. But the past does not exist in the same way as the present. Bergson argues that the past exists virtually in contrast to the present which always exists actually. The virtual is structured differently. The virtual is not the possible, the transcendent, or a copy, or even a type. It is real. But it is not what has happened. Otherwise, we would be back to a linear conception. Instead, the past is understood as that which is always different and cannot be subsumed under

18 Todd May, *Gilles Deleuze: An Introduction* (Cambridge: Cambridge University Press, 2005), 44.

19 May, *Gilles Deleuze*, 45.

20 Aleida Assmann, *Cultural Memory and Western Civilization: Functions, Media, Archives* (Cambridge: Cambridge University Press, 2011), 23–29.

21 Gilles Deleuze, *Bergsonism*, trans. Hugh Tomlinson and Barbara Habberjam (New York: Zone Books, 1988), 59.

identity because it is always an effect of an ongoing differing present.[22] The past is coiled into every present resulting in only potentiality and differences, each of which is identity. For Bergson, memory is not simply psychological, but is a wider single ontological condition wherein its innumerable expressions function.[23] The present and the past exist "at the same time." Todd May summarizes Bergson's main points this way: "There is no present that does not actualize the past. It is all of the past that is actualized at every moment. The past that is actualized exists."[24] Halbwachs carries this idea into his understanding of social memory, arguing that the received past is influential for meaning-making in the present, especially if the tradition is older, is adopted by a large number of adherents, and is widespread. Since the past serves the present, the present determines how the past is remembered.[25] The past for Halbwachs was the past as it was variously remembered.

When texts are viewed as memory texts, they are media of suspended expressions, capturing a snapshot of the unfolding rhizome. As a distinct model of text production, social memory theory collapses tradition and reception into an integrated process whereby constructs of the present and the anticipated future are shaped by culturally significant remembrances of the past. When tradition and memory are conflated, we can assume a past, but it is always a past that has always been received. To clarify, the object for social memory theorists is not the storage or recitation (*Erinnerung*) of select data from the past, but rather involuntary acts of internalization and identity construction (*Gedächtnis*) where remembering and forgetting are inextricably bound in the service of relevance.[26] Social memory theory challenges linear models of transmission and proposes that traditions, as products of memory, are more pliable, situational, temporally conditioned and disconnected from some underlying transcendent reality that serves as a standard. Its capital lies in its explanatory value for making sense of how and why authors of texts perceived the past in competing ways.

The process of remembering which accounts for the product of the zombie episode can be understood in light of Jan and Aleida Assmann's distinction between *collective* memory and *cultural* memory which underscores how temporal frameworks can impinge on the relationship between the past and present in the transmission process. Sandra Huebenthal has perceptively

22 May, *Gilles Deleuze*, 53.

23 Deleuze, *Bergsonism*, 56.

24 May, *Gilles Deleuze*, 52–55.

25 Maurice Halbwachs, *On Collective Memory*, trans. L. A. Coser (Chicago: University of Chicago Press, 1992), 183.

26 Assmann, *Cultural Memory and Western Civilization*, 19–20.

appropriated the Assmanns' distinction by drawing attention to its respective temporal frameworks which include gaps or temporal partitions that divide generations.[27] While her focus is on the diversity of identity construction within early Christianity, the attention to temporality is particularly useful for understanding the zombie episode as a synthesis of two commemorative frameworks, one of which being scripture and the other being remembrances of Jesus.

I turn first to collective (or short-term) remembrance which is formed over two generations, each lasting 30–50 years. If the second generation appropriates the remembrances after the passing of the first generation, it does so in different times and different contexts, potentially facing entirely different issues. Within this framework, if Matthew is dated to around 90 CE, then as a second-generation remembrance, it appropriates the receptions of the first generation. The point is that Matthew's frame of reference does not lie in the actual past of the late 20s, but in its receptions. It is generally agreed that the second generation marked a necessary transition that led to substantial shifts in early Christian thought and structure. After the death of the original followers of Jesus in the early 60s CE (namely James, Peter and Paul), which marks a generational gap, the continuation of the emerging movement required answers to new questions in a way that maintained legitimacy by means of a continuity with the authoritative voices of the past, one of which may well be represented by "Matthew" if indeed the name was attached to the Gospel at this stage. At this stage, remembrance is, and indeed must be, much more pliable and constructive in the shaping of potential frames of identity formation in the service of relevance which is open-ended, lest it is lost in the past and forgotten. Prevailing iconic mental images (such as receptions of the resurrected Jesus) appear to override temporal factors such as the truth of their origins, which results in reducing events to mythical archetypes that primarily function to persuade so as to control the future. Since the meanings of Jesus during the first two generations are not yet standardized or institutionally sanctioned at the level of cultural memory, they are necessarily entangled with imagination and forgetting because prevailing bits of phenomena require order and connectivity.[28]

27 Sandra Huebenthal, "'Frozen Moments'—Early Christianity through the Lens of Social Memory Theory," in *Memory and Memories in Early Christianity*, ed. Simon Butticaz and Enrico Morelli, WUNT 1.398 (Tübingen: Mohr Siebeck, 2018), 17–43.

28 On the relationship between imagination and memory, see Paul Ricoeur, *Memory, History, Forgetting*, trans. Kathleen Blamey and David Pellauer (Chicago: The University of Chicago Press, 2004), 5–55.

By comparison, within the temporal framework of cultural (or long-term) memory, shared group identities stem from inherited remembrances that are framed within a larger cultural system or web of significance. Barry Schwartz observes that this frequently occurs among the evangelists' use of scripture. He writes, "The Gospels key the activities and fate of Jesus to statements in the Hebrew Scriptures an estimated three hundred times, which affirms both the Gospel writers' mastery of Scripture and their listeners' identification with the history the sacred texts describe."[29] What needs to be emphasized, however, is that keying, which usually highlights a patriarch, prophet, or event, is concerned with memories themselves, and not the texts on which they are cited, which in the zombie episode appear to be conceptions of restoration, vindication, and even vengeance in Ezekiel 14, Zecheriah 12, Isaiah 29, 52, and Daniel 12, and the like.[30] The allusions are symbols that point to existentially experienced myths. As a result, otherwise unrelated texts which refer to a common past (event or figure) can be merged into coherent and simplified plotlines that re-narrate the past in a relevant way.[31] What we find in the entirety of Matthew is scripture that is newly remembered, bridged seamlessly from one era to another. Social memory theory has come to challenge the modernist sense of temporal distance by bringing attention to the fluid intertextuality of meaning making, which leads to a better representation of the prophetic framework of antiquity where events are viewed as symbols of renewal that always lead to a prescribed *telos*.[32] Prophetic miscalculations do not require containment because they can always be renewed within a framework that is fixated on a religiously conceived *telos* and not subject to time.[33]

29 Barry Schwartz, "Where There's Smoke, There's Fire: Memory and History," in *Memory and Identity in Ancient Judaism and Early Christianity: A Conversation with Barry Schwartz*, ed. Tom Thatcher, Semeia 78 (Atlanta: SBL Press, 2014), 15–16.

30 Catrin H. Williams, "Patriarchs and Prophets Remembered: Framing Israel's Past in the Gospel of John," in *Abiding Words: The Use of Scripture in the Gospel of John*, ed. Alicia D. Myers and Bruce G. Schuchard, RBS 81 (Atlanta: SBL Press, 2012), 189.

31 Eviatar Zerubavel, *Time Maps: Collective Memory and the Social Space of the Past* (Chicago: University of Chicago Press, 2003), 13–14.

32 This is one of the key points in Jeffrey K. Olick, V. Vinitzky-Seroussi, and D. Levy, eds., *Collective Memory Reader* (Oxford: Oxford University Press, 2011).

33 Reinhart Koselleck, *Futures Past: On the Semantics of Historical Time*, trans. Keith Tribe (Cambridge: MIT Press, 1985), 14–16.

Toward A Method: Exegeting the Zombie Episode

As an ethnic Jew, the evangelist could not but use scripture to legitimize his story. His reception of the scriptures was pressured by the synchronic context, which is accessible to us primarily through the product of his narrative. This brings us to a relatively unchartered area of negotiating the evangelist's present, which necessitates a transference from hermeneutics to method. I suggest that since the zombie episode and the story in which it is found is viewed as a suspended expression, or snapshot of a rhizome, it requires a synchronic approach. One of the obvious options is narrative criticism, since it focuses on the text as a unified literary whole that conveys its own narrative world, people, places, events, plot structures, characterization and points of view, all of which fix the social situation of the evangelist's existential present. When it comes to the raised saints in the zombie episode, whatever the evangelist's conception, they are literary figures who occupy a character-space whereby the implied persons behind the literary figure (if there are any) can only be partially reflected because the identity construction is radically dependent on the narrative, which in terms of process overlaps with commemoration. In Alex Woloch's words, "our sense of the human figure (*as* implied person) is inseparable from the space that he or she occupies within the narrative totality."[34]

Synchronic interpretations are more open-ended than diachronic ones because they are oriented toward a coherence within the perimeters that the text itself sets up. Even if a narrative is presented as a history, the events, structure, and formal features are not arbitrary, but have a teleological purpose. While the narrative approach acknowledges polyvalence, it operates within a set of contextual limits which allows for some testability that can curb otherwise insatiable exegetical desires. Yet, diachronic inquiry still remains necessary for a fuller contribution to exegesis, but it does so in the service of the synchronic. Werner Kelber, like an increasing number of Gospel critics, regards both the historical and narrative approaches as "mutually enriching and corrective enterprises" since the Gospels are not only working out of and responding to tradition, but in the process form their own related tradition in narrative form.[35] Of particular value for social memory theorists, is the necessity of diachronic methods in the construction of memory frames.

34 Alex Woloch, *The One vs. the Many. Minor Characters and the Space of the Protagonist in the Novel* (Princeton: Princeton University Press, 2003), 13.

35 Werner H. Kelber, "Narrative as Interpretation and Interpretation of Narrative: Hermeneutical Reflections on the Gospels," *Semeia* 39 (1987): 124–25.

While the internal integrity of the narrative must be maintained, we need to be cognizant that at every turn the diachronically derived supplement may in fact distort the very integrity we want to preserve, and hermeneutically have to preserve. It is, in the end, potentially the problem that David Hoy and other literary theorists call the "critical circle."[36] The possibility of its escape, however, is a long-standing issue which will undoubtedly continue to be debated by philosophers and literary theorists for some time to come. While there is a tendency to advocate for narrative criticism in contemporary Gospels studies, the traditional weight of diachronic inquiry is still dominant, even for some advocates of social memory.[37]

My reading of the zombie episode is structured according to the common exegetical convention, which considers first the identity of the raised saints, and second, their role in Jerusalem *after* the resurrection of Jesus.

Who Are the Raised Saints?

This indeed is a perplexing question which has led to much speculation as I noted earlier. From a synchronic angle, I do not view the saints from a Pauline two-stage resurrection or other conceptions that supposedly represented a standard. We are told that there were "*many* bodies of the saints," not *all*. And we are told that their "bodies" (σώματα) were raised, which is the same way that the evangelist describes the resurrection of Jesus in 27:58–59 (τὸ σωμᾶ τοῦ Ἰησοῦ). This implies that the same corporeal event that leaves the tombs empty is probably distinct from the raising of the girl earlier in 9:25 and in the reference to the dead being raised in 11:5. These earlier events clearly function as signs of the messiah's presence among his people and point forward to Jesus' resurrection. While some have suggested that the passive "they were made visible" (ἐνεφανίσθησαν) indicates that the raised had glorified bodies, there is nothing in the narrative to substantiate this.[38] The evangelist's reference to the "tombs" (μνημεῖα) in connection with and use of "saints" (ἅγιοι) is most significant for identifying them. It leaves us with two options. On the one hand, the reference to the tombs connects us with the "tombs of the righteous" (μνημεῖα τῶν δικαίων) in 23:29, where Jesus casts blame on the descendants of the scribes and Pharisees for their murder. As a result, many have suggested that the raised saints are the murdered prophets who are now vindicated. In this scenario, the

---

36 David C. Hoy, *The Critical Circle: Literature and History in Contemporary Hermeneutics* (Berkeley: University of California Press, 1978).

37 E.g., Mary B. Spaulding, *Commemorative Identities: Jewish Social Memory and the Johannine Feast of Booths*, LNTS 396 (London: T&T Clark, 2009).

38 Stephanus P. Botha, "'n Opstanding met verheerlikte liggame in Matteus 27:51b–53? 'n Noukeurige lees van die teks," *HvTSt* 52 (1996): 270–84.

saints, like Jesus, are the vindicated victims of Jerusalem. The problem is that there is no mention of the "holy ones" in the "woes" of Matthew 23.[39] On the other hand, the term ἅγιος is used adjectively of Jerusalem, the sanctuary, and sacred objects,[40] but most distinctly of the spirit in whom Jesus will baptize his followers (3:11) and in whom the disciples will baptize new followers in the great commission (28:19). It seems logical to infer that the evangelist, who along with other Jesus followers in his community would have been baptized in the name of the "Father, Son, and Holy Spirit," would have called his fellow believers "holy ones." If we push the distinction far enough, it is tempting to argue that the "saints" are the followers of Jesus who have come back to Jerusalem after the war as part of a missionary tour. Accordingly, the opening of the tombs functions metaphorically to convey profundity, as do the cosmic portents here and in chapter 24. However, the saints cannot be the Twelve in light of the sequence of events in Matthew 28, but they can be the missionaries who are baptized εἰς τὸ ὄνομα τοῦ πατρὸς καὶ τοῦ υἱοῦ καὶ τοῦ ἁγίου πνεύματος (28:19), and with whom abides the risen Jesus. If this is the case, then the evangelist would have read the scriptural stories about the restoration of the Israelites (e.g., Ezekiel 37; Zechariah 14; Daniel 12) from the perspective of the restoration of the new people of God, namely the followers of Jesus within his postwar setting. Interestingly, while Tertullian connects the zombie episode with the stories about Christ's victory in the underworld as many early receptions did,[41] the middle recension of Ignatius' *Letter to the Magnesians* 9.2 identifies the raised prophets as Jesus' "disciples in the Spirit."[42]

Diachronically, this reading coheres with the breadth of Jewish-Hellenistic conceptions of resurrection in the first century which would have provided the necessary cultural language and symbols. Jon Levinson has provided one of the best definitions of resurrection highlighting its divinely directed eschatological

39 That this is the only use of ἅγιος as a reference to Israel's prophets and/or patriarchs may not be as problematic as might first appear since Matthew uses 667 *hapax legomena* within a total of 1,068 verses and is not shy in using synonyms and new vocabulary in unexpected places, such as ἔγερσις (27:53) and τὴν ἁγιάν πόλιν as a reference to Jerusalem (4:5; 27:53), which occur nowhere else in the NT. Jerusalem as the ἁγιάν city occurs several times in the LXX (e.g. Neh 11:1; Joel 4:17; Isa 48:2; 52:1; 66:20; Dan 3:28). See also Quarles, "Matthew 27:51–53," 221.

40 1:18, 20; 3:11; 4:5; 7:6; 12:32; 24:15; 28:19.

41 Tertullian, *An.* 55.4; *Acts Thad.* 5; Eusebius, *Hist. eccl.* 1.13.20; Origen, *Comm. Rom.* 5.10; *Gos. Nic.* 19:12; 20:2; 21:2; cf. *Odes Sol.* 42:15–26. W. R. Schoedel and Helmut Koester, *Ignatius of Antioch: A Commentary on the Letters of Ignatius of Antioch* (Philadelphia: Fortress Press, 1985), 124.

42 Translation is taken from Michael Holmes, ed., *The Apostolic Fathers*, 2nd edn (Grand Rapids: Baker, 1999), 154–55.

significance. He writes, "Resurrection we must define as an eschatological event, that is, one that is expected to occur in history but also to transform and redeem history and to open onto a barely imaginable world beyond anything that preceded it." He further adds that it inaugurates a qualitatively different, exalted life into which the dead are raised, which distinguishes it from resuscitation and reincarnation.[43] In Geza Vermes' definition, it is the bestowal of divine grace upon the dead who experience the "reversal of death."[44] Beyond these kinds of definitions, however, the expression of resurrection in early Jewish literature is diverse and betrays deep-seeded creativity and imagination in relation to the mortal life. Some Jews emphasized the new form of embodiment; others saw it as a restoration of the same body (2 Macc); a few emphasized the location of the cosmos as the sphere of new existence whereas for others still it was on earth (*1 En.* 24–25). What is more, some focused on the contrast between mortal life and everlasting life; others compared the new life to the life of angels with no concern for mortal bodies (*1 En.* 91–108); others still compared the new life with an idealized past. Some even underscored the new life as a representation of the new creation.[45] C. D. Elledge points to the *Messianic Apocalypse* as a summary of the unprecedented events, which includes the resurrection that will inaugurate the eschatological age: "wondrous things which have not existed, the Lord will do, even as he [aid. For he will heal the slain, and the dead he will cause to live" (4Q521 frgs. 2 II + 4 lines 11–12).[46] As a general reflection on early Jewish conceptions of resurrection, Elledge observes that emphasis is placed on transference from one realm to another as opposed to the nature or the embodiment of the raised. It is often cosmic-spatial transference of the dead to a location where they will be restored and will thrive. An often-cited text is Dan 12:1–3 which describes the dead as being exalted from the "land of dust" to the dazzling "firmament" and "stars."[47]

When we investigate to see if there was some cohesive idea about the resurrection of the dead in early Christianity which may have served as a frame for Matthew, we find ourselves in a variegated world of ambiguity. Outi Lehtipuu has convincingly shown that the resurrection of the dead is not always

43 John D. Levinson, *Resurrection and the Restoration of Israel: The Ultimate Victory of the God of Life* (New Haven: Yale University Press, 2006), 20.

44 Geza Vermes, *The Resurrection: History and Myth* (New York: Doubleday, 2008), 3.

45 Elledge, Resurrection of the Dead, 3–6.

46 Translation is from Émile Puech, *Qumran Cave 4.XVIII: Textes hébreux (4Q521–4Q528, 4Q576–4Q579)* (DJD 25; Oxford: Clarendon, 1998), 10–11.

47 Elledge, *Resurrection of the Dead*, 6.

conceived as a physical phenomenon nor is it always limited to post-mortem existence (e.g., John 5:25–29). It may refer to a transformed existence, but not the ultimate goal of humanity. Clearly, the nature of the resurrected form dominated the debate in early Christian thought.[48]

Most scholars who study the concept of resurrection in antiquity assume that it is preceded by a literal or biological death that leads to new forms of embodiment.[49] Our traditional notion of death in antiquity, however, should be expanded. Like the concept of resurrection, the concept of death was not limited to biological death, but rather could include a range of "lifeless" states of existence, experienced in sickness, persecution, economic ruin, national decline, and personal tragedy, all of which could lead to biological death. Furthermore, even biological death was not always viewed as annihilation (Matt 22:32). Being in the state of death, and even in the grave, did not always mean that the deceased is fully dead, without a future, since death was sometimes viewed as lifeless existence in Sheol that one can call a state of afterlife that awaits resurrection.[50]

Closely related to the existential ambiguity of the resurrected state and form is the temporal ambiguity. In particular, how was resurrection manifested in the life of the Jesus follower? Will it occur when Christ returns? Does it happen at the moment of death? Or is it a spiritual experience prior to death? Emphases varied. Those who argued for the resurrection of the earthly body (flesh) associated it with the general resurrection in the future at the Parousia, yet they still had to make sense of the resurrection virtues in the present life. Whereas those who rejected the notion of a resurrected earthly body argued either for the heavenly ascent of the "spirit/soul," which still assumed a nebulous non-earthly "form/body" or the transformation of the believer in the present, before physical death. Yet, they still needed to incorporate some kind of change in the post-mortem state. Despite the lack of an overriding timetable, Christians were unique in the sense that they wrestled with this temporal paradox.[51]

Lehtipuu shows that one of the ways that Christian conception incorporated a temporal paradox that enabled them to participate in resurrection was through ritual, notably baptism. While Paul only associated baptism with a

---

48 Outi Lehtipuu, *Debates over the Resurrection of the Dead: Constructing Early Christian Identity* (Oxford: Oxford University Press, 2015).

49 George W. E. Nickelsburg, *Ancient Judaism and Christian Origins: Diversity, Continuity, and Transformation* (Minneapolis: Fortress Press, 2003), 151.

50 Elledge, *Resurrection of the Dead*, 4.

51 Lehtipuu, *Debates over the Resurrection of the Dead*, 159–60.

new life freed from the bondage of sin before resurrection, some of his followers viewed baptism as a participation in the resurrected life (Col 2:12–13). Others, however, appeared to have opposed the idea that "the resurrection is already past" (2 Tim. 2:16–18). This idea of baptism as an initiation into the resurrected life may be connected with Matthew's command to baptize in the name of the Father, son and Holy Spirit (28:19). Does Matthew's community see itself as already living in this resurrected state since it is presumably already baptized? Would this present reality inform their memory (*Gedächtnis*) of the significance of the crucifixion of Jesus? Without getting mired in the vast theological and historical discussion on the relationship between resurrection, ritual, and sacrament, I do want to stress that the ritual practice of baptism as a symbol of inclusion within a group that shares new identity in Matthew, connects the devotee with the risen Christ who commands the practice at the end of the Gospel. The commission sends the reader back to the baptism of Jesus at the beginning of his ministry, which implies that they not only carry on his work, but become like him. The difference is that they are baptized in the name of not only the Father and the Holy Spirit, but of the risen Son. Are we to assume that the opening of the heavens and divine declaration of Jesus as God's son at his baptism (3:17) is a shared identity of the risen life even before death? If so, then can this principle be applied to his followers? What makes this proposal even more possible is the Baptist's prediction that Jesus will "baptize in the Holy Spirit and fire" (3:11).

The Role of the Raised Saints

If the raised saints are literary and proleptic representations of missionaries from Matthew's community, what purpose do they serve in being seen in Jerusalem? Here again the synchronic approach determines our potential directions. Many scholars have argued that the zombie episode functions as a preparation for Jesus' resurrection in the next chapter.[52] Davies and Allison refer to it as a miniature dawning of the day of Lord.[53] The widespread concerns in the scholarly literature whether the zombie episode is or is not an eschatological account, a day of the Lord, the dawn of the new age, or the general resurrection is precisely the thinking that social memory theory within an ontological system of difference can avoid. If Matthew's account of the impact

52 W. D. Davies and Dale C. Allison, *A Critical and Exegetical Commentary on the Gospel According to Saint Matthew. Volume III: Commentary on Matthew XIX–XXVIII*, ICC (Edinburgh: T & T Clark, 1997), 640–41; Weren, *Studies in Matthew's Gospel*, 81.

53 Davies and Allison, *Matthew XIX–XXVIII*, 639.

of Jesus' crucifixion in relation to resurrection is a suspended expression in an ever-changing web of intersections, then we must allow for wider options, without transcendent ideas determining the so-called different ones.

Synchronically, despite the zombie episode taking place *after* the resurrection of Jesus, its location in the narrative links it directly with his crucifixion. This link can be explained as conveying both vengeance and vindication when we again take into account the series of scathing condemnations against the Jerusalem establishment, represented by the scribes and Pharisees, from chapter 23 onward. Without citing them all, they are not only portrayed as the murderers of Israel's Messiah, who is righteous and innocent, but they are aligned with the murderers of the prophets. Of particular note is Jesus' condemnation in ironic form that they build the tombs of the prophets (23:29). Are these tombs to be linked with the metaphorical tombs of the raised saints? Furthermore, the irony in Matt 27:25 of the self-assurance by the religious leaders that if Jesus is guilty, his blood should be on "us and our children's heads" has been pointed out numerous times. The interplay of guilt and innocence in the passion account is second to none in Matthew. In addition to Jesus' *post-eventu* prediction of the Temple's destruction in Matthew 24, the "woes" of Matthew 23 carry the same theme, culminating in "Jerusalem, Jerusalem, the city that kills the prophets and stones those who are sent to it ... See, your house is left to you, desolate" (vv. 37–38).

The main point is that the guilt is associated with the leadership and residents of Jerusalem. While the city is the object of divine devotion, it is once again guilty of murdering God's agent. Since the zombie episode functions within the immediate judgment metaphors and at the end of an extended condemnation against Jerusalem, Ulrich Luz correctly argues that the visibility of the raised saints is a prediction of the punishment due to those who have killed the messiah is significant.[54] Talbert has argued that a possible precedent lies in 2 Bar. 50.3–4 which depicts the raising of the righteous as a sign of judgment to the wicked.[55]

From a diachronic vantage point, it is highly probable that the evangelist is framing the crucifixion scene through the lens of the destruction of Jerusalem which would have been virtually present in light of the narrative. It would not have been a problem for the evangelist to temporally conflate the crucifixion of Jesus in ca. 30 CE with the destruction of the city in 70 CE. Bergson's

54 Luz, *Matthew 21–28*, 567–68.
55 Talbert, *Matthew*, 307.

conception of time gives the conflation explanation. Social memory theorists have commonly noted that the effects of trauma, conflict, and displacement have a lasting impact on how the past is narrated. If Matthew's community comprises of refugees escaping the post war conditions, as many scholars argue, then this diachronically constructed frame would account for the remembrance of the crucifixion and its aftermath. In this case, the destruction of Jerusalem is interpreted as divine vengeance for the murder of Jesus, and by extension the prophets. The visibility of the raised saints in the aftermath of the war is vindication since it demonstrates the city that has killed the prophets has not prevailed.

Do the risen saints, who are the missionaries from Matthew's community, represent a new age that has dawned? I think that they represent the end of the judgment, which is predicted throughout the Gospel as being imminent (especially in chapter 22). Though it need not be eschatological judgment as could be argued in Mark. The audience knows that it occurred in the destruction of Jerusalem. Many have lost family members, (24:36–44) and it occurred after a generation (24:34). To say more, forces us to extrapolate beyond the synchronic and diachronic data.

Implications

A social memory approach, within an ontology of difference, affects how we might conceive ideas of afterlife. It challenges us to no longer view them as dichotomies of accuracy and inaccuracy, originality and interpretation, or historical and remembered. Rather, they lend themselves to the vast array of interconnections which help us to better understand why the evangelist presented the zombie episode in the way he did. It also challenges us to think about the relationship between the past, present, and future as a collapsing of frames. The evangelist collapses his culturally inherited frame which can be called "scripture" in a general sense with the collectively inherited frame of Jesus. Both of these are collapsed into a communicative frame, which is the inherited first-hand experience of the trauma from the destruction of Jerusalem. All of these frames exist virtually in the production of Matthew's zombie episode as a snapshot, an identification, or a suspended expression within a web of interconnections that cannot be replicated in another expression. For this reason, theological systems that require consistency and continuity in conceptions of afterlife face a significant challenge that requires attention.

Bibliography

Allison Jr., Dale C. "The Scriptural Background of a Matthean Legend: Ezekiel 37, Zechariah 14, and Matthew 27." Pages 153–88 in *Life beyond Death in Matthew's Gospel: Religious Metaphor or Bodily Reality?* Edited by Wim Weren, Huub van de Sandt, and Joseph Verheyden. BTS 13. Leuven: Peeters, 2011.

Assmann, Aleida. *Cultural Memory and Western Civilization: Functions, Media, Archives*. Cambridge: Cambridge University Press, 2011.

Botha, Stephanus P. "'n Opstanding met verheerlikte liggame in Matteus 27:51b–53? 'n Noukeurige lees van die teks." *HvTSt* 52 (1996): 270–84.

Crossan, John Dominic. "The Resurrection of Jesus in Its Jewish Context." *Neot* 37 (2003): 29–57.

Davies, W. D., and Dale C. Allison. *A Critical and Exegetical Commentary on the Gospel According to Saint Matthew. Volume* III*: Commentary on Matthew XIX–XXVIII*. ICC. Edinburgh: T & T Clark, 1997.

Deleuze, Gilles. *Bergsonism*. Translated by Hugh Tomlinson and Barbara Habberjam. New York: Zone Books, 1988.

Deleuze Gilles, and Felix Guattari. *A Thousand Plateaus*. Translated by Brian Massumi. Minneapolis: University of Minnesota Press, 1987.

Elledge, C. D. *Resurrection of the Dead in Early Judaism 200 BCE–CE 200*. Oxford: Oxford University Press, 2017.

Goodenough, Erwin R. *Jewish Symbols in the Greco-Roman Period*. New York: Pantheon, 1964.

Grassi, J. "The Resurrection and the Ezechiel Panel of the DuraEuropos Synagogue." TBT 11 (1964): 721–726.

Halbwachs, Maurice. *On Collective Memory*. Translated by L. A. Coser. Chicago: University of Chicago Press, 1992.

Holmes, Michael, ed. *The Apostolic Fathers*. 2nd edn. Grand Rapids: Baker, 1999.

Hoy, David C. *The Critical Circle: Literature and History in Contemporary Hermeneutics*. Berkeley: University of California Press, 1978.

Huebenthal, Sandra. "'Frozen Moments'—Early Christianity through the Lens of Social Memory Theory." Pages 17–43 in *Memory and Memories in Early Christianity*. Edited by Simon Butticaz and Enrico Morelli. WUNT 1.398. Tübingen: Mohr Siebeck, 2018.

Kelber, Werner H. "Narrative as Interpretation and Interpretation of Narrative: Hermeneutical Reflections on the Gospels." *Semeia* 39 (1987): 107–33.

Koselleck, Reinhart. *Futures Past: On the Semantics of Historical Time*. Translated by Keith Tribe Cambridge: MIT Press, 1985.

Lehtipuu, Outi. *Debates over the Resurrection of the Dead: Constructing Early Christian Identity*. Oxford: Oxford University Press, 2015.

Levinson, John D. *Resurrection and the Restoration of Israel: The Ultimate Victory of the God of Life*. New Haven: Yale University Press, 2006.
Luz, Ulrich. *Matthew 21–28*. Hermeneia. Minneapolis: Fortress, 2005.
May, Todd. *Gilles Deleuze: An Introduction*. Cambridge: Cambridge University Press, 2005.
Nickelsburg, George W. E. *Ancient Judaism and Christian Origins: Diversity, Continuity, and Transformation*. Minneapolis: Fortress Press, 2003.
Olick, Jeffery K., V. Vinitzky-Seroussi, and D. Levy, eds. *Collective Memory Reader*. Oxford: Oxford University Press, 2011.
Puech, Émile. *Qumran Cave 4.XVIII: Textes hébreux (4Q521–4Q528, 4Q576–4Q579)*. DJD 25. Oxford: Clarendon, 1998.
Quarles, Charles L. "Matthew 27:51–53: Meaning, Genre, Intertextuality, Theology, and Reception History." JETS 59 (2016): 271–86.
Ricoeur, Paul. *Memory, History, Forgetting*. Translated by Kathleen Blamey and David Pellauer. Chicago: The University of Chicago Press, 2004.
Riesenfeld, Harald. *The Resurrection in Ezekiel xxxvii and in the Dura-Europos Paintings*. Upsala: Lundaquistilca Bokhandeln, 1948.
Schoedel, W. R., and Helmut Koester. *Ignatius of Antioch: A Commentary on the Letters of Ignatius of Antioch*. Hermeneia. Philadelphia: Fortress Press, 1985.
Schwartz, Barry. "Where There's Smoke, There's Fire: Memory and History." Pages 7–37 in *Memory and Identity in Ancient Judaism and Early Christianity: A Conversation with Barry Schwartz*. Semeia 78. Edited by Tom Thatcher. Atlanta: SBL Press, 2014.
Spaulding, Mary B. *Commemorative Identities: Jewish Social Memory and the Johannine Feast of Booths*. LNTS 396. London: T&T Clark, 2009.
Strauss, David F. *The Life of Jesus Critically Examined*. Edited and translated by Peter Hodgson. Lives of Jesus Series. Philadelphia: Fortress, 1972.
Talbert, Charles H. *Matthew*. Grand Rapids: Baker Academic, 2010.
Troxel, Ronald L. "Matthew 27.51–4 Reconsidered: Its Role in the Passion Narrative, Meaning and Origin." *NTS* 48 (2002): 30–47.
Vermes, Geza. *The Resurrection: History and Myth*. New York: Doubleday, 2008.
Wardle, Timothy. "Resurrection and the Holy City: Matthew's Use of Isaiah in 27:51–53." *CBQ* 78 (2016): 666–81.
Weren, Wim J. C. *Studies in Matthew's Gospel: Literary Design, Intertextuality, and Social Setting*. BIS 130. Leiden: Brill, 2014.
Weren, Wim, Huub van de Sandt, and Joseph Verheyden, eds. *Life beyond Death in Matthew's Gospel: Religious Metaphor or Bodily Reality?* BTS 13. Leuven: Peeters, 2011.
Williams, Catrin H. "Patriarchs and Prophets Remembered: Framing Israel's Past in the Gospel of John." Pages 187–212 in *Abiding Words: The Use of Scripture in the Gospel of John*. RBS 81. Edited by Alicia D. Myers and Bruce G. Schuchard. Atlanta: SBL Press, 2012.

Woloch, Alex. *The One vs. the Many. Minor Characters and the Space of the Protagonist in the Novel.* Princeton: Princeton University Press, 2003.
Wright, N. T. *The Resurrection of the Son of God.* Minneapolis: Fortress, 2003.
Zangenberg, Jürgen K. "Bodily Resurrection of Jesus in Matthew?" Pages 217–31 in *Life beyond Death in Matthew's Gospel: Religious Metaphor or Bodily Reality?* Edited by Wim Weren, Huub van de Sandt, and Joseph Verheyden. BTS 13. Leuven: Peeters, 2011.
Zerubavel, Eviatar. *Time Maps: Collective Memory and the Social Space of the Past.* Chicago: University of Chicago Press, 2003.

List of Contributors

Bradford A. Anderson
Associate Professor of Hebrew Bible, Dublin City University, Ireland

Craig C. Broyles
Professor of Religious Studies, Trinity Western University, Langley, British Columbia, Canada

David Cielontko
Postdoctoral Research Fellow, Protestant Theological Faculty, Charles University, Prague, Czech Republic
Postdoctoral Research Fellow, Centre for Classical Studies, Czech Academy of Sciences, Prague, Czech Republic

Zeba Crook
Professor of Religious Studies, Carleton University, Ottawa, Canada

Christian Handschuh
Professor of Ecclesiastical History and Christian Identities, Universität Passau, Germany

Thomas R. Hatina
Professor of Religion and Culture, Chair of the Religious Studies Department, Director of the Graduate Program in Biblical Studies & Christian Thought, Trinity Western University, Langley, British Columbia, Canada
Visiting Professor, Charles University, Prague, Czech Republic

Sandra Huebenthal
Professor and Chair of Exegesis and Biblical Theology, Universität Passau, Germany

Jiří Janák
Associate Professor of Egyptology, Czech Institute of Egyptology, Faculty of Arts, Charles University, Prague, Czech Republic

Anthony Le Donne
Professor of New Testament, United Theological Seminary, Dayton, Ohio, USA

Jiří Lukeš
Lecturer in Biblical Studies, Hussite Theological Faculty, Charles University, Prague, Czech Republic

Tobias Nicklas
Professor of New Testament, Director of the Centre for Advanced Studies "Beyond Canon", Universität Regensburg, Germany
Research Associate, University of the Free State, Bloemfontein, South Africa

Kyle R. L. Parsons
Instructor in Religious Studies, Trinity Western University, Langley, British Columbia, Canada

Michael Sommer
Privatdozent, Faculty for Catholic Theology, University of Regensburg, Germany

Stu Talené
Instructor in Religious Studies, Trinity Western University, Langley, British Columbia, Canada

Frederick S. Tappenden
Principal, Dean, and Professor of Theology, St. Stephen's College, University of Alberta, Edmonton, Alberta, Canada

Index of Ancient Sources

*References from footnotes included

Index of Modern Authors